California
REAL ESTATE
PRINCIPLES

Walt Huber

NEW EXAM EDITION

10th Edition

COPYRIGHT 1976, 1977, 1978, 1979, 1985, 1989, 1994, ,1995, 2003, 2004 10th Edition
Educational Textbook Company, Inc.
P. O. Box 3597
Covina, California 91722
(626)339-7733
(626)332-4744 (Fax)
www.etcbooks.com

Library of Congress Cataloging-in-Publication Data

California Real Estate Principles - Walt Huber

Summary: Covers all material in Real Estate Principles classes with special emphasis on California real estate laws. Very clear and simple language, easy-to-read format with photographs, charts, and graphs. Includes glossary and index. Suitable for consumers, students, and teachers wishing information about personal real estate transactions. This textbook is designed to fulfill the course requirement necessary to take the California Real Estate Salespersons and Broker's Exams.

ISBN 0-916772-06-3

Preface

The 10th edition of *CALIFORNIA REAL ESTATE PRINCIPLES* is an excellent beginning real estate text and also an essential review and reference book for those students planning to take the California Real Estate License Examination.

This new edition covers all matters related to the ownership and transfer of real property, from deposit receipt to completed escrow, and beyond. All the commonly used forms used are shown and explained in detail, including the CAR 8-page deposit receipt. Each chapter includes a multiple choice quiz to test the reader's comprehension of material contained in the preceding pages. We also have a vocabulary test at the end of every chapter so students can match important real estate terms with concise definitions. Correct quiz answers appear (inverted) at the end of each quiz section.

I want to express my appreciation to the many people who helped to make this text possible. I received advice and helpful suggestions from the **California Department of Real Estate** (www.dre.ca.gov) and advice and forms from the **California Association of Realtors®** (www.car.org).

We would like to thank Levin P. Messick, IFAC, President, AC Appraisals, Inc. and instructor at Mt. San Antonio College, and Arlette Lyons, CRS, GRI, President and owner of Lyons and Associates, Inc. Realtor®, and instructor at Mt. San Antonio College. We would also like to thank Fred Martinez, instructor, City College of San Francisco.

Special thanks for the valuable assistance given by the people who helped design and produce this book: Philip Dockter, art director; Melinda Winters, cover design; Colleen Taber, executive editor; Linda Serra and Andrea Atkins, editors; and Rick Lee, pre-press editor and layout.

Acknowledgments

This book contains the input of many prominent educators and real estate professionals. Their involvement as contributing advisors has made it possible for us to cover a wide range of material in detail and, at the same time, offer practical perspectives based upon their extensive classroom and industry experience. Their contributions werre invaluable and merit my most sincere thanks.

Hal Madson
Allan Hancock College

Alfred J. Guetling
American River College

Ryan M. Polstra
American River College

Steve Sodergren
Antelope Valley College

Joe Newton
Bakersfield College

Thurza B. Andrew
Butte College

Donald T. Brown
Butte College

Joseph F. Belohlavek
Cabrillo College

Robin Sherman
Cabrillo College

Melvin Brady
Cerritos College

John T. Martinez
Chabot College

Richard McCartney
Chabot College

John A. Culver
Chabot College

Robert Andersen
Chabot College

Earl H. Bond
Chaffey College

J. O. Wright
Chaffey College

Frederick A. Henning
Citrus College

Keith H. Kerr
City College San Francisco

Fred Martinez
City College San Francisco

Hal Bouley
Coastline College

Bart J. Kearney
College Of San Mateo

Allen C. Shute
College Of The Canyons

Stan Reyburn
College Of The Desert

Jeff Eddy
College Of The Sequoias

John A. Miller
Contra Costa College

Ronald G. Rueb
Contra Costa College

Mike Hoey
Cosumnes River College

D. Blazej
Cuesta College

John R. Morrissey
Diablo Valley College

Tim Murphy
Diablo Valley College

Leo Saunders, GRI, CRB
Diablo Valley College

Dr. Elliott J. Dixon
East Los Angeles College

Olivia Vasquez Anderson
East Los Angeles College

Frances K. Jackson
E.C.C., San Diego

Michael Botello
El Camino College

Donna Grogan, CPM
El Camino College

Charles W. Leonhardt
Feather River College

Dr. Eugene C. Azamber
Fresno City College

Peter Kirianoff
Fullerton College

Karen Obuljen
Golden West College

Dino Vlachos
Golden West College

Frank Pangborn
Irvine Valley College

Doug Rosner
Lake Tahoe Community College

Larry R. Hoffman
Long Beach City College

Sherry F. Tunison
Long Beach City College

Bill Monroe
Los Angeles City College

Alex Yguado
Los Angeles Mission College

John J. Meichtry
Los Angeles Mission College

Thomas Morehouse
Los Angeles Pierce College

Harold Lerner
Los Angeles Pierce College

Robert R. Enger
Los Angeles Pierce College

Table of Contents

CHAPTER *2*: *Estates, Transfers, and Titles*   27

CHAPTER 3: *Encumbrances* 57

CHAPTER 4: *Agency and Its Responsibilities* 83

CHAPTER 5: Contracts

129

CHAPTER 7: Escrows and Title Insurance — 207

CHAPTER 8:   Real Estate Finance

CHAPTER 9: *Financial Institutions*   293

Table of Contents

CHAPTER *10: Appraisal Basics*　　　　　　337

CHAPTER 12: Subdivisions and Government Control 401

CHAPTER 13: Taxation of Real Estate   447

CHAPTER 14: Licensing, Education, and Associations   481

SUNSET BROKERS

Scott Chapin

http://www.bankhomes.com

493-4357

Chapter 1
Introduction to Real Estate

I. California's Real Estate Market

A. CALIFORNIA DEPARTMENT OF REAL ESTATE (DRE)

Each state has its own real estate licensing laws, governed by its own state regulatory commission.

In California that regulatory body is the Department of Real Estate (DRE), which is headed by the real estate commissioner. The California DRE is widely recognized as a progressive organization whose example is followed by other states. The most current and accurate information from the DRE can be found at their website: **www.dre.ca.gov**

B. HIGH COST OF REAL ESTATE

Due to increased job opportunities, higher birthrates, immigration, and migration, California's population growth rate is expected to practically double that of the national average in the next decade. For a variety of reasons, the number of new houses and condominiums being constructed is low. As a result, demand is already outpacing supply.

CALIFORNIA DEPARTMENT OF REAL ESTATE (DRE)

The California Department of Real Estate (DRE) is on the Internet. They supply all the procedural information (See **Chapter 14** of this book) you need to know about a license; for example, the successful completion of a college level course in real estate principles is required to take the salesperson exam. We advise you to look at the section called **"Examinees."**

The DRE is constantly improving their website and adding valuable services via the Internet. Now, not only can you research what's new at the DRE and access valuable information on most subjects involving real estate, you can conduct DRE licensing transactions online as well! The following transactions can now be performed online, using the "eLicensing" system:

1. Acquire Testing Schedules
2. Check Test Results
3. Salesperson and Broker License Renewals
4. File Mailing Address Changes
5. Salesperson Changes of Employing Broker
6. Continuing Education Extension/Exemption Request

It dosen't get much easier than this! Check out DRE's website for further improvements!

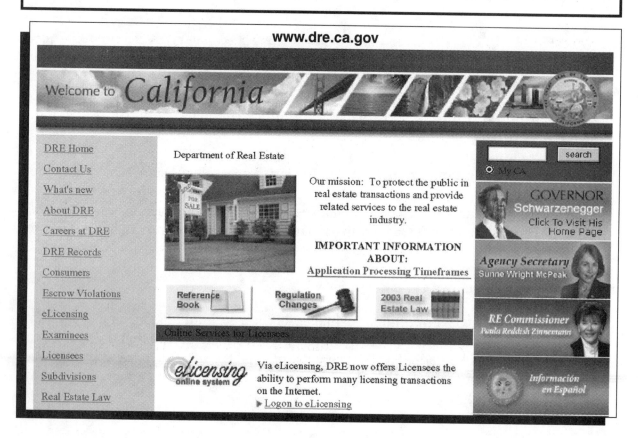

With the state's abundance of community colleges and universities generating so many educated professionals, is it any wonder the personal incomes in California are the envy of the rest of the nation?

California's remarkable expansion is due no doubt to our dominance in the areas of: 1) high technology and biotechnology; 2) foreign trade; 3) tourism and entertainment; 4) agriculture; as well as 5) professional services. Projections indicate that California will nearly double the national average in 1) job creations; 2) income increases; 3) household formation; and 4) population increases. This has created a demand for housing, and a scarcity of buildable land close to urban areas, which means the price of real estate will continue to be driven higher over the next decade.

A home is an expensive venture that includes a home loan payment. This payment usually equals 25 percent to 28 percent of the wages earned monthly by the homeowner. The monthly payment is only part of owning a home. Property taxes, fire insurance, repairs, and furnishings are expenses that will further increase the monthly cost of maintaining a home.

A home is often the largest and most important purchase a person makes in his or her lifetime.

C. REAL ESTATE: A PROFITABLE PROFESSION

With the high cost of real estate comes the potential for high profits in the selling of real estate. A purchase as important as a home requires a great deal of knowledge and usually entails the services of a real estate professional. Because brokers and real estate salespeople are paid by commission, the higher the cost of housing, the higher the price of their services. A *COMMISSION is an amount paid, usually as a percentage of the selling price, to a broker for services.* The broker is responsible for paying his or her salespeople their part of any commissions.

Commissions paid to licensees are fully negotiable.

Real estate brokers in California normally receive around five or six percent of the sales price of a home as their commission. For example, if a home sells for $500,000 and the broker involved in the sale receives a 6 percent commission, he or she would collect a total of $30,000 ($500,000 x .06).

As you can see, the real estate business is a profitable one. It requires a person who is helpful, ambitious, willing to work and familiar with computer programs and the Internet. There is always a need for knowledgeable, well-trained salespeople and professionals in related fields, such as loan brokers, appraisers, and escrow officers.

II. Historical Influence

www.ca.gov
Welcome To California
www.calhist.org
California History

A. NATIVE AMERICAN INDIANS WERE FIRST

California's colorful history gives a unique flavor to its customs and lifestyles. The first Europeans to actively settle California were Spaniards. In 1769, they began the famous mission system along El Camino Real, now known as U.S. Highway 101 and California 1. *They established fortified trading posts, called **PRESIDIOS**,* at San Diego, San Francisco and Monterey.

*The first cities, called **PUEBLOS**,* were Los Angeles and San Jose. Spain's king granted vast ranchos to favored civil and military officers. Many streets, towns and landmarks in California still bear their names. The state's distinct architectural style, the rambling, cool, thick-walled adobe structure with red tile roof, dates from the Spanish period.

In the early 1800s, California became a self-governing province of newly independent Mexico. The ruling government attempted land reform, breaking up the huge Spanish ranchos and giving ownership to Mexican citizens. This disturbed the large American population in California and led to war with Mexico.

The United States war with Mexico ended on February 2, 1848, with the Treaty of Guadalupe Hidalgo. As part of the settlement, the United States purchased from Mexico more than 500,000 square miles of land, including the present states of Nevada, Utah and California. In an extraordinary example of political-economic timing, Mexico deeded over all rights to this province within a few weeks of John Sutter's explosive discovery of gold near Sacramento.

The Gold Rush brought thousands of new citizens swarming to the west coast. Many settled permanently, founding towns and businesses, and expanding the already well-established orchards, vineyards and cattle ranches. Foreign trade crowded the coastal cities with goods and increased immigration. California achieved full statehood on September 9, 1850, and from that time on the state's population increased until it could boast of having the largest population in the nation (over 12.5%). The newly-established legislature adopted a land ownership recording system that recognized and protected the early land grants. This recording system provides an interesting and complete history of the ownership of California lands and their subsequent division and subdivision.

California statehood: September 9, 1850. In 1917, California created the first licensing law in the country, which was declared unconstitutional. This led to the Real Estate Act of 1919.

In 1917 California passed the first real estate licensing law in the nation. Although this first law was declared unconstitutional, the Real Estate Act of 1919 was upheld by the State Supreme Court. Licensing laws are a reasonable exercise by the state to regulate the conduct of its citizens in the interest of the public good.

III. Real and Personal Property

A. OWNERSHIP IS A BUNDLE OF RIGHTS

In the historical legal sense, property refers to "all the rights" or interests one has in the "thing" owned, rather the thing itself. Commonly referred to as a "bundle of rights," some of these rights include possession, enjoyment, control, and disposition. See **Figure 1-1** for more details.

Figure 1-1

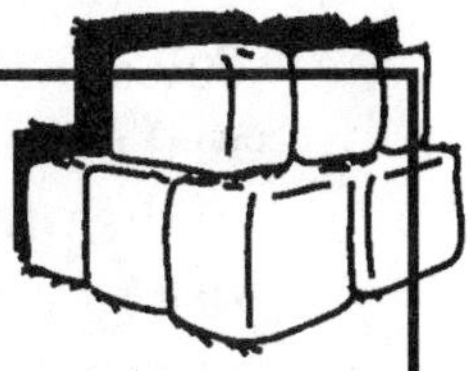

OWNERSHIP IS A "BUNDLE OF RIGHTS"

Bundle of Rights Theory

The bundle of rights theory views property ownership rights as a large bundle of sticks, where each "stick" is a property right. Individually, these rights represent various, specific forms of ownership; the more of these you hold the more completely you own the property. So if you lease the property to someone, you give up one of your "sticks" (the right of possession). The basic rights of ownership include the following:

1. **Possession** — is the right to occupy, rent or keep others out.

2. **Enjoyment** — is the right to "peace and quiet" without interference from past owners and others.

3. **Control** — is the right to physically change or keep the property the way you like it.

4. **Disposition** — is the right to transfer all or part of your property to others as you see fit.

All of your ownership rights are, of course, subject to governmental limitations and restrictions.

There are two types of property: **REAL PROPERTY** *(immovable)* and **PERSONAL PROPERTY** *(movable),* formerly called "chattel" or "chattel real."

Real property is "immovable"; title to real property is passed with a deed.

B. REAL PROPERTY

REAL PROPERTY *is the right or interest that a person has in the land or anything attached to the land.*

Real property is legally defined as:

1. *Land*
2. *Anything permanently attached or affixed to the land*
3. *Anything incidental or appurtenant to the land*
4. *That which is immovable by law*

1. Land

LAND *ownership is commonly thought of as owning the surface of the earth;* in other words, the ground we walk and build upon. But ownership also gives us rights to the space that is above our land and extends below our feet to the center of the earth, as **Figure 1-2** illustrates.

An **AIRSPACE** *is the right to the use of the air space above the surface of the earth.* It is real property. In reality, the courts have restricted, to a reasonable height, the right of the property owner to use this space. An example for allowing only **reasonable use** of airspace is the need for airlines to have public "air highways" to provide us with transportation.

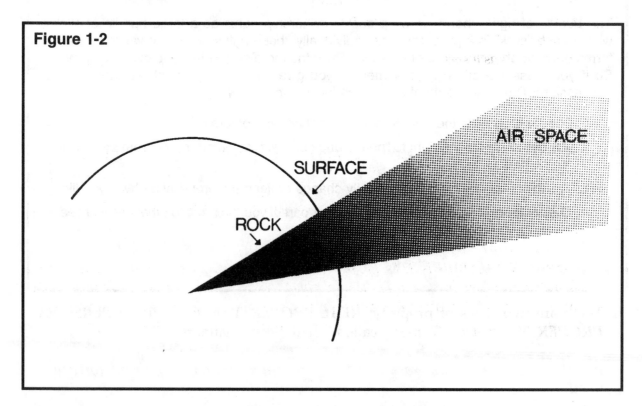

Figure 1-2

This airspace above the ground can be leased or sold in the same manner that mineral rights can be leased or sold. Airspace is an effective way to fully utilize the prime construction sites in many of our larger cites by building "up" instead of "out." An example of effective airspace use is storage space leased under our freeway overpasses by Caltrans, our state highway maintenance division.

Condominiums are another good example of airspace use. Inside a condominium, one only owns the airspace (area within the finished walls). The owner also owns a fractional share of the entire project (common area). Each owner may use the airspace within his or her unit in any manner he or she wishes, unless it violates the by-laws of the homeowner's group.

Generally, all that is beneath the surface of the earth belongs to the owner as real property. *MINERAL RIGHTS, such as gold, silver and borax, are solids that are part of the real property, but can be removed.* However, there are some exceptions: oil and other minerals can be claimed by the owner as personal property when removed from the ground. This is because they are considered, by law, to be "fugitive (meaning moving) substances." As an owner, you may sell your mineral rights below 500 feet; or you may exercise your "right of surface entry" above the 500 foot level.

A *LITTORAL RIGHT is the right of an owner of land bordering a lake or pond to reasonable usage of that non-flowing body of water,* whereas a *RIPARIAN RIGHT is the right of the owner of land bordering a river or stream to reasonable usage of that moving, free flowing water source.* Neither riparian nor littoral rights are automatic. *PERCOLATING WATER refers to water seeping up from the soil from an underground source, such as a spring.*

A "riparian right" is the right to reasonable use of running water from a river, stream, or water course, if the land borders it.

A landowner has the right, in common with others, to take his or her share of underground (percolating) waters for beneficial use. *When the state (not city or county) takes surplus underground water for beneficial use of non-owners, it is called ALLOCATION or APPROPRIATION. POTABLE WATER refers to water that is suitable for human consumption.*

SURFACE WATER RIGHTS prohibit the diversion of runoff from rain unless confined to a channel (river or stream) to the property of another. An owner can use reasonable means to protect against floodwater, but not at the expense of his neighbor.

The "degrees of flood hazard" include: 1) inundation (the most severe), 2) sheet overflow, and 3) ponding. Flooding that occurs twice in ten years is considered "frequent flooding."

2. Attached to the Land ("Improvements")

Anything attached to the land, such as buildings, fences, walls, walks and shrubs, are called **IMPROVEMENTS**, and become **real property** when they are permanently incorporated, integrated in, affixed or attached to the land. Buildings that rest on the land or anything attached by cement, nails, screws, and plaster are examples of real property, as is a bearing wall that supports the upper part of a structure.

Real property is the land and anything attached to the land (called "improvements"). Natural growth (vegetation attached by roots) is real property as are industrial crops produced by labor and industry until they are severed, mortgaged, or sold.

3. Incidental or Appurtenant to the Land

Anything that is incidental or appurtenant to the land is real property. *APPURTENANT means attached to and runs with the land.* Certain things that are a part of the land must be sold with the land or else the usefulness of the land is reduced. For example, some small communities own shares of stock in their own mutual water companies that supply them with water. When the land is sold, the shares in the water company go with the land. Easements that allow the use of someone else's land, such as a driveway to enter your land, also go with the land being sold if it is the only way to access the land.

Appurtenant means ownership "runs with the land"; it transfers automatically, without the need of a separate conveyance. Stock in a mutual water company is usually an appurtenance (and is therefore considered real property).

4. Immovable by Law

That which by law is considered immovable is real property. Under California law, established crops and trees are a part of the land. Growing vegetables or fruits are considered **personal property**. Trees are sold with the land. The only exception is when a contract of sale for these items is made before the land is sold. If you have such a contract, it is a good idea to record it at the appropriate county recorder's office to assure that everyone has notice of the sale.

Title to real property is passed with a "deed," whereas title to personal property is passed with a "bill of sale."

C. PERSONAL PROPERTY

PERSONAL PROPERTY is any property that is movable and cannot be properly classified under the definition of real property. Items such as clothes, furniture and automobiles are tangible and easily movable. Personal property can also be documents that represent value, such as stocks, bonds, or leases.

Personal property is "movable," like a refrigerator, washer, or dryer. The seller takes his or her personal property with them, unless negotiated otherwise. Any personal property meant to be included in the sale should be written in the sales contract (deposit receipt).

*Planted growing crops are called **EMBLEMENTS** if they are cultivated annually by a tenant farmer on leased land. These crops belong to the tenant even after the expiration of the lease. Such crops are considered personal property because they are harvested yearly (removed from the ground).*

Unlike harvested crops, vegetation (or landscaping) is permanent, attached by roots and therefore considered real property.

When buying personal property, your receipt is called a "Bill of Sale." The Bill of Sale states that the goods have been paid for and that no outstanding loans exist on the personal property. It is always considered good practice to obtain a Bill of Sale. **Figure 1-3** is an example of a Bill of Sale.

A lease is personal property, as are stocks and bonds. Trust deeds (loans) are personal property.

Figure 1-3   **TRANSFERS TITLE OF PERSONAL PROPERTY**

BILL OF SALE

In consideration for the sum of ___Three hundred fifty and ....no/100___

_____$350.00_____ as payment in full is hereby acknowledged from

_(Mr. John Q. Smart)___ for the purchase of _____(A Maytag washer

and dryer, serial numbers #H02257 and #D376240).____

Executed on ___April 19, 20XX___

in the county of ____Sacramento,____ California.

___Robert Seller___
Signature of Seller

Personal property can be sold, can be used as security for a debt, or can be changed into real property by becoming "affixed" to the land.

D. FIXTURES

FIXTURES are items of personal property that are attached to, or incorporated into, the land in such a manner as to become real property. The courts use these five tests to determine if an item is a fixture:

M 1. **Method of attachment**
A 2. **Adaptability**
R 3. **Relationship of the parties**
I 4. **Intention**
A 5. **Agreement**

> We sometimes place an acronym in front of a word to help you remember! MARIA stands for the first letter.

1. Method of Attachment

If an item can be removed by simply being unplugged, it is probably personal property. On the other hand, if it is attached by cement, plaster, screws, nails or plumbing, it is probably real property. If removal of an item would leave permanent damage or an unusable area, it is surely real property. A rug lying in a living room would be considered personal property; carpet affixed to the floor would be considered real property.

Cost, size, and time installed are not tests in determining if something is a fixture.

2. Adaptability

The second test is adaptability of the personal property (attached to be essential for ordinary use in connection with the land). If well adapted, the item is probably a fixture.

3. Relationship of the Parties

If a fixture is not mentioned in a contract, and is affixed to the property, most courts will give the seller the benefit of the doubt. A refrigerator that is just plugged in would be considered personal property and would remain with the seller. To protect yourself, any questionable fixtures should be mentioned in the purchase agreement (deposit receipt). **Real estate salespeople remember: your client should secure a bill of sale for personal items.** In the case of a tenant and landlord, the court usually rules in favor of the tenant. There are, however, no set rules. A court decision is dependent upon the facts of each individual case.

4. Intention

The intention of the person attaching the personal property to the land is the most important test in a court of law.

If you plan to remove an item of personal property, you may not permanently attach it to the land.

5. Agreement

Disputes between buyers and sellers often arise regarding fixtures and what remains with the property. It is advisable to secure, in writing, any personal property that you want to remain as personal property. If you are buying a house, list all items you want to accompany the house, such as light fixtures, drapes or a fireplace screen. If you are selling, list only the items that will remain with the house. Remember: if in doubt, put it in writing!

The five tests stated above are used to determine facts, and the facts are what the courts use to settle disputes.

E. TRADE FIXTURES (Always Personal Property) (Removable - Exception to the Rule)

TRADE FIXTURES are personal property used in the normal course of business, such as shelving or refrigeration units. A tenant may remove any trade fixture he or she installed provided the real property is left in the same condition as he or she found it. In this sense, trade fixtures are an exception to the rules of personal property.

Tenants own trade fixtures (built-in business furniture), so they are removed by tenants when they leave. Any damage caused by these removals must be repaired by the tenant.

IV. Methods of Land Description

A *COMMON ADDRESS is the address that is used for mail delivery, or the address posted on the property.* For example, let us assume that you live at 732 MAIN STREET, SAN DIEGO, CALIFORNIA. There may be several Main Streets in San Diego. Does the street run north and south or east and west? What are the boundaries of the property? As you can see, in a real estate transaction it is important to identify a property more precisely. A common address does not give all the information needed to properly describe or locate a property.

In California, every parcel of land must be properly described or identified. If the property is to be sold, financed or leased, a recognized legal description is required. The following three methods are accepted as means of property identification:

A. Metes and Bounds (Surveyor's Maps — Irregular Parcels)
B. Sections and Townships (U.S. Government Survey — Rural)
C. Lots, Blocks and Tracts (Recorded Subdivision — Cities)

A. METES AND BOUNDS (SURVEYOR'S MAPS)

*METES AND BOUNDS (**measuring boundaries**) is the method of identifying (describing) property by its boundaries, distances, and angles from a given starting point.* In the past, surveyors often used natural objects as a starting point in their descriptions. *A MONUMENT is a fixed object and point set in the earth by surveyors to establish land locations.* An outdated surveyor's report might read:

> *"Starting at the old oak tree at the stream, go 300 feet north along the river bed, then make a 90 degree right turn and proceed 100 feet..."*

The weakness in this type of description is that when natural objects are used as starting points, there is a chance that time, or man, many move or destroy these objects. Modern day surveying is a complicated method of property description better left to the professionals. It is also unnecessary for the average real estate salesperson to study this method in depth, but a basic working knowledge can be helpful. The following (**Figure 1-4**) is an example of how a simple surveyor's report might look.

Figure 1-4 **True Point of Beginning (Starting Point)**

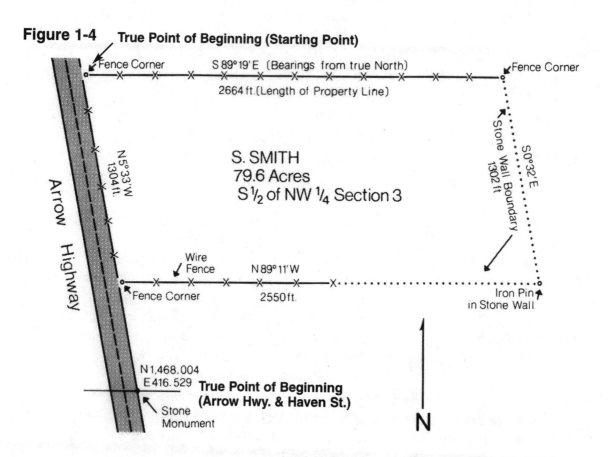

B. SECTIONS AND TOWNSHIPS (U.S. GOVERNMENT SURVEYS)

The United States Government Survey system was established to identify all public lands by the use of "base lines" and "meridians" starting from a precise surveying point. There are many such starting points throughout the country. There are 3 main starting points in California **(See Figure 1-5)**. The three starting points are:

1. **Humboldt Base Line and Meridian** in Northern California;
2. **Mt. Diablo Base Line and Meridian** in Central California; and
3. **San Bernardino Base Line and Meridian** in Southern California.

From these three starting points, all of California may be described using sections, townships and ranges to define any given parcel.

1. Base Lines and Meridian Lines

A *BASE LINE is a horizontal line that runs east and west from any one of three starting points in California.* Each base line is marked in six-mile increments. Every 6 mile increment is called a range and each range is 6 miles in width. It is possible to move east or west a designated number of ranges from any starting point.

MERIDIAN LINES are vertical lines that run north and south from any one of the three starting points in California. Meridians are also marked off in increments of 6 miles each, but each 6 mile increment north or south on a meridian is called a township or tier.

2. Tiers, Ranges, and Townships

Each rectangular survey grid consists of a series of lines that run parallel to the principal meridian and the base line, at intervals of six miles. The *east-west lines (running parallel to the base line) are called TIER LINES. The north-south lines (parallel to the principal meridian) are referred to as RANGE LINES.*

Township lines divide the land into a series of east-west strips, called TIERS. Range lines divide the land into north-south strips called RANGES. Where a tier intersects with a range, the result is a six miles by six miles square of land known as a TOWNSHIP. Thus, each township contains 36 square miles. Townships are the main divisions of land in the rectangular survey system. Each township is identified according to its distance from the principal meridian and base line.

The location of any township is determined by its distance from the nearest base line and meridian line. For example, see **Figure 1-6** to determine the location of a township northeast of the San Bernardino Base Line and Meridian (T. 4N, R. 3E).

The following steps are used:

Figure 1-5

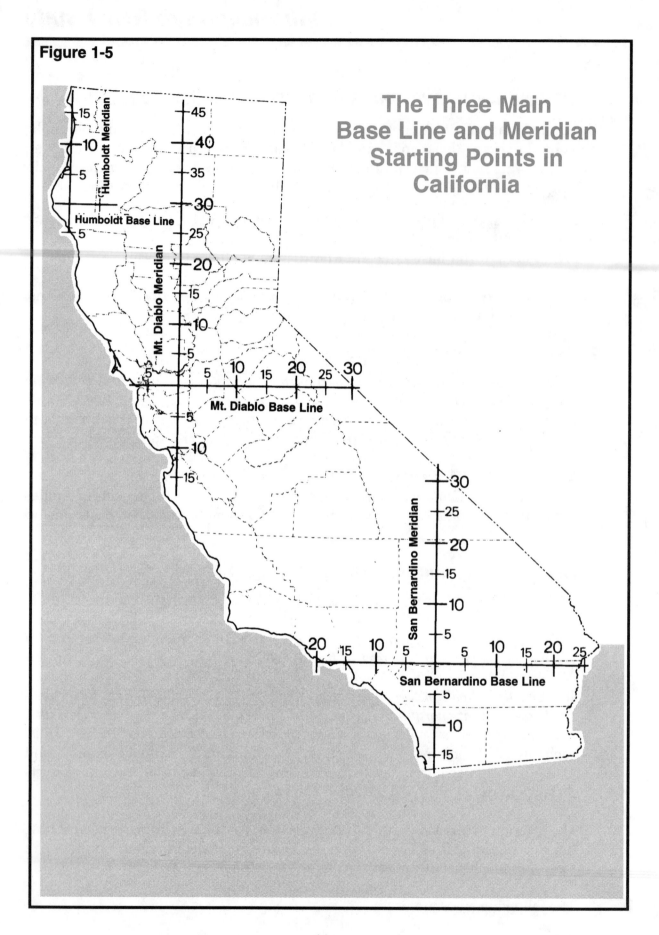

The Three Main
Base Line and Meridian
Starting Points in
California

Figure 1-6

TIERS, RANGES, AND TOWNSHIPS

				MERIDIAN LINE		Fig. 1-7	Tier 4 North	

(Diagram showing the grid of tiers, ranges, and townships)

Tier 4 North — Fig. 1-7
Tier 3 North
6 Miles x 6 Miles — Tier 2 North
Tier 1 North
San Bernardino — BASE LINE — Tier 1 South

Ranges labeled: Range 1 West, Range 1 East, Range 2 East, Range 3 East, Range 4 East

MERIDIAN LINE (vertical)

N (with north arrow)

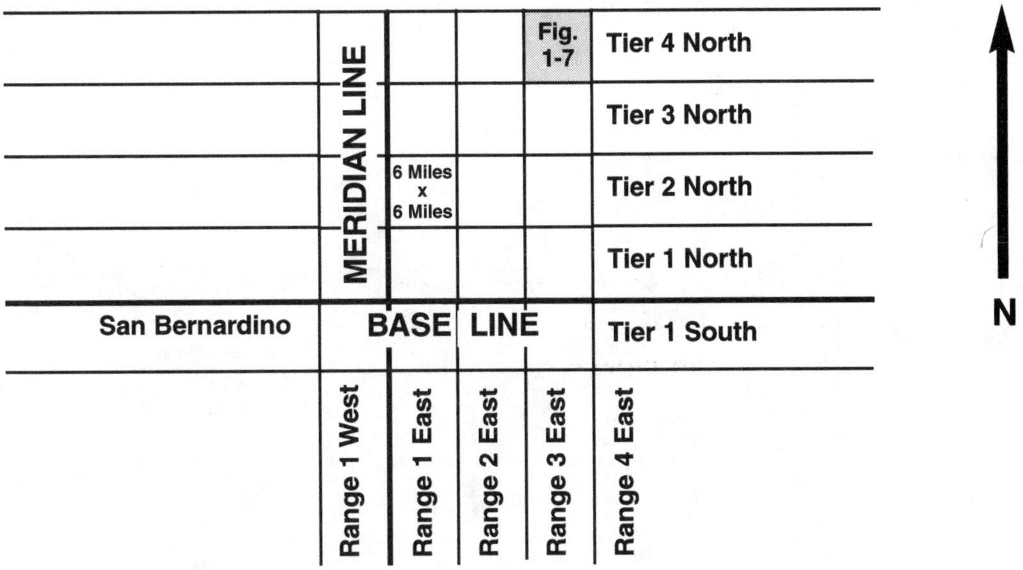

First, move east along the San Bernardino Base Line three ranges. This is the range located between the 2nd and 3rd range lines east of the San Bernardino Meridian. Second, move north from the San Bernardino Base Line four tiers (townships). This is the township located between the 3rd and 4th tier (township) lines north of the base line.

a. Reading Tier (Township) and Section Descriptions

The above description would be written:

T. 4N, R. 3E San Bernardino Base Line and Meridian.

In this form "R" represents the word range and "3E" tells you to move three ranges east of the meridian. Likewise, "T" means township, and "4N" tells you to go four townships (tiers) north of the San Bernardino Base Line.

To locate a property, work backwards on the description. When reading a description, read it from right to left. A verbal interpretation of our above description would read: "Starting from the San Bernardino Base Line and Meridian, go three ranges east and four townships north." You have located the township in which the property is located.

3. Sections (A Section is One Mile Square)

Each township is divided into 36 sections. A *SECTION is one mile square of land consisting of 640 acres.* There are 36 sections in a township.

A section contains 640 acres; 1/2 section, 320 acres; 1/4 section, 160 acres.

These sections are numbered in sequential order starting at the upper right-hand corner, as illustrated in **Figure 1-7**. Since each township is 6 miles square and consists of 36 sections, each section measures 1 mile square.

Figure 1-7

36	31	32	33	34	35	36	31
1	6	5	4	3	2	1	6
12	7	8	9	10	11	12	7
13	18	17	16	15	14	13	18
24	19	20	21	22	23	24	19
25	30	29	28	27	26	25	30
36	31	32	33	34	35	36	31
1	6	5	4	3	2	1	6

If we wanted to located section 29, the description would read:

Section 29, T. 4N, R. 3E San Bernardino Base Line and Meridian.

Each section measures one mile square and consists of 640 acres. A section can be broken down into halves or quarters. For example, the description for the northeast quarter of section 29 (**See Figure 1-8**) would read:

Figure 1-8   SECTION 29

| | | (NW ¼ NE ¼) | (NE ¼ NE ¼) |
| NORTHWEST QUARTER (NW ¼) 160 ACRES | | (SW ¼ NE ¼) | (SE ¼ NE ¼) |

(Figure table)

NORTHWEST QUARTER (NW ¼) 160 ACRES

(NW ¼ NE ¼) (NE ¼ NE ¼)
(SW ¼ NE ¼) (SE ¼ NE ¼)

WEST HALF OF SOUTHWEST QUARTER (W ½ SW ¼) 80 Acres

EAST HALF OF SOUTHWEST QUARTER (E ½ SW ¼) 80 Acres

40 Acres

10 Acres | 2½ Acres | 2½ Acres
| 2½ Acres | 2½ Acres
10 Acres | 10 Acres

40 Acres   40 Acres

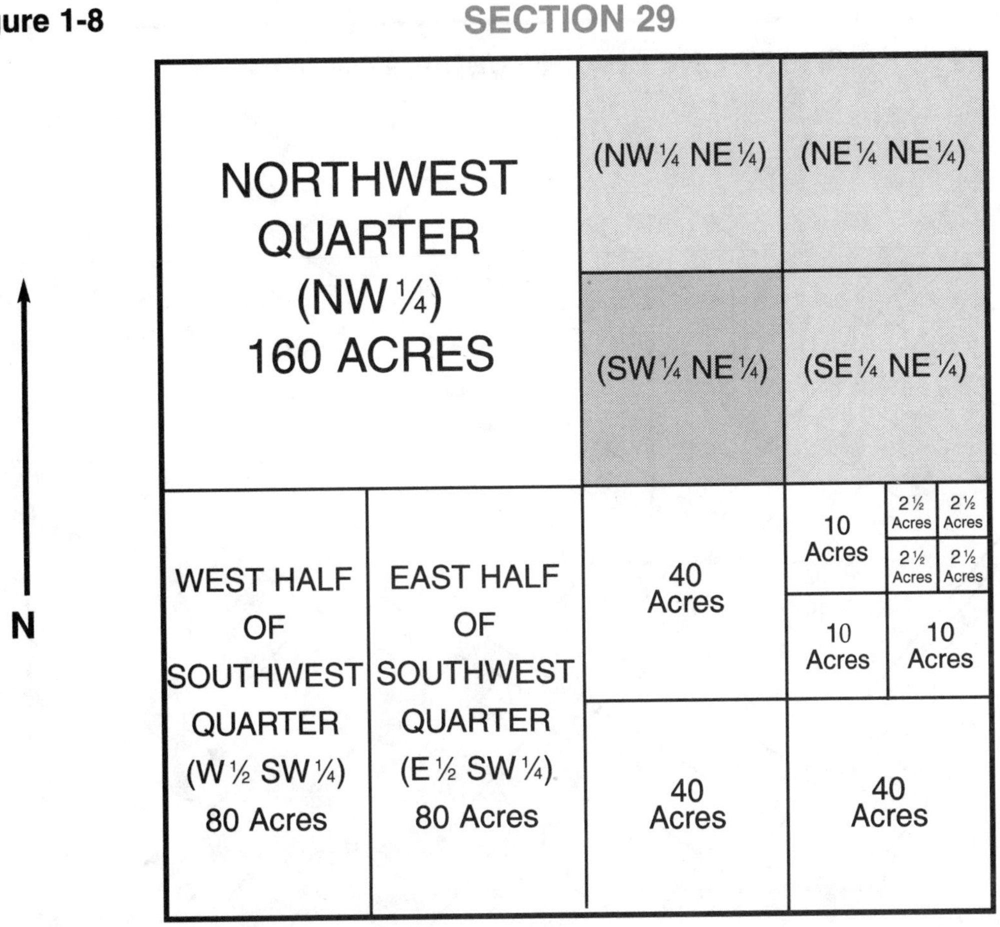

NE 1/4 of Section 29, T. 4N, R. 3E San Bernardino Base Line and Meridian.

That quarter can then be broken down further into halves or quarters. The description of the southwest quarter of the northeast quarter of section 29 would read:

SW 1/4 of the NE 1/4 of section 29, T. 4N, R. 3E San Bernardino Base Line and Meridian.

This procedure can continue until the property is completely described.

C. LOTS, BLOCKS, AND TRACTS (Recorded Subdivisions)

In California, subdivisions are granted by the Department of Real Estate. The subdivision map, however, is approved by the county or city in which the property is located. The approved subdivision map is recorded at the County Recorder's Office, and given a book and page number. Once it is recorded, all future transactions can be referenced to that map. *This subdivision map is also referred to as a PLAT MAP.* As an example, **Figure 1-9** is a description of a home located in Venice, California.

See **Figure 1-10** for a handy reference table and **Figure 1-11** for math problems.

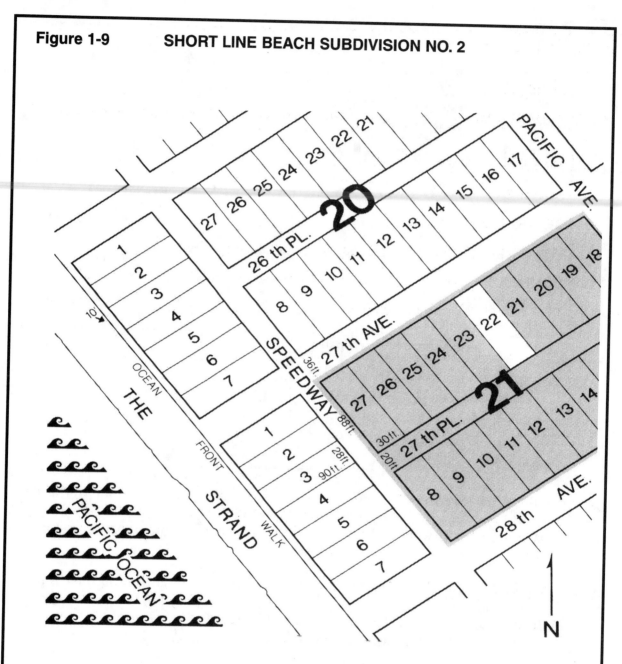

Figure 1-9   **SHORT LINE BEACH SUBDIVISION NO. 2**

LOT 22 in BLOCK 21 of *Short line Beach Subdivision No. 2, as per map recorded in Book 4, Page 42 of Maps, in the office of the County Recorder of Los Angeles.*

Figure 1-10   REFERENCE TABLE

One **ACRE** is 43,560 square feet.

One **SQUARE ACRE** is 208.71 feet on each side, but this number is generally rounded off to 209 feet.

One **MILE** is 5,280 feet long.

One **SQUARE MILE** contains 640 acres.

One **SECTION** is one square mile.

One **TOWNSHIP** (standard) is six miles square (36 square miles).

One **COMMERCIAL ACRE** is an acre minus any required public dedications.

One **ROD** is 16.5 feet long (5.5 yards).

V. California Facts

A. CALIFORNIA LAND

California, which is the largest state in population, is also one of the largest states in size with 101,803,000 acres. The Pacific Ocean touches over 840 miles of the California coastline, and the inland waterways account for 2,332 square miles of water. Nearly 45% of all the land (mostly National Forest and park land) in the state is owned by the Federal Government. Unfortunately, the federal government pays no taxes to the state, so California receives little compensation.

B. LAND OWNERSHIP

OWNERSHIP	ACRES	PERCENTAGE OF TOTAL
Federal	46,183,000	45%
State	3,125,000	3%
Local	2,059,000	2%
Private	50,436,000	**50%**
	101,803,000	100%

California, in recent decades, has become the most popular state. The Mediterranean climate has enticed millions to settle down in California. Because winters are mild for work or play, and because there is a great variety of lifestyles available, California will continue to be a magnet for the people of the United States and the World.

Figure 1-11

How Do You Find The Dimensions Of An Acre?

An **ACRE** is an area of land that contains 43,560 square feet. So if the area of a lot has more than 43,560 square feet, there is more than an acre of land. On the other hand, if there is less than 43,560 square feet in a lot it is smaller than an acre.

AREA is a definite amount of space within a shape. In America area is usually measured in square feet, but may also be measured in square yards or square meters in other parts of the world. Most test questions about area refer to a rectangular or square shape. The area of a rectangular or square shape is obtained by multiplying length x (times) width. The answer is in square feet. The area of a square lot 100 feet x 100 feet is 10,000 square feet.

Example (1): How many acres is a parcel of land that measures 330 feet by 660 feet?

Answer:

Area   = Length x Width
217,800 = 330 feet x 660 feet

Note: 1 acre = 43,560 square feet

$\dfrac{217,800}{43,560}$ = **5 ACRES** (Round if necessary)

Example (2): If an acre is divided into four equal lots, with each lot placed parallel to the other and having a depth of 240 feet, what is the width of each lot?

Answer:

Area   = Length x Width
43,560 = 240 feet (x 4 lots)   x   ? feet
43,560 = 960 feet   x   ? feet

$\dfrac{43,560}{960}$ = **45.375 feet wide (Round to 45.4 feet wide)**

See Chapter 15 (Math) for more problems.

C. CALIFORNIA IS NOW THE 5th LARGEST ECONOMY

California has a favorable future. We have the largest population in the United States and we're still growing! Because of our variable climate, California enjoys agricultural superiority, a thriving tourist trade and unchallenged status as the center of the entertainment industry. We also dominate in high technology, such as the computer industry. Our strategic trade position on the Pacific Rim gives us excellent access to such booming economic centers as Japan, Korea, Taiwan, Singapore, and Australia.

In 2003, the number of people living in California was 35 million. Population estimates forecast the following population trends:

By 2010, 40 million people, over 12% of the U.S. population (one in eight Americans), will live and play in California.

VI. SUMMARY

California was purchased by the United States from Mexico as part of the **Treaty of Guadalupe Hidalgo** in 1848, just weeks before the discovery of gold by John Sutter, and became a state on **September 9, 1850**. California's Legislature passed the nation's first real estate licensing law in 1917.

Simply stated, in order to sell, lease, or loan money on real estate owned by others, a license is required from the **California Department of Real Estate (DRE)**. A salesperson must work for a broker, both of whom must pass their respective state exams to be issued a license by the DRE. (See chapter 14 for more license details.) Commission rates are fully negotiable between broker and buyer/seller, with the broker responsible for paying his or her salespeople their part of any commissions.

Real property is generally immovable, passed by deed, and includes the right or interests in the 1) land; 2) anything permanently attached or affixed to the land; 3) anything incidental or appurtenant to the land; and 4) that which is immovable by law. Anything attached to the land, like fences, walls, etc., become real property when they are permanently incorporated or integrated in, affixed, or attached to the land (called **improvements**). Land ownership is not only the surface of the earth but the **air space** above it and that which is below, like **mineral rights**. Real property can be thought of as a **bundle of rights**, which includes the rights of possession, enjoyment, control, and disposition.

Personal property is movable, like a refrigerator or washing machine, but can include **emblements** (annually harvested crops) and some substances beneath the land, like oil and minerals when they have been removed from the land. Anything that is **appurtenant** to the land means it runs with the land and must be sold with the land. An example is stock in a mutual water company. (Water suitable for drinking is referred to as **potable water.**) **Title** to real property is passed with a **deed**, while title to personal property is passed with a **bill of sale.**

A **fixture** is an item of personal property that is attached to or incorporated into the land in such a way as to become real property. The courts use the **MARIA** method to determine if an item is a fixture: Method of attachment, Adaptability, Relationship of the parties, Intention, and Agreement. **Trade fixtures** are personal property used in the normal course of business, such as shelving or refrigeration units, which can be removed by tenants, who are responsible for any damage caused by their removal.

In California, every parcel of land must be properly described and identified. The three methods of identification include the Metes and Bounds method, the Section and Township method, and the Lots, Blocks, and Tracts method. **Metes and Bounds** is the method of identifying property in relationship to its boundaries, distances, and angles from a given starting point.

Sections and Townships are used in a government survey system used to identify public and private lands. This system uses base lines (running east and west) and meridian lines (running north and south), as well as defining townships (36 square mile sections of land, where each section is 640 acres). **Lots, Blocks, and Tracts** make up subdivisions, which are approved by the Department of Real Estate and the city, and then recorded on a **Subdivision Map** in the County Recorder's Office.

California is the most populated state in the nation, and one of the largest at 101,803,000 acres. Approximately 45% of the land is owned by the Federal Government (a huge amount considering they pay no taxes) and consists mostly of national forest and parkland. The state owns 3% of the land, city and counties own 2%, and only 50% is privately owned.

There are more than 35 million people living in California. This state is so big that it makes up 12.5% of the United States' population (one in eight live in California).

VII. TERMINOLOGY - CHAPTER 1

A. Acre
B. Admission Date
C. Air Space
D. Base Lines
E. Bill of Sale
F. Bundle of Rights
G. Chattel or Chattel Real
H. Commission

I. Condominium
J. Emblements
K. Fixtures
L. Meridian Lines
M. Metes and Bounds
N. Personal Property
O. Potable Water
P. Range

Q. Real Property
R. Riparian Rights
S. Rod
T. Section
U. Township
V. Trade Fixtures

1.____ A column of land six miles wide, determined by a government survey, running in a north-south direction, lying east or west of a principal meridian.

2.____ Personal property that has become permanently attached to the land or improvements that are legally treated as real property; examples: plumbing fixtures, or built in range, etc..

3.____ Personal property used in a business, attached to the property, but removable by the tenant.

4.____ A structure of two or more units where the interior air space of each unit is individually owned; the balance of land and improvements is owned in common by all the owners.

5.____ Imaginary north-south lines used in U.S. government surveys.

6.____ Property that is movable and not real property.

7.____ A written instrument that passes title of personal property from vendor (seller) to the vendee (buyer).

8.____ An amount, usually a percentage, paid to a broker as compensation for his or her services.

9.____ A legal description of land, setting forth all the boundary lines with their terminal points and angles.

10.____ All of the legal rights relevant to ownership of property including rights of use, possession, encumbering and disposition.

11.____ In the survey of public lands, a territorial subdivision six miles long, six miles wide and containing 36 sections, each one mile square.

12.____ Land, improvements, items permanently attached to the land, appurtenances and that which is immovable by law.

13._G_ A personal property interest in real property. An old term meaning personal property.

14.____ An area of land equaling 43,560 square feet, or a tract about 208.71 feet square.

15.____ The right of a landowner, whose land borders a stream or waterway, to use and enjoy the water, provided such use does not injure the rights of other owners.

16.____ A square of land (U.S. government survey) that contains 640 acres and is one mile square.

17.____ This old unit of measurement is 16 1/2 feet long (5.5 yards).

18.____ The reasonable space above a parcel or in a condominium; the cubic area of a space within the walls.

19.____ Imaginary east-west lines that intersect meridian lines to form a starting point for the measurement of land.

20.____ Water that is suitable for human consumption.

21.____ Crops (produced on leased land by a tenant farmer) from an annual cultivation considered personal property.

22.____ September 9, 1850.

Answers to the matching terminology are found on page 612.

VIII. MULTIPLE CHOICE

1. How many square miles are there in a section?

    a. 6

    b. 9

    c. 4

    d. 1

2. Which of the following are considered improvements?

    a. Buildings

    b. Fences

    c. Trees and shrubs

    d. All of the above

3. What percentage of California land is owned by the federal government?

    a. 2%

    b. 3%

    c. 45%

    d. 50%

4. The number of the section just below section one is:

    a. 7.

    b. 8.

    c. 12.

    d. 36.

5. A township is:

    a. 1 square mile.

    b. 6 square miles.

    c. 36 square miles.

    d. 640 acres.

6. California became a state on September 9,:

    a. 1825.

    b. 1849.

    c. 1850.

    d. 1878.

7.As long as it does NOT infringe on the rights of neighboring properties, landowners may claim a "riparian right" to what substance on, under or adjacent to his or her land?

    a. Water
    b. Silver
    c. Gold
    d. None of the above

8. Emblements are considered:

    a. annually cultivated crops by tenant farmers.
    b. designs on houses.
    c. transfer of ownership documents.
    d. none of the above.

9. The commission paid for the sale of a condominium is:

    a. 6%.
    b. 10%.
    c. set by law.
    d. fully negotiable.

10. The address posted on a property is the:

    a. legal address.
    b. common address.
    c. assessor's address.
    d. lot, block, and tract.

ANSWERS: 1. d.; 2. d.; 3. c.; 4. c.; 5. c.; 6. c.; 7. a.; 8. a.; 9. d.; 10. b

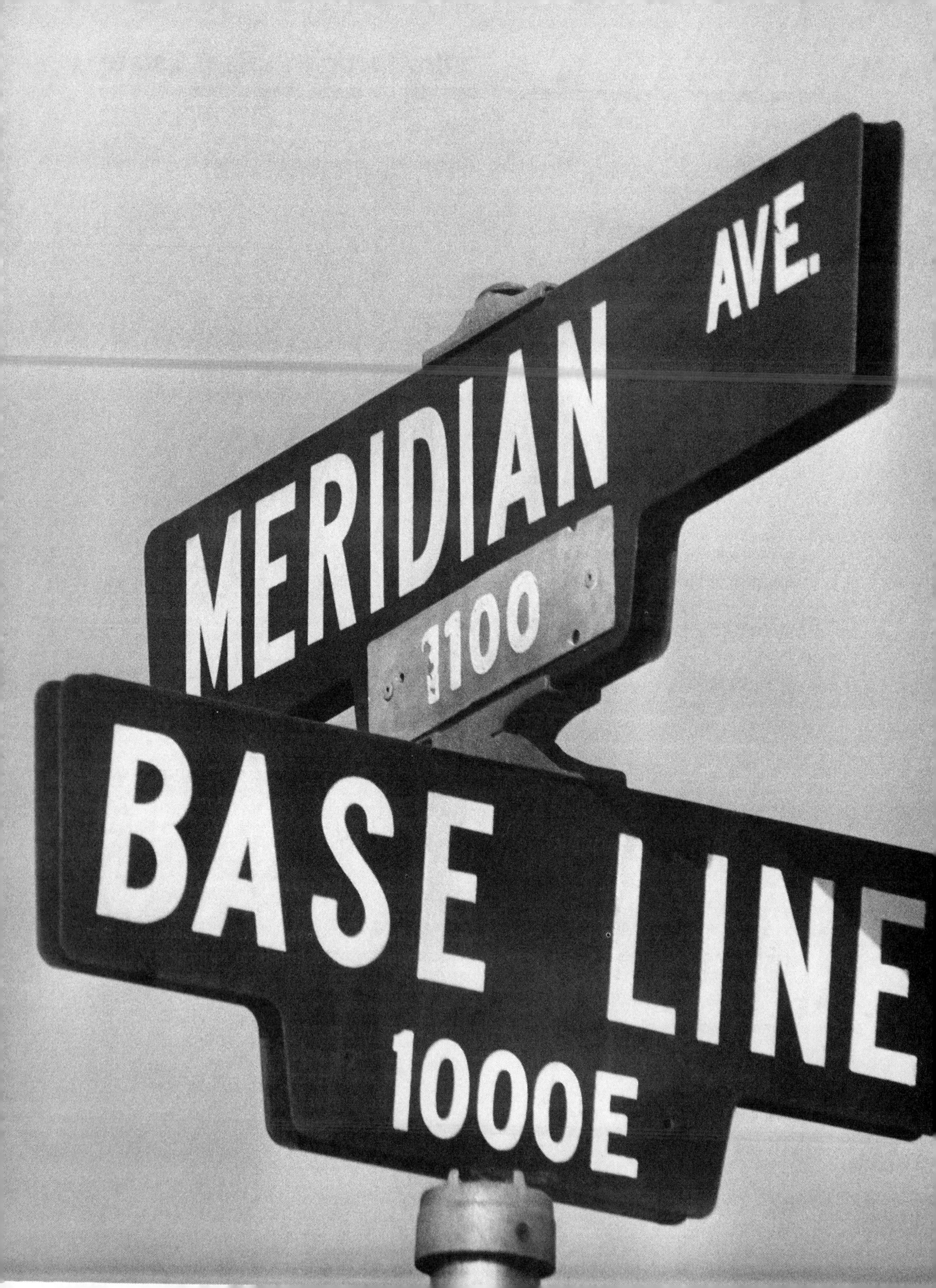
MERIDIAN AVE.
BASE LINE
1000E

Chapter 2
Estates, Transfers, and Titles

The previous chapter explained the differences between real and personal property. This chapter illustrates the types of estates (ownership) that you may have, the ways in which you can hold title and the methods of transferring real property.

I. Estate Ownership

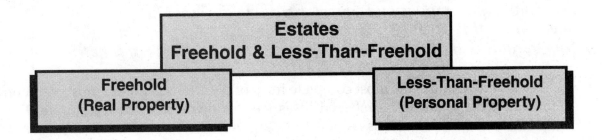

Estates
Freehold & Less-Than-Freehold

Freehold	**Less-Than-Freehold**
(Real Property)	**(Personal Property)**

A. ESTATES (OWNERSHIP)

*An **ESTATE** is an interest, share, right or equity in real estate that varies from the minimal right of a renter to the maximum right of a full owner.*

Estates are either **(1) freehold** or **(2) less-than-freehold**, depending upon the degree of ownership and the duration of interest. Freehold estates are real property and less-than-freehold estates are personal property. Less-than-freehold estates come with certain rights for the use of real property. **See Figure 2-1**.

Figure 2-1

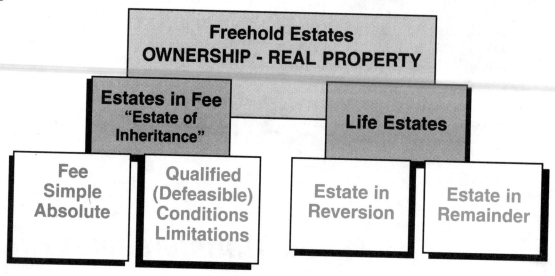

B. FREEHOLD ESTATE (Real Property)

Freehold estates are 1) fee simple estates or 2) life estates.

The two types of freehold estates are: 1) a fee simple estate or 2) a life estate. These freehold estates are the greatest degree of ownership you can have under the law.

Freehold estates receive title.

1. Estates in Fee

Fee simple (paramount and superior title) is the most interest (greatest) one can hold; it is of "indefinite duration" (perpetual), "freely transferable," and "inheritable" (referred to as an estate of inheritance).

A fee simple estate is the most complete form of ownership and the most common in California. This can be referred to as fee, fee ownership, or fee simple. *FEE SIMPLE means an owner has transferred all rights of a property to a new owner for an indefinite duration of time (perpetual).* All transfers are assumed to be fee simple unless the grant part of the deed limits, by the use of conditions, the property's use.

a. Conditions That Restrict a Fee Estate (Fee Simple Defeasible)

A *FEE SIMPLE DEFEASIBLE ESTATE (or qualified fee estate) is a fee estate that is subject to particular limitations imposed by the grantor of the estate.* **Breaking any**

condition of the transfer may be grounds for terminating or revoking the property transfer.

There are three categories of conditions: 1) condition precedent; 2) condition subsequent; and 3) determinable.

In the case of a *CONDITION PRECEDENT, title will not take effect until a condition is performed.* For example, a property owner will give the state a parcel of land on the condition that the state agrees to build a college on the site. If the state does not agree, the owner will not transfer the property.

A *CONDITION SUBSEQUENT gives the grantor the "right" to terminate the estate.* In other words, by stating that "if construction of the college has not started within five years, the property will revert to the grantor," the example becomes a condition subsequent.

A *FEE SIMPLE DETERMINABLE ESTATE determines the duration of the estate by the deed itself.* For example, the property owner can donate the parcel of land to the state "so long as" the land is used as a college campus. The key phrase is "so long as." If some other use is made of the land, it **automatically** reverts back to the grantor, or someone else named by the grantor.

A "fee simple defeasible estate" is an estate that can be defeated if a condition placed upon the estate is violated.

For example, if a person takes title subject to a condition that liquor NOT be served on the premises, and then turns around and breaks this promise, the previous title holder has grounds to reclaim title through a court action.

A fee simple defeasible estate, with a condition (precedent or subsequent) hanging over it, has less value than a fee simple estate.

In this chapter we have briefly discussed conditions, as in CC&Rs (Covenants, Conditions & Restrictions). For a more complete discussion of other types of private restrictions, please see Chapter 3.

2. Life Estate (Indefinite Period)

"Life" and "fee simple" are the two types of freehold estates.

A *LIFE ESTATE is an ownership interest in real property that only exists for the life of any designated person or persons (grantee).* The usual intent of this type of estate is to provide a lifetime residence for an individual. A life estate can be created by either a will or a deed.

A "life estate" is a freehold estate with a limited duration based upon someone's lifetime. This can be the lifetime of the person granting the estate or any other person so designated. The term "pur autre vie" refers to the "life of another."

When that designated person dies, the estate reverts back to the original owner. A person holding a life estate is free to lease the property to someone else, but this lease is also subject to the lifetime limitation. If the designated person dies, the estate ends and all rights, including any tenant rights, revert back to the original owner.

The owner of a life estate cannot grant more rights than he or she holds. A life estate may lease the property to someone, but the lease terminates when the life estate ends.

The life tenant usually has certain interests and obligations as long as the life estate is in effect. The life tenant:

1. has the right of physical possession of the property;
2. has the right to all rents and profits, but this terminates when the life estate holder dies;
3. can usually lease, sell or finance the property, but not beyond the time frame of the life estate;
4. is obligated to keep the property in good repair, although he or she is not required to make improvements;
5. may not damage or destroy any permanent part of the property to the detriment of succeeding interests; and
6. is usually responsible for all annual costs and expenses.

The property returns (reverts back) to the grantor when the life estate holder dies.

The party (grantor) granting a life estate is said to hold an **ESTATE IN REVERSION**.

If I give you a life estate, you hold "possession" for as long as you live. You can lease it out. However if you lease it out, the property interest is subject to how long you live. When you die, possession reverts back to me, or any specified person (estate in remainder).

If an owner granting a life estate names another person to receive title upon the death of the current life estate holder, that other person claims an **ESTATE IN REMAINDER**. The holder of an estate in remainder or estate in reversion has no right to the use and enjoyment of the property until the current life tenant dies.

An uncle deeds his property to his niece, but reserves the right to live in it until he dies. This is "reserving a life estate." Alway talk to a tax advisor before deeding over any property!

C. LESS-THAN-FREEHOLD ESTATES (No Title to Real Property) (A Leasehold is Personal Property)

LESS-THAN-FREEHOLD ESTATES are personal rights to the use of real property for a period of time. They are more commonly referred to as leases or rental agreements, which give tenants various rights to use real property for a specified period.

The lease or rental agreement is personal property because there is no true ownership in the property.

The tenant only has possession of the property. **See Figure 2-2**.

Figure 2-2

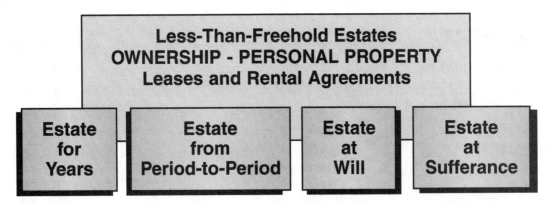

A lease is a less-than-freehold estate because it is for a definite period of time. The lease is the personal property of the lessee (renter).

1. Estate For Years

An *ESTATE FOR YEARS is a lease for a fixed period of time, agreed to in advance.* This period can be from a few days up to 99 years. No notice to terminate is necessary.

A "definite period of time," fixed in advance, from three hours at a wedding chapel to a 99-year lease, is called an estate for years.

2. Estate From Period-To-Period

An *ESTATE FROM PERIOD-TO-PERIOD is a renewable agreement to rent or lease a property for a period of time,* where the rental or lease amount is fixed at an agreed to sum per week, month, or year. A notice to terminate must be given. If annual rent is paid in advance and the tenant has been in possession for more than one year, a 60-day notice to vacate must be given.

3. Estate At Will

An *ESTATE AT WILL is a rental agreement that can be terminated by either party at any time,* although by California law, there must be at least a 60-day notice to vacate.

4. Estate At Sufferance

An **ESTATE AT SUFFERANCE** *occurs when the person renting or leasing a particular property remains after the expiration of the stated term.*

The four main types of less-than-freehold estates are explained in further detail in Chapter 6, "Landlord and Tenant."

II. Acquisitions and Transfers

"Acquisition" means to acquire, buy, or pull in, whereas "alienation" means to transfer, sell, or push away.

A. TRANSFERS

A sale is the means by which real estate is usually transferred. A sale is the most familiar way of transferring property, but it is not the only way. The seven basic ways to transfer real property are:

1. Deed	5. Accession
2. Will	6. Occupancy
3. Probate	7. Dedication
4. Intestate succession (no will)	

Figure 2-3 illustrates the six methods of transferring real property.

1. Transfer by Deed

The deed is NOT the title, but is "evidence" of the title.

The most common method of acquiring title to a property is by deed transfer. In California, **CONVEYANCE** *is the document used to effect the transfer of title to property*

Figure 2-3

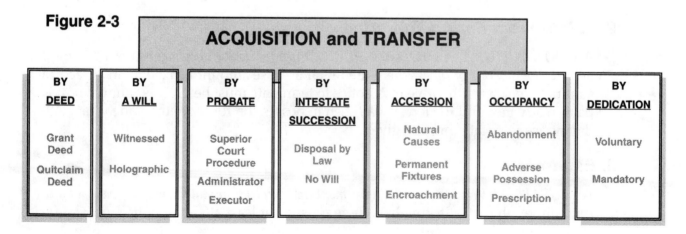

ACQUISITION and TRANSFER						
BY **DEED**	BY **A WILL**	BY **PROBATE**	BY **INTESTATE SUCCESSION**	BY **ACCESSION**	BY **OCCUPANCY**	BY **DEDICATION**
Grant Deed	Witnessed	Superior Court Procedure	Disposal by Law	Natural Causes	Abandonment	Voluntary
Quitclaim Deed	Holographic	Administrator	No Will	Permanent Fixtures	Adverse Possession	Mandatory
		Executor		Encroachment	Prescription	

from one person to another. This is usually accomplished by a simple written document known as a deed. A *DEED is a written instrument that conveys and evidences title.*

The *GRANTOR is the person who grants property or property rights (seller).* The *GRANTEE is the person to whom the grant is made (buyer).* A grantee cannot be a fictitious person (i.e., Batman or Catwoman), but it can be a person with a fictitious name (i.e., Microsoft, Inc.).

All deeds must have a "granting" clause (action clause). The grantor is the person transferring real property. Both grant deeds and quitclaim deeds are signed only by the grantor, at which time they are considered to be "executed."

There are two basic types of deeds: (1) grant deed and (2) quitclaim deed. All other deeds are versions of these two deeds.

A *GRANT DEED is a document that transfers title (evidence of property ownership),* with the key word being "grant." **See Figure 2-4.**

The grant (or warranty) aspect of the deed is a promise that:

a. The owner (grantor) has not conveyed title to the property to any other person (grantee).

b. The property is free of any encumbrances (liens or other restrictions) other than those already disclosed to the grantee. A grant deed also transfers any **after-acquired title,** meaning that rights obtained after the sale has been completed are also conveyed.

These warranties are part of the grant deed, although they are not written into the deed. They are called *IMPLIED WARRANTIES because they are not expressed in writing, but are present.*

Grant deeds contain "implied warranties" although they are NOT expressed in writing.

It should be noted that the grant deed does not necessarily give one all the rights to a property. Easements, rights of way, mineral rights, building restrictions and other types of restrictions may still restrict the use of the property.

A person who transfers title to real property is the grantor; therefore anyone who signs a grant deed or a quitclaim deed is a "grantor." The person receiving property is the "grantee."

Figure 2-4

RECORDING REQUESTED BY

320

827367

WHEN RECORDED MAIL TO

NAME Philip S. Dockter
Street Address 1212 Lincoln Avenue
City & State Pomona, California 91767

#61638

RECORDED IN OFFICIAL RECORDS
OF LOS ANGELES COUNTY, CALIF.
FOR TITLE INSURANCE & TRUST CO
MAY 19 1971 AT 8 A.M.

Registrar-Recorder

FEE $2 c

MAIL TAX STATEMENTS TO

NAME SAME AS SHOWN ABOVE:
Street Address
City & State

SPACE ABOVE THIS LINE FOR RECORDER'S USE

DOCUMENTARY TRANSFER TAX $33.00
...Computed on full value of property conveyed
...Or computed on full value less liens and encumbrances remaining at time of sale.
WILSHIRE ESCROW COMPANY
Signature of Declarant or Agent determining Tax. Firm name

Grant Deed

FOR A VALUABLE CONSIDERATION, receipt of which is hereby acknowledged,

HENRY W. SPLITTER, a widower, who acquired title as HENRY SPLITTER, does hereby

GRANT to   Philip S. Dockter , a single man,

the real property in the   City of Los Angeles   County of   Los Angeles
State of California, described as:

Lot 22 in Block 21 of Short Line Beach Subdivision No. 2, as per map recorded in Book 4 Page 42 of Maps, in the office of the County Recorder of said County.

RESERVING UNTO THE GRANTOR 50% of all oil, minerals, coals, petroleum, gas and kindred substances in and under said land, from a depth below 500 feet from the surface of said land, but without the right of entry of the surface thereof.

SUBJECT TO:
1. General and Special Taxes for the fiscal year 1971-72.
2. Covenants, conditions, restrictions, reservations, easements, rights and rights of way of record, if any.
3. Trust Deed to file concurrently herewith.

Dated   April 15, 1971

STATE OF CALIFORNIA
COUNTY OF   Los Angeles   }SS.
On   May 4, 1971   before me, the undersigned, a Notary Public in and for said State, personally appeared
Henry W. Splitter

_____, known to me
to be the person   whose name is subscribed to the within
instrument and acknowledged that he executed the same.
WITNESS my hand and official seal.

Signature _____

Donald R. Shewfelt
Name (Typed or Printed)

Henry W. Splitter

OFFICIAL SEAL
DONALD R. SHEWFELT
NOTARY PUBLIC — CALIFORNIA
PRINCIPAL OFFICE IN
LOS ANGELES COUNTY
My Commission Expires Aug. 17, 1971

(This area for official notarial seal)

320

MAIL TAX STATEMENTS AS DIRECTED ABOVE

A *QUITCLAIM DEED* is a deed that conveys all the present rights or interest that a person may have in a property, without any warranty, title, or interest.

A quitclaim deed can give absolute ownership or only such title as one may hold. If there is no ownership interest, then nothing can be acquired. Read the quitclaim deed in **Figure 2-5**. Note that there are no warranties; just the clause, I quitclaim. This deed is used primarily to clear a cloud on title from the records. A *CLOUD ON TITLE* is a claim, encumbrance or condition that impairs the title to real property until removed or eliminated, as, for example, through a quitclaim deed or a quiet title legal action. A *QUIET TITLE ACTION* is a court proceeding to remove a cloud on title to real property. It is usually a minor defect that requires a quitclaim deed before a title insurance company will clear the transfer. A quitclaim deed is often used in divorce actions, so that one party may have clear title.

Quitclaim deeds make NO "covenants" (promises); they guarantee nothing, only convey whatever rights the grantor may have.

A **VALID DEED** has all the following eight essential elements:

1. It must be in writing.
2. The parties must be properly described (grantee and grantor).
3. Grantor must competent to convey real property.
4. The property must be adequately described (need not be legal description).
5. There must be a granting clause (action clause).
6. It must be signed by the granting party (grantor).
7. The grantee must be capable of holding title to real property (living).
8. A deed does not take effect until it is delivered and accepted.

Some subtypes of grant or quitclaim deeds used in California are:

GIFT DEED—Granted as a gift of love and affection. No other consideration is necessary, but is void if given to defraud creditors.

TAX DEED—Given if property is sold as payment of past-due property taxes.

ADMINISTRATOR'S DEED OR EXECUTOR'S DEED—Given to the purchaser of the deceased person's real property.

SHERIFF'S DEED—Granted to the purchaser at a court-ordered sale.

TRUSTEE'S DEED—Given to the purchaser of property at a trust deed foreclosure sale.

GUARDIAN'S DEED—Used by a guardian to transfer the real property of minors or incompetents.

LAND PATENT—Used by the government to grant public land to an individual.

Figure 2-5

RECORDING REQUESTED BY

AND WHEN RECORDED MAIL THIS DEED AND. UNLESS OTHER-
WISE SHOWN BELOW. MAIL TAX STATEMENTS TO:

NAME
ADDRESS
CITY &
STATE
ZIP

Title Order No.   Escrow No.

—— SPACE ABOVE THIS LINE FOR RECORDER'S USE ——

Quitclaim Deed

The undersigned declares that the documentary transfer tax is $ .... and is
☐ computed on the full value of the interest or property conveyed, or is
☐ computed on the full value less the value of liens or encumbrances remaining thereon at the time of sale. The land, tenements or realty
is located in
☐ unincorporated area   ☐ city of ....

FOR A VALUABLE CONSIDERATION, receipt of which is hereby acknowledged,

do   . hereby remise, release and forever quitclaim to

the following described real property in the   county of
state of California:

Dated _____   _____

                                                _____

STATE OF CALIFORNIA   _____
                                    } SS
COUNTY OF _____   _____
On this the _____ day of _____ 19 ___, before me,
the undersigned, a Notary Public in and for said County and State,   _____
personally appeared _____
_____
_____
_____, personally known to me
or proved to me on the basis of satisfactory evidence to be the   ┌─────────────────────────────┐
person_____ whose name_____ subscribed to the within instrument   │   FOR NOTARY SEAL OR STAMP   │
and acknowledged that _____ executed the same.   │   │
                                                                      │   │
_____   │   │
        Signature of Notary   │   │
                                                                      └─────────────────────────────┘

MAIL TAX STATEMENTS TO PARTY SHOWN ON FOLLOWING LINE; IF NO PARTY SO SHOWN, MAIL AS DIRECTED ABOVE
_____
            Name   Street Address   City & State
SAFECO Stock No. **CAL-0011A**

36

TRUST DEEDS ARE LOANS, NOT DEEDS

A **TRUST DEED** *is a security device; it pledges real property as security for the payment of a loan.*

A trust deed is NOT a deed, but rather a conveyance; it gives legal (bare naked) title to a trustee with the power to sell.

A **RECONVEYANCE** *is a document granted by a trustee to clear a trustor's debt from the recorded title after a trust deed has been paid in full.* (See Chapter 8.)

A reconveyance deed is used to convey legal title to the borrower.

The following are the three basic methods of delivery.

1. *MANUAL DELIVERY is a direct transfer of the deed from the grantor to the grantee.*

2. *DELIVERY THROUGH RECORDING is the act of putting the title of record in the grantee's name at the county recorder's office.* The grantee must have agreed to the recording.

3. *CONDITIONAL DELIVERY requires that a specific event take place before title can be passed,* and must be passed through a third party.

A deed delivered by "grantor to grantee" with a condition involved is a manual delivery, NOT a conditional delivery, because there is no third party involved. Delivery and acceptance of the deed conveys title even if "intentional."

2. Transfer By Will (Testate)

A **WILL** *is a document, created by a person, stating how that person's property is to be conveyed or distributed upon his or her death.* It also leaves instructions as to the disposition of the body upon death. This is known as dying *TESTATE, which means having made and left a valid will.*

There are two types of wills that can legally dispose of real and personal property:

a. Witnessed will (typed)
b. Holographic will (handwritten)

A **WITNESSED WILL** *is a typed document usually prepared by an attorney, dated, signed by the property owners and declared to be a will by at least two witnesses (three signatures total).*

A *HOLOGRAPHIC WILL* is entirely handwritten by the owner, dated and signed. Since it is in the owner's own handwriting, no other formalities and no witnesses are required, unless the will is signed with an "X", in which case it must be witnessed.

A *CODICIL* is a change in a will before the maker's death.

A holographic will signed with an "X" must be witnessed.

Note: *A REVOCABLE LIVING TRUST is a trust that is effective during the life of the owner, rather than upon his or her death.* It can eliminate probate (to prove a will) cost and serve the same function as a will. The property is placed in a trust created for the heirs and may consist of both real and personal property. It is revocable at the discretion of the benefactor (owner), but becomes fully enforceable upon that person's death. There can be a considerable estate tax savings under this arrangement, depending on the size of the estate. At the very least, a revocable living trust protects the interests of everyone involved while avoiding the time and expense of probate. This type of trust is, however, rather complicated to set up, so an attorney specializing in this field should be consulted.

3. Transfer by Probate (Superior Court Approval)

PROBATE is a Superior Court procedure to determine a will's validity, any creditors' claims, and establish the identity of the beneficiaries. The first accepted offer must be for at least 90% of the court appraiser's evaluation. There are charges for the court probate action and fees for any related attorney costs.

After a person dies, an **administrator (male)** or **administratrix (female)** is appointed by the court to temporarily take possession of the property until probate is finalized. If the will has appointed a particular person to administer the estate, that person is known as an **executor (male)** or an **executrix (female)**.

When real estate is sold through probate, the amount of sales commission is determined by the court.

Note: *Wills and living trusts are legal devices for transferring property at death. To protect yourself, have an attorney draw up a will or living trust that reflects your desires, or leave your own handwritten (holographic) will.*

4. Transfer by Intestate Succession (No Will)

If there is no will, the procedure used for transferring the deceased's property to his or her heirs is called INTESTATE SUCCESSION. The law of intestate succession provides for the disposition of the property. The rules for dividing the property are complex and dependent upon the relationship of the kin.

Separate property: If the decedent leaves a spouse and one child, property is divided equally, 50-50. If there is a surviving spouse and two or more children, 1/3 to spouse and 2/3 to children. If no surviving spouse, property is divided equally among the children.

ESCHEAT is the term used if there is no will and there are no heirs; the property lapses to the state of California. This is not automatic. The state must wait **5 years** to make a formal request to claim the property.

Individuals do NOT acquire property by escheat; if there are NO heirs, it goes only to the state.

5. Transfer by Accession (Natural Causes)

ACCESSION occurs when an owner acquires title to additional land by natural causes, that is, additions to the property by natural growth. The addition to land from natural causes, such as earthquakes, volcanoes or the action of moving water is known as ACCRETION. For example, a river over time may slowly deposit soil on one of its banks. *These deposits of earth made through the natural action of water, called ALLUVIUM,* become the real property of the landowner who holds title to the river bank. *AVULSION is the sudden, violent tearing away of land by, for example, a river.* Title to that land is lost by the property owner.

Permanent fixtures attached to the land or buildings by residential tenants must be left with the building. Any improvements that are mistakenly placed on the property must also remain. *Placement of improvements and permanent fixtures on property that does not legally belong to the person who placed them is called ENCROACHMENT.*

6. Transfer by Occupancy

Ownership of real property, or the use of real property, can be gained through three types of occupancy:

  a. Abandonment
  b. Adverse Possession
  c. Prescription (by use)

a. Abandonment

ABANDONMENT is the relinquishing of a right or interest with the intention of never again reclaiming it. One cannot acquire title to abandoned real property without court action, but a landlord can acquire possession of a property that is left (abandoned) by a tenant simply by gaining full control of the property. In the case of a lease, a financially troubled tenant might negotiate a release or abandon the property, thereby forfeiting part of the deposit.

b. Adverse Possession

ADVERSE POSSESSION is acquiring title to another's property through continuous and notorious occupancy under a claim of title. It is the legal way to acquire title without a deed. Title may be obtained through adverse possession only if certain conditions are met:

1. **Property taxes** – The adverse possessor must have paid all taxes levied and assessed on the property for five consecutive years. (The owner may also be paying taxes.)

2. **Open and notorious occupancy** – The adverse possessor must live on, or openly use, the property in such a way that the titled owners might easily detect his or her presence.

3. **Uninterrupted use for five years** – The adverse possessor must use the property continuously for at least five consecutive years.

4. **Claim of title (color of title)**– The adverse possessor must have some reasonable claim of right or color of title (perhaps a defective written instrument) as a basis for his or her assertion. For example, a person could claim that his uncle gave the property to him before he died, but the deed is missing.

5. **Hostile** – The adverse possessor must possess the property hostile to the legal owner, without his or her permission or any rental payment (consideration).

NO fighting please, just confrontation in the legal sense.

The courts will require substantial proof before ruling there is adverse possession. To obtain marketable title, or before a title insurance company can insure a property, clear title must be obtained by a court decree. This essentially means that a "quiet title" action is brought in court to prove that all requirements have been fulfilled. In the peoples' interest, adverse possession is not possible against public or government lands, but only against privately owned lands.

c. Prescription

PRESCRIPTION is an easement, or the right to use another's land, which can be obtained through five years of continuous use. Its requirements are similar to those of adverse possession, the differences being that: by prescription, 1) only the use of the property has been obtained; and 2) taxes are still paid by the property owner; paying the property taxes is not a requirement for an easement by prescription.

Prescription is acquiring the "use" of a property, NOT the title. It is an easement.

7. Transfer by Dedication

DEDICATION is the gift (appropriation) of land, by its owner, for some public use. To be fully dedicated, the land must be accepted for such use by authorized public officials. Dedication may be either (1) voluntary or (2) mandated by statute.

A developer will "dedicate land" for a street to the city.

III. Title (Forms of Ownership)

A. TITLE

TITLE is the right to ownership of land and the evidence of that ownership. There are six distinct methods of holding title. **Figure 2-6** displays the six ways a person, or persons, may hold title to real property and whether a single title holder has the right to will or sell his or her share independent of the other owners. *VESTING is the placing of a person's (or persons') name on the deed and the description of the method by which that person will hold title.*

Figure 2-6 **Methods of Holding Title (Vesting) Concurrently or in Severalty**		
A SINGLE TITLE HOLDER	**WILL**	**SELL**
SEVERALTY	YES	YES
TENANCY IN COMMON	YES	YES
JOINT TENANCY	NO	YES
TENANCY IN PARTNERSHIP	NO	NO
COMMUNITY PROPERTY	YES	NO
COMMUNITY PROPERTY (w/ Right of Survivorship)	NO	NO

Vesting is the method by which one holds title. A deed to a fictitious name is valid; a deed to a fictitious person is void.

1. Severalty (Separate Ownership)

SEVERALTY is the sole and separate ownership of property by one individual or by a corporation. The word "severed" means to sever, to cut off or separate. The name severalty is misleading; it means single.

Title can be held by a corporation (legal person) or individual (natural person). Severalty means ownership by "only one."

Property held by corporations is owned in severalty, as if by a single individual. A **CORPORATION** *is a body of persons treated by law as a single "legal person," having a personality and existence distinct from that of its shareholders.* A corporation can go on forever; it does not die.

Examples to show ownership by severalty are:

as a natural person, a real person

"Mary Smith, a single woman"

or

"Mary Smith, an unmarried woman"

or as a legal person; charter granted by the state

"Urban Analysis Inc., a corporation"

Sometimes married people wish to keep ownership to certain properties as separate property (in severalty). They may then use the phrase:

"Mary Smith, a married women, as her sole and separate property"

or

"Jim Smith, a married man, as his sole and separate property"

2. Tenancy In Common

Two or more people hold ownership concurrently, with the right to individually possess, will, or sell. (Undivided, but not necessarily equal, interest.)

*When two or more people own property together with the right to will or sell it (however, without survivorship rights or community property rights), it is called **TENANCY IN COMMON.*** If there is no other agreement, they will each share an equal interest in the property. All tenants in common have "unity of possession," which means they each have the right to occupy the property. Often, the property is rented to one of the owners or to a tenant. Tenancy in common gives all owners a share of the income and expenses of the property. An example of the wording illustrating this would be:

"Jim Smith and Mary Smith, husband and wife, as tenants in common"

Each owner may sell or transfer his or her interest separately from the others. For example, if one of the four owners of a building was to sell his or her / interest, there would be no restrictions. More commonly, if one of the owners dies, his or her heirs will inherit a one-quarter interest in the property.

If the owners do not agree on the ownership or management, and persistent disagreements exist, it would probably be best to sell the property and divide the profits accordingly. If an agreement cannot be reached by the owners, a court of law will sell the property and decide what is best for all concerned. *When the courts have the responsibility of selling the property, it is referred to as a PARTITION ACTION.* It is obviously better for the owners to sell the property themselves, as attorney's fees and court costs would be involved. Furthermore, the court would probably sell the land at a lower price to expedite the sale.

3. Joint Tenancy

JOINT TENANCY occurs when two or more people have identical interests in the whole property with the same right of possession and the right of survivorship. If one of the joint tenancy owners should die, his or her interest is then split evenly with the surviving owners. Joint tenancy can never be willed.

Joint tenants have the right of "survivorship." A joint tenancy cannot be willed.

When a joint tenancy is established, there are four necessary unities (T-Tip):

    T **1. Title** — All owners are granted title by the same instrument.
    T **2. Time** — All owners obtain title at the same time.
    I **3. Interest** — All owners share an equal interest.
    P **4. Possession** — All owners have an equal right to possess the property.

To create joint tenancy, there must be intention by the owners. The deed must be in writing and contain the phrase:

"as joint tenants" or "in joint tenancy"

If it does not "state" that it is a joint tenancy, joint tenancy does not exist. Since this form of ownership is most common between married people, the usual phrase would read:

"Jim Smith and Mary Smith, husband and wife, as joint tenants"

If one of the parties should die, the property is automatically transferred to the remaining parties without having to go through the superior court procedure known as *PROBATE (to prove a will).* The transferred portion conveys the ownership and all debts on the property at the moment of death. Upon death, that debt does not transfer to the surviving joint tenants until it is foreclosed. Although probate costs may be avoided in joint tenancy, the surviving owners may end up paying higher income taxes later.

A lien placed on one joint tenant's interest does not sever a joint tenancy until the debt is foreclosed. Until then, surviving joint tenants are not liable to creditors of a deceased joint tenant.

A joint tenant can sell or transfer his or her ownership interest. Any portion of joint tenancy transferred or sold to a nonowner will bring the nonowner into tenancy in common with the other owners, who remain as joint tenants. If A, B and C own a property together and C sells his interest to D, then D gets only the tenancy in common interest with A and B (who continue to be joint tenants).

Because a corporation could, conceivably, go on forever, it is not permitted to enter into joint tenancies. Such a situation would give corporations an unfair survivorship advantage.

4. Tenancy in Partnership

TENANCY IN PARTNERSHIP refers to two or more people who are co-owners in a business. A GENERAL PARTNERSHIP is where the partners share all profits and losses and share management responsibilities. All partners must agree to a sale or transfer of real property. Each has a right to possess the partnership property. If a partner should die, his or her interest passes to any heirs who then have a right in the partnership, but not in any particular property. If an agreement cannot be reached with the heirs, the partnership may have to be dissolved.

The amount invested in a partnership need not be equal, but must be agreed upon mutually. The partnership agreement states the amount of money to be contributed by each, the duties of each, and sets the proportional distribution of profits or losses.

A *LIMITED PARTNERSHIP is one consisting of one or more general partners and limited partners.* A limited partner's losses are limited to the amount of his or her investment. A limited partner does not share management responsibilities.

5. Community Property

COMMUNITY PROPERTY refers to all the property acquired by a husband and wife during their marriage. California is a community property state, which means that any property acquired during a marriage is shared equally. This practice is derived from Spanish law and became incorporated into our legal system when California was a part of Mexico. Both husband and wife must sign all transfer documents to convey community real property. If only one spouse signs a transfer document, the "injured" spouse could void the sale within a one-year period. **Salespeople should make certain that both husband and wife sign all real estate documents such as listings, deposit receipts and escrow instructions if the property being transferred is community property. Both signatures are required when selling, borrowing money, or leasing community property for more than one year.**

The right to manage the community property is shared by both the husband and wife. Each can will his or her respective half to whomever they wish. If there is no will, the half belonging to the deceased would go to the surviving spouse. If willed to an heir, the heir and the remaining spouse would then be tenants in common.

Community property (husband and wife) vesting has equal interest.

Debts can become a liability if they are incurred after marriage. Debts incurred by either spouse before marriage cannot be converted to the debts of the community property. The law also allows some community property to be transferred without going through probate. Questions about debts or probate should be directed to an attorney, as this issue is quite complex.

Any property obtained by either the husband or wife before marriage may remain as separate property. Both may inherit or receive gifts of property, which can remain as separate property. **However, any proceeds from the property held separately, such as rents or profit, cannot be commingled with community property, as this would cause them to become community property**.

Do NOT advise a buyer how to hold title—that is giving legal advice. However, you can explain the different ways to take title. How a person holds title has a big impact upon income tax planning and estate planning.

6. Community Property With Right of Survivorship

The California legislature enacted legislation which allows married couples in California to hold title to real and personal property as "community property with right of survivorship." *COMMUNITY PROPERTY WITH RIGHT OF SURVIVORSHIP transfers ownership to the spouse at death, with income tax benefits.* The goal of the legislation was to combine the right of survivorship benefit of joint tenancy with the favorable tax status of community property under federal tax law. The survivorship benefit allows title to pass to the surviving spouse at the death of one spouse. The surviving spouse also gets the benefit of a stepped up basis for 100% of the property upon the death of a spouse. The surviving spouse may use an affidavit of death of spouse to satisfy title company underwriting requirements to convey or encumber title. Probate proceedings are not necessary to transfer title to the surviving spouse.

IV. Recording and Acknowledgment

A deed does NOT have to be "acknowledged" or "recorded" to be valid, although it is wise to do both.

A. RECORDING

RECORDING is the legal process of making an instrument an official part of the records of a county, after it has been acknowledged. Instruments that affect real property are legal

documents, such as deeds, mortgages, trust deeds, leases and contracts of sale. Recording gives constructive notice of the existence and content of these instruments to the public.

CONSTRUCTIVE NOTICE *is notice presumed by law to have been acquired by a person and thus imputed to that person.* Any recorded notice that can be obtained from the county recorder's office can be considered constructive notice (and therefore public knowledge).

The first to possess or record (without notice of the rights of others) gets the property.

ACTUAL NOTICE *is knowing (or one's responsibility for knowing) that a transaction has taken place.* If you have found, for example, that someone other than the owner is living in a house you are buying, you should have been aware of the existence of a signed lease. This is actual notice, whereas public records are representative of constructive notice. The act of taking possession (holding an unrecorded deed) gives constructive notice.

The recording process is a privilege rather than a legal requirement. **Some documents have to be recorded to be valid. These include mechanic's liens and declarations of homestead.** You may record an acknowledged instrument at any time. However, failure to utilize the privilege of recording at the earliest possible date can result in a question of legal or rightful title. **If the same property is sold to more than one party, the individual who has recorded first will usually be recognized as the rightful owner.** Therefore, time of recording is very important to a bona fide purchaser who is protected only if he or she records first.

If there are NO prior arrangements, such as a subordination clause, the deed having priority is the one recorded first (so long as the owner had no constructive or actual notice of the rights of others).

In order to establish priority, the documents affecting real property must be recorded by the county recorder in the county where the property is located. If the property is located in two counties, it should be recorded in both counties.

B. PRIORITY OF RECORDING

Under the recording system in California, "The first in time is the first in right." If an owner sells his or her house twice, the first deed recorded would be considered the valid deed. This person must not have knowledge of the rights of the other party. This is the reward granted in California for recording any real estate transaction. However, there are four exceptions to the rule that protects a person from later recordings. They are:

1. Government liens, property taxes and special assessments
2. Actual or constructive notice of another person's prior rights

www.finance.saccounty.net/ccr/

DEPARTMENT OF FINANCE
COUNTY CLERK-RECORDER
County of Sacramento Web Site ... www.saccounty.net

Craig A. Kramer, Assistant County Clerk-Recorder

The mission of the County Clerk-Recorder is to serve as custodian of public records and recorder of real property documents for Sacramento County, and to issue and register marriage licenses, notaries public, vital statistics, and other public documents while providing the highest level of courtesy, efficiency, and cost-effective service to all customers.

Program Description:

▶ Serves as custodian of public records.
▶ Issues and registers marriage licenses.
▶ Registers notaries public.
▶ Receives, verifies, and records documents regarding land ownership, vital statistics, and various other public documents.

▶ Search of Previously Recorded Document Index

3. Mechanic's liens
4. Agreements to the contrary

C. ACKNOWLEDGMENT (or Notary)

All documents must be acknowledged before they are recorded by the county recorder. *ACKNOWLEDGMENT refers to a signed statement by the named person that he or she has signed that document of his or her own free will, in other words, that person "acknowledges" his or her signature.* This acknowledgment must be performed in the presence of a witness, usually a notary public, authorized by law to witness acknowledgments.

A deed does NOT have to be acknowledged to be valid, but must be acknowledged to be recorded.

A *NOTARY PUBLIC is a person who is authorized by the Secretary of State to witness the acknowledgment of documents.* All notarized documents must be stamped with a notary seal. The seal must contain the following information:

1. The word "Notary Public"
2. The name of the county
3. The name of the notary
4. The state seal
5. The expiration date

Any person signing a **grant deed**, **quitclaim deed** or **trust deed** is required to place a right thumb print on the notary's sequential journal. This is because of a high rate of fraud by the use of false deeds. Additionally, a notary must immediately notify the Secretary of State if the notary's sequential journal is stolen, lost, misplaced, destroyed, damaged or otherwise rendered unusable.

State, county, city or district officers and their deputies may also acknowledge a document. They include: court clerks, county clerks, court commissioners, municipal judges and county recorders.

VERIFICATION is an oath or affirmation made before a notary public that the content of an instrument is true. Notices of completion, non-responsibility and the statements used in filing a mechanic's lien are among instruments that must be verified rather than simply acknowledged.

An *AFFIRMATION is a solemn and legally binding declaration made by a person whose religious or other beliefs prohibit the taking of an oath.*

An *AFFIDAVIT is a written statement of circumstances, submitted under verification.*

D. DO NOT GIVE LEGAL ADVICE

A real estate salesperson or broker may not give legal advice, as the law is a highly complex and specialized profession that requires years of preparation and training. In the state of California, only a licensed attorney who is a member of the State Bar is allowed to practice law. A broker cannot give legal advice, unless he or she is also an attorney, and must realize the truth in the saying:

"A man who is his own lawyer has a fool for a client."

Uniform Electronic Transactions Act
(Record Retention)

A real estate broker who obtains documents in any transaction for which a real estate broker license is required, when such documents contain an electronic signature pursuant to the Uniform Electronic Transaction Act, must retain a copy of such documents by: 1) Causing a paper copy of the document to be made or 2) By using electronic image storing media. The broker may retain copies of such documents at a location other than the broker's place of business.

RE AD

What appears to be a minor difficulty can often be the tip of the iceberg of concealed hazards. Any legal advice, counsel or preparation of legal instruments must, therefore, be handled by an attorney. An enterprising broker should establish a relationship with a local attorney specializing in real estate. If any problems arise, they can be cleared up in the shortest time possible to facilitate the sale.

It is illegal for an agent, except an attorney, to draw up legal documents. For this reason, real estate brokers use preprinted fill-in forms. These standard forms are drawn up by licensed attorneys who are familiar with the legalities involved in contracts.

V. SUMMARY

An **estate** is an interest, share, right or equity in real estate, and can be either **freehold** (real property) or **less-than-freehold** (personal property). A freehold estate includes fee estates or life estates.

A **fee simple** is the most complete form of ownership as it is of indefinite duration, freely transferable, and inheritable. If a **precedent** (before) or **subsequent** (future) condition is attached to a property's use, it is a **fee simple defeasible estate**.

A **life estate** is a freehold estate with a limited duration based upon someone's lifetime, with the property reverting back to the original owner (who holds an **estate in reversion**) upon the death of the life estate holder. If someone other than the owner is to receive title, that person is said to hold an **estate in remainder**.

A property owner may reserve a life estate for the duration of his or her lifetime. Although the estate is deeded to a designated party, he or she doesn't take possession until the death of the owner.

A **lease** or **rental agreement** is a less-than-freehold estate, where the tenant is given rights to use the real property for a period of time. It's personal property because no real ownership exists. An **estate for years** is a lease for a fixed period of time, agreed to in advance. Other less-than-freehold estates include **estates from period-to-period**, **estates at will**, and **estates at sufferance**.

Property can be sold or transferred by: 1) **deed** (grant deed transfers title), 2) **will** (witnessed or holographic), 3) **probate** (after death through the courts), 4) **intestate succession** (no will, divided among family or state), 5) **accession** (land increases through natural causes), 6) **occupancy** (**abandonment, adverse possession**, and **prescription**), and 7) **dedication** (gift to public).

A **grant deed** is a document that transfers title (evidence of the right to possess property). The method (tenancy) under which you hold that title is called **vesting**. The methods of **tenancy** include **severalty, tenants in common, joint tenancy, tenancy in partnership, community property,** and **community property with right of survivorship**.

Although severalty means separate ownership, title can be held by an individual or a corporation and can be willed or sold. When two or more people own property concurrently, it is called a **tenancy in common,** and it too can be willed or sold (although there are no survivorship or community property rights).

If there is the right of survivorship it is called **joint tenancy,** and that title cannot be willed. The four unities for joint tenancy are: 1) **title**, 2) **time**, 3) **interest**, and 4) **possession** (Remember: "T-TIP").

Tenancy in partnership refers to two or more people who are co-owners in a business, and can be a **general partnership** (losses and management duties shared) or **limited partnership** (losses limited and no management duties).

Community property refers to all the property acquired by a husband and wife during their marriage, and it can be willed, but if no heir exists, it goes to the remaining spouse. **Community property with right of survivorship** allows the property to pass to the surviving spouse without probate administration, and the property will receive a full step-up basis, which means no capital gains tax to the surviving spouse if the property is sold.

All deeds must be **acknowledged** (witnessed by a notary public) to be recorded, and are not valid unless recorded with the county. **Generally, the deed recorded first has priority over any that follow.**

VI. TERMINOLOGY - CHAPTER 2

A. Abandonment
B. Accession
C. Actual Notice
D. Adverse Possession
E. Affirmation, Affidavit, Verification
F. Community Property
G. Condition Precedent
H. Condition Subsequent
I. Constructive Notice
J. Corporation
K. Dedication

L. Delivery
M. Encroachment
N. Escheat
O. Freehold Estate
P. General and Limited Partnerships
Q. Grant Deed
R. Holographic Will
S. Intestate Succession
T. Joint Tenancy
U. Life Estate
V. Notary Public

W. Prescription
X. Probate
Y. Quitclaim Deed
Z. Recording
AA. Remainder
BB. Reversion
CC. Severalty
DD. Tenancy in Common
EE. Witnessed Will

1.____ The giving of private land by its owner for a public use; most commonly, the developer who gives it to a city.

2.____ The reverting of private property to the state when there are no valid heirs.

3.____ A voluntary association between two or more people to carry on a business with general and limited partners.

4.____ A deed using the word "grant," or like words, containing warranties against prior conveyances and encumbrances. This is the most commonly used deed in California.

5.____ An estate of indeterminable duration, e.g., fee simple or life estate.

6.____ Undivided ownership of a property interest by two or more persons, each of whom has a right to an equal share in the interest and a right of survivorship.

7.____ It is notice that is actually and expressly given or implied.

8.____ A person authorized by the state to witness the signatures of persons executing documents, sign the certificate and affix the official seal.

9.____ An event that must happen before title is passed.

10.____ Documents filed with the County Recorder in such a way as are considered open notice to the world.

11.____ Co-ownership of property by two or more persons who hold undivided interest, without right of survivorship. The interests need not be equal.

12.____ An unlawful intrusion onto another's property by making improvements to real property, e.g., a swimming pool built across a property line.

13.____ A legal entity, sanctioned by the state, with rights and liabilities, distinct and apart from those of the persons composing it.

14.____ The intentional and voluntary relinquishment of any ownership interest (such as an easement) or possession of real property.

15.____ The means of acquiring interests in land, usually an easement, by continued use.

16.____ A condition attached to an estate whereby the estate is defeated or changed through the failure or non-performance of the condition.

17.____ A process of law by which the state lays out the correct succession of inheritance when a person dies without leaving a valid will.

18.____ Many different types of statements made before a professional witness.

19.____ An estate that reverts back to the grantor after the life of the tenant expires.

20.____ The court procedure of proving that a will is valid.

21.____ A method of acquiring title to real property, through possession of the property for a statutory period under certain conditions, by a person other than the owner.

22.____ A deed to relinquish any interest in property, which the grantor may have, without any warranty of title or interest.

23.____ An estate that is transferred to a third party (anyone other than the grantor) upon the death of the life estate holder.

24.____ A formal expression of a person's desires, witnessed by others, as to the disposition of his or her property after death.

25.____ Property acquired by husband and/or wife during marriage that is not acquired as separate property. Each spouse has equal rights of management, alienation and disposition.

26.____ An estate of a single entity held by a single person alone.

27.____ An estate or interest in real property that is held for the duration of the life of some certain person. It may be the person holding title to the estate or some other person.

28.____ A handwritten expression of a person's desires as to the disposition of their property after death.

29.____ Placing a document in the official records of the county.

30.____ The act of receiving a deed.

31.____ The acquiring of additional property.

VII. MULTIPLE CHOICE

1. The most complete form of land ownership is:

    a. fee, simple, absolute estate.
    b. estate for years.
    c. estate at will.
    d. none of the above.

2. The two types of freehold estates are:

    a. life estate and estate at will.
    b. fee simple and life estate.
    c. fee simple and estate for years.
    d. fee qualified and estate at will.

3. A lease for a fixed period of time, agreed to in advance and requiring NO notice of termination is called a (an):

    a. estate for years.
    b. estate from period-to-period.
    c. estate at sufferance.
    d. perpetual estate.

4. A lease for a period of time that is renewable and requires a notice of termination is called a (an):

    a. life estate.
    b. estate for years.
    c. estate from period-to-period.
    d. estate in reversion.

5. A grant deed must be signed by:

    a. the grantee.
    b. both the grantor and grantee.
    c. neither if the grantee takes possession.
    d. the grantor of the property.

6. A holographic will that is signed with an "X":

    a. is not legal.
    b. must be reviewed by an attorney.
    c. requires no other formalities to be legal.
    d. must be witnessed.

7. A legal way to acquire title without a deed is through:

   a. adverse possession.
   b. prescription.
   c. encroachment.
   d. dedication.

8. Smart, Black, and Curtis have a joint tenancy. Curtis sells his interest to Jones. A short time later, Smart dies. What method of holding title do Black and Jones have?

   a. Joint tenancy
   b. Tenancy in common
   c. Tenancy in partnership
   d. Severalty

9. Frank and Margaret Sharp purchased an income producing property through broker Finch. The Sharps asked Finch how they should hold title. Finch suggested they hold title as tenants in common. Finch's advice is:

   a. legal as long as the buyers asked him.
   b. legal as long as community property is not involved.
   c. legal if Finch is a member of NAR.
   d. against the law; Finch is not an attorney.

10. Frank is a life estate holder. He leases the property to Mary for a five-year period. After two years of the lease, Frank dies. The original grantor orders Mary to move out. Mary's lease was:

   a. not legal to begin with.
   b. legal and valid until Frank's death.
   c. legal and valid for the full five years.
   d. valid only if confirmed by the administrator of the deceased's will.

ANSWERS: 1. a; 2. b; 3. a; 4. c; 5. d; 6. d; 7. a; 8. b; 9. d; 10. b

THE MIND

Chapter 3
Encumbrances

I. Encumbrances – An Overview

An encumbrance burdens the property (affects or limits title) by either:

1) money owed (liens) or
2) items that affect the physical use of the property (non-money).

The term encumbrance is usually new to the beginner in real estate. An **ENCUMBRANCE** *is a right or interest in real property other than an owner or tenancy interest.* It is a burden to the property that limits its use and may lessen its value. The two main types of encumbrances, shown in **Figure 3-1** and **Figure 3-3**, are: (1) liens and (2) items that affect the physical condition or use of the property. All liens are encumbrances but not all encumbrances are liens.

An encumbrance affects the fee simple title; all liens are "encumbrances" but NOT all encumbrances are liens.

When an owner encumbers more than one lot under a single lien, that owner has created a blanket encumbrance. A **BLANKET ENCUMBRANCE** *is a voluntary lien (money owed) placed over more than one parcel.* A **RELEASE CLAUSE** *releases portions of the property.*

Figure 3-1

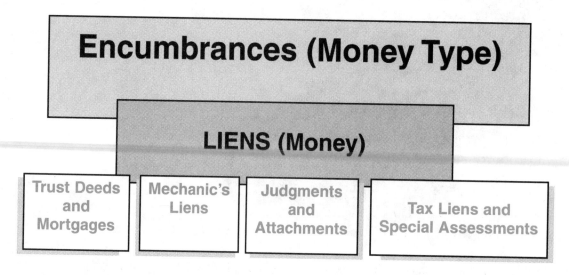

Encumbrances (Money Type)

LIENS (Money)

| Trust Deeds and Mortgages | Mechanic's Liens | Judgments and Attachments | Tax Liens and Special Assessments |

A blanket encumbrance (one lien on several properties) usually has a "release clause" so that one or more of the parcels can be released under certain conditions.

II. Liens (Money Owed)

Liens ("money owed") are money encumbrances.

A **LIEN** *is a document that uses a property to secure the payment of a debt or the discharge of an obligation.* It is money owed for one reason or another on a property. Liens include trust deeds or mortgages, tax liens, special assessments, mechanic's liens, judgments, attachments and bankruptcies.

Liens are either:

1. voluntary or
2. involuntary; and
3. specific or
4. general

A. VOLUNTARY AND INVOLUNTARY LIENS

VOLUNTARY LIENS are money debts that an owner agrees to pay. A lien is created when the buyer takes out a loan to finance the purchase of real estate. He or she voluntarily agrees to pay for the money borrowed.

INVOLUNTARY LIENS are money obligations that create a burden on a property by government taxes or legal action because of unpaid bills. Both involuntary liens and voluntary liens must be paid, or assumed, in full before the owner can sell or refinance the property.

Liens are encumbrances against a property that can be either 1) voluntary or 2) involuntary.

B. SPECIFIC AND GENERAL LIENS

SPECIFIC LIENS are liens against just one property. Property taxes assessed against real property automatically become a specific lien on only that property on July 1st of each year.

GENERAL LIENS are liens on all the properties of the owner, not just one. Federal or state income taxes and judgment liens can become a general lien on all your real property.

C. TRUST DEED (Security Device – Voluntary and Specific)

A *TRUST DEED is a written instrument that makes real property collateral for a loan.* The evidence of debt is created by the promissory note that accompanies the trust deed. The trust deed pledges (hypothecates) the property as collateral, or security, for the note. In California, the trust deed is the usual security device for real property. In eastern states, the mortgage is the typical financing instrument. See Chapter 8 for details on trust deeds.

Trust deeds and mortgages are security devices that make property security for the debt. The accompanying promissory note is the evidence of the debt. Trust deeds and mortgages are personal property as well as examples of voluntary liens; therefore, a lien can be created by recording.

D. MORTGAGE (Security Device – Voluntary and Specific)

A *MORTGAGE is a lien that secures real property for the payment of a promissory note (debt).* Mortgages are rarely employed in financing California homes, but because of their wide use in other states, they are emphasized in the real estate licensing examination. In California many people use the term "mortgage" to mean a property loan, but they usually are talking about trust deeds. Therefore, it is essential to understand the difference between mortgages and trust deeds since almost every property transfer in California is financed through a trust deed. Details on mortgages are discussed further in Chapter 8.

Mortgages are covered on the state DRE exam, but are rare in California.

E. MECHANIC'S LIENS (Involuntary and Specific)

MECHANIC'S LIENS *are liens that may be filed against a property by a person who was not paid after furnishing labor or materials for construction work on that property.* The form used to enforce a mechanic's lien action must be recorded to be effective. A mechanic's lien is a lien against the property itself. The property cannot be transferred until the obligation is paid and the title cleared. This gives a subcontractor, craftsman or general contractor, employed by an owner, the right to protect his or her interest. The same right applies to material suppliers who furnish such items as lumber, plumbing or roofing supplies. To determine the start time, the mechanic's lien dates back to the commencement of the project (see below).

A mechanic's lien is filed (recorded) against an individual's property; it is a specific (one property) and involuntary lien. If unpaid, architects, pool repair companies, plumbers, and truck drivers (among others) can file mechanic's liens on a property.

1. Preliminary Notice (To Protect Your Rights)

A **PRELIMINARY NOTICE** *is a written notice that must be given before filing a mechanic's lien and within 20 days of supplying labor or services.* This notice must be given, either by mail or in person, to the owner, general contractor and the lender. The notice must contain a general description of the labor or materials furnished, who supplied them and the person who contracted for these services. Failure to give the preliminary notice within 20 days does not restrict a supplier's right to file, but he or she may have allowed other claimants to file before him or her, which gives those claimants priority. As a matter of good practice, most suppliers include a preliminary notice as part of the original contract.

Lenders want to be first in priority.

2. Determining the Start Time for Mechanic's Liens

An important determination, when considering a mechanic's lien, is **the date that work started**. Mechanic's liens, once recorded, have priority over all other liens except taxes, special assessments and trust deeds. To lenders, this is critical because lenders want their trust deeds recorded before any work starts. Before they will lend money, lenders will conduct a physical inspection of the property to make sure no construction has started.

A mechanic's lien must be recorded to become effective.

A mechanic's lien (labor or materials) dates back to the beginning (commencement) of work on the project. This is known as the SCHEME OF IMPROVEMENTS.

3. Notice of Completion and Cessation (Limits Time to File)

A "Notice of Completion" (Shown in **Figure 3-2**), in order to be valid, should be recorded by the owner within 10 days of completion, thereby limiting the original contractors to 60 days to file a claim and all others to 30 days. This gives everyone constructive notice. Completion technically occurs when the owner accepts the finished work of the contractor, but in some instances, the job is never completed. Guidelines have been set up by the state to allow suppliers of services and materials a filing period of up to 90 days if the owner doesn't file a valid notice of completion. If one of these four alternatives occurs, the work is considered to be complete:

1. Occupation or use by owner after cessation of labor.

2. Acceptance of work improvements by owner.

3. A cessation of labor for 60 continuous days.

4. A cessation of labor for 30 continuous days if the owner files a "notice of cessation" with the county recorder's office.

An unpaid pool contractor who supplied labor and materials could file a mechanic's lien in the county in which the work was done. The encumbrance created would be an unwelcome, involuntary and specific lien.

4. Filing Time

The filing period is very important because the rights of a person filing a mechanic's lien are valid for only a short time. A suit can be filed later, but it would not automatically become a lien against the real property. A mechanic's lien may be filed any time after the preliminary notice and until 30 days after completion, if you are a supplier or subcontractor, and 60 days after completion if you are the general contractor. **If there is no notice of completion recorded for the project, all parties have 90 days after completion of the job to file.**

Filing time = 30 days (subcontractor), 60 days (general contractor), and 90 days (all parties, if no notice of completion). A "Completion Bond" may be required by a lender to insure that insurance companies will pay to complete the job if the contractor cannot.

5. Notice of Non-Responsibility (Must be Recorded and Posted)

An owner may file a notice of non-responsibility within 10 days of discovering that an unauthorized person is performing construction service on his or her property. A recorded and verified *NOTICE OF NON-RESPONSIBILITY is posted on the property stating that the owner is not responsible for the work being done.* This action releases an owner from any liability caused by the unauthorized activity. This notice of non-responsibility prevents suppliers from filing a valid mechanic's lien.

Figure 3-2   **To be Recorded by the Owner**

RECORDING REQUESTED BY

AND WHEN RECORDED MAIL TO

Name

Street
Address

City &
State

——————— SPACE ABOVE THIS LINE FOR RECORDER'S USE ———————

INDIVIDUAL FORM

Notice of Completion

TO 1927 CA (3-75)   Before execution, refer to title company requirements stated on reverse side.   A. P. N. ____ ____ ____ ____

Notice is hereby given that:

1. The undersigned is owner of the interest or estate stated below in the property hereinafter described.
2. The full name of the undersigned is _____
3. The full address of the undersigned is _____
4. The nature of the title of the undersigned is: In fee. _____
     (If other than fee, strike "In fee" and insert, for example, "purchaser under contract of purchase," or "lessee".)
5. The full names and full addresses of all persons, if any, who hold title with the undersigned as joint tenants or as tenants in common are:

       NAMES   ADDRESSES

6. The names of the predecessors in interest of the undersigned, if the property was transferred subsequent to the commencement of the work of improvement herein referred to:

       NAMES   ADDRESSES

                 (If no transfer made, insert "none".)

7. A work of improvement on the property hereinafter described was completed on _____
8. The name of the contractor, if any, for such work of improvement was _____

         (If no contractor for work of improvement as a whole, insert "none".)

9. The property on which said work of improvement was completed is in the City of _____ , County of _____ , State of California, and is described as follows:

10. The street address of said property is _____
              (If no street address has been officially assigned, insert "none".)

Signature of
owner named
Dated: _____   in paragraph 2 _____
                 (Also sign verification below at X)

STATE OF CALIFORNIA,
COUNTY OF _____ } SS.   _____

The undersigned, being duly sworn, says: That ___he is the owner of the aforesaid interest or estate in the property described in the foregoing notice; that ___he has read the same, and knows the contents thereof, and that the facts stated therein are true.

Signature of
owner named
SUBSCRIBED AND SWORN TO before me   in paragraph 2   X _____

on _____

Signature _____

     Notary Public in and for said State

Title Order No. _____
Escrow or Loan No. _____

SEE REVERSE SIDE FOR
TITLE COMPANY REQUIREMENTS AS TO NOTICE OF COMPLETION

                              (This area for official notarial seal)

An apartment tenant may ask a painter, plumber or electrician to do work without the landlord's authorization and may try to charge the owner for the work done. This is the time for a landlord to file a notice of non-responsibility with the county recorder's office. If a tenant is installing carpet in your apartment without your authorization, a notice of non-responsibility would protect you against the claims of the carpet supplier.

Mechanic's liens have priority over any other liens except taxes and special assessments, like the 1911 Street Improvement Bond.

F. TAX LIENS (Specific or General Liens)

If any government tax is not paid, it may become a lien, through law or a court action, on real property. If the lien is not settled, the property can be sold to pay back-taxes. Tax liens are either: (1) specific liens or (2) general liens.

Example: Property taxes, mechanic's liens = specific liens
Income taxes, judgments = general liens

G. SPECIAL ASSESSMENTS

Local improvements are paid for by the property owners in a given district through SPECIAL ASSESSMENTS. Improvements such as streets, sewers, street lighting and irrigation projects are generally paid for by the property owners who have benefited from the work. If these assessments are not paid, they become a lien against the property. Most special assessments are 10-to-30-year bonds. This allows the property owner a reasonable amount of time to pay them off. Real property cannot be transferred until an outstanding bond is paid, unless there is an agreement between the parties involved in the transaction.

Special assessments are levied for the cost of specific local improvements, while property tax revenue goes into the general fund.

H. JUDGMENTS (Involuntary and General Liens)

A JUDGMENT is a court decision determining the rights of the parties involved and the amount of compensation. A judgment can be appealed.

For a judgment to become a lien, an *ABSTRACT OF JUDGMENT, or formal filing of the judgment,* must be recorded. The judgment then becomes a lien upon all nonexempt property of the debtor. It also becomes a lien on all future property he or she later acquires until the lien is paid. A judgment lien is good for ten years. So, if any property is transferred within this ten year period, the lien must first be paid off. Under additional court action, the judgment holder may be able to force the debtor to sell the real property to pay off the lien.

A judgment is a general and involuntary lien against all real property in the county in which the judgment is recorded. Once recorded, it is good for 10 years.

1. Small Claims Court

At this point, it is important that you understand the use of the Small Claims Court. Anyone can take someone else to court regarding civil cases for a $6 filing fee plus the fee for serving the subpoena. Neither party is allowed to be represented in the courtroom by legal counsel. The current maximum amount of a judgment is $5,000. This limit will be adjusted periodically by the state legislature to meet inflationary trends. Night court is also available in some districts, making this process even more accessible. You should be aware, however, that for a plaintiff, the judge's decision in a small claims action is final. The defendant, though, has the right of appeal. This is an excellent way to settle a dispute with a minimal amount of time and expense.

A judgment is not final until the appeal period has elapsed. In municipal court, the appeal period is up to 30 days. In a superior or federal court, the appeal period is up to 60 days. Only a defendant can appeal an unfavorable verdict.

I. TERMINATION OF JUDGMENT LIEN

Most judgment liens are terminated by the satisfaction of the judgment. *SATISFACTION OF JUDGMENT is compensation made by the payment of money or the return of property.* A notice that the judgment has been satisfied should be filed with the clerk of the court. It clears the lien from the record. Sometimes certain properties may be released from the judgment, but only with the judgment holder's consent. This partial release enables an owner to sell a property to satisfy a part of the judgment. A judgment may also be terminated if a bond is posted or if the judge grants a new trial.

Satisfaction of judgment clears the lien from the record.

J. ATTACHMENT (Court-Seized Property)

ATTACHMENT (LIEN) is a process of the law that creates a lien. It gives custody of real or personal property to the courts to assure payment of a pending lawsuit in that county. This is to assure that there will be enough property to satisfy the judgment should the plaintiff prevail. The *PLAINTIFF is the person filing a court action to obtain an attachment lien. The DEFENDANT is the person who is being sued.* During an unlawful detainer action for collection of past due rents, for instance, it may be advantageous for a plaintiff to obtain an attachment against the defendant. This type of lien is good for three years, and is extended only if the plaintiff wins the court case. Use of the attachment lien is not very common because there are many rules and formalities involved in obtaining this type of lien. This is another area that requires the help of an attorney. The important thing to remember about an attachment lien is that it does exist, and can be a lien on real property.

An attachment creates a specific and involuntary lien on one property, which is good for 3 years, even if the property owner dies.

K. LIS PENDENS ("Lawsuit is Pending")

LIS PENDENS *is the recording of a notice with the county recorder's office warning all persons that a lawsuit is pending concerning a particular property.* Attorneys often file a lis pendens before a court date is set in order to stop the transfer of the property. A lis pendens places a cloud on the title, and is effective when filed. The property is not marketable until the lis pendens is removed.

A lis pendens is notice of a pending lawsuit that affects title or possession of real property (clouds title) and remains on the public record until judgment is rendered or suit is dismissed. A bankruptcy is a lis pendens.

L. SHERIFF'S SALE (Court Order to Sell—Execution)

A "writ of execution" is a court order to sell property to satisfy a judgment. The state controls lien and attachment laws, cities and counties do NOT.

A **WRIT OF EXECUTION** *is a court order requiring the sale of certain property to satisfy a judgment.* The writ of execution extends the lien against the real property for one year. If the judgment has already been recorded as a lien on the property, the writ of execution will not create a new lien. The county sheriff, or other local officials, are then ordered to secure and sell the real or personal property to satisfy the lien.

If a person refuses to pay off the judgment, the sheriff's sale is the next step. A **SHERIFF'S SALE** *is the forced sale of a debtor's property to satisfy a judgment under a writ of execution.* In California, the sheriff's sale is the usual method of forcing someone to sell property to pay off a judgment.

Taxes and assessment liens have the priority to any proceeds from a sheriff's sale.

Mechanic's liens and any previously recorded judgments have priority over paying the expenses of the sale. If these expenses are paid, a first trust deed is next to be satisfied. Any amount left over is applied toward a second trust deed and any subsequent liens, in the order of their recording, until the proceeds are exhausted.

M. INJUNCTION (Court Order to Stop)

An **INJUNCTION** *is a court order to stop doing something.* For example, the court may order a developer to stop damming up a river.

III. Items That Affect Physical Use
(Non-Money Encumbrances)

A. ITEMS THAT AFFECT PHYSICAL USE

ITEMS THAT AFFECT PHYSICAL USE *are non-money encumbrances that affect the physical use of real property.* They include: easements, building restrictions, zoning and encroachments, which are conditions that limit the physical use of the property. **See Figure 3-3.**

Figure 3-3

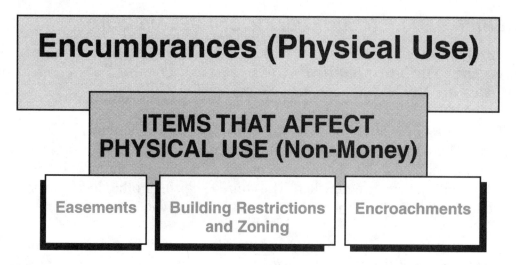

Encumbrances (Physical Use)

ITEMS THAT AFFECT
PHYSICAL USE (Non-Money)

Easements

Building Restrictions and Zoning

Encroachments

Some encumbrances affect the physical use of the property. They are:

1. Easements
2. Building Restrictions and Zoning
3. Encroachments
4. Leases (see Chapter 6).

1. Easements (The Right to Use Another's Land)

An easement is an interest in another's land; it is a right. Easements are non-money encumbrances; they are NOT liens. Land that is burdened with an easement is said to be "encumbered."

An ***EASEMENT*** *is an interest in land owned by another person consisting in the right to use or control the land, or an area above or below it, for a specific, limited purpose. The right to enter is called **INGRESS** and the right to exit is **EGRESS**.* Included in this definition is the right to profit from the easement, such as the right to take minerals, oil and gas. Easements are of two types: (1) easements appurtenant and (2) easements in gross.

An easement is the right to use another's land. It is a right, interest or privilege, but NOT an estate.

a. Easement Appurtenant (Runs with the Land)

An easement is said to be appurtenant, which means the easement "belongs to" or "runs with the land." (Easements are non-exclusive, meaning the owner can still use the land.) The new buyer would have the "same rights" to the easement as did the seller.

An **EASEMENT APPURTENANT** *is an easement "created for and beneficial to" the owner of adjoining or attached lands.* An easement is real property, not personal property, but it is not an estate. In this case there are two parcels of land, with one owner giving another owner an easement. The **DOMINANT TENEMENT** *is the land that obtains the benefits of an easement.* **Figure 3-4** is an illustration of a driveway easement. Owner A's land is the dominant tenement and Owner B's land is the servient tenement.

Figure 3-4

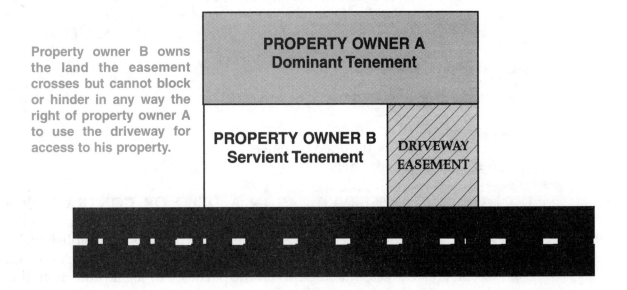

Property owner B owns the land the easement crosses but cannot block or hinder in any way the right of property owner A to use the driveway for access to his property.

PROPERTY OWNER A
Dominant Tenement

PROPERTY OWNER B
Servient Tenement

DRIVEWAY EASEMENT

The dominant tenement is the land that benefits; the owner is the party who can terminate the easement, which does not expire for non-use.

A **SERVIENT TENEMENT** *is the land that gives the easement (use of the land) for the benefit of another.* The appurtenant easement belongs to the land and is transferred with the land. This easement cannot be transferred separately from the land.

The owner of the servient tenement CANNOT revoke the easement; it must "serve" the dominant tenement, even if not used.

b. Easement in Gross (Does Not Benefit Adjoining Landowner)

An example of an easement in gross would be an easement for the telephone company (utility company) to enter the property to run telephone lines. Easements in gross do NOT benefit adjoining lands.

An **EASEMENT IN GROSS** *is not attached to any particular land or dominant tenement. It is an easement created for the benefit of others who do not own adjoining or attached lands.* It is a personal property right. Even though it is a personal right, there are still servient tenements. An example of an easement in gross would be a utility company obtaining the right to run natural gas lines across your land. In this instance your land would become a servient tenement.

Other not-so-common easements are: rights to take water, wood or minerals; rights to transact business or conduct sports upon the land; rights to receive light, air or heat from the land; and the right to use a wall as a common party wall.

An easement that does not specify a special area for a right-of-way is also valid. *A property owner could give the right to cross his land and not limit how or where a person would have to cross. This is known as an* **UNLOCATED EASEMENT**.

c. Creation of an Easement

Easements are created in three basic ways:

1. Express Grant (in writing)
2. Implication of Law (implied easement)
3. Long Use (prescription)

1. IN WRITING (RESERVED), AS IN A DEED OR CONTRACT. If a property is transferred as part of the deed, an easement appurtenant to the land would be included in the grant. The same thing is accomplished by transferring a property, but **reserving an easement** over the land. A written contract can create an easement between the parties. For legal protection, this contract should be acknowledged and recorded.

2. IMPLICATION OF LAW (IMPLIED EASEMENT). If an easement is implied in a transfer, or if it is necessary for use of the land, then the easement is said to be implied by law. The right to use the land for obtaining minerals implies that you have the right of surface entry in order to extract the minerals.

If surface entry is denied to someone with an implied easement, the damaged party should file a quiet title action in court to perfect title.

EASEMENT BY NECESSITY (LANDLOCKED) is an easement that is absolutely necessary for access. If a person is sold property that landlocks that person, he or she may acquire an easement by necessity. When the grantor transfers a portion of his or her land that leaves the grantee totally surrounded by the grantor (transferor), the grantor can be forced to give an easement of access to the grantee. An easement by necessity does not have to be the most convenient way of entering the property. If the grantee later acquires another access to his or her property, the easement by necessity is then terminated.

3. LONG USE (EASEMENT BY PRESCRIPTION). Prescription is an easement to continue using land by virtue of having used it for a long period of time.

A prescriptive easement can be obtained after five years of uninterrupted use of another's land; NO confrontation with the owner or property tax payments required.

Possession for five continuous years can create a prescriptive easement, as long as there is:

1. Open and notorious use
2. Uninterrupted use for five years
3. Hostile (without permission of the owner)
4. Under a claim of right.

An easement obtained by prescription can be terminated if NOT used for five years.

d. Transfer of an Easement

Easements are transferred automatically if they are easements appurtenant. Easements in gross can be transferred only by express agreement, providing the easement is not made to a specific individual. An easement should be recorded. If it is not recorded, and the purchaser does not have knowledge of an easement, then the easement may not be considered to have been transferred with the property.

e. Termination of an Easement

Easements may be terminated in several ways:

1. EXPRESS RELEASE – Any written agreement can terminate an easement, but the usual form is a quitclaim deed. The servient tenement is the only one that could benefit from the termination of an easement.

2. MERGER OF DOMINANT AND SERVIENT TENEMENTS – An easement is automatically terminated when the dominant and servient tenements merge into a common, or single, ownership. The easement can be created again if any part of the property is later transferred to a "separate owner."

3. EXCESSIVE USE – The courts have held that excessive use of an easement that increases the burden on the servient tenement may be forfeited through a court injunction. If the dominant tenement refuses to correct the excessive use, and misuses of the easement can be established, the easement can be terminated. An example would be a dominant tenement owner allowing the entire neighborhood to use the easement as a through-street.

4. ABANDONMENT AND NON-USE – If there is an obvious intent of an easement holder to abandon his or her easement, then that person may lose the easement through court action. In this way, an easement gained through prescription may be extinguished if non-use exists for a period of five continuous years.

Non-use can only terminate an easement created by prescription (long use). However, non-use of an easement appurtenant would NOT terminate the easement, unless it is abandoned.

5. DESTRUCTION OF SERVIENT TENEMENT – When a governing body, by exercising the right of eminent domain, takes servient tenement property for its own use, the dominant tenement easement is considered automatically terminated.

Summary:

Easements are a right to use land (NOT an estate)
Easements are NOT liens, they are encumbrances
Easements are usually created by deed or prescription
Easements are appurtenant or in gross

2. Building Restrictions (CC&Rs) and Zoning

Restrictions are: 1) "private deed restrictions," such as those placed on a property by the grantor or developer, or 2) public restrictions, such as city zoning laws. The restrictions that are the most restrictive will always control the use of the property.

PRIVATE DEED RESTRICTIONS limit the use or occupancy of the land. A typical restriction would be to limit the types of buildings on a given piece of land to single family residences. Also, a restriction might require future construction to meet specific standards. For example, all houses erected on a property must be at least 5,000 square feet. Another example might be a setback requirement, which would require any structure to be set back so many feet from the street or adjoining property.

There are three types of private building restrictions: Covenants, Conditions and Restrictions (CC&Rs). They are usually included in the deed at the time the property is subdivided, or may be created by a written contract and are listed in the recorded "Declaration of Restrictions." Their main purpose is to keep use of the land uniform throughout certain tracts of land. Subdivisions and condominiums usually include deed restrictions as a method to promote the aesthetics and economics of the project. These private deed restrictions and bylaws are usually recorded separately, and are only referenced in the original grant deeds.

Private restrictions are written agreements to establish private land use controls which are part of a developer's general plan.

a. Covenants (Promise Broken, Sue for Damages)

A *COVENANT is a promise to do or not to do a certain thing.* For instance, a property could sell with a covenant stating that the property shall never be used to sell alcoholic beverages. If the covenant is broken, the usual court remedy would be an action for money damages. A court may also grant an injunction requiring compliance with the covenant.

Deed restrictions are NOT liens.

b. Conditions (More Stringent than Breaking a Covenant—Can Lose Title)

CONDITIONS are promises to do or not to do something, the failure of which may terminate the contract. **The penalty for not following the set conditions is the reversion of the property to the grantor.** This penalty is so stiff that most courts will treat a condition as a covenant unless the terms are clearly stated in the deed or other contract. For a complete discussion of conditions, refer back to Chapter 2.

A condo association cannot prohibit the placing of a "for sale" sign (a restraint of trade), but can dictate the size, color, and location of sign.

c. Governmental Restrictions (Zoning)

PUBLIC RESTRICTIONS are limits made by governmental agencies, usually by cities and counties, in the form of zoning.

"Public restrictions" promote health, safety, morals, and general welfare of the public. This is the use of police power.

Private restrictions are made by the present or previous landowners and are created only for their benefit. On the other hand, **zoning restrictions** are created by and for the benefit of the general public to insure its health, safety, comfort, and morals.

Cities and counties can divide land into districts for control over local property through local laws that enforce zoning, rent control, building codes and other subdivision land use regulations.

Zoning is the restriction on the use of private property by the local government agency. Zoning dictates how the property can be used, the setbacks required and the height limit on any structures.

Private restrictions are placed on the property by the grantor or developer. If there are two restrictions, the most restrictive of the two will take precedence. For example, if a developer sets a deed restriction of 15,000 square feet to a lot but zoning only allows 10,000 square feet per lot, the zoning is more restrictive and would prevail. This area is covered in depth in Chapter 12 under "Government Control."

d. Race Restrictions (Illegal)

In 1961 the California State Legislature enacted a law that voided all restrictions as to race. Any race deed restriction before that law or after that law is now void. By law, we cannot erase recorded restrictions, but the 1961 law did make such restrictions illegal. It is illegal to restrict the right of an individual to sell, rent, lease, use or otherwise occupy a property because of race or membership in a certain ethnic group.

Race restrictions on a property by a grantor (past or present) are unenforceable and illegal.

3. Encroachments (3 years to Act)

As stated earlier, an **ENCROACHMENT** *is the wrongful, unauthorized placement of improvements or permanent fixtures on property by a nonowner of that property.* You must pursue the right to have an encroachment removed within 3 years or lose your right. If someone encroaches on your property, he or she is limiting the use of your property.

If one neighbor builds a driveway over another neighbor's property, it is considered an encroachment, which is a form of "trespass." The owner of the encroached land has three years to sue his neighbor to have the encroachment removed.

Often fences, walls or buildings may extend over the recognized boundary line. The encroaching party may possibly gain legal title to the property through adverse possession, or legal use through an easement by prescription, if there is legal justification. In any event, encroachment may legally limit the use of your property.

LICENSE is the revocable permission to enter a licensor's land to do something that would otherwise be illegal, such as hunting game.

Unlike an easement, a license can be revoked.

IV. Homesteading Your Residence (Protects Against Judgment Liens)

Although a homestead is not an encumbrance, it is appropriately discussed at this point. A *HOMESTEAD is a special provision of the California law that allows homeowners to protect their homes from forced sale to satisfy their debts, within certain limits.* There are two types of homesteads: (1) Head of the household and (2) Federal Homestead Act of 1862, whereby the government encouraged settlements (gave land free to those who made certain improvements—this is not discussed here). It is basic to our society that a homeowner should have some protection against losing his or her home because of debts. A homestead consists of the house and adjoining dwellings in which the owner resides. This can include condominiums, farm and life estates. A homestead cannot include "unimproved" land such as vacant lots or a residence under construction.

A. DECLARATION OF HOMESTEAD

A *DECLARATION OF HOMESTEAD, after acknowledgment and recording, protects a residence from judgments that become liens.* **See Figure 3-5.** This protects you for $75,000 if you are the head of a family. Persons who are mentally or physically disabled or over the age of 65 are entitled to protection for up to $125,000. Any resident who does not qualify under either of these conditions has a homestead valued at $50,000. It is a loose provision and almost everyone qualifies. If the equity exceeds the exemption, the home may be sold to satisfy creditors, but the exemption amount is protected for six months for reinvestment in another home. When a person files a homestead, it does not protect that person against trust deeds, mechanic's liens, or liens owed prior to homestead filing.

You may only have one homestead at a time. A homestead is NOT an encumbrance.

In order for a declaration of homestead to be valid, there are certain requirements that must be met. Omissions of any one of these will make the homestead void. The requirements are:

1. A statement showing the claimant is the head of a family and stating the name of the spouse. "Head of family" may be anyone who lives in the home and provides for any relative living in the same house.

2. A statement that the claimant is residing on the premises and claims it as his or her homestead.

Figure 3-5

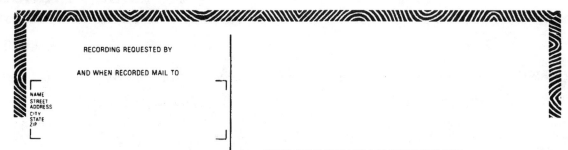

RECORDING REQUESTED BY

AND WHEN RECORDED MAIL TO

NAME
STREET
ADDRESS
CITY
STATE
ZIP

————————(SPACE ABOVE THIS LINE FOR RECORDER'S USE)————————

HOMESTEAD DECLARATION

—————— ◄ ► ——————

I, _____
(Full Name of Declarant)

do hereby certify and declare as follows:

(1) I hereby claim as a declared homestead the premises located in the City of _____.

County of _____ , State of _____ commonly known as
_____
(Street Address)

and more particularly described as follows [Give complete legal description]

(2) I am the declared homestead owner of the above declared homestead.

(3) I own the following interest in the above declared homestead:

(4) The above declared homestead is [strike inapplicable clause] my principal dwelling, the principal dwelling of my spouse, and
[strike inapplicable clause] I am / my spouse is currently residing on that declared homestead.

(5) The facts stated in this Declaration are true as of my personal knowledge.

Dated: _____ , 19____   _____
(Signature of Declarant)

STATE OF _____ }
COUNTY OF _____ } ss.

On _____ before me, _____
(Name, title of officer-i.e. "Jane Doe Notary Public")

personally appeared _____
_____

personally known to me (or proved to me on the basis of satisfactory evidence) to
be the person(s) whose name(s) is/are subscribed to the within instrument and
acknowledged to me that he/she/they executed the same in his/her/their authorized capacity(ies), and that by his/her/their signature(s) on the instrument the
person(s), or the entity upon behalf of which the person(s) acted, executed the
instrument.

WITNESS my hand and official seal.

_____
Signature

(Seal)

WOLCOTTS FORM 756—HOMESTEAD DECLARATION —Rev 1-93
(price class 3)

© 1993 WOLCOTTS FORMS, INC

This standard form is intended for the typical situations encountered in the field indicated. However, before you sign, read it, fill in all blanks, and make
whatever changes are appropriate and necessary to your particular transaction. Consult a lawyer if you doubt the form's fitness for your purpose and use

3. A description of the premises and an estimate of cash value.

4. It further provides that the declaration of homestead may need to contain a statement as to the character of the property; that no former declaration has been made and that it is within the limits prescribed by law.

The homeowner has time to file a declaration of homestead prior to court approval for a writ of execution. As part of the judicial process, the defendant must be informed of his or her right to file a declaration of homestead. This law, in effect, reduces the necessity of filing a homestead declaration until the homeowner is in financial trouble.

Recording a homestead has no impact on property taxes.

B. TERMINATION OF HOMESTEAD

A homestead may be terminated by a DECLARATION OF ABANDONMENT. The declaration of abandonment must be acknowledged and recorded by the involved parties. A sale or other conveyance of the property also terminates the homestead. The removal or destruction of the dwelling does not terminate the homestead. The reason for abandoning a homestead is to allow the homeowner the privilege of obtaining another homestead on a new residence.

A homestead is terminated by 1) Declaration of Abandonment or 2) the sale of the homesteaded property.

V. SUMMARY

An **encumbrance** is a burden to a property that limits its use by either 1) money owed (liens) or 2) items that affect the physical use of the property (non-money). All liens are "encumbrances," but not all encumbrances are liens. A **blanket encumbrance** is a voluntary lien placed over more than one property, and usually has a release clause for one or more of the parcels.

A **lien** is a document that uses a property to secure the payment of a debt or the discharge of an obligation. Liens are either 1) **voluntary**, 2) **involuntary**, 3) **specific**, or 4) **general**.

Trust deeds and **mortgages** (mortgages are rare in California) are security devices that make property security for a debt, and are considered personal property. The accompanying **promissory note** is the evidence of the debt.

If the people who supply labor or materials for construction on a property are not paid, they can file a **mechanic's lien** against that individual property. It is a **specific and involuntary lien,** and once recorded has priority over all other liens except taxes, special assessments, and trust deeds. Before filing a mechanic's lien, **Preliminary Notice** must be given (within 20 days of supplying labor or services).

It is important to establish the starting time and completion date of the work or materials supplied. A **Notice of Completion** should be recorded by the owner within ten days of completion, or a **Notice of Cessation** in order to stop work being done. If a person is unauthorized to do construction on a property, an owner needs to file and post a **Notice of Non-Responsibility** on the property, releasing him or her from liability and preventing suppliers from filing a valid mechanic's lien.

Property taxes and mechanic's liens are **specific liens**, meaning against just one property, whereas income taxes and judgments are **general liens**, covering all the properties of an owner. A **judgment** is a **general and involuntary lien** against all real property in the county in which the judgment is recorded, and is good for ten years. A **satisfaction of judgment** is made by payment of money or return of property and clears the lien from the record.

An **attachment** (lien), which is good for three years, creates a **specific and involuntary lien** on one property to assure payment of a pending lawsuit. A **lis pendens** is a notice of a pending lawsuit that affects title (**clouds** title) and remains on the public record until judgment is rendered or suit is dismissed. If a person does not pay off a judgment, he or she may be forced to sell the property in a **sheriff's sale** under a court order called a **Writ of Execution**.

Items that affect **physical use** of a property are **non-money encumbrances** and include: 1) **easements**, 2) **restrictions**, 3) **encroachments**, and 4) **leases**.

An **easement** is the right to enter, use and exit another person's land for certain purpose. If it runs with the land it is an **easement appurtenant**. The **dominant tenant** is the land that benefits from the easement that the **servient tenement** gives up. An **easement in gross** benefits others who do not own adjoining or attached lands (like a utility company running gas line across a property).

Easements can be created by 1) **deed** (writing), 2) **implication of law** (implied easement or easement by necessity), or 3) **prescription** (long use). They can also be terminated in several ways, including: 1) **express release**, 2) **merger** of dominant and servient tenements, 3) **excessive use**, 4) **abandonment and non-use**, and 5) **destruction of servient tenement**.

Restrictions can be private deed restrictions, or public restrictions. **Covenants, conditions, and restrictions (CC&Rs)** are private building restrictions. **Public restrictions** are limits made by governmental agencies and are meant to promote health, safety, morals, and general welfare of the public (**police power**). **Zoning** is a public restriction dictating how property can be used. An **encroachment** is the wrongful, unauthorized placement of improvements or permanent fixtures on a property by a non-owner.

A **homestead** is not an encumbrance, but a special provision of California law that allows homeowners to protect their homes from forced sale to satisfy their debts. A homestead is terminated by 1) **declaration of abandonment** or 2) **the sale of the homesteaded property**.

VI. TERMINOLOGY - CHAPTER 3

A. Abstract of Judgment
B. Attachment
C. Blanket Encumbrance
D. Conditions
E. Covenant
F. Declaration of Abandonment
G. Declaration of Homestead
H. Defendant
I. Dominant Tenement
J. Easement
K. Easement Appurtenant

L. Easement in Gross
M. Encroachment
N. Encumbrance
O. General Lien
P. Homestead
Q. Lien
R. Lis Pendens
S. Mechanic's Lien
T. Mortgage
U. Notice of Nonresponsibility
V. Plaintiff

W. Preliminary Notice
X. Restrictions
Y. Satisfaction
Z. Servient Tenement
AA. Sheriff's Sale
BB. Specific Lien
CC. Trust Deed
DD. Writ of Execution

1.____ A right, limited to a specific use, that one party has in the land of another.

2.____ A statutory protection of a home from the claims of certain creditors and judgments up to a specified amount.

3.____ Anything that affects or limits the fee simple title to, or value of, property, e.g., mortgages or easements.

4.____ A notice, recorded and posted by the property owner to relieve them of responsibility for the cost of unauthorized work done on his or her property or materials furnished.

5.____ A limitation on the use of real property. These limitations fall into two general classifications -- public and private. Zoning ordinances are public, while a clause in the deed requiring the roof to be made of Spanish red title would be a private limitation.

6.____ The process by which real or personal property is seized by the court for the purpose of assuring payment.

7.____ A form of encumbrance that usually makes specific property security for the payment of a debt.

8.____ Discharge of a mortgage or trust deed from the records upon payment of the debt. Make sure you receive a Deed of Reconveyance to prove that you paid off the deed of trust.

9.____ A limiting restriction stating that upon the happening or not happening of some stated event, the estate shall be changed in some manner.

10.____ A promise to do or not to do a particular thing.

11.____ A person against whom a civil or criminal action is taken.

12.____ An instrument, recognized by law, by which property is hypothecated to secure the payment of a debt. This instrument is not commonly used in California, but is popular on the East coast.

13.____ In a court action, the one who sues; the complainant.

14.____ A recorded document of the essential provisions of a court judgment.

15.____ A lien, created by statute, which exists against real or personal property in favor of persons who have performed work or furnished materials for the improvement of real property.

16.____ A legal document by which a borrower pledges certain real property as collateral for the repayment of a loan. In addition to the buyer and seller, there is a third party to the transaction known as a trustee.

17.____ A formal statement that protects the head of the household from losing the property to the claims of creditors, usually up to a set maximum amount.

18.____ A lien, usually a trust deed in California, covering more than one property of the borrower.

19.____ A notice that informs or warns owners, lenders and general contractors that subcontractors have been hired, or materials have been supplied, to a particular job site.

20.____ A statement declaring the intent to give up a homestead, usually to declare a homestead on a new residence.

21.____ A court ordered sale of real or personal property by the sheriff pursuant to the execution of a judgment.

22.____ The construction of improvements on the property of another.

23.____ An easement for the benefit of the owner of an adjacent parcel of land.

24.____ Real property that benefits from an easement.

25.____ A writ to carry out a court order, usually arising from a judgment.

26.____ A property that is burdened by an easement.

27.____ An easement for the benefit of a person or utility company rather than for the benefit of adjacent landowners.

28.____ A notice filed or recorded for the purpose of warning all persons that the title to certain real property is in litigation.

29.____ A lien such as a tax lien or judgment lien that attaches to all property of the debtor rather than a specific property.

30.____ A lien that attaches to a specific property rather than all the property of the debtor.

VII. MULTIPLE CHOICE

1. A mechanic's lien:

    a. is a general lien.
    b. is a voluntary lien.
    c. is a non-money encumbrance.
    d. must be recorded to be effective.

2. Income taxes would be an example of a(n):

    a. voluntary lien.
    b. attachment lien.
    c. general lien.
    d. specific lien.

3. An easement appurtenant:

    a. runs with the land.
    b. cannot be transferred.
    c. has a separate conveyance.
    d. does not benefit the adjoining land.

4. If you fail to pay a subcontractor and he or she files a mechanic's lien, the lien is:

    a. specific.
    b. general.
    c. voluntary.
    d. both a and b.

5. Homesteads allow homeowners, in some cases, to protect their homes from forced:

    a. robbery.
    b. sale to pay bad debts.
    c. condemnation.
    d. eminent domain.

6. A sheriff's sale CANNOT be the result of a(n):

    a. judgment.
    b. court action.
    c. writ of execution.
    d. easement.

7. Which of the following is true with regard to a filed homestead?

    a. The home must be used as a residence.
    b. It must be acknowledged and recorded to be in effect.
    c. One property at a time can be homesteaded.
    d. All of the above.

8. A document using property to secure the payment of debt is called a:

   a. lien.
   b. cloud on title.
   c. grant deed.
   d. reconveyance.

9. Which of the following would be considered a voluntary lien?

   a. Special assessment
   b. Tax lien
   c. Attachment
   d. Mortgage

10. Local improvements that are paid for by the property owners who benefit from the work are called:

   a. special assessments.
   b. tax liens.
   c. property taxes.
   d. district assessments.

ANSWERS: 1. d; 2. c; 3. a; 4. a; 5. b; 6. d; 7. d; 8. a; 9. d; 10. a

SALESPERSON WANTED

Chapter 4
Agency and Its Responsibility

www.dre.ca.gov
California Department of Real Estate
www.car.org
California Association of Realtors
www.inman.com/index.asp
Inman News Features

I. Agency Overview

A. AGENT, PRINCIPAL, AND THIRD PARTY

Agency is the relationship between a seller, a broker (and his or her salespeople), and a buyer.

1. Agent

AGENCY *is the authority (or power) to act for or in place of another, a principal (person who hires), in a specified act for a stated period of time.* An **AGENT** *is one who acts for and with authority from another, called the principal.*

AGENT, BROKER, SALESPERSON, ASSOCIATE
Who Holds a Real Estate License?

REAL ESTATE AGENT

A *REAL ESTATE AGENT is a person, licensed by the Department of Real Estate (DRE), who holds either a broker or salesperson license and negotiates sales for other people.*

REAL ESTATE BROKER AND SALESPERSON

A *REAL ESTATE BROKER is a license holder (boss/owner) and therefore permitted by law to employ those individuals holding a salesperson license (or another broker). A REAL ESTATE SALESPERSON is an individual holding a salesperson license who must be employed by a real estate broker to perform any of the activities of a real estate broker.*

REAL ESTATE ASSOCIATE

A *REAL ESTATE ASSOCIATE or ASSOCIATE LICENSEE is another name for a real estate salesperson.* An associate works for a broker as either an employee or an independent contractor.

An agent or licensee is either a broker or a salesperson who works for a broker.

DEPARTMENT OF REAL ESTATE (DRE)

Checking the Status of a Real Estate Salesperson or Broker

To check the status of a real estate salesperson or broker, connect with the following Department of Real Estate Internet address:

www.dre.ca.gov/licstats.htm
Department of Real Estate - Licensee Status Inquires

Click on LICENSE RECORDS ON-LINE and enter the name or license number, and the DRE will do the rest.

Agents (brokers) usually select and control their own professional approach to selling a property. Sellers are responsible for their representations to the buyer. While brokers share this responsibility, they also have a responsibility for their individual representations. Agency is a fiduciary relationship based on trust. The agent representing the seller must disclose all pertinent facts to the seller and must not take advantage of, or gain from, this relationship in an unethical manner.

2. Principal

A *PRINCIPAL (CLIENT) is a person who hires or employs an agent to work for him or her.* If the principal is a buyer, the agent represents the buyer. On the other hand, if the principal is a seller, the agent represents the seller.

The principal is the person who hires an agent.

3. Third Party

A *THIRD PARTY is the other person in a contractual negotiation, other than the principal and his or her agent.* If an agent works for the seller, the third party is the buyer, but if the agent works for the buyer, the third party is the seller. In effect, the agent is the second party to the transaction.

In the agency relationship, the broker and other salespeople are required to make certain representations about the property they are selling. They are expected to do what is necessary, proper, and usual to sell the real estate being offered. They must also make truthful representations to the buyer as to the condition of the property that may materially affect the value or desirability and the terms of the sale. This is spelled out in the Disclosure Regarding Real Estate Agency Relationships Form (discussed later).

The agency of a real estate broker may be established by express agreement, implied agreement, ratification, or estoppel. Express (written) agreement is by far the best way to establish agency!

OSTENSIBLE or IMPLIED AUTHORITY is the authority which a third person reasonably believes an agent possesses because of the acts or omissions of the principal. This authority is conferred when a principal gives a third party reason to believe that another person is his or her agent even if that person is unaware of the appointment. If the third party accepts this as true, the principal may well be bound by the acts of his or her agent.

Example: If you tell a prospective buyer to see Agent Ramos about seeing the property even though the listing has expired and Ramos sells the house, the buyer has every reason to believe that Miss Ramos had the authority to sell your home.

An agency relationship may also come about by estoppel or ratification, although it is **not** advisable. *ESTOPPEL prohibits the principal from denying that a person is his or her*

agent if the principal has misled another to his prejudice into believing that person is the agent. In the above example, you, the owner, would be "estopped" from denying that Miss Ramos was your agent, based on your past actions or words. **RATIFICATION** *is approval of a transaction which has already taken place.* For example, when you authorize a broker to have acted for you after he or she has already done so, the action is called ratification.

The best evidence of an agency relationship is a written agreement.

In California, most real estate transactions involve the use of a broker and his or her salespeople. To run a real estate office, a broker's license is required, and a licensed salesperson can only work for a licensed real estate broker (one broker at a time). In California, any person in real estate who is acting in return for compensation from others must have a Department of Real Estate license to:

1. Sell or offer to sell

2. Buy or offer to buy

3. Solicit prospective buyers or sellers

4. Negotiate the purchase, sale, loan, or exchange of business opportunities or real estate

5. Negotiate leases and collect rents.

Real estate license requirements are explained fully in Chapter 14.

You may buy, sell, or lease your own property without a real estate license as often as you like in a given year because there is no agency involved.

B. LAW OF AGENCY

Real estate brokers are agents because they represent an interest other than their own (buyer's or seller's). A written agency contract (listing) exists, for which they may receive compensation if there is a sale. Whenever one person represents another in a business transaction, the "Law of Agency" applies.

The Law of Agency that defines agents' duties and responsibilities is found in the California Civil Code. Any grounds for professional discipline of a licensed real estate agent are dealt with under the Business and Professions Code.

Because the real estate broker is an agent, the California Civil Code, governing the law of Agency, defines his or her duties and responsibilities. Further, since the broker is a licensed real estate agent, he or she must comply with the rules and regulations of the California Real Estate Commissioner, which is enforced by the Commissioner. Both codes and regulations can be enforced against all brokers and their salespeople. Throughout this chapter, when we speak of a broker we are also referring to any salesperson (or broker) who may be working for that company broker.

The broker must supervise his or her salespeople and any brokers working as salespeople for his or her agency.

A salesperson and broker may also be referred to as real estate agents. Since they are in an agency relationship, it is only logical to refer to them as agents.

C. RESPONSIBILITIES OF AGENCY

The California Civil Code boils the law of agency down to three basic rules applying to licensed brokers and licensed salespeople:

1. The agent must inform the principal of all facts pertaining to the handling of the principal's property. Agent must put client's interest above interest of self or others.

2. The agent may not gain any monetary interest in the property without the principal's prior consent.

3. An agent may not use the principal's property to his or her own advantage.

1. Fiduciary Relationship

A *FIDUCIARY is a person acting in a position of trust and confidence in a business relationship. A FIDUCIARY RELATIONSHIP requires the highest good faith from the agent to his or her principal.* An agent must act as though he or she is the principal and always seek to represent the principal's best interest. In this case, the agent takes on the responsibility of diligently finding a buyer or seller. **See Figure 4-1**.

The broker (agent) works for the principal and forms a fiduciary relationship with him or her. The broker also must maintain an honest and truthful relationship with the third party (including full disclosure of material facts affecting value or desirability).

The broker (agent) owes certain duties, rights, and responsibilities to both the principal and third party. The broker owes a fidcuiary duty of (including, but not limited to) honesty, utmost care, integrity, accounting, disclosure, and loyalty to the principal. To a third party, an agent owes honesty and disclosure of material facts in a timely fashion.

An agent must exercise honesty, reasonable skill and care, fair dealing and good faith in dealing with a third party. An agent of the principal must disclose to the

Figure 4-1

BROKER'S DUTIES, RIGHTS, AND RESPONSIBILITIES	
FIDUCIARY RELATIONSHIP	**TRUTHFUL RELATIONSHIP**
PRINCIPAL *Honest good Faith.* 1. Honest—Disclose Material Facts 2. Utmost Care 3. Integrity—Accounting for Actions 4. Loyalty 5. Obey—Lawful Instructions 6. No Secret Profits	**THIRD PARTIES** 1. Honest—Disclose Material Facts 2. Reasonable Skill and Care 3. Fair Dealing 4. Good Faith

third party any facts known to the agent that could materially affect the value or desirability of the property.

D. LISTING AND SELLING AGENTS

When a salesperson obtains a listing agreement to sell a particular property, he or she is referred to as the "listing salesperson." That salesperson's broker is referred to as the "listing broker." If a different brokerage company negotiates the sale, that agency is the "selling broker" and "selling salesperson." A broker or salesperson who both lists and sells the same property is referred to as the "listing and selling broker or salesperson."

In a real estate transaction, agents are identified as the "listing agent" or "selling agent." A salesperson employed by a listing broker is an agent of the owner/seller.

II. Real Estate Agency Relationship Disclosure

A. AGENCY DISCLOSURE LAW

According to the Disclosure Regarding Real Estate Agency Relationships form, the first thing the agent must do is establish if he or she is an agent for the seller, buyer or both.

TOP AGENTS HIRE TOP ASSISTANTS

It is estimated that 80 percent of the real estate business is handled by 10 percent of the agents. To handle the workload, more top agents are hiring personal assistants to take over the day-to-day brokerage chores, leaving the agents free to concentrate on sales. **PERSONAL ASSISTANTS** *handle such things as clerical tasks, paperwork, marketing, tickler files, and conduct computer research.* More and more real estate licensees are working as assistants.

The growth in personal assistants is not without criticism. Among the complaints are that using assistants entrusts too many high-level tasks to unskilled employees and makes the agents inaccessible. It is important that the broker establish who is employing the assistants, and that unlicensed assistants do not act as agents. There is a wealth of educational materials available to improve the quality of real estate assistants.

The Disclosure Regarding Real Estate Agency Relationships form states that an agent must disclose an agency relationship as soon as practical. An agent can represent a seller, a buyer, or both. The three steps to agency disclosure are: disclose, elect, confirm.

The Disclosure Regarding Real Estate Agency Relationships Form states that both the listing broker and the selling broker must declare in writing, as soon as possible, whom they represent:

1. The seller/owner (seller's agency)
2. The buyer (buyer's agency) or
3. Both the seller and buyer (dual agency).

The only requirement is that the listing broker must at least represent the seller (owner). **This law applies to all sales of residential property of from one-to-four units.**

Be aware: agency disclosure law, which differs from state to state, will profoundly affect the way brokers represent their clients and the way we, as an industry, are perceived by the public at large.

Figure 4-2 shows a Disclosure Regarding Real Estate Agency Relationships form used by the California Association of Realtors®. Civil law requires that both parties to a transaction be informed of the various options they have regarding agency representation. Both the buyer and the seller must sign the upper part of this form as an acknowledgment that they understand their rights and have received a copy of this disclosure. In addition, agency disclosure must again be confirmed on the Residential Purchase Agreement ("Deposit Receipt"—see Chapter 5). If it is not confirmed on the Deposit Receipt, then it must be confirmed on a separate form. This

Figure 4-2

CALIFORNIA ASSOCIATION OF REALTORS®

DISCLOSURE REGARDING REAL ESTATE AGENCY RELATIONSHIPS
(As required by the Civil Code)
(C.A.R. Form AD-11, Revised 10/01)

When you enter into a discussion with a real estate agent regarding a real estate transaction, you should from the outset understand what type of agency relationship or representation you wish to have with the agent in the transaction.

SELLER'S AGENT

A Seller's agent under a listing agreement with the Seller acts as the agent for the Seller only. A Seller's agent or a subagent of that agent has the following affirmative obligations:
To the Seller:
    A Fiduciary duty of utmost care, integrity, honesty, and loyalty in dealings with the Seller.
To the Buyer and the Seller:
    (a) Diligent exercise of reasonable skill and care in performance of the agent's duties.
    (b) A duty of honest and fair dealing and good faith.
    (c) A duty to disclose all facts known to the agent materially affecting the value or desirability of the property that are not known to, or within the diligent attention and observation of, the parties.

An agent is not obligated to reveal to either party any confidential information obtained from the other party that does not involve the affirmative duties set forth above.

BUYER'S AGENT

A selling agent can, with a Buyer's consent, agree to act as agent for the Buyer only. In these situations, the agent is not the Seller's agent, even if by agreement the agent may receive compensation for services rendered, either in full or in part from the Seller. An agent acting only for a Buyer has the following affirmative obligations:
To the Buyer:
    A fiduciary duty of utmost care, integrity, honesty, and loyalty in dealings with the Buyer.
To the Buyer and the Seller:
    (a) Diligent exercise of reasonable skill and care in performance of the agent's duties.
    (b) A duty of honest and fair dealing and good faith.
    (c) A duty to disclose all facts known to the agent materially affecting the value or desirability of the property that are not known to, or within the diligent attention and observation of, the parties.

An agent is not obligated to reveal to either party any confidential information obtained from the other party that does not involve the affirmative duties set forth above.

AGENT REPRESENTING BOTH SELLER AND BUYER

A real estate agent, either acting directly or through one or more associate licensees, can legally be the agent of both the Seller and the Buyer in a transaction, but only with the knowledge and consent of both the Seller and the Buyer.

In a dual agency situation, the agent has the following affirmative obligations to both the Seller and the Buyer:
    (a) A fiduciary duty of utmost care, integrity, honesty and loyalty in the dealings with either the Seller or the Buyer.
    (b) Other duties to the Seller and the Buyer as stated above in their respective sections.

In representing both Seller and Buyer, the agent may not, without the express permission of the respective party, disclose to the other party that the Seller will accept a price less than the listing price or that the Buyer will pay a price greater than the price offered.

The above duties of the agent in a real estate transaction do not relieve a Seller or Buyer from the responsibility to protect his or her own interests. You should carefully read all agreements to assure that they adequately express your understanding of the transaction. A real estate agent is a person qualified to advise about real estate. If legal or tax advice is desired, consult a competent professional.

Throughout your real property transaction you may receive more than one disclosure form, depending upon the number of agents assisting in the transaction. The law requires each agent with whom you have more than a casual relationship to present you with this disclosure form. You should read its contents each time it is presented to you, considering the relationship between you and the real estate agent in your specific transaction.

This disclosure form includes the provisions of Sections 2079.13 to 2079.24, inclusive, of the Civil Code set forth on the reverse hereof. Read it carefully.

I/WE ACKNOWLEDGE RECEIPT OF A COPY OF THIS DISCLOSURE.

BUYER/SELLER _____ Date _____ Time _____ AM/PM

BUYER/SELLER _____ Date _____ Time _____ AM/PM

AGENT _____ By _____ Date _____
      (Please Print)   (Associate-Licensee or Broker Signature)

THIS FORM SHALL BE PROVIDED AND ACKNOWLEDGED AS FOLLOWS (Civil Code §2079.14):
•When the listing brokerage company also represents the Buyer, the Listing Agent shall give one AD-11 form to the Seller and one to the Buyer.
•When Buyer and Seller are represented by different brokerage companies, then the Listing Agent shall give one AD-11 form to the Seller and the Buyer's Agent shall give one AD-11 form to the Buyer and one AD-11 form to the Seller.

SEE REVERSE SIDE FOR FURTHER INFORMATION

Published and Distributed by:
REAL ESTATE BUSINESS SERVICES, INC.
a subsidiary of the CALIFORNIA ASSOCIATION OF REALTORS®
525 South Virgil Avenue, Los Angeles, California 90020

Reviewed by _____

Broker or Designee _____ Date _____

EQUAL HOUSING OPPORTUNITY

AD-11 REVISED 10/01 (PAGE 1 OF 1) Print Date

DISCLOSURE REGARDING REAL ESTATE AGENCY RELATIONSHIPS (AD-11 PAGE 1 OF 1)

confirmation will protect the licensee against any future charges of misrepresentation in the agency relationship. It should be completed as soon as possible.

The seller's agent cannot keep silent about any material facts that affect the value of the property (for example, the property is in an earthquake zone or backs up to a freeway or school).

But, the seller's agent cannot tell the buyer that the seller is insolvent because this would lower the offering price, violating the duty of loyalty in a fiduciary relationship.

Traditionally, the principal was usually a seller. Brokers are now free to represent the buyer, the seller, and sometimes both. **Figure 4-3** illustrates the agency options.

It is legal for an agent to work as a dual agent for both the buyer and seller if the agent has the written acknowledgment and consent of all parties to the transaction.

Figure 4-3

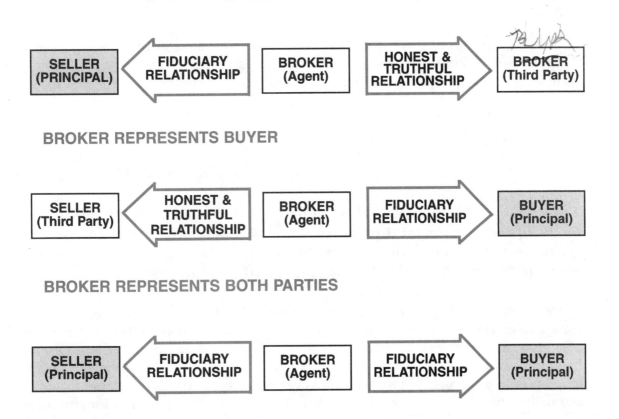

BROKER REPRESENTS SELLER

SELLER (PRINCIPAL) — FIDUCIARY RELATIONSHIP — BROKER (Agent) — HONEST & TRUTHFUL RELATIONSHIP — BROKER (Third Party)

BROKER REPRESENTS BUYER

SELLER (Third Party) — HONEST & TRUTHFUL RELATIONSHIP — BROKER (Agent) — FIDUCIARY RELATIONSHIP — BUYER (Principal)

BROKER REPRESENTS BOTH PARTIES

SELLER (Principal) — FIDUCIARY RELATIONSHIP — BROKER (Agent) — FIDUCIARY RELATIONSHIP — BUYER (Principal)

THE GROWTH OF "BUYER BROKERAGES"

A large number of brokers are responding to a need that a buyer be represented diligently by offering exclusive buyer's services. More than a fad, it is estimated that buyer's agents will represent 25% or more of the industry within the next ten years.

It is believed that good buyer representation will cut down on disputes and lawsuits. In the future, the trend will be toward brokers working for either the seller or buyer, not just the seller. No longer do brokers have to exclude themselves from one entire side of the market.

A broker who is helping a relative negotiate a lease/purchase option on a seller's home must inform the seller of this fact.

As you can see, there may be several brokers involved in a single transaction. In California, the seller (owner) and the buyer are usually represented by different brokers. The listing broker always represents the seller but may represent both. Traditionally, the selling broker, who procures the buyer, customarily represents the buyer. In some other states, all the brokers and salespeople represent only the seller (owner).

B. SALESPEOPLE MAY BE INDEPENDENT CONTRACTORS OR EMPLOYEES

In California most salespeople working under a broker are considered employees for the purposes of administration of the real estate law, even if they act as independent contractors for other purposes, such as income tax wage withholding, social security, or worker's compensation claim coverage.

An **INDEPENDENT CONTRACTOR** *sells results rather than time, and his or her physical conduct is not subject to the control of another. An* **EMPLOYEE**, *on the other hand, works under the direct control (designated hours and breaks) and supervision of the employer.*

The Department of Real Estate considers a salesperson an employee of the broker for the administration of the real estate broker law, even if he or she is an independent contractor. This makes the broker responsible for the real estate activities of the salesperson.

In most real estate offices the salespeople are treated as independent contractors. They come and go at will, working no fixed hours and pay their own payroll taxes (Federal and State Income Taxes, Social Security, Unemployment Insurance, and State Disability Insurance). More strictly supervised workers, such as secretaries, are generally considered employees. **The broker is required, however, to carry workman's compensation and public liability insurance for salespeople in the same way that they do for employees.**

TECHNOLOGY AND THE BROKER

The evolution of the computer (both in the home and in the office) and the Internet has revolutionized the way brokers do business. The majority of the public may now transmit loan applications, check out credit histories and view color photos of properties, both in and out-of-state.

Customers must have the perception that the REALTOR® utilizes the latest technological trends. Customers will not feel confident in using an agent who is not up to speed.

C. WRITTEN BROKER-ASSOCIATE CONTRACTS

As required by the Real Estate Commissioner's Regulations, brokers must have a written contract with each licensed member of the sale's staff. A copy of this contract must be retained by all parties for three years from the date of termination. This is also required of salespeople who are themselves brokers but are working under another broker's license. The agreement shall be dated and signed by the parties and shall cover material aspects of the relationship between the parties, including supervision of licensed activities, duties, and compensation.

Signed "broker-salesperson contracts" must be kept for "three years" from the date of termination of the contract by both parties.

Figure 4-4 shows the three-page CAR® Independent Contractor Agreement (Between Broker and Associate-Licensee). It outlines the duties, responsibilities, and compensation to be provided and must be signed and dated by both the broker and the salesperson.

Other specific rules and policies for handling procedures at a specific brokerage firm are usually set down in the company POLICY MANUAL. This manual must be read by all salespeople.

III. Listings and the Multiple Listing Service (MLS)

A. LISTING AGREEMENTS

A listing is an employment contract for personal service between a broker (represented by the salesperson) and a principal that creates an agency relationship.

The usual way to establish a broker's right to negotiate a sale of property is through a written contract, commonly called a listing. A *LISTING is a contract to employ a*

Figure 4-4

CALIFORNIA
ASSOCIATION
OF REALTORS®

INDEPENDENT CONTRACTOR AGREEMENT
(Between Broker and Associate-Licensee)

This Agreement, dated _____ is made between _____
_____ ("Broker") and
_____ ("Associate-Licensee").
In consideration of the covenants and representations contained in this Agreement, Broker and Associate-Licensee agree as follows:

1. **BROKER:** Broker represents that Broker is duly licensed as a real estate broker by the State of California, ☐ doing business as _____
   _____ (firm name), ☐ a sole proprietorship, ☐ a partnership, ☐ a corporation.
   Broker is a member of the _____
   Association(s) of REALTORS®, and a subscriber to the _____ multiple
   listing service(s). Broker shall keep Broker's license current during the term of this Agreement.

2. **ASSOCIATE-LICENSEE:** Associate-Licensee represents that, (a) he/she is duly licensed by the State of California as a ☐ real estate broker,
   ☐ real estate salesperson, and (b) he/she has not used any other names within the past five years, except _____
   _____. Associate-Licensee shall keep his/her license current during
   the term of this Agreement, including satisfying all applicable continuing education and provisional license requirements.

3. **INDEPENDENT CONTRACTOR RELATIONSHIP:**
   A. Broker and Associate-Licensee intend that, to the maximum extent permissible by law: **(i)** This Agreement does not constitute an employment agreement by either party; **(ii)** Broker and Associate-Licensee are independent contracting parties with respect to all services rendered under this Agreement; **(iii)** This Agreement shall not be construed as a partnership.
   B. Broker shall not: **(i)** restrict Associate-Licensee's activities to particular geographical areas or, **(ii)** dictate Associate-Licensee's activities with regard to hours, leads, open houses, opportunity or floor time, production, prospects, sales meetings, schedule, inventory, time off, vacation, or similar activities, except to the extent required by law.
   C. Associate-Licensee shall not be required to accept an assignment by Broker to service any particular current or prospective listing or parties.
   D. Except as required by law: **(i)** Associate-Licensee retains sole and absolute discretion and judgment in the methods, techniques, and procedures to be used in soliciting and obtaining listings, sales, exchanges, leases, rentals, or other transactions, and in carrying out Associate-Licensee's selling and soliciting activities, **(ii)** Associate-Licensee is under the control of Broker as to the results of Associate-Licensee's work only, and not as to the means by which those results are accomplished, **(iii)** Associate-Licensee has no authority to bind Broker by any promise or representation and **(iv)** Broker shall not be liable for any obligation or liability incurred by Associate-Licensee.
   E. Associate-Licensee's only remuneration shall be the compensation specified in paragraph 8.
   F. Associate-Licensee shall not be treated as an employee with respect to services performed as a real estate agent, for state and federal tax purposes.
   G. The fact the Broker may carry worker compensation insurance for Broker's own benefit and for the mutual benefit of Broker and licensees associated with Broker, including Associate-Licensee, shall not create an inference of employment.

4. **LICENSED ACTIVITY:** All listings of property, and all agreements, acts or actions for performance of licensed acts, which are taken or performed in connection with this Agreement, shall be taken and performed in the name of Broker. Associate-Licensee agrees to and does hereby contribute all right and title to such listings to Broker for the benefit and use of Broker, Associate-Licensee, and other licensees associated with Broker. Broker shall make available to Associate-Licensee, equally with other licensees associated with Broker, all current listings in Broker's office, except any listing which Broker may choose to place in the exclusive servicing of Associate-Licensee or one or more other specific licensees associated with Broker. Associate-Licensee shall provide and pay for all professional licenses, supplies, services, and other items required in connection with Associate-Licensee's activities under this Agreement, or any listing or transaction, without reimbursement from Broker except as required by law. Associate-Licensee shall work diligently and with his/her best efforts: **(a)** To sell, exchange, lease, or rent properties listed with Broker or other cooperating Brokers; **(b)** To solicit additional listings, clients, and customers; and **(c)** To otherwise promote the business of serving the public in real estate transactions to the end that Broker and Associate-Licensee may derive the greatest benefit possible, in accordance with law. Associate-Licensee shall not commit any unlawful act under federal, state or local law or regulation while conducting licensed activity. Associate-Licensee shall at all times be familiar, and comply, with all applicable federal, state and local laws, including, but not limited to, anti-discrimination laws and restrictions against the giving or accepting a fee, or other thing of value, for the referral of business to title companies, escrow companies, home inspection companies, pest control companies and other settlement service providers pursuant to the California Business and Professions Code and the Real Estate Settlement Procedures Acts (RESPA). Broker shall make available for Associate-Licensee's use, along with other licensees associated with Broker, the facilities of the real estate office operated by Broker at _____
   _____ and the facilities of any other office
   locations made available by Broker pursuant to this Agreement.

Broker and Associate-Licensee acknowledge receipt of copy of this page, which constitutes Page 1 of _____ Pages.
   Broker's Initials (_____) (_____) Associate-Licensee's Initials (_____) (_____)

REVISED 10/98

OFFICE USE ONLY
Reviewed by Broker
or Designee _____
Date _____

EQUAL HOUSING
OPPORTUNITY

INDEPENDENT CONTRACTOR AGREEMENT (ICA-11 PAGE 1 OF 3)

5. **PROPRIETARY INFORMATION AND FILES:** **(a)** All files and documents pertaining to listings, leads and transactions are the property of Broker and shall be delivered to Broker by Associate-Licensee immediately upon request or termination of their relationship under this Agreement. **(b)** Associate-Licensee acknowledges that Broker's method of conducting business is a protected trade secret. **(c)** Associate-Licensee shall not use to his/her own advantage, or the advantage of any other person, business, or entity, except as specifically agreed in writing, either during Associate-Licensee's association with Broker, or thereafter, any information gained for or from the business, or files of Broker.

6. **SUPERVISION:** Associate-Licensee, within 24 hours (or ☐ _____) after preparing, signing, or receiving same, shall submit to Broker, or Broker's designated licensee: **(a)** All documents which may have a material effect upon the rights and duties of principals in a transaction, **(b)** Any documents or other items connected with a transaction pursuant to this Agreement in the possession of or available to Associate-Licensee and, **(c)** All documents associated with any real estate transaction in which Associate-Licensee is a principal.

7. **TRUST FUNDS:** All trust funds shall be handled in compliance with the Business and Professions Code, and other applicable laws.

8. **COMPENSATION:**
   A. TO BROKER: Compensation shall be charged to parties who enter into listing or other agreements for services requiring a real estate license:
   ☐ as shown in "Exhibit A" attached, which is incorporated as a part of this Agreement by reference, or
   ☐ as follows: _____
   _____
   _____
   Any deviation which is not approved in writing in advance by Broker, shall be (1) deducted from Associate-Licensee's compensation, if lower than the amount or rate approved above; and, (2) subject to Broker approval, if higher than the amount approved above. Any permanent change in commission schedule shall be disseminated by Broker to Associate-Licensee.

   B. TO ASSOCIATE-LICENSEE: Associate-Licensee shall receive a share of compensation actually collected by Broker, on listings or other agreements for services requiring a real estate license, which are solicited and obtained by Associate-Licensee, and on transactions of which Associate-Licensee's activities are the procuring cause, as follows:
   ☐ as shown in "Exhibit B" attached, which is incorporated as a part of this Agreement by reference, or
   ☐ other: _____
   _____
   _____

   C. PARTNERS, TEAMS, AND AGREEMENTS WITH OTHER ASSOCIATE-LICENSEES IN OFFICE: If Associate-Licensee and one or more other Associate-Licensees affiliated with Broker participate on the same side (either listing or selling) of a transaction, the commission allocated to their combined activities shall be divided by Broker and paid to them according to their written agreement. Broker shall have the right to withhold total compensation if there is a dispute between associate-licensees, or if there is no written agreement, or if no written agreement has been provided to Broker.

   D. EXPENSES AND OFFSETS: If Broker elects to advance funds to pay expenses or liabilities of Associate-Licensee, or for an advance payment of, or draw upon, future compensation, Broker may deduct the full amount advanced from compensation payable to Associate-Licensee on any transaction without notice. If Associate-Licensee's compensation is subject to a lien, garnishment or other restriction on payment, Broker shall charge Associate-Licensee a fee for complying with such restriction.

   E. PAYMENT: **(1)** All compensation collected by Broker and due to Associate-Licensee shall be paid to Associate-Licensee, after deduction of expenses and offsets, immediately or as soon thereafter as practicable, except as otherwise provided in this Agreement, or a separate written agreement between Broker and Associate-Licensee. **(2)** Compensation shall not be paid to Associate-Licensee until both the transaction and file are complete. **(3)** Broker is under no obligation to pursue collection of compensation from any person or entity responsible for payment. Associate-Licensee does not have the independent right to pursue collection of compensation for activities which require a real estate license which were done in the name of Broker. **(4)** Expenses which are incurred in the attempt to collect compensation shall be paid by Broker and Associate-Licensee in the same proportion as set forth for the division of compensation (paragraph 8(B)). **(5)** If there is a known or pending claim against Broker or Associate-Licensee on transactions for which Associate-Licensee has not yet been paid, Broker may withhold from compensation due Associate-Licensee on that transaction amounts for which Associate-Licensee could be responsible under paragraph 14, until such claim is resolved. **(6)** Associate-Licensee shall not be entitled to any advance payment from Broker upon future compensation.

   F. UPON OR AFTER TERMINATION: If this Agreement is terminated while Associate-Licensee has listings or pending transactions that require further work normally rendered by Associate-Licensee, Broker shall make arrangements with another associate-licensee to perform the required work, or Broker shall perform the work him/herself. The licensee performing the work shall be reasonably compensated for completing work on those listings or transactions, and such reasonable compensation shall be deducted from Associate-Licensee's share of compensation. Except for such offset, Associate-Licensee shall receive the compensation due as specified above.

9. **TERMINATION OF RELATIONSHIP:** Broker or Associate-Licensee may terminate their relationship under this Agreement at any time, with or without cause. After termination, Associate-Licensee shall not solicit **(a)** prospective or existing clients or customers based upon company-generated leads obtained during the time Associate-Licensee was affiliated with Broker, or (b) any principal with existing contractual obligations to Broker, or (c) any principal with a contractual transactional obligation for which Broker is entitled to be compensated. Even after termination, this Agreement shall govern all disputes and claims between Broker and Associate-Licensee connected with their relationship under this Agreement, including obligations and liabilities arising from existing and completed listings, transactions, and services.

Broker and Associate-Licensee acknowledge receipt of copy of this page, which constitutes Page 2 of _____ Pages.
Broker's Initials (_____) (_____)   Associate-Licensee's Initials (_____) (_____)

REVISED 10/98

OFFICE USE ONLY
Reviewed by Broker
or Designee _____
Date _____

Page 2 of ___ Pages.

PRINT DATE

INDEPENDENT CONTRACTOR AGREEMENT (ICA-11 PAGE 2 OF 3)

10. **DISPUTE RESOLUTION:**
    A. Mediation: Mediation is recommended as a method of resolving disputes arising out of this Agreement between Broker and Associate-Licensee.
    B. Arbitration: All disputes or claims between Associate-Licensee and other licensee(s) associated with Broker, or between Associate-Licensee and Broker, arising from or connected in any way with this Agreement, which cannot be adjusted between the parties involved, shall be submitted to the Association of REALTORS® of which all such disputing parties are members for arbitration pursuant to the provisions of its Bylaws, as may be amended from time to time, which are incorporated as a part of this Agreement by reference. If the Bylaws of the Association do not cover arbitration of the dispute, or if the Association declines jurisdiction over the dispute, then arbitration shall be pursuant to the rules of California law. The Federal Arbitration Act, Title 9, U.S. Code, Section 1, et seq., shall govern this Agreement.

11. **AUTOMOBILE:** Associate-Licensee shall maintain automobile insurance coverage for liability and property damage in the following amounts $_____/$_____. Broker shall be named as an additional insured party on Associate-Licensee's policies. A copy of the endorsement showing Broker as an additional insured shall be provided to Broker.

12. **PERSONAL ASSISTANTS:** Associate-Licensee may make use of a personal assistant, provided the following requirements are satisfied. Associate-Licensee shall have a written agreement with the personal assistant which establishes the terms and responsibilities of the parties to the employment agreement, including, but not limited to, compensation, supervision and compliance with applicable law. The agreement shall be subject to Broker's review and approval. Unless otherwise agreed, if the personal assistant has a real estate license, that license must be provided to the Broker. Both Associate-Licensee and personal assistant must sign any agreement that Broker has established for such purposes.

13. **OFFICE POLICY MANUAL:** If Broker's office policy manual, now or as modified in the future, conflicts with or differs from the terms of this Agreement, the terms of the office policy manual shall govern the relationship between Broker and Associate-Licensee.

14. **INDEMNITY AND HOLD HARMLESS:** Associate-Licensee agrees to indemnify, defend and hold Broker harmless from all claims, disputes, litigation, judgments, awards, costs and attorney's fees, arising from any action taken or omitted by Associate-Licensee, or others working through, or on behalf of Associate-Licensee in connection with services rendered. Any such claims or costs payable pursuant to this Agreement, are due as follows:
    ☐ Paid in full by Associate-Licensee, who hereby agrees to indemnify and hold harmless Broker for all such sums, or
    ☐ In the same ratio as the compensation split as it existed at the time the compensation was earned by Associate-Licensee
    ☐ Other: _____
    _____
    _____

    Payment from Associate-Licensee is due at the time Broker makes such payment and can be offset from any compensation due Associate-Licensee as above. Broker retains the authority to settle claims or disputes, whether or not Associate-Licensee consents to such settlement.

15. **ADDITIONAL PROVISIONS:** _____
    _____
    _____

16. **DEFINITIONS:** As used in this Agreement, the following terms have the meanings indicated:
    (A) "Listing" means an agreement with a property owner or other party to locate a buyer, exchange party, lessee, or other party to a transaction involving real property, a mobile home, or other property or transaction which may be brokered by a real estate licensee, or an agreement with a party to locate or negotiate for any such property or transaction.
    (B) "Compensation means compensation for acts requiring a real estate license, regardless of whether calculated as a percentage of transaction price, flat fee, hourly rate, or in any other manner.
    (C) "Transaction" means a sale, exchange, lease, or rental of real property, a business opportunity, or a manufactured home, which may lawfully be brokered by a real estate licensee.

17. **ATTORNEY FEES:** In any action, proceeding, or arbitration between Broker and Associate-Licensee arising from or related to this Agreement, the prevailing Broker or Associate-Licensee shall be entitled to reasonable attorney fees and costs.

18. **ENTIRE AGREEMENT; MODIFICATION:** All prior agreements between the parties concerning their relationship as Broker and Associate-Licensee are incorporated in this Agreement, which constitutes the entire contract. Its terms are intended by the parties as a final and complete expression of their agreement with respect to its subject matter, and may not be contradicted by evidence of any prior agreement or contemporaneous oral agreement. This Agreement may not be amended, modified, altered, or changed except by a further agreement in writing executed by Broker and Associate-Licensee.

Broker:

_____
(Brokerage firm name)

By _____
Its Broker/Office manager (circle one)

_____
(Print name)

_____
(Address)

_____
(City, State, Zip)

_____
(Telephone)   (Fax)

Associate-Licensee:

_____
(Signature)

_____
(Print name)

_____
(Address)

_____
(City, State, Zip)

_____
(Telephone)   (Fax)

REVISED 10/98

Page 3 of ___ Pages.

OFFICE USE ONLY
Reviewed by Broker
or Designee _____
Date _____

EQUAL HOUSING OPPORTUNITY

INDEPENDENT CONTRACTOR AGREEMENT (ICA-11 PAGE 3 OF 3)

broker, legally referred to as an agent, to do certain things for the owner/seller. It is an employment contract for personal service.

Listings are NOT assignable and death of the seller or broker cancels a listing, unless the seller is a corporation (which may live forever).

There are four basic types of listings used in California. They are:

1. Open Listing (non-exclusive)
2. Exclusive Agency Listing
3. Exclusive Right to Sell Listing
4. Net Listing (rare)

A listing may be for any period of time. If NO beginning date is specified, the effective date is the date when the listing is signed. Real estate law requires that exclusive listings must have a definite, final termination date. If NOT, the agent may lose the commission and possibly his or her license.

You should also know: all real estate listing agreements or contracts should be in writing, and must be in writing to assure collection of a commission.

All listings belong to the broker, NOT the salesperson. If you move, few brokers will allow you to take your (their) listings.

1. Open Listing (Unilateral, Non-Exclusive Contract)

An *OPEN LISTING is an authorization to sell a property. It may be given to several brokers or the property may be sold by the owner.* If the owner sells the property, he or she is not required to pay a commission. Usually, no time limit is placed on an open listing. A description of the property is included in the agreement along with the selling price and other terms.

Open listings are the simplest form of broker authorization. They can be given to several brokers concurrently, and no notice of sale is required to terminate the listing. A broker should make sure an open listing is still valid before pursuing it. When an open listing is given to more than one broker, the first broker who finds a qualified buyer is entitled to the commission. On the other hand, if an owner finds his or her own buyer, that owner has no obligation to pay a commission to a broker.

NOT all listings are a promise for a promise (bilateral). The open listing is unilateral (only seller promises). Exclusive listings are bilateral.

Few brokers use this type of listing because of its uncertainty and the expense of advertising when working an open listing.

2. Exclusive Agency Listing (No Commission if Owner Sells)

The *EXCLUSIVE AGENCY LISTING is a listing providing that one agent has the right to be the only person, other than the owner, to sell the property during a specified period.* The owner, however, still has the right to independently sell the property without paying a commission to the listing broker. The drawback with this type of listing is that the broker is, or could be, in competition with the owner for the sale. These listings are entered into the MLS.

An exclusive agency listing and exclusive right to sell listing both require a definite termination date.

3. Exclusive Right to Sell Listing (Commission if Sold Within the Listing Period)

The most common type of listing is the exclusive right to sell listing. Only the *EXCLUSIVE RIGHT TO SELL LISTING entitles the listing broker named in the agency contract to a commission even if the owner sells the property.* **Figure 4-5** shows the CAR® Residential Listing Agreement (Exclusive Authorization and Right to Sell).

With an exclusive agency listing, the broker competes with the owner; with an exclusive right to sell listing, the broker is entitled to a commission even if the owner sells the property. An exclusive right to sell is the "strongest listing."

This type of listing often contains a section referred to as a safety clause. A *SAFETY CLAUSE in a listing is a negotiated period (any agreed to time period) after the termination of a listing in which the listing broker may still be entitled to a commission.* To protect themselves, brokers must furnish the owner/seller with a written list of persons to whom they have shown the property during the listing period. If the owner or a new broker sells the property to someone on the list within the negotiated period, the original broker may be entitled to a commission. **If a seller signs, for example, a 90-day exclusive right to sell listing with one broker, cancels it two weeks later, and gives an open listing to another broker who brings in an offer that is accepted, both brokers are entitled to a full commission.**

4. Net Listing (Must Be Used With Other Listing—Seldom Used)

A *NET LISTING is an agreement providing that the agent agrees to sell the owner's property for a set minimum price, any amount over the minimum being retained by the agent as commission.* This authorization to sell must be used with one of the other three listings, taking the form of an open listing, an exclusive agency listing, or an exclusive right to sell listing.

With this type of listing it is imperative for the broker to explain, in writing, the exact meaning of a net listing so that there is no confusion about any earned

Figure 4-5

CALIFORNIA
ASSOCIATION
OF REALTORS®

RESIDENTIAL LISTING AGREEMENT
(Exclusive Authorization and Right to Sell)
(C.A.R. Form LA, Revised 10/02)

1. **EXCLUSIVE RIGHT TO SELL:** _____ ("Seller")
   hereby employs and grants _____ ("Broker")
   beginning (date) _____ and ending at 11:59 P.M. on (date) _____ ("Listing Period")
   the exclusive and irrevocable right to sell or exchange the real property in the City of _____,
   County of _____, California, described as: _____
   _____ ("Property").

2. **ITEMS EXCLUDED AND INCLUDED:** Unless otherwise specified in a real estate purchase agreement, all fixtures and fittings that are attached to the Property are included, and personal property items are excluded, from the purchase price.
   ADDITIONAL ITEMS EXCLUDED: _____.
   ADDITIONAL ITEMS INCLUDED: _____.
   Seller intends that the above items be excluded or included in offering the Property for sale, but understands that: **(i)** the purchase agreement supersedes any intention expressed above and will ultimately determine which items are excluded and included in the sale; and **(ii)** Broker is not responsible for and does not guarantee that the above exclusions and/or inclusions will be in the purchase agreement.

3. **LISTING PRICE AND TERMS:**
   A. The listing price shall be: _____
   _____ Dollars ($ _____).
   B. Additional Terms: _____
   _____

4. **COMPENSATION TO BROKER:**
   Notice: The amount or rate of real estate commissions is not fixed by law. They are set by each Broker individually and may be negotiable between Seller and Broker (real estate commissions include all compensation and fees to Broker).
   A. Seller agrees to pay to Broker as compensation for services irrespective of agency relationship(s), either ☐ _____ percent of the listing price (or if a purchase agreement is entered into, of the purchase price), or ☐ $ _____,
   AND _____, as follows:
   (1) If Broker, Seller, cooperating broker, or any other person procures a buyer(s) who offers to purchase the Property on the above price and terms, or on any price and terms acceptable to Seller during the Listing Period, or any extension.
   (2) If Seller, within _____ calendar days after the end of the Listing Period or any extension, enters into a contract to sell, convey, lease or otherwise transfer the Property to anyone ("Prospective Buyer") or that person's related entity: **(i)** who physically entered and was shown the Property during the Listing Period or any extension by Broker or a cooperating broker; or **(ii)** for whom Broker or any cooperating broker submitted to Seller a signed, written offer to acquire, lease, exchange or obtain an option on the Property. Seller, however, shall have no obligation to Broker under paragraph 4A(2) unless, not later than **3 calendar days** after the end of the Listing Period or any extension, Broker has given Seller a written notice of the names of such Prospective Buyers.
   (3) If, without Broker's prior written consent, the Property is withdrawn from sale, conveyed, leased, rented, otherwise transferred, or made unmarketable by a voluntary act of Seller during the Listing Period, or any extension.
   B. If completion of the sale is prevented by a party to the transaction other than Seller, then compensation due under paragraph 4A shall be payable only if and when Seller collects damages by suit, arbitration, settlement or otherwise, and then in an amount equal to the lesser of one-half of the damages recovered or the above compensation, after first deducting title and escrow expenses and the expenses of collection, if any.
   C. In addition, Seller agrees to pay Broker: _____
   D. **(1)** Broker is authorized to cooperate with and compensate brokers participating through the multiple listing service(s) ("MLS"): **(i)** in any manner; **OR (ii)** (if checked) by offering MLS brokers: either ☐ _____ percent of the purchase price, or ☐ $ _____.
   (2) Broker is authorized to cooperate with and compensate brokers operating outside the MLS in any manner.
   E. Seller hereby irrevocably assigns to Broker the above compensation from Seller's funds and proceeds in escrow. Broker may submit this agreement, as instructions to compensate Broker pursuant to paragraph 4A, to any escrow regarding the Property involving Seller and a buyer, Prospective Buyer or other transferee.
   F. **(1)** Seller represents that Seller has not previously entered into a listing agreement with another broker regarding the Property, unless specified as follows: _____.
   (2) Seller warrants that Seller has no obligation to pay compensation to any other broker regarding the Property unless the Property is transferred to any of the following individuals or entities: _____
   _____.
   (3) If the Property is sold to anyone listed above during the time Seller is obligated to compensate another broker: **(i)** Broker is not entitled to compensation under this agreement; and **(ii)** Broker is not obligated to represent Seller in such transaction.

LA REVISED 10/02 (PAGE 1 OF 3)   Print Date

Seller acknowledges receipt of a copy of this page.
Seller's Initials (_____)(_____)

| Reviewed by _____ Date _____ |

EQUAL HOUSING OPPORTUNITY

RESIDENTIAL LISTING AGREEMENT-EXCLUSIVE (LA PAGE 1 OF 3)

Property Address: _____ Date: _____

5. **OWNERSHIP, TITLE AND AUTHORITY:** Seller warrants that: **(i)** Seller is the owner of the Property; **(ii)** no other persons or entities have title to the Property; and **(iii)** Seller has the authority to both execute this agreement and sell the Property. Exceptions to ownership, title and authority are as follows: _____.

6. **MULTIPLE LISTING SERVICE:** Information about this listing will (or ☐ will not) be provided to the MLS of Broker's selection. All terms of the transaction, including financing, if applicable, will be provided to the selected MLS for publication, dissemination and use by persons and entities on terms approved by the MLS. Seller authorizes Broker to comply with all applicable MLS rules. MLS rules allow MLS data to be made available by the MLS to additional Internet sites unless Broker gives the MLS instructions to the contrary.

7. **SELLER REPRESENTATIONS:** Seller represents that, unless otherwise specified in writing, Seller is unaware of: **(i)** any Notice of Default recorded against the Property; **(ii)** any delinquent amounts due under any loan secured by, or other obligation affecting, the Property; **(iii)** any bankruptcy, insolvency or similar proceeding affecting the Property; **(iv)** any litigation, arbitration, administrative action, government investigation or other pending or threatened action that affects or may affect the Property or Seller's ability to transfer it; and **(v)** any current, pending or proposed special assessments affecting the Property. Seller shall promptly notify Broker in writing if Seller becomes aware of any of these items during the Listing Period or any extension thereof.

8. **BROKER'S AND SELLER'S DUTIES:** Broker agrees to exercise reasonable effort and due diligence to achieve the purposes of this agreement. Unless Seller gives Broker written instructions to the contrary, Broker is authorized to order reports and disclosures as appropriate or necessary and advertise and market the Property by any method and in any medium selected by Broker, including MLS and the Internet, and, to the extent permitted by these media, control the dissemination of the information submitted to any medium. Seller agrees to consider offers presented by Broker, and to act in good faith to accomplish the sale of the Property by, among other things, making the Property available for showing at reasonable times and referring to Broker all inquiries of any party interested in the Property. Seller is responsible for determining at what price to list and sell the Property. **Seller further agrees to indemnify, defend and hold Broker harmless from all claims, disputes, litigation, judgments and attorney fees arising from any incorrect information supplied by Seller, or from any material facts that Seller knows but fails to disclose.**

9. **DEPOSIT:** Broker is authorized to accept and hold on Seller's behalf any deposits to be applied toward the purchase price.

10. **AGENCY RELATIONSHIPS:**
    A. **Disclosure:** If the Property includes residential property with one-to-four dwelling units, Seller shall receive a "Disclosure Regarding Agency Relationships" form prior to entering into this agreement.
    B. **Seller Representation:** Broker shall represent Seller in any resulting transaction, except as specified in paragraph 4F.
    C. **Possible Dual Agency With Buyer:** Depending upon the circumstances, it may be necessary or appropriate for Broker to act as an agent for both Seller and buyer, exchange party, or one or more additional parties ("Buyer"). Broker shall, as soon as practicable, disclose to Seller any election to act as a dual agent representing both Seller and Buyer. If a Buyer is procured directly by Broker or an associate licensee in Broker's firm, Seller hereby consents to Broker acting as a dual agent for Seller and such Buyer. In the event of an exchange, Seller hereby consents to Broker collecting compensation from additional parties for services rendered, provided there is disclosure to all parties of such agency and compensation. Seller understands and agrees that: **(i)** Broker, without the prior written consent of Seller, will not disclose to Buyer that Seller is willing to sell the Property at a price less than the listing price; **(ii)** Broker, without the prior written consent of Buyer, will not disclose to Seller that Buyer is willing to pay a price greater than the offered price; and **(iii)** except for (i) and (ii) above, a dual agent is obligated to disclose known facts materially affecting the value or desirability of the Property to both parties.
    D. **Other Sellers:** Seller understands that Broker may have or obtain listings on other properties, and that potential buyers may consider, make offers on, or purchase through Broker, property the same as or similar to Seller's Property. Seller consents to Broker's representation of sellers and buyers of other properties before, during and after the end of this agreement.
    E. **Confirmation:** If the Property includes residential property with one-to-four dwelling units, Broker shall confirm the agency relationship described above, or as modified, in writing, prior to or concurrent with Seller's execution of a purchase agreement.

11. **SECURITY AND INSURANCE:** Broker is not responsible for loss of or damage to personal or real property, or person, whether attributable to use of a keysafe/lockbox, a showing of the Property, or otherwise. Third parties, including, but not limited to, appraisers, inspectors, brokers and prospective buyers, may have access to, and take videos and photographs of, the interior of the Property. Seller agrees: **(i)** to take reasonable precautions to safeguard and protect valuables that might be accessible during showings of the Property; and **(ii)** to obtain insurance to protect against these risks. Broker does not maintain insurance to protect Seller.

12. **KEYSAFE/LOCKBOX:** A keysafe/lockbox is designed to hold a key to the Property to permit access to the Property by Broker, cooperating brokers, MLS participants, their authorized licensees and representatives, authorized inspectors, and accompanied prospective buyers. Broker, cooperating brokers, MLS and Associations/Boards of REALTORS® are **not** insurers against injury, theft, loss, vandalism or damage attributed to the use of a keysafe/lockbox. Seller does (or if checked ☐ does not) authorize Broker to install a keysafe/lockbox. If Seller does not occupy the Property, Seller shall be responsible for obtaining occupant(s)' written permission for use of a keysafe/lockbox.

13. **SIGN:** Seller does (or if checked ☐ does not) authorize Broker to install a FOR SALE/SOLD sign on the Property.

14. **EQUAL HOUSING OPPORTUNITY:** The Property is offered in compliance with federal, state and local anti-discrimination laws.

15. **ATTORNEY FEES:** In any action, proceeding or arbitration between Seller and Broker regarding the obligation to pay compensation under this agreement, the prevailing Seller or Broker shall be entitled to reasonable attorney fees and costs from the non-prevailing Seller or Broker, except as provided in paragraph 19A.

16. **ADDITIONAL TERMS:** _____
    _____
    _____
    _____

17. **MANAGEMENT APPROVAL:** If an associate licensee in Broker's office (salesperson or broker-associate) enters into this agreement on Broker's behalf, and Broker or Manager does not approve of its terms, Broker or Manager has the right to cancel this agreement, in writing, within 5 days after its execution.

18. **SUCCESSORS AND ASSIGNS:** This agreement shall be binding upon Seller and Seller's successors and assigns.

Seller acknowledges receipt of a copy of this page.
Seller's Initials (_____)(_____)

LA REVISED 10/02 (PAGE 2 OF 3)

| Reviewed by _____ Date _____ |

EQUAL HOUSING OPPORTUNITY

RESIDENTIAL LISTING AGREEMENT-EXCLUSIVE (LA PAGE 2 OF 3)

Property Address: _____ Date: _____

19. DISPUTE RESOLUTION:

  A. MEDIATION: Seller and Broker agree to mediate any dispute or claim arising between them out of this agreement, or any resulting transaction, before resorting to arbitration or court action, subject to paragraph 19B(2) below. Paragraph 19B(2) below applies whether or not the arbitration provision is initialed. Mediation fees, if any, shall be divided equally among the parties involved. If, for any dispute or claim to which this paragraph applies, any party commences an action without first attempting to resolve the matter through mediation, or refuses to mediate after a request has been made, then that party shall not be entitled to recover attorney fees, even if they would otherwise be available to that party in any such action. THIS MEDIATION PROVISION APPLIES WHETHER OR NOT THE ARBITRATION PROVISION IS INITIALED.

  B. ARBITRATION OF DISPUTES: (1) Seller and Broker agree that any dispute or claim in Law or equity arising between them regarding the obligation to pay compensation under this agreement, which is not settled through mediation, shall be decided by neutral, binding arbitration, including and subject to paragraph 19B(2) below. The arbitrator shall be a retired judge or justice, or an attorney with at least 5 years of residential real estate law experience, unless the parties mutually agree to a different arbitrator, who shall render an award in accordance with substantive California Law. The parties shall have the right to discovery in accordance with Code of Civil Procedure §1283.05. In all other respects, the arbitration shall be conducted in accordance with Title 9 of Part III of the California Code of Civil Procedure. Judgment upon the award of the arbitrator(s) may be entered in any court having jurisdiction. Interpretation of this agreement to arbitrate shall be governed by the Federal Arbitration Act.
  (2) EXCLUSIONS FROM MEDIATION AND ARBITRATION: The following matters are excluded from mediation and arbitration hereunder: **(i)** a judicial or non-judicial foreclosure or other action or proceeding to enforce a deed of trust, mortgage, or installment land sale contract as defined in Civil Code §2985; **(ii)** an unlawful detainer action; **(iii)** the filing or enforcement of a mechanic's lien; and **(iv)** any matter that is within the jurisdiction of a probate, small claims, or bankruptcy court. The filing of a court action to enable the recording of a notice of pending action, for order of attachment, receivership, injunction, or other provisional remedies, shall not constitute a waiver of the mediation and arbitration provisions.
  "NOTICE: BY INITIALING IN THE SPACE BELOW YOU ARE AGREEING TO HAVE ANY DISPUTE ARISING OUT OF THE MATTERS INCLUDED IN THE 'ARBITRATION OF DISPUTES' PROVISION DECIDED BY NEUTRAL ARBITRATION AS PROVIDED BY CALIFORNIA LAW AND YOU ARE GIVING UP ANY RIGHTS YOU MIGHT POSSESS TO HAVE THE DISPUTE LITIGATED IN A COURT OR JURY TRIAL. BY INITIALING IN THE SPACE BELOW YOU ARE GIVING UP YOUR JUDICIAL RIGHTS TO DISCOVERY AND APPEAL, UNLESS THOSE RIGHTS ARE SPECIFICALLY INCLUDED IN THE 'ARBITRATION OF DISPUTES' PROVISION. IF YOU REFUSE TO SUBMIT TO ARBITRATION AFTER AGREEING TO THIS PROVISION, YOU MAY BE COMPELLED TO ARBITRATE UNDER THE AUTHORITY OF THE CALIFORNIA CODE OF CIVIL PROCEDURE. YOUR AGREEMENT TO THIS ARBITRATION PROVISION IS VOLUNTARY."
  "WE HAVE READ AND UNDERSTAND THE FOREGOING AND AGREE TO SUBMIT DISPUTES ARISING OUT OF THE MATTERS INCLUDED IN THE 'ARBITRATION OF DISPUTES' PROVISION TO NEUTRAL ARBITRATION."

Seller's Initials _____ / _____	Broker's Initials _____ / _____

20. ENTIRE CONTRACT: All prior discussions, negotiations and agreements between the parties concerning the subject matter of this agreement are superseded by this agreement, which constitutes the entire contract and a complete and exclusive expression of their agreement, and may not be contradicted by evidence of any prior agreement or contemporaneous oral agreement. If any provision of this agreement is held to be ineffective or invalid, the remaining provisions will nevertheless be given full force and effect. This agreement and any supplement, addendum or modification, including any photocopy or facsimile, may be executed in counterparts.

By signing below, Seller acknowledges that Seller has read, understands, accepts and has received a copy of this agreement.

Seller _____ Date _____
Address _____ City _____ State _____ Zip _____
Telephone _____ Fax _____ E-mail _____

Seller _____ Date _____
Address _____ City _____ State _____ Zip _____
Telephone _____ Fax _____ E-mail _____

Real Estate Broker (Firm) _____
By (Agent) _____ Date _____
Address _____ City _____ State _____ Zip _____
Telephone _____ Fax _____ E-mail _____

SURE TRAC
The System for Success™

Published by the
California Association of REALTORS®

Reviewed by _____ Date _____

EQUAL HOUSING OPPORTUNITY

LA REVISED 10/02 (PAGE 3 OF 3)

RESIDENTIAL LISTING AGREEMENT-EXCLUSIVE (LA PAGE 3 OF 3)

Photo Reality: Seeing is Believing

Imagine having an open house where clients can do a "walk through" without personally visiting the property. Streaming video tours on the Web allow your clients to see the listed properties anytime they want.

While "virtual tours" may never replace a good old fashion walk through, internet screening may very well eliminate the real estate "drive-by" and "looky-loo" phenomenon. Potential homebuyers no longer need to drive-by a home to get a feel for such things as the neighborhood, condition of the house, curbside appeal, interior layout, spacial relationships, an kitchen design. Because of digital technology, a prospective buyer can zoom in and out, follow the camera to another room, check out the ceiling, and get a 360 degree view of a living room or bedroom. Once a client has seen a video of both the inside and outside of a home, they can decide if they're interested before contacting an agent.

"Streaming video tours" may encompass not only the house for sale, but also show the surrounding area, including schools, churches, shopping districts, and parks. If a picture is worth a thousand words, imagine how valuable a picture tour on a Website could be. Picture tours are an effective means to attract both buyers and sellers.

You may want to lend a hand and prepare Web pictures for busy and non-computer oriented salespeople in your office, as it will benefit you and your company in the long run. In fact, many will be willing to pay you for this service. Because you offer picture tours on the Web, sellers will prefer to list properties with you. Not only will your listings increase, but they will get more attention from buyers.

A real estate licensee who can provide photo or video services to real estate agents will always be in demand. He or she can take digital photos and videos of a property without the listing agent present and speed up the process of getting that property listed on the company's Web tours. Panoramic videos are valuable visual aides for a buyer to see size and scale, and a walking video tour provides an unparalleled viewing experience for all to get the feel of space and flow.

SERVICES

www.ipix.com (Internet Pictures Corp.)
www.home-view.com/ (HomeView.com)
www.evox.com eVox Productions)
www.virtualpr perties.com (Virtual Tours)

SOFTWARE

www.enroute.com (Immersive Video)
www.smoothmove.com
(iMove Spherical Imaging Systems)
www.apple.com/quicktime/
(Quicktime)

Property Address: _____ Date: _____

19. DISPUTE RESOLUTION:

A. MEDIATION: Seller and Broker agree to mediate any dispute or claim arising between them out of this agreement, or any resulting transaction, before resorting to arbitration or court action, subject to paragraph 19B(2) below. Paragraph 19B(2) below applies whether or not the arbitration provision is initialed. Mediation fees, if any, shall be divided equally among the parties involved. If, for any dispute or claim to which this paragraph applies, any party commences an action without first attempting to resolve the matter through mediation, or refuses to mediate after a request has been made, then that party shall not be entitled to recover attorney fees, even if they would otherwise be available to that party in any such action. THIS MEDIATION PROVISION APPLIES WHETHER OR NOT THE ARBITRATION PROVISION IS INITIALED.

B. ARBITRATION OF DISPUTES: (1) Seller and Broker agree that any dispute or claim in Law or equity arising between them regarding the obligation to pay compensation under this agreement, which is not settled through mediation, shall be decided by neutral, binding arbitration, including and subject to paragraph 19B(2) below. The arbitrator shall be a retired judge or justice, or an attorney with at least 5 years of residential real estate law experience, unless the parties mutually agree to a different arbitrator, who shall render an award in accordance with substantive California Law. The parties shall have the right to discovery in accordance with Code of Civil Procedure §1283.05. In all other respects, the arbitration shall be conducted in accordance with Title 9 of Part III of the California Code of Civil Procedure. Judgment upon the award of the arbitrator(s) may be entered in any court having jurisdiction. Interpretation of this agreement to arbitrate shall be governed by the Federal Arbitration Act.

(2) EXCLUSIONS FROM MEDIATION AND ARBITRATION: The following matters are excluded from mediation and arbitration hereunder: **(i)** a judicial or non-judicial foreclosure or other action or proceeding to enforce a deed of trust, mortgage, or installment land sale contract as defined in Civil Code §2985; **(ii)** an unlawful detainer action; **(iii)** the filing or enforcement of a mechanic's lien; and **(iv)** any matter that is within the jurisdiction of a probate, small claims, or bankruptcy court. The filing of a court action to enable the recording of a notice of pending action, for order of attachment, receivership, injunction, or other provisional remedies, shall not constitute a waiver of the mediation and arbitration provisions.

"NOTICE: BY INITIALING IN THE SPACE BELOW YOU ARE AGREEING TO HAVE ANY DISPUTE ARISING OUT OF THE MATTERS INCLUDED IN THE 'ARBITRATION OF DISPUTES' PROVISION DECIDED BY NEUTRAL ARBITRATION AS PROVIDED BY CALIFORNIA LAW AND YOU ARE GIVING UP ANY RIGHTS YOU MIGHT POSSESS TO HAVE THE DISPUTE LITIGATED IN A COURT OR JURY TRIAL. BY INITIALING IN THE SPACE BELOW YOU ARE GIVING UP YOUR JUDICIAL RIGHTS TO DISCOVERY AND APPEAL, UNLESS THOSE RIGHTS ARE SPECIFICALLY INCLUDED IN THE 'ARBITRATION OF DISPUTES' PROVISION. IF YOU REFUSE TO SUBMIT TO ARBITRATION AFTER AGREEING TO THIS PROVISION, YOU MAY BE COMPELLED TO ARBITRATE UNDER THE AUTHORITY OF THE CALIFORNIA CODE OF CIVIL PROCEDURE. YOUR AGREEMENT TO THIS ARBITRATION PROVISION IS VOLUNTARY."

"WE HAVE READ AND UNDERSTAND THE FOREGOING AND AGREE TO SUBMIT DISPUTES ARISING OUT OF THE MATTERS INCLUDED IN THE 'ARBITRATION OF DISPUTES' PROVISION TO NEUTRAL ARBITRATION."

| Seller's Initials _____ / _____ | Broker's Initials _____ / _____ |

20. ENTIRE CONTRACT: All prior discussions, negotiations and agreements between the parties concerning the subject matter of this agreement are superseded by this agreement, which constitutes the entire contract and a complete and exclusive expression of their agreement, and may not be contradicted by evidence of any prior agreement or contemporaneous oral agreement. If any provision of this agreement is held to be ineffective or invalid, the remaining provisions will nevertheless be given full force and effect. This agreement and any supplement, addendum or modification, including any photocopy or facsimile, may be executed in counterparts.

By signing below, Seller acknowledges that Seller has read, understands, accepts and has received a copy of this agreement.

Seller _____ Date _____
Address _____ City _____ State _____ Zip _____
Telephone _____ Fax _____ E-mail _____

Seller _____ Date _____
Address _____ City _____ State _____ Zip _____
Telephone _____ Fax _____ E-mail _____

Real Estate Broker (Firm) _____
By (Agent) _____ Date _____
Address _____ City _____ State _____ Zip _____
Telephone _____ Fax _____ E-mail _____

THIS FORM HAS BEEN APPROVED BY THE CALIFORNIA ASSOCIATION OF REALTORS® (C.A.R.). NO REPRESENTATION IS MADE AS TO THE LEGAL VALIDITY OR ADEQUACY OF ANY PROVISION IN ANY SPECIFIC TRANSACTION. A REAL ESTATE BROKER IS THE PERSON QUALIFIED TO ADVISE ON REAL ESTATE TRANSACTIONS. IF YOU DESIRE LEGAL OR TAX ADVICE, CONSULT AN APPROPRIATE PROFESSIONAL.

This form is available for use by the entire real estate industry. It is not intended to identify the user as a REALTOR®. REALTOR® is a registered collective membership mark which may be used only by members of the NATIONAL ASSOCIATION OF REALTORS® who subscribe to its Code of Ethics.

SURE TRAC
The System for Success™

Published by the
California Association of REALTORS®

LA REVISED 10/02 (PAGE 3 OF 3)

Reviewed by _____ Date _____

EQUAL HOUSING OPPORTUNITY

RESIDENTIAL LISTING AGREEMENT-EXCLUSIVE (LA PAGE 3 OF 3)

Photo Reality: Seeing is Believing

Imagine having an open house where clients can do a "walk through" without personally visiting the property. Streaming video tours on the Web allow your clients to see the listed properties anytime they want.

While "virtual tours" may never replace a good old fashion walk through, internet screening may very well eliminate the real estate "drive-by" and "looky-loo" phenomenon. Potential homebuyers no longer need to drive-by a home to get a feel for such things as the neighborhood, condition of the house, curbside appeal, interior layout, spacial relationships, an kitchen design. Because of digital technology, a prospective buyer can zoom in and out, follow the camera to another room, check out the ceiling, and get a 360 degree view of a living room or bedroom. Once a client has seen a video of both the inside and outside of a home, they can decide if they're interested before contacting an agent.

"Streaming video tours" may encompass not only the house for sale, but also show the surrounding area, including schools, churches, shopping districts, and parks. If a picture is worth a thousand words, imagine how valuable a picture tour on a Website could be. Picture tours are an effective means to attract both buyers and sellers.

You may want to lend a hand and prepare Web pictures for busy and non-computer oriented salespeople in your office, as it will benefit you and your company in the long run. In fact, many will be willing to pay you for this service. Because you offer picture tours on the Web, sellers will prefer to list properties with you. Not only will your listings increase, but they will get more attention from buyers.

A real estate licensee who can provide photo or video services to real estate agents will always be in demand. He or she can take digital photos and videos of a property without the listing agent present and speed up the process of getting that property listed on the company's Web tours. Panoramic videos are valuable visual aides for a buyer to see size and scale, and a walking video tour provides an unparalleled viewing experience for all to get the feel of space and flow.

SERVICES

www.ipix.com (Internet Pictures Corp.)
www.home-view.com/ (HomeView.com)
www.evox.com eVox Productions)
www.virtualpr perties.com (Virtual Tours)

SOFTWARE

www.enroute.com (Immersive Video)
www.smoothmove.com
(iMove Spherical Imaging Systems)
www.apple.com/quicktime/
(Quicktime)

compensation. Since this is a vague type of listing and the possibility of wide variations in commission, a net listing is seldom used in California.

The best way to create an agency relationship is in writing. In order to be entitled to a commission, it must be in writing.

B. LISTING AGREEMENT COPIES (Give Copy When Signed)

Always give the buyer and seller a copy of any agreement when signed. Couples who are considered "one legal person" receive one copy; so if there are six couples, give six copies.

A copy of the listing agreement or any other real estate agreement, including the agency relationship and the transfer disclosure statements, must be given to the signing party immediately after they are signed. This is a requirement of the Commissioner's Regulations and a violation could result in license suspension or revocation.

C. MULTIPLE LISTING SERVICE (MLS)
(Subagents and Cooperating Brokers)

A **MULTIPLE LISTING SERVICE (MLS)** *is an association of real estate brokers that provides a pooling of listings, recent sales, and the sharing of commissions on a specified basis.* The advantage to the seller is that his or her home or property will receive wider market exposure because it will be shown by other cooperating brokers.

A **MULTIPLE LISTING** *is a listing, usually an exclusive right to sell, taken by a member of a multiple listing service, with the provision that all members of the multiple listing service have the opportunity to find an interested buyer.* Sometimes in exclusive areas, sellers will request that their listing not be put into the multiple listing service. This would limit the number of people (looky-loos) who just look at their properties for curiosity's sake.

A "pocket listing" is the unethical practice of NOT giving a new listing to the MLS until the listing broker first tries to sell that listed property through only the other agents within the company.

An agent can delegate some authority to his or her salespeople or other brokers and their salespeople. This is known as subagency. A **SUBAGENT** *is a licensed broker or salesperson upon whom the powers of an agent have been conferred, not by the principal, but by the agent with the principal's authorization.* The agent can delegate purely mechanical acts such as typing to anyone, but a subagency can only be created with the principal's consent. The subagent has the same duties and responsibilities as the agent.

Subagents have only the powers that are given to them by the listing agent. They have the same fiduciary relationship as that of the listing agent and seller. To avoid conflict and liability issues, most agents choose to act as cooperating agents.

> *Generally, real estate agents will have to spend less time with clients who are better informed and have searched the Multiple Listing Services (MLSs)*
>
> The "Internet generation" will probably be searching MLSs on the Net for their "dream home" before they first see a real estate broker or his or her salespeople. Clients can click on **www.ca.realtor.com** or **www.realtor.com** to search through every multiple listing service and every listed property in California by region and zip code. Customers can now see on the Internet what agents used to have to wait a week to see when the MLS printed the books of the current listings. The following is only a partial list of MLS Web sites:
>
>
> **www.ca.realtor.com (California Living Network)**
> **www.car.org (California Association of Realtors)**
> **www.sucasa.net (Spanish Version)**
> **www.realtor.com (NAR Home Finder Sites)**

D. MULTIPLE LISTING SERVICES ON THE INTERNET

Internet Multiple Listing Services are here to stay. Some are independent but most are still controlled by the local Boards of Realtors®. The California Association of Realtors® has the most complete system linking the MLS services of the entire state into one Internet address. *WWW.CAR.ORG or WWW.CA.REALTOR.COM is a source of California Multiple Listing Services' databases that links and provides the largest directory of homes for sale in California.* This has become the main source of available California home listings on the Internet. It breaks down California by regions, maps, and counties in order to help locate the Multiple Listing Service that covers whatever geographical area the user wants. It is the gateway to real estate listing information.

E. COOPERATING BROKERS

A broker acting as a subagent for the seller has a fiduciary duty to both the seller and the appointing broker.

A listing agreement usually authorizes the principal's agent to use cooperating brokers. A *COOPERATING BROKER is a non-listing broker who also works to sell the listed property.* The cooperating broker performs the same acts as the agent to find a buyer. Cooperating brokers and salespeople represent the buyer if it is disclosed to all parties. The purpose of a multiple listing service is to authorize and encourage cooperation within the real estate industry. Their members can act as cooperating brokers, thus sharing listings and commissions.

Agreements between brokers (considered experts) need NOT always be in writing, although it is obviously preferred. Agreements between brokers and salespeople, however, must be in writing.

"Comps" are the recent sales prices of similar properties in a neighborhood. It's the most important information a real estate salesperson can provide a buyer to pick a "realistic asking price" or a seller to "understand current market pricing."

A salesperson can quickly obtain a fairly accurate estimate of the probable selling price of a property to be listed or sold by knowing and comparing **recent selling prices (comps)**. Comps are proprietary information, the most comprehensive versions of which are given out only to members of the Multiple Listing Service (MLS) associations. As such, it can be difficult for buyers and sellers to access current comps—although similar information may be obtained by visiting the websites listed below.

Because it can be so difficult to obtain accurate comps, buyers, and sellers usually seek out the professional services of real estate salespeople.

Most sellers are not realistic about the "probable selling price" of their property. Sellers do not always realize that informed buyers will normally purchase only the lowest priced house among similarly priced homes. Comps are used by the buyers as a basis to determine a realistic offering price. Often a property owner mistakenly believes he or she can get 10% or more over what recent comps indicate a property is worth. Realistically, there is little chance a buyer will pay more than 3% over the probable selling price, the result of which is that the overpriced property is often overlooked by brokers and remains unsold for a long period of time.

While the MLS comps may be more accurate and detailed, surfing the Net can turn up alternative methods for finding similar information. The Internet company listed below can give a rough estimate of comps based on secondary sales information statistically averaged by recorded tracks or zip codes.

www.expercent.com
Expercent Online Real Estate

1. Selling in Other States

Since each state has its own licensing laws, how can a cooperating broker sell a property, for commission, in another state? The answer is simple. Find a licensed, cooperating broker in that state.

IV. Commissions

A **COMMISSION** *in real estate is a fee paid, usually as a percentage, to a broker/agent as compensation for his or her services.* Traditionally, it is payment from the seller to the agent who finds a ready, willing, and able buyer to purchase the seller's property, according to the listing terms or any other terms acceptable to the seller. A broker/agent can pay a "finder's fee" to an unlicensed individual only for introducing a client to the broker/agent (non-broker services).

A **COMMISSION SPLIT** *is a previously agreed to split between a broker and his or her salesperson of a commission earned on a sale.* Commission rates vary by negotiation throughout California, but usually range from 3% to 10% of the selling price. The listing agreement states that a commission is to be paid only when all the terms of the listing or other acceptable terms of the sale are met.

Commission rates are negotiable between principal and broker; the listing must have this statement printed in TEN POINT BOLD. Note: NO documents can imply commissions are NOT negotiable.

When a broker lists a property for sale and a cooperating broker sells it, the commission is shared. Although the ratio for dividing the commission varies, it is often 50% to the listing broker, and 50% to the selling broker. If a salesperson is involved, he or she shares in the employing broker's part of the commission.

Salespeople only receive compensation for real estate transactions from their employing brokers. All persons performing real estate activities for compensation must hold a valid real estate license.

A commission can be earned even if the sale is not finalized. **The broker is entitled to a commission if all the "exact" terms of the listing agreement are met**, provided the buyer is ready, willing, and able to complete the transaction. This is true even if the seller changes his or her mind and refuses to sell. If there is a valid listing agreement and the exact terms are met, the seller is still responsible for the commission. See **Figure 4-6** for facts about commissions from auctions.

If an offer meets the "exact terms" of the listing, the agent has earned the commission even if the owner refuses to sell to the buyer.

A broker or his or her salesperson must be the procuring cause of a sale to earn a commission. **PROCURING CAUSE** *is defined as a series of unbroken events that lead to an acceptable agreement with the seller.* If there are several brokers trying to sell the same property, the one who is the procuring cause of the sale is entitled to the selling broker's portion of the commission.

The commission paid to a broker selling agricultural land can be in the form of a trust deed on the property, cash or check, or funds paid from escrow.

V. Transfer Disclosure Statement

A. EASTON v. STRASSBURGER

The agent has a duty to inspect and disclose. Both the listing and selling agents must conduct a reasonable, competent, and diligent

Figure 4-6

Real Estate Auction ...
Another Way to Sell and Receive Commissions

A *REAL ESTATE AUCTION is a meeting where interested parties come together and continue to offer higher bids (purchase prices) until only one bidder is left, to whom the property is sold.* The person making the highest bid buys the property. The time and place are always stated on the announcement, but the amount of advertising depends on the type of auction.

An auction is one of the quickest ways to unload a piece of property. Auctions are very popular with government agencies and builders in over-built or economically depressed communities. This can be a great way to pick up a real bargain property, as long as you bid using your head, not your heart. Auctions are emotional events where the excitement keeps rising until the property is sold. The best buys are at foreclosure sales, which are put on by public agencies, banks, or savings banks.

Be forewarned: you will be bidding against seasoned professionals at most of these auctions. Be careful!

An *ABSOLUTE AUCTION is an auction where the property must be sold to the highest bidder no matter how low the final bid.* A *NO-SALE AUCTION is where there is a minimum bid underlying each property so that a certain price must be reached before the property will be sold.* In legitimate auctions, the starting bid is the minimum bid. But if that fact is not stated, make sure the minimum bid is stated clearly before the auction starts, or do not bid.

Do not attend a real property auction if you have not first seen the property and decided what you would be willing to pay for it. The broker auctioneers will be glad to give you maps or help you view the properties. Remember, don't get caught up in auction fever, because you should never go beyond your maximum bid price established well in advance of the auction.

An auction salesperson represents the seller and is required to have a real estate license.

www.cwsmarketing.com (Online Auctions)
www.jpking.com (JP King Auction Company)

In New Zealand, auctions are the most common method of selling real estate!

inspection of residential property. They must disclose, on the Transfer Disclosure Statement (TDS), any relevant facts that materially affect the value or desirability of the property.

A 1984 California Court of Appeals decision in the case of **Easton v. Strassburger** greatly extended the liability of brokers engaged in real estate sales. **Be warned:** Brokers are required to be aware (or should be aware) of all material facts negatively influencing the value or desirability of the property (**"red flags"**), by a reasonable visual inspection, and must disclose these facts to all prospective buyers.

A buyer has two years to sue an agent for failure to make proper disclosures in the Transfer Disclosure Statement.

B. TRANSFER DISCLOSURE STATEMENT
(Seller and Selling Broker Must Provide This Form)

The law requires sellers of residential property of from one-to-four units to provide prospective buyers with a Real Estate Transfer Disclosure Statement.

The **REAL ESTATE TRANSFER DISCLOSURE STATEMENT** *identifies items of value attached to the structure or land and states whether these items are operational* (**See Figure 4-7**). It also asks the seller to identify any structural or material defects. This form provides an opportunity for the seller to completely disclose problems of any kind that might adversely affect the value of the property. The obligation to prepare and deliver the Transfer Disclosure Statement to the prospective buyer is imposed upon the **seller and the seller's broker**. (See Civil Code 1102.6 for exemptions.)

Legally, the listing broker and the buyer's broker must conduct a reasonably competent, diligent, and visual inspection of accessible areas of the property and disclose to a prospective buyer all material facts affecting value and desirability.

The following sequence of events may help explain how the four parties (seller, seller's agent, buyer, and buyer's agent) fill in and sign the Transfer Disclosure Statement form:

1. The Transfer Disclosure Statement form should be filled out and signed completely by the seller at the time of listing the property. Since the seller is the one most familiar with the property, he or she must be encouraged to be forthright and honest about all known defects.

2. The seller's agent makes a visual, diligent inspection of the property, fills out the appropriate section of the Transfer Disclosure Statement, and signs at the same time the seller lists the property for sale.

Figure 4-7

CALIFORNIA ASSOCIATION OF REALTORS®

REAL ESTATE TRANSFER DISCLOSURE STATEMENT
(CALIFORNIA CIVIL CODE §1102, ET SEQ.)
(C.A.R. Form TDS, Revised 10/03)

THIS DISCLOSURE STATEMENT CONCERNS THE REAL PROPERTY SITUATED IN THE CITY OF _____
_____, COUNTY OF _____, STATE OF CALIFORNIA,
DESCRIBED AS _____.
THIS STATEMENT IS A DISCLOSURE OF THE CONDITION OF THE ABOVE DESCRIBED PROPERTY IN COMPLIANCE
WITH SECTION 1102 OF THE CIVIL CODE AS OF (date) _____. IT IS NOT A WARRANTY OF ANY
KIND BY THE SELLER(S) OR ANY AGENT(S) REPRESENTING ANY PRINCIPAL(S) IN THIS TRANSACTION, AND IS
NOT A SUBSTITUTE FOR ANY INSPECTIONS OR WARRANTIES THE PRINCIPAL(S) MAY WISH TO OBTAIN.

I. COORDINATION WITH OTHER DISCLOSURE FORMS

This Real Estate Transfer Disclosure Statement is made pursuant to Section 1102 of the Civil Code. Other statutes require disclosures, depending upon the details of the particular real estate transaction (for example: special study zone and purchase-money liens on residential property).

Substituted Disclosures: The following disclosures and other disclosures required by law, including the Natural Hazard Disclosure Report/Statement that may include airport annoyances, earthquake, fire, flood, or special assessment information, have or will be made in connection with this real estate transfer, and are intended to satisfy the disclosure obligations on this form, where the subject matter is the same:

☐ Inspection reports completed pursuant to the contract of sale or receipt for deposit.
☐ Additional inspection reports or disclosures: _____
_____

II. SELLER'S INFORMATION

The Seller discloses the following information with the knowledge that even though this is not a warranty, prospective Buyers may rely on this information in deciding whether and on what terms to purchase the subject property. Seller hereby authorizes any agent(s) representing any principal(s) in this transaction to provide a copy of this statement to any person or entity in connection with any actual or anticipated sale of the property.

THE FOLLOWING ARE REPRESENTATIONS MADE BY THE SELLER(S) AND ARE NOT THE REPRESENTATIONS OF THE AGENT(S), IF ANY. THIS INFORMATION IS A DISCLOSURE AND IS NOT INTENDED TO BE PART OF ANY CONTRACT BETWEEN THE BUYER AND SELLER.

Seller ☐ is ☐ is not occupying the property.

A. The subject property has the items checked below (read across):

☐ Range	☐ Oven	☐ Microwave
☐ Dishwasher	☐ Trash Compactor	☐ Garbage Disposal
☐ Washer/Dryer Hookups		☐ Rain Gutters
☐ Burglar Alarms	☐ Smoke Detector(s)	☐ Fire Alarm
☐ TV Antenna	☐ Satellite Dish	☐ Intercom
☐ Central Heating	☐ Central Air Conditioning	☐ Evaporator Cooler(s)
☐ Wall/Window Air Conditioning	☐ Sprinklers	☐ Public Sewer System
☐ Septic Tank	☐ Sump Pump	☐ Water Softener
☐ Patio/Decking	☐ Built-in Barbecue	☐ Gazebo
☐ Sauna		
☐ Hot Tub	☐ Pool	☐ Spa
☐ Locking Safety Cover*	☐ Child Resistant Barrier*	☐ Locking Safety Cover*
☐ Security Gate(s)	☐ Automatic Garage Door Opener(s)*	☐ Number Remote Controls ____
Garage: ☐ Attached	☐ Not Attached	☐ Carport
Pool/Spa Heater: ☐ Gas	☐ Solar	☐ Electric
Water Heater: ☐ Gas	☐ Water Heater Anchored, Braced, or Strapped*	
Water Supply: ☐ City	☐ Well	☐ Private Utility or
Gas Supply: ☐ Utility	☐ Bottled	Other _____
☐ Window Screens	☐ Window Security Bars ☐ Quick Release Mechanism on Bedroom Windows*	

Exhaust Fan(s) in _____ 220 Volt Wiring in _____ Fireplace(s) in _____
☐ Gas Starter _____ ☐ Roof(s): Type: _____ Age: _____ (approx.)
☐ Other: _____
Are there, to the best of your (Seller's) knowledge, any of the above that are not in operating condition? ☐ Yes ☐ No. If yes, then describe. (Attach additional sheets if necessary): _____
_____

(*see footnote on page 2)

TDS REVISED 10/03 (PAGE 1 OF 3) Print Date

Buyer's Initials (_____)(_____)
Seller's Initials (_____)(_____)

Reviewed by _____ Date _____

EQUAL HOUSING OPPORTUNITY

REAL ESTATE TRANSFER DISCLOSURE STATEMENT (TDS PAGE 1 OF 3)

Property Address: _____ Date: _____

B. Are you (Seller) aware of any significant defects/malfunctions in any of the following? ☐ Yes ☐ No. If yes, check appropriate space(s) below.

☐ Interior Walls ☐ Ceilings ☐ Floors ☐ Exterior Walls ☐ Insulation ☐ Roof(s) ☐ Windows ☐ Doors ☐ Foundation ☐ Slab(s) ☐ Driveways ☐ Sidewalks ☐ Walls/Fences ☐ Electrical Systems ☐ Plumbing/Sewers/Septics ☐ Other Structural Components

(Describe: _____
_____
_____
_____)

If any of the above is checked, explain. (Attach additional sheets if necessary.): _____
_____
_____
_____
_____

*This garage door opener or child resistant pool barrier may not be in compliance with the safety standards relating to automatic reversing devices as set forth in Chapter 12.5 (commencing with Section 19890) of Part 3 of Division 13 of, or with the pool safety standards of Article 2.5 (commencing with Section 115920) of Chapter 5 of Part 10 of Division 104 of, the Health and Safety Code. The water heater may not be anchored, braced, or strapped in accordance with Section 19211 of the Health and Safety Code. Window security bars may not have quick release mechanisms in compliance with the 1995 edition of the California Building Standards Code.

C. Are you (Seller) aware of any of the following:

1. Substances, materials, or products which may be an environmental hazard such as, but not limited to, asbestos, formaldehyde, radon gas, lead-based paint, mold, fuel or chemical storage tanks, and contaminated soil or water on the subject property . . . . ☐ Yes ☐ No
2. Features of the property shared in common with adjoining landowners, such as walls, fences, and driveways, whose use or responsibility for maintenance may have an effect on the subject property . . . . ☐ Yes ☐ No
3. Any encroachments, easements or similar matters that may affect your interest in the subject property . . . . ☐ Yes ☐ No
4. Room additions, structural modifications, or other alterations or repairs made without necessary permits . . . . ☐ Yes ☐ No
5. Room additions, structural modifications, or other alterations or repairs not in compliance with building codes . . . ☐ Yes ☐ No
6. Fill (compacted or otherwise) on the property or any portion thereof . . . . ☐ Yes ☐ No
7. Any settling from any cause, or slippage, sliding, or other soil problems . . . . ☐ Yes ☐ No
8. Flooding, drainage or grading problems . . . . ☐ Yes ☐ No
9. Major damage to the property or any of the structures from fire, earthquake, floods, or landslides . . . . ☐ Yes ☐ No
10. Any zoning violations, nonconforming uses, violations of "setback" requirements . . . . ☐ Yes ☐ No
11. Neighborhood noise problems or other nuisances . . . . ☐ Yes ☐ No
12. CC&R's or other deed restrictions or obligations . . . . ☐ Yes ☐ No
13. Homeowners' Association which has any authority over the subject property . . . . ☐ Yes ☐ No
14. Any "common area" (facilities such as pools, tennis courts, walkways, or other areas co-owned in undivided interest with others) . . . . ☐ Yes ☐ No
15. Any notices of abatement or citations against the property . . . . ☐ Yes ☐ No
16. Any lawsuits by or against the Seller threatening to or affecting this real property, including any lawsuits alleging a defect or deficiency in this real property or "common areas" (facilities such as pools, tennis courts, walkways, or other areas co-owned in undivided interest with others) . . . . ☐ Yes ☐ No

If the answer to any of these is yes, explain. (Attach additional sheets if necessary.): _____
_____
_____
_____
_____

Seller certifies that the information herein is true and correct to the best of the Seller's knowledge as of the date signed by the Seller.

Seller_____ Date _____

Seller_____ Date _____

Buyer's Initials (_____)(_____)
Seller's Initials (_____)(_____)

Copyright © 1991-2003, CALIFORNIA ASSOCIATION OF REALTORS®, INC.
TDS REVISED 10/03 (PAGE 2 OF 3)

Reviewed by _____ Date _____

☐ EQUAL HOUSING OPPORTUNITY

REAL ESTATE TRANSFER DISCLOSURE STATEMENT (TDS PAGE 2 OF 3)

Property Address: _____ Date: _____

III. AGENT'S INSPECTION DISCLOSURE
(To be completed only if the Seller is represented by an agent in this transaction.)

THE UNDERSIGNED, BASED ON THE ABOVE INQUIRY OF THE SELLER(S) AS TO THE CONDITION OF THE PROPERTY AND BASED ON A REASONABLY COMPETENT AND DILIGENT VISUAL INSPECTION OF THE ACCESSIBLE AREAS OF THE PROPERTY IN CONJUNCTION WITH THAT INQUIRY, STATES THE FOLLOWING:

☐ Agent notes no items for disclosure.

☐ Agent notes the following items: _____
_____
_____
_____
_____

Agent (Broker Representing Seller) _____ By _____ Date _____
             (Please Print)   (Associate Licensee or Broker Signature)

IV. AGENT'S INSPECTION DISCLOSURE
(To be completed only if the agent who has obtained the offer is other than the agent above.)

THE UNDERSIGNED, BASED ON A REASONABLY COMPETENT AND DILIGENT VISUAL INSPECTION OF THE ACCESSIBLE AREAS OF THE PROPERTY, STATES THE FOLLOWING:

☐ Agent notes no items for disclosure.

☐ Agent notes the following items: _____
_____
_____
_____

Agent (Broker Obtaining the Offer) _____ By _____ Date _____
             (Please Print)   (Associate Licensee or Broker Signature)

V. BUYER(S) AND SELLER(S) MAY WISH TO OBTAIN PROFESSIONAL ADVICE AND/OR INSPECTIONS OF THE PROPERTY AND TO PROVIDE FOR APPROPRIATE PROVISIONS IN A CONTRACT BETWEEN BUYER AND SELLER(S) WITH RESPECT TO ANY ADVICE/INSPECTIONS/DEFECTS.

I/WE ACKNOWLEDGE RECEIPT OF A COPY OF THIS STATEMENT.

Seller _____ Date _____ Buyer _____ Date _____

Seller _____ Date _____ Buyer _____ Date _____

Agent (Broker Representing Seller) _____ By _____ Date _____
             (Please Print)   (Associate Licensee or Broker Signature)

Agent (Broker Obtaining the Offer) _____ By _____ Date _____
             (Please Print)   (Associate Licensee or Broker Signature)

SECTION 1102.3 OF THE CIVIL CODE PROVIDES A BUYER WITH THE RIGHT TO RESCIND A PURCHASE CONTRACT FOR AT LEAST THREE DAYS AFTER THE DELIVERY OF THIS DISCLOSURE IF DELIVERY OCCURS AFTER THE SIGNING OF AN OFFER TO PURCHASE. IF YOU WISH TO RESCIND THE CONTRACT, YOU MUST ACT WITHIN THE PRESCRIBED PERIOD.

A REAL ESTATE BROKER IS QUALIFIED TO ADVISE ON REAL ESTATE. IF YOU DESIRE LEGAL ADVICE, CONSULT YOUR ATTORNEY.

SURE TRAC
The System for Success™

Published by the
California Association of REALTORS®

Reviewed by _____ Date _____

EQUAL HOUSING OPPORTUNITY

TDS REVISED 10/03 (PAGE 3 OF 3)

REAL ESTATE TRANSFER DISCLOSURE STATEMENT (TDS PAGE 3 OF 3)

3. The buyer should receive a copy of the Transfer Disclosure Statement and sign that he or she has received it before making a written offer.

4. The buyer's agent must also visually inspect the property, fill out the appropriate section of the statement, and sign it.

5. If the buyer fails to receive the Transfer Disclosure Statement form prior to signing the contractual offer (Deposit Receipt), he or she has the right to cancel, after receipt of the Transfer Disclosure Statement, for any reason (three days if delivered by hand or five days if mailed). A written notice of termination must be delivered to the seller or to the seller's broker.

The Transfer Disclosure Statement (or amended Disclosure Statement) must be given to the prospective buyer as soon as practicable before or after the offer (Deposit Receipt) is signed.

VI. Agents' Other Responsibilities

A. TRUST ACCOUNTS (Other People's Money)

A broker, when receiving a buyer's money deposit (and instructions), either opens an escrow, gives it to the principal, or puts it in the broker's trust fund account. If NOT instructed otherwise, the money must go into the broker's trust fund account no later than three business days following receipt of the funds by the broker.

A broker accepting a money deposit (and instructions) is required to: 1) give it to the principal; 2) place it in a trust account; or 3) give it to an escrow company. **Deposits other than the intial deposit (usually around $200) to start the account are never the personal property of the broker**. Any moneys accepted should go, within three business days, into an independent bank trust account in the name of the broker as trustee. Most trust accounts are non-interest-bearing because all overages must be explained. Placing a buyer's cash or check in the broker's personal account is called commingling.

COMMINGLING is the mixing together of the funds of a principal and a licensee. Commingling is a violation of the Commissioner's Regulations. Commingling is the opposite of segregating (keeping separate).

Commingling is the illegal practice of mixing a client's money with the agent's private funds. By law, each entry in the broker's trust fund account (bank) must be identified.

CONVERSION is the unlawful misappropriation and use of a client's funds by a licensee. A broker who upon receipt spends his or her principal's deposit without the principal's authorization, has not commingled funds with his or her own funds in a technical sense, but has converted them. This is a much more serious violation than commingling, with heavy criminal penalties.

An unlicensed employee can make withdrawals if bonded for at least the amount of funds to which the employee has access at any given time.

B. TRANSACTION FILE (Keep for Three Years)

A *TRANSACTION FILE is the file or folder (**all documents**) kept for three years by the broker for each real estate transaction in which the broker or his or her salespeople participated.*

The commissioner of real estate has the right to inspect this file. Maintaining a complete, up-to-date transaction file is not only good business practice, **it is the law**. A licensed broker must retain for three years copies of all listings, deposit receipts, canceled checks, trust fund records and other documents executed by the broker or obtained by him or her in connection with any real estate transaction. The retention period shall run from the date of the closing of the transaction or from the date of the listing, if the transaction is not consummated.

The Real Estate Commissioner requires that all records of a broker or salesperson be kept a minimum of three years.

C. AGENTS WHO BUY AND SELL FOR THEIR OWN ACCOUNT (Disclose You Have a Real Estate License)

Many real estate professionals buy and sell property for themselves as part of their own personal investments (acting as a principal and not as an agent). The Real Estate Commissioner created a regulation requiring disclosure of license status (buyer and seller) which has the full force and effect of law. The commissioner has strongly suggested that it would be in the licensee's best interest to disclose this fact, in writing, as soon as possible. This protects the purchasers and others involved. Everyone should be aware that they are dealing with a person knowledgeable in real estate and that he or she is representing his or her own interests.

D. POWER OF ATTORNEY

A *POWER OF ATTORNEY is an acknowledged, written authorization of one person to act for another.* There are two categories of power of attorney: 1) a general power of attorney, and 2) a special power of attorney.

A *GENERAL POWER OF ATTORNEY allows the person so authorized to perform any act the principal could perform.* The person thus authorized to act on behalf of the principal is called the attorney in fact.

An *ATTORNEY IN FACT*, *under a "general" power of attorney, is an agent who may have the power to transact all of a principal's business.* The specific powers conferred must be set down in writing, duly acknowledged and recorded with the county recorder's office in the county where the property is located, in order for the agency to take effect. **Death of either party or an acknowledged declaration from the principal may revoke this power**. An attorney in fact cannot deed his client's property to himself.

The power of attorney must be recorded in the county where the property is located in order to be properly exercised.

A *SPECIAL POWER OF ATTORNEY* *allows the person so authorized to perform only a specific act (for example, sell your house).* The *ATTORNEY IN FACT*, *under a "special" power of attorney, has the authorization to perform only a specific act.*

A real estate agent under a special power of attorney is an "attorney in fact" who is usually authorized to find a ready, willing, and able buyer.

A listing agreement makes the broker a special agent to perform the authorized act of selling, exchanging, or otherwise transferring real property. Usually an agent is given expressed authority, by written agreement (listing), to sell a home. If not otherwise expressed in writing, the agent is allowed to delegate parts of that authority under three circumstances:

1. If the act to be performed is purely mechanical, such as typing out a standard form.

2. If the agent is not legally qualified to do something, such as notarizing a document that requires a state license.

3. If it is customary to delegate authority for that task in that business or locality.

E. TORTS BY AN AGENT (Broker/Salesperson)

A *TORT* *is any civil injury or wrong committed upon a person or that person's property.* Fraud, misrepresentation, negligence, and secret profit all stem from a breach of an agent's duty. In some cases they can even be considered criminal acts. The broker and his or her salespeople, as professionals, are expected to maintain a high standard of ethics. They are responsible for their own acts and representations even when following the seller's directions.

F. MISREPRESENTATION OF A MATERIAL FACT

A misrepresentation by a broker or salesperson may be material or immaterial. If the representation is slight, or would not have a measurable effect on the people relying on it, it is not a material fact. When a broker misrepresents his or her authority to act as an agent for someone else, he or she may be liable to the person who relies on the misrepresentation. A statement such as "I think this is the best house on the street" is a statement of opinion and is not considered a misrepresentation.

"Puffing" is a statement of opinion (not fact) that exaggerates a property's benefits. It is common practice, but an agent should never misrepresent a material fact. It would be a misrepresentation if a reasonable person would consider it a statement of fact.

The misrepresentation of a material fact can financially injure someone, and may be punishable under the Civil Code or the Commissioner's Regulations.

There are three types of misrepresentations:

1. Innocent Misrepresentations,
2. Negligent Misrepresentations, and
3. Fraudulent Misrepresentations (nondisclosures).

The first misrepresentation usually has no broker liability. The second and third are subject to civil penalties and the Real Estate Commissioner's actions. *INNOCENT MISREPRESENTATIONS are false statements that are not known to be false at the time they are made.* These statements do not usually warrant legal liability for the broker but can cause a rescission of any contract. Everyone involved would then be reinstated to their original positions.

An agent who sells the wrong condo because a prankster switched the condo unit's number is an example of an innocent misrepresentation.

NEGLIGENT MISREPRESENTATIONS are statements believed to be true but made without reasonable grounds, and are false. This is breach of duty without fraudulent intent. The broker is liable for any negligent statements made to a buyer or seller. Such statements are in effect a form of deceit.

An agent mistakenly confirms that a property is within a particular school district without checking. This would be negligent misrepresentation.

FRAUDULENT MISREPRESENTATIONS are statements made at a time when the broker knows the statement to be false, or statements in which the broker does not disclose material facts (conceals). This is actual fraud. Any contract made under the influence of fraudulent information may become void, and the person making the fraudulent statements may be liable for civil or even criminal fraud.

"Intentional deceptions" or the "concealment of material facts" are fraudulent misrepresentations, which are immoral and unlawful.

If a broker presented a full price offer to a seller, which the seller accepted, but the seller discovers, during escrow, that the buyer is the brother of the broker, the seller can cancel the transaction without any liability for the commission.

G. SECRET PROFIT

An agent may not make any secret profit. This is a breach of the fiduciary relationship between the principal and the real estate agent. All financial offers, whether legitimate or not, must be presented to the seller. So, if a real estate agent is offered a secret profit, he or she has a duty to inform his or her principal of this. In addition, the broker may not allow others (friends and relatives) to make a secret profit with his or her knowledge.

H. WARRANTY OF AUTHORITY

The broker, as an agent, warrants that he or she has the authority to represent another person. *If there is a written listing between the seller and the broker, he or she has an* **EXPRESSED WARRANTY OF AUTHORITY** *to offer the property for sale.* The problem arises when the broker offers to sell a property, without the listing, to an unsuspecting buyer who relies on the fact that the agent has certain authority. In such cases, the broker could be liable for this untrue representation. A broker gives **IMPLIED WARRANTY OF AUTHORITY** *to act for a seller by the mere fact that he or she shows the seller's property.*

When a broker represents a seller, he or she does not warrant that the seller has the capacity to sell. If, in fact, the seller does not have the capacity to contract, then the broker is not liable, as long as he or she did not have knowledge of the fact. However, if the broker has knowledge that the seller could not contract, then the broker could be liable to the buyer.

The prosecution of an unlicensed salesperson, acting as a licensed salesperson, would be handled by the district attorney's office.

I. DISCLOSURE OF AIDS AND DEATH

An occupant's death from AIDS or AIDS-related illness, or any other contagious disease, is a highly emotional issue. Brokers must strive to balance the principle of full disclosure against the right to privacy of an AIDS victim. Disclosing casually that a tenant or former tenant (owner or occupant) died, or is dying, from AIDS might very well be in violation of that person's civil rights and might expose the broker to civil or criminal penalties. By law, sellers, brokers, and landlords have no liability for failure to disclose a prior occupant's death or its cause after three years. On the other hand, intentional misrepresentation concerning an occupant's death on the property, in response to direct inquiry, is illegal.

The broker does NOT have to disclose cause of death unless there is a direct inquiry.

VII. Required Agent Disclosures—Summary (One-to-Four Unit Residential Sales)

A. VISUAL INSPECTION

A listing and selling broker must each conduct a reasonably competent and diligent inspection of the property and disclose to the prospective buyer all material facts affecting the value, desirability, and intended use of the property. The real estate agent does not have to inspect; (a) areas not reasonably accessible; (b) areas off the site of the property; (c) public records or permits concerning the title or use of the property; or (d) in a common interest development and the seller or broker complies by furnishing controlling documents and a financial statement.

B. DISCLOSURE OF AGENCY RELATIONSHIP

A real estate agent must disclose, in writing, the duties which arise from certain agency relationships, the broker's status as agent of the seller, agent of the buyer, or agent of both the seller and the buyer (dual agent).

C. DISCLOSURE OF THE NEGOTIABILITY OF REAL ESTATE COMMISSIONS

The listing or sales agreement must contain the following disclosure in not less than 10-point boldface: NOTICE: The rate of real estate commissions is not fixed by law. They are set by each broker individually and may be negotiable between the seller and the broker. (See **Chapter 1**)

D. NO DISCLOSURE REQUIRED FOR MANNER/OCCURRENCE OF DEATH; AFFLICTION OF OCCUPANT WITH AIDS

Any death, which occurred within a 3-year period, should be disclosed if it is "material." If the death occurred more than 3 years before the date of the offer to buy, there is no liability for failing to disclose the fact of death. The seller and his agent need not voluntarily disclose affliction with AIDS or death from AIDS, but cannot make any misrepresentations to a direct question about death on the property.

VIII. Terminating an Agency Relationship

A. REASONS FOR TERMINATION OF AGENCY

An agency relationship between a seller and a real estate broker can be terminated by operation of law or by the acts of either the broker or the seller. **Figure 4-8** shows the six subcategories of these methods.

Figure 4-8

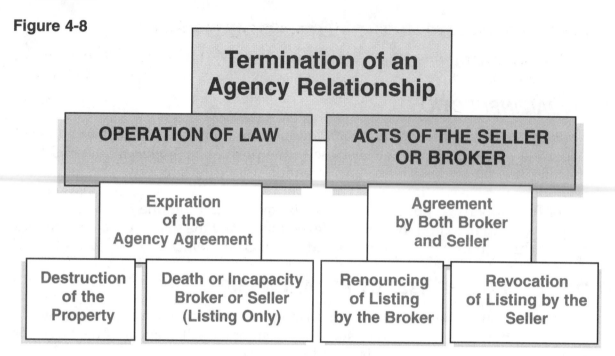

1. Expiration of the Agency (Listing) Agreement

The Exclusive Agency Listing Agreement and the Exclusive Authorization and Right to Sell Listing Agreement have a definite termination date. These listings will end automatically on the stated date if not terminated in some other way before that date. The other type of listing, an open listing, does not require a termination date because it can be terminated at any time.

2. Destruction of the Property

If the property is destroyed or damaged by certain causes, such as earthquake or fire, the listing agreement is terminated.

3. Death or Incapacity of the Broker or Seller

If either the agent or seller is not mentally or physically able to complete the agency relationship (personal service contract), it is terminated.

4. Agreement by Both the Broker and Seller

If both parties to a contract want to end it, it may be terminated by mutual agreement.

5. Renouncement of the Listing Agreement by the Broker

The broker can refuse to fulfill the listing agreement but may be subject to damages for breach of contract.

6. Revocation of the Listing Agreement by the Seller

The seller can refuse to sell the listed property but may be liable for the commission if the broker has found a buyer who is ready, willing and able to purchase the property.

IX. A Brokerage Must be Run Like a Business

A "company dollar" is the dollar (income and commissions) a broker receives after all salespersons' commissions have been paid.

A **GROSS DOLLAR** is all the income that is received by the office before paying out commissions. A **COMPANY DOLLAR** is the amount left to management after payment of all commissions, including in-house salespeople and other multiple listings brokers and salespeople. **See Figure 4-9.** The concept of the company dollar allows the brokerage to examine and focus on how their after-commission income is spent.

Figure 4-9

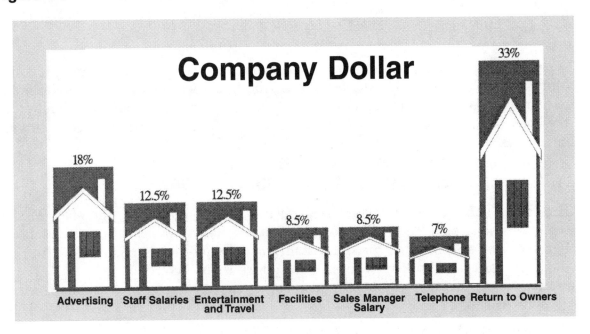

The following is a general list of how a brokerage spends its company dollar after paying commissions:

1. 15 to 21%   Advertising—newspapers, signs
2. 10 to 15%   Staff Salaries—secretary and receptionist
3. 10 to 15%   Entertainment and Travel
4. 7   to 10%   Facilities—interest, property taxes, and maintenance

5. 7 to 10%   Sales Manager Salary
6. 5 to 9%   Telephone
7. 24 to 41%   Return to Owners—profit, training, and income taxes

"TOE" is the acronym for Total Operating Expense.

T **Total**
O **Operating**
E **Expense**

The **DESK COST** *is the total operating expenses divided by the number of salespeople.* The desk cost tells the broker the financial loss caused by an empty desk or an unproductive salesperson.

A. ONE-STOP SHOPPING

When the real estate market goes "soft," it means shrinking profit margins and fewer company dollars. Some brokerages respond to this by offering one-stop shopping. **ONE-STOP SHOPPING** *means the brokerage is involved in multiple facets of property transactions, including escrow and title services, property management, and mortgage brokerage.*

A recent trend has shown significant increases in large real estate brokerages providing mortgages and trust deeds to buyers. Often, though, sales agents would prefer not to use an in-house lender. The reason? If something goes wrong in-house, it will reflect on the sales agent. Brokerages are countering this by hiring experienced mortgage executives and top-notch processing and closing staff.

B. ALLIANCE ASSOCIATION (NEW ASSOCIATIONS)

An **ALLIANCE** *is an association (cooperative) of members who seek to reduce their costs by negotiating service discounts with a company and then refer their members to that company.* For example, a large retail discount chain may charge their members $100 to refer them to real estate brokers who in turn reduce their commissions by 35%. A real estate broker may refer clients to a good carpet cleaner if his or her clients receive a genuine discount.

X. SUMMARY

Agency is the relationship between a seller, broker (and his or her salespeople), and a buyer. A **principal** is the person who hires the agent. The agency of a real estate broker may be established by **express agreement, implied agreement, ratification**, or **estoppel**. The best evidence of an agency relationship is a **written agreement (listing)**.

Agents can be identified as the **listing agents** or **selling agents**. A broker (agent) working for a principal owes him or her a **fiduciary duty**, including honesty, utmost care, integrity, accounting, disclosure, and loyalty. An agent owes a third party (the "other" party in a negotiation) an obligation of honesty and timely disclosure of material facts.

An agent can represent a seller, a buyer, or both (**dual agency**), if all parties consent to the transaction. The **Disclosure Regarding Real Estate Agency Relationships Form** states that the agency relationship must be disclosed as soon as practical. **Termination of agency** can be by operation of law or by acts of the seller or broker.

Salespeople can be **independent contractors** or **employees**, although the DRE considers them employees of the broker, making the broker responsible for their activities. A broker must immediately notify the DRE in writing of the hiring or firing of a salesperson. Signed **broker-salesperson contracts** must be kept for **three years** after termination of the contract (as well as all transactions files).

A **listing** is a personal service contract between and agent and a principal creating an **agency relationship**. It may be for any period of time, but must have a definite, final termination date. An **open listing** may be given to several brokers, or the property may be sold by the owner without obligation to pay a commission. It is **unilateral**, because only the seller makes a promise, whereas an **exclusive listing and exclusive right to sell are bilateral** (a promise for a promise).

An **exclusive agency listing** entitles only the listing broker to a commission, unless the owner sells the property, in which case, no commission is owed. An **exclusive right to sell listing** entitles the listing broker to a commission even if the owner sells the property.

The rarely used **net listing** sets the broker's commission at whatever amount a property sells for above the selling price set by the owner. A **multiple listing** is an exclusive right to sell held by all the members of a **Multiple Listing Service (MLS)**.

A copy of the **listing agreement** (and any other real estate agreement) should be given to the buyer and seller immediately after signing. All listings belong to the broker, not the salesperson.

An agent can delegate authority to a **subagent** or to a **cooperating agent or broker**. While agreements between brokers don't need to be in writing, they must be in writing between brokers and salespeople.

Real estate commissions are negotiable. If an offer meets the exact terms of a listing, the agent has earned the commission even if the owner refuses to sell. The agent who is the **procuring cause** (series of unbroken events that lead to an acceptable agreement with the seller) is entitled to the commission.

The *Easton v. Strassburger* case extended the liabilities of brokers to include a duty to inspect and disclose any relevant facts that might materially affect the value or desirability of a property. The **Transfer Disclosure Statement** must be provided by both seller and broker and must be given to the prospective buyer as soon as practicable before or within three days after the **Deposit Receipt** is signed. A broker does not have to disclose a cause of death unless there is a direct inquiry, and no liability to disclose an occupant's cause of death after three years.

When a broker receives a buyer's money deposit he must 1) place the deposit in escrow, 2) give it to the principal, or 3) put it in the broker's trust fund account. All funds must be kept segregated, as **commingling**, or mixing the client's money with private funds, is illegal.

A real estate agent, under a **special power of attorney** is an attorney in fact, authorized to find a ready, willing, and able buyer. As an agent, the broker warrants that he or she has the authority to represent another person. He or she is obligated maintain a high standard of ethics, and refrain from either material or immaterial misrepresentation. **Misrepresentations** can be innocent, negligent, or fraudulent. Intentional deceptions or concealment of material facts are examples of **fraudulent misrepresentations**. Agents are also prohibited from making **secret profits**.

A brokerage must be run like a business. A **gross dollar** is all the income received by the office, and the company dollar is all the money left after paying commissions. **"TOE"** is an easy way to remember **Total Operating Expense**.

Agency and Its Responsibility

XI. TERMINOLOGY - CHAPTER 4

A. Agency
B. Agency Disclosure Form
C. Commingling
D. Conversion
E. Dual Agency
F. Easton Decision
G. Employee
H. Estoppel
 I. Exclusive Agency Listing
J. Exclusive Right to Sell Listing
K. Fiduciary Relationship
L. Fraudulent Misrepresentation

M. General Attorney in Fact
N. Independent Contractor
O. Innocent Misrepresentation
P. Multiple Listing Service (MLS)
Q. Negligent Misrepresentation
R. Net Listing
S. Open Listing
T. Policy Manual
U. Principal
V. Ratification
W. Secret Profit
X. Special Attorney in Fact

Y. Subagent
Z. Third Party
AA. Tort
BB. Transfer Disclosure Statement

1.____ The mixing of funds held in trust with personal funds.

2.____ Authorization from a property owner giving a real estate agent the non-exclusive right to secure a purchaser. Other brokers, or the owners themselves, may also solicit a purchaser.

3.____ The unlawful taking and use of another's property placed in your trust, as an agent, by that person.

4.____ The person(s) who employs a real estate agent, usually through a listing agreement.

5.____ The relationship between the principal and the principal's agent that arises out of a contract, either expressed or implied, written or oral, wherein the agent is employed by the principal to do certain acts dealing with a third party.

6.____ A person upon whom the powers of an agent have been conferred, not by the principal, but by an agent authorized by the principal.

7.____ A civil wrong committed against a person or property, independent of any contractual agreement.

8.____ The theory of law that states a person cannot suddenly assert a legal right when that person has neglected to assert it previously. For example: If someone claims to be your agent and you know about it and don't stop that person, you can't later claim that person was not acting on your behalf.

9.____ A person who acts for another, selling final results and using his or her own judgment to achieve those results.

10.____ The approval of an act performed on behalf of a person without previous authorization, such as the approval by a principal of a previously unauthorized act of an agent.

11.____ An agency relationship in which the agent acts concurrently for both of the principals (buyer and seller), with their consent, in a transaction.

12.____ An association of real estate agents that provides a pooling of listings and the sharing of commissions.

13.____ Any party to a transaction other than the principal with whom you have an agency relationship.

14.____ One who is authorized to perform many acts for another under a power of attorney.

15.____ A listing agreement employing a broker as the sole agent for the seller of real property, under the terms of which the broker is entitled to a commission unless the homeowner sells the property.

16.____ A listing agreement employing a broker to act as an agent for the seller of real property. Under the terms of this agreement, the broker is entitled to a commission if the property is sold during the duration of the listing by the broker or by the owner without an agent.

17.____ A listing that provides for the agent to retain, as compensation for his or her services, all sums received over and above a net price to the owner.

18.____ The major court decision which requires an agent to disclose any physical defects or evidence of defects that could affect the value of real property.

19.____ An agent's making of additional money in a real estate transaction without disclosing it to the principal and third party.

20.____ Knowingly making false and deceptive statements to help sell a property.

21.____ Making false statements about a property, without realizing it.

22.____ Making false statements regarding a property that could have been checked out or verified.

23.____ A form that notifies buyers of any physical defects to a property and requires the seller and the agent to list any evidence of defects of which they are aware.

24.____ A form presented to the principal(s) in a transaction stating exactly who the agent is working for: the buyer, the seller, or both.

25.____ The relationship between the agent and the principal that requires the highest level of trust and good faith.

26.____ One who works directly for another person and is told what to do and is controlled in how they do it.

27.____ A written book of procedures explaining how a broker expects the agents working under him or her to conduct business and handle routine problems.

28.____ Someone authorized to represent a principal in a specific task, such as selling a property.

XII. MULTIPLE CHOICE

1. The Real Estate Commissioner's regulations require a broker to have a signed employment agreement for each of his or her salespeople. A copy of this agreement must be kept by both parties for:

    a. one year from the date of termination.
    b. two years from the date of termination.
    c. three years from the date of termination.
    d. the parties do not have to keep copies.

2. A broker is required, by law, to make certain representations about the property he or she is selling. These requirements are spelled out in the:

    a. Agency Disclosure Form.
    b. Listing Agreement.
    c. Transfer Disclosure Statement.
    d. Business and Professional Code.

3. The Agency Disclosure Law went into effect in:

    a. 1986.
    b. 1988.
    c. 1990.
    d. 1991.

4. Real estate law (Civil Code Section 2013) requires that an exclusive listing:

    a. must have a definite starting time.
    b. be unilateral in nature.
    c. be printed in ten point bold.
    d. must have a definite termination date.

5. The unethical practice of NOT giving a new listing to an MLS until the listing broker first tries to sell it within the company is called a(n):

    a. negligent misrepresentation.
    b. secret profit.
    c. pocket listing.
    d. illegal conversion.

6. In any real estate transaction, the salesperson would receive his or her commission from:

    a. the listing agent.
    b. his or her broker.
    c. the selling agent.
    d. the buyer's broker.

7. A statement that exaggerates a property's benefits is called:

    a. innocent misrepresentation.

    b. steering.

    c. negligent misrepresentation.

    d. puffing.

8. The salesperson, who is required to work for a broker by law, is technically called a:

    a. subagent.

    b. principal.

    c. third party.

    d. all of the above.

9. Real estate salespeople are:

    a. employees of the seller.

    b. employees of the buyer.

    c. agents of the buyer, the seller, or both.

    d. agents of the title company.

10. The proper way to create an agency relationship is by:

    a. estoppel.

    b. written agreement.

    c. ratification.

    d. implication.

ANSWERS: 1. c; 2. c; 3. b; 4. d; 5. c; 6. b; 7. d; 8. a; 9. c; 10. b

Chapter 5
Contracts

I. Contracts in General

Nothing is as important to the real estate broker and his or her salespeople than the law of contracts. Because every phase of a real estate transaction involves one or more contracts, it is important to understand the basic rules that govern the creation and life of a contract. This chapter will explain the elements of contracts and illustrate, in detail, the important parts of a deposit receipt (the Residential Purchase Agreement).

 www.leginfo.ca.gov/calaw.html **(California Law)**
www.leginfo.ca.gov/statute.html **(State Statutes)**
www.courtinfo.ca.gov **(California Courts)**
www.ce9.uscourts.gov **(9th Circuit Court)**
www.calbar.org **(State Bar of California)**

A *CONTRACT is an agreement to do or not to do a certain act or service.* Every contract consists of a promise or a set of promises that are enforceable by law. These promises may be created in two ways, either in an express manner or in an implied manner.

An *EXPRESS CONTRACT is an agreement that is made either orally or in writing.* Listings, deposit receipts, and leases are all express contracts.

Real estate contracts may be either oral (ill-advised) or in writing. Any important contract should be written, even if not required by law.

On the other hand, an **IMPLIED CONTRACT** *is created when an agreement is made by acts and conduct (implication) rather than by words.* For example, suppose you entered a hardware store where you had an account, picked up an $8 paint brush, and waved it at the clerk as you departed. The clerk, judging from your conduct, would assume that you wanted the paint brush charged to your account and would bill you accordingly. An implied contract would have been formed. Implied contracts are not used in the practice of real estate.

Contracts are "express" by explicit words (written or oral) or "implied" by conduct. Implied contracts are discouraged in real estate.

A **BILATERAL CONTRACT** *is a promise made by one party in exchange for the promise of another party.* It is a promise for a promise. For instance, if a homeowner offers a painter $2,000 to paint his or her garage and the painter agrees to do it, a bilateral contract is formed: The painter promises to paint the garage, while the homeowner promises to give the painter $2,000. *When only one party makes a promise for an act of another, the agreement is called a* **UNILATERAL CONTRACT**. It is a promise for an act. If someone acts upon an offer, the one making the offer is obligated to complete his or her promise.

Suppose Mr. Bentley offers a reward to any person who can identify the arsonist who set his home on fire. Because this is a unilateral contract, Mr. Bentley is required to give the reward to any person who can fulfill the obligation.

A contract can be either bilateral (two promises) or unilateral (one promise for an act).

A. CLASSIFICATION OF CONTRACTS

Contracts may be classified in any of these four ways:

1. Valid

A contract that is binding and enforceable in a court of law.

Performance is expected, or legal action can be filed.

2. Voidable

Valid on its face, but one or more of the parties may reject it.

Victim can rescind, cancel, or annul. A contract signed under duress is voidable.

3. Void

Has no legal force or effect.

Essential elements of a contract are lacking.

4. Unenforceable

The contract cannot be proved or sued upon.

If a law has changed, for example, performance may be unenforceable.

B. LIFE OF A CONTRACT

A Contract Has Three Basic Phases.

1. Phase 1 - Negotiation

This is the negotiation period. During this period the buyer and seller discuss the possibility of a contract. If there is mutual interest between the parties, then an offer, or perhaps several offers, can be made. The offer becomes a contract when accepted, provided that all the other elements necessary for the creation of a contract are present.

2. Phase 2 - Performance

This is the performance stage of the contract. An *EXECUTORY CONTRACT is a legal agreement, the provisions of which have yet to be completely fulfilled.* A deposit receipt is executory until payment is made and title is transferred. Then it becomes executed. A land contract might be executory for years.

An exclusive listing just signed by an owner is an example of an express, bilateral, executory contract.

3. Phase 3 - Completed Performance

This stage occurs after a contract has been completed. An *EXECUTED CONTRACT is one that has either been discharged or performed.* After a contract has been completed, there is the warranty that every aspect of the contract has been properly performed.

This term should not be confused with the execution of a contract. To *EXECUTE a contract is to sign a contract*, while the *EXECUTION of a contract is the act of performing or carrying out the contract.*

A contract to be performed is called "executory"; a completely performed contract has been "executed." The contract lives on until legal right to bring legal action has expired. This is called the "statute of limitations."

II. Elements of a Contract

According to the California Civil Code, there must be four elements to any valid contract whether it involves real estate or not. However, in real estate, contracts generally must be in writing. **See Figure 5-1.**

Figure 5-1

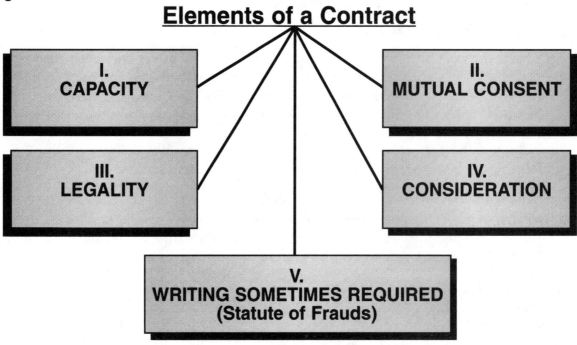

Elements of a Contract

| I. CAPACITY | II. MUTUAL CONSENT |
| III. LEGALITY | IV. CONSIDERATION |

V.
WRITING SOMETIMES REQUIRED
(Statute of Frauds)

These are the four elements of any contract: 1) capacity, 2) mutual consent, 3) legality, and 4) consideration. Sometimes in real estate writing is required, making this the fifth element. The following are NOT essential elements of a valid contract:

1) money (can be other consideration),
2) writing (real estate contracts sometimes require it), and
3) performance.

A. CAPACITY

For a contract to be valid, there must be two or more parties who have the legal capacity to contract. Everyone is capable of contracting, except for the following persons: 1) minors, 2) incompetents, and 3) convicts.

1. Minor

A **MINOR** *is a person under the age of eighteen.* A minor cannot make contracts relating to real property or property not in his or her immediate possession or control, and does not have the right to employ an agent, **unless the minor is emancipated**. An *EMANCIPATED MINOR is one who has the contractual rights of an adult.* The three ways that a minor becomes emancipated are:

1. through marriage,
2. a member or former member of the armed forces, and
3. declared to be self-supporting by the courts.

A minor who has been "emancipated" has legal capacity. Once emancipated, always emancipated. Otherwise, a contract or deed signed by a minor would be void. Any minor can acquire property by gift or inheritance.

A contract with a minor is void because a minor cannot delegate authority. A minor may, however, buy and sell real estate through a guardian if the action is given court approval.

2. Incompetent

An **INCOMPETENT** *is a person who is judged to be of unsound mind.* Such a person has no capacity (power) to contract; any contract made is void. In real estate transactions with incompetents, it is necessary to have the guardian's decision approved by the court. However, both minors and incompetents may acquire real property by gift or inheritance.

Both minors and incompetents may acquire real property by gift or inheritance.

3. Convicts

CONVICTS *are persons who have lost their civil rights during their imprisonment.* Convicts are incapable of contracting, but they do not forfeit any property in their possession. They may acquire property by gift, inheritance, or will, but can only convey property if the action is ratified by the California Adult Authority.

Criminal acts (illegal acts) are prosecuted by the city or county prosecutor.

> *ALIENS are not citizens of the United states, but they have the right to own property in California.* This surprises some people, but it is true that any person, whether he or she is a U.S. citizen or not, may buy, hold or transfer real property.

B. MUTUAL CONSENT

Mutual consent is an offer by one party and acceptance by the other party.

This is the second major requirement of a valid contract. **MUTUAL CONSENT** *is an offer of one party and acceptance of that offer by the other party.* This acceptance need not be a true "meeting of the minds" of the parties because they are bound only by an objective standard (their apparent intentions as evidenced by words or acts). Since courts cannot read minds, any secret or unexpressed intentions are immaterial. The consent must be genuine and free from fraud or mistake, and there must be a true intention to be obligated or it may be voidable by one or both of the parties.

Death does NOT cancel most contracts; they are binding on the estate, except a listing agreement, which is an employment (personal service) contract.

1. The Offer

An **OFFER** *expresses a person's willingness to enter into a contract. The* **OFFEROR** *is the person (buyer) who has made the offer, and the* **OFFEREE** *is the person (seller) to whom the offer has been made.* The offer made by the offeror must be communicated to the offeree. Every offer must have contractual intent. **CONTRACTUAL INTENT** *exists when a party communicates an offer to another with the intention of forming a binding contract.* For example, a social invitation to attend a party is not meant to be a contract and therefore lacks contractual intent. Likewise, an advertisement in the newspaper is not an offer, but merely an invitation to deal.

A buyer can withdraw his or her offer anytime prior to receiving communication—in writing, personally, or by registered mail—of its acceptance and receive a refund of the money deposited.

Finally, an offer must be definite and certain in its terms. **DEFINITE AND CERTAIN** *means that the precise acts to be performed must be clearly stated.* A court can neither create contracts for parties nor fix the terms and conditions of any contract. An **ILLUSORY CONTRACT** *is one in which the terms are uncertain, therefore the contract is unenforceable.*

An "illusory contract" appears to be a contract but it is NOT definite and certain, so it is unenforceable.

2. Acceptance

ACCEPTANCE is the consent to the terms by the offeree. Acceptance of an offer must be in the manner specified in the offer, but if no particular manner of acceptance is specified, then acceptance may be made by any reasonable or usual mode.

If an offer is accepted by the offeree and communicated to the offeror, it is a legally binding contract. Should the buyer or seller now die, there is still a legally binding contract.

Silence cannot be interpreted as an acceptance of an offer because acceptance must be communicated. One cannot say "If I do not hear from you in 10 days, the offer is considered accepted." There must be a communicated acceptance of an offer in writing.

The broker who has communicated acceptance of the offer is most likely to earn the commission.

The acceptance must be absolute and unqualified, because if it modifies the terms of the offer, it becomes a counter offer. A *COUNTER OFFER is the rejection of an original offer and the proposal of a new offer.* The offeree rejects the offer then becomes the offeror of the counter offer. **Once there is a counter offer, the previous offer is automatically terminated**. The counter offer is discussed later in the chapter. (**See Counter Offer form, Figure 5-8.**)

3. Termination of an Offer

The hope of the offeror is that the other party will accept and that a contract will be formed, but most initial offers are rejected. Here are six ways an offer can be terminated:

1. **Lapse of Time.** The offer is terminated if the offeree fails to accept within a prescribed period.
2. **Communication of Revocation.** An offer can be withdrawn anytime before the other party has communicated his or her acceptance.
3. **Failure of Offeree to Fulfill a Condition.** A specified condition must be satisfied in a prescribed manner or the offer is terminated.
4. **Rejection.** If the offer is rejected, it is terminated.
5. **Death or Insanity of the Offeror or Offeree.** This would void the offer. The death of the offeror or offeree constitutes a revocation of the offer—the offer died with the death of the offeror.
6. **Illegality of Purpose.** If the conditions or the purpose of a contract are illegal, then the contract is void.

4. Genuine Consent (Contract is Void or Voidable by Victim)

The final requirement for mutual consent is that the offer and acceptance must be given freely. If not, the contract is void or voidable by the victim. Genuine consent does not exist if any of the following conditions are present:

1. *FRAUD occurs when a person misrepresents a material fact, knowing it is not true, or is carelessly indifferent to the truth of the stated facts.* The contract is void or voidable, depending on the degree of fraud.

2. *MISTAKE exists when both parties are mistaken as to the matter of the agreement, or where the subject matter of the contract ceases to exist. A mistake is also void or voidable.*

    Example: I offer to buy your mountain cabin but neither of us knows it has burned down.

3. *DURESS is the unlawful detention of a person and/or that person's property.*

4. *MENACE is a threat to commit duress,* but it also can be a threat of unlawful violent injury to a person and/or his or her character as a party to the contract.

5. *UNDUE INFLUENCE occurs when a person in a position of authority uses that authority to an unfair advantage.* This is usually found in a confidential relationship.

If a contract was entered into under pressure, as with duress, menace, and undue influence, it is voidable.

C. LEGALITY

A contract that forces one to break the law is void.

A contract must be legal in its formation and operation. **Both the consideration and its objective must also be lawful**. The objective refers to what the contract requires the parties to do or not to do. If the contract consists of a single objective that is unlawful in whole or in part, then the contract is void. If there are several objectives, the contract is normally valid as to those parts that are lawful.

The law will not enforce an illegal contract. If an illegal contract is not completed, the courts will not force its completion. Even if an illegal contract is completed, the courts will rarely enforce it unless the law violated was designed to protect one of the parties.

Example: A contract to bribe a city building inspector to accept substandard work for $5,000 is illegal and void.

D. CONSIDERATION (Anything of Value)

VALUABLE CONSIDERATION in a contract is anything of value given by one party to another party to make the agreement binding. A valid contract must have sufficient consideration, which is any amount of valued consideration. Consideration need not be money. It may: (1) benefit the person making the contract or another person, (2) be a loss suffered or agreed to be suffered, or (3) be an agreement not to bring a legal suit. If the price paid is a promise, consideration may be a promise for a promise. The important point is that the consideration must be of some value.

Payment of money is NOT needed as consideration. It can also be a benefit, like the performance of an act or the nonperformance (forbearance) of an act.

Some rare types of contracts require that consideration be adequate. In such contracts the condition of adequate consideration must be met for those contracts to be enforceable. Other contracts, without such a condition, are enforceable no matter what the consideration is, as long as it is agreed on by all parties.

A contract based on unlawful consideration is void.

E. PROPER WRITING (Real Estate Contracts)

Certain real estate contracts must be in writing to prevent fraud or perjury.

All contracts may be oral except those specifically required by the Statute of Frauds to be in writing. A contract for personal property can be oral or written, but the Statute of Frauds requires that most real estate contracts be in writing. **See Figure 5-2.**

A listing agreement must be in writing to enforce the payment of a commission. Oral agreements between brokers to share commissions are binding.

Personal property contracts, like rental agreements, for one year or less, need NOT be in writing. Any contract that can't be performed within a year from the date of signing must be in writing.

1. Parol Evidence Rule

PAROL EVIDENCE refers to prior oral or written agreements of the parties, or even oral agreements concurrent (contemporaneous) with a written contract. Under the "parol evidence rule," a contract expressed in writing is intended to be a complete and final expression of the rights and duties of the contracting parties. The parol evidence rule means that prior oral or written agreements of the parties **cannot** be

Figure 5-2

STATUTE OF FRAUDS

Most contracts, which by statute are required to be in writing, are found under the Statute of Frauds. The Statute of Frauds was first adopted in England in 1677 and became part of English common law. Subsequently, it was introduced into this country and has become part of California's law. The main purpose of this law is to prevent forgery, perjury, and dishonest conduct by unscrupulous people, thus improving the existence and terms of certain important types of contracts.

The statute provides that certain contracts are invalid unless those contracts are in writing and signed by either the parties to be charged or their agents. Under California's Civil Code, the following contracts must be in writing:

1. Any agreement where the terms will not be performed within one year following the making of the contract.

2. A special promise to answer for the debt, default, or nonperformance of another, except in cases provided for by the Civil Code.

3. Agreement made upon the consideration of marriage, other than a mutual promise to marry.

4. An agreement for the leasing of real property for a period longer than one year (one year and one day), or for the sale of real property or of interest therein. It also applies to any agreement authorizing an agent to perform the above acts.

5. An agreement authorizing or employing an agent, broker, or any other person to purchase, sell, or lease real estate for more than one year. It is also an agreement to find a buyer, seller, or lessee for more than one year, in return for compensation.

6. An agreement, which by its terms is not to be performed during the lifetime of the promisor, or an agreement that devises or bequeaths any property, or makes provision for any reason by will.

7. An agreement by a purchaser of real estate to pay a debt secured by a trust deed or mortgage upon the property purchased, unless assumption of that debt by the purchaser is specifically provided for in the conveyance of such property.

The Statute of Frauds also applies to personal property. If the sales price of an item is more than $500, the contract must be in writing. Furthermore, if several items are purchased with the intent that the agreement be a single contract, the contract should be in writing if the total sales price is $500 or more.

introduced as evidence to contradict or modify the terms of the written contract. The courts, however, will permit such outside evidence to be introduced when the written contract is incomplete, ambiguous, or it is necessary to show that the contract is not enforceable because of mistake or fraud.

Rarely will the courts allow prior "oral parts or an entire oral contract" to be substituted for a later written contract. The courts would be jammed with people who wanted to change their contracts. So do it properly. Make only written real estate contracts.

III. Performance, Discharge, and Breach of Contract

Acts described in a contract must be performed in a TIMELY MANNER (within time limits described in the contract). Most contracts are properly performed and discharged without any legal complications. If difficulties do arise, the parties, either by themselves or with the aid of legal counsel, usually work out an agreeable settlement. If there is no settlement, the courts are available for the resolution of any contractual conflicts.

In a contract, the "time is of the essence" clause applies to the entire contract.

A. PERFORMANCE OF A CONTRACT

PERFORMANCE is the successful completion of a contractual duty, usually resulting in the performer's release from any past or future liability. Sometimes with performance of a contract, one of the parties would prefer to drop out of the picture without terminating the contract. He or she may, under proper circumstances, accomplish this by assignment. An *ASSIGNMENT is the transfer of a person's right in a contract to another party.* An assignment happens when the *ASSIGNOR, the party to the original contract, transfers his or her rights in the contract to another party, called an ASSIGNEE.* Any contract, unless it calls for some personal service, can be assigned if the contract does not state otherwise. For example, listings are not assignable because they are personal service contracts. If the assignee does not perform, the assignor remains liable (secondary liability) for the contract.

In some cases, the original contracting party may want to drop out of the contract completely. This can be done by novation. A *NOVATION is the substitution or exchange (by mutual agreement of the parties) of a new obligation or contract for an existing one with intent to cancel the old contract.* Since it is a new contract, it requires consideration and the other essentials of a valid contract.

Novation replaces the old contract with a new contract.

Time is often significant in a contract and is usually stated in the contract. By statute, if no time is specified for the performance of an act, a reasonable time is allowed. If an act, by its nature, can be done instantly (such as the payment of money) it must be done. If the last day for the performance of an act falls upon a holiday or weekend, the period is extended to include the next business day. *REVOCATION is the cancelling of an offer to contract by the the original offeror.*

B. DISCHARGE OF A CONTRACT

The *DISCHARGE OF A CONTRACT occurs when the contract has been terminated.* Contracts can be discharged in many ways, from the extreme of full performance (which is the usual pattern) to breach of contract (nonperformance). **Figure 5-3** illustrates these extremes and the variety of possibilities that may exist between them. A brief description of these possibilities follows.

Figure 5-3

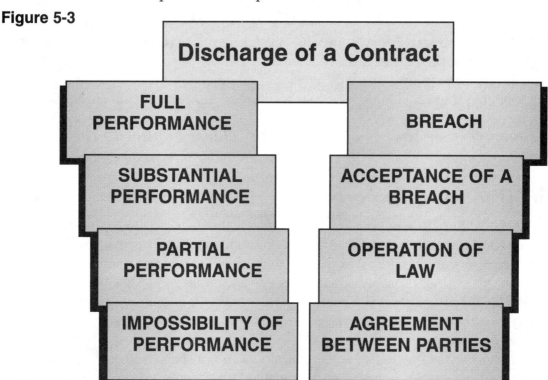

1. Full Performance

The contract is completed according to the terms specified in the original agreement.

2. Substantial Performance

Sometimes one party attempts to discharge a contract when the contract has almost, but not entirely, been completed. In certain cases the courts will accept this as a discharge of the contract. Otherwise there are usually slight monetary charges for damages.

3. Partial Performance

If both parties agree to the value of the work partially completed, the contract is discharged. This agreement should be in writing. However if a dispute arises, the courts will determine the obligations of the defaulting party. Damages are one of the hardest things to prove, and the courts usually lean towards the non-defaulting party. A judge will most likely award the non-defaulting party any amount necessary to complete the contract.

4. Impossibility of Performance

Under certain circumstances, the contract, for one reason or another, may be impossible to perform. An obvious example is where a painting contractor can no longer paint a house because it was destroyed by fire. In other cases, legality of the purpose may be challenged.

5. Agreement Between the Parties

If a contract is not completed, the usual way to discharge the contract is by mutual agreement (agree to disagree). A mutual agreement not to complete the contract is also a contract. Most knowledgeable contractors include ways for the contract to be discharged if one of the parties defaults on the original contract.

When a contract is mutually rescinded, the deposit must be returned to the buyer immediately.

6. Operation of Law (According to Statutes)

Whenever a contract or parts of a contract become illegal, the contract is discharged by operation of law.

7. Acceptance of a Breach

A *BREACH is the failure to perform a contract, in part or in whole, without legal excuse.* Sometimes a person will accept a breach. If time is important, the anxious party will usually discharge the contract and try to find a new party to perform the task. Contesting the contract sometimes only creates more problems, such as expensive interruption of work in progress and postponement of other contracts.

8. Breach (Nonperformance)

This is the nonperformance by one of the contracting parties. The performing party has his or her choice of several legal remedies.

The most common breaches, from the agent's point of view, are: (1) the buyers who decide not to buy after signing the deposit receipt or (2) the seller who decides not to sell after signing the listing and/or deposit receipt.

If a buyer backs out, the seller can exercise the "right of rescission" and must return anything of value received from the buyer, sue the buyer, and try to find a new buyer to mitigate damages.

9. Statute of Limitations (For Breach of Contract)

According to the Statute of Limitations, a civil action for a breach of contract must be started within a certain period of time. If the civil action has not been started within that given time, no legal recourse will be possible. This policy of law states that a person who "sleeps upon his rights" may find himself barred from any legal action. **See Figure 5-4**.

IV. Remedies for Breach of a Contract

A breach of contract occurs when one party fails to perform his or her contractual obligations. By law, the party who has been wronged has only four choices. Action for dollar damages is the most common remedy for breach of a contract because most people prefer to receive money (cash) for their damages. **Figure 5-5** illustrates the four alternatives.

A. ACCEPTANCE OF BREACH

A discharge of a contract may be simply the acceptance of the breach. In an *ACCEPTANCE OF BREACH, the wronged party does not pursue legal action.* Sometimes he or she may feel that the damages recoverable are too limited to justify litigation. Perhaps the person considers the other party judgment-proof, which means that the other party does not have enough assets available to satisfy a judgment. Moreover, the legal cost of a lawsuit, the time, the effort, and the psychological effect may not be worth the possible outcome.

B. UNILATERAL RESCISSION

In a **UNILATERAL RESCISSION** *the wronged party (1) discloses the wrong and (2) restores everything of value to the offended party.* The legal grounds for a rescission are: fraud, mistake, duress, menace, undue influence, and faulty consideration. Rescission is possible when the contract is unlawful for causes not apparent on its face, when the parties are not equally at fault, or when the public interest would be hurt. Minors or incompetents may generally rescind their contracts.

C. ACTION FOR DOLLAR DAMAGES

An *ACTION FOR DOLLAR DAMAGES occurs when a court suit for a breach requests payment of a fixed amount of money as compensation.* If a party to a contract causes you to lose money, it is only fair for you to receive compensation. In most deposit receipts (contract to purchase), there is usually a liquidated damages agreement. A

Figure 5-4

STATUTE OF LIMITATIONS

Actions Which Must Be Brought Within 90 Days

CIVIL ACTION FOR THE RECOVERY OF PERSONAL PROPERTY, such as trunks or baggage left in a hotel or other furnished establishment, must be started within 90 days after being left by the owner of the personal property.

Within Six Months

AN ACTION AGAINST AN OFFICER TO RECOVER ANY GOODS, WAGES, MERCHANDISE, OR OTHER PROPERTY seized by any officer in his or her official capacity as tax collector. To recover the value of such goods, as well as compensation for damage done to the property seized and further actions against the county, an action must be started within six months of the seizure.

Within Two Years

AN ACTION FOR LIBEL, SLANDER, INJURY, OR DEATH caused by the neglect of another or against a bank for the payment of a forged check must be started within one year of the alleged wrong.

ACTION MUST BE TAKEN WITHIN TWO YEARS AGAINST CONTRACTS OR OBLIGATIONS THAT WERE NOT MADE IN WRITING. Actions against contracts that have been founded on title insurance policies, certificates, or abstracts of title for real property must be made within two years from the date the cause of these actions is discovered. This does not include contracts made for accounts receivable.

Action for **misleading transfer disclosure statements** made by broker or agent must be taken within two years.

Within Three Years (Attachments)

ACTIONS UPON LIABILITIES CREATED BY STATUTE (other than penalties) for trespass upon, or damage to, real property; for taking or damaging goods (including action for the recovery of specific personal property); and actions on the grounds of fraud or mistake caused before discovery by the injured party must be brought within three years.

Within Four Years (Listings and Deposit Receipts)

ACTIONS WHICH MUST BE MADE ON ANY WRITTEN CONTRACT WITHIN FOUR YEARS include most real estate contracts such as deposit receipts and listings, except for notes or obligations of publicly held corporations (where the limit is specified as being six years). Other exceptions exist when specific limitations are written into a contract. These exceptions include actions on a money judgment for the balance due upon a trust deed or mortgage, actions following the exercise of the power of sale (which may not be brought later than three months after the sale), and actions to recover upon accounts receivable.

Within Five Years

ANY ACTION FOR INTERMEDIATE PROFITS OF REAL ESTATE from wrongful occupancy and any action for the recovery of real property may be started anytime within five years.

Within Ten Years (Judgments)

AN ACTION UPON A JUDGMENT OF ANY COURT OF THE UNITED STATES or of any state within the United States must be brought within ten years.

Figure 5-5

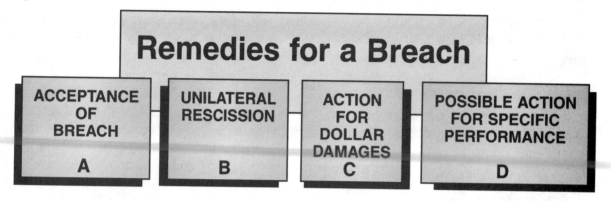

Remedies for a Breach

ACCEPTANCE OF BREACH	UNILATERAL RESCISSION	ACTION FOR DOLLAR DAMAGES	POSSIBLE ACTION FOR SPECIFIC PERFORMANCE
A	B	C	D

LIQUIDATED DAMAGES AGREEMENT sets, in advance, a specified amount of money as compensation if there is a breach. This clause is used because it is usually impractical or difficult to determine the actual damages caused by a breach.

The current award for liquidated damages on a deposit receipt form is a maximum of 3% (by law) of the home purchase price. Any deposit amount in excess of 3% must be refunded to the offeror.

D. SPECIFIC PERFORMANCE

The final remedy for a breach of contract is specific performance. *SPECIFIC PERFORMANCE means that the party causing the breach is, through court action, forced to perform.* For the most part, courts are skeptical of forcing a person to sell their real property and as a result this type of remedy is seldom used. Courts of equity will consider this action only if dollar damages cannot provide an adequate remedy. If specific performance is ordered, the remedy must be mutual. That is, neither party to a contract can be compelled specifically to perform unless the other party has performed or is also specifically compelled to perform.

As discussed in Chapter 2, community real property must be transferred by both husband and wife. A buyer who does not realize the existence of a marriage relationship in which the husband alone holds all titles may have his or her rights enforced through specific performance without the wife's signature. This, however, requires court action. An agreement to obtain a spouse's consent cannot be specifically enforced until one year's spousal silence on the matter has passed. So it is extremely important for a **salesperson** to acquire the signatures of both husband and wife. In fact, the signatures of both spouses should always be obtained if the contract relates to community real property.

To obtain specific performance, the plaintiff must show that the contract was just and reasonable. The contract must have been based on adequate consideration, meaning that the price received for the property must have been fair and reasonable. In addition, specific performance cannot be forced against a party if the contract was obtained by misrepresentation, concealment, circumvention, or any other unfair practice.

V. The Residential Purchase Agreement

A. THE OFFER AND ACCEPTANCE (WITH DEPOSIT)

A deposit of money or items of value accompany a deposit receipt to be a valid offer. If a postdated check or promissory note is given as consideration for a deposit with an offer (deposit receipt), the agent must disclose this fact to the seller.

The deposit receipt is the most important contract in the real estate field! A California *CALIFORNIA RESIDENTIAL PURCHASE AGREEMENT AND JOINT ESCROW INSTRUCTIONS is an offer and deposit to purchase a specific property on certain terms and conditions.* When acceptance is communicated to the buyer, this becomes a binding contract on the buyer and seller, and, generally, this becomes the date of the purchase agreement. Acceptance is communicated in writing, in person, by mail, or fax.

In addition, the deposit receipt discloses (as in the listing agreement) the percentage of commission to be paid to the brokers involved. (**See Figure 5-6**, CAR® California Residential Purchase Agreement and Joint Escrow Instructions.)

The Deposit Receipt is also called "The Contract" or "California Residential Purchase Agreement," but it is most commonly referred to as the "Deposit Receipt."

The deposit receipt is neater and more polished if it is typed, but there is nothing wrong with filling it in with a pen. Each form has three copies: a master copy, a buyer's copy, and a seller's copy.

An agent must always give a copy of a signed contract to the parties involved.

NOTE: When using preprinted forms, the handwritten parts have control over the printed parts, and all corrections must be initialed by both parties.

B. THE DEPOSIT (Consideration for Deposit Receipt)

The deposit is collected as consideration from a prospective buyer on behalf of the seller for the deposit receipt contract. Suppose the seller accepts the offer on the CAR® Deposit Receipt form and the buyer later defaults on the transaction. If the liquidated

Figure 5-6

CALIFORNIA
ASSOCIATION
OF REALTORS®

CALIFORNIA
RESIDENTIAL PURCHASE AGREEMENT
AND JOINT ESCROW INSTRUCTIONS
For Use With Single Family Residential Property — Attached or Detached
(C.A.R. Form RPA-CA, Revised 10/02)

Date _JUNE 14, 2003_____, at _Costa Mesa_____, California.
1. **OFFER:**
   A. THIS IS AN OFFER FROM _Walter and Debbie Buyer_____ ("Buyer").
   B. THE REAL PROPERTY TO BE ACQUIRED is described as _264 Beach Lane_____
   _____, Assessor's Parcel No. _____, situated in
   _Costa Mesa_____, County of _Orange_____, California, ("Property").
   C. THE PURCHASE PRICE offered is _Eight Hundred Thousand ✓———No/100—————_
   _____ Dollars $ _800,000_____
   D. CLOSE OF ESCROW shall occur on _____ (date)(or ☒ _90_ **Days** After Acceptance).
2. **FINANCE TERMS:** Obtaining the loans below **is a contingency** of this Agreement unless: **(i)** either 2K or 2L is checked below; or **(ii)** otherwise agreed in writing. Buyer shall act diligently and in good faith to obtain the designated loans. Obtaining deposit, down payment and closing costs **is not a contingency.** Buyer represents that funds will be good when deposited with Escrow Holder.
   A. INITIAL DEPOSIT: Buyer has given a deposit in the amount of . . . .$ _10,000_
   to the agent submitting the offer (or to ☐ _____), by personal check
   (or ☐ _____), made payable to _ABC Escrow_____
   which shall be held uncashed until Acceptance and then deposited within **3** business days after
   Acceptance (or ☐ _____), with
   Escrow Holder, (or ☐ into Broker's trust account).
   B. INCREASED DEPOSIT: Buyer shall deposit with Escrow Holder an increased deposit in the amount of . . .$ _____
   within _____ **Days** After Acceptance, or ☐ _____.
   C. FIRST LOAN IN THE AMOUNT OF . . . .$ _640,000_
   (1) NEW First Deed of Trust in favor of lender, encumbering the Property, securing a note payable at
   maximum interest of _8_% fixed rate, or _____% initial adjustable rate with a maximum
   interest rate of _____%, balance due in _____ years, amortized over _30_ years. Buyer
   shall pay loan fees/points not to exceed _2_. (These terms apply whether the designated loan
   is conventional, FHA or VA.)
   (2) ☐ FHA ☐ VA: (The following terms only apply to the FHA or VA loan that is checked.)
   Seller shall pay _____% discount points. Seller shall pay other fees not allowed to be paid by
   Buyer, ☐ not to exceed $_____. Seller shall pay the cost of lender required Repairs
   (including those for wood destroying pest) not otherwise provided for in this Agreement, ☐ not to
   exceed $ _____. (Actual loan amount may increase if mortgage insurance premiums,
   funding fees or closing costs are financed.)
   D. ADDITIONAL FINANCING TERMS: ☐ Seller financing, (C.A.R. Form SFA); ☐ secondary financing, ...$ _____
   (C.A.R. Form PAA, paragraph 4A); ☐ assumed financing (C.A.R. Form PAA, paragraph 4B)
   _____
   _____
   E. BALANCE OF PURCHASE PRICE (not including costs of obtaining loans and other closing costs) in the amount of . . .$ _150,000_
   to be deposited with Escrow Holder within sufficient time to close escrow.
   F. PURCHASE PRICE (TOTAL): . . . .$ _800,000_
   G. LOAN APPLICATIONS: Within **7 (or ☐ _____) Days** After Acceptance, Buyer shall provide Seller a letter from lender or
   mortgage loan broker stating that, based on a review of Buyer's written application and credit report, Buyer is prequalified or
   preapproved for the NEW loan specified in 2C above.
   H. VERIFICATION OF DOWN PAYMENT AND CLOSING COSTS: Buyer (or Buyer's lender or loan broker pursuant to 2G) shall, within
   7 (or ☐ _____) Days After Acceptance, provide Seller written verification of Buyer's down payment and closing costs.
   I. LOAN CONTINGENCY REMOVAL: **(i)** Within **17 (or ☐ _____) Days** After Acceptance, Buyer shall, as specified in paragraph
   14, remove the loan contingency or cancel this Agreement; **OR (ii)** (if checked) ☐ the loan contingency shall remain in effect
   until the designated loans are funded.
   J. APPRAISAL CONTINGENCY AND REMOVAL: This Agreement is (**OR**, if checked, ☐ is NOT) contingent upon the Property
   appraising at no less than the specified purchase price. Buyer shall, as specified in paragraph 14, remove the appraisal
   contingency or cancel this Agreement when the loan contingency is removed (or, if checked, ☐ within **17 (or ☐ _____) Days**
   After Acceptance).
   K. ☐ NO LOAN CONTINGENCY (If checked): Obtaining any loan in paragraphs 2C, 2D or elsewhere in this Agreement is NOT
   a contingency of this Agreement. If Buyer does not obtain the loan and as a result Buyer does not purchase the Property, Seller
   may be entitled to Buyer's deposit or other legal remedies.
   L. ☐ ALL CASH OFFER (If checked): No loan is needed to purchase the Property. Buyer shall, within **7 (or ☐ _____) Days** After Acceptance,
   provide Seller written verification of sufficient funds to close this transaction.
3. **CLOSING AND OCCUPANCY:**
   A. Buyer intends (or ☐ does not intend) to occupy the Property as Buyer's primary residence.
   B. Seller-occupied or vacant property: Occupancy shall be delivered to Buyer at _11_ AM/PM, ☒ on the date of Close Of
   Escrow; ☐ on _____; or ☐ no later than _____ **Days** After Close Of Escrow. (C.A.R. Form PAA, paragraph 2.) If
   transfer of title and occupancy do not occur at the same time, Buyer and Seller are advised to: **(i)** enter into a written occupancy
   agreement; and **(ii)** consult with their insurance and legal advisors.

RPA-CA REVISED 10/02 (PAGE 1 OF 8) Print Date

Buyer's Initials (_WB_)(_DB_)
Seller's Initials (_TA._)(_vp._)

Reviewed by _JR_ Date _6/14/03_

EQUAL HOUSING
OPPORTUNITY

CALIFORNIA RESIDENTIAL PURCHASE AGREEMENT (RPA-CA PAGE 1 OF 8)

Property Address: *264 Beach Lane, Costa Mesa, CA 92627*   Date: *JUNE 14, 2003*

C. **Tenant-occupied property: (i) Property** shall be vacant at least 5 (or ☐ _____) **Days** Prior to Close Of Escrow, unless otherwise agreed in writing. **Note to Seller: If you are unable to deliver Property vacant in accordance with rent control and other applicable Law, you may be in breach of this Agreement.**

OR **(ii)** (if checked) ☐ **Tenant to remain in possession.** The attached addendum is incorporated into this Agreement (C.A.R. Form PAA, paragraph 3.);

OR **(iii)** (if checked) ☐ **This Agreement is contingent** upon Buyer and Seller entering into a written agreement regarding occupancy of the Property within the time specified in paragraph 14. If no written agreement is reached within this time, either Buyer or Seller may cancel this Agreement in writing.

D. At Close Of Escrow, Seller assigns to Buyer any assignable warranty rights for items included in the sale and shall provide any available Copies of such warranties. Brokers cannot and will not determine the assignability of any warranties.

E. At Close Of Escrow, unless otherwise agreed in writing, Seller shall provide keys and/or means to operate all locks, mailboxes, security systems, alarms and garage door openers. If Property is a condominium or located in a common interest subdivision, Buyer may be required to pay a deposit to the Homeowners' Association ("HOA") to obtain keys to accessible HOA facilities.

4. **ALLOCATION OF COSTS (If checked):** Unless otherwise specified here, this paragraph only determines who is to pay for the report, inspection, test or service mentioned. If not specified here or elsewhere in this Agreement, the determination of who is to pay for any work recommended or identified by any such report, inspection, test or service shall be by the method specified in paragraph 14.

A. **WOOD DESTROYING PEST INSPECTION:**
(1) ☐ Buyer ☒ Seller shall pay for an inspection and report for wood destroying pests and organisms ("Report") which shall be prepared by _**BUG-R-GONE**_____, a registered structural pest control company. The Report shall cover the accessible areas of the main building and attached structures and, if checked: ☐ detached garages and carports, ☐ detached decks, ☐ the following other structures or areas _____. The Report shall not include roof coverings. If Property is a condominium or located in a common interest subdivision, the Report shall include only the separate interest and any exclusive-use areas being transferred and shall not include common areas, unless otherwise agreed. Water tests of shower pans on upper level units may not be performed without consent of the owners of property below the shower.

OR **(2)** ☐ (If checked) The attached addendum (C.A.R. Form WPA) regarding wood destroying pest inspection and allocation of cost is incorporated into this Agreement.

B. **OTHER INSPECTIONS AND REPORTS:**
(1) ☐ Buyer ☐ Seller shall pay to have septic or private sewage disposal systems inspected _____.
(2) ☐ Buyer ☐ Seller shall pay to have domestic wells tested for water potability and productivity _____.
(3) ☐ Buyer ☐ Seller shall pay for a natural hazard zone disclosure report prepared by _____.
(4) ☐ Buyer ☐ Seller shall pay for the following inspection or report _____.
(5) ☐ Buyer ☐ Seller shall pay for the following inspection or report _____.

C. **GOVERNMENT REQUIREMENTS AND RETROFIT:**
(1) ☐ Buyer ☒ Seller shall pay for smoke detector installation and/or water heater bracing, if required by Law. Prior to Close Of Escrow, Seller shall provide Buyer a written statement of compliance in accordance with state and local Law, unless exempt.
(2) ☐ Buyer ☐ Seller shall pay the cost of compliance with any other minimum mandatory government retrofit standards, inspections and reports if required as a condition of closing escrow under any Law. _____.

D. **ESCROW AND TITLE:**
(1) ☒ Buyer ☒ Seller shall pay escrow fee _50% / 50%_____.
Escrow Holder shall be _ABC ESCROW_____.
(2) ☒ Buyer ☐ Seller shall pay for **owner's** title insurance policy specified in paragraph 12 _____.
Owner's title policy to be issued by _____.
(Buyer shall pay for any title insurance policy insuring Buyer's **lender**, unless otherwise agreed in writing.)

E. **OTHER COSTS:**
(1) ☐ Buyer ☐ Seller shall pay County transfer tax or transfer fee _____.
(2) ☐ Buyer ☐ Seller shall pay City transfer tax or transfer fee _____.
(3) ☐ Buyer ☐ Seller shall pay HOA transfer fee _____.
(4) ☐ Buyer ☐ Seller shall pay HOA document preparation fees _____.
(5) ☐ Buyer ☐ Seller shall pay the cost, not to exceed $ _____, of a one-year home warranty plan, issued by _____
with the following optional coverage: _____.
(6) ☐ Buyer ☐ Seller shall pay for _____.
(7) ☐ Buyer ☐ Seller shall pay for _____.

5. **STATUTORY DISCLOSURES (INCLUDING LEAD-BASED PAINT HAZARD DISCLOSURES) AND CANCELLATION RIGHTS:**
A. (1) Seller shall, within the time specified in paragraph 14, deliver to Buyer, if required by Law: (i) Federal Lead-Based Paint Disclosures and pamphlet ("Lead Disclosures"); and (ii) disclosures or notices required by sections 1102 et. seq. and 1103 et. seq. of the California Civil Code ("Statutory Disclosures"). Statutory Disclosures include, but are not limited to, a Real Estate Transfer Disclosure Statement ("TDS"), Natural Hazard Disclosure Statement ("NHD"), notice or actual knowledge of release of illegal controlled substance, notice of special tax and/or assessments (or, if allowed, substantially equivalent notice regarding the Mello-Roos Community Facilities Act and Improvement Bond Act of 1915) and, if Seller has actual knowledge, an industrial use and military ordnance location disclosure (C.A.R. Form SSD).
(2) Buyer shall, within the time specified in paragraph 14, return Signed Copies of the Statutory and Lead Disclosures to Seller.
(3) In the event Seller, prior to Close Of Escrow, becomes aware of adverse conditions materially affecting the Property, or any material inaccuracy in disclosures, information or representations previously provided to Buyer of which Buyer is otherwise unaware, Seller shall promptly provide a subsequent or amended disclosure or notice, in writing, covering those items. **However, a subsequent or amended disclosure shall not be required for conditions and material inaccuracies disclosed in reports ordered and paid for by Buyer.**

Buyer's Initials (WB)(DB)
Seller's Initials (TP)(yp)

Reviewed by _SR_ Date _6/14/03_

EQUAL HOUSING OPPORTUNITY

CALIFORNIA RESIDENTIAL PURCHASE AGREEMENT (RPA-CA PAGE 2 OF 8)

Property Address: 264 Beach Lane, Costa Mesa, CA 92627   Date: JUNE 14, 2003

(4) If any disclosure or notice specified in 5A(1), or subsequent or amended disclosure or notice is delivered to Buyer after the offer is Signed, Buyer shall have the right to cancel this Agreement within **3 Days** After delivery in person, or **5 Days** After delivery by deposit in the mail, by giving written notice of cancellation to Seller or Seller's agent. (Lead Disclosures sent by mail must be sent certified mail or better.)

(5) Note to Buyer and Seller: Waiver of Statutory and Lead Disclosures is prohibited by Law.

B. NATURAL AND ENVIRONMENTAL HAZARDS: Within the time specified in paragraph 14, Seller shall, if required by Law: **(i)** deliver to Buyer earthquake guides (and questionnaire) and environmental hazards booklet; **(ii)** even if exempt from the obligation to provide a NHD, disclose if the Property is located in a Special Flood Hazard Area; Potential Flooding (Inundation) Area; Very High Fire Hazard Zone; State Fire Responsibility Area; Earthquake Fault Zone; Seismic Hazard Zone; and **(iii)** disclose any other zone as required by Law and provide any other information required for those zones.

C. DATA BASE DISCLOSURE: NOTICE: The California Department of Justice, sheriff's departments, police departments serving jurisdictions of 200,000 or more and many other local law enforcement authorities maintain for public access a data base of the locations of persons required to register pursuant to paragraph (1) of subdivision (a) of Section 290.4 of the Penal Code. The data base is updated on a quarterly basis and a source of information about the presence of these individuals in any neighborhood. The Department of Justice also maintains a Sex Offender Identification Line through which inquiries about individuals may be made. This is a "900" telephone service. Callers must have specific information about individuals they are checking. Information regarding neighborhoods is not available through the "900" telephone service.

6. CONDOMINIUM/PLANNED UNIT DEVELOPMENT DISCLOSURES:

A. SELLER HAS: 7 (or ☐ _____) Days After Acceptance to disclose to Buyer whether the Property is a condominium, or is located in a planned unit development or other common interest subdivision.

B. If the Property is a condominium or is located in a planned unit development or other common interest subdivision, Seller has **3 (or ☐ _____) Days** After Acceptance to request from the HOA (C.A.R. Form HOA): **(i)** Copies of any documents required by Law; **(ii)** disclosure of any pending or anticipated claim or litigation by or against the HOA; **(iii)** a statement containing the location and number of designated parking and storage spaces; **(iv)** Copies of the most recent 12 months of HOA minutes for regular and special meetings; and **(v)** the names and contact information of all HOAs governing the Property (collectively, "CI Disclosures"). Seller shall itemize and deliver to Buyer all CI Disclosures received from the HOA and any CI Disclosures in Seller's possession. Buyer's approval of CI Disclosures is a contingency of this Agreement as specified in paragraph 14.

7. CONDITIONS AFFECTING PROPERTY:

A. Unless otherwise agreed: **(i) the Property is sold (a) in its PRESENT physical condition as of the date of Acceptance and (b) subject to Buyer's Investigation rights; (ii)** the Property, including pool, spa, landscaping and grounds, is to be maintained in substantially the same condition as on the date of Acceptance; and **(iii)** all debris and personal property not included in the sale shall be removed by Close Of Escrow.

B. SELLER SHALL, within the time specified in paragraph 14, **DISCLOSE KNOWN MATERIAL FACTS AND DEFECTS** affecting the Property, including known insurance claims within the past five years, **AND MAKE OTHER DISCLOSURES REQUIRED BY LAW.**

C. NOTE TO BUYER: You are strongly advised to conduct investigations of the entire Property in order to determine its present condition since Seller may not be aware of all defects affecting the Property or other factors that you consider important. Property improvements may not be built according to code, in compliance with current Law, or have had permits issued.

D. NOTE TO SELLER: Buyer has the right to inspect the Property and, as specified in paragraph 14, based upon information discovered in those inspections: **(i)** cancel this Agreement; or **(ii)** request that you make Repairs or take other action.

8. ITEMS INCLUDED AND EXCLUDED:

A. NOTE TO BUYER AND SELLER: Items listed as included or excluded in the MLS, flyers or marketing materials are **not** included in the purchase price or excluded from the sale unless specified in 8B or C.

B. ITEMS INCLUDED IN SALE:

(1) All EXISTING fixtures and fittings that are attached to the Property;

(2) Existing electrical, mechanical, lighting, plumbing and heating fixtures, ceiling fans, fireplace inserts, gas logs and grates, solar systems, built-in appliances, window and door screens, awnings, shutters, window coverings, attached floor coverings, television antennas, satellite dishes, private integrated telephone systems, air coolers/conditioners, pool/spa equipment, garage door openers/remote controls, mailbox, in-ground landscaping, trees/shrubs, water softeners, water purifiers, security systems/alarms;

(3) The following items: _____

_____ .

(4) Seller represents that all items included in the purchase price, unless otherwise specified, are owned by Seller.

(5) All items included shall be transferred free of liens and without Seller warranty.

C. ITEMS EXCLUDED FROM SALE: _____

_____ .

9. BUYER'S INVESTIGATION OF PROPERTY AND MATTERS AFFECTING PROPERTY:

A. Buyer's acceptance of the condition of, and any other matter affecting the Property, is a contingency of this Agreement as specified in this paragraph and paragraph 14. Within the time specified in paragraph 14, Buyer shall have the right, at Buyer's expense unless otherwise agreed, to conduct inspections, investigations, tests, surveys and other studies ("Buyer Investigations"), including, but not limited to, the right to: **(i)** inspect for lead-based paint and other lead-based paint hazards; **(ii)** inspect for wood destroying pests and organisms; **(iii)** review the registered sex offender database; **(iv)** confirm the insurability of Buyer and the Property; and **(v)** satisfy Buyer as to any matter specified in the attached Buyer's Inspection Advisory (C.A.R. Form BIA). Without Seller's prior written consent, Buyer shall neither make nor cause to be made: **(i)** invasive or destructive Buyer's Investigations; or **(ii)** inspections by any governmental building or zoning inspector or government employee, unless required by Law.

B. Buyer shall complete Buyer Investigations and, as specified in paragraph 14, remove the contingency or cancel the Agreement. Buyer shall give Seller, at no cost, complete Copies of all Buyer Investigation reports obtained by Buyer. Seller shall make the Property available for all Buyer Investigations. Seller shall have water, gas, electricity and all operable pilot lights on for Buyer's Investigations and through the date possession is made available to Buyer.

Buyer's Initials (WB)(DB)
Seller's Initials (TP.)(yp.)

Reviewed by _____ Date 6/14/63

CALIFORNIA RESIDENTIAL PURCHASE AGREEMENT (RPA-CA PAGE 3 OF 8)

Property Address: **264 Beach Lane, Costa Mesa, CA 92627**   Date: **JUNE 14, 2003**

10. **REPAIRS:** Repairs shall be completed prior to final verification of condition unless otherwise agreed in writing. Repairs to be performed at Seller's expense may be performed by Seller or through others, provided that the work complies with applicable Law, including governmental permit, inspection and approval requirements. Repairs shall be performed in a good, skillful manner with materials of quality and appearance comparable to existing materials. It is understood that exact restoration of appearance or cosmetic items following all Repairs may not be possible. Seller shall: **(i)** obtain receipts for Repairs performed by others; **(ii)** prepare a written statement indicating the Repairs performed by Seller and the date of such Repairs; and **(iii)** provide Copies of receipts and statements to Buyer prior to final verification of condition.

11. **BUYER INDEMNITY AND SELLER PROTECTION FOR ENTRY UPON PROPERTY:** Buyer shall: **(i)** keep the Property free and clear of liens; **(ii)** Repair all damage arising from Buyer Investigations; and **(iii)** indemnify and hold Seller harmless from all resulting liability, claims, demands, damages and costs. Buyer shall carry, or Buyer shall require anyone acting on Buyer's behalf to carry, policies of liability, workers' compensation and other applicable insurance, defending and protecting Seller from liability for any injuries to persons or property occurring during any Buyer Investigations or work done on the Property at Buyer's direction prior to Close Of Escrow. Seller is advised that certain protections may be afforded Seller by recording a "Notice of Non-responsibility" (C.A.R. Form NNR) for Buyer Investigations and work done on the Property at Buyer's direction. Buyer's obligations under this paragraph shall survive the termination of this Agreement.

12. **TITLE AND VESTING:**
    A. Within the time specified in paragraph 14, Buyer shall be provided a current preliminary (title) report, which is only an offer by the title insurer to issue a policy of title insurance and may not contain every item affecting title. Buyer's review of the preliminary report and any other matters which may affect title are a contingency of this Agreement as specified in paragraph 14.
    B. Title is taken in its present condition subject to all encumbrances, easements, covenants, conditions, restrictions, rights and other matters, whether of record or not, as of the date of Acceptance except: **(i)** monetary liens of record unless Buyer is assuming those obligations or taking the Property subject to those obligations; and **(ii)** those matters which Seller has agreed to remove in writing.
    C. Within the time specified in paragraph 14, Seller has a duty to disclose to Buyer all matters known to Seller affecting title, whether of record or not.
    D. At Close Of Escrow, Buyer shall receive a grant deed conveying title (or, for stock cooperative or long-term lease, an assignment of stock certificate or of Seller's leasehold interest), including oil, mineral and water rights if currently owned by Seller. Title shall vest as designated in Buyer's supplemental escrow instructions. THE MANNER OF TAKING TITLE MAY HAVE SIGNIFICANT LEGAL AND TAX CONSEQUENCES. CONSULT AN APPROPRIATE PROFESSIONAL.
    E. Buyer shall receive a CLTA/ALTA Homeowner's Policy of Title Insurance. A title company, at Buyer's request, can provide information about the availability, desirability, coverage, and cost of various title insurance coverages and endorsements. If Buyer desires title coverage other than that required by this paragraph, Buyer shall instruct Escrow Holder in writing and pay any increase in cost.

13. **SALE OF BUYER'S PROPERTY:**
    A. This Agreement is NOT contingent upon the sale of any property owned by Buyer.
 OR B. ☐ (If checked): The attached addendum (C.A.R. Form COP) regarding the contingency for the sale of property owned by Buyer is incorporated into this Agreement.

14. **TIME PERIODS; REMOVAL OF CONTINGENCIES; CANCELLATION RIGHTS: The following time periods may only be extended, altered, modified or changed by mutual written agreement. Any removal of contingencies or cancellation under this paragraph must be in writing (C.A.R. Form RRCR).**
    A. **SELLER HAS: 7 (or ☐ _____) Days** After Acceptance to deliver to Buyer all reports, disclosures and information for which Seller is responsible under paragraphs 4, 5A and B, 6A, 7B and 12.
    B. **(1) BUYER HAS: 17 (or ☐ _____) Days** After Acceptance, unless otherwise agreed in writing, to:
        (i) complete all Buyer Investigations; approve all disclosures, reports and other applicable information, which Buyer receives from Seller; and approve all matters affecting the Property (including lead-based paint and lead-based paint hazards as well as other information specified in paragraph 5 and insurability of Buyer and the Property); and
        (ii) return to Seller Signed Copies of Statutory and Lead Disclosures delivered by Seller in accordance with paragraph 5A.
        (2) Within the time specified in 14B(1), Buyer may request that Seller make repairs or take any other action regarding the Property. Seller has no obligation to agree to or respond to Buyer's requests. (C.A.R. Form RR)
        (3) By the end of the time specified in 14B(1) (or 2I for loan contingency or 2J for appraisal contingency), Buyer shall, in writing, remove the applicable contingency (C.A.R. Form RRCR) or cancel this Agreement. However, if the following inspections, reports or disclosures are not made within the time specified in 14A, then Buyer has **5 (or ☐ _____) Days** after receipt of any such items, or the time specified in 14B(1), whichever is later, to remove the applicable contingency or cancel this Agreement in writing: **(i)** government-mandated inspections or reports required as a condition of closing; or **(ii)** Common Interest Disclosures pursuant to paragraph 6B.
    C. **CONTINUATION OF CONTINGENCY OR CONTRACTUAL OBLIGATION; SELLER RIGHT TO CANCEL:**
        (1) Seller right to Cancel; Buyer Contingencies: Seller, after first giving Buyer a Notice to Buyer to Perform (as specified below), may cancel this Agreement in writing and authorize return of Buyer's deposit if, by the time specified in this Agreement, Buyer does not remove in writing the applicable contingency or cancel this Agreement. Once all contingencies have been removed, failure of either Buyer or Seller to close escrow on time may be a breach of this Agreement.
        (2) Continuation of Contingency: Even after the expiration of the time specified in 14B(1), Buyer retains the right to make requests to Seller, remove in writing the applicable contingency or cancel this Agreement until Seller cancels pursuant to 14C(1). Once Seller receives Buyer's written removal of all contingencies, Seller may not cancel this Agreement pursuant to 14C(1).
        (3) Seller right to Cancel; Buyer Contract Obligations: Seller, after first giving Buyer a Notice to Buyer to Perform (as specified below), may cancel this Agreement in writing and authorize return of Buyer's deposit for any of the following reasons: **(i)** if Buyer fails to deposit funds as required by 2A or 2B; **(ii)** if the funds deposited pursuant to 2A or 2B are not good when deposited; **(iii)** if Buyer fails to provide a letter as required by 2G; **(iv)** if Buyer fails to provide verification as required by 2H or 2L; **(v)** if Seller reasonably disapproves of the verification provided by 2H or 2L; **(vi)** if Buyer fails to return Statutory and Lead Disclosures as required by paragraph 5A(2); or **(vii)** if Buyer fails to sign or initial a separate liquidated damage form for an increased deposit as required by paragraph 16. **Seller is not required to give Buyer a Notice to Perform regarding Close of Escrow.**
        (4) Notice To Buyer To Perform: The Notice to Buyer to Perform (C.A.R. Form NBP) shall: **(i)** be in writing; **(ii)** be signed by Seller; and **(iii)** give Buyer at least **24 (or ☐ _____) hours** (or until the time specified in the applicable paragraph, whichever occurs last) to take the applicable action. A Notice to Buyer to Perform may not be given any earlier than **2 Days** Prior to the expiration of the applicable time for Buyer to remove a contingency or cancel this Agreement or meet a 14C(3) obligation.

Buyer's Initials (WB)(DB)
Seller's Initials (T.P.)(up.)

Reviewed by _____ Date 6/14/03

CALIFORNIA RESIDENTIAL PURCHASE AGREEMENT   (RPA-CA PAGE 4 OF 8)

Property Address: _264 Beach Lane, Costa Mesa, CA 92627_ Date: _JUNE 14, 2003_

D. EFFECT OF BUYER'S REMOVAL OF CONTINGENCIES : If Buyer removes, in writing, any contingency or cancellation rights, unless otherwise specified in a separate written agreement between Buyer and Seller, Buyer shall conclusively be deemed to have: **(i)** completed all Buyer Investigations, and review of reports and other applicable information and disclosures pertaining to that contingency or cancellation right; **(ii)** elected to proceed with the transaction; and **(iii)** assumed all liability, responsibility and expense for Repairs or corrections pertaining to that contingency or cancellation right, or for inability to obtain financing.

E. EFFECT OF CANCELLATION ON DEPOSITS: If Buyer or Seller gives written notice of cancellation pursuant to rights duly exercised under the terms of this Agreement, Buyer and Seller agree to Sign mutual instructions to cancel the sale and escrow and release deposits, less fees and costs, to the party entitled to the funds. Fees and costs may be payable to service providers and vendors for services and products provided during escrow. **Release of funds will require mutual Signed release instructions from Buyer and Seller, judicial decision or arbitration award. A party may be subject to a civil penalty of up to $1,000 for refusal to sign such instructions if no good faith dispute exists as to who is entitled to the deposited funds (Civil Code §1057.3).**

15. FINAL VERIFICATION OF CONDITION: Buyer shall have the right to make a final inspection of the Property within **5 (or _____) Days** Prior to Close Of Escrow, NOT AS A CONTINGENCY OF THE SALE, but solely to confirm: **(i)** the Property is maintained pursuant to paragraph 7A; **(ii)** Repairs have been completed as agreed; and **(iii)** Seller has complied with Seller's other obligations under this Agreement.

16. LIQUIDATED DAMAGES: If Buyer fails to complete this purchase because of Buyer's default, Seller shall retain, as liquidated damages, the deposit actually paid. If the Property is a dwelling with no more than four units, one of which Buyer intends to occupy, then the amount retained shall be no more than 3% of the purchase price. Any excess shall be returned to Buyer. Release of funds will require mutual, Signed release instructions from both Buyer and Seller, judicial decision or arbitration award.
BUYER AND SELLER SHALL SIGN A SEPARATE LIQUIDATED DAMAGES PROVISION FOR ANY INCREASED DEPOSIT. (C.A.R. FORM RID)

Buyer's Initials _WB_ _DB_	Seller's Initials _TA_ _up_

17. DISPUTE RESOLUTION:

A. MEDIATION: Buyer and Seller agree to mediate any dispute or claim arising between them out of this Agreement, or any resulting transaction, before resorting to arbitration or court action. Paragraphs 17B(2) and (3) below apply whether or not the Arbitration provision is initialed. Mediation fees, if any, shall be divided equally among the parties involved. If, for any dispute or claim to which this paragraph applies, any party commences an action without first attempting to resolve the matter through mediation, or refuses to mediate after a request has been made, then that party shall not be entitled to recover attorney fees, even if they would otherwise be available to that party in any such action. THIS MEDIATION PROVISION APPLIES WHETHER OR NOT THE ARBITRATION PROVISION IS INITIALED.

B. ARBITRATION OF DISPUTES: (1) Buyer and Seller agree that any dispute or claim in Law or equity arising between them out of this Agreement or any resulting transaction, which is not settled through mediation, shall be decided by neutral, binding arbitration, including and subject to paragraphs 17B(2) and (3) below. The arbitrator shall be a retired judge or justice, or an attorney with at least 5 years of residential real estate Law experience, unless the parties mutually agree to a different arbitrator, who shall render an award in accordance with substantive California Law. The parties shall have the right to discovery in accordance with California Code of Civil Procedure §1283.05. In all other respects, the arbitration shall be conducted in accordance with Title 9 of Part III of the California Code of Civil Procedure. Judgment upon the award of the arbitrator(s) may be entered into any court having jurisdiction. Interpretation of this agreement to arbitrate shall be governed by the Federal Arbitration Act.
(2) EXCLUSIONS FROM MEDIATION AND ARBITRATION: The following matters are excluded from mediation and arbitration: **(i)** a judicial or non-judicial foreclosure or other action or proceeding to enforce a deed of trust, mortgage or installment land sale contract as defined in California Civil Code §2985; **(ii)** an unlawful detainer action; **(iii)** the filing or enforcement of a mechanic's lien; and **(iv)** any matter that is within the jurisdiction of a probate, small claims or bankruptcy court. The filing of a court action to enable the recording of a notice of pending action, for order of attachment, receivership, injunction, or other provisional remedies, shall not constitute a waiver of the mediation and arbitration provisions.
(3) BROKERS: Buyer and Seller agree to mediate and arbitrate disputes or claims involving either or both Brokers, consistent with 17 A and B, provided either or both Brokers shall have agreed to such mediation or arbitration prior to, or within a reasonable time after, the dispute or claim is presented to Brokers. Any election by either or both Brokers to participate in mediation or arbitration shall not result in Brokers being deemed parties to the Agreement.

"NOTICE: BY INITIALING IN THE SPACE BELOW YOU ARE AGREEING TO HAVE ANY DISPUTE ARISING OUT OF THE MATTERS INCLUDED IN THE 'ARBITRATION OF DISPUTES' PROVISION DECIDED BY NEUTRAL ARBITRATION AS PROVIDED BY CALIFORNIA LAW AND YOU ARE GIVING UP ANY RIGHTS YOU MIGHT POSSESS TO HAVE THE DISPUTE LITIGATED IN A COURT OR JURY TRIAL. BY INITIALING IN THE SPACE BELOW YOU ARE GIVING UP YOUR JUDICIAL RIGHTS TO DISCOVERY AND APPEAL, UNLESS THOSE RIGHTS ARE SPECIFICALLY INCLUDED IN THE 'ARBITRATION OF DISPUTES' PROVISION. IF YOU REFUSE TO SUBMIT TO ARBITRATION AFTER AGREEING TO THIS PROVISION, YOU MAY BE COMPELLED TO ARBITRATE UNDER THE AUTHORITY OF THE CALIFORNIA CODE OF CIVIL PROCEDURE. YOUR AGREEMENT TO THIS ARBITRATION PROVISION IS VOLUNTARY."

"WE HAVE READ AND UNDERSTAND THE FOREGOING AND AGREE TO SUBMIT DISPUTES ARISING OUT OF THE MATTERS INCLUDED IN THE 'ARBITRATION OF DISPUTES' PROVISION TO NEUTRAL ARBITRATION."

Buyer's Initials _WB_ _DB_	Seller's Initials _TA_ _up_

Buyer's Initials (_WB_)(_DB_)
Seller's Initials (_TA_)(_up._)

Reviewed by _[initials]_ Date _6/14/03_

CALIFORNIA RESIDENTIAL PURCHASE AGREEMENT (RPA-CA PAGE 5 OF 8)

Property Address: 264 Beach Lane, Costa Mesa, CA 92627   Date: JUNE 14, 2003

18. **PRORATIONS OF PROPERTY TAXES AND OTHER ITEMS:** Unless otherwise agreed in writing, the following items shall be PAID CURRENT and prorated between Buyer and Seller as of Close Of Escrow: real property taxes and assessments, interest, rents, HOA regular, special, and emergency dues and assessments imposed prior to Close Of Escrow, premiums on insurance assumed by Buyer, payments on bonds and assessments assumed by Buyer, and payments on Mello-Roos and other Special Assessment District bonds and assessments that are now a lien. The following items shall be assumed by Buyer WITHOUT CREDIT toward the purchase price: prorated payments on Mello-Roos and other Special Assessment District bonds and assessments and HOA special assessments that are now a lien but not yet due. Property will be reassessed upon change of ownership. Any supplemental tax bills shall be paid as follows: **(i)** for periods after Close Of Escrow, by Buyer; and **(ii)** for periods prior to Close Of Escrow, by Seller. TAX BILLS ISSUED AFTER CLOSE OF ESCROW SHALL BE HANDLED DIRECTLY BETWEEN BUYER AND SELLER. Prorations shall be made based on a 30-day month.

19. **WITHHOLDING TAXES:** Seller and Buyer agree to execute any instrument, affidavit, statement or instruction reasonably necessary to comply with federal (FIRPTA) and California withholding Law, if required (C.A.R. Forms AS and AB).

20. **MULTIPLE LISTING SERVICE ("MLS"):** Brokers are authorized to report to the MLS a pending sale and, upon Close Of Escrow, the terms of this transaction to be published and disseminated to persons and entities authorized to use the information on terms approved by the MLS.

21. **EQUAL HOUSING OPPORTUNITY:** The Property is sold in compliance with federal, state and local anti-discrimination Laws.

22. **ATTORNEY FEES:** In any action, proceeding, or arbitration between Buyer and Seller arising out of this Agreement, the prevailing Buyer or Seller shall be entitled to reasonable attorney fees and costs from the non-prevailing Buyer or Seller, except as provided in paragraph 17A.

23. **SELECTION OF SERVICE PROVIDERS:** If Brokers refer Buyer or Seller to persons, vendors, or service or product providers ("Providers"), Brokers do not guarantee the performance of any Providers. Buyer and Seller may select ANY Providers of their own choosing.

24. **TIME OF ESSENCE; ENTIRE CONTRACT; CHANGES:** Time is of the essence. All understandings between the parties are incorporated in this Agreement. Its terms are intended by the parties as a final, complete and exclusive expression of their Agreement with respect to its subject matter, and may not be contradicted by evidence of any prior agreement or contemporaneous oral agreement. If any provision of this Agreement is held to be ineffective or invalid, the remaining provisions will nevertheless be given full force and effect. **Neither this Agreement nor any provision in it may be extended, amended, modified, altered or changed, except in writing Signed by Buyer and Seller.**

25. **OTHER TERMS AND CONDITIONS,** including attached supplements:
    A. ☑ Buyer's Inspection Advisory (C.A.R. Form BIA)
    B. ☐ Purchase Agreement Addendum (C.A.R. Form PAA paragraph numbers: _____)
    C. _____
    _____
    _____

26. **DEFINITIONS:** As used in this Agreement:
    A. **"Acceptance"** means the time the offer or final counter offer is accepted in writing by a party and is delivered to and personally received by the other party or that party's authorized agent in accordance with the terms of this offer or a final counter offer.
    B. **"Agreement"** means the terms and conditions of this accepted California Residential Purchase Agreement and any accepted counter offers and addenda.
    C. **"C.A.R. Form"** means the specific form referenced or another comparable form agreed to by the parties.
    D. **"Close Of Escrow"** means the date the grant deed, or other evidence of transfer of title, is recorded. If the scheduled close of escrow falls on a Saturday, Sunday or legal holiday, then close of escrow shall be the next business day after the scheduled close of escrow date.
    E. **"Copy"** means copy by any means including photocopy, NCR, facsimile and electronic.
    F. **"Days"** means calendar days, unless otherwise required by Law.
    G. **"Days After"** means the specified number of calendar days after the occurrence of the event specified, not counting the calendar date on which the specified event occurs, and ending at 11:59PM on the final day.
    H. **"Days Prior"** means the specified number of calendar days before the occurrence of the event specified, not counting the calendar date on which the specified event is scheduled to occur.
    I. **"Electronic Copy"** or **"Electronic Signature"** means, as applicable, an electronic copy or signature complying with California Law. Buyer and Seller agree that electronic means will not be used by either party to modify or alter the content or integrity of this Agreement without the knowledge and consent of the other.
    J. **"Law"** means any law, code, statute, ordinance, regulation, rule or order, which is adopted by a controlling city, county, state or federal legislative, judicial or executive body or agency.
    K. **"Notice to Buyer to Perform"** means a document (C.A.R. Form NBP), which shall be in writing and Signed by Seller and shall give Buyer at least 24 hours **(or as otherwise specified in paragraph 14C(4))** to remove a contingency or perform as applicable.
    L. **"Repairs"** means any repairs (including pest control), alterations, replacements, modifications or retrofitting of the Property provided for under this Agreement.
    M. **"Signed"** means either a handwritten or electronic signature on an original document, Copy or any counterpart.
    N. **Singular and Plural** terms each include the other, when appropriate.

Buyer's Initials (WB)(OB)
Seller's Initials (TR)(yp.)
Reviewed by ____ Date 6/14/03

CALIFORNIA RESIDENTIAL PURCHASE AGREEMENT (RPA-CA PAGE 6 OF 8)

Property Address: _264 Beach Lane, Costa Mesa, CA 92627_   Date: _JUNE 14, 2003_

27. AGENCY:

A. DISCLOSURE: Buyer and Seller each acknowledge prior receipt of C.A.R. Form AD "Disclosure Regarding Real Estate Agency Relationships."

B. POTENTIALLY COMPETING BUYERS AND SELLERS: Buyer and Seller each acknowledge receipt of a disclosure of the possibility of multiple representation by the Broker representing that principal. This disclosure may be part of a listing agreement, buyer-broker agreement or separate document (C.A.R. Form DA). Buyer understands that Broker representing Buyer may also represent other potential buyers, who may consider, make offers on or ultimately acquire the Property. Seller understands that Broker representing Seller may also represent other sellers with competing properties of interest to this Buyer.

C. CONFIRMATION: The following agency relationships are hereby confirmed for this transaction:
Listing Agent _Sail Realty_ (Print Firm Name) is the agent of (check one): ☒ the Seller exclusively; or ☐ both the Buyer and Seller.
Selling Agent _Ramos Realty_ (Print Firm Name) (if not same as Listing Agent) is the agent of (check one): ☒ the Buyer exclusively; or ☐ the Seller exclusively; or ☐ both the Buyer and Seller. Real Estate Brokers are not parties to the Agreement between Buyer and Seller.

28. JOINT ESCROW INSTRUCTIONS TO ESCROW HOLDER:

A. The following paragraphs, or applicable portions thereof, of this Agreement constitute the joint escrow instructions of Buyer and Seller to Escrow Holder, which Escrow Holder is to use along with any related counter offers and addenda, and any additional mutual instructions to close the escrow: 1, 2, 4, 12, 13B, 14E, 18, 19, 24, 25B and C, 26, 28, 29, 32A, 33 and paragraph D of the section titled Real Estate Brokers on page 8. If a Copy of the separate compensation agreement(s) provided for in paragraph 29 or 32A, or paragraph D of the section titled Real Estate Brokers on page 8 is deposited with Escrow Holder by Broker, Escrow Holder shall accept such agreement(s) and pay out from Buyer's or Seller's funds, or both, as applicable, the Broker's compensation provided for in such agreement(s). The terms and conditions of this Agreement not set forth in the specified paragraphs are additional matters for the information of Escrow Holder, but about which Escrow Holder need not be concerned. Buyer and Seller will receive Escrow Holder's general provisions directly from Escrow Holder and will execute such provisions upon Escrow Holder's request. To the extent the general provisions are inconsistent or conflict with this Agreement, the general provisions will control as to the duties and obligations of Escrow Holder only. Buyer and Seller will execute additional instructions, documents and forms provided by Escrow Holder that are reasonably necessary to close escrow.

B. A Copy of this Agreement shall be delivered to Escrow Holder within **3** business days after Acceptance (or ☐ _____). Buyer and Seller authorize Escrow Holder to accept and rely on Copies and Signatures as defined in this Agreement as originals, to open escrow and for other purposes of escrow. The validity of this Agreement as between Buyer and Seller is not affected by whether or when Escrow Holder Signs this Agreement.

C. Brokers are a party to the escrow for the sole purpose of compensation pursuant to paragraphs 29, 32A and paragraph D of the section titled Real Estate Brokers on page 8. Buyer and Seller irrevocably assign to Brokers compensation specified in paragraphs 29 and 32A, respectively, and irrevocably instruct Escrow Holder to disburse those funds to Brokers at Close Of Escrow or pursuant to any other mutually executed cancellation agreement. Compensation instructions can be amended or revoked only with the written consent of Brokers. Escrow Holder shall immediately notify Brokers: (i) if Buyer's initial or any additional deposit is not made pursuant to this Agreement, or is not good at time of deposit with Escrow Holder; or (ii) if Buyer and Seller instruct Escrow Holder to cancel escrow.

D. A Copy of any amendment that affects any paragraph of this Agreement for which Escrow Holder is responsible shall be delivered to Escrow Holder within **2** business days after mutual execution of the amendment.

29. BROKER COMPENSATION FROM BUYER: If applicable, upon Close Of Escrow, **Buyer** agrees to pay compensation to Broker as specified in a separate written agreement between Buyer and Broker.

30. TERMS AND CONDITIONS OF OFFER:

This is an offer to purchase the Property on the above terms and conditions. All paragraphs with spaces for initials by Buyer and Seller are incorporated in this Agreement only if initialed by all parties. If at least one but not all parties initial, a counter offer is required until agreement is reached. Seller has the right to continue to offer the Property for sale and to accept any other offer at any time prior to notification of Acceptance. Buyer has read and acknowledges receipt of a Copy of the offer and agrees to the above confirmation of agency relationships. If this offer is accepted and Buyer subsequently defaults, Buyer may be responsible for payment of Brokers' compensation. This Agreement and any supplement, addendum or modification, including any Copy, may be Signed in two or more counterparts, all of which shall constitute one and the same writing.

Buyer's Initials (_wB_)(_DB_)
Seller's Initials (_tA_)(_yp_)

Reviewed by _JR_ Date _6/14/03_

CALIFORNIA RESIDENTIAL PURCHASE AGREEMENT (RPA-CA PAGE 7 OF 8)

Property Address: _264 Beach Lane, Costa Mesa, CA 92627_   Date: _JUNE 14, 2003_

31. EXPIRATION OF OFFER: This offer shall be deemed revoked and the deposit shall be returned unless the offer is Signed by Seller and a Copy of the Signed offer is personally received by Buyer, or by _____, who is authorized to receive it by 5:00 PM on the third calendar day after this offer is signed by Buyer (or, if checked) ☐ by _____ (date), at _____ AM/PM).

Date _JUNE 14, 2003_   Date _JUNE 14, 2003_

BUYER _Walter Buyer_   BUYER _Debbie Buyer_

Walter Buyer   _Debbie Buyer_
(Print name)   **(Print name)**
100 Boat Lane, Marina del Rey, CA 90292
(Address)

32. BROKER COMPENSATION FROM SELLER:
   A. Upon Close Of Escrow, **Seller** agrees to pay compensation to Broker as specified in a separate written agreement between Seller and Broker.
   B. If escrow does not close, compensation is payable as specified in that separate written agreement.
33. ACCEPTANCE OF OFFER: Seller warrants that Seller is the owner of the Property, or has the authority to execute this Agreement. Seller accepts the above offer, agrees to sell the Property on the above terms and conditions, and agrees to the above confirmation of agency relationships. Seller has read and acknowledges receipt of a Copy of this Agreement, and authorizes Broker to deliver a Signed Copy to Buyer.
   ☐ **(If checked) SUBJECT TO ATTACHED COUNTER OFFER, DATED** _____.

Date _JUNE 15, 2003_   Date _JUNE 15, 2003_

SELLER _Tony Seller_   SELLER _Yolanda Seller_

TONY SELLER   _YOLANDA SELLER_
(Print name)   **(Print name)**
264 Beach Lane, Costa Mesa, CA 92627
(Address)

_(WB DB)_ **CONFIRMATION OF ACCEPTANCE:** A Copy of Signed Acceptance was personally received by Buyer or Buyer's authorized
(Initials) agent on (date) _6/15/03_ at _3_ AM/PM. **A binding Agreement is created when a Copy of Signed Acceptance is personally received by Buyer or Buyer's authorized agent whether or not confirmed in this document. Completion of this confirmation is not legally required in order to create a binding Agreement; it is solely intended to evidence the date that Confirmation of Acceptance has occurred.**

REAL ESTATE BROKERS:
A. Real Estate Brokers are not parties to the Agreement between Buyer and Seller.
B. Agency relationships are confirmed as stated in paragraph 27.
C. If specified in paragraph 2A, Agent who submitted the offer for Buyer acknowledges receipt of deposit.
D. COOPERATING BROKER COMPENSATION: Listing Broker agrees to pay Cooperating Broker **(Selling Firm)** and Cooperating Broker agrees to accept, out of Listing Broker's proceeds in escrow: **(i)** the amount specified in the MLS, provided Cooperating Broker is a Participant of the MLS in which the Property is offered for sale or a reciprocal MLS; or **(ii)** ☐ (if checked) the amount specified in a separate written agreement (C.A.R. Form CBC) between Listing Broker and Cooperating Broker.

Real Estate Broker (Selling Firm) _Ramos Realty_
By _Joseph Ramos_   Date _6/14/03_
Address _777 Newport Blvd._   City _Newport Beach_   State _CA_   Zip _92663_
Telephone _714-647-0000_   Fax _714-647-0001_   E-mail _jr@ramosrealty.com_

Real Estate Broker (Listing Firm) _Sail Realty_
By _Carmen Caro_   Date _6/15/03_
Address _227 Harbor Blvd._   City _Costa Mesa_   State _CA_   Zip _92627_
Telephone _714-626-2828_   Fax _714-646-2829_   E-mail _carmen@sailreal.com_

ESCROW HOLDER ACKNOWLEDGMENT:
Escrow Holder acknowledges receipt of a Copy of this Agreement, (if checked, ☐ a deposit in the amount of $ _____), counter offer numbers _____ and _____, and agrees to act as Escrow Holder subject to paragraph 28 of this Agreement, any supplemental escrow instructions and the terms of Escrow Holder's general provisions.

Escrow Holder is advised that the date of Confirmation of Acceptance of the Agreement as between Buyer and Seller is _____

Escrow Holder _____   Escrow # _____
By _____   Date _____
Address _____
Phone/Fax/E-mail _____
Escrow Holder is licensed by the California Department of ☐ Corporations, ☐ Insurance, ☐ Real Estate. License # _____

THIS FORM HAS BEEN APPROVED BY THE CALIFORNIA ASSOCIATION OF REALTORS® (C.A.R.). NO REPRESENTATION IS MADE AS TO THE LEGAL VALIDITY OR ADEQUACY OF ANY PROVISION IN ANY SPECIFIC TRANSACTION. A REAL ESTATE BROKER IS THE PERSON QUALIFIED TO ADVISE ON REAL ESTATE TRANSACTIONS. IF YOU DESIRE LEGAL OR TAX ADVICE, CONSULT AN APPROPRIATE PROFESSIONAL.
This form is available for use by the entire real estate industry. It is not intended to identify the user as a REALTOR®. REALTOR® is a registered collective membership mark which may be used only by members of the NATIONAL ASSOCIATION OF REALTORS® who subscribe to its Code of Ethics.

SURE TRAC
The System for Success™
Published by the
California Association of REALTORS®

Reviewed by _JR_ Date _6/14/03_   **EQUAL HOUSING OPPORTUNITY**

RPA-CA REVISED 10/02 (PAGE 8 OF 8)

CALIFORNIA RESIDENTIAL PURCHASE AGREEMENT (RPA-CA PAGE 8 OF 8)

California Residential Purchase Agreement and Joint Escrow Instructions – Highlights

1. Includes fixed times for delivery of disclosures and removal of contingencies.

2. Allows the Buyer to cancel, within a set time, without first requesting Seller to make repairs.

3. Requires written removal of contingencies.

4. Requires Seller to give Notice to Buyer to Perform before Seller may cancel.

5. Gives Seller a cancellation right if Buyer does not meet certain contractual obligations.

6. Refers to separate agreement for broker compensation.

7. No pre-allocation of costs to cure problems with wood destroying pests.

8. Use of addendum required to accommodate pre-allocation requests.

---

damages clause is initialed by both the buyer and seller, the seller may retain the deposit (up to three percent of the sale price). This would then be split 50-50 between the seller and the listing broker, unless otherwise stated in the deposit receipt.

Deposits are always the property of the seller (after the removal of contingencies on the binding Deposit Receipt contract); never the broker.

1. Covenants (A Promise in the Deposit Receipt)

COVENANTS are promises between the parties to a contract. Covenants represent promises, obligations and considerations exchanged to fulfill a contract.

If you break a contractual promise, the other party can sue for damages.

Failure to perform a stipulated covenant does not release either party from his or her responsibility. The contract is still in effect, although the offended party may sue for damages.

2. Contingencies, Conditions, or Subject To (An "If" Clause in the Deposit Receipt)

CONTINGENCIES, CONDITIONS or SUBJECT TO are provisions by which all parties are released from any obligations of a contract if some stated condition fails to happen. For example, purchase offers may be made contingent upon the availability of financing, or subject to the successful sale of another property. If the contingency falls through, the contract is voidable by the buyer.

A contingency clause is an "if" situation, so it should be used sparingly. Example: Only if I qualify for the loan will I purchase the property. They are also referred to as conditions or "subject to" provisions.

Items that are usually found in contingency clauses include:

1. Obtaining financing at a certain interest rate or less.
2. Subject to the approval of my CPA and attorney within 20 days.
3. Conditional upon inspection and approval of each apartment.
4. Subject to property appraisal at no less than the specified price.

C. THE PURCHASE AGREEMENT ADDENDUM

The *PURCHASE AGREEMENT ADDENDUM form is used as an addendum to either the Residential Purchase Agreement, another offer form, or the counter offer form.* Only the paragraphs that are checked are included as part of the contract. The CAR® two-page addendum (**See Figure 5-7**) covers six separate topics that are occasionally relevant to a transaction:

1. The cancellation of prior sale; back-up offers.
2. Seller to remain in possession after close of escrow.
3. Tenant to remain in possession.
4. Junior or assumed financing.
5. Short pay.
6. Court confirmation.

ERRORS AND OMISSIONS INSURANCE is the liability insurance that brokers and salespeople should carry in order to pay for any costly lawsuits.

D. THE COUNTER OFFER (Replaces Original Offer With Changes in Terms)

A counter offer automatically cancels the original offer if terms of the new offer vary from the original. The different terms stated on the counter offer must be accepted by the other party.

Rather than preparing a whole new deposit receipt when presenting a counter offer, most sellers prefer to use a standard counter offer form like the sample CAR® form

Figure 5-7

CALIFORNIA
ASSOCIATION
OF REALTORS®

PURCHASE AGREEMENT ADDENDUM
May Also Be Used With Counter Offer
(C.A.R. Form PAA, Revised 10/02)

This is an addendum to the ☐ California Residential Purchase Agreement, ☐ Counter Offer No._____, ☐ Other _____
_____, ("Agreement"), dated _____
on property known as _____ ("Property"),
between _____ ("Buyer"),
and _____ ("Seller").
(The definitions in the California Residential Purchase Agreement are applicable to this Purchase Agreement Addendum.)

1. ☐ **CANCELLATION OF PRIOR SALE; BACK-UP OFFER** (If checked): This Agreement is in back-up position number _____, and is contingent upon written cancellation of any prior contracts and related escrows ("Prior Contracts") between Seller and other buyers. Seller and other buyers may mutually agree to modify or amend the terms of Prior Contracts. Buyer may cancel this Agreement in writing at any time before Seller provides Buyer Copies of written cancellations of Prior Contracts Signed by all parties to those contracts. If Seller is unable to provide such written Signed cancellations to Buyer by _____ (date), then either Buyer or Seller may cancel the Agreement in writing.

   A. **BUYER'S DEPOSIT CHECK** shall be: **(i)** held uncashed until Copies of the written cancellations Signed by all parties to the Prior Contracts are provided to Buyer; OR **(ii)** (if checked) ☐ immediately handled as provided in the Agreement.

   B. **TIME PERIODS** in the Agreement for Investigations, contingencies, covenants and other obligations **(i)** shall begin on the Day After Seller provides Buyer Copies of Signed cancellations of Prior Contracts; OR **(ii)** (if checked) ☐ all time periods shall begin as provided in this Agreement. However, if the date for Close Of Escrow is a specific calendar date, that date shall NOT be extended, unless agreed to in writing by Buyer and Seller.

2. ☐ **SELLER TO REMAIN IN POSSESSION AFTER CLOSE OF ESCROW** (If checked): This provision is intended for short-term occupancy (i.e. less than 30 Days). If occupancy is intended to be for 30 Days or longer, use Residential Lease After Sale (C.A.R. Form RLAS). **Note: Local rent control or other Law regarding tenant's rights may impact Buyer's and Seller's rights and obligations.**

   A. **TERM:** Seller to remain in possession of Property for ____ Days After Close Of Escrow (or ☐ _____).

   B. **COMPENSATION:** Seller agrees to pay Buyer $_____ per Day (or ☐ _____), which **(i)** Seller shall deposit with escrow holder prior to Close Of Escrow; or **(ii)** shall be withheld from Seller's proceeds. Seller agrees to pay $_____ per Day for any holding over.

   C. **LATE CHARGE/NSF CHECKS:** If any payment from Seller to Buyer is required outside of escrow, and any such payment is not received by Buyer within **5 (or ☐ _____) Days** After date due, Seller shall pay to Buyer an additional sum of $_____ as a Late Charge. If a check is returned for non-sufficient fund ("NSF"), Seller shall pay to Buyer $25.00 as an NSF charge. Seller and Buyer agree that these charges represent a fair and reasonable estimate of the costs Buyer may incur by reason of Seller's late or NSF payment. Buyer's acceptance of any Late Charge or NSF fee shall not constitute a waiver as to any default by Seller.

   D. **UTILITIES:** Seller agrees to pay for all utilities and services, and the following charges: _____ _____ except _____, which shall be paid for by Buyer.

   E. **ENTRY:** Seller shall make Property available to Buyer for the purpose of entering to make necessary or agreed repairs, or to supply necessary or agreed services, or to show Property to prospective or actual purchasers, tenants, mortgagees, lenders, appraisers or contractors. Buyer and Seller agree that 24 hours notice (oral or written) shall be reasonable and sufficient notice. In an emergency, Buyer may enter Property at any time without prior notice.

   F. **MAINTENANCE:** Seller shall maintain the Property, including pool, spa, landscaping and grounds, and all personal property included in the sale in substantially the same condition as on the date of Acceptance of the Agreement. Except as provided in the Agreement, Seller shall not make alterations to the Property without Buyer's written consent.

   G. **ASSIGNMENT; SUBLETTING:** Seller shall not assign or sublet all or any part of the Property, or assign or transfer the right to occupy the Property. Any assignment, subletting or transfer of the Property by voluntary act of Seller, by operation of Law or otherwise, without Buyer's prior written consent shall give Buyer the right to terminate Seller's right to possession.

   H. **SELLER'S OBLIGATIONS UPON DELIVERY OF POSSESSION:** Upon delivery of possession to Buyer, Seller shall deliver the Property in the condition and on the terms provided in the Agreement.

   I. **INSURANCE:** Seller's personal property (including vehicles) are not insured by Buyer, and, if applicable, owner's association, against loss or damage due to fire, theft, vandalism, rain, water, criminal or negligent acts of others, or any other cause. Seller is to carry Seller's own insurance to protect Seller from such loss.

   J. **WAIVER:** The waiver of any breach shall not be construed as a continuing waiver of the same or any subsequent breach.

   K. **OTHER TERMS AND CONDITIONS/SUPPLEMENTS:** _____
   _____
   _____
   _____

Buyer's Initials (_____)(_____)
Seller's Initials (_____)(_____)

Reviewed by _____ Date _____

EQUAL HOUSING OPPORTUNITY

PURCHASE AGREEMENT ADDENDUM (PAA PAGE 1 OF 2)

Property Address: _____ Date: _____

3. ☐ **TENANT TO REMAIN IN POSSESSION** (If checked): Buyer shall take Property subject to the rights of existing tenants. Seller shall, within **7 (or ☐ _____) Days** After Acceptance, deliver to Buyer Copies of all: estoppel certificates sent to and received back from tenants; leases; rental agreements; and current income and expense statements ("Rental Documents"). Seller shall give Buyer written notice of any changes to existing leases or tenancies or new agreements to lease or rent ("Proposed Changes") at least **7 (or ☐ _____) Days** prior to any Proposed Changes. Buyer's approval of the Rental Documents and Proposed Changes is a contingency of the Agreement. Buyer shall, within **5 (or ☐ _____) Days** After receipt of Rental Documents or Proposed Changes remove the applicable contingency or cancel the Agreement. Seller shall transfer to Buyer, through escrow, all unused tenant deposits. No warranty is made concerning compliance with governmental restrictions, if any, limiting the amount of rent that can lawfully be charged, and/or the maximum number of persons who can lawfully occupy the Property, unless otherwise agreed in writing.

4. ☐ **SECONDARY OR ASSUMED LOAN** (If checked): Obtaining the secondary loan or assumption below and approval of such financing is a contingency of this Agreement. Buyer shall act diligently and in good faith to obtain the designated financing.

   A. ☐ **SECONDARY LOAN**

     (1) New second deed of trust in favor of LENDER encumbering the Property, securing a note payable at maximum interest of _____% fixed rate or _____% initial adjustable rate, with a maximum interest rate of _____%, balance due in _____ years. Buyer shall pay loan fees/points not to exceed _____. (These terms apply whether the designated loan is conventional, FHA or VA.)

     (2) Within **17 (or ☐ _____ Days)** After Acceptance, Buyer shall, as specified in the Agreement, remove this contingency or cancel this Agreement; OR (if checked) ☐ secondary loan contingency shall remain in effect until the loan is funded.

   B. ☐ **ASSUMPTION OF EXISTING LOAN:**

     (1) Assumption of existing deed of trust encumbering the Property, securing a note payable at maximum interest of _____% fixed rate or _____% initial adjustable rate, with a maximum interest rate of _____%, balance due in _____ years. Buyer shall pay loan fees/points not to exceed _____. Seller shall, within **5 (or ☐ _____) Days** After Acceptance, request from Lender, and upon receipt provide to Buyer, Copies of all applicable notes and deeds of trust, loan balances and current interest rates. Differences between estimated and actual loan balances shall be adjusted at Close Of Escrow by cash down payment. Impound accounts, if any, shall be assigned and charged to Buyer and credited to Seller. If this is an assumption of a VA Loan, the sale is contingent upon Seller being provided a release of liability and substitution of eligibility, unless otherwise agreed in writing.

     (2) Within **17 (or ☐ _____ Days)** After Acceptance, Buyer shall, as specified in the Agreement, remove this contingency or cancel this Agreement. However, if the assumed loan documents are not provided to Buyer within 7 Days After Acceptance, Buyer has **5 (or ☐ _____) Days** after receipt of these documents, or the fixed time specified in 4B(2), whichever occurs last, to remove this contingency or cancel the Agreement; OR (if checked) ☐ assumed loan contingency shall remain in effect until the assumption is approved.

5. ☐ **SHORT PAY** (If checked): This Agreement is contingent upon Seller's receipt of written consent from all existing secured lenders and lienholders ("Short-Pay Lenders"), no later than 5:00 P.M. on _____ (date) ("Short-Pay Contingency Date"), to reduce their respective loan balances by an amount sufficient to permit the proceeds from the sale of the Property, without additional funds from Seller, to pay the existing balances on loans, real property taxes, brokerage commissions, closing costs, and other monetary obligations the Agreement requires Seller to pay at Close Of Escrow (including, but not limited to, escrow charges, title charges, documentary transfer taxes, prorations, retrofit costs and Repairs). If Seller fails to give Buyer written notice of all existing Short-Pay Lenders' consent by the Short-Pay Contingency Date, either Seller or Buyer may cancel the Agreement in writing. Seller shall reasonably cooperate with existing Short-Pay lenders in the short-pay off process. Buyer and Seller understand that Lenders are not obligated to accept a short-pay off and may accept other offers, and that Seller, Buyer and Brokers do not have control over whether Short-Pay Lenders will consent to a short-pay off, or any act, omission, or decision by any Short-Pay Lender in the short-pay off process. Seller is informed that a short-pay may create credit or legal problems, or may result in taxable income to Seller. Seller may present to Short-Pay Lender any additional offers that are received on the Property. **Seller is advised to seek advice from an attorney, certified public accountant or other expert regarding such potential consequences of a short-pay off.**

6. ☐ **COURT CONFIRMATION** (If checked): This Agreement is contingent upon court confirmation on or before _____ (date). If court confirmation is not obtained by that date, Buyer may cancel this Agreement in writing. Court confirmation may be required in probate, conservatorship, guardianship, receivership, bankruptcy, or other proceedings. The court may allow open, competitive bidding, resulting in Property being sold to the highest bidder. Broker recommends that Buyer appear at court confirmation hearing. Buyer understands that **(i)** Broker and others may continue to market the Property and **(ii)** Broker may represent other competitive bidders prior to and at the court confirmation.

Date _____ Date _____

Buyer _____ Seller _____

Buyer _____ Seller _____

SURE TRAC
The System for Success™

Published by the
California Association of REALTORS®

Reviewed by _____ Date _____

EQUAL HOUSING OPPORTUNITY

PAA REVISED 10/02 (PAGE 2 OF 2)

PURCHASE AGREEMENT ADDENDUM (PAA PAGE 2 OF 2)

shown in **Figure 5-8**. This form is used to change some of the terms of the original deposit receipt and allows the seller and buyer to accept the remaining agreed-to terms and conditions of the original agreement. Plenty of blank space is provided to list these exceptions that formally amend the deposit receipt without the necessity of completing an entirely new deposit receipt.

In a counter offer, the offeree becomes the offeror. A contract negotiation may involve several counter offers.

If there is only a minor change in a term (like sale's price), the counter offer can be written on the back of the original deposit receipt and signed by the buyer and seller. **The seller can never change the deposit receipt on its face by crossing out sections or adding new information**. The counter offer must contain a clause stating that all of the conditions of the original deposit receipt are acceptable except for the listed new terms. If there are major changes, the formal counter offer form may be required. Finally, if there are significant changes it may be better to start the process again by filling out a new deposit receipt.

A seller's acceptance of an offer must be a "mirror" image of the offer. Changing any terms in the acceptance makes it a counter offer. It is illegal and unethical for an agent to make changes to an offer without his or her principal's knowledge and consent.

E. INSPECTION ADVISORY FOR BUYERS

Property inspection is important. The physical condition of the land and improvements being purchased are not guaranteed by either sellers or brokers, except as specifically set forth in the purchase agreement. For this reason, most salespeople are required by their brokers to "advise" buyers of their right to have a personal and professional inspection of the property they are purchasing. Furthermore, brokers have been advised by their attorneys to have potential buyers sign the Buyer's Inspection Advisory Form to protect themselves. This form expressly states in bold print:

"YOU ARE STRONGLY ADVISED TO INVESTIGATE THE CONDITION AND SUITABILITY OF ALL ASPECTS OF THE PROPERTY. IF YOU DO NOT DO SO, YOU ARE ACTING AGAINST THE ADVICE OF BROKERS."

As professionals, we have a duty to advise buyers to exercise reasonable care to protect themselves. The buyer acknowledges receipt of a copy of the Buyer's Inspection Advisory CAR® form (**See Figure 5-9**) by signing a copy.

If an agent fails to disclose known defects in a property to the buyer, the buyer can file civil action against the agent for up to two years.

Figure 5-8

CALIFORNIA
ASSOCIATION
OF REALTORS®

COUNTER OFFER No. _____

For use by Seller or Buyer. May be used for Multiple Counter Offer.

(C.A.R. Form CO, Revised 10/02)

Date _____, at _____, California.
This is a counter offer to the: ☐ California Residential Purchase Agreement, ☐ Counter Offer, or ☐ Other _____ ("Offer"),
dated _____, on property known as _____ ("Property"),
between _____ ("Buyer") and _____ ("Seller").

1. **TERMS:** The terms and conditions of the above referenced document are **accepted subject to the following:**

    A. **Paragraphs in the Offer that require initials by all parties, but are not initialed by all parties, are excluded from the final agreement unless specifically referenced for inclusion in paragraph 1C of this or another Counter Offer.**

    B. **Unless otherwise agreed in writing, down payment and loan amount(s) will be adjusted in the same proportion as in the original Offer.**

    C. _____
       _____
       _____
       _____
       _____
       _____
       _____
       _____
       _____

    D. **The following attached supplements are incorporated in this Counter Offer:** ☐ Addendum No. _____
       ☐ _____   ☐ _____

2. **RIGHT TO ACCEPT OTHER OFFERS:** Seller has the right to continue to offer the Property for sale or for other transaction, and to accept any other offer at any time prior to notification of acceptance, as described in paragraph 3. If this is a Seller Counter Offer, Seller's acceptance of another offer prior to Buyer's acceptance and communication of notification of this Counter Offer, shall revoke this Counter Offer.

3. **EXPIRATION:** This Counter Offer shall be deemed revoked and the deposits, if any, shall be returned unless this Counter Offer is Signed by the Buyer or Seller to whom it is sent and a Copy of the Signed Counter Offer is personally received by the person making this Counter Offer or _____,
who is authorized to receive it, by 5:00 PM on the third Day After this Counter Offer is made or, (if checked)
by ☐ _____ (date), at _____ AM/PM. This Counter Offer may be executed in counterparts.

4. ☐ **(If checked:) MULTIPLE COUNTER OFFER:** Seller is making a Counter Offer(s) to another prospective buyer(s) on terms that may or may not be the same as in this Counter Offer. Acceptance of this Counter Offer by Buyer shall **not** be binding unless and until it is subsequently re-Signed by Seller in paragraph 7 below and a Copy of the Counter Offer Signed in paragraph 7 is personally received by Buyer or by _____, who is authorized to receive it. Prior to the completion of all of these events, Buyer and Seller shall have no duties or obligations for the purchase or sale of the Property.

5. **OFFER: BUYER OR SELLER MAKES THIS COUNTER OFFER ON THE TERMS ABOVE AND ACKNOWLEDGES RECEIPT OF A COPY.**
    _____ Date _____
    _____ Date _____

6. **ACCEPTANCE: I/WE** accept the above Counter Offer **(If checked ☐ SUBJECT TO THE ATTACHED COUNTER OFFER)** and acknowledge receipt of a Copy.
    _____ Date _____ Time _____ AM/PM
    _____ Date _____ Time _____ AM/PM

7. **MULTIPLE COUNTER OFFER SIGNATURE LINE: By signing below, Seller accepts this Multiple Counter Offer.**
    NOTE TO SELLER: Do NOT sign in this box until after Buyer signs in paragraph 6. (Paragraph 7 applies only if paragraph 4 is checked.)
    _____ Date _____ Time _____ AM/PM
    _____ Date _____ Time _____ AM/PM

8. (_____/_____) (Initials) **Confirmation of Acceptance:** A Copy of Signed Acceptance was personally received by the maker of the Counter Offer, or that person's authorized agent as specified in paragraph 3 (or, if this is a Multiple Counter Offer, the Buyer or Buyer's authorized agent as specified in paragraph 4) on (date) _____, at _____ **AM/PM. A binding Agreement is created when a Copy of Signed Acceptance is personally received by the the maker of the Counter Offer, or that person's authorized agent (or, if this is a Multiple Counter Offer, the Buyer or Buyer's authorized agent) whether or not confirmed in this document. Completion of this confirmation is not legally required in order to create a binding Agreement; it is solely intended to evidence the date that Confirmation of Acceptance has occurred.**

SURE TRAC
The System for Success™

Published by the
California Association of REALTORS®

Reviewed by _____ Date _____

EQUAL HOUSING
OPPORTUNITY

CO REVISED 10/02 (PAGE 1 OF 1) Print Date

COUNTER OFFER (CO PAGE 1 OF 1)

Figure 5-9

CALIFORNIA
ASSOCIATION
OF REALTORS®

BUYER'S INSPECTION ADVISORY

(C.A.R. Form BIA, Revised 10/02)

Property Address: 264 Beech Lane, Costa Mesa, CA 92627 ("Property").

A. IMPORTANCE OF PROPERTY INVESTIGATION: The physical condition of the land and improvements being purchased is not guaranteed by either Seller or Brokers. For this reason, you should conduct thorough investigations of the Property personally and with professionals who should provide written reports of their investigations. A general physical inspection typically does not cover all aspects of the Property nor items affecting the Property that are not physically located on the Property. If the professionals recommend further investigations, including a recommendation by a pest control operator to inspect inaccessible areas of the Property, you should contact qualified experts to conduct such additional investigations.

B. BUYER RIGHTS AND DUTIES: You have an affirmative duty to exercise reasonable care to protect yourself, including discovery of the legal, practical and technical implications of disclosed facts, and the investigation and verification of information and facts that you know or that are within your diligent attention and observation. The purchase agreement gives you the right to investigate the Property. If you exercise this right, and you should, you must do so in accordance with the terms of that agreement. This is the best way for you to protect yourself. It is extremely important for you to read all written reports provided by professionals and to discuss the results of inspections with the professional who conducted the inspection. You have the right to request that Seller make repairs, corrections or take other action based upon items discovered in your investigations or disclosed by Seller. If Seller is unwilling or unable to satisfy your requests, or you do not want to purchase the Property in its disclosed and discovered condition, you have the right to cancel the agreement if you act within specific time periods. If you do not cancel the agreement in a timely and proper manner, you may be in breach of contract.

C. SELLER RIGHTS AND DUTIES: Seller is required to disclose to you material facts known to him/her that affect the value or desirability of the Property. However, Seller may not be aware of some Property defects or conditions. Seller does not have an obligation to inspect the Property for your benefit nor is Seller obligated to repair, correct or otherwise cure known defects that are disclosed to you or previously unknown defects that are discovered by you or your inspectors during escrow. The purchase agreement obligates Seller to make the Property available to you for investigations.

D. BROKER OBLIGATIONS: Brokers do not have expertise in all areas and therefore cannot advise you on many items, such as soil stability, geologic or environmental conditions, hazardous or illegal controlled substances, structural conditions of the foundation or other improvements, or the condition of the roof, plumbing, heating, air conditioning, electrical, sewer, septic, waste disposal, or other system. The only way to accurately determine the condition of the Property is through an inspection by an appropriate professional selected by you. If Broker gives you referrals to such professionals, Broker does not guarantee their performance. You may select any professional of your choosing. In sales involving residential dwellings with no more than four units, Brokers have a duty to make a diligent visual inspection of the accessible areas of the Property and to disclose the results of that inspection. However, as some Property defects or conditions may not be discoverable from a visual inspection, it is possible Brokers are not aware of them. If you have entered into a written agreement with a Broker, the specific terms of that agreement will determine the nature and extent of that Broker's duty to you. **YOU ARE STRONGLY ADVISED TO INVESTIGATE THE CONDITION AND SUITABILITY OF ALL ASPECTS OF THE PROPERTY. IF YOU DO NOT DO SO, YOU ARE ACTING AGAINST THE ADVICE OF BROKERS.**

E. YOU ARE ADVISED TO CONDUCT INVESTIGATIONS OF THE ENTIRE PROPERTY, INCLUDING, BUT NOT LIMITED TO THE FOLLOWING:
1. **GENERAL CONDITION OF THE PROPERTY, ITS SYSTEMS AND COMPONENTS:** Foundation, roof, plumbing, heating, air conditioning, electrical, mechanical, security, pool/spa, other structural and non-structural systems and components, fixtures, built-in appliances, any personal property included in the sale, and energy efficiency of the Property. (Structural engineers are best suited to determine possible design or construction defects, and whether improvements are structurally sound.)
2. **SQUARE FOOTAGE, AGE, BOUNDARIES:** Square footage, room dimensions, lot size, age of improvements and boundaries. Any numerical statements regarding these items are APPROXIMATIONS ONLY and have not been verified by Seller and cannot be verified by Brokers. Fences, hedges, walls, retaining walls and other natural or constructed barriers or markers do not necessarily identify true Property boundaries. (Professionals such as appraisers, architects, surveyors and civil engineers are best suited to determine square footage, dimensions and boundaries of the Property.)
3. **WOOD DESTROYING PESTS:** Presence of, or conditions likely to lead to the presence of wood destroying pests and organisms and other infestation or infection. Inspection reports covering these items can be separated into two sections: Section 1 identifies areas where infestation or infection is evident. Section 2 identifies areas where there are conditions likely to lead to infestation or infection. A registered structural pest control company is best suited to perform these inspections.

BIA REVISED 10/02 (PAGE 1 OF 2) Print Date

Buyer's Initials (WB)(DB)
Seller's Initials (TA)(yp.)
Reviewed by _____ Date 6/15/03

EQUAL HOUSING OPPORTUNITY

BUYER'S INSPECTION ADVISORY (BIA PAGE 1 OF 2)

Property Address: 264 Beach Lane, Costa Mesa, CA 92627   Date: JUNE 14, 2005

4. **SOIL STABILITY:** Existence of fill or compacted soil, expansive or contracting soil, susceptibility to slippage, settling or movement, and the adequacy of drainage. (Geotechnical engineers are best suited to determine such conditions, causes and remedies.)
5. **ROOF:** Present condition, age, leaks, and remaining useful life. (Roofing contractors are best suited to determine these conditions.)
6. **POOL/SPA:** Cracks, leaks or operational problems. (Pool contractors are best suited to determine these conditions.)
7. **WASTE DISPOSAL:** Type, size, adequacy, capacity and condition of sewer and septic systems and components, connection to sewer, and applicable fees.
8. **WATER AND UTILITIES; WELL SYSTEMS AND COMPONENTS:** Water and utility availability, use restrictions and costs. Water quality, adequacy, condition, and performance of well systems and components.
9. **ENVIRONMENTAL HAZARDS:** Potential environmental hazards, including, but not limited to, asbestos, lead-based paint and other lead contamination, radon, methane, other gases, fuel oil or chemical storage tanks, contaminated soil or water, hazardous waste, waste disposal sites, electromagnetic fields, nuclear sources, and other substances, materials, products, or conditions (including mold (airborne, toxic or otherwise), fungus or similar contaminants). (For more information on these items, you may consult an appropriate professional or read the booklets "Environmental Hazards: A Guide for Homeowners ,Buyers, Landlords and Tenants," "Protect Your Family From Lead in Your Home" or both.)
10. **EARTHQUAKES AND FLOODING:** Susceptibility of the Property to earthquake/seismic hazards and propensity of the Property to flood. (A Geologist or Geotechnical Engineer is best suited to provide information on these conditions.)
11. **FIRE, HAZARD AND OTHER INSURANCE:** The availability and cost of necessary or desired insurance may vary. The location of the Property in a seismic, flood or fire hazard zone, and other conditions, such as the age of the Property and the claims history of the Property and Buyer, may affect the availability and need for certain types of insurance. Buyer should explore insurance options early as this information may affect other decisions, including the removal of loan and inspection contingencies. (An insurance agent is best suited to provide information on these conditions.)
12. **BUILDING PERMITS, ZONING AND GOVERNMENTAL REQUIREMENTS:** Permits, inspections, certificates, zoning, other governmental limitations, restrictions, and requirements affecting the current or future use of the Property, its development or size. (Such information is available from appropriate governmental agencies and private information providers. Brokers are not qualified to review or interpret any such information.)
13. **RENTAL PROPERTY RESTRICTIONS:** Some cities and counties impose restrictions that limit the amount of rent that can be charged, the maximum number of occupants, and the right of a landlord to terminate a tenancy. Deadbolt or other locks and security systems for doors and windows, including window bars, should be examined to determine whether they satisfy legal requirements. (Government agencies can provide information about these restrictions and other requirements.)
14. **SECURITY AND SAFETY:** State and local Law may require the installation of barriers, access alarms, self-latching mechanisms and/or other measures to decrease the risk to children and other persons of existing swimming pools and hot tubs, as well as various fire safety and other measures concerning other features of the Property. Compliance requirements differ from city to city and county to county. Unless specifically agreed, the Property may not be in compliance with these requirements. (Local government agencies can provide information about these restrictions and other requirements.)
15. **NEIGHBORHOOD, AREA, SUBDIVISION CONDITIONS; PERSONAL FACTORS:** Neighborhood or area conditions, including schools, proximity and adequacy of law enforcement, crime statistics, the proximity of registered felons or offenders, fire protection, other government services, availability, adequacy and cost of any speed-wired, wireless internet connections or other telecommunications or other technology services and installations, proximity to commercial, industrial or agricultural activities, existing and proposed transportation, construction and development that may affect noise, view, or traffic, airport noise, noise or odor from any source, wild and domestic animals, other nuisances, hazards, or circumstances, protected species, wetland properties, botanical diseases, historic or other governmentally protected sites or improvements, cemeteries, facilities and condition of common areas of common interest subdivisions, and possible lack of compliance with any governing documents or Homeowners' Association requirements, conditions and influences of significance to certain cultures and/or religions, and personal needs, requirements and preferences of Buyer.

Buyer and Seller acknowledge and agree that Broker: **(i)** Does not decide what price Buyer should pay or Seller should accept; **(ii)** Does not guarantee the condition of the Property; **(iii)** Does not guarantee the performance, adequacy or completeness of inspections, services, products or repairs provided or made by Seller or others; **(iv)** Shall not be responsible for identifying defects that are not known to Broker and **(a)** are not visually observable in reasonably accessible areas of the Property; **(b)** are in common areas; or **(c)** are off the site of the Property; **(v)** Shall not be responsible for inspecting public records or permits concerning the title or use of Property; **(vi)** Shall not be responsible for identifying the location of boundary lines or other items affecting title; **(vii)** Shall not be responsible for verifying square footage, representations of others or information contained in Investigation reports, Multiple Listing Service, advertisements, flyers or other promotional material; **(viii)** Shall not be responsible for providing legal or tax advice regarding any aspect of a transaction entered into by Buyer or Seller; and **(ix)** Shall not be responsible for providing other advice or information that exceeds the knowledge, education and experience required to perform real estate licensed activity. Buyer and Seller agree to seek legal, tax, insurance, title and other desired assistance from appropriate professionals.

By signing below, Buyer and Seller each acknowledge that they have read, understand, accept and have received a Copy of this Advisory. Buyer is encouraged to read it carefully.

Mattie Buyer	6/14/03	_Della Buyer_	6/14/03
Buyer Signature	Date	Buyer Signature	Date
Tony Seller	6/15/03	_Yolanda Seller_	6/15/03
Seller Signature	Date	Seller Signature	Date

THIS FORM HAS BEEN APPROVED BY THE CALIFORNIA ASSOCIATION OF REALTORS® (C.A.R.). NO REPRESENTATION IS MADE AS TO THE LEGAL VALIDITY OR ADEQUACY OF ANY PROVISION IN ANY SPECIFIC TRANSACTION. A REAL ESTATE BROKER IS THE PERSON QUALIFIED TO ADVISE ON REAL ESTATE TRANSACTIONS. IF YOU DESIRE LEGAL OR TAX ADVICE, CONSULT AN APPROPRIATE PROFESSIONAL.

This form is available for use by the entire real estate industry. It is not intended to identify the user as a REALTOR®. REALTOR® is a registered collective membership mark which may be used only by members of the NATIONAL ASSOCIATION OF REALTORS® who subscribe to its Code of Ethics.

SURE TRAC The System for Success™

Published by the
California Association of REALTORS®

BIA REVISED 10/02 (PAGE 2 OF 2)

Reviewed by _____ Date 6/15/03

BUYER'S INSPECTION ADVISORY (BIA PAGE 2 OF 2)

VI. Seller and Agent Required Disclosures

A. AGENCY RELATIONSHIP DISCLOSURE

The Disclosure Regarding Real Estate Agency Relationships form states that both the listing broker and selling broker must declare in writing, as soon as practicable, if they represent the seller, the buyer, or both (see Chapter 4).

B. CIVIL CODE § 1102 "DISCLOSURES UPON THE SALE OF REAL PROPERTY"

Real Estate Transfer Disclosure Statement. The seller and his agent make disclosures. The Transfer Disclosure Statement provides details of the condition of the property. It is given to transferee as soon as practicable before transfer of title. **(See Chapter 4.)**

Mold Disclosure. The Transfer Disclosure Statement prompts sellers to disclose their awareness of mold to buyers.

"Drug Lab"—Illegal Controlled Substance. If a seller has actual knowledge that an illegal controlled substance has been released on the property, he/she must provide written notice to a prospective buyer.

Local Option Real Estate Transfer Disclosure Statement. The seller may be required by a city or county to provide specific information about the neighborhood or community in the Transfer Disclosure Statement.

Natural Hazards Disclosure. The seller or his or her real estate agent is required to provide prospective buyers a revised Natural Hazard Disclosure statement disclosing that the property is located within one or more of the six specified natural hazard zones.

Mello-Roos Bonds and Taxes. If the property is subject to a continuing lien securing the levy of special taxes to finance designated public facilities and services under the Mello-Roos Community Facilities Act and/or a 1915 Bond Act assessment, the seller must attempt to obtain a notice from an appropriate local agency disclosing details of the tax. Because of the technological nature of the information required, most sellers opt to have a professional company provide this information to the buyers.

Military Ordnance Location. Seller must give written notice of any knowledge of former state or federal ordnance locations (possible contaminants) within one mile of the property.

Window Security Bars. Seller must disclose existence of window security bars and safety release mechanisms on the Transfer Disclosure Statement.

C. EARTHQUAKE GUIDES

Seller and agent provide transferee with a copy of *Homeowner's Guide to Earthquake Safety* from the Seismic Safety Commission. **Important:** If a buyer receives a copy of the booklet, neither the seller nor agent are required to provide additional information regarding geologic and seismic hazards. Seller and agent must, however, disclose that a property is in an earthquake zone.

D. SMOKE DETECTOR STATEMENT OF COMPLIANCE

Seller must provide buyer with a written statement that the property complies with California smoke detector's law.

E. DISCLOSURE REGARDING LEAD-BASED PAINT HAZARDS

Sellers must disclose the presence of lead-based paint or lead-based hazards and any known information and reports, e.g., location and condition of painted surfaces.

F. CALIFORNIA'S ENVIRONMENTAL HAZARDS PAMPHLET

The Real Estate Transfer Disclosure Statement provided to the buyer by the seller and his real estate agent must specify environmental hazards of which the seller is aware. If the buyer is given a pamphlet entitled *Environmental Hazards: A Guide for Homeowners, Buyers, Landlords, and Tenants*, neither the seller nor his real estate agent is required to furnish any more information concerning such hazards unless the seller or agent has actual knowledge of the existence of an environmental hazard on or affecting the property. *The Environmental Hazards Pamphlet includes sections on asbestos, radon, lead, mold, and formaldehyde.* **Radon can be detected with a spectrometer.**

G. DELIVERY OF STRUCTURAL PEST CONTROL INSPECTION AND CERTIFICATION REPORTS

If required by contract or by the lender, the seller or his agent must deliver to the buyer before transfer of title a report and written certification by a registered structural pest control company, regarding the presence of wood-destroying organisms.

The Structural Pest Control Board collects termite reports, copies of which can be obtained by anyone upon request and payment of a fee.

H. FOREIGN INVESTMENT IN REAL PROPERTY TAX ACT

A buyer of real property must withhold and send to the IRS 10% of the gross sales price if seller is a "foreign person."

I. NOTICE AND DISCLOSURE TO BUYER OF STATE TAX WITHHOLDING OR DISPOSITION OF CALIFORNIA REAL PROPERTY

The buyer must withhold 3.33% of the total sale price as state income tax in certain transactions.

J. FURNISHING CONTROLLING DOCUMENTS AND A FINANCIAL STATEMENT REGARDING COMMON INTEREST DEVELOPMENTS

The seller or his or her agent must provide a prospective buyer with the following: (a) copy of governing documents of development; (b) copy of most recent financial statement of the homeowner's association; (c) a written statement from the association specifying the amount of the current, regular, and special assessments and any unpaid assessments.

K. NOTICE REGARDING THE ADVISABILITY OF TITLE INSURANCE

Where no title insurance is to be issued, the buyer must receive and sign or acknowledge a statutory notice regarding the advisability of obtaining title insurance with the close of escrow.

L. CERTIFICATION REGARDING WATER HEATER'S (AND SMOKE ALARM) SECURITY AGAINST EARTHQUAKE

A seller must certify in writing to the prospective buyer that a water heater has been braced, anchored, or strapped to resist movement due to earthquake motion.

M. DATA BASE REGARDING LOCATION OF REGISTERED SEX OFFENDERS (MEGAN'S LAW)

A statutorily defined notice regarding the existence of public access to database information regarding sex offenders is required in every real property sales contract.

Note: See box on page 168 for more disclosures.

VII. Purchase Options

A. OPTIONS (A Unilateral Contract)

An *OPTION is a right to purchase a property upon specified terms within a specific time period, which is granted in exchange for money.* (**See Figure 5-10** for the CAR® three-page Option Agreement). An option is normally purchased to take a property off the open market. The prospective purchaser holds an exclusive right to buy during the option period.

An option contract CANNOT be revoked by optionor who could be forced to sell the property by specific performance.

An *OPTIONOR is a property owner who gives an interested buyer an exclusive right to purchase a property.* An *OPTIONEE is a potential buyer who purchases an agreed-to amount of time to buy a specific property upon set terms.* The optionee does not have to go through with the purchase.

Figure 5-10

CALIFORNIA
ASSOCIATION
OF REALTORS®

OPTION AGREEMENT
To be used with a purchase agreement. May also be used with a lease.

Date_____, at _____, California
_____, ("Optionor"), grants to
_____, ("Optionee"),
an option ("Agreement") to purchase the real property and improvements situated in (city) _____
_____, County of _____,
California, described as _____ ("Property") as specified in the
attached: ☐ Real Estate Purchase Agreement ☐ Other_____, which is incorporated
by this reference as a part of this Agreement, on the following terms and conditions.

1. **OPTION CONSIDERATION:**
   A. _____ Dollars $_____,
   ☐ (if checked) and/or (circle one), the amount specified in paragraph 6B.
   B. By ☐ cash, ☐ cashier's check, ☐ personal check, or ☐ _____
   _____
   made payable to _____.
   C. ☐ Payable upon execution of this Agreement,
   OR ☐ Payable within _____ days after acceptance of this Agreement, by which time Optionee shall have completed a
   due diligence investigation and accepted the condition of the Property. At least 5 (or _____) days before expiration of this time
   period, Optionor shall provide to Optionee (i) any mandatory disclosures (such as those required by paragraph 7), (ii) a
   preliminary title report, and (iii) _____.
   OR ☐ _____
   D. If payment is not made by the time specified in paragraph 1C above, this Agreement shall become immediately null and void.
   E. If this Option is exercised, ☐ all, or ☐ $_____ of the Option Consideration shall be applied toward
   Optionee's down payment obligations under the terms of the attached purchase agreement, upon close of escrow of that
   agreement. Optionee is advised that the full amount of the option consideration applied toward any down payment may not be
   counted by a lender for financing purposes.

2. **OPTION PERIOD:** The Option shall begin on (date) _____, and shall end at 11:59 p.m.
   (or at ☐ _____), on (date) _____.

3. **MANNER OF EXERCISE:** Optionee may exercise the Option **only** by delivering a written unconditional notice of exercise, signed
   by Optionee, to Optionor, or _____, who is authorized to receive it, no earlier than
   _____ and no later than _____.
   A copy of the unconditional notice of exercise shall be delivered to the Brokers identified in this Agreement.

4. **EFFECT OF DEFAULT ON OPTION:** Optionee shall have no right to exercise this Option if Optionee has not performed any
   obligation imposed by, or is in default of, any obligation of this Agreement, any addenda, or any document incorporated by reference.

5. **NON-EXERCISE:** If the Option is not exercised in the manner specified, within the option period or any written extension thereof,
   or if it is terminated under any provision of this Agreement, then:
   A. The Option and all rights of Optionee to purchase the Property shall immediately terminate without notice; and
   B. All Option Consideration paid, rent paid, services rendered to Optionor, and improvements made to the Property, if any, by
   Optionee, shall be retained by Optionor in consideration of the granting of the Option; and
   C. Optionee shall execute, acknowledge, and deliver to Option or, within 5 (or ☐ _____) calendar days of Optionor's request, a
   release, quitclaim deed, or any other document reasonably required by Optionor or a title insurance company to verify the
   termination of the Option.

Optionee and Optionor acknowledge receipt of copy of this page, which constitutes Page 1 of _____ Pages.
Optionee's Initials (_____) (_____)   Optionor's Initials (_____) (_____)

Published and Distributed by:
REAL ESTATE BUSINESS SERVICES, INC.
a subsidiary of the CALIFORNIA ASSOCIATION OF REALTORS®
525 South Virgil Avenue, Los Angeles, California 90020

REVISED 10/98

OFFICE USE ONLY
Reviewed by Broker
or Designee _____
Date _____

EQUAL HOUSING OPPORTUNITY

PRINT DATE

OPTION AGREEMENT (OA-11 PAGE 1 OF 3)

Property Address: _____ Date: _____

6. ☐ **LEASE (If checked):**
   A. The attached lease agreement, dated _____, between Optionee as Tenant and Optionor as Landlord, is incorporated by reference as part of this Agreement.
   B. $_____ per month of rent actually paid by Optionee shall be treated as Option Consideration pursuant to paragraph 1.
   C. The lease obligations shall continue until termination of the lease. If the Option is exercised, the lease shall continue until the earliest of (i) the date scheduled for close of escrow under the purchase agreement, or as extended in writing, (ii) the close of escrow of the purchase agreement, or (iii) mutual cancellation of the purchase agreement.
   D. In addition to the reason stated in paragraph 4, Optionee shall have no right to exercise this Option if Optionor, as landlord, has given to Optionee, as tenant, two or more notices to cure any default or non-performance under the terms of the lease.

7. **DISCLOSURE STATEMENTS:** Unless exempt, if the Property contains one-to-four residential dwelling units, Optionor must comply with Civil Code §1102 et seq., by providing Optionee with a Real Estate Transfer Disclosure Statement and Natural Hazard Disclosure Statement.

8. **RECORDING:** Optionor or Optionee shall, upon request, execute, acknowledge, and deliver to the other a memorandum of this Agreement for recording purposes. All resulting fees and taxes shall be paid by the party requesting recordation.

9. **DAMAGE OR DESTRUCTION:** If, prior to exercise of this Option, by no fault of Optionee, the Property is totally or partially damaged or destroyed by fire, earthquake, accident or other casualty, Optionee may cancel this Agreement by giving written notice to Optionor, and is entitled to the return of all Option Consideration paid. However, if, prior to Optionee giving notice of cancellation to Optionor, the Property has been repaired or replaced so that it is in substantially the same condition as of the date of acceptance of this Agreement, Optionee shall not have the right to cancel this Agreement.

10. **PURCHASE AGREEMENT:** All of the time limits contained in the attached purchase agreement, which begin on the date of Acceptance of the purchase agreement, shall instead begin to run on the date the Option is exercised. After exercise of this Option, if any contingency in the attached purchase agreement, including but not limited to any right of inspection or financing provision, is not satisfied or is disapproved by Optionee at any time, all option consideration paid, rent paid, services rendered to Optionor, and improvements to the Property, if any, by Optionee, shall be retained by Optionor in consideration of the granting of the Option.

11. **NOTICES:** Unless otherwise provided in this Agreement, any notice, tender, or delivery to be given by either party to the other may be performed by personal delivery or by registered or certified mail, postage prepaid, return receipt requested, and shall be deemed delivered when mailed (except for acceptance of the offer to enter into this Agreement, which must be done in the manner specified in paragraph 16). Mailed notices shall be addressed as shown below, but each party may designate a new address by giving written notice to the other.

12. **DISPUTE RESOLUTION:** Optionee and Optionor agree that any dispute or claim arising between them out of this Agreement shall be decided by the same method agreed to for resolving disputes in the attached purchase agreement.

13. **OTHER TERMS AND CONDITIONS,** including attached supplements: _____
_____
_____
_____
_____
_____
_____
_____
_____
_____
_____
_____
_____
_____
_____
_____

14. **ATTORNEY'S FEES:** In any action, proceeding, or arbitration between Optionee and Optionor arising out of this Agreement, the prevailing Optionee or Optionor shall be entitled to reasonable attorney's fees and costs from the non-prevailing Optionee or Optionor.

Optionee and Optionor acknowledge receipt of copy of this page, which constitutes Page 2 of _____ Pages.
Optionee's Initials (_____) (_____)   Optionor's Initials (_____) (_____)

OFFICE USE ONLY
Reviewed by Broker
or Designee _____
Date _____

REVISED 10/98

PRINT DATE

OPTION AGREEMENT (OA-11 PAGE 2 OF 3)

Property Address: _____ Date: _____

15. TIME OF ESSENCE; ENTIRE CONTRACT; CHANGES: Time is of the essence. All understandings between the parties are incorporated in this Agreement. Its terms are intended by the parties as a final, complete, and exclusive expression of their agreement with respect to its subject matter, and may not be contradicted by evidence of any prior agreement or contemporaneous oral agreement. **This Agreement may not be extended, amended, modified, altered, or changed, except in writing signed by Optionee and Optionor.**

16. OFFER: This is an offer for an Option to purchase Property on the above terms and conditions. Unless Acceptance of Offer is signed by Optionor, and a signed copy delivered in person, by mail, or facsimile, and personally received by Optionee, or by _____, who is authorized to receive it, by (date) _____, at _____ AM/PM, the offer shall be deemed revoked. Optionee has read and acknowledges receipt of a copy of the offer. This Agreement and any supplement, addendum, or modification, including any photocopy or facsimile, may be signed in two or more counterparts, all of which shall constitute one and the same writing.

OPTIONEE _____

OPTIONEE _____
Address _____
_____
Telephone _____ Fax _____

17. BROKER COMPENSATION: Optionor agrees to pay compensation for services as follows:
_____, to _____, Broker, and
_____, to _____, Broker,
payable upon execution of this Agreement.

18. ACCEPTANCE OF OPTION: Optionor warrants that Optionor is the owner of the Property or has the authority to execute this Agreement. Optionor accepts and agrees to grant an Option to purchase the Property on the above terms and conditions.

If checked: ☐ **SUBJECT TO ATTACHED COUNTER OFFER, DATED** _____.

OPTIONOR _____

OPTIONOR _____
Address _____
_____
Telephone _____ Fax _____

Real Estate Brokers are not parties to the Agreement between Optionee and Optionor.

Broker _____ By _____ Date _____
Address _____
Telephone _____ Fax _____

Broker _____ By _____ Date _____
Address _____
Telephone _____ Fax _____

Page 3 of _____ Pages.

REVISED 10/98

OFFICE USE ONLY
Reviewed by Broker
or Designee _____
Date _____

EQUAL HOUSING
OPPORTUNITY

OPTION AGREEMENT (OA-11 PAGE 3 OF 3)

It is a good practice to obtain a preliminary title report or otherwise verify that the owner will be able to convey marketable title.

If the optionee decides to buy the property during his or her option period, the optionor must sell. In this case, the option will become a sales contract and both parties are bound by its terms.

A salesperson who has a listing and an option to purchase a property at the same time must disclose all offers, material information, and obtain consent of any anticipated profits from the seller before exercising the option to purchase.

The optionee may also secure another buyer for the property (sell his or her option to another party) during its term. Thus, all rights and interests may be transferred without the consent of the optionor, unless stated otherwise.

If an optionee has, for example, a one year recorded option and, after six months decides not to exercise his or her option, the property owner should see to it that a quitclaim deed is recorded so that the option might be removed from the records.

An agent who exercises an option to buy his own listing has a conflict of interest. He or she must disclose the full amount of his or her commission and profit and obtain the seller's approval before buying the property.

ADDITIONAL DISCLOSURE REQUIREMENTS

FLOOD HAZARD ZONE – Seller's agent must disclose the flood hazard zone in which the property is located. Flood insurance rate maps are issued by the Federal Emergency Management Agency (FEMA).

WILDLAND FIRE AREA – Seller must disclose to buyer if property is located in an officially designated State Fire Responsibility area. These areas are found on maps issued by the California Department of Forestry and Fire Protection and are generally wild areas.

LANDSLIDE INVENTORY REPORT – Since this may be a material fact, seller should provide this report. County records will disclose if property is or is not located in an area with a high or moderately high potential for bedrock landslide, or mud-debris flows during periods of exceptionally high rainfall or seismic shaking.

VIII. SUMMARY

A **contract** is an agreement to perform or not perform a certain act or service. It can be **express** (verbal or written) or **implied** (by actions). A **bilateral contract** obligates two people, whereas a **unilateral contract** only obligates one party. A **valid contract** is binding and enforceable, but a **voidable contract** can be disavowed by its maker. A contract can also be **void** (no contract exists) and **unenforceable** if it's now against the law, for example.

A contract has three phases: **negotiation, performance,** and **completion**. If some provision of a contract is not yet fulfilled, it's called an **executory contract**. If it has been discharged or performed, it's considered an **executed contract**.

The four elements of a contract are 1) **capacity**, 2) **mutual assent**, 3) **legality**, and 4) **consideration**. (Money, writing, and performance are NOT necessary for a contract to be valid.) Every offer must be made with **contractual intent**, although a buyer can withdraw an offer before acceptance. If the offer is rejected and a new offer is proposed, it's known as a **counter offer**, and automatically terminates the previous offer. The offeree becomes the offeror in a counter offer.

If any of the following conditions exist, a contract is void or voidable: **fraud, misrepresentation, mistake, duress, menace,** or **undue influence**.

A contract for personal property can be oral or written but the **Statute of Frauds** requires that most real estate contracts be in **writing**. Any contract that can't be performed **within a year** from the date of signing must also be in writing.

A contract can be discharged by **performance** (full, substantial, and partial), **breach, acceptance of breach, operation of law,** or **agreement between parties**.

The remedies for a breach of contract include **acceptance of breach, unilateral rescission, action for money damages,** and **specific performance**. (The current liquidated damages on a CAR deposit receipt form is a maximum of 3% of the home purchase price.) Remedies for a breach must be sought within a certain period of time called the **Statute of Limitations**.

The California **Residential Purchase Agreement and Joint Escrow Instructions - and Receipt For Deposit** is the contract, and is also called the residential purchase agreement. A deposit of money or items of value (always the property of the seller, not the buyer) must accompany a deposit receipt to be a valid offer.

Chapter 5

A **covenant** in a deposit receipt is a promise between the parties to contract. A **contingency clause** is an "if" situation, also referred to as **conditions** or **"subject to"** provisions that, if not met, can make the contract voidable.

An **option** allows a prospective purchaser to hold the exclusive right to buy during a specified period, in exchange for a money. It cannot be revoked by the **optionor** (seller) who could be forced to sell the property by specific performance to the **optionee** (buyer). To avoid a conflict of interest, an agent with a listing and an option to purchase must disclose all offers, material information, and obtain consent of any anticipated profits from the seller before exercising the option.

IX. TERMINOLOGY - CHAPTER 5

A. Acceptance
B. Assignee
C. Assignment
D. Assignor
E. Bilateral Contract
F. Breach
G. Capable Parties
H. Consideration
I. Contingencies
J. Contract
K. Counter Offer
L. Covenant
M. Definite and Certain

N. Deposit Receipt
O. Dollar Damages
P. Execute
Q. Executory Contract
R. Expressed Contract
S. Fraud, Duress, Menace
T. Implied Contract
U. Incompetent
V. Liquidated Damages
W. Minors
X. Mutual Consent
Y. Novation
Z. Offer

AA. Offeree
BB. Offeror
CC. Option
DD. Optionee
EE. Optionor
FF. Pest Control Report
GG. Rescission
HH. Specific Performance
II. Undue Influence
JJ. Unilateral Contract
KK. Valid Contract
LL. Void, Voidable, Unenforceable

1.____ A court action to compel the performance of an agreement, e.g., sale of land.
2.____ Anything given or promised by a party to induce another to enter into a contract.
3.____ A contract in which something remains to be done by one or both the parties.
4.____ A right given, for consideration, to purchase a property upon specified terms within a specified time period, without obligating the party to purchase the property.
5.____ A written offer to purchase real property upon stated terms and conditions, accompanied by a deposit toward the purchase price, which becomes the contract for the sale of the property upon acceptance.
6.____ All persons under 18 years of age.
7.____ The act of agreeing or consenting to the terms of an offer, thereby establishing "the meeting of the minds" that is an essential element of a contract; genuine assent from both parties.
8.____ One who assigns his or her right in a contract.
9.____ A person to whom property or interests therein shall have been assigned.
10.____ One who is mentally incapable of managing or taking care of self or property and therefore cannot enter into a contract without a guardian.
11.____ A promise to do or not to do a particular act.

12.____ The substitution or exchange of a new contract for an old one by the mutual agreement of the parties.

13.____ A transfer by a person of that person's rights under a contract.

14.____ An agreement to do or not to do a certain thing. It must have four essential elements: parties capable of contracting, consent of the parties, a lawful object, and consideration.

15.____ The terms and provisions of a contract, which are clear, definite and set forth, as opposed to implied.

16.____ A binding contract created by the actions of the principals rather than by written or oral agreement.

17.____ A contract under which the parties expressly enter into mutual promises, such as sales contracts.

18.____ A contract under which only one party expressly makes a promise.

19.____ Having no legal force or binding effect, or cannot be enforced for one reason or another.

20.____ One making an offer.

21.____ One to whom an offer is made.

22.____ A proposal for acceptance, in order to form a contract. It must be definite as to price and terms.

23.____ Voluntarily agreeing to the price and terms of an offer. Offer and acceptance create a contract.

24.____ An offer in response to an offer.

25.____ Failure to perform a contract, in whole or part, without legal excuse.

26.____ Annulling a contract and placing the parties to it in a position as if there had not been a contract.

27.____ A definite amount of damage, set forth in a contract, to be paid by the party breaching the contract. A predetermined estimate of actual damages from a breach.

28.____ An inspection report required, in the sale of property, to determine if termites are present within a building.

29.____ One who, for consideration, receives an option.

30.____ One who, for consideration, gives an option.

31.____ A contract under which the parties expressly enter into mutual promises.

32.____ The dependence upon a stated event before a contract becomes binding.

33.____ An action that abandons all other remedies and simply asks for money.

34.____ Influence used to destroy the will of another so that any decision is not his or her free act.

35.____ To complete a contract by signing it.

36.____ Legally binding, the terms of which can be sued for in a court of law.

37.____ Deceptive statements or acts used to wrongfully obtain money or property.

38.____ Individuals who have a legal capacity to contract, as opposed to minors, convicts and incompetents.

X. MULTIPLE CHOICE

1. An agreement that is created by acts and conduct, rather than by words, is known as a(n):

   a. bilateral agreement.
   b. unilateral contract.
   c. expressed contract.
   d. implied contract.

2. When using pre-printed forms, what is the order of control over the parts?

   a. Typed, handwritten, printed
   b. Handwritten, typed, printed
   c. Printed, typed, handwritten
   d. None of the above

3. Misrepresentation of a material fact that is known to be false is called:

   a. mistake.
   b. duress.
   c. fraud.
   d. undue influence.

4. What restrictions are placed on aliens with regard to buying real property in California?

   a. Must be at least 21 years of age
   b. Must live in California for at least 10 years
   c. Cannot transfer property for at least 1 year
   d. There are no unusual restrictions

5. An initial counter offer has the effect of:

   a. amending the original offer.
   b. terminating the original offer.
   c. modifying the original offer.
   d. no effect on the original offer.

6. Which of the following can terminate an original offer?

   a. Counter offer
   b. Lapse of time
   c. Withdrawal before acceptance
   d. All of the above

7. A bilateral contract is a(n):

   a. promise for an act.
   b. promise for a promise.
   c. implied contract.
   d. contract made in writing.

8. What is the most commonly requested court action for remedy for a breach?

    a. Action for dollar damages
    b. Unilateral rescission
    c. Specific performance
    d. Acceptance of breach

9. A contract that is NOT definite and certain, and therefore unenforceable, is a(n):

    a. implied contract.
    b. illusory contract.
    c. partially completed contract.
    d. emancipated contract.

10. Which of the following do the courts consider to be grounds for emancipation?

    a. Married minors
    b. Minors serving in the armed forces
    c. Court-declared self-supporting minors
    d. All of the above

ANSWERS: 1. d; 2. b; 3. c; 4. d; 5. b; 6. d; 7. b; 8. a; 9. b; 10. d

Chapter 6
Landlord and Tenant (Lessor and Lessee)

I. Landlord and Tenant – An Overview

A landlord and tenant relationship is created when the owner gives the possession and use of his or her property to another for rent or other consideration. The *LANDLORD (LESSOR) is the owner of the property being rented or leased.* The landlord, or his or her agent, may lease only the land, the land and buildings, or only the buildings or parts of the buildings. The *TENANT (LESSEE) is the person or persons renting or leasing the property.*

A *LEASE is a contract for a set time, typically one year or longer.* A *RENTAL AGREEMENT is different in that it is usually made on a monthly basis and is renewable at the end of each period (week-to-week, month-to-month, or any period-to-period up to one year).* Because a rental agreement is a type of lease, the principles are the same as those of the lease, except for the time periods involved.

II. Leasehold Estates (Less-than-Freehold)

A. TYPES OF LEASEHOLD ESTATES (Tenancies)

A leasehold is a personal property right in real property.

As discussed before, with less-than-freehold estates, there is no direct ownership of real estate. They are chattel real estates. A ***CHATTEL REAL*** *is a personal property estate, such as a lease.* We call this type of interest in a property a lease or leasehold. A ***LEASEHOLD*** *is an exclusive right to occupy and use the property on a temporary basis.* There are no ownership rights in real property. The owner has ***REVERSIONARY INTEREST***, *which means that he or she can regain possession at the end of the leasehold period.* **Figure 6-1** shows the four types of leasehold estates.

1. Estate For Years (A Lease for a Predetermined Amount of Time)

An estate for years (lease) is usually for a year or more, but can be for any predetermined time, agreed to in advance, from one month up to 99 years. The term estate for years is gradually being replaced by the term "tenancy for a fixed term."

*A conveyance of an estate in real property, such as a lease, to someone for a certain length of time is called a **DEMISE**. An **ESTATE FOR YEARS** is an agreement, in advance, between a lessee and a lessor for use of a property for a fixed (predetermined) period of time.*

Figure 6-1

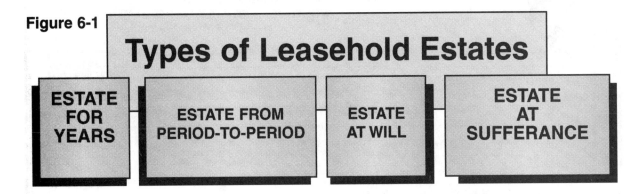

Types of Leasehold Estates

| ESTATE FOR YEARS | ESTATE FROM PERIOD-TO-PERIOD | ESTATE AT WILL | ESTATE AT SUFFERANCE |

A *LEASE* is a contractual agreement to possess and use a property for an agreed to (predetermined) period of time. If the lease period is longer than one year from the date of the signing, it must be in writing and signed by the lessor. The *LESSOR* is the owner, sometimes referred to as the landlord, and the *LESSEE* is the tenant.

The lessor is the owner of a fee estate or a holder of a life estate who gives up possession to all or part of his or her estate and holds a reversionary interest.

2. Estate From Period-To-Period (Periodic Tenancy) (Renewable Each Period)

An *ESTATE FROM PERIOD-TO-PERIOD* is periodic tenancy that continues from year-to-year, month-to-month, week-to-week, or from any other designated period-to-period. This period-to-period tenancy, which is automatically renewable, is called a rental agreement. As previously stated, a rental agreement is an agreement between a tenant and landlord for continuing periods of time, usually from month-to-month. Rental agreements do not expire; notice must be given by one of the parties.

Written rental agreements have become the most commonly used real estate agreements in the United States. They are used frequently when renting apartments, duplexes, houses, condominiums, and other types of residential property. The California Association of Realtors® (CAR) has a Residential Lease or Month-To-Month Rental Agreement Form that covers all the basic conditions desired in such a contract (**see Figure 6-2**). **Figure 6-3** is an Application To Rent, Receipt For Deposit/Screening Fee Form to be filled out by the prospective tenant.

Unless otherwise stated, a 30-Day Notice by the renter and a 60-Day Notice by the landlord is required to terminate a month-to-month tenancy when the tenant has lived on the property for more than one year. (There are some exceptions for a landlord who has a bona fide buyer.)

A landlord holds a reversionary right to the property. A *REVERSIONARY RIGHT* means the landlord grants the tenant the right to occupy (possess) the property, but retains the

177

Figure 6-2

CALIFORNIA
ASSOCIATION
OF REALTORS®

RESIDENTIAL LEASE OR
MONTH-TO-MONTH RENTAL AGREEMENT
(C.A.R. Form LR, Revised 4/03)

_____ ("Landlord") and
_____ ("Tenant") agree as follows:

1. PROPERTY:
   A. Landlord rents to Tenant and Tenant rents from Landlord, the real property and improvements described as: _____
   _____ ("Premises").
   B. The Premises are for the sole use as a personal residence by the following named person(s) **only**: _____
   _____
   C. The following personal property, maintained pursuant to paragraph 11, is included: _____
   _____ or ☐ (if checked) the personal property on the attached addendum.

2. TERM: The term begins on (date) _____ ("Commencement Date"), **(Check A or B):**
   ☐ **A. Month-to-Month:** and continues as a month-to-month tenancy. Tenant may terminate the tenancy by giving written notice at least 30 days prior to the intended termination date. Landlord may terminate the tenancy by giving written notice as provided by law. Such notices may be given on any date.
   ☐ **B. Lease:** and shall terminate on (date) _____ at _____ ☐ AM/☐ PM. Tenant shall vacate the Premises upon termination of the Agreement, unless: **(i)** Landlord and Tenant have in writing extended this agreement or signed a new agreement; **(ii)** mandated by local rent control law; or **(iii)** Landlord accepts Rent from Tenant (other than past due Rent), in which case a month-to-month tenancy shall be created which either party may terminate as specified in paragraph 2A. Rent shall be at a rate agreed to by Landlord and Tenant, or as allowed by law. All other terms and conditions of this Agreement shall remain in full force and effect.

3. RENT: "Rent" shall mean all monetary obligations of Tenant to Landlord under the terms of the Agreement, except security deposit.
   A. Tenant agrees to pay $ _____ per month for the term of the Agreement.
   B. Rent is payable in advance on the **1st (or** _____**) day** of each calendar month, and is delinquent on the next day.
   C. If Commencement Date falls on any day other than the day Rent is payable under paragraph 3B, and Tenant has paid one full month's Rent in advance of Commencement Date, Rent for the second calendar month shall be prorated based on a 30-day period.
   D. PAYMENT: Rent shall be paid by ☐ cash, ☐ personal check, ☐ money order, ☐ cashier check, ☐ other _____,
   to (name) _____ (phone) _____ at
   (address) _____, (or at any other location specified by Landlord in writing to Tenant) between the hours of _____ and _____ on the following days _____. If any payment is returned for non-sufficient funds ("NSF") or other reason then all future Rent shall be paid by ☐ cash, ☐ money order, ☐ cashier check.

4. SECURITY DEPOSIT:
   A. Tenant agrees to pay $ _____ as a security deposit. Security deposit will be ☐ transferred to and held by the Owner of the Premises, or ☐ held in Owner's Broker's trust account.
   B. All or any portion of the security deposit may be used, as reasonably necessary, to: **(i)** cure Tenant's default in payment of Rent (which includes Late Charges, NSF fees or other sums due); **(ii)** repair damage, excluding ordinary wear and tear, caused by Tenant or by a guest or licensee of Tenant; **(iii)** clean Premises, if necessary, upon termination of the tenancy; and **(iv)** replace or return personal property or appurtenances. **SECURITY DEPOSIT SHALL NOT BE USED BY TENANT IN LIEU OF PAYMENT OF LAST MONTH'S RENT.** If all or any portion of the security deposit is used during the tenancy, Tenant agrees to reinstate the total security deposit within five days after written notice is delivered to Tenant. Within three weeks after Tenant vacates the Premises, Landlord shall: **(1)** furnish Tenant an itemized statement indicating the amount of any security deposit received and the basis for its disposition; and **(2)** return any remaining portion of the security deposit to Tenant.
   C. Security deposit will not be returned until all Tenants have vacated the Premises. Any security deposit returned by check shall be made out to all Tenants named on this Agreement, or as subsequently modified.
   D. No interest will be paid on security deposit unless required by local law.
   E. If the security deposit is held by Owner, Tenant agrees not to hold Broker responsible for its return. If the security deposit is held in Owner's Broker's trust account, **and** Broker's authority is terminated before expiration of this Agreement, **and** security deposit is released to someone other than Tenant, **then** Broker shall notify Tenant, in writing, where and to whom security deposit has been released. Once Tenant has been provided such notice, Tenant agrees not to hold Broker responsible for the security deposit.

5. MOVE-IN COSTS RECEIVED/DUE: Move-in funds made payable to _____
shall be paid by ☐ cash, ☐ personal check, ☐ money order, ☐ cashier check.

Category	Total Due	Payment Received	Balance Due	Date Due
Rent from _____ to _____ (date)				
*Security Deposit				
Other _____				
Other _____				
Total				

*The maximum amount Landlord may receive as security deposit, however designated, cannot exceed two months' Rent for unfurnished premises, or three months' Rent for furnished premises.

LR REVISED 4/03 (PAGE 1 OF 6) Print Date

Tenant's Initials (_____)(_____)
Landlord's Initials (_____)(_____)

Reviewed by _____ Date _____

EQUAL HOUSING OPPORTUNITY

RESIDENTIAL LEASE OR MONTH-TO-MONTH RENTAL AGREEMENT (LR PAGE 1 OF 6)

Premises: ______________________ Date: ____________

6. LATE CHARGE;RETURNED CHECKS:

A. Tenant acknowledges either late payment of Rent or issuance of a returned check may cause Landlord to incur costs and expenses, the exact amounts of which are extremely difficult and impractical to determine. These costs may include, but are not limited to, processing, enforcement and accounting expenses, and late charges imposed on Landlord. If any installment of Rent due from Tenant is not received by Landlord within **5 (or ☐ ______) calendar days** after the date due, or if a check is returned, Tenant shall pay to Landlord, respectively, an additional sum of $ ________ or ______% of the Rent due as Late Charge and $25.00 as a NSF fee for the first returned check and $35.00 as a NSF fee for each additional returned check, either or both of which shall be deemed additional Rent.

B. Landlord and Tenant agree that these charges represent a fair and reasonable estimate of the costs Landlord may incur by reason of Tenant's late or NSF payment. Any Late Charge or NSF fee due shall be paid with the current installment of Rent. Landlord's acceptance of any Late Charge or NSF fee shall not constitute a waiver as to any default of Tenant. Landlord's right to collect a Late Charge or NSF fee shall not be deemed an extension of the date Rent is due under paragraph 3 or prevent Landlord from exercising any other rights and remedies under this Agreement and as provided by law.

7. PARKING: (Check A or B)

☐ **A.** Parking is permitted as follows: ______________________

The right to parking ☐ is ☐ is not included in the Rent charged pursuant to paragraph 3. If not included in the Rent, the parking rental fee shall be an additional $ ____________ per month. Parking space(s) are to be used for parking properly licensed and operable motor vehicles, except for trailers, boats, campers, buses or trucks (other than pick-up trucks). Tenant shall park in assigned space(s) only. Parking space(s) are to be kept clean. Vehicles leaking oil, gas or other motor vehicle fluids shall not be parked on the Premises. Mechanical work or storage of inoperable vehicles is not permitted in parking space(s) or elsewhere on the Premises.

OR ☐ **B.** Parking is not permitted on the Premises.

8. STORAGE: (Check A or B)

☐ **A.** Storage is permitted as follows: ______________________

The right to storage space ☐ is, ☐ is not, included in the Rent charged pursuant to paragraph 3. If not included in the Rent, storage space fee shall be an additional $ ____________ per month. Tenant shall store only personal property Tenant owns, and shall not store property claimed by another or in which another has any right, title or interest. Tenant shall not store any improperly packaged food or perishable goods, flammable materials, explosives, hazardous waste or other inherently dangerous material, or illegal substances.

OR ☐ **B.** Storage is not permitted on the Premises.

9. UTILITIES: Tenant agrees to pay for all utilities and services, and the following charges: ____________ except ______________________, which shall be paid for by Landlord. If any utilities are not separately metered, Tenant shall pay Tenant's proportional share, as reasonably determined and directed by Landlord. If utilities are separately metered, Tenant shall place utilities in Tenant's name as of the Commencement Date. Landlord is only responsible for installing and maintaining one usable telephone jack and one telephone line to the Premises. Tenant shall pay any cost for conversion from existing utilities service provider.

10. CONDITION OF PREMISES: Tenant has examined Premises and, if any, all furniture, furnishings, appliances, landscaping and fixtures, including smoke detector(s).

(Check all that apply:)

☐ **A.** Tenant acknowledges these items are clean and in operable condition, with the following exceptions: ____________

☐ **B.** Tenant's acknowledgment of the condition of these items is contained in an attached statement of condition (C.A.R. Form MIMO).

☐ **C.** Tenant will provide Landlord a list of items that are damaged or not in operable condition within **3 (or ☐ ______) days** after Commencement Date, not as a contingency of this Agreement but rather as an acknowledgment of the condition of the Premises.

☐ **D.** Other: ______________________

11. MAINTENANCE:

A. Tenant shall properly use, operate and safeguard Premises, including if applicable, any landscaping, furniture, furnishings and appliances, and all mechanical, electrical, gas and plumbing fixtures, and keep them and the Premises clean, sanitary and well ventilated. Tenant shall be responsible for checking and maintaining all smoke detectors and any additional phone lines beyond the one line and jack that Landlord shall provide and maintain. Tenant shall immediately notify Landlord, in writing, of any problem, malfunction or damage. Tenant shall be charged for all repairs or replacements caused by Tenant, pets, guests or licensees of Tenant, excluding ordinary wear and tear. Tenant shall be charged for all damage to Premises as a result of failure to report a problem in a timely manner. Tenant shall be charged for repair of drain blockages or stoppages, unless caused by defective plumbing parts or tree roots invading sewer lines.

B. ☐ Landlord ☐ Tenant shall water the garden, landscaping, trees and shrubs, except: ______________________

C. ☐ Landlord ☐ Tenant shall maintain the garden, landscaping, trees and shrubs, except: ______________________

D. ☐ Landlord ☐ Tenant shall maintain ______________________

E. Tenant's failure to maintain any item for which Tenant is responsible shall give Landlord the right to hire someone to perform such maintenance and charge Tenant to cover the cost of such maintenance.

F. The following items of personal property are included in the Premises without warranty and Landlord will not maintain, repair or replace them: ______________________

Tenant's Initials (________)(________)
Landlord's Initials (________)(________)

LR REVISED 4/03 (PAGE 2 OF 6)

Reviewed by ______ Date ______

RESIDENTIAL LEASE OR MONTH-TO-MONTH RENTAL AGREEMENT (LR PAGE 2 OF 6)

______________________ Date: ____________

RHOOD CONDITIONS: Tenant is advised to satisfy him or herself as to neighborhood or area conditions, chools, proximity and adequacy of law enforcement, crime statistics, proximity of registered felons or fire protection, other governmental services, availability, adequacy and cost of any speed-wired, wireless nnections or other telecommunications or other technology services and installations, proximity to l, industrial or agricultural activities, existing and proposed transportation, construction and development ffect noise, view, or traffic, airport noise, noise or odor from any source, wild and domestic animals, other hazards, or circumstances, cemeteries, facilities and condition of common areas, conditions and influences nce to certain cultures and/or religions, and personal needs, requirements and preferences of Tenant.

ess otherwise provided in California Civil Code § 54.2, no animal or pet shall be kept on or about the without Landlord's prior written consent, except: ______________________

GULATIONS:

agrees to comply with all Landlord rules and regulations that are at any time posted on the Premises or ed to Tenant. Tenant shall not, and shall ensure that guests and licensees of Tenant shall not, disturb, annoy, jer or interfere with other tenants of the building or neighbors, or use the Premises for any unlawful es, including, but not limited to, using, manufacturing, selling, storing or transporting illicit drugs or other contraband, or violate any law or ordinance, or commit a waste or nuisance on or about the Premises.

B. **(If applicable, check one)**

☐ **1.** Landlord shall provide Tenant with a copy of the rules and regulations within ________ days or ____________

OR ☐ **2.** Tenant has been provided with, and acknowledges receipt of, a copy of the rules and regulations.

15. ☐ (If checked) **CONDOMINIUM;PLANNED UNIT DEVELOPMENT:**

A. The Premises is a unit in a condominium, planned unit development, common interest subdivision or other development governed by a homeowners' association ("HOA"). The name of the HOA is ____________. Tenant agrees to comply with all HOA covenants, conditions and restrictions, bylaws, rules and regulations and decisions. Landlord shall provide Tenant copies of rules and regulations, if any. Tenant shall reimburse Landlord for any fines or charges imposed by HOA or other authorities, due to any violation by Tenant, or the guests or licensees of Tenant.

B. **(Check one)**

☐ **1.** Landlord shall provide Tenant with a copy of the HOA rules and regulations within ________ days or ____________.

OR ☐ **2.** Tenant has been provided with, and acknowledges receipt of, a copy of the HOA rules and regulations.

16. ALTERATIONS;REPAIRS: Unless otherwise specified by law or paragraph 27C, without Landlord's prior written consent, **(i)** Tenant shall not make any repairs, alterations or improvements in or about the Premises including: painting, wallpapering, adding or changing locks, installing antenna or satellite dish(es), placing signs, displays or exhibits, or using screws, fastening devices, large nails or adhesive materials; **(ii)** Landlord shall not be responsible for the costs of alterations or repairs made by Tenant; **(iii)** Tenant shall not deduct from Rent the costs of any repairs, alterations or improvements; and **(iv)** any deduction made by Tenant shall be considered unpaid Rent.

17. KEYS;LOCKS:

A. Tenant acknowledges receipt of (or Tenant will receive ☐ prior to the Commencement Date, or ☐ ____________):

☐ ________ key(s) to Premises, ☐ ________ remote control device(s) for garage door/gate opener(s).
☐ ________ key(s) to mailbox, ☐ ______________________
☐ ________ key(s) to common area(s), ☐ ______________________

B. Tenant acknowledges that locks to the Premises ☐ have, ☐ have not, been re-keyed.

C. If Tenant re-keys existing locks or opening devices, Tenant shall immediately deliver copies of all keys to Landlord. Tenant shall pay all costs and charges related to loss of any keys or opening devices. Tenant may not remove locks, even if installed by Tenant.

18. ENTRY:

A. Tenant shall make Premises available to Landlord or Landlord's representative for the purpose of entering to make necessary or agreed repairs, decorations, alterations, or improvements, or to supply necessary or agreed services, or to show Premises to prospective or actual purchasers, tenants, mortgagees, lenders, appraisers, or contractors.

B. Landlord and Tenant agree that 24-hour written notice shall be reasonable and sufficient notice. However, if the purpose of the entry is to: (i) show the Premises to actual or prospective purchasers, the notice may be given orally provided Tenant has been notified in writing within 120 days preceding the oral notice that the Premises are for sale and that oral notice may be given to show the Premises; or (ii) conduct an inspection of the Premises prior to the Tenant moving out, 48-hour written notice is required unless the Tenant waives the right to such notice; or (iii) enter in case of an emergency, Landlord or Landlord's representative may enter Premises at any time without prior notice.

C. ☐ (If checked) Tenant authorizes the use of a keysafe/lockbox to allow entry into the Premises and agrees to sign a keysafe/lockbox addendum (C.A.R. Form KLA).

19. SIGNS: Tenant authorizes Landlord to place FOR SALE/LEASE signs on the Premises.

20. ASSIGNMENT;SUBLETTING: Tenant shall not sublet all or any part of Premises, or assign or transfer this Agreement or any interest in it, without Landlord's prior written consent. Unless such consent is obtained, any assignment, transfer or subletting of Premises or this Agreement or tenancy, by voluntary act of Tenant, operation of law or otherwise, shall be null and void and, at the option of Landlord, terminate this Agreement. Any proposed assignee, transferee or sublessee shall submit to Landlord an application and credit information for Landlord's approval and, if approved, sign a separate written agreement with Landlord and Tenant. Landlord's consent to any one assignment, transfer or sublease, shall not be construed as consent to any subsequent assignment, transfer or sublease and does not release Tenant of Tenant's obligations under this Agreement.

21. JOINT AND INDIVIDUAL OBLIGATIONS: If there is more than one Tenant, each one shall be individually and completely responsible for the performance of all obligations of Tenant under this Agreement, jointly with every other Tenant, and individually, whether or not in possession.

Tenant's Initials (________)(________)
Landlord's Initials (________)(________)

LR REVISED 4/03 (PAGE 3 OF 6)

Reviewed by ______ Date ______

RESIDENTIAL LEASE OR MONTH-TO-MONTH RENTAL AGREEMENT (LR PAGE 3 OF 6)

Premises: ______________________________ Date: ______________

22. ☐ **LEAD-BASED PAINT (If checked):** Premises was constructed prior to 1978. In accordance with federal law, Landlord gives and Tenant acknowledges receipt of the disclosures on the attached form (C.A.R. Form FLD) and a federally approved lead pamphlet.

23. ☐ **MILITARY ORDNANCE DISCLOSURE:** (If applicable and known to Landlord) Premises is located within one mile of an area once used for military training, and may contain potentially explosive munitions.

24. ☐ **PERIODIC PEST CONTROL:** Landlord has entered into a contract for periodic pest control treatment of the Premises and shall give Tenant a copy of the notice originally given to Landlord by the pest control company.

25. **DATABASE DISCLOSURE: NOTICE:** The California Department of Justice, sheriff's departments, police departments serving jurisdictions of 200,000 or more, and many other local law enforcement authorities maintain for public access a database of the locations of persons required to register pursuant to paragraph (1) of subdivision (a) of Section 290.4 of the Penal Code. The data base is updated on a quarterly basis and a source of information about the presence of these individuals in any neighborhood. The Department of Justice also maintains a Sex Offender Identification Line through which inquiries about individuals may be made. This is a "900" telephone service. Callers must have specific information about individuals they are checking. Information regarding neighborhoods is not available through the "900" telephone service.

26. **POSSESSION:** If Landlord is unable to deliver possession of Premises on Commencement Date, such Date shall be extended to the date on which possession is made available to Tenant. If Landlord is unable to deliver possession within 5 (or ☐ ________) **calendar days** after agreed Commencement Date, Tenant may terminate this Agreement by giving written notice to Landlord, and shall be refunded all Rent and security deposit paid. Possession is deemed terminated when Tenant has returned all keys to the Premises to Landlord. ☐ Tenant is already in possession of the Premises.

27. **TENANT'S OBLIGATIONS UPON VACATING PREMISES:**

A. Upon termination of the Agreement, Tenant shall: **(i)** give Landlord all copies of all keys or opening devices to Premises, including any common areas; **(ii)** vacate and surrender Premises to Landlord, empty of all persons; **(iii)** vacate any/all parking and/or storage space; **(iv)** clean and deliver Premises, as specified in paragraph C below, to Landlord in the same condition as referenced in paragraph 10; **(v)** remove all debris; **(vi)** give written notice to Landlord of Tenant's forwarding address; and **(vii)** ______________________________.

B. All alterations/improvements made by or caused to be made by Tenant, with or without Landlord's consent, become the property of Landlord upon termination. Landlord may charge Tenant for restoration of the Premises to the condition it was in prior to any alterations/improvements.

C. **Right to Pre-Move Out Inspection and Repairs as follows: (i)** After giving or receiving notice of termination of a tenancy (C.A.R. Form NTT), or before the end of a lease, Tenant has the right to request that an inspection of the Premises take place prior to termination of the lease or rental (C.A.R. Form NRI). If Tenant requests such an inspection, Tenant shall be given an opportunity to remedy identified deficiencies prior to termination, consistent with the terms of this Agreement. **(ii)** Any repairs or alterations made to the Premises as a result of this inspection (collectively, "Repairs") shall be made at Tenant's expense. Repairs may be performed by Tenant or through others, who have adequate insurance and licenses and are approved by Landlord. The work shall comply with applicable law, including governmental permit, inspection and approval requirements. Repairs shall be performed in a good, skillful manner with materials of quality and appearance comparable to existing materials. It is understood that exact restoration of appearance or cosmetic items following all Repairs may not be possible. **(iii)** Tenant shall: **(a)** obtain receipts for Repairs performed by others; **(b)** prepare a written statement indicating the Repairs performed by Tenant and the date of such Repairs; and **(c)** provide copies of receipts and statements to Landlord prior to termination.

28. **BREACH OF CONTRACT;EARLY TERMINATION:** In addition to any obligations established by paragraph 27, in the event of termination by Tenant prior to completion of the original term of the Agreement, Tenant shall also be responsible for lost Rent, rental commissions, advertising expenses and painting costs necessary to ready Premises for re-rental. Landlord may withhold any such amounts from Tenant's security deposit.

29. **TEMPORARY RELOCATION:** Subject to local law, Tenant agrees, upon demand of Landlord, to temporarily vacate Premises for a reasonable period, to allow for fumigation (or other methods) to control wood destroying pests or organisms, or other repairs to Premises. Tenant agrees to comply with all instructions and requirements necessary to prepare Premises to accommodate pest control, fumigation or other work, including bagging or storage of food and medicine, and removal of perishables and valuables. Tenant shall only be entitled to a credit of Rent equal to the per diem Rent for the period of time Tenant is required to vacate Premises.

30. **DAMAGE TO PREMISES:** If, by no fault of Tenant, Premises are totally or partially damaged or destroyed by fire, earthquake, accident or other casualty that render Premises totally or partially uninhabitable, either Landlord or Tenant may terminate the Agreement by giving the other written notice. Rent shall be abated as of the date Premises become totally or partially uninhabitable. The abated amount shall be the current monthly Rent prorated on a 30-day period. If the Agreement is not terminated, Landlord shall promptly repair the damage, and Rent shall be reduced based on the extent to which the damage interferes with Tenant's reasonable use of Premises. If damage occurs as a result of an act of Tenant or Tenant's guests, only Landlord shall have the right of termination, and no reduction in Rent shall be made.

31. **INSURANCE:** Tenant's or guest's personal property and vehicles are not insured by Landlord, manager or, if applicable, HOA, against loss or damage due to fire, theft, vandalism, rain, water, criminal or negligent acts of others, or any other cause. **Tenant is advised to carry Tenant's own insurance (renter's insurance) to protect Tenant from any such loss or damage.** Tenant shall comply with any requirement imposed on Tenant by Landlord's insurer to avoid: **(i)** an increase in Landlord's insurance premium (or Tenant shall pay for the increase in premium); or **(ii)** loss of insurance.

32. **WATERBEDS:** Tenant shall not use or have waterbeds on the Premises unless: **(i)** Tenant obtains a valid waterbed insurance policy; **(ii)** Tenant increases the security deposit in an amount equal to one-half of one month's Rent; and **(iii)** the bed conforms to the floor load capacity of Premises.

Tenant's Initials (________)(________)
Landlord's Initials (________)(________)

LR REVISED 4/03 (PAGE 4 OF 6)

Reviewed by ______ Date ______

RESIDENTIAL LEASE OR MONTH-TO-MONTH RENTAL AGREEMENT (LR PAGE 4 OF 6)

______________________________ Date: ______________

ER: The waiver of any breach shall not be construed as a continuing waiver of the same or any subsequent breach.

E: Notices may be served at the following address, or at any other location subsequently designated:

rd: ______________________ Tenant: ______________________

NT ESTOPPEL CERTIFICATE: Tenant shall execute and return a tenant estoppel certificate delivered to by Landlord or Landlord's agent within 3 days after its receipt. Failure to comply with this requirement shall med Tenant's acknowledgment that the tenant estoppel certificate is true and correct, and may be relied upon nder or purchaser.

NT REPRESENTATIONS; CREDIT: Tenant warrants that all statements in Tenant's rental application are te. Tenant authorizes Landlord and Broker(s) to obtain Tenant's credit report periodically during the tenancy in connection with the modification or enforcement of this Agreement. Landlord may cancel this Agreement: **(i)** before occupancy begins; **(ii)** upon disapproval of the credit report(s); or **(iii)** at any time, upon discovering that information in Tenant's application is false. A negative credit report reflecting on Tenant's record may be submitted to a credit reporting agency if Tenant fails to fulfill the terms of payment and other obligations under this Agreement.

37. **MEDIATION:**

A. Consistent with paragraphs B and C below, Landlord and Tenant agree to mediate any dispute or claim arising between them out of this Agreement, or any resulting transaction, before resorting to court action. Mediation fees, if any, shall be divided equally among the parties involved. If, for any dispute or claim to which this paragraph applies, any party commences an action without first attempting to resolve the matter through mediation, or refuses to mediate after a request has been made, then that party shall not be entitled to recover attorney fees, even if they would otherwise be available to that party in any such action.

B. The following matters are excluded from mediation: **(i)** an unlawful detainer action; **(ii)** the filing or enforcement of a mechanic's lien; and **(iii)** any matter within the jurisdiction of a probate, small claims or bankruptcy court. The filing of a court action to enable the recording of a notice of pending action, for order of attachment, receivership, injunction, or other provisional remedies, shall not constitute a waiver of the mediation provision.

C. Landlord and Tenant agree to mediate disputes or claims involving Listing Agent, Leasing Agent or property manager ("Broker"), provided Broker shall have agreed to such mediation prior to, or within a reasonable time after, the dispute or claim is presented to such Broker. Any election by Broker to participate in mediation shall not result in Broker being deemed a party to the Agreement.

38. **ATTORNEY FEES:** In any action or proceeding arising out of this Agreement, the prevailing party between Landlord and Tenant shall be entitled to reasonable attorney fees and costs, except as provided in paragraph 37A.

39. **CAR FORM: C.A.R. Form** means the specific form referenced or another comparable form.

40. **OTHER TERMS AND CONDITIONS;SUPPLEMENTS:** ______________________________

The following ATTACHED supplements are incorporated in this Agreement: ☐ Keysafe/Lockbox Addendum (C.A.R. Form KLA); ☐ Interpreter/Translator Agreement (C.A.R. Form ITA); ☐ Lead-Based Paint and Lead-Based Paint Hazards Disclosure (C.A.R. Form FLD)

41. **TIME OF ESSENCE; ENTIRE CONTRACT; CHANGES:** Time is of the essence. All understandings between the parties are incorporated in the Agreement. Its terms are intended by the parties as a final, complete and exclusive expression of their Agreement with respect to its subject matter, and may not be contradicted by evidence of any prior agreement or contemporaneous oral agreement. If any provision of the Agreement is held to be ineffective or invalid, the remaining provisions will nevertheless be given full force and effect. Neither this Agreement nor any provision in it may be extended, amended, modified, altered or changed except in writing. The Agreement and any supplement, addendum or modification, including any copy, may be signed in two or more counterparts, all of which shall constitute one and the same writing.

42. **AGENCY:**

A. **CONFIRMATION:** The following agency relationship(s) are hereby confirmed for this transaction:
Listing Agent: (Print firm name) ______________________________
is the agent of (check one): ☐ the Landlord exclusively; or ☐ both the Landlord and Tenant.
Leasing Agent: (Print firm name) ______________________________
(if not same as Listing Agent) is the agent of (check one): ☐ the Tenant exclusively; or ☐ the Landlord exclusively; or ☐ both the Tenant and Landlord.

B. **DISCLOSURE:** ☐ (If checked): The term of this lease exceeds one year. A disclosure regarding real estate agency relationships (C.A.R. Form AD) has been provided to Landlord and Tenant, who each acknowledge its receipt.

43. ☐ **TENANT COMPENSATION TO BROKER:** Upon execution of this Agreement, Tenant agrees to pay compensation to Broker as specified in a separate written agreement between Tenant and Broker.

44. ☐ **INTERPRETER/TRANSLATOR:** The terms of this Agreement have been interpreted/translated for Tenant into the following language: ______________________. Landlord and Tenant acknowledge receipt of the attached interpretation/translation agreement (C.A.R. Form ITA).

45. **FOREIGN LANGUAGE NEGOTIATION:** If this Agreement has been negotiated primarily in Spanish, Tenant has been provided a Spanish language translation of this Agreement pursuant to the California Civil Code (C.A.R. Form LR-S).

Tenant's Initials (________)(________)
Landlord's Initials (________)(________)

LR REVISED 4/03 (PAGE 5 OF 6)

Reviewed by ______ Date ______

RESIDENTIAL LEASE OR MONTH-TO-MONTH RENTAL AGREEMENT (LR PAGE 5 OF 6)

Premises: _____ Date: _____

Landlord and Tenant acknowledge and agree Brokers: **(a)** do not guarantee the condition of the Premises; **(b)** cannot verify representations made by others; **(c)** cannot provide legal or tax advice; **(d)** will not provide other advice or information that exceeds the knowledge, education or experience required to obtain a real estate license. Furthermore, if Brokers are not also acting as Landlord in this Agreement, Brokers: **(e)** do not decide what rental rate a Tenant should pay or Landlord should accept; and **(f)** do not decide upon the length or other terms of tenancy. Landlord and Tenant agree that they will seek legal, tax, insurance and other desired assistance from appropriate professionals.

Tenant _____ Date _____
Address _____ City _____ State _____ Zip _____
Telephone _____ Fax _____ E-mail _____

Tenant _____ Date _____
Address _____ City _____ State _____ Zip _____
Telephone _____ Fax _____ E-mail _____

46. ☐ **GUARANTEE:** In consideration of the execution of the Agreement by and between Landlord and Tenant and for valuable consideration, receipt of which is hereby acknowledged, the undersigned ("Guarantor") does hereby: **(i)** guarantee unconditionally to Landlord and Landlord's agents, successors and assigns, the prompt payment of Rent or other sums that become due pursuant to this Agreement, including any and all court costs and attorney fees included in enforcing the Agreement; **(ii)** consent to any changes, modifications or alterations of any term in this Agreement agreed to by Landlord and Tenant; and **(iii)** waive any right to require Landlord and/or Landlord's agents to proceed against Tenant for any default occurring under this Agreement before seeking to enforce this Guarantee.

Guarantor (Print Name) _____
Guarantor _____ Date _____
Address _____ City _____ State _____ Zip _____
Telephone _____ Fax _____ E-mail _____

47. **OWNER COMPENSATION TO BROKER:** Upon execution of this Agreement, Owner agrees to pay compensation to Broker as specified in a separate written agreement between Owner and Broker (C.A.R. Form LCA).

48. **RECEIPT**: If specified in paragraph 5, Landlord or Broker, acknowledges receipt of move-in funds.

Landlord _____ Date _____
(Owner or Agent with authority to enter into this Agreement)

Landlord _____ Date _____
(Owner or Agent with authority to enter into this Agreement)

Landlord Address _____ City _____ State _____ Zip _____
Telephone _____ Fax _____ E-mail _____

REAL ESTATE BROKERS:
A. Real estate brokers who are not also Landlord under the Agreement are not parties to the Agreement between Landlord and Tenant.
B. Agency relationships are confirmed in paragraph 42.
C. **COOPERATING BROKER COMPENSATION:** Listing Broker agrees to pay Cooperating Broker (**Leasing Firm**) and Cooperating Broker agrees to accept: **(i)** the amount specified in the MLS, provided Cooperating Broker is a Participant of the MLS in which the Property is offered for sale or a reciprocal MLS; or **(ii)** ☐ (if checked) the amount specified in a separate written agreement between Listing Broker and Cooperating Broker.

Real Estate Broker (Leasing Firm) _____
By (Agent) _____ Date _____
Address _____ City _____ State _____ Zip _____
Telephone _____ Fax _____ E-mail _____

Real Estate Broker (Listing Firm) _____
By (Agent) _____ Date _____
Address _____ City _____ State _____ Zip _____
Telephone _____ Fax _____ E-mail _____

SURE TRAC
The System for Success™

Published by the
California Association of REALTORS®

Reviewed by _____ Date _____

EQUAL HOUSING OPPORTUNITY

LR REVISED 4/03 (PAGE 6 OF 6)

RESIDENTIAL LEASE OR MONTH-TO-MONTH RENTAL AGREEMENT (LR PAGE 6 OF 6)

Figure 6-3

CALIFORNIA
ASSOCIATION
OF REALTORS®

APPLICATION TO RENT/SCREENING FEE
(C.A.R. Form LRA, Revised 4/03)

I. APPLICATION TO RENT

THIS SECTION TO BE COMPLETED BY APPLICANT. A SEPARATE APPLICATION TO RENT IS REQUIRED FOR EACH OCCUPANT 18 YEARS OF AGE OR OVER, OR AN EMANCIPATED MINOR.

Applicant is completing Application as a (check one) ☐ tenant, ☐ tenant with co-tenant(s) or ☐ guarantor/co-signor.
Total number of applicants _____

PREMISES INFORMATION

Application to rent property at _____ ("Premises")
Rent: $_____ per _____ Proposed move-in date _____

PERSONAL INFORMATION

FULL NAME OF APPLICANT _____
Social security No. _____ Driver's license No. _____ State _____ Expires _____
Phone number: Home _____ Work _____ Other _____
Email _____
Name(s) of all other proposed occupant(s) and relationship to applicant _____

Pet(s) or service animals (number and type) _____
Auto: Make _____ Model _____ Year _____ License No. _____ State _____ Color _____
Other vehicle(s): _____
In case of emergency, person to notify _____ Relationship _____
Address _____ Phone _____
Does applicant or any proposed occupant plan to use liquid-filled furniture? ☐ No ☐ Yes Type _____
Has applicant been a party to an unlawful detainer action or filed bankruptcy within the last seven years? ☐ No ☐ Yes
If yes, explain _____
Has applicant or any proposed occupant ever been convicted of or pleaded no contest to a felony? ☐ No ☐ Yes
If yes, explain _____
Has applicant or any proposed occupant ever been asked to move out of a residence? ☐ No ☐ Yes
If yes, explain _____

RESIDENCE HISTORY

Current address _____ | Previous address _____
City/State/Zip _____ | City/State/Zip _____
From _____ to _____ | From _____ to _____
Name of Landlord/Manager _____ | Name of Landlord/Manager _____
Landlord/Manager's phone _____ | Landlord/Manager's phone _____
Do you own this property? ☐ No ☐ Yes | Did you own this property? ☐ No ☐ Yes
Reason for leaving current address _____ | Reason for leaving this address _____

EMPLOYMENT AND INCOME HISTORY

Current employer _____ | Supervisor _____ From _____ To _____
Employer's address _____ | Supervisor's phone _____
Position or title _____ | Phone number to verify employment _____
Employment gross income $_____ per ____ | Other $_____ per ____ Source _____
Previous employer _____ | Supervisor _____ From _____ To _____
Employer's address _____ | Supervisor's phone _____
Position or title _____ | Employment gross income $_____ per ____

LRA REVISED 4/03 (PAGE 1 OF 2) Print Date

Applicant's Initials (_____)(_____)

Reviewed by _____ Date _____

EQUAL HOUSING
OPPORTUNITY

APPLICATION TO RENT/SCREENING FEE (LRA PAGE 1 OF 2)

Property Address: _____ Date: _____

CREDIT INFORMATION

Name of creditor	Account number	Monthly payment	Balance due

Name of bank/branch	Account number	Type of account	Account balance

PERSONAL REFERENCES

Name _____ Address _____
Phone _____ Length of acquaintance _____ Occupation _____
Name _____ Address _____
Phone _____ Length of acquaintance _____ Occupation _____

NEAREST RELATIVE(S)

Name _____ Address _____
Phone _____ Relationship _____
Name _____ Address _____
Phone _____ Relationship _____

Applicant understands and agrees: **(i)** this is an application to rent only and does not guarantee that applicant will be offered the Premises; and **(ii)** Landlord or Manager or Agent may accept more than one application for the Premises and, at using their sole discretion, will select the best qualified applicant.

Applicant represents the above information to be true and complete, and hereby authorizes Landlord or Manager or Agent to: **(i)** verify the information provided; and **(ii)** obtain credit report on applicant.

If application is not fully completed, or received without the screening fee: (i) the application will not be processed, and (ii) the application and any screening fee will be returned.

Applicant _____ Date _____ Time _____

Return your completed application and any applicable fee not already paid to: _____
Address _____ City _____ State _____ Zip _____

II. SCREENING FEE

THIS SECTION TO BE COMPLETED BY LANDLORD, MANAGER OR AGENT.

Applicant has paid a **nonrefundable** screening fee of $ _____, applied as follows: (The screening fee may not exceed $30.00 (adjusted annually from 1-1-98 commensurate with the increase in the Consumer Price Index).)

$ _____ for credit reports prepared by _____;
$ _____ for _____ (other out-of-pocket expenses); and
$ _____ for processing.
The undersigned has read the foregoing and acknowledges receipt of a copy.

_____ Date _____
Applicant Signature

The undersigned has received the screening fee indicated above.

_____ Date _____
Landlord or Manager or Agent Signature

SURE TRAC
The System for Success™

Published by the
California Association of REALTORS®

Reviewed by _____ Date _____

EQUAL HOUSING OPPORTUNITY

LRA REVISED 4/03 (PAGE 2 OF 2)

APPLICATION TO RENT/SCREENING FEE (LRA PAGE 2 OF 2)

right to retake possession after the lease or rental term has expired. Periodic tenancy is usually terminated when the appropriate party gives a 30- or 60-day notice, because most rental agreements are month-to-month. If the rental period is less than one month, then only one period (that is, agreed length of the tenancy) notice is required. For example, if tenancy was from week-to-week, only seven days notice would be necessary.

3. Estate At Will (Tenancy at Will - Uncommon)

An *ESTATE AT WILL can be terminated at the will of either the lessor or the lessee, and has no fixed duration period.* By California statute, 1) the parties involved must give at least a 30-day notice of termination and 2) since a periodic tenancy is automatically created when a landlord accepts rent, there is no true estate at will in California.

4. Estate At Sufferance

An *ESTATE AT SUFFERANCE occurs when a lessee, who has rightfully come into possession of the land, retains possession after the expiration of his or her term.* (In other words, the tenant does not leave after expiration of the lease.) An estate at sufferance does not require a notice of termination because the expiration of the lease is an automatic termination. If the landlord accepts any payment of rent, the lease reverts to periodic tenancy.

A court action called an "unlawful detainer" is used to evict a tenant who stays past the expiration of his or her lease. This is NOT the same as dealing with a trespasser.

B. MINIMUM REQUIREMENTS OF A LEASE (Or Rental Agreement)

As long as there is intent to rent property, the creation of a lease requires no particular language and can be either a written or an oral agreement. A lease or rental agreement must, at a minimum, include these four items:

1. **L**ength or duration of the lease.
2. **A**mount of rent.
3. **N**ames of parties.
4. **D**escription of property.

Think of
L.A.N.D.!

Leases for one year or less do not need to be in writing, but it makes good business sense to have all real estate agreements in writing. Under the Statute of Frauds, any lease lasting longer than one year from the date of signing must be in writing. California courts have held that in the event the lease is written, it must be signed by the lessor. It is not necessary for the lessee to sign if the lease has been delivered to, and accepted by, the lessee. The payment of rent and possession of the property is sufficient acceptance. Hotels, motels, and other types of lodging fall into the category of leases, even though the duration of use may be for a much shorter time and eviction or termination is handled differently for these daily or weekly rentals.

A lease for more than one year must be in writing and signed by the lessor; but if the lessee does NOT sign, moves in and pays rent, he or she is bound to the terms of the lease.

C. RIGHTS AND OBLIGATIONS OF THE PARTIES

In addition to the minimum requirements, a number of contractual matters between a landlord and tenant should be considered before entering into a lease. The importance of these factors increases as the time period covered by the contract increases. Certain points that should be covered are:

1. duration of lease
2. amount of rent and manner of payment
3. security deposits
4. assignment and subleasing provisions
5. liabilities for injuries and repairs
6. conditions and provisions of a lease
7. termination of a lease or rental agreement
8. renewal or extension provisions in bold type.

1. Duration of Lease

There are certain statutory restrictions on the terms of certain leases:

1. Agricultural lands cannot be leased for more than 51 years
2. Property situated in a city or town cannot be leased for more than 99 years
3. A mineral, oil, or gas lease cannot be longer than 99 years after work begins
4. A minor or incompetent can possess property only for the time a court has approved

2. Amount of Rent

RENT is the amount of money paid for the use of a property. It is important to state both the specific amount of rent and when the rent is to be paid to the landlord. With a periodic tenancy, if the rent is to be paid in advance, or any time other than the end of the term, it should be stated in the agreement. **By law, rent becomes due only at the end of the term, unless the lease agreement states otherwise.** Preprinted lease forms normally specify that rent is due on the first day of each calendar month.

Warning: With an estate for years, if the due date is NOT stated in the agreement, it is due on the last business day of the calendar year.

The actual amount of rent to be paid is called contract rent. *CONTRACT RENT is the payment designated in a lease contract, at the time the lease is signed, for the use of the property.* This amount must be distinguished from the economic rent.

ECONOMIC RENT is the amount of rent a property might be expected to yield if it were available for lease in the current market. The economic rent and contract rent of a given property might differ if the lessor is receiving more or less rent than the property should reasonably yield.

If a rental property is sold, the rents of the tenants are prorated in escrow.

For income tax purposes, the amount of rent paid in advance must be included in the landlord's income for that year. If the landlord collects the first month and a security deposit, both are considered current year income.

3. Security Deposits (Refundable)

A *SECURITY DEPOSIT provides the landlord with funds to pay for damages or unpaid rent when the tenant vacates.* It is in the landlord's and tenant's best interests to have an inspection of the premises before the tenant moves in and before the tenant moves out.

A *STATEMENT OF PROPERTY CONDITION is a report filled out by the landlord, in the presence of the tenant, that states the condition of the premises on moving in and moving out.* If both parties to a lease or rental agreement complete this form together, the chances of any disputes arising, with regard to damages and the security deposit, are greatly reduced.

Maximum rental agreement security deposits for residential properties (in addition to first month's rent) are:

Unfurnished = 2 months rent
Furnished = 3 months rent

Security (and "cleaning") deposits for residential leases in California must be refunded, in full, within twenty-one days of the tenant vacating the premises unless there is damage to the property or required cleaning. If part (or all) of the security deposit is to be withheld from the tenant, the landlord must furnish the tenant an itemized, written statement within the same twenty-one day period. There are a limited number of areas in California that require a minimal amount of interest to be paid on deposits.

4. Assignment and Subleasing Provisions

A sublease or assignment transfers possession, but not ownership.

The tenant, without a clause to the contrary in the lease, may assign or sublease the property. An *ASSIGNMENT of a lease is a transfer of the entire lease,* whereas a *SUBLEASE is a transfer of less than the entire time or space of the lease.* For example, if there is a two-year lease, then an assignment could be for those two years, or a sublease could be for one year of the two-year lease, as long as it's not forbidden in the lease contract.

In a sublease, the lessee is still obligated for the original lease, whereas in an assignment, all the rights and obligations are transferred to the new tenant (assignee).

When a lessee or sublessee subleases a property, he or she holds a sandwich lease. A *SANDWICH LEASE is a leasehold interest in a property that lies between the primary (ownership) interest and the operating (tenancy) interest.* The lessee or sublessee with a sandwich lease is both a tenant and landlord to the same property.

If a developer leases land for 70 years, builds apartments, and then leases the units out individually, the developer has a "sandwich lease."

5. Liabilities for Injuries and Repairs

Generally, when the entire property is leased, the landlord is not liable for injuries to the tenant or any guests that resulted from a defective condition on the premises. This is true even if reasonable care would have disclosed the defects. In apartments or situations where the tenant does not lease the entire property, the liability for injury in the common areas belongs to the landlord. Therefore, it is the landlord's responsibility to either repair defective conditions in the common areas or be liable for injuries resulting from them. If a landlord has knowledge of such defects or disrepair but conceals the fact from the tenant, the landlord is liable for any resulting injuries.

It's easy to see why landlords should carry a large amount of liability insurance. Building defects may cause serious injury that could result in a lawsuit against the landlord. The tenant may also carry a renter's liability policy to protect against injuries sustained by others while visiting his or her apartment. This type of protection is usually contained in a "renters" or "content's" policy, which protects the tenants from most losses, including liability and personal property damages.

6. Conditions and Provisions of a Lease

The California State Bar Association, in conjunction with CAR, has developed a standard combination lease and rental agreement form (**Refer back to Figures 6-2 and 6-3**). This lease contains a number of conditions and provisions that both groups believe provide a good lease contract. As well as explaining who is responsible for any breach, this lease covers most of the common problems that may arise.

Possessory rights belong to the lessee, while reversionary rights belong to the lessor. A lease form, just like any other contract, is very important. Therefore, you should take time to carefully read each of its provisions.

187

III. Termination of a Lease (or Rental Agreement)

A lease or rental agreement can be terminated for a variety of reasons. **Figure 6-4** lists the seven most common reasons for termination. A lease ends at the expiration of the term and without notice. Rental agreements terminate by a written notice that must be at least one rental period in length. For example, if a tenancy is on a two-week basis, and the rent is paid for that period, then two week's notice is required.

Figure 6-4

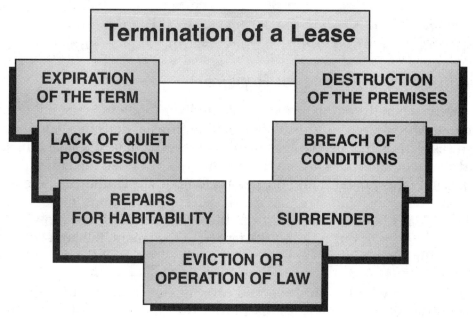

Termination of a Lease

EXPIRATION OF THE TERM

DESTRUCTION OF THE PREMISES

LACK OF QUIET POSSESSION

BREACH OF CONDITIONS

REPAIRS FOR HABITABILITY

SURRENDER

EVICTION OR OPERATION OF LAW

A. TERMINATION: EXPIRATION OF THE TERM (Most Common Reason)

A lease ends, without notice, at the expiration of the term. Rental agreements are usually terminated by either party with a 30-day written notice, unless a longer period is agreed to by both parties. (60-day notice is required by landlord if tenant has been there over a year.) As stated before, if the rental period is less than a month, only that much time is required. "Tenancies at Will" require no less than a 30-day written "notice to vacate" to be served upon the tenant, or a 30-day notice given to the landlord by a vacating tenant. The 30-day notice may be made at any time during the rental period, with the balance of the rent due prorated. **Any condition in a rental agreement may be changed with a 30-day written notice.**

B. TERMINATION: LACK OF QUIET POSSESSION

A tenant is entitled to the quiet possession and enjoyment of the premises without interference. The lease or rental agreement is made with the assumption that the tenant will have use of the premises and enjoy a quiet, uninterrupted stay. The landlord has the responsibility to maintain reasonable quiet on the premises for his or her tenants, and must not harass them unduly. Failure in either responsibility can give a tenant grounds for terminating a lease.

A lessor (landlord) owes "quiet enjoyment" to the lessee (tenant), who is currently in possession of the real property. This means without disturbance from the owner/landlord (not the neighbors).

The California Civil Code permits the landlord to enter a tenant's unit under the following conditions:

1. Emergencies
2. Necessary repairs
3. To show premises to prospective tenants, buyers, or appraisers
4. If the tenant has abandoned the premises
5. With a court order to enter

No notice to the tenant is required if the landlord believes the tenant has abandoned the premises or it is an emergency. Otherwise, 24 hours is considered sufficient notice.

C. TERMINATION: REPAIRS FOR HABITABILITY

The landlord of a rented home, whether the home is a house, a condominium or an apartment, has the implied responsibility to keep the premises maintained in a condition that meets at least bare living requirements: Hazardous conditions cannot exist that threaten the tenant's health or safety. **See Figure 6-5**.

If the landlord does not live up to this implied warranty of habitability, the tenant is not obligated to pay all the rent. However, a tenant must give notice of any necessary repairs to the landlord. The landlord has a reasonable amount of time to make any necessary repairs. A "reasonable amount of time" is determined by the type of repair needed. If the landlord, after a reasonable amount of time, has failed to make the necessary repairs, the tenant has two methods of recourse:

1. Spend up to (maximum) one month's rent in repairs, up to twice in a twelve consecutive month period. (A tenant cannot charge for his or her labor.)
2. Abandon the premises, which terminates the lease or rental agreement.

D. TERMINATION: EVICTION OR OPERATION OF LAW

If a tenant does not pay the rent, or the tenant does illegal acts on the premises, legal action is available to the landlord. *EVICTION is the legal process of removing a tenant because there is a breach of the lease or rental agreement.* **Figure 6-6** shows the life of an eviction process. An alternative would be for the landlord to sue for each payment (installment) as it becomes due. This is true whether the tenant remains in possession

Figure 6-5

Habitability Obligations
(Civil Code Section 1941.1)

LANDLORD'S LEGAL MINIMUM OBLIGATIONS

The landlord's minimum habitability obligations are:

1. Effective waterproofing of roof and exterior walls, including unbroken windows and doors.
2. Plumbing and gas facilities installation maintained in good working order.
3. A water supply capable of hot and cold running water, fixtures, and connection to a sewage disposal system.
4. Heating facilities maintained in good working order.
5. Electrical lighting maintained in good working order.
6. Building and grounds kept clean and sanitary, free from all accumulations of debris, filth, rubbish, garbage, and rodents.
7. An adequate number of rubbish receptacles.
8. Floors, stairways and railings maintained in good repair.

TENANT'S LEGAL OBLIGATIONS

Tenant's Legal Obligations for Care of Premises. A tenant's affirmative obligations to a landlord for reasonable care and habitability are:

1. Keep his or her part of the premises as clean and sanitary as possible.
2. Dispose of garbage and trash in a clean and sanitary manner.
3. Properly use the plumbing, electrical and gas fixtures and keep them as clean as their condition permits.
4. Not permit any person on the premises to willfully destroy, deface, damage, impair or remove any part of the structure, facilities or equipment.
5. Occupy the premises for sleeping, cooking, dining or other purposes for which they were designed or intended.

Figure 6-6

Life of an Eviction Process

3 Days	1 Day	5 Days	1 Day	5 Days
3 Day Notice to Pay or Quit	**Grace Period**	Unlawful Detainer	**Grace Period**	Writ of Possession

Minimum Time Span

or abandons the premises. But at this point most landlords elect to evict the lessee. If the tenant moves and the landlord leases the property, the landlord can only sue for the rent lost while the property was vacant. A ***RETALIATORY EVICTION*** *is the process whereby a landlord evicts a tenant in response to complaint lodged, or a repair deducted from rent, by the tenant.*

Remember: it is unlawful for the landlord to lock out tenants, take the tenants' property, remove doors, shut off utilities, or trespass. The landlord must protect the health and safety of tenants, obey fair housing laws, and give 24 hours' notice before entering a rental.

When the tenant refuses to give up possession but does not pay the rent, the landlord normally serves a "three-day notice" and, if necessary, files an "unlawful detainer" action. A ***THREE-DAY NOTICE TO PAY*** *is a legal document that informs the tenant that he or she has three business days to pay all past due rent or vacate the property. A **THREE-DAY NOTICE TO QUIT** states that the tenant has breached the lease or rental agreement and has three business days to surrender (quit) the premises or face an unlawful detainer court action.* (**See Figure 6-7.**) It is referred to as an eviction notice. After serving the three-day notice, a minimum one-day grace period is recommended to ensure proper service.

An ***UNLAWFUL DETAINER*** *is a legal action in which a complaint is filed with the court asserting charges against the tenant.* After it is served, the tenant has five days to surrender possession or answer the complaint. Once again, it is suggested that at least a one-day grace period be allowed.

An unlawful detainer action is used by the offended lessor (landlord) to gain possession.

191

Figure 6-7

Notice to Pay Rent or Quit

STATE OF CALIFORNIA \
COUNTY OF_____ } ss

TO_____, John Doe, Jane Doe, \
and to all others in possession of the accommodations described below.

    PLEASE TAKE NOTICE that you are hereby required to pay rent for the accommodations described below in the amount stated below or you are hereby required to QUIT and DELIVER UP POSSESSION of the said accommodations within three (3) days after service upon you of this notice.

    The undersigned, as landlord, hereby elects to declare a forfeiture of the lease or agreement under which you occupy the said accommodations and, unless you pay the rent or vacate the premises as required by this notice, will institute legal proceedings against you to recover possession of the premises plus court costs and three times the amount of rent and damages due as provided by California Law*.

Description of Accommodations

Address_____, _____, Calif.

Unit No_____ Rental Due Date_____ Rental Rate per_____ $_____

Amount Due $_____ From_____, 19____ Through_____, 19____

Date_____, 19____

_____
Landlord/Agent

*Code of Civil Procedure Annotated, State of California, Section 1174.

FORM NO. 110 - NOTICE TO PAY RENT OR QUIT · COPYRIGHT 1976 · APARTMENT SERVICE CO., 3921 WILSHIRE BLVD., SUITE 402, LOS ANGELES, CALIFORNIA 388-6136

If the tenant loses or does not answer the unlawful detainer complaint (defaults), a judge may issue a writ of possession. A **WRIT OF POSSESSION** *is a court order directing the sheriff to remove the tenant from the premises within five days.* Often, the landlord will have to account for the storage of the tenant's personal property. This can be complicated, so a landlord should consult an attorney before obtaining an unlawful detainer or writ of possession. Although an entire eviction process could take only fifteen working days, it will most likely take a longer period of time. If the tenant answers the complaint, the matter could take several months.

A lessor goes to court to get possession.

E. TERMINATION: SURRENDER

SURRENDER is the giving up of a lease or other estate, thus terminating any further obligations. Leases may be surrendered either by mutual agreement of the parties or through operation of law.

A lease or rental agreement may be terminated, at any time, by the mutual agreement of both parties. If you are thinking about breaking a lease, it is a good idea to talk to the landlord first. He or she may want to terminate the agreement just as much as you do, or at least suggest a way to sublease the unit.

It is generally considered a good idea to try to negotiate your way out of a rental contract dispute instead of creating hard feelings with a breach of the contract. It is only natural to feel guilty about breaking a lease or rental agreement. If you do not try to communicate your problems or circumstances to the landlord, he or she cannot help feeling that you do not care. Most people will be more sympathetic if you explain the situation to them. This will give them a chance to help you. Allow the landlord a chance to minimize any loss either of you might suffer.

If a tenant abandons a property without cause, he or she has, by "operation of law," surrendered the property back to the landlord. Any cost for legal action by the landlord, plus the cost of any rental loss, may be charged to the tenant. The losses will be minimized if the landlord recovers possession and re-leases the premises quickly. A landlord can bring a lawsuit against the tenant for the lost rents, advertising expenses, and repairs or cleaning.

If a tenant's rent is 14 days delinquent and the landlord has reasonable cause to believe that the lessee has abandoned the premises, the lessor may bring action to reclaim the property. The lease is terminated 15 to 18 days after the lessor posts a **Notice of Belief of Abandonment** in a conspicuous place (door, window) on the premises. This will occur unless the lessee pays the rent or notifies the landlord that the premises has not been abandoned and he or she does not wish to surrender the leasehold estate.

F. TERMINATION: BREACH OF CONDITIONS

The violation of any conditions of the lease is a breach of contract and may terminate the agreement. Both the lessee and lessor have the responsibility of being informed of all contractual conditions and understand that violation of the conditions may cause termination.

G. TERMINATION: DESTRUCTION OF THE PREMISES

If a structure is destroyed, there is usually a clause in the contract that automatically terminates the lease. If the damage is light, the tenant may stay while the landlord makes repairs. The lessee has the right to vacate the lease if the property is condemned.

Selling an apartment is "subject to the rights of tenants in possession." It does NOT terminate leases.

IV. Special Purpose Leases

In this section we will cover several unique types of leases designed to meet specific needs.

A. SALE-LEASEBACK

A *SALE-LEASEBACK occurs when an owner sells his or her property to another party and leases it back for a stated period of time; the original owner becomes the lessee.* This is also a financing device, but it is used mostly for commercial buildings where large business concerns are involved. The main reason for this type of lease is that a large company usually builds structures to its specifications. A large amount of money is required, therefore the company sells the building to get back most of its invested capital. By doing this, the company increases its working capital.

Large investors, such as insurance companies and pension funds, will purchase or build such a property, provided they get a well written, long-term lease. Of course the credit rating and financial position of the lessee must be outstanding. This is one device that nets a high rental income to the investor and allows the business concern a better cash flow. Chain stores, such as department stores and discount stores, use this device frequently.

The original owner of property in a sale-leaseback becomes the lessee. All lease payments are deductible from taxable income if it is business property (nonresidential).

B. LEASE-PURCHASE OPTION

A *LEASE-PURCHASE OPTION exists only when a tenant leases a property with the option to purchase it at some future date.* This gives the lessee the chance to occupy the property and to decide if it suits his or her needs before purchasing it. This is the "try before you buy" idea.

This type of option can also be used as a financing device. If current interest rates for financing are high, it gives the tenant an additional period of time during which interest rates may decrease. Time may also be needed to raise enough money for the down payment. This option must be carefully written and all terms must be clear and definite to be legally enforceable. See Chapter 5 for more details on options.

C. GROUND LEASE

Large business concerns have several different kinds of leases designed to conform to specific purposes. A *GROUND LEASE is for the exclusive use and possession of a specific parcel of land.* The ground lease allows a company to build on a parcel of land without investing a large amount of money for the purchase of the land, because the lessor retains ownership of the land. Ground leases can run for 99 years. In other instances, the land may be used for parking spaces, trailer parks, farming, or as recreational land, such as a golf course or motorcycle park.

When leasing industrial space, the landlord and property manager must make certain that the property being leased complies with all local building and health codes.

D. GRADUATED LEASE

A *GRADUATED LEASE provides for a varying rental rate.* It is often based upon future determination, such as periodic appraisals. Also called a "stair-step" lease.

The Consumer Price Index (CPI) might be used to adjust the rent of a graduated lease.

E. GROSS LEASE (Income Property)

A *GROSS LEASE is a lease where the lessee pays only a flat rental fee for the use of the property.* The lessor is responsible for property taxes, insurance, and other property expenses.

F. NET LEASE (Income Property)

A *NET LEASE is one where the lessee pays the property taxes, insurance and other operating costs in addition to rental payments.* The lessor receives only a net amount and does not pay the other related property expenses. Sometimes the net lease is referred to as a **"triple net lease"** because the lessee pays for (1) property taxes, (2) fire and hazard insurance, and (3) assessments or other operating expenses.

The lessor benefits from a net lease because it generates a fixed income.

G. PERCENTAGE LEASE (Retail Sales Property)

A *PERCENTAGE LEASE is a commercial (retail sales) lease in which the lessee pays, or may pay, a certain percentage of the monthly gross sales to the lessor.* The idea is that if the lessee has a good or excellent location, the lessor will also benefit. Most percentage leases are written for a base rental amount, paid in advance, with an additional amount due if a predetermined percentage of the gross income receipts exceeds the base rental amount.

Percentage lease payments are based upon monthly gross income receipts (with a fixed minimum rental).

H. CONSUMER PRICE INDEX (CPI)

The *CONSUMER PRICE INDEX (CPI) is a government indicator (also called the "cost of living index") that shows changes in the cost of living from period-to-period.* As one of the largest expenses for consumers, **housing expenses are one of the largest denominators used when calculating the CPI**. Leases are often tied to the CPI, so that rents will adjust to give the lessor the same relative purchasing power from rents during a period of inflation. Long-term commercial leases generally include an *ESCALATOR CLAUSE whereby rents increase with inflation.*

The most frequently used standard (index) for making commercial lease adjustments is the Consumer Price Index for Wage Earners and Clerical Workers ((CPI-W).

I. LICENSE

A **LICENSE** *is a personal non-ownership right to use personal or real property for a specific period of time.* It is nontransferable and can be revoked. Think of it as a ticket to a movie.

If a landowner grants permission to hunt on his property, it is considered a license.

V. Property Management
(Real Estate License Required)

In ever growing numbers, real estate brokers are now functioning as real property managers. A **PROPERTY MANAGER** *is a licensed real estate person who is paid to oversee the proper management and operations of rental and commercial property.* A property management company in California must be run by a licensed real estate broker and may include licensed salespeople working as property managers. Property managers include, for example, those who only engage in the management of one and two-family homes as well as agents who oversee large projects such as office and industrial complexes, apartment buildings, and condominiums.

Property managers must also be familiar with rent control laws in their city. See **Figure 6-8** for an explanation of rent control.

A. MANAGEMENT CONTRACT

It is good business practice for a property manager, managing properties for an owner, to have a well written contract with the property owner that sets forth the responsibilities of both parties. (**See Figure 6-9 for the CAR Property Management Agreement Form.**) This should include the terms and period of the contract, policies pertaining to the management of the premises, management fees, and the powers granted the agent by the owner.

Property management contracts usually provide for the property manager to be compensated through a flat fee plus a percentage of the gross income.

B. RESIDENTIAL MANAGER

California law requires that rental unit buildings of 16 units or more must have an on-site resident manager in the employ of the owner or property management

Figure 6-8

RENT CONTROL
(Editorial)

Residential

RENT CONTROL *is government regulation of the amount of rent a landlord may charge tenants*. In its usual form the government restricts, by percentage, annual increases in rental payments. Such restrictions may be applied at the city, county and even the state level. Commercial, industrial and luxury rentals are generally exempt from this control.

In the opinion of many informed real estate analysts, rent control is a form of economic suicide. It discourages new construction by removing economic incentives for developers. This results in a limited supply of new units available to deserving renters.

Landlords, victimized by this profit squeeze, are often forced to convert their apartments into condominiums. This further reduces the number of units available in the open market.

Rent control was originated by well-meaning politicians to relieve an inflated rental market. However it has, in effect, worsened the situation by reducing the supply in the face of an ever increasing demand.

The real solution to the rental crunch will not involve more government regulation. **The answer lies in the government providing more incentives and increased profits to developers, thereby increasing availability and allowing rents to settle at their natural level on the open market.**

Commercial Rent Control Prohibited

By California law, no governmental agency can adopt any rent control restrictions on nonresidential property. Nonresidential property is defined as all rental space except dwelling units, manufactured housing parks and residential hotels. However, public entities can establish requirements for notice relating to the termination of a nonresidential lease.

Figure 6-9

CALIFORNIA
ASSOCIATION
OF REALTORS®

PROPERTY MANAGEMENT AGREEMENT

(C.A.R. Form PMA, Revised 4/03)

_____ ("Owner"), and
_____ ("Broker"), agree as follows:

1. **APPOINTMENT OF BROKER:** Owner hereby appoints and grants Broker the exclusive right to rent, lease, operate and manage the property(ies) known as _____
_____,
_____ and any additional property that may later be added to this Agreement ("Property"), upon the terms below, for the period beginning (date) _____ and ending (date) _____, at 11:59 PM. (If checked:) ☐ Either party may terminate this Property Management Agreement ("Agreement") on at least 30 days written notice _____ months after the original commencement date of this Agreement. After the exclusive term expires, this Agreement shall continue as a non-exclusive agreement that either party may terminate by giving at least 30 days written notice to the other.

2. **BROKER ACCEPTANCE:** Broker accepts the appointment and grant, and agrees to:
   A. Use due diligence in the performance of this Agreement.
   B. Furnish the services of its firm for the rental, leasing, operation and management of the Property.

3. **AUTHORITY AND POWERS:** Owner grants Broker the authority and power, at Owner's expense, to:
   A. **ADVERTISING:** Display FOR RENT/LEASE and similar signs on the Property and advertise the availability of the Property, or any part thereof, for rental or lease.
   B. **RENTAL;LEASING:** Initiate, sign, renew, modify or cancel rental agreements and leases for the Property, or any part thereof; collect and give receipts for rents, other fees, charges and security deposits. Any lease or rental agreement executed by Broker for Owner shall not exceed _____ year(s) or ☐ shall be month-to-month. Unless Owner authorizes a lower amount, rent shall be: ☐ at market rate; OR ☐ a minimum of $ _____ per _____; OR ☐ see attachment.
   C. **TENANCY TERMINATION:** Sign and serve in Owner's name notices that are required or appropriate; commence and prosecute actions to evict tenants; recover possession of the Property in Owner's name; recover rents and other sums due; and, when expedient, settle, compromise and release claims, actions and suits and/or reinstate tenancies.
   D. **REPAIR;MAINTENANCE:** Make, cause to be made, and/or supervise repairs, improvements, alterations and decorations to the Property; purchase, and pay bills for services and supplies. Broker shall obtain prior approval of Owner for all expenditures over $ _____ for any one item. Prior approval shall not be required for monthly or recurring operating charges or, if in Broker's opinion, emergency expenditures over the maximum are needed to protect the Property or other property(ies) from damage, prevent injury to persons, avoid suspension of necessary services, avoid penalties or fines, or suspension of services to tenants required by a lease or rental agreement or by law, including, but not limited to, maintaining the Property in a condition fit for human habitation as required by Civil Code §§ 1941 and 1941.1 and Health and Safety Code §§ 17920.3 and 17920.10.
   E. **REPORTS, NOTICES AND SIGNS:** Comply with federal, state or local law requiring delivery of reports or notices and/or posting of signs or notices.
   F. **CONTRACTS;SERVICES:** Contract, hire, supervise and/or discharge firms and persons, including utilities, required for the operation and maintenance of the Property. Broker may perform any of Broker's duties through attorneys, agents, employees, or independent contractors and, except for persons working in Broker's firm, shall not be responsible for their acts, omissions, defaults, negligence and/or costs of same.
   G. **EXPENSE PAYMENTS:** Pay expenses and costs for the Property from Owner's funds held by Broker, unless otherwise directed by Owner. Expenses and costs may include, but are not limited to, property management compensation, fees and charges, expenses for goods and services, property taxes and other taxes, Owner's Association dues, assessments, loan payments and insurance premiums.
   H. **SECURITY DEPOSITS:** Receive security deposits from tenants, which deposits shall be ☐ given to Owner, or ☐ placed in Broker's trust account and, if held in Broker's trust account, pay from Owner's funds all interest on tenants' security deposits if required by local law or ordinance. Owner shall be responsible to tenants for return of security deposits and all interest due on security deposits held by Owner.
   I. **TRUST FUNDS:** Deposit all receipts collected for Owner, less any sums properly deducted or disbursed, in a financial institution whose deposits are insured by an agency of the United States government. The funds shall be held in a trust account separate from Broker's personal accounts. Broker shall not be liable in event of bankruptcy or failure of a financial institution.
   J. **RESERVES:** Maintain a reserve in Broker's trust account of $ _____.
   K. **DISBURSEMENTS:** Disburse Owner's funds held in Broker's trust account in the following order:
      (1) Compensation due Broker under paragraph 6.
      (2) All other operating expenses, costs and disbursements payable from Owner's funds held by Broker.
      (3) Reserves and security deposits held by Broker.
      (4) Balance to Owner.
   L. **OWNER DISTRIBUTION:** Remit funds, if any are available, monthly (or ☐ _____), to Owner.
   M. **OWNER STATEMENTS:** Render monthly (or ☐ _____), statements of receipts, expenses and charges for each Property.
   N. **BROKER FUNDS:** Broker shall not advance Broker's own funds in connection with the Property or this Agreement.
   O. ☐ (If checked) Owner authorizes the use of a keysafe/lockbox to allow entry into the Property and agrees to sign a keysafe/lockbox addendum (C.A.R. Form KLA).

PMA REVISED 4/03 (PAGE 1 OF 3) Print Date

Owner's Initials (_____)(_____)
Broker's Initials (_____)(_____)

Reviewed by _____ Date _____

EQUAL HOUSING OPPORTUNITY

PROPERTY MANAGEMENT AGREEMENT (PMA PAGE 1 OF 3)

4. **OWNER RESPONSIBILITIES:** Owner shall:

   A. Provide all documentation, records and disclosures as required by law or required by Broker to manage and operate the Property, and immediately notify Broker if Owner becomes aware of any change in such documentation, records or disclosures, or any matter affecting the habitability of the Property.

   B. Indemnify, defend and hold harmless Broker, and all persons in Broker's firm, regardless of responsibility, from all costs, expenses, suits, liabilities, damages, attorney fees and claims of every type, including but not limited to those arising out of injury or death of any person, or damage to any real or personal property of any person, including Owner, for: **(i)** any repairs performed by Owner or by others hired directly by Owner; or **(ii)** those relating to the management, leasing, rental, security deposits, or operation of the Property by Broker, or any person in Broker's firm, or the performance or exercise of any of the duties, powers or authorities granted to Broker.

   C. Maintain the Property in a condition fit for human habitation as required by Civil Code §§ 1941 and 1941.1 and Health and Safety Code §§ 17920.3 and 17920.10 and other applicable law.

   D. Pay all interest on tenants' security deposits if required by local law or ordinance.

   E. Carry and pay for: **(i)** public and premises liability insurance in an amount of no less than $1,000,000; and **(ii)** property damage and worker's compensation insurance adequate to protect the interests of Owner and Broker. Broker shall be, and Owner authorizes Broker to be, named as an additional insured party on Owner's policies.

   F. Pay any late charges, penalties and/or interest imposed by lenders or other parties for failure to make payment to those parties, if the failure is due to insufficient funds in Broker's trust account available for such payment.

   G. Immediately replace any funds required if there are insufficient funds in Broker's trust account to cover Owner's responsibilities.

5. **LEAD-BASED PAINT DISCLOSURE:**

   A. ☐ The Property was constructed on or after January 1, 1978.

OR B. ☐ The Property was constructed prior to 1978.

     (1) Owner has no knowledge of lead-based paint or lead-based paint hazards in the housing except: _____.

     (2) Owner has no reports or records pertaining to lead-based paint or lead-based paint hazards in the housing, except the following, which Owner shall provide to Broker: _____.

6. **COMPENSATION:**

   A. Owner agrees to pay Broker fees in the amounts indicated below for:

     (1) Management: _____.

     (2) Renting or Leasing: _____.

     (3) Evictions: _____.

     (4) Preparing Property for rental or lease: _____.

     (5) Managing Property during extended periods of vacancy: _____.

     (6) An overhead and service fee added to the cost of all work performed by, or at the direction of, Broker: _____.

     (7) Other: _____.

   B. This Agreement does not include providing on-site management services, property sales, refinancing, preparing Property for sale or refinancing, modernization, fire or major damage restoration, rehabilitation, obtaining income tax, accounting or legal advice, representation before public agencies, advising on proposed new construction, debt collection, counseling, attending Owner's Association meetings or _____.

   If Owner requests Broker to perform services not included in this Agreement, a fee shall be agreed upon before these services are performed.

   C. Broker may divide compensation, fees and charges due under this Agreement in any manner acceptable to Broker.

   D. Owner further agrees that:

     (1) Broker may receive and keep fees and charges from tenants for: **(i)** requesting an assignment of lease or sublease of the Property; **(ii)** processing credit applications; **(iii)** any returned checks and/or (☐ if checked) late payments; and **(iv)** any other services that are not in conflict with this Agreement.

     (2) Broker may perform any of Broker's duties, and obtain necessary products and services, through affiliated companies or organizations in which Broker may own an interest. Broker may receive fees, commissions and/or profits from these affiliated companies or organizations. Broker has an ownership interest in the following affiliated companies or organizations: _____.

     Broker shall disclose to Owner any other such relationships as they occur. Broker shall not receive any fees, commissions or profits from unaffiliated companies or organizations in the performance of this Agreement, without prior disclosure to Owner.

     (3) Other: _____.

7. **AGENCY RELATIONSHIPS:** Broker shall act, and Owner hereby consents to Broker acting, as dual agent for Owner and tenant(s) in any resulting transaction. If the Property includes residential property with one-to-four dwelling units and this Agreement permits a tenancy in excess of one year, Owner acknowledges receipt of the "Disclosure Regarding Agency Relationships" (C.A.R. Form AD). Owner understands that Broker may have or obtain property management agreements on other property, and that potential tenants may consider, make offers on, or lease through Broker, property the same as or similar to Owner's Property. Owner consents to Broker's representation of other owners' properties before, during and after the expiration of this Agreement.

8. **NOTICES:** Any written notice to Owner or Broker required under this Agreement shall be served by sending such notice by first class mail or other agreed-to delivery method to that party at the address below, or at any different address the parties may later designate for this purpose. Notice shall be deemed received three (3) calendar days after deposit into the United States mail OR ☐ _____.

PMA REVISED 4/03 (PAGE 2 OF 3)

Owner's Initials (_____)(_____)
Broker's Initials (_____)(_____)

Reviewed by _____ Date _____

EQUAL HOUSING
OPPORTUNITY

PROPERTY MANAGEMENT AGREEMENT (PMA PAGE 2 OF 3)

Owner Name: _____ Date: _____

9. DISPUTE RESOLUTION

   A. MEDIATION: Owner and Broker agree to mediate any dispute or claim arising between them out of this Agreement, or any resulting transaction before resorting to arbitration or court action, subject to paragraph 9B(2) below. Paragraph 9B(2) below applies whether or not the arbitration provision is initialed. Mediation fees, if any, shall be divided equally among the parties involved. If, for any dispute or claim to which this paragraph applies, any party commences an action based on a dispute or claim to which this paragraph applies, without first attempting to resolve the matter through mediation, or refuses to mediate after a request has been made, then that party shall not be entitled to recover attorney fees, even if they would otherwise be available to that party in any such action. THIS MEDIATION PROVISION APPLIES WHETHER OR NOT THE ARBITRATION PROVISION IS INITIALED.

   B. ARBITRATION OF DISPUTES: (1) Owner and Broker agree that any dispute or claim in law or equity arising between them regarding the obligation to pay compensation under this agreement, which is not settled through mediation, shall be decided by neutral, binding arbitration, including and subject to paragraph 9B(2) below. The arbitrator shall be a retired judge or justice, or an attorney with at least 5 years of residential real estate law experience, unless the parties mutually agree to a different arbitrator, who shall render an award in accordance with substantive California Law. The parties shall have the right to discovery in accordance with Code of Civil Procedure § 1283.05. In all other respects, the arbitration shall be conducted in accordance with Title 9 of Part III of the California Code of Civil Procedure. Judgment upon the award of the arbitrator(s) may be entered in any court having jurisdiction. Interpretation of this agreement to arbitrate shall be governed by the Federal Arbitration Act.

   (2) EXCLUSIONS FROM MEDIATION AND ARBITRATION: The following matters are excluded from mediation and arbitration hereunder: **(i)** a judicial or non-judicial foreclosure or other action or proceeding to enforce a deed of trust, mortgage, or installment land sale contract as defined in Civil Code § 2985; **(ii)** an unlawful detainer action; **(iii)** the filing or enforcement of a mechanic's lien; and **(iv)** any matter that is within the jurisdiction of a probate, small claims, or bankruptcy court. The filing of a court action to enable the recording of a notice of pending action, for order of attachment, receivership, injunction, or other provisional remedies, shall not constitute a waiver of the mediation and arbitration provisions.

      "NOTICE: BY INITIALING IN THE SPACE BELOW YOU ARE AGREEING TO HAVE ANY DISPUTE ARISING OUT OF THE MATTERS INCLUDED IN THE 'ARBITRATION OF DISPUTES' PROVISION DECIDED BY NEUTRAL ARBITRATION AS PROVIDED BY CALIFORNIA LAW AND YOU ARE GIVING UP ANY RIGHTS YOU MIGHT POSSESS TO HAVE THE DISPUTE LITIGATED IN A COURT OR JURY TRIAL. BY INITIALING IN THE SPACE BELOW YOU ARE GIVING UP YOUR JUDICIAL RIGHTS TO DISCOVERY AND APPEAL, UNLESS THOSE RIGHTS ARE SPECIFICALLY INCLUDED IN THE 'ARBITRATION OF DISPUTES' PROVISION. IF YOU REFUSE TO SUBMIT TO ARBITRATION AFTER AGREEING TO THIS PROVISION, YOU MAY BE COMPELLED TO ARBITRATE UNDER THE AUTHORITY OF THE CALIFORNIA CODE OF CIVIL PROCEDURE. YOUR AGREEMENT TO THIS ARBITRATION PROVISION IS VOLUNTARY."

      "WE HAVE READ AND UNDERSTAND THE FOREGOING AND AGREE TO SUBMIT DISPUTES ARISING OUT OF THE MATTERS INCLUDED IN THE 'ARBITRATION OF DISPUTES' PROVISION TO NEUTRAL ARBITRATION."

Owner's Initials _____ / _____	Broker's Initials _____ / _____

10. EQUAL HOUSING OPPORTUNITY: The Property is offered in compliance with federal, state and local anti-discrimination laws.

11. ATTORNEY FEES: In any action, proceeding or arbitration between Owner and Broker regarding the obligation to pay compensation under this Agreement, the prevailing Owner or Broker shall be entitled to reasonable attorney fees and costs from the non-prevailing Owner or Broker, except as provided in paragraph 9A.

12. ADDITIONAL TERMS: ☐ Keysafe/Lockbox Addendum (C.A.R. Form KLA); ☐ Lead-Based Paint and Lead-Based Paint Hazards Disclosure (C.A.R. Form FLD)
_____

13. TIME OF ESSENCE; ENTIRE CONTRACT; CHANGES: Time is of the essence. All understandings between the parties are incorporated in this Agreement. Its terms are intended by the parties as a final, complete and exclusive expression of their Agreement with respect to its subject matter, and may not be contradicted by evidence of any prior agreement or contemporaneous oral agreement. If any provision of this Agreement is held to be ineffective or invalid, the remaining provisions will nevertheless be given full force and effect. Neither this Agreement nor any provision in it may be extended, amended, modified, altered or changed except in writing. This Agreement and any supplement, addendum or modification, including any copy, may be signed in two or more counterparts, all of which shall constitute one and the same writing.

Owner warrants that Owner is the owner of the Property or has the authority to execute this contract. Owner acknowledges Owner has read, understands, accepts and has received a copy of the Agreement.

Owner _____ Date _____
Owner _____
     Print Name   Social Security/Tax ID # (for tax reporting purposes
Address _____ City _____ State _____ Zip _____
Telephone _____ Fax _____ E-mail _____

Owner _____ Date _____
Owner _____
     Print Name   Social Security/Tax ID # (for tax reporting purposes
Address _____ City _____ State _____ Zip _____
Telephone _____ Fax _____ E-mail _____

Real Estate Broker (Firm) _____ Date _____
By (Agent) _____
Address _____ City _____ State _____ Zip _____
Telephone _____ Fax _____ E-mail _____

SURE TRAC
The System for Success™

Published by the
California Association of REALTORS®

| Reviewed by _____ Date _____ |

PMA REVISED 4/03 (PAGE 3 OF 3)

PROPERTY MANAGEMENT AGREEMENT (PMA PAGE 3 OF 3)

company living on the premises. ***RESIDENTIAL MANAGERS*** *are tenants of the property who rent units, handle tenants' complaints, and maintain the premises.* They are not required to have a real estate license.

An on-site residential manager does NOT need a real estate license to manage property where he or she is living, but does need one if he or she manages other properties.

VI. Professional Associations

A. INSTITUTE OF REAL ESTATE MANAGEMENT® (IREM)

The Institute of Real Estate Management® (IREM) was created by the National Association of Realtors® as a professional society for real property managers. To bolster professionalism within the industry, they offer the designation Certified Property Manager® (CPM) to qualified candidates who can demonstrate a high standard of competence, ethics, and experience. Property management companies may apply for the Accredited Management Organization® (AMO) designation, while residential on-site managers, who live up to the education and experience guidelines, are bestowed with the Accredited Resident Managers® (ARM) designation.

www.irem.org
Institute of Real Estate Management

B. CALIFORNIA APARTMENT ASSOCIATION® (CAA)

The California Apartment Association® has many local associations to assist property owners with forms and credit checks. Their professional designation for resident managers is Certified Apartment Manager® (CAM) for on-site managers.

VII. SUMMARY

A **less-than-freehold** (chattel) estate is a **personal property** estate in real property, with no ownership rights, such as a lease or leasehold. A **leasehold** is an exclusive right to occupy and use a property on a temporary basis. The types of leasehold estates include: 1) an **estate for years**, 2) an **estate from period-to-period**, 3) an **estate at will**, and 4) an **estate at sufferance**.

The minimum requirements of a lease (or rental agreement) can be remembered by the acronym **LAND** for 1) length of time or duration of lease, 2) amount of rent, 3) names of parties, and 4) descriptions of property.

Contract rent is actual rent, whereas **economic rent** is the amount a property might get if it was for lease in the current market. **Rent control** is a governmental regulation of the amount of rent a landlord may charge tenants.

A tenant may be required to pay a **security deposit** of two months rent for an unfurnished property (three months for furnished) to cover any damage repair necessary when he or she moves out. A **statement of property condition** ensures that both parties are aware of the condition of the premises before the tenant moves in.

Without a clause disallowing it, a tenant may **assign** (transfer entire lease) or **sublease** (for less than the entire time or space) to another. If the old tenant (assignor) signs a new valid lease with an assignee, the assignee is the tenant. An owner who is a landlord and a tenant (like a developer who rents out his apartment complex) has a **sandwich lease. Possessory rights** belong to the lessee, **reversionary rights** to the lessor.

A lease or rental agreement can be terminated by 1) **expiration of the term**, 2) **lack of quiet possession**, 3) **repairs for habitability**, 4) **eviction or operation of law**, 5) **destruction of the premises**, 6) **breach of conditions**, or 7) **surrender**. A landlord has a legal minimum obligation to maintain **habitability**, and a tenant has a legal obligation to care for the premises. Selling an apartment does not terminate a lease.

In the case of **eviction**, it is unlawful for a landlord to lock out tenants, take their property, remove doors, shut off utilities, or trespass. First, the landlord must give a **3-Day Notice to Pay or Quit** (eviction notice), then file an **unlawful detainer** with the court, who issues a **writ of possession**, directing the sheriff to remove the tenant in five days.

Sale-leasebacks, lease purchase options, ground leases, graduated leases, gross leases, net leases, and percentage leases are all **specialty leases**.

A **property manager** is a licensed real estate person paid to oversee the proper management and operations of rental and commercial property. A **residential manager** is a tenant of the property, and as an on-site manager, does not need to have a real estate license. The **Institute of Real Estate Management (IREM)** offers the designation of **Certified Property Manager (CPM)**, **Accredited Management Organization (AMO)**, and **Accredited Resident Manager (ARM)**.

VIII. TERMINOLOGY - CHAPTER 6

A. Assignment
B. Contract Rent
C. Economic Rent
D. Estate at Sufferance
E. Estate at Will
F. Estate for Years
G. Estate From Period-to-Period
H. Eviction Process
I. Ground Lease
J. Landlord

K. Lease
L. Lease Purchase Option
M. Lessee
N. Lessor
O. Net Lease
P. Percentage Lease
Q. Rent
R. Rent Control
S. Rental Agreement
T. Sale-Leaseback

U. Sandwich Lease
V. Sublease
W. Surrender
X. Tenant
Y. Unlawful Detainer or Notice to Quit
Z. Writ of Possession

1.____ A financial arrangement in which, at the time of sale, the seller retains occupancy by concurrently agreeing to lease the property back from the purchaser.
2.____ One who pays rent under a lease agreement.
3.____ Lease on the property, the rental payment for which is determined by a percentage of gross receipts from the business.
4.____ The amount of rent expected if the property were currently available for renting.
5.____ One who rents his or her property to another under a lease or rental agreement.
6.____ An owner who enters into a lease agreement with a tenant.
7.____ A lease requiring a lessee to pay charges against the property, such as taxes, insurance, and maintenance costs, in addition to rental payments.
8.____ The party who pays rent for a lease or rental agreement.
9.____ An agreement for the use of the land, only.
10.____ The occupation of property by a tenant for an indefinite period, terminable by one or both parties (not common in California).
11.____ The general name of the process, from beginning to end, that serves to remove a person from the possession of real property.
12.____ A lease given by a lessee.
13.____ A leasehold interest that lies between the primary lease and the operating lease.
14.____ The concept of possessing an interest in real property by virtue of a contract for a fixed and definite period of time.
15.____ A transfer of a person's entire rights under a contract.
16.____ An estate contract between owner and tenant, setting forth conditions of a period-to-period tenancy.

17.____ A contract between an owner and tenant, setting forth conditions of tenancy for a fixed period of time.

18.____ An estate arising when the tenant wrongfully holds over after the expiration of the term.

19.____ A contract for the monthly rental of residential property.

20.____ Consideration paid for the occupancy and use of real property.

21.____ Rent paid under a lease: the actual rent as opposed to the market rental value of the property.

22.____ The name of the legal process to initiate the removal of a tenant.

23.____ The giving up of an estate, such as a lease. A contractual agreement, having the consent of both parties, such as lessor and lessee, as opposed to abandonment.

24.____ A legal maximum on rental price.

25.____ The court order physically expelling a tenant.

26.____ A lease that includes the right to purchase later.

IX. MULTIPLE CHOICE

1. The lessor is more commonly known as the:

    a. tenant.

    b. landlord.

    c. renter.

    d. agent.

2. Whatever remains of a lessee's (tenant's) security and cleaning deposit must be refunded within how many days after he or she vacates the premises?

    a. 21

    b. 30

    c. 45

    d. 60

3. A transfer of less than the entire time or space of a lease is called a(n):

    a. assignment.

    b. sublease.

    c. estate from period-to-period.

    d. defeasable transfer.

4. What document, filed with the court, asserts nonpayment of rent or other illegal acts by the tenant?

    a. Writ of possession

    b. Three-day notice

    c. Notice to vacate

    d. Unlawful detainer

5. With a sale-leaseback, the original owner assumes the role of:

    a. landlord.

    b. lessee.

    c. lessor.

    d. seller.

6. Percentage lease payments are based upon:

    a. gross income receipts.

    b. a predetermined lease amount.

    c. an amount due after taxes and other expenses have been deducted.

    d. an amount due including all taxes and operating expenses.

7. Can a landlord check the credit rating of a prospective tenant?

    a. No

    b. Only if a prospect is from out of town

    c. Yes

    d. Only with prospect's approval

8. If a large investment group leases a regional shopping center from the developer and subleases to retailers, the second lease is called a(n):

    a. sandwich lease.

    b. blanket lease.

    c. assignment.

    d. double lease.

9. California law requires that an apartment building have an on-site resident manager when it consists of:

    a. 4 units or more.

    b. 16 units or more.

    c. 20 units or more.

    d. 50 units or more.

10. Rent control in California CANNOT be imposed on which of the following?

    a. Retail stores

    b. Office buildings

    c. Manufacturing sites

    d. All of the above

ANSWERS: *1. b; 2. a; 3. b; 4. d; 5. b; 6. a; 7. d; 8. a; 9. b; 10. d*

Chapter 7
Escrows and Title Insurance

I. Escrows in General

An escrow is the processing, by a neutral party, of the paperwork and money involved in a sale or other real estate transaction. The purpose of an escrow is to assure that the appropriate parties perform the terms of the contract.

An **ESCROW** *is created when a new written agreement instructs a neutral third party to hold funds and only proceed when all the agreed to conditions have been performed.* In California, an escrow is usually a requirement for the sale of a home or any other real estate. Although it is not always required by law, it is an indispensable process by which an independent third party handles the legal paperwork of a real estate sale. An escrow is not only an effective tool for handling normal real estate transactions like sales or refinancing, but is also for the sale of trust deeds, exchanges, and transfer of liquor licenses, businesses, securities, and court-required transfers. The legally required and recommended uses of an escrow are illustrated in **Figure 7-1.**

Figure 7-1

Highly Recommended	Required By Law
1. Sales of Real Property	1. Liquor License Transfers
2. Loans	2. Security Sales (Impound Accounts)
3. Exchanges	3. Court Ordered Transfers (Probate Sales)

A. REQUIREMENTS FOR A VALID ESCROW

The Escrow Act is found in the Financial Code.

The three requirements for a valid escrow are:

1. Signed escrow instructions, forming a binding contract between two or more parties: usually a buyer and seller.

2. A neutral party, which is the escrow company, acting as a dual agent of the buyer and seller.

3. Conditional delivery of funds and documents when all the conditions in the escrow are met.

When escrow closes, dual agency (representing both parties, usually buyers and sellers, at once) changes to separate agency (handling each party's separate paperwork requirements).

An escrow may be initiated with a written contract, such as a deposit receipt, or through oral instructions. It is important to have agreed upon the written instructions drawn by the escrow company. Since this may be a new experience for most people, the escrow agent will, when necessary, explain each step to a buyer or seller. A helpful escrow officer can point out possible problems, suggest alternatives, but cannot give legal advice.

B. ESCROW OFFICER

An escrow holder can be: 1) a corporation, 2) an attorney, or 3) a real estate broker who acts as a real estate agent in the transaction.

A *NEUTRAL DEPOSITORY* is an escrow business conducted by a licensed escrow holder. An *ESCROW OFFICER, HOLDER, OR AGENT*, though not licensed by the state, is an employee of a licensed escrow company who acts as the agent. Escrow law is found in the California Financial Code. An independent escrow corporation must be licensed by the Department of Corporations to handle escrows. Corporations that are exempt from the escrow law but can handle escrows include: banks, savings banks, and title insurance companies, because they are under the supervision of their respective authorizing agencies.

There are two other types of escrow holders. They are attorneys who perform escrow duties as a part of their practice, and real estate brokers who handle their own escrows (must be the broker in the transaction). Regardless of the type of escrow company, each performs three essential duties. (Diagrammed in **Figure 7-2**.)

Figure 7-2

Conditional	Confidentiality	Deposit Holder
Delivery of all funds and documents when the conditions of the escrow have been met.	All escrow instructions are confidential, and disclosure can be authorized only by the buyer or seller.	The escrow company can disburse funds and documents only when all conditions have been met and both parties have reached an agreement.

The complete sequence of events in an escrow is:

1. Preliminary title search and report
2. Lender's demand (amount owed, pay-off statement)
3. Request for new loan documents
4. Completion of conditions and depositing of funds
5. Adjustments and prorations
6. Transfer of existing fire policies or creation of new ones
7. Recording and issuing of title policy
8. Disbursement of funds
9. Escrow statement sent to each party

After these steps have been completed and all other escrow conditions have been met, the closing of an escrow is usually routine. **See Figure 7-3**.

The escrow agent is authorized to call for a buyer's documents and funds.

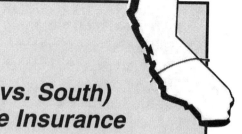

Figure 7-3

California Customs (North vs. South) for Escrow Services and Title Insurance

When are signed escrow instructions delivered?

Customarily in Southern California, the (bilateral) escrow instructions are signed by both the buyer and seller just after the **start of escrow**.

Customarily in Northern California, the (unilateral) escrow instructions are given to the escrow officer just before the **close of escrow**.

Who performs the escrow services?

Escrow services in Southern California are traditionally performed by **independent escrow companies (corporations) or financial institutions**.

Escrow services in Northern California are traditionally performed by **title insurance companies**.

Who pays the escrow fees?

Escrow service fees in Southern California are usually **split 50-50 between the buyer and the seller**.

Escrow service fees in Northern California are usually **paid for by the buyer**.

Who traditionally pays title insurance fees?

Customarily in Southern California, the **seller pays for the California Land Title Association (CLTA) policy (standard policy)**.

Customarily in Northern California, the **buyer pays for the California Land Title Association (CLTA) policy (standard policy)**.

In both the North and the South, the buyers pay for any coverage above the California Standard Title Insurance (CLTA) policy.

C. REAL ESTATE BROKERS CAN CONDUCT ESCROWS

A broker can handle escrows for a fee only if the broker is acting as a real estate agent or principal in that transaction.

A licensed broker can handle an escrow for a fee only if he or she is acting as a broker in that real estate transaction. This right is personal to the broker, and the broker shall not delegate any duties other than escrow duties normally performed under the direct supervision of the broker.

All written escrow instructions executed by a buyer or seller must contain a statement, in not less than 10-point type, that includes the licensee's name and the fact that he or she is licensed by the Department of Real Estate.

II. How Escrows Work

Escrow amendments must be signed by the parties to change the escrow.

A. ESCROW RULES

Once the escrow instructions have been drawn from the original contract (deposit receipt) and signed by each party, neither party may change the escrow instructions without the written agreement of the other. (All time frames commence from the time the contract became binding; usually the deposit receipt has a provision for escrow to acknowledge receipt of this document.) The escrow is complete when: 1) all conditions of the escrow have been met, 2) all conditions of the parties have been met, and 3) the parties have received an accounting of the procedure. If both parties mutually agree to change the instructions, the change can be put into effect at any time. However, if a dispute should arise, the escrow company will not proceed until both parties come to terms. If the parties cannot agree to terms, an escrow company will bring an interpleader action (court action) to determine where the money or consideration goes. **Figure 7-4** illustrates the three ways in which an escrow can be terminated.

If the seller thinks he or she can obtain more money and wants to rescind an escrow, remember: the seller cannot rescind an escrow without the consent of the buyer.

B. WHO SELECTS THE ESCROW COMPANY?

A real estate licensee is prohibited by law from receiving any "kickback" for solicitation of escrow business.

Selection of an escrow company and an escrow officer are part of the negotiation between buyer and seller. Like any other item in a real estate transaction, it is part of the negotiated

Figure 7-4

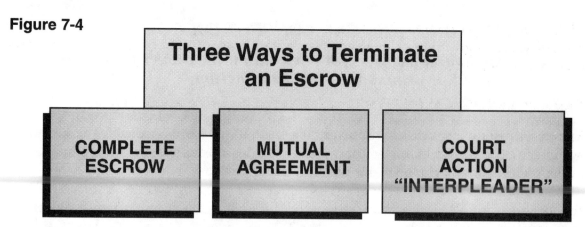

agreement. Either one of the parties may choose the escrow company, which should be explained when completing the deposit receipt. The salesperson may certainly make suggestions as to a preferred escrow company for both the buyer and seller. When the escrow company is named in the listing agreement, the real estate listing agent cannot change the escrow company without the consent of the seller or the seller's agent. If the buyer and seller each desire a different escrow company, then the salesperson must work for a mutual agreement before there can be an offer and acceptance of the sale.

Death does NOT cancel an escrow; it is binding on the heirs (estate) because of the prior agreed-to contract.

It is imperative that the salesperson disclose in writing any shared interest that salesperson or his or her broker has with the selected escrow company. This disclosure must be made either at the time of listing or whenever the escrow company is selected. Disciplinary action will be taken against any salesperson or broker who, in bad faith and against the wishes of the buyer and seller, attempts to force the use of a particular escrow company. Furthermore, a real estate licensee is prohibited by law from receiving any "kickback" for solicitation of escrow business.

C. ESCROW INSTRUCTIONS

Escrow instructions and the deposit receipt are interpreted together, but if a conflict arises, the latest signed document will prevail (unless otherwise specified).

ESCROW INSTRUCTIONS *are formal instructions drawn from the information contained in the original agreement, usually the signed deposit receipt.* When these instructions are drawn and signed, they become an enforceable contract binding on all parties.

Since the escrow instructions supplement the original contract, both are interpreted together whenever possible. If a conflict should arise between the content of the instructions and the original contract, the instructions will usually prevail.

Therefore, all parties to the escrow should read the escrow instructions very carefully, and sign them only after every detail is absolutely correct and the terms meet with their approval.

D. FINANCING IS AN IMPORTANT ASPECT OF THE ESCROW

Most escrows for the sale of a home include obtaining a new loan and the payoff or assumption of an old loan. The brokers and their salespeople can be helpful to the buyer obtaining new financing by providing the necessary loan documentation to the escrow company in a timely manner. Keeping the buyer and seller informed about the progress of the financing and escrow helps to maintain good client-agent communication and trust.

The *PAYOFF DEMAND STATEMENT is a formal demand statement from the lender that details the amounts owed, as calculated by the lender, for the purpose of paying off the loan in full.* The failure to obtain a payoff or beneficiary statement in a timely manner could hold up the escrow. A payoff demand statement is different from a beneficiary's statement. A *BENEFICIARY'S (LENDER'S) STATEMENT is a demand statement by a lender, under a deed of trust, that provides information, such as the unpaid balance, monthly payment, and interest rate, necessary if the loan is to be assumed.* The lender may charge up to $100 for furnishing the payoff or beneficiary statement, except when the loan is insured by the FHA or guaranteed by the VA.

During escrow, if a buyer receives loan approval and requests to move into the property before escrow closes, he or she must obtain permission from the seller, with written autorization.

E. ESCROW EXAMPLE

To help illustrate the closing statements used in a simple escrow, let's assume the following facts:

Figure 7-5 illustrates the buyer's escrow statement, and **Figure 7-6** illustrates the seller's statement. These statements include many other miscellaneous costs that are a usual part of the escrow.

F. CLOSING DATE IS THE DATE OF RECORDATION

Closing is the process of signing, transfer of documents, and distribution of funds. When time is not specified, the escrow will close by mutual consent or within a reasonable period.

The *CLOSING DATE is the date that the documents are recorded.* Escrow usually approximates the closing date, but the actual date is when all the conditions of the escrow have been completed, the buyer's remaining money (cashier's checks) is received, and

An Escrow Example

BUYER   John Buyer and Jane Buyer
SELLER   John Seller and Jane Seller
SALES PRICE $800,000
1ST TRUST DEED $640,000
2ND TRUST DEED . . . . $ 80,000
DOWN PAYMENT . . . . $ 80,000
BROKER   J.Q. Smart . . . . $ 48,000
EXISTING LIENS
    1) 1ST TRUST DEED $290,000
    2) STREET ASSESSMENT BOND . . . . $ 1,300
CLTA TITLE POLICY PAID BY SELLER . . . . $ 2,165
Date of Closing is June 1, 2020

---

when all the documents are recorded. Most escrows are for handling the paperwork of property sale and loan financing, but escrows can be for almost any purpose.

At the close of escrow, if a seller decides not to pay the commission, the broker/agent can file civil action in court.

Note: In closing statements, the buyer's and seller's totals are different. However, each closing statement must balance within itself. In the "buyer's closing statement, the purchase price is debited."

III. Proration

Property taxes, interest, fire insurance, and rents are prorated, but NOT title insurance and non-recurring fees.

PRORATION *is the process of proportionately dividing expenses or income to the precise date that escrow closes, or any other date previously agreed upon.* It enables the buyer and seller to pay or receive their proportionate share of expenses or income. Items that are commonly prorated include:

1. property taxes,
2. fire insurance,
3. interest, and
4. rents.

Figure 7-5   BUYER'S ESCROW STATEMENT

601 East Glenoaks Blvd. Suite 210
Glendale, CA 91207
P.O. Box 433 Glendale, CA 91209-0433
Tel: (818) 500-1633
Fax: (818) 500-0862

BUYER FINAL SETTLEMENT STATEMENT

PROPERTY: 123 Purchase Lane   CLOSING DATE: 06/01/20
          Glendale, CA   ESCROW NO.: 1-10533
BUYER: John Buyer and Jane Buyer

	DEBITS	CREDITS
FINANCIAL		
Total Consideration	$ 800,000.00	$
Cash Deposit		5,000.00
Cash Deposit		86,000.00
New 1st Trust Deed		640,000.00
New 2nd Trust Deed		80,000.00
PRORATIONS AND ADJUSTMENTS		
Taxes at 4000.00/6 mo. from 06/01/20 to 07/01/20	666.67	
OTHER DISBURSEMENTS		
Property Insurance, Inc. for Fire Insurance	1,000.00	
TITLE CHARGES TO AMERICAN COAST TITLE		
Title Policy Premium	628.50	
Sub Escrow Fee	75.00	
Recording Grant Deed	8.00	
Recording Trust Deed(s)	20.00	
Title Endorsement Fee(s)	50.00	
ESCROW CHARGES TO COLONIAL ESCROW, INC.		
Escrow Fee	900.00	
Messenger Fee	50.00	
Loan Tie In Fee	125.00	
NEW 1ST TRUST DEED TO GET SMART SAVINGS AND LOAN		
Loan Fees	6,400.00	
Credit Report	45.00	
Appraisal	350.00	
Tax Service	89.00	
Document Fee	250.00	
Interest at 7.5000% from 05/31/20 to 06/01/20	131.51	
REFUND	211.32	
TOTALS	811,000.00	811,000.00

SAVE FOR INCOME TAX PURPOSES

Figure 7-6   SELLER'S ESCROW STATEMENT

601 East Glenoaks Blvd. Suite 210
Glendale, CA 91207
P.O. Box 433 Glendale, CA 91209-0433
Tel: (818) 500-1633
Fax: (818) 500-0862

SELLER FINAL SETTLEMENT STATEMENT

PROPERTY: 123 Purchase Lane
         Glendale, CA
SELLER: John Seller and Jane Seller

CLOSING DATE: 06/01/20
ESCROW NO.: 1-10533

	DEBITS	CREDITS
FINANCIAL		
Total Consideration	$	$ 800,000.00
New 2nd Trust Deed	**80,000.00**	
PRORATIONS AND ADJUSTMENTS		
Taxes at 4000.00/6 mo. from 06/01/20 to 07/01/20		666.67
PAYOFF CHARGES TO MOST SUPERIOR		
SAVINGS AND LOAN		
Principal Balance	490,000.00	
Interest on Principal Balance at 10.0000% from 05/01/20 to 06/01/20	4,161.64	
Forwarding Fee	50.00	
Reconveyance Fee	60.00	
OTHER DISBURSEMENTS		
Pest Control, Inc. for Termite Report/Work	1,000.00	
Home Warranty, Inc. for Home Protection Policy	400.00	
COMMISSION		
Listing Broker: J. Q. Smart	48,000.00	
TITLE CHARGES TO AMERICAN COAST		
TITLE		
Title Policy Premium	2,165.00	
Sub Escrow Fee	75.00	
Documentary Transfer Tax	880.00	
Recording Reconveyance	5.00	
Street Assessment Bond	1,300.00	
ESCROW CHARGES TO COLONIAL ESCROW, INC.		
Escrow Fee	900.00	
Processing Demands	35.00	
Document Fee	85.00	
NET PROCEEDS	**171,550.03**	
TOTALS	**800,666.67**	**800,666.67**

SAVE FOR INCOME TAX PURPOSES

A. 30 DAYS IS THE BASIS FOR PRORATION

All escrow companies use 30 days as a base month. For example, if an escrow closes on the 10th day of the month, all prepaid rents for that month would constitute 9/30 of the rent left for the seller, and 21/30 of the rent would go to the buyer. If the rent is $2,000, the seller's portion would be 9/30 of $2,000, or $600, and the buyer's portion would be 21/30 of $2,000 or $1,400. (Rents belong to the buyer as of the closing date.)

The two rules of proration: (1) date escrow closes and (2) date item is paid.

The date used in calculating proration is usually assumed to be the date of closing, but any date may be used if agreed upon by all parties. This is the case when the possession date differs from the closing date.

Property tax prorations are based on the amount the seller is paying. Escrow uses the old assessed valuation when prorating.

Taxes are prorated either from July 1, which marks the beginning of the county fiscal year, or January 1, the middle of the fiscal year. If the property taxes on a home, amounting to $2,400 per year, have been paid up to July 1, what is the proration if escrow is to be closed on June 1? In this case, the buyer would reimburse the seller for one month's taxes (or $2,400 divided by twelve months, equaling $200 per month). The seller would then be credited for the $200 in property taxes that he or she had already paid in advance.

IV. Termites and Other Problems

A. STRUCTURAL PEST CONTROL CERTIFICATION REPORT (Report and Clearance)

A Structural Pest Control Report is usually a condition of the escrow.

Pest control inspection reports are not required by law in California, but many lenders will require this report. A *STRUCTURAL PEST CONTROL CERTIFICATION REPORT is a written report given by a licensed pest control company identifying any wood-destroying pests or conditions likely to cause pest infestation. The report states the condition and correction cost of any pest, dry rot, excessive moisture, earth-wood contacts, or fungus damage in accessible areas of a structure.* Who pays for the (1) pest control inspection report and (2) any required or recommended repair work is up to the buyer and seller, although they are usually paid for by the seller. There may sometimes be a local custom that dictates who will pay, while in other instances financial institutions or financing agencies will decide which one of the parties will pay.

ESCROW COMPANY REPORTS INFORMATION TO THE I.R.S.

All real estate transactions must be reported to the Internal Revenue Service. This is done by the escrow company or whoever handles the closing. A 1099 Form is required for any sale or exchange.

Escrow reports real estate transactions to the I.R.S. using the seller's social security number.

The escrow officer accepts and holds the pest control report and awaits further instructions from both parties. If there is Section I infestation damage (required work), it is usually paid for by the seller. If there is only Section II potential for infestation damage (recommended work), the extent of repairs is up to the parties.

Most lenders require a pest control inspection report before making a loan, and every VA and FHA loan application requires an inspection report. The usual cost for an inspection report is about $65. The cost, in some areas, may be as high as $175 to $195.

If escrow holds two pest control reports, escrow will notify the broker and get instructions from both buyer and seller.

The question of which party pays for any necessary repairs to obtain a "Notice of Work Completed" report is also a matter of local custom. In most areas the seller usually pays. However, FHA and VA termite certificates and repairs are always paid for by the seller. The seller is allowed to include a clause stating what the maximum cost of repairs will be as a condition of the sale.

The best time for a seller to have a termite report issued is before putting the home on the market.

California law requires that the seller must receive a copy of the pest control certificate before the close of escrow. For a few dollars, any person may request certified copies of any certificate inspection report, filed during the preceding two years, from the State Structural Pest Control Board.

B. BROKER MAINTAINS PEST CONTROL DOCUMENTATION

The Civil Code requires that the broker shall deliver a copy of the Structural Pest Control Certification Report and Notice of Work Completed to the buyer, if such a report is a condition of the deposit receipt or is a requirement imposed as a condition of financing. If more than one broker is acting as an agent in the transaction, the broker who obtained the offer (selling broker) made by the buyer shall deliver the required documents to the buyer.

V. Fire Insurance

When one party agrees to indemnify another for loss in return for periodic premium payments, it is called "insurance."

A. FIRE INSURANCE . . . A MUST!

Fire insurance is very inexpensive compared to the possible dollar loss due to fire, and all property owners should have this financial protection. A lending institution will require coverage for the amount of its loan. However, it is in the owner's best interest to carry sufficient fire insurance to replace the structure if it is totally destroyed. It is only necessary to insure the current replacement value of the dwelling, since the land itself cannot be destroyed by fire.

The *CALIFORNIA STANDARD FORM FIRE INSURANCE POLICY insures the dwelling against (1) fire and (2) lightning.* If you so desire, you may procure an *EXTENDED COVERAGE ENDORSEMENT that will insure you against the additional perils of windstorm, explosion, hail, aircraft, smoke, riot, and vehicles not attributed to a strike or civil commotion.* Other types of endorsements may insure you against vandalism, malicious mischief, floods, and other damage. Coverage depends on your needs and the perils common to your area.

B. FIRE INSURANCE PRORATION

If the old policy is canceled, the seller is charged a higher rate. It is said to be "short-rated."

When purchasing property, a buyer usually obtains a new policy. **If the seller/owner has filed an insurance claim during the previous three years, he or she must disclose this to the buyer in writing**. This may cause some hardship to the new owner/buyer in obtaining his or her own insurance. Cancellation of the seller's insurance must be initiated by the seller after close of escrow, with any unused premium to be prorated and reimbursed to the seller. It is always the buyer's choice to select his or her own house insurance. Condo insurance is chosen by the association.

Whenever you are buying insurance, review the policy carefully to determine if you have the correct type of coverage and are carrying an adequate amount of insurance, particularly when your property value has increased.

C. COINSURANCE CLAUSE

A *COINSURANCE CLAUSE is a provision in an insurance policy requiring a property owner to carry separate insurance up to an amount stated in the policy to qualify for full coverage. That amount is usually 80% of the value of the dwelling in order to receive full insurance benefits.* The percentage paid represents the actual percentage of insurance carried (up to 80%), which is then divided by the required 80%. **See Figure 7-7**.

Figure 7-7

HOW NONRESIDENTIAL COINSURANCE WORKS

1. Actual value of your improvements	=	$200,000
2. 80% coinsurance clause requires you to carry fire insurance on 80% of the actual value of the dwelling. (80% of $200,000)	=	$160,000
3. Amount of fire insurance carried (Face amount on your policy)	=	**$120,000**
4. Ratio of loss payment $120,000 (actual amount) $160,000 (required amount)	=	75%
5. If your actual fire loss is	=	$80,000
6. Your insurance would pay 75% of actual loss (75% of $80,000)	=	$60,000
7. Your out-of-pocket cost would be the loss less insurance payments ($80,000 - $60,000)	=	**$20,000**

VI. Title Insurance

A. CHAIN OF TITLE (Recorded Public History)

Abstract of title: a written summary of a property's documents that evidences title.

If one person sells a property to another person, *a recorded public history of a specific property called the CHAIN OF TITLE* is compiled. These public records include files at the county recorder's office, various tax agencies, federal court clerk, and the Secretary of State. *All such information about people and their real property is stored in computers (within a grantor-grantee index) and is referred to as a TITLE PLANT.*

A title insurance company is primarily concerned with a search of the public records, which includes: the Federal Lands Office, the County Clerk's Office, the County Recorder's Office and other sources. This search establishes what is called the "chain of title."

B. TITLE INSURANCE (Has Four Functions)

Title insurance companies are regulated by the California Insurance Commissioner. Fee schedules must be available to the general public upon request. To guarantee solvency, each title insurance company must set aside reserves.

Because many things outside the public record can affect the legality of title, title insurance functions to protect the insured.

TITLE INSURANCE also insures a lender (and property owner for an additional fee) against losses that result from imperfections in title. Title insurance companies examine the records documenting chain of title, review any risks that might not be found in the public records, interpret legality, help the seller correct any defects, and insure marketable title to the property. Title insurance is only paid once, unlike auto or fire insurance, which must be paid annually. **Figure 7-8** emphasizes the four most important functions of title insurance.

C. PRELIMINARY TITLE REPORT (Ordered First)

The first step in a title search is the ordering of the preliminary title report by the escrow officer. After the buyer or borrower completes a statement of information, a title search can begin. **See Figure 7-9.** A *PRELIMINARY TITLE REPORT is a report showing the condition of title before a sale or loan transaction.* After completion of the transaction, a title insurance policy is issued. The preliminary title report consists of the following items:

Figure 7-8

Title Insurance

A SEARCH OF RECORDS	EXAMINES "OFF" RECORD RISKS	INTERPRETS LEGALITY OF RECORDS	INSURES AGAINST ECONOMIC LOSS

1. The name of the owner and a description of the property.

2. A list of any outstanding taxes, bonds, or other assessments.

3. The identity of any covenants, conditions or restrictions.

4. Any recorded liens or other encumbrances that must be eliminated before any loan is made.

A "preliminary title report" gives the current status of items from the county records that affect the property's title.

VII. Types of Title Insurance Policies

All title insurance policies in California cover policyholders as of the date of the policy.

A. CALIFORNIA LAND TITLE ASSOCIATION (CLTA)
(Standard Coverage Policy)

In California, the standard title insurance policy is the CLTA. The **CALIFORNIA LAND TITLE ASSOCIATION (CLTA)** *policy is the basic title insurance policy.* It may be issued to insure a lender only, or an owner only, or it may insure both the lender and the owner (a joint-protection standard coverage policy). This standard policy insures the lender only, unless the owner requests and pays for owner coverage.

CLTA is the acronym for the state trade association, California Land Title Association®.

Figure 7-10 is a sample of a standard CLTA policy form.

Besides insuring against all items of record, the CLTA policy offers protection against many off-record risks. Some of these off-record risks include forgeries, acts of minors

Figure 7-9   **PRELIMINARY TITLE REPORT**

Complete, Sign and Return
STATEMENT OF INFORMATION

Order No. 5278

To expedite the completion of your escrow, please fill out and return this form at your earliest convenience. This information is for confidential use by North American Title Company in searching the land records in connection with the order number shown above. Further explanation of the need for this information is printed on the reverse side of this form.

Please Print all information

PERSONAL IDENTIFICATION

Name

_____
FIRST NAME   FULL MIDDLE NAME—IF NONE, INDICATE   LAST NAME

Year of Birth _____ Birthplace _____ Social Security No. _____

Full name of Wife
Husband _____
FIRST NAME   FULL MIDDLE NAME—IF NONE, INDICATE   LAST NAME

Year of Birth _____ Birthplace _____ Social Security No. _____

We were married on _____ at _____
DATE   CITY AND STATE

Wife's maiden name _____

RESIDENCES DURING PAST 10 YEARS

NUMBER AND STREET	CITY	FROM (DATE)	TO (DATE)
NUMBER AND STREET	CITY	FROM (DATE)	TO (DATE)
NUMBER AND STREET	CITY	FROM (DATE)	TO (DATE)

(If more space is needed, use reverse side of form)

OCCUPATIONS DURING PAST 10 YEARS

Husband's

OCCUPATION	FIRM NAME	STREET AND CITY	FROM (DATE) TO (DATE)
OCCUPATION	FIRM NAME	STREET AND CITY	FROM (DATE) TO (DATE)
OCCUPATION	FIRM NAME	STREET AND CITY	FROM (DATE) TO (DATE)

Wife's

OCCUPATION	FIRM NAME	STREET AND CITY	FROM (DATE) TO (DATE)
OCCUPATION	FIRM NAME	STREET AND CITY	FROM (DATE) TO (DATE)

(If more space is needed, use reverse side of form)

FORMER MARRIAGE(S), IF ANY

If no former marriages, write "None" _____ Otherwise, please complete the following:

Name of former wife _____

Deceased ☐   Divorced ☐   When _____ Where _____

Name of former husband _____

Deceased ☐   Divorced ☐   When _____ Where _____

(If more space is needed, use reverse side of form)

Buyer intends to reside on the property in this transaction   Yes ☐   No ☐

THIS PORTION IS TO BE COMPLETED BY THE SELLER

The Street Address of the property in this transaction is _____
(LEAVE BLANK IF NONE)

The land is unimproved ☐ or improved with a structure of the following type;

IMPROVEMENTS: ☐ SINGLE RESIDENCE OR 1-4 FAMILY   ☐ MULTIPLE RESIDENCE   ☐ COMMERCIAL

OCCUPIED BY: ☐ OWNER   ☐ LESSEE   ☐ TENANTS

ANY PORTION OF NEW LOAN FUNDS TO BE USED FOR CONSTRUCTION

IMPROVEMENTS, REMODELING OR REPAIRS TO THIS PROPERTY HAVE BEEN MADE WITHIN THE PAST SIX MONTHS   ☐ YES   ☐ NO

IF YES,

HAVE ALL COSTS FOR LABOR AND MATERIALS ARISING IN CONNECTION THEREWITH BEEN PAID IN FULL?   ☐ YES   ☐ NO

The undersigned declare, under penalty of perjury, that the foregoing is true and correct.

DATE _____   _____

HOME   BUSINESS
PHONE _____ PHONE _____   _____
                                          (IF MARRIED, BOTH HUSBAND AND WIFE SHOULD SIGN)

NAT 44 (5/88)

Figure 7-10

POLICY OF TITLE INSURANCE

ISSUED BY

SUBJECT TO THE EXCLUSIONS FROM COVERAGE, THE EXCEPTIONS FROM COVERAGE CONTAINED IN SCHEDULE B AND THE CONDITIONS AND STIPULATIONS, NORTH AMERICAN TITLE INSURANCE COMPANY, a California corporation, herein called the Company, insures, as of Date of Policy shown in Schedule A, against loss or damage, not exceeding the Amount of Insurance stated in Schedule A, sustained or incurred by the insured by reason of:

1. Title to the estate or interest described in Schedule A being vested otherwise than as stated therein;
2. Any defect in or lien or encumbrance on such title;
3. Unmarketability of the title;
4. Lack of a right of access to and from the land;
5. The invalidity or unenforceability of the lien of the insured mortgage upon the title;
6. The priority of any lien or encumbrance over the lien of the insured mortgage;
7. Lack of priority of the lien of the insured mortgage over any statutory lien for services, labor or material:
    (a) arising from an improvement or work related to the land which is contracted for or commenced prior to Date of Policy; or
    (b) arising from an improvement or work related to the land which is contracted for or commenced subsequent to Date of Policy and which is financed in whole or in part by proceeds of the indebtedness secured by the insured mortgage which at Date of Policy the insured has advanced or is obligated to advance.
8. Any assessments for street improvements under construction or completed at Date of Policy which now have gained or hereafter may gain priority over the insured mortgage; or
9. The invalidity or unenforceability of any assignment of the insured mortgage, provided the assignment is shown in Schedule A, or the failure of the assignment shown in Schedule A to vest title to the insured mortgage in the named insured assignee free and clear of all liens.

The Company will also pay the costs, attorneys' fees and expenses incurred in defense of the title or the lien of the insured mortgage, as insured, but only to the extent provided in the Conditions and Stipulations.

NORTH AMERICAN TITLE INSURANCE COMPANY

BY *Gerald B Beery* PRESIDENT

ATTEST _____ SECRETARY

FORM NO. 6056-87 (4-6-90)
ALTA LOAN POLICY
FORM 1

SCHEDULE A

POLICY NO. 116823   FILE NO.: 14-15360-63

AMOUNT OF INSURANCE: $296,800.00   PREMIUM: $1,161.75

DATE OF POLICY: JULY 22, 1992 AT 8:00 A.M.

1. **NAME OF INSURED:**

   SYCAMORE FINANCIAL GROUP, INC., A CALIFORNIA CORPORATION

2. **THE ESTATE OR INTEREST IN THE LAND WHICH IS ENCUMBERED BY THE INSURED MORTGAGE IS:**

   A CONDOMINIUM, AS DEFINED IN SECTION 783 OF THE CALIFORNIA CIVIL CODE, IN FEE

3. **TITLE TO THE ESTATE OR INTEREST IN THE LAND IS VESTED IN:**

   WALTER ROY HUBER AND DEBBIE R. HUBER, HUSBAND AND WIFE AS COMMUNITY PROPERTY

4. **THE INSURED MORTGAGE AND ASSIGNMENTS THEREOF, IF ANY, ARE DESCRIBED AS FOLLOWS:**

   A DEED OF TRUST TO SECURE AN INDEBTEDNESS IN THE AMOUNT SHOWN BELOW AND ANY OTHER OBLIGATIONS SECURED THEREBY:

   RECORDED: JULY 22, 1992 AS INSTRUMENT NO. 92-1329290 OF OFFICIAL RECORDS
   AMOUNT: $296,800.00
   DATED: JULY 13, 1992
   TRUSTOR: WALTER ROY HUBER AND DEBBIE R. HUBER, HUSBAND AND WIFE AS COMMUNITY PROPERTY
   TRUSTEE: UTICA ESCROW INC., A CALIFORNIA CORPORATION
   BENEFICIARY: SYCAMORE FINANCIAL GROUP, INC., A CALIFORNIA CORPORATION

5. **THE LAND REFERRED TO IN THIS POLICY IS DESCRIBED AS FOLLOWS:**

   PARCEL 1:

   THAT PORTION OF PARCEL A OF PARCEL MAP L.A. NO. 3111, IN THE CITY OF LOS ANGELES, COUNTY OF LOS ANGELES, STATE OF CALIFORNIA, AS PER MAP FILED IN BOOK 72 PAGE 26 OF PARCEL MAPS, IN THE OFFICE OF THE COUNTY RECORDER OF SAID COUNTY, SHOWN AND DEFINED AS UNIT 1 AND AIR SPACE A ON THE CONDOMINIUM PLAN, RECORDED DECEMBER 17, 1976 AS INSTRUMENT NO. 5334, OF OFFICIAL RECORDS OF SAID COUNTY.

   PARCEL 2:

   AN UNDIVIDED 1/4 INTEREST IN AND TO PARCEL A OF SAID PARCEL MAP LOS ANGELES NO. 3111.

   EXCEPT THEREFROM THOSE PORTIONS SHOWN AND DEFINED AS UNITS 1 TO 4 AND AIR SPACE A AND B ON SAID CONDOMINIUM PLAN.

EXCLUSIONS FROM COVERAGE

The following matters are expressly excluded from the coverage of this policy and the Company will not pay loss or damage, costs, attorneys' fees or expenses which arise by reason of:

1. (a) Any law, ordinance or governmental regulation (including but not limited to building and zoning laws, ordinances, or regulations) restricting, regulating, prohibiting or relating to (i) the occupancy, use, or enjoyment of the land; (ii) the character, dimensions or location of any improvement now or hereafter erected on the land; (iii) a separation in ownership or a change in the dimensions or area of the land or any parcel of which the land is or was a part; or (iv) environmental protection, or the effect of any violation of these laws, ordinances or governmental regulations, except to the extent that a notice of the enforcement thereof or a notice of a defect, lien or encumbrance resulting from a violation or alleged violation affecting the land has been recorded in the public records at Date of Policy.
   (b) Any governmental police power not excluded by (a) above, except to the extent that a notice of the exercise thereof or a notice of a defect, lien or encumbrance resulting from a violation or alleged violation affecting the land has been recorded in the public records at Date of Policy.
2. Rights of eminent domain unless notice of the exercise thereof has been recorded in the public records at Date of Policy, but not excluding from coverage any taking which has occurred prior to Date of Policy which would be binding on the rights of a purchaser for value without knowledge.
3. Defects, liens, encumbrances, adverse claims or other matters:
   (a) created, suffered, assumed or agreed to by the insured claimant;
   (b) not known to the Company, not recorded in the public records at Date of Policy, but known to the insured claimant and not disclosed in writing to the Company by the insured claimant prior to the date the insured claimant became an insured under this policy;
   (c) resulting in no loss or damage to the insured claimant;
   (d) attaching or created subsequent to Date of Policy (except to the extent that this policy insures the priority of the lien of the insured mortgage over any statutory lien for services, labor or material or the extent insurance is afforded herein as to assessments for street improvements under construction or completed at Date of Policy); or
   (e) resulting in loss or damage which would not have been sustained if the insured claimant had paid value for the insured mortgage.
4. Unenforceability of the lien of the insured mortgage because of the inability or failure of the insured at Date of Policy, or the inability or failure of any subsequent owner of the indebtedness, to comply with applicable doing business laws of the state in which the land is situated.
5. Invalidity or unenforceability of the lien of the insured mortgage, or claim thereof, which arises out of the transaction evidenced by the insured mortgage and is based upon usury or any consumer credit protection or truth in lending law.
6. Any statutory lien for services, labor or materials (or the claim of priority of any statutory lien for services, labor or materials over the lien of the insured mortgage) arising from an improvement or work related to the land which is contracted for and commenced subsequent to Date of Policy and is not financed in whole or in part by proceeds of the indebtedness secured by the insured mortgage which at Date of Policy the insured has advanced or is obligated to advance.
7. Any claim, which arises out of the transaction creating the interest of the mortgagee insured by this policy, by reason of the operation of federal bankruptcy, state insolvency, or similar creditors' rights laws.

CONDITIONS AND STIPULATIONS

1. DEFINITION OF TERMS.

The following terms when used in this policy mean:

(a) "insured": the insured named in Schedule A. The term "insured" also includes

(i) the owner of the indebtedness secured by the insured mortgage and each successor in ownership of the indebtedness except a successor who is an obligor under the provisions of Section 12(c) of these Conditions and Stipulations (reserving, however, all rights and defenses as to any successor that the Company would have had against any predecessor insured, unless the successor acquired the indebtedness as a purchaser for value without knowledge of the asserted defect, lien, encumbrance, adverse claim or other matter insured against by this policy as affecting title to the estate or interest in the land);

(ii) any governmental agency or governmental instrumentality which is an insurer or guarantor under an insurance contract or guaranty insuring or guaranteeing the indebtedness secured by the insured mortgage, or any part thereof, whether named as an insured herein or not;

(iii) the parties designated in Section 2(a) of these Conditions and Stipulations.

(b) "insured claimant": an insured claiming loss or damage.

(c) "knowledge" or "known": actual knowledge, not constructive knowledge or notice which may be imputed to an insured by reason of the public records as defined in this policy or any other records which impart constructive notice of matters affecting the land.

(d) "land": the land described or referred to in Schedule (A), and improvements affixed thereto which by law constitute real property. The term "land" does not include any property beyond the lines of the area described or referred to in Schedule (A), nor any right, title, interest, estate or easement in abutting streets, roads, avenues, alleys, lanes, ways or waterways, but nothing herein shall modify or limit the extent to which a right of access to and from the land is insured by this policy.

(e) "mortgage": mortgage, deed of trust, trust deed, or other security instrument.

(f) "public records": records established under state statutes at Date of Policy for the purpose of imparting constructive notice of matters relating to real property to purchasers for value and without knowledge. With respect to Section 1(a)(iv) of the Exclusions From Coverage, "public records" shall also include environmental protection liens filed in the records of the clerk of the United States district court for the district in which the land is located.

(g) "unmarketability of the title": an alleged or apparent matter affecting the title to the land, not excluded or excepted from coverage, which would entitle a purchaser of the estate or interest described in Schedule A or the insured mortgage to be released from the obligation to purchase by virtue of a contractual condition requiring the delivery of marketable title.

2. CONTINUATION OF INSURANCE.

(a) **After Acquisition of Title.** The coverage of this policy shall continue in force as of Date of Policy in favor of (i) an insured who acquires all or any part of the estate or interest in the land by foreclosure, trustee's sale, conveyance in lieu of foreclosure, or other legal manner which discharges the lien of the insured mortgage; (ii) a transferee of the estate or interest so acquired from an insured corporation, provided the transferee is the parent or wholly-owned subsidiary of the insured corporation, and their corporate successors by operation of law and not by purchase, subject to any rights or defenses the Company may have against any predecessor insureds; and (iii) any governmental agency or governmental instrumentality which acquires all or any part of the estate or interest pursuant to a contract of insurance or guaranty insuring or guaranteeing the indebtedness secured by the insured mortgage.

settlement, and (ii) in any other lawful act which in the opinion of the Company may be necessary or desirable to establish the title to the estate or interest or the lien of the insured mortgage, as insured. If the Company is prejudiced by the failure of the insured to furnish the required cooperation, the Company's obligations to the insured under the policy shall terminate, including any liability or obligation to defend, prosecute, or continue any litigation, with regard to the matter or matters requiring such cooperation.

5. PROOF OF LOSS OR DAMAGE.

In addition to and after the notices required under Section 3 of these Conditions and Stipulations have been provided the Company, a proof of loss or damage signed and sworn to by the insured claimant shall be furnished to the Company within 90 days after the insured claimant shall ascertain the facts giving rise to the loss or damage. The proof of loss or damage shall describe the defect in, or lien or encumbrance on the title, or other matter insured against by this policy which constitutes the basis of loss or damage and shall state, to the extent possible, the basis of calculating the amount of the loss or damage. If the Company is prejudiced by the failure of the insured claimant to provide the required proof of loss or damage, the Company's obligations to the insured under the policy shall terminate, including any liability or obligation to defend, prosecute, or continue any litigation, with regard to the matter or matters requiring such proof of loss or damage.

In addition, the insured claimant may reasonably be required to submit to examination under oath by any authorized representative of the Company and shall produce for examination, inspection and copying, at such reasonable times and places as may be designated by any authorized representative of the Company, all records, books, ledgers, checks, correspondence and memoranda, whether bearing a date before or after Date of Policy, which reasonably pertain to the loss or damage. Further, if requested by any authorized representative of the Company, the insured claimant shall grant its permission, in writing, for any authorized representative of the Company to examine, inspect and copy all records, books, ledgers, checks, correspondence and memoranda in the custody or control of a third party, which reasonably pertain to the loss or damage. All information designated as confidential by the insured claimant provided to the Company pursuant to this Section shall not be disclosed to others unless, in the reasonable judgment of the Company, it is necessary in the administration of the claim. Failure of the insured claimant to submit for examination under oath, produce other reasonably requested information or grant permission to secure reasonably necessary information from third parties as required in this paragraph, unless prohibited by law or governmental regulation, shall terminate any liability of the Company under this policy as to that claim.

the insured was and continued to be obligated to advance at and after Date of Policy.

9. REDUCTION OF INSURANCE; REDUCTION OR TERMINATION OF LIABILITY.

(a) All payments under this policy, except payments made for costs, attorneys' fees and expenses, shall reduce the amount of the insurance pro tanto. However, any payments made prior to the acquisition of title to the estate or interest as provided in Section 2(a) of these Conditions and Stipulations shall not reduce pro tanto the amount of the insurance afforded under this policy except to the extent that the payments reduce the amount of the indebtedness secured by the insured mortgage.

(b) Payment in part by any person of the principal of the indebtedness, or any other obligation secured by the insured mortgage, or any voluntary partial satisfaction or release of the insured mortgage, to the extent of the payment, satisfaction or release, shall reduce the amount of insurance pro tanto. The amount of insurance may thereafter be increased by accruing interest and advances made to protect the lien of the insured mortgage and secured thereby, with interest thereon, provided in no event shall the amount of insurance be greater than the amount of insurance stated in Schedule A.

(c) Payment in full by any person or the voluntary satisfaction or release of the insured mortgage shall terminate all liability of the Company except as provided in Section 2(a) of these Conditions and Stipulations.

10. LIABILITY NONCUMULATIVE.

If the insured acquires title to the estate or interest in satisfaction of the indebtedness secured by the insured mortgage, or any part thereof, it is expressly understood that the amount of insurance under this policy shall be reduced by any amount the Company may pay under any policy insuring a mortgage to which exception is taken in Schedule B or to which the insured has agreed, assumed, or taken subject, or which is hereafter executed by an insured and which is a charge or lien on the estate or interest described or referred to in Schedule A, and the amount so paid shall be deemed a payment under this policy.

11. PAYMENT OF LOSS.

(a) No payment shall be made without producing this policy for endorsement of the payment unless the policy has been lost or destroyed, in which case proof of loss or destruction shall be furnished to the satisfaction of the Company.

(b) When liability and the extent of loss or damage has been definitely fixed in accordance with these Conditions and Stipulations, the loss or damage shall be payable within 30 days thereafter.

(b) **After Conveyance of Title.** The coverage of this policy shall continue in force as of Date of Policy in favor of an insured only so long as the insured retains an estate or interest in the land, or holds an indebtedness secured by a purchase money mortgage given by a purchaser from the insured, or only so long as the insured shall have liability by reason of covenants of warranty made by the insured in any transfer or conveyance of the estate or interest. This policy shall not continue in force in favor of any purchaser from the insured of either (i) an estate or interest in the land, or (ii) an indebtedness secured by a purchase money mortgage given to the insured.

(c) **Amount of Insurance:** The amount of insurance after the acquisition or after the conveyance shall in neither event exceed the least of:

(i) the amount of insurance stated in Schedule A;

(ii) the amount of the principal of the indebtedness secured by the insured mortgage as of Date of Policy, interest thereon, expenses of foreclosure, amounts advanced pursuant to the insured mortgage to assure compliance with laws or to protect the lien of the insured mortgage prior to the time of acquisition of the estate or interest in the land and secured thereby and reasonable amounts expended to prevent deterioration of improvements, but reduced by the amount of all payments made; or

(iii) the amount paid by any governmental agency or governmental instrumentality, if the agency or instrumentality is the insured claimant, in the acquisition of the estate or interest in satisfaction of its insurance contract or guaranty.

3. NOTICE OF CLAIM TO BE GIVEN BY INSURED CLAIMANT.

The insured shall notify the Company promptly in writing (i) in case of any litigation as set forth in Section 4(a) below, (ii) in case knowledge shall come to an insured hereunder of any claim of title or interest which is adverse to the title to the estate or interest or the lien of the insured mortgage, as insured, and which might cause loss or damage for which the Company may be liable by virtue of this policy, or (iii) if title to the estate or interest or the lien of the insured mortgage, as insured, is rejected as unmarketable. If prompt notice shall not be given to the Company, then as to the insured all liability of the Company shall terminate with regard to the matter or matters for which prompt notice is required; provided, however, that failure to notify the Company shall in no case prejudice the rights of any insured under this policy unless the Company shall be prejudiced by the failure and then only to the extent of the prejudice.

4. DEFENSE AND PROSECUTION OF ACTIONS; DUTY OF INSURED CLAIMANT TO COOPERATE.

(a) Upon written request by the insured and subject to the options contained in Section 6 of these Conditions and Stipulations, the Company, at its own cost and without unreasonable delay, shall provide for the defense of an insured in litigation in which any third party asserts a claim adverse to the title or interest as insured, but only as to those stated causes of action alleging a defect, lien or encumbrance or other matter insured against by this policy. The Company shall have the right to select counsel of its choice (subject to the right of the insured to object for reasonable cause) to represent the insured as to those stated causes of action and shall not be liable for and will not pay the fees of any other counsel. The Company will not pay any fees, costs or expenses incurred by the insured in the defense of those causes of action which allege matters not insured against by this policy.

(b) The Company shall have the right, at its own cost, to institute and prosecute any action or proceeding or to do any other act which in its opinion may be necessary or desirable to establish the title to the estate or interest or the lien of the insured mortgage, as insured, or to prevent or reduce loss or damage to the insured. The Company may take any appropriate action under the terms of this policy, whether or not it shall be liable hereunder, and shall not thereby concede liability or waive any provision of this policy. If the Company shall exercise its rights under this paragraph, it shall do so diligently.

(c) Whenever the Company shall have brought an action or interposed a defense as required or permitted by the provisions of this policy, the Company may pursue any litigation to final determination by a court of competent jurisdiction and expressly reserves the right, in its sole discretion, to appeal from any adverse judgment or order.

(d) In all cases where this policy permits or requires the Company to prosecute or provide for the defense of any action or proceeding, the insured shall secure to the Company the right to so prosecute or provide defense in the action or proceeding, and all appeals therein, and permit the Company to use, at its option, the name of the insured for this purpose. Whenever requested by the Company, the insured, at the Company's expense, shall give the Company all reasonable aid (i) in any action or proceeding, securing evidence, obtaining witnesses, prosecuting or defending the action or proceeding, or effecting

6. OPTIONS TO PAY OR OTHERWISE SETTLE CLAIMS; TERMINATION OF LIABILITY.

In case of a claim under this policy, the Company shall have the following options:

(a) To Pay or Tender Payment of the Amount of Insurance or to Purchase the Indebtedness.

(i) to pay or tender payment of the amount of insurance under this policy together with any costs, attorneys' fees and expenses incurred by the insured claimant, which were authorized by the Company, up to the time of payment or tender of payment and which the Company is obligated to pay; or

(ii) to purchase the indebtedness secured by the insured mortgage for the amount owing thereon together with any costs, attorneys' fees and expenses incurred by the insured claimant which were authorized by the Company up to the time of purchase and which the Company is obligated to pay.

If the Company offers to purchase the indebtedness as herein provided, the owner of the indebtedness shall transfer, assign, and convey the indebtedness and the insured mortgage, together with any collateral security, to the Company upon payment therefor.

Upon the exercise by the Company of either of the options provided for in paragraphs a(i) or (ii), all liability and obligations to the insured under this policy, other than to make the payment required in those paragraphs, shall terminate, including any liability or obligation to defend, prosecute, or continue any litigation, and the policy shall be surrendered to the Company for cancellation.

(b) To Pay or Otherwise Settle With Parties Other than the Insured or With the Insured Claimant.

(i) to pay or otherwise settle with other parties for or in the name of an insured claimant any claim insured against under this policy, together with any costs, attorneys' fees and expenses incurred by the insured claimant which were authorized by the Company up to the time of payment and which the Company is obligated to pay; or

(ii) to pay or otherwise settle with the insured claimant the loss or damage provided for under this policy, together with any costs, attorneys' fees and expenses incurred by the insured claimant which were authorized by the Company up to the time of payment and which the Company is obligated to pay.

Upon the exercise by the Company of either of the options provided for in paragraphs b(i) or (ii), the Company's obligations to the insured under this policy for the claimed loss or damage, other than the payments required to be made, shall terminate, including any liability or obligation to defend, prosecute or continue any litigation.

7. DETERMINATION AND EXTENT OF LIABILITY.

This policy is a contract of indemnity against actual monetary loss or damage sustained or incurred by the insured claimant who has suffered loss or damage by reason of matters insured against by this policy and only to the extent herein described.

(a) The liability of the Company under this policy shall not exceed the least of:

(i) the amount of insurance stated in Schedule A, or, if applicable, the amount of insurance as defined in Section 2 (c) of these Conditions and Stipulations;

(ii) the amount of the unpaid principal indebtedness secured by the insured mortgage as limited or provided under Section 8 of these Conditions and Stipulations or as reduced under Section 9 of these Conditions and Stipulations, at the time the loss or damage insured against by this policy occurs, together with interest thereon; or

(iii) the difference between the value of the insured estate or interest as insured and the value of the insured estate or interest subject to the defect, lien or encumbrance insured against by this policy.

(b) In the event the insured has acquired the estate or interest in the manner described in Section 2(a) of these Conditions and Stipulations or has conveyed the title, then the liability of the Company shall continue as set forth in Section 7(a) of these Conditions and Stipulations.

(c) The Company will pay only those costs, attorneys' fees and expenses incurred in accordance with Section 4 of these Conditions and Stipulations.

8. LIMITATION OF LIABILITY.

(a) If the Company establishes the title, or removes the alleged defect, lien or encumbrance, or cures the lack of a right of access to or from the land, or cures the claim of unmarketability of title, or otherwise establishes the lien of the insured mortgage, all as insured, in a reasonably diligent manner by any method, including litigation and the completion of any appeals therefrom, it shall have fully performed its obligations with respect to that matter and shall not be liable for any loss or damage caused thereby.

(b) In the event of any litigation, including litigation by the Company or with the Company's consent, the Company shall have no liability for loss or damage until there has been a final determination by a court of competent jurisdiction, and disposition of all appeals therefrom, adverse to the title or to the lien of the insured mortgage, as insured.

(c) The Company shall not be liable for loss or damage to any insured for liability voluntarily assumed by the insured in settling any claim or suit without the prior written consent of the Company.

(d) The Company shall not be liable for:

(i) any indebtedness created subsequent to Date of Policy except for advances made to protect the lien of the insured mortgage and secured thereby and reasonable amounts expended to prevent deterioration of improvements; or

(ii) construction loan advances made subsequent to Date of Policy, except construction loan advances made subsequent to Date of Policy for the purpose of financing in whole or in part the construction of an improvement to the land which at Date of Policy were secured by the insured mortgage and which

12. SUBROGATION UPON PAYMENT OR SETTLEMENT.

(a) The Company's Right of Subrogation.

Whenever the Company shall have settled and paid a claim under this policy, all right of subrogation shall vest in the Company unaffected by any act of the insured claimant.

The Company shall be subrogated to and be entitled to all rights and remedies which the insured claimant would have had against any person or property in respect to the claim had this policy not been issued. If requested by the Company, the insured claimant shall transfer to the Company all rights and remedies against any person or property necessary in order to perfect this right of subrogation. The insured claimant shall permit the Company to sue, compromise or settle in the name of the insured claimant and to use the name of the insured claimant in any transaction or litigation involving these rights or remedies.

If a payment on account of a claim does not fully cover the loss of the insured claimant, the Company shall be subrogated to all rights and remedies of the insured claimant after the insured claimant shall have recovered its principal, interest, and costs of collection.

(b) The Insured's Rights and Limitations.

Notwithstanding the foregoing, the owner of the indebtedness secured by the insured mortgage, provided the priority of the lien of the insured mortgage or its enforceability is not affected, may release or substitute the personal liability of any debtor or guarantor, or extend or otherwise modify the terms of payment, or release a portion of the estate or interest from the lien of the insured mortgage, or release any collateral security for the indebtedness.

When the permitted acts of the insured claimant occur and the insured has knowledge of any claim of title or interest adverse to the title to the estate or interest or the priority or enforceability of the lien of the insured mortgage, as insured, the Company shall be required to pay only that part of any losses insured against by this policy which shall exceed the amount, if any, lost to the Company by reason of the impairment by the insured claimant of the Company's right of subrogation.

(c) The Company's Rights Against Non-insured Obligors.

The Company's right of subrogation against non-insured obligors shall exist and shall include, without limitation, the rights of the insured to indemnities, guaranties, other policies of insurance or bonds, notwithstanding any terms or conditions contained in those instruments which provide for subrogation rights by reason of this policy.

The Company's right of subrogation shall not be avoided by acquisition of the insured mortgage by an obligor (except an obligor described in Section 1(a)(ii) of these Conditions and Stipulations) who acquires the insured mortgage as a result of an indemnity, guarantee, other policy of insurance, or bond and the obligor will not be an insured under this policy, notwithstanding Section 1(a)(i) of these Conditions and Stipulations.

13. ARBITRATION.

Unless prohibited by applicable law, either the Company or the insured may demand arbitration pursuant to the Title Insurance Arbitration Rules of the American Arbitration Association. Arbitrable matters may include, but are not limited to, any controversy or claim between the Company and the insured arising out of or relating to this policy, any service of the Company in connection with its issuance or the breach of a policy provision or other obligation. All arbitrable matters when the Amount of Insurance is $1,000,000 or less shall be arbitrated at the option of either the Company or the insured. All arbitrable matters when the Amount of Insurance is in excess of $1,000,000 shall be arbitrated only when agreed to by both the Company and the insured. Arbitration pursuant to this policy and under the Rules in effect on the date the demand for arbitration is made or, at the option of the insured, the Rules in effect at Date of Policy shall be binding upon the parties. The award may include attorneys' fees only if the laws of the state in which the land is located permit a court to award attorneys' fees to a prevailing party. Judgment upon the award rendered by the Arbitrator(s) may be entered in any court having jurisdiction thereof.

The law of the situs of the land shall apply to an arbitration under the Title Insurance Arbitration Rules.

A copy of the Rules may be obtained from the Company upon request.

14. LIABILITY LIMITED TO THIS POLICY; POLICY ENTIRE CONTRACT.

(a) This policy together with all endorsements, if any, attached hereto by the Company is the entire policy and contract between the insured and the Company. In interpreting any provision of this policy, this policy shall be construed as a whole.

(b) Any claim of loss or damage, whether or not based on negligence, and which arises out of the status of the lien of the insured mortgage or of the title to the estate or interest covered hereby or by any action asserting such claim, shall be restricted to this policy.

(c) No amendment of or endorsement to this policy can be made except by a writing endorsed hereon or attached hereto signed by either the President, a Vice President, the Secretary, an Assistant Secretary, or validating officer or authorized signatory of the Company.

15. SEVERABILITY.

In the event any provision of this policy is held invalid or unenforceable under applicable law, the policy shall be deemed not to include that provision and all other provisions shall remain in full force and effect.

16. NOTICES, WHERE SENT.

All notices required to be given the Company and any statement in writing required to be furnished the Company shall include the number of this policy and shall be addressed to the Company at 114 East Fifth Street, Santa Ana, California 92701, or to the office which issued this policy.

and incompetents, acts of an agent whose authority has terminated, invalid deed delivery, unrecorded federal estate tax liens, undisclosed rights of husband and wife when the chain of title states "unmarried," and the expenses (including attorneys' fees) incurred in defending title.

The "standard" and most common title insurance policy in California is the CLTA policy (no survey). The CLTA policy protects against: 1) Someone else who owns a recorded interest in your title; 2) A document not properly signed; 3) Forgery, fraud, duress, incompetency; 4) Defective recording of a document; 5) Unmarketability of title; 6) Restrictive covenants; 7) Lack of a right of access to and from the land.

It is very important to note those items not included in the standard policy. The items not included are:

1. Easements, encumbrances, and liens that are not shown by the public record.
2. Rights or claims of persons in physical possession of the land.
3. Unrecorded claims not shown by the public record that could be ascertained by physical inspection or correct survey.
4. Mining claims, reservations in patents, water rights, and government actions, such as zoning ordinances.

Standard title insurance (CLTA) does NOT insure against undisclosed liens placed on a property by a grantor (although it is warranted in a grant deed). NO title insurance policy covers everything.

---

www.clta.org

Alliance for Open Real Estate Records

California Land Title Association
PO Box 13968, Sacramento CA 95853-3968
1110 K Street, #100, Sacramento, CA 95814-3905
tel: 916-444-2647 * fax: 916-444-2851
web: www.clta.org * email: mail@clta.org

email CLTA

Insuring the American Dream

News

Get Acrobat Reader
Click here to download Acrobat Reader.

This is required to view all "PDF" files found on this website. Clicking on the link above will take you to the Adobe Acrobat Reader download page which provides complete instructions on how to download and install the plug-in. Once this has been completed you will be able to view acrobat files ("pdf")

Administrative Law Judge Ruling Protects Consumers - California DOI Cease-and-Desist Order Affirmed - News Express.
An Administrative Law Judge affirmed state laws that protect consumers by ruling against the Radian Corporation's attempt to introduce unregulated, unlicensed, and incomplete title insurance products to the California market. The California Land Title Association, which sets and monitors professional standards and education for the title insurance industry, praised the judge's decision

DOI Privacy Regulations Adopted - News Express.
The Department of Insurance filed privacy regulations with the California Office of Administrative Law on November 22, 2002 which become effective

B. AMERICAN LAND TITLE ASSOCIATION (ALTA)
(Extended Coverage Policy - Survey Included)

Most lenders require more protection than provided for by the standard coverage (CLTA) policy. They require the extended coverage (ALTA) policy.

The **AMERICAN LAND TITLE ASSOCIATION (ALTA)** *policy is an extended coverage policy that insures against many exclusions of the standard coverage (CLTA) policy.* The ALTA policy (which includes a competent survey or physical inspection) is usually required by California lenders and by out-of-state lenders who are not able to make a personal physical inspection of the property.

An extended ALTA title insurance policy is a lender's policy. It protects only the lender. If an owner wants this kind of protection, he or she should request the extended ALTA Owner's Policy.

Purchasers should note that there are still certain exceptions to the CLTA standard policy and even to the ALTA extended policy. There is no insurance coverage for the following:

1) Defects known to the insured at the time the policy was issued, but not designated in writing, and 2) government regulations regarding occupancy and use (zoning).

NO title insurance protects against governmental regulations (zoning changes) or defects known to the insured.

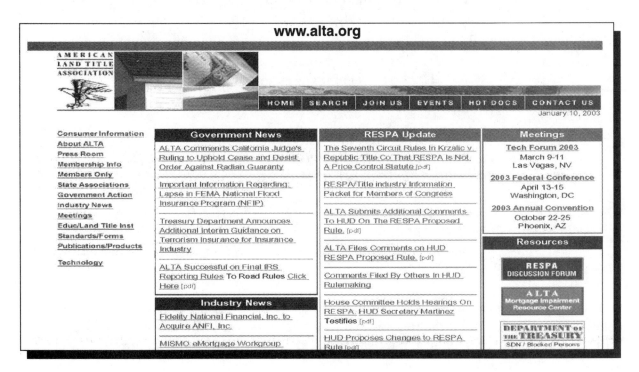

C. ALTA-R (One-to-Four Residential Units)

The **ALTA-R POLICY** *is recommended by title companies for one-to-four unit owner-occupied residential dwellings.* It doesn't include a survey because the property lines are already established by a recorded subdivision map. Since the title company does not have to do a survey, it gives the buyer more coverage for the same price. The CAR® deposit receipt includes the ALTA-R as the preferred residential title policy choice.

D. WHO PAYS TITLE INSURANCE FEES?

Title insurance fees are a part of the escrow closing costs. Title insurance companies are required to publish rate schedules and charge according to the published rates. Who assumes payment of the fees, however, varies depending upon the area in which one lives.

In Southern California it is customary for the seller to pay the title fees, whereas in Northern California it is usually the buyer who assumes the cost. Because there is no law determining who must pay, it should be stated in the deposit receipt to prevent any misunderstanding. This, however, covers only the standard CLTA policy. The additional cost of the ALTA extended policy is usually charged to the party purchasing the property (the buyer).

E. TITLE INSURANCE DISCLOSURE

In any escrow transaction for the purchase or exchange of real property where a title insurance policy will not be issued to the buyer (or exchanger), the buyer (or exchanger) must sign and acknowledge a disclosure statement stating that it may be advisable to obtain title insurance.

VIII. Real Estate Settlement Procedures Act (RESPA)

RESPA allows borrowers to shop for settlement services. The law covers first loans on one-to-four unit residential dwellings.

The **REAL ESTATE SETTLEMENT PROCEDURES ACT (RESPA)** *is a law for the sale or transfer of one-to-four residential units requiring: 1) specific procedures and 2) forms for settlements (closing costs) involving most home loans from financial institutions with federally insured deposits, including FHA and VA loans.*

This law, although amended several times, states that the closing settlement cost of a real estate transaction must be made known to the borrower, on or before the settlement date, although, at the buyer's request, it must be provided one business day before escrow closes.

Before this law was passed, buyers were unaware of the exact amount needed until the actual escrow closing day. Sometimes the buyers were surprised to find that more money than expected was needed to complete the procedure. The current law alleviates this problem.

RESPA disclosure requirements are for federally related lenders. This means almost all lenders.

Other provisions required by the Real Estate Settlement Procedures Act include the following:

1. At the time of loan application, or within three business days, the lender must give a good faith estimate of the total closing charges to the borrower.

2. At the same time, the lender must furnish the buyer with an information booklet.

3. The escrow agent must give a uniform settlement statement to the borrower, the seller, and the lender. **Figure 7-11** illustrates the settlement statement. It must be furnished by the time of settlement, except when the borrower waives it, or in areas where the HUD (Department of Housing and Urban Development) permits a later date for supplying it.

The settlement statement must be delivered on or before the date of settlement, at no charge. The buyer can request it one business day before closing.

4. Individuals are prohibited from receiving kickbacks and unearned fees. Payments to cooperating brokerages and referral agreements between brokers are exempt.

5. No seller may require a buyer to purchase title insurance from any particular company as a condition of sale.

There are penalties for "kickbacks" and unearned fees. The seller may request a specific title insurer, but only the buyer can require a specific insurance company.

IX. California Escrow Association

The California Escrow Association has developed a statewide program to promote professional service and educational opportunities for its members. Many community colleges have also adopted certificate courses for escrow personnel and real estate brokers to provide a better understanding of the highly technical escrow field.

Figure 7-11

A. U.S. DEPARTMENT OF HOUSING AND URBAN DEVELOPMENT SETTLEMENT STATEMENT	B. TYPE OF LOAN 1. [ ] FHA 2. [ ] FmHA 3. [X] Conv. unis 4. [ ] VA 5. [ ] Conv. ins

B. TYPE OF LOAN	
6. ESCROW NUMBER: 1-10533	7. LOAN NUMBER:
8. MORTGAGE INSURANCE NUMBER:	

THIS NOTE IS FURNISHED TO GIVE YOU A STATEMENT OF THE ACTUAL SETTLEMENT COSTS. AMOUNTS PAID TO AND BY THE SETTLEMENT AGENT ARE SHOWN. ITEMS MARKED "(P.O.C.)" WERE PAID OUTSIDE OF THE CLOSING; THEY ARE SHOWN HERE FOR INFORMATIONAL PURPOSES AND ARE NOT INCLUDED IN THE TOTALS.

D. NAME OF BORROWER: JOHN BUYER JANE BUYER 123 Purchase Lane Glendale, CA	E. NAME OF SELLER: JOHN SELLER JANE SELLER	F. NAME OF LENDER: GET SMART SAVINGS AND LOAN 123 Lending Lane Beverly Hills, CA 91020
G. PROPERTY LOCATION: 123 PURCHASE LANE GLENDALE, CA	H. SETTLEMENT AGENT: COLONIAL ESCROW, INC. PLACE OF SETTLEMENT: 601 EAST GLENOAKS BLVD. SUITE 210 GLENDALE, CA 91207 P.O. BOX 433 GLENDALE, CA 91209-0433	I. SETTLEMENT DATE: 06/01/20

J. SUMMARY OF BORROWER'S TRANSACTIONS		K. SUMMARY OF SELLER'S TRANSACTIONS	
100. GROSS AMOUNT DUE FROM BORROWER		**400. GROSS AMOUNT DUE TO SELLER**	
101. CONTRACT SALES PRICE	800,000.00	401. CONTRACT SALES PRICE	800,000.00
102. PERSONAL PROPERTY		402. PERSONAL PROPERTY	
103. SETTL. CHRGS. TO BORROWER (LINE 1400)	10,122.01	403. DEPOSITS	
104.		404.	
105.		405.	
Adjustments: items paid by seller in advance		Adjustments: items paid by seller in advance	
106. CITY/TOWN TAXES		406. CITY/TOWN TAXES	
107. COUNTY TAXES		407. COUNTY TAXES	
108. ASSESSMENTS		408. ASSESSMENTS	
109. TAXES : 06/01/20 TO 07/01/20	666.67	409. TAXES : 06/01/20 TO 07/01/20	666.67
110.		410.	
111.		411.	
112.		412.	
120. GROSS AMOUNT DUE FROM BORROWER	810,788.68	420. GROSS AMOUNT DUE TO SELLER	800,666.67
200. AMOUNTS PAID BY OR IN BEHALF OF BORROWER		**500. REDUCTIONS IN AMOUNT DUE TO SELLER**	
201. DEPOSITS	91,000.00	501. EXCESS DEPOSIT	
202. PRINCIPAL AMOUNT OF NEW LOAN(S)	640,000.00	502. SETTL. CHRGS. TO SELLER (LINE 1400)	54,845.00
203. EXISTING LOAN(S) TAKEN SUBJECT TO		503. EXISTING LOAN(S) TAKEN SUBJECT TO	
204. NEW 2ND TRUST DEED	80,000.00	504. PAYOFF TO MOST SUPERIOR SAVINGS AND L	490,000.00
205.		505. INTEREST FROM 05/01/20 TO 06/01/20	4,161.64
206.		506. FORWARDING FEE	50.00
207.		507. RECONVEYANCE FEE	60.00
208.		508. NEW 2ND TRUST DEED	80,000.00
209.		509.	
Adjustments: Items unpaid by seller		Adjustments: Items unpaid by seller	
210. CITY/TOWN TAXES		510. CITY/TOWN TAXES	
211. COUNTY TAXES		511. COUNTY TAXES	
212. ASSESSMENTS		512. ASSESSMENTS	
213.		513.	
214.		514.	
215.		515.	
216.		516.	
217.		517.	
218.		518.	
219.		519.	
220. TOTAL PAID BY/FOR BORROWER	811,000.00	520. TOTAL REDUCTION AMOUNT DUE SELLER	629,116.64
300. CASH AT SETTLEMENT FROM/TO BORROWER		**600. CASH AT SETTLEMENT TO/FROM SELLER**	
301. Gross amounts due from borrower (line 120)	810,788.68	601. Gross amount due to seller (line 420)	800,666.67
302. Less amounts paid by/for borrower (line 220)	811,000.00	602. Less reductions in amount due seller (line 520)	629,116.64
303. CASH FROM[ ] TO[X] BORROWER	211.32	603. CASH FROM[ ] TO[X] SELLER	171,550.03

232

L. SETTLEMENT STATEMENT

700. TOTAL SALES/BROKER'S COMMISSION	PAID FROM BORROWER'S FUNDS AT SETTLEMENT	PAID FROM SELLER'S FUNDS AT SETTLEMENT
BASED ON PRICE $ 800,000.00 @ 6.00%		
701. BROKER: J. Q. SMART 48,000.00		
702.		
703.		
704. COMMISSIONS PAID AT SETTLEMENT		48,000.00
800. ITEMS PAYABLE IN CONNECTION WITH LOAN		
801. LOAN FEE	6,400.00	
802. LOAN DISCOUNT		
803. APPRAISAL	350.00	
804. CREDIT REPORT	45.00	
805. LENDER'S INSPECTION FEE		
806. MORTGAGE INSURANCE APPLICATION FEE		
807. ASSUMPTION FEE		
808. TAX SERVICE	89.00	
809. DOCUMENT FEE	250.00	
810.		
811.		
900. ITEMS REQUIRED BY LENDER TO BE PAID IN ADVANCE		
901. INTEREST AT 7.5000% FROM 05/31/20 TO 06/01/20	131.51	
902. MORTGAGE INSURANCE		
903. PROPERTY INSURANCE, INC. FOR FIRE INSURANCE	1,000.00	
904.		
905.		
1000. RESERVES DEPOSITED WITH LENDER		
1001. HAZARD INSURANCE		
1002. MORTGAGE INSURANCE		
1003. CITY PROPERTY TAXES		
1004. COUNTY PROPERTY TAXES		
1005. ANNUAL ASSESSMENTS		
1006.		
1007.		
1008.		
1100. ESCROW AND TITLE CHARGES		
1101. ESCROW FEE TO COLONIAL ESCROW, INC.	900.00	900.00
1102. ABSTRACT OR TITLE SEARCH		
1103. TITLE EXAMINATION		
1104. TITLE INSURANCE BINDER		
1105. DOCUMENT PREPARATION TO COLONIAL ESCROW, INC.		
1106. MESSENGER FEE TO COLONIAL ESCROW, INC.	50.00	
1107. ATTORNEY'S FEES		
1108. TITLE POLICY TO AMERICAN COAST TITLE	628.50	2,165.00
1109. LENDERS COVERAGE $ 640,000.00		
1110. OWNERS COVERAGE $ 800,000.00		
1111. PROCESSING DEMANDS TO COLONIAL ESCROW, INC.		35.00
1112. DOCUMENT FEE TO COLONIAL ESCROW, INC.		85.00
1113. LOAN TIE IN FEE TO COLONIAL ESCROW, INC.	125.00	
1200. GOVERNMENT RECORDING AND TRANSFER CHARGES		
1201. RECORDING FEES: DEED $8.00; MORTGAGE $20.00; RELEASES $5.00	28.00	5.00
1202. DOCUMENTARY TRANSFER TAX		880.00
1203. STATE TAX/STAMPS		
1204.		
1205.		
1300. ADDITIONAL SETTLEMENT CHARGES		
1301. SURVEY		
1302. PEST CONTROL, INC. FOR TERMITE REPORT/WORK		1,000.00
1303. SUB ESCROW FEE TO AMERICAN COAST TITLE	75.00	75.00
1304. TITLE ENDORSEMENT FEE(S) TO AMERICAN COAST TITLE	50.00	
1305. STREET ASSESSMENT BOND TO AMERICAN COAST TITLE		1,300.00
1306. HOME WARRANTY, INC. FOR HOME PROTECTION POLICY		400.00
1307.		
1400. TOTAL SETTLEMENT CHARGES (ENTER ON LINES 102 SECTION J AND 501 SECTION K)	10,122.01	54,845.00

**California Escrow Association
530 Bercut Drive, Suite G
Sacramento, CA 95814**

X. SUMMARY

An **escrow** is created when a written agreement (usually from a **Deposit Receipt**) instructs a neutral third party to hold funds and proceed only when all the agreed to conditions have been completed. An escrow is strongly recommended in connection with real estate sales, loan agreements, or exchanges made in California. But escrows are required for liquor license transfers, security sales, and court ordered transfers (**probate sales**).

A valid escrow requires: 1) signed escrow instructions (a written escrow contract) between the buying and selling parties; 2) a neutral escrow company acting as a dual agent for the buyer and the seller; and 3) conditional delivery of funds until the escrow conditions are completed.

An **escrow holder** can be a corporation, an attorney, or a real estate broker acting as a real estate agent in the transaction. An escrow officer, holder, or agent, though not licensed by the state, must be an employee of a licensed escrow company acting as agent. The duties of an escrow company include conditional delivery of funds until escrow conditions are met, confidentiality of escrow instructions, and acting as a deposit holder until funds are disbursed when escrow closes.

A real estate broker can handle escrow for a fee, but only if the broker acts as a real estate agent in that transaction, or if the broker is a principal (buyer or seller).

The escrow is complete when: 1) all escrow conditions of the parties have been met and 2) the parties have received an accounting of the procedure. Escrows can be terminated in three ways: by **completion**, **mutual agreement**, or court action **interpleader**.

Amendments changing escrow instructions must be signed by both parties. The seller cannot rescind escrow without consent of the buyer, but the salesperson may recommend an escrow company. **Selection of an escrow company and officer is negotiated between buyer and seller**. It is illegal for a real estate licensee to receive a kickback for solicitation of escrow business.

Escrow instructions for the sale of a house are formal instructions drawn from the information contained in the Deposit Receipt. They are usually interpreted together, but if a conflict arises, the latest signed document will usually prevail. Most escrows for home sales include getting a new loan and the payoff or assumption of an old one. The **payoff demand statement** details the lender's calculations of the amounts owed for the purpose of paying off the loan in full. If a loan is to be assumed, a **beneficiary's (lender's) statement** under a deed of trust provides information, such as the unpaid balance, monthly payment and interest rate.

Closing escrow is the process of signing various documents, transfer of documents, recordation of deed and trust deeds, and distribution of funds. The **closing date** is the date that the documents are recorded.

Proration is the process of dividing expenses or income proportionately between buyer and seller to the precise date that escrow closes, or an agreed date. Items commonly prorated include: **property taxes**, **fire insurance**, **interest** and **rents**. All escrow companies use 30 days as a "base month." The two important dates in determining proration amounts are the dates escrow closes and when the item is paid.

A **Structural Pest Control Report** (termite report) is usually a condition of the escrow. This report is given by a licensed pest control company to identify any wood-destroying pests or conditions likely to cause pest infestation. It also states the conditions and correction costs of any pest, dry rot, excessive moisture, earth-wood contacts, or fungus damage in accessible areas of a structure. Payment for the report is negotiated between parties, but is usually made by the seller, as indicated in the allocation of costs signed by both parties. **Required repairs** are usually paid for by the seller, then a notice of work completed is obtained. But **recommended repairs** are negotiated between the parties.

Most lenders require a pest control inspection before making a loan. Every VA and FHA loan application requires one. A copy of the pest control report and notice of work completed must be delivered to the buyer if it's a condition of the deposit receipt or financing.

Fire insurance is a necessity. A lending institution requires fire coverage for the amount of its loan. **California Standard Form Fire Insurance Policy** insures the dwelling **only against fire and lightning**. An **Extended Coverage Endorsement** insures against windstorms, explosions, hail aircraft, smoke, riot, and vehicles not attributed to a strike or civil commotion. Buyers can assume existing fire insurance policies or obtain new ones. When assuming fire insurance policies, the premium amount will be prorated in escrow. A coinsurance clause in a policy requires that 80% of the value of a commercial dwelling be insured or only a percentage of the insurance value will be payable.

Chain of title is the recorded public history of a specific property. Information about people and their real property is stored in computers in a grantor-grantee index and referred to as a **title plant**. Title insurance companies examine chain of title records, review any risks not found in public records, seek legal interpretation of deeds or other real estate documents, help the seller correct any defects, and insure marketable title to the property.

A **preliminary title report** is the first step in a title search. It shows the condition of title before a sale or loan transaction.

Title insurance policies in California include the **California Land Title Association (CLTA) Policy**, the more comprehensive **American Land Title Association (ALTA) Policy**, or the **ALTA-R Policy**.

The **CLTA policy** is the most common and basic title insurance policy. The standard CLTA policy insures only the lender, unless the owner pays for "owner" coverage. It protects against lack of capacity of a party in a the chain of title, deeds not properly delivered, and forgery.

The **ATLA policy** is an extended coverage policy that insures against many exclusions in the standard coverage (CTLA) policy. The ALTA policy (which includes a competent survey or physical inspection) is usually required by California lenders and out of state lenders unable to make personal inspections of the property. Neither ALTA or CTLA covers unwritten **title defects known** to the insured at the time of policy issuance or **zoning changes**.

The **ALTA-R policy** is recommended by title companies for one-to-four owner-occupied residential dwellings. It offers more coverage for less money because no survey is necessary.

Payment for the CTLA policy insurance fees is negotiable, but the deposit receipt must state who pays the insurance fees to prevent any misunderstanding. In Southern California, the seller customarily pays for the CTLA policy. In Northern California, the buyer pays. The fees to upgrade the coverage from a CTLA to an ALTA policy are paid by the buyer in either part of the state.

Escrow service fees are usually split 50-50 in Southern California. The buyer usually pays in Northern California.

The **Real Estate Settlement Procedures Act (RESPA)** involves most federally insured home loans. It is a Federal law relating to the sale or transfer of one-to-four residential units requiring specific procedures and forms for settlements closing costs. All settlement closing costs must be disclosed to the borrower one business day before escrow closes.

XI. TERMINOLOGY - CHAPTER 7

A. ALTA
B. Chain of Title
C. CLTA
D. Coinsurance
E. Date of Closing

F. Escrow
G. Escrow Instructions
H. Escrow Officer
I. Payoff Demand Statement
J. Pest Control Report

K. Preliminary Title Report
L. Proration
M. RESPA
N. Title Insurance
O. Title Plant

1.____ Insurance to protect a real property owner or lender up to a specified amount against certain types of loss; e.g., defective or unmarketable title.

2.____ The process of depositing instruments, funds, and instructions, with a third neutral party who finalizes the transaction.

3.____ A history of conveyances and encumbrances affecting the title from the time the original patent was granted, or as far back as records are available, used to determine how title came to be vested in current owner.

4.____ Adjustments of interest, taxes, and insurance, etc., on a prorated basis as of the closing or agreed upon date.

5.____ The person at the escrow company who handles the paperwork of the escrow.

6.____ The written instructions of the escrow, prepared by the escrow officer and approved by both the buyer and the seller.

7.____ The most all inclusive title insurance policy. It requires a property survey and is usually required by most lenders.

8.____ The minimum standard title insurance policy in California that does NOT require a property survey.

9.____ The requirement by a lender that a property be insured up to its full value, or only a proportion of any loss will be reimbursed.

10.____ A report from a structural pest control company stating the termite or other type of pest damage found and the cost of repairing it.

11.____ The date documents are recorded and title insurance is written.

12.____ A federal statute requiring disclosure of certain costs in the sale of residential property.

13.____ A report showing the condition of title before a sale or loan transaction.

14.____ Written instructions by a lender stating and demanding the amount necessary to pay off a loan.

15.____ A filing of all recorded information to real property.

XII. MULTIPLE CHOICE

1. When a trust deed is sold, the parties often use an escrow (agent) in order to:

   a. obey the civil code.
   b. serve as a witness.
   c. assure conditions are met.
   d. provide a legal service.

2. Which of the following is NOT a requirement of a valid escrow?

   a. Escrow officer must be licensed
   b. Signed instructions
   c. Neutral third party
   d. Conditional delivery

3. Of the following, which would be the last function in an escrow sequence of events?

   a. Recording and issuing of title policy
   b. Lender's demand (amount owed on property)
   c. Request of new loan documents
   d. Adjustments and prorations

4. If a new owner cancels the fire insurance policy belonging to the seller and buys a new policy that carries a higher rate, the new policy is said to be :

   a. short-insured.
   b. short-rated.
   c. pro-rated.
   d. none of the above.

5. The only way that escrow instructions can be changed, once they have been drawn and signed by each party, is by:

   a. the escrow officer.
   b. mutual consent of the parties.
   c. the listing broker.
   d. operation of law.

6. The California Standard Form Fire Insurance Policy would NOT insure your property against:

   a. fire.
   b. windstorm.
   c. lightning.
   d. any of the above.

7. Escrow companies use what base period when calculating prorations?

    a. 31 days

    b. 30 days

    c. 28 days

    d. Depends on the month being prorated.

8. What title policy would cover most of the exclusions of a standard policy?

    a. ALTA

    b. MLTA

    c. CLTA

    d. BLTA

9. Who selects the escrow company?

    a. Agent only

    b. Buyer only

    c. Seller only

    d. Buyer and seller

10. Which of the following is NOT a one-time fee, but is in fact a recurring charge?

    a. Property tax fees

    b. Title insurance fees

    c. Escrow fees

    d. County recording fees

ANSWERS: 1. c; 2. a; 3. a; 4. b; 5. b; 6. b; 7. b; 8. a; 9. d; 10. a

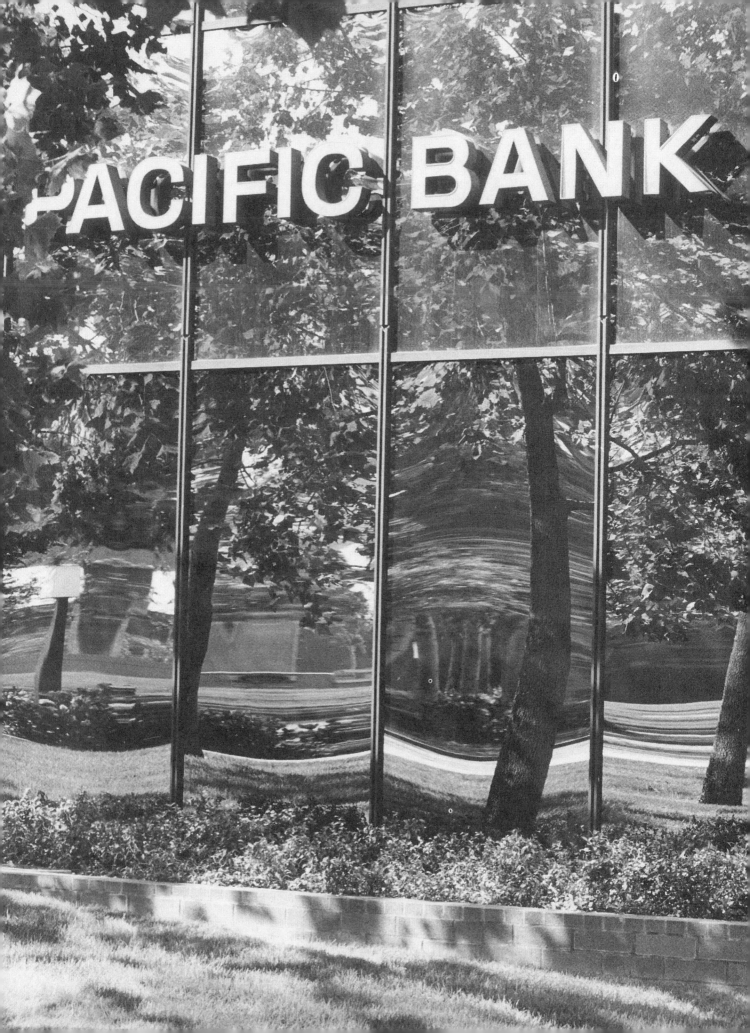

Chapter 8
Real Estate Finance

Real estate is expensive compared to most other possessions. A person or business seldom has enough cash to buy the real estate outright, and therefore must borrow the necessary money to help finance the transaction. If a buyer makes a cash down payment of 20% for example, he or she must then obtain a loan for the remaining 80% of the purchase price. Most buyers must finance at least part of the purchase, so a good rule to remember is, "If you can't finance a property, you probably can't sell it later." If a property can't be easily financed, don't waste time with it: find another, more easily financed, property.

To utilize the "principle of leverage," an investor would use the maximum amount of borrowed money.

Even buyers with large amounts of cash rarely purchase real estate outright. An investment principle known as "leverage" favors buying real estate using borrowed funds. *LEVERAGE is the practice of purchasing real estate using a small amount of your own money and a larger proportion of borrowed funds.* The more money borrowed to buy a property, the greater the leverage.

Example: If you buy a $300,000 house with 20% down, the down payment is $60,000. If inflation increases the value by 30% over 10 years, you have increased the market value by $90,000 on a $60,000 investment.

As you can see, employing leverage makes it possible for real estate investors to reap the same profits as those buying entirely with their own funds without having to tie up as much cash. This chapter explores the different ways in which real estate can be financed. Each type of financing instrument will be discussed, including the many clauses in the note and trust deed.

I. Hypothecation
(Property as Collateral)

Real estate finance is based on the principle of hypothecation. To **HYPOTHECATE** *is to provide title to a property as security for a loan without giving up possession.* Although one can hypothecate or "pledge" stocks as security for a bank loan, most real property buyers hypothecate their property as security for a real estate loan. In neither case does the person surrender the use or possession of the property. The hypothecation principle is fundamental to the major instruments of real estate finance: the trust deed in California and the less common mortgage. Each of these instruments uses the promissory note as the primary evidence of debt, which creates a lien on the property.

II. The Promissory Note

A **PROMISSORY NOTE** *is the basic instrument used to evidence the obligation or debt.* It is an unconditional promise, in writing, by one person to another, promising to pay on demand, or over a fixed determinable time, a certain sum of money. Borrowers hypothecate real property as security for payment of the promissory note. The trust deed or mortgage is used with the promissory note to hypothecate the property as security for the note.

Co-borrowers responsible for each other's debts sign the promissory note as "jointly and severally obligated."

A loan payment on a note is made up of principal and interest. **PRINCIPAL** *is the dollar amount of the loan.* Commonly we call it the amount of money remaining to be paid off on a promissory note (the loan balance). **INTEREST** *is the rent charged for the use of money.*

Interest on most real estate loans is "simple interest." Simple interest is interest paid only on the principal amount owed.

Figure 8-1 illustrates the three basic kinds of promissory notes that affect real estate financing.

Figure 8-1

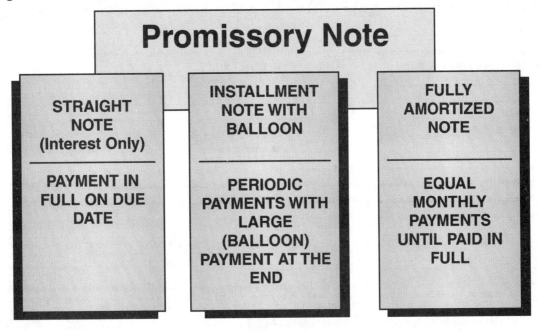

A. STRAIGHT NOTE (Interest Only)

A *STRAIGHT NOTE is a promissory note in which a borrower repays the principal in one lump sum, at maturity, while interest is paid in installments or at maturity.* The parties could agree that interest be paid monthly, quarterly, annually, or any agreed-to term, but the principal is a lump sum payment. In real estate, this type of note is usually for relatively small amounts of money being borrowed for a short time.

B. INSTALLMENT NOTE WITH A BALLOON PAYMENT

An *INSTALLMENT NOTE WITH A BALLOON PAYMENT (PARTIALLY AMORTIZED NOTE) is a promissory note with periodic payments of principal and interest and a large payment at the end (maturity date or due date).* This type of note and the straight note are usually in the form of secondary financing (second trust deeds). **See Figure 8-2**.

C. FULLY AMORTIZED INSTALLMENT NOTE

A *FULLY AMORTIZED INSTALLMENT NOTE is a promissory note for which both the principal and interest are paid in equal installments until the debt is paid in full.* Installments make it easy to pay off a note, and there is no balloon payment at the end of the loan period.

For real estate financing in California, the fully amortized installment note is the most commonly used type of note. Loan payments are either fixed or adjustable.

Figure 8-2   **Installment Note With a Balloon Payment**

$_____ _____, California_____, 19_____

In installments as herein stated, for value received, I promise to pay to_____

_____, or order,

at_____

the sum of _____ DOLLARS,

with interest from_____ on unpaid principal at the

rate of_____ per cent per annum; principal and interest payable in installments of

_____ Dollars

or more on the_____day of each _____month, beginning

on the_____ day of _____, 19_____. _____

_____

_____

_____

_____and continuing until said principal and interest have been paid.

   Each payment shall be credited first on interest then due and the remainder on principal; and interest shall thereupon cease upon the principal so credited. Should default be made in payment of any installment when due the whole sum of principal and interest shall become immediately due at the option of the holder of this note. Principal and interest payable in lawful money of the United States. If action be instituted on this note I promise to pay such sum as the Court may fix as attorney's fees. I promise to pay Servicing Agent a late payment charge of $5 or 10% of installment due of principal and interest, whichever is greater. For First Trust Deed loans of $16,000 or more; and for Junior Lien loans of $8,000 or more, the following clause governs: $5 or 6% of installment due of principal and interest, whichever is greater. For all loans, regardless of principal amount, no late payment charge will be made if the installment is paid or tendered in full within 10 days after its scheduled due date. This note is secured by a DEED OF TRUST to _____

_____ _____

_____ _____

DEED OF TRUST NOTE-INSTALLMENT NOTE-WOLCOTTS FORM 1458 REV.

To amortize is to slowly reduce the principal owed. Fully amortized loans are seldom foreclosed on because the principal is reduced with each payment.

A fully amortized loan has equal monthly payments except for the last payment, which is slightly higher or lower. With *EQUAL MONTHLY PAYMENTS, the monthly payment amount, including principal and interest, is constant, but as the loan is paid off, the amount of the payment attributed to interest decreases and the amount attributed to principal increases.*

III. Negotiable Instruments

A. (PROMISSORY NOTES, CHECKS, OTHERS)

Negotiable instruments are easily transferable from one person to another. Promissory notes are negotiable. The most common example is a personal check.

A **NEGOTIABLE INSTRUMENT** is any financial document (promissory note, check or other) that can be passed easily from one person to another, if it meets certain legal requirements. Any promissory note may be a negotiable instrument that is freely transferable. A negotiable instrument must be:

1. an unconditional promise
2. in writing
3. made by one person to another
4. signed by the maker
5. payable on demand or on a set date
6. for a set amount of money.

B. HOLDER IN DUE COURSE (No Knowledge of Defect)

The new owner of the check or note has become an innocent third party.

A **HOLDER IN DUE COURSE** is one who has taken a negotiable instrument from another.

IV. Important Clauses in Financial Instruments

The following financial instrument clauses are the most commonly used terms, and they have definite meanings that affect the financial obligations of both a lender and borrower.

A. ACCELERATION CLAUSE (Entire Amount Due)

In an **ACCELERATION CLAUSE,** *upon the occurrence of a* **specific event***, the lender has the right to demand immediate payment of the entire note.* An acceleration clause is used to demand immediate payment in full because of a default in loan payments, property taxes, fire insurance, or upon the transfer of property. The main purpose of an acceleration clause is to make the entire balance of the loan due and payable at once. A **LATE PAYMENT** *is a payment that is, unless otherwise stated, more than ten days past due.*

An acceleration clause "speeds up" the balance due based on the occurrence of a specific event.

B. ALIENATION CLAUSE (Due on Sale)

An *ALIENATION CLAUSE is a form of the acceleration clause, stating that the entire loan becomes due and payable when the property is sold, assigned, transferred, or otherwise alienated.* The lender, whether a financial institution or a private party, is given the right to full payment when the original borrower transfers the property. This is also commonly referred to as a **"due on sale"** clause.

With an alienation clause, the lender demands that the entire balance of the loan is due when the owner is alienating, transferring (selling), or "conveying" the property.

C. ASSUMPTION

In order to assume an existing loan, the promissory note cannot include an alienation clause.

If a buyer *ASSUMES a loan on a property that is already encumbered, he or she accepts responsibility, with the lender's consent, for the full payment of the loan.* The name on the loan is changed to that of the buyer. With a true assumption, the seller has **secondary responsibility**. To end his or her liability and put the loan in the name of the buyer, the seller files a Substitution of Liability form.

A seller is protected from liability for payments on an existing loan when the buyer "assumes" the trust deed (and note liability).

When a buyer purchases a property "subject to," he or she has no responsibility in the event of a default; the seller retains responsibility. "Subject to" benefits the buyer.

Taking title *SUBJECT TO a prior loan constitutes an agreement to take over and make the payments or lose the property.* The current seller (the buyer to whom the loan was originally made) remains legally responsible for the note, but the new buyer makes the payments.

D. SUBORDINATION CLAUSE
(Current Loan Stands Still; New Loan Moves Ahead)

A subordination clause gives the borrower (buyer) the ability to obtain additional loans on the property that become a higher priority.

A *SUBORDINATION CLAUSE is part of a trust deed or mortgage that allows for a future change in the priority of financial liens*. It is used when the buyer wants future financial liens to have priority over a lien he or she is now acquiring. The seller of vacant land will sometimes lend money to the buyer as part of the transaction and will allow the subordination of that loan to any new construction loans.

The subordination clause is used to change the priority on one or more financial liens, but the terms of a subordination clause must be clear and definite. The courts are skeptical about loosely written subordination clauses. Subordination clauses are not used that often, but a salesperson must know and understand them.

E. PREPAYMENT PENALTIES (Fee for Early Payment)

A *PREPAYMENT PENALTY is a charge to the borrower for paying off all or part of a loan balance before the due date.*

Most financial institutions use a prepayment penalty clause on fixed rate loans, but they are rarely employed with the adjustable rate loans. A prepayment penalty is only enforceable during the first five years of a (one-to-four unit) home loan. The penalty is usually six months' interest on the amount prepaid (each year) that exceeds 20% of the original principal amount of the loan. However, penalties do vary among lenders. After negotiating, a lender may sometimes waive the prepayment penalty if the borrower obtains a new loan from that institution, or if the money market is tight and the lender needs to use the money to lend out at a higher interest rate.

A prepayment penalty is only enforceable during the first five years of a one-to-four unit home loan.

F. IMPOUND ACCOUNTS (Reserves)

IMPOUND ACCOUNTS (RESERVES) are moneys collected in advance from borrowers to assure the payment of recurring costs, such as property taxes and fire insurance. Some lenders require impound accounts. Impound accounts are especially appropriate when there is a relatively low down payment.

Impounds are reserves (money) on hand for recurring costs, such as property taxes and fire insurance. Impounds CANNOT be used to pay interest.

G. ASSIGNMENT OF RENTS (Take Possession)

An *ASSIGNMENT OF RENTS clause allows a lender, upon default of the borrower, to take possession of the property, collect rents, and pay expenses.*

V. Interest and Types of Loans

A. INTEREST (Simple Interest)

INTEREST *is the charge for borrowing money.* In real estate we use simple interest, not compound interest. Interest can be thought of as a rental charge for the use of money.

The "Nominal Interest Rate" is the rate stated in the note. The "Effective Interest Rate" is the rate the borrower is actually paying (including interest, points, and loan fees).

The formula for calculating interest is:

$$I = P \times R \times T$$
$$\text{or}$$
$$\textbf{Interest} = \textbf{Principal} \times \textbf{Rate} \times \textbf{Time}$$

To find the interest on an $80,000 loan at 12 percent interest for 3 years, we would make the following calculation:

$$I = P \times R \times T$$
$$\$28,800 = \$80,000 \times .12 \times 3 \text{ years}$$

(See Chapter 15 for a more detailed discussion of interest calculations.)

B. FIXED INTEREST RATES (Fixed Rate)

A **FIXED INTEREST RATE LOAN** *is a loan for which the payments are the same each month for the life of the loan.* The equal monthly payment includes both the principal and the interest. A loan with this kind of fixed rate of interest is said to be a "fully amortized fixed rate loan."

C. AMORTIZATION PAYMENTS

Amortization is the liquidation of a note including principal and interest.

AMORTIZATION *is the repaying of a loan (principal and interest), in regular payments, over the term of the loan.* This repayment is usually in monthly payments but can be paid quarterly or semi-annually.

NEGATIVE AMORTIZATION *means the interest rate charges are higher than the monthly payment.* Negative amortization means that the loan payment does not cover the interest charges, and the amount of unpaid interest is added to the unpaid loan balance.

Real estate salespeople should always have amortization books handy so that they can figure out the monthly payment on any loan. The *AMORTIZATION (SCHEDULE) BOOK shows the monthly payments necessary to amortize a loan, over a given number of years, at different interest rates and for different loan amounts.* This amortization table book is usually given free, upon request, to salespeople by title insurance companies or financial institutions. Salespeople can also use specially programmed, hand-held calculators to instantly determine the monthly payment amount.

Figure 8-3 on the next page is an example of an amortization table at 7% interest per annum for 20, 25, 30, and 40 years at different loan amounts. The loan amounts range from $100 to $100,000, but any loan amount can be obtained by adding the necessary increments. If, for example, we want to determine the monthly payments for a $155,000 loan at 7% interest for 30 years, this is what we would do:

1. Check the 30 years' column for the monthly payment on $100,000.

2. Next, determine the monthly payment for $50,000 and $5,000 using the same method.

3. Lastly, add the monthly payment amounts together.

Amount	Payment
$100,000.00	$665.30
50,000.00	332.65
5,000.00	33.27

TOTAL LOAN $155,000.00　　　**$1,031.22 Monthly Payment**

Lenders determine monthly payments by using amortization tables.

www.bankrate.com/gookeyword/mortgage-calculator.asp
Bankrate.com Mortgage calculator
www.interest.com/hugh/calc/
Hugh's Mortgage and Financial Calculators

D. ADJUSTABLE RATE MORTGAGE (ARM)

Many lenders will allow the borrower a choice of either 1) a fixed interest rate loan or 2) an adjustable rate mortgage (ARM) loan. An ARM allows the interest rate to fluctuate (go up or down) depending on money market conditions. Rather than making equal monthly payments as with a fixed rate loan, the ARM payments will vary over the term of the loan.

An *ADJUSTABLE RATE MORTGAGE "ARM" (OR TRUST DEED) is a loan in which the interest rate fluctuates periodically, based on a specific index, which makes the payment amount also change.* Each lending institution has its own ARM terms and provisions.

Figure 8-3	**Monthly Payments Necessary To Amortize a Loan**			**7%**
TERM AMOUNT	**20 YEARS**	**25 YEARS**	**30 YEARS**	**40 YEARS**
$100	0.78	0.71	0.67	0.62
200	1.55	1.41	1.33	1.24
300	2.33	2.12	2.00	1.86
400	3.10	2.83	2.66	2.49
500	3.88	3.53	3.33	3.11
600	4.65	4.24	3.99	3.73
700	5.43	4.95	4.66	4.35
800	6.20	5.65	5.32	4.97
900	6.98	6.36	5.99	5.59
1,000	7.75	7.07	6.65	6.21
2,000	15.51	14.14	13.31	12.43
3,000	23.26	21.20	19.96	18.64
4,000	31.01	28.27	26.61	24.86
5,000	38.76	35.34	33.27	31.07
6,000	46.52	42.41	39.92	37.29
7,000	54.27	49.47	46.57	43.50
8,000	62.02	56.54	53.22	49.71
9,000	69.78	63.61	59.88	55.93
10,000	77.53	70.68	66.53	62.14
20,000	155.06	141.36	133.06	124.29
30,000	232.59	212.03	199.59	186.43
40,000	310.12	282.71	266.12	248.57
50,000	387.65	353.39	332.65	310.72
100,000	775.30	706.78	665.30	621.43

Figure 8-4 illustrates how an adjustable rate mortgage (ARM) works. The interest rate, and therefore the payments, will change often over the term of the loan. ARM lenders attempt to make this type of loan more attractive to a potential borrower by offering the loan at a much lower starting interest rate than with a fixed interest rate loan.

www.loanpage.com
The LoanPage

E. SOME SPECIAL PURPOSE TYPES OF LOANS

1. Graduated Payment Mortgage (For First Time Buyers)

A GRADUATED PAYMENT MORTGAGE (TRUST DEED) is a type of fixed interest rate loan for which the monthly payments start out lower and then gradually increase (for example,

Figure 8-4

How ARMs Work

THE INDEX

The **INDEX** *is the starting interest rate used as the indicator so that changes from it can be calculated.* If the index rises 1%, the ARM interest rate you pay goes up 1%. The index must be: 1) beyond the control of the lender, and 2) available and verifiable by the public. Examples of indexes used are the Cost of Living Index, the 11th District Cost of Funds Index, the One Year T-Bill, and the London Interbank Offered Rate (LIBOR).

THE ADJUSTABLE INTERVAL

The **ADJUSTABLE INTERVAL** *is the frequency with which interest rates are reset.* This period can be monthly, quarterly, every six months, or even once a year. If the index has risen .3% by the end of the interval period, the interest rate you pay goes up .3%.

THE CAP

The **CAP** *is a percentage rate ceiling or restriction on the 1) periodic (adjustable) interval; and 2) lifetime change in interest rates or payments.* An adjustable interval cap limits the percentage of change upward or downward to, for example, 1/2% every quarter. The lifetime cap is often around a maximum of 5% above or below the initial agreed-to contract rate.

THE MARGIN

The **MARGIN** *is the spread between the index rate and the initial contract rate from which the lender will make a profit and cover its costs.* It is the agreed to, in advance, amount of profit for the lender. If the index rate is 4% and the margin is 3%, then the current interest rate paid by the borrower is 7%. Even if the index rate moves up to 5%, the margin will always remain at 3% and the new interest rate will be 8%. Some adjustables have **teaser rates** that are even below the starting rate to entice the borrower into the transaction. The borrower is qualified based on the teaser rate, which only lasts for a short period of time and then goes up to the agreed upon rate.

ADVANTAGES OF ARMS

The main advantage of an ARM is a lower interest rate than can be found with a fixed rate loan because the lender is protected if interest rates rise over the loan period. This makes an ARM more affordable, thus more people can qualify for it. Generally there are no prepayment penalties, and an assumption is usually permitted if the new buyer meets credit standards. ARMs benefit first-time buyers and short-term investors who just want a lower interest rate, because interest rates are initially lower.

after five years the payments will be higher for the remainder of the loan payment). Although the final level of payments is higher than the payments would have been had the loan been fully amortized, the initial payments are much lower than the fully amortized rate.

2. Biweekly Mortgage (26 Payments)

A *BIWEEKLY mortgage (trust deed) is a fixed interest rate loan for which the payments are made every two weeks, but each payment is one-half the amount of a regular monthly payment.* Since there are 52 weeks in a year, the borrower pays a total of 26 payments.

3. 15-Year Fixed and Adjustable Rate Loans

Fifteen-year fixed-rate loans are gaining in popularity because, for a slight increase in the monthly payment, the loan can be paid off in only 15 years, usually at a lower interest rate than 30-year loans.

4. Reverse Annuity Loans (Seniors Who Need Income)

REVERSE ANNUITY LOANS are loans in which the lender pays the borrower a fixed monthly payment based on the value of the property. The loan is not repaid until the last owner dies or the property is sold, at which time it is paid back through probate. This type of loan is good for senior citizens who need a monthly income and have a large amount of equity in their homes. The senior citizens can pay off the loans earlier if they so desire.

VI. Points, Loan Fees, and Usury

A. POINTS (1 POINT = 1% OF THE LOAN AMOUNT)

A point is one percent of the loan amount. Five points on a $300,000 loan is $15,000. It is also called an "origination fee."

A *POINT is an origination fee of 1% of the amount borrowed, charged by the lender.* Most financial institutions charge the borrower points when he or she obtains a new loan. Points vary, but generally range from 1% to 7% of the loan amount. They are usually paid by the buyer but, if so negotiated, the seller may also pay.

If you purchase a home for $150,000 and obtain a loan for $120,000 plus two points, the loan points will cost you $2,400 ($120,000 x .02). These points are an additional cost and are added to the down payment and other closing costs required to complete the transaction at the time of purchase.

Points paid are usually adjustments to the interest rate. If the interest rate quoted is lower than what is currently being charged, more points are charged to make up the difference, which is paid to the lender. If a savings bank wants to quote a lower interest rate, the borrower can expect a larger point charge.

B. LOAN FEES

There is usually a loan fee in addition to points. A **LOAN FEE** *is the fee charged by the lender in order to apply for a loan*. This charge runs about $250 to $400. Other charges may include the appraisal and credit report.

The FHA charges a 1 percent loan fee, which is usually paid by the seller.

C. USURY

USURY *is charging more than the legally allowed percentage of interest*. In California the maximum interest rate charged for various loans is set by law. Anyone charging more than the designated rate is committing usury and is breaking the law. In determining whether an interest charge is usurious or not, all loan fees and points are added to the interest rate. Prepayment penalties are not included in the usury law test.

The constitutional usury rate in California is ten percent, or five percent above the discount rate charged by the Federal Reserve Bank of San Francisco, whichever is higher. This limit only applies to lenders who are not exempt from the law. Nearly every conventional source of real estate financing, however, has been exempted from the usury limit. Banks, savings banks, and other institutional lenders are all exempt. Sellers carrying back a purchase money trust deed as part of their equity in a real estate sale are exempt. **Any transaction made through a licensed broker is also exempt from usury laws**. The problem arises when a private individual lends money to another private individual. Check with an attorney first.

www.frbsf.org **(Federal Reserve Bank of San Francisco, 12th District)**
www.fdic.gov **(Federal Deposit Insurance Corporation - FDIC)**

---

www.frbsf.org

Explore frbsf.org ... your digital gateway to the
Federal Reserve Bank of San Francisco

Home | What's New | Careers | Glossary | FAQ | E-Mail Us | Site Map

About the Fed

News and Events

Economic Research & Data

Publications

Educational Resources

Community Development

Consumer Information

Banking Information

Services for Financial

Welcome to the
Federal Reserve Bank of San Francisco

The Federal Reserve Bank of San Francisco is one of twelve regional Federal Reserve Banks across the U.S. that, together with the Board of Governors in Washington, D.C., serve as our nation's central bank.

The Twelfth Federal Reserve District includes the nine western states--Alaska, Arizona, California, Hawaii, Idaho, Nevada, Oregon, Utah, and Washington--and American Samoa, Guam, and the Northern Mariana Islands. Branches are located in Los Angeles, Portland, Salt Lake City, and Seattle. The largest District, it covers 35 percent of the nation's landmass, ranks first in the size of its economy, and is home to approximately 20 percent of the nation's population.

Chapter 8

VII. Security Devices

SECURITY DEVICES (FINANCIAL INSTRUMENTS) *are written documents that pledge real property as security for a promissory note.*

The three financial instruments (security devices to collateralize real property) used in California are: mortgages, trust deeds, and land contracts.

In California we have three common types of security devices (financing instruments). **See Figure 8-5**. Any of the three previously mentioned notes may be used in conjunction with these financial instruments.

Figure 8-5

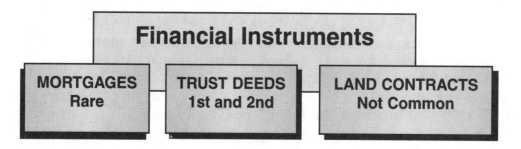

Financial Instruments

MORTGAGES	TRUST DEEDS	LAND CONTRACTS
Rare	1st and 2nd	Not Common

A. MORTGAGES

A ***MORTGAGE*** *is a financial instrument, in the form of a lien, that secures a property for payment of a promissory note.* It is not common in California. The ***MORTGAGOR*** *is the buyer/owner who is borrowing,* and the ***MORTGAGEE*** *is the lender.* If the mortgagor defaults in his or her payments, a foreclosure action may be started. After the foreclosure sale, the borrower has one year to redeem (buy back) the property, pay all the accumulated charges, or pay the mortgagee rent. **Figure 8-6** is a two-page comparison of the differences between mortgages and trust deeds.

Mortgagee = Lender; Mortgagor = Buyer/Owner who is borrowing

1. Power of Sale Clause

Some mortgages have a power of sale clause. A ***POWER OF SALE CLAUSE*** *allows the mortgagee to sell the property without a court proceeding (much like a trustee's sale) if the mortgagor is in default.* But it still requires a lengthy proceeding. If there is no power of sale clause, court (judicial) action is required for a foreclosure.

In a trust deed, the "power of sale" clause is given from the trustor to the trustee.

Figure 8-6

TRUST DEED

1. Parties:

   a. Trustor - Borrower who conveys title to trustee who holds as security for debt.

   b. Trustee - Receiver of naked legal title who will reconvey it when debt is paid or will sell if foreclosure necessary (must be a corporation or division of an escrow company).

   c. Beneficiary - Lender who holds note and trust deed.

2. Legal Title - Conveyed to trustee with trustor retaining possession of the property.

3. Statute of Limitations - Since security for the debt (title) is held by trustee, rights of creditor are not ended when statute has run out on note.

4. Remedy for Default - Foreclosure can be instituted through:

   a. Trustee's Sale, or

   b. Court Foreclosure.

5. Right of Redemption - When title has been sold by trustee at Trustee's Sale, no right of redemption previously existed, but in rare cases the courts now say it does.

6. Satisfaction - Trustor has beneficiary send original note and trust deed to trustee with request for full reconveyance. Upon payment of fees, trustee issues reconveyance deed, which must be recorded.

7. Foreclosure by Trustee's Sale:

   a. Beneficiary notifies trustee of default, who in turn notifies trustor and also records notice. Anyone with recorded "Request for Notice of Default" must also be notified.

   b. Trustee waits at least three months. During three-month period, trustor can reinstate loan.

   c. Trustee advertises "Notice of Sale" once a week for three weeks and posts notice on property.

   d. Trustee conducts sale and issues Trustee's Deed to highest bidder.

8. Deficiency Judgment - No judgment available:

   a. if foreclosure by Trustee's Sale.

   b. on purchase money trust deeds, even if by court foreclosure. (Deficiency judgments may be obtained on FHA and VA first purchase money trust deeds.)

MORTGAGE

1. Parties:

    a. Mortgagor - Borrower who retains title but gives lender a lien on the property as the security for debt.

    b. Mortgagee - Lender who holds the mortgage.

2. Title - Retained by mortgagor together with possession.

3. Statute of Limitations - Foreclosure is barred if no action is taken within four years of delinquency. Mortgage is said to have "outlawed."

4. Remedy for Default - Court foreclosure is usually the only remedy.

5. Right of Redemption - Mortgagor has one year to redeem following court foreclosure; called "Equity of Redemption."

6. Satisfaction of Mortgage - Upon final payment and on demand, mortgagee signs certificate that debt is satisfied. Certificate or release is recorded.

7. Foreclosure by Court:

    a. Court action commenced by mortgagee. Court issues decree of foreclosure and order of sale.

    b. Commissioner appointed by court sells to highest bidder after publication and posting of sale notice.

    c. Certificate of Sale issued by Commissioner. Mortgagor has one year to redeem property and to remain in possession.

    d. Sheriff's Deed issued after one year.

8. Deficiency Judgment - Available in court foreclosure unless mortgage was purchase money mortgage as noted below.

Note: Purchase money is defined as:

    1. Mortgage or trust deed or real property sales contract given to seller as part of purchase price, or
    2. Mortgage or trust deed given to lender to finance purchase of owner-occupied dwelling of four or fewer units.

2. Mortgages Compared to Trust Deeds

a. Parties

In the mortgage there are two parties: the mortgagor (borrower) and the mortgagee (lender). The deed of trust has three: trustor (borrower), trustee (third party), and beneficiary (lender).

b. Title

A mortgage does not convey title; it creates a lien. In a deed of trust the title is conveyed to a trustee (third party) for the benefit of the lender (beneficiary) and is in effect a lien.

c. Statute of Limitations

In a mortgage, an action to foreclose is subject to the statute of limitations. Since it is a promissory note, the mortgagee has four years from the date of the last payment to start foreclosure. With a trust deed, there is no time limit because the third party (trustee) has title and power of sale.

d. Remedy for Default

In a mortgage, the only remedy of the mortgagee (lender) is judicial (court) foreclosure, unless the mortgage contains a power of sale clause. Although the actual mortgage foreclosure takes a short period of time, the redemption period is very long (1 year). The **REDEMPTION PERIOD** *is the legally acceptable time period for buying back one's property after a judicial sale.* In a deed of trust the entire process, including any redemption or sale, requires a short period of time (4 months).

During the one-year mortgage redemption period, (four months for a trust deed), the right of possession remains with the the mortgagor (borrower).

3. Trust Deeds are Preferred to Mortgages

In California, the trust deed is preferred to the mortgage as the usual financing device. The lender has fewer restrictions when using a trust deed. There is: 1) A short period to reinstate prior to the sale and the fact that the sale, once made, is usually absolute. The purchaser can take possession at once, which is not true for a mortgage; 2) The ease and convenience, without having to resort to court action, with which the property may be sold to satisfy the debt if the borrower defaults. California laws favor lenders who use the trust deed, which allows them more freedom in granting loans to deserving buyers.

MORGAGE: A GENERAL TERM

Although mortgages are rarely used in California, the term "mortgage" is so ingrained in the tradition of lending that often trust deeds and other loans are referred to as "mortgages." Adjustable Rate Mortgages and Fixed Rate Mortgages, for example, are deeds of trust. We will use the general words mortgage and deed of trust interchangeably, but mortgagee or mortgagor refer only to mortgages and trustee, trustor, and beneficiary refer only to trust deeds.

B. TRUST DEEDS

1. Trust Deeds are Used in California

Trust deeds (deeds of trust loans) are personal property.

In California the trust deed, sometimes called a deed of trust, is the usual financing instrument. The **TRUST DEED** *is a security device that makes the real property collateral for the promissory note.* **Figure 8-7** shows a copy of a trust deed.

A trust deed needs a note for security, but a note does NOT need a trust deed. A trust deed is not a negotiable instrument; the note is. If the conditions of a note and the trust deed are in conflict, the note prevails.

2. Parties to a Trust Deed

In a trust deed there are three parties. The **TRUSTOR** *is the party that is borrowing the money.* This is usually the buyer, but may also be the owner if the property is being refinanced. The **BENEFICIARY** *is the lender who is lending money for the purchase of real property.* Home lenders in California are usually savings banks, but may also be banks. The **TRUSTEE** *is the third, disinterested party (usually a corporation) who holds title to the property, but only in so far as the trustee may have to sell the property for the beneficiary, should the trustor default.* This is normally a title insurance company. **Figure 8-8** illustrates this three-party relationship.

A trustor signs the promissory note and trust deed, as he or she owes the debt. The promissory note is evidence of the amount owed and the trust deed makes the real estate security for the loan.

A trust deed must have all three parties: trustor, trustee, and beneficiary. The trust deed and note form the lien, which conveys the "bare naked title" of the property to the trustee. The trustee holds title to the real property until the trust deed is paid in full, at which time the title is reconveyed to the trustor through a reconveyance. If the trustor defaults in payments, the beneficiary will instruct the trustee to start the default period, which could ultimately lead to a trustee foreclosure sale.

Figure 8-7

RECORDING REQUESTED BY

ORDER #
APN

WHEN RECORDED MAIL TO

Name
Street
Address
City &
State

SPACE ABOVE THIS LINE FOR RECORDER'S USE

SHORT FORM DEED OF TRUST AND ASSIGNMENT OF RENTS

ALL   PTN.

This Deed of Trust, made this _____ day of _____ , between _____

, herein called TRUSTOR,

whose address is _____
(number and street)   (city)   (state)   (zip)

OLD REPUBLIC TITLE COMPANY, a California corporation, herein called TRUSTEE, and

, herein called BENEFICIARY,

Witnesseth: That Trustor IRREVOCABLY GRANTS, TRANSFERS AND ASSIGNS TO TRUSTEE IN TRUST, WITH POWER OF SALE, that property in _____ County, California, described as:

TOGETHER WITH the rents, issues and profits thereof, SUBJECT, HOWEVER, to the right, power and authority given to and conferred upon Beneficiary by paragraph (10) of the provisions incorporated herein by reference to collect and apply such rents, issues and profits.

For the Purpose of Securing: 1. Performance of each agreement of Trustor incorporated by reference or contained herein. 2. Payment of the indebtedness evidenced by one promissory note of even date herewith, and any extension or renewal thereof, in the principal sum of $_____ executed by Trustor in favor of Beneficiary or order. 3. Payment of such further sums as the then record owner of said property hereafter may borrow from Beneficiary, when evidenced by another note (or notes) reciting it is so secured.

To Protect the Security of This Deed of Trust, Trustor Agrees: By the execution and delivery of this Deed of Trust and the note secured hereby, that provisions (1) to (14), inclusive, of the fictitious deed of trust recorded in Santa Barbara County and Sonoma County October 18, 1961, and in all other counties October 23, 1961, in the book and at the page of Official Records in the office of the county recorder of the county where said property is located, noted below opposite the name of such county, viz.:

COUNTY	BOOK	PAGE	COUNTY	BOOK	PAGE	COUNTY	BOOK	PAGE	COUNTY	BOOK	PAGE
Alameda	435	684	Kings	792	833	Placer	895	301	Sierra	29	335
Alpine	1	250	Lake	362	39	Plumas	151	5	Siskiyou	468	181
Amador	104	348	Lassen	171	471	Riverside	3005	523	Solano	1105	182
Butte	1145	1	Los Angeles	T2055	899	Sacramento	4331	62	Sonoma	1851	689
Calaveras	145	152	Madera	810	170	San Benito	271	383	Stanislaus	1715	456
Colusa	296	617	Marin	1508	339	San Bernardino	5567	61	Sutter	572	297
Contra Costa	3978	47	Mariposa	77	292	San Francisco	A332	905	Tehama	401	289
Del Norte	78	414	Mendocino	579	530	San Joaquin	2470	311	Trinity	93	366
El Dorado	568	456	Merced	1547	538	San Luis Obispo	1151	12	Tulare	2294	275
Fresno	4626	572	Modoc	184	851	San Mateo	4078	420	Tuolumne	135	47
Glenn	422	184	Mono	52	429	Santa Barbara	1878	860	Ventura	2062	386
Humboldt	657	527	Monterey	2194	538	Santa Clara	5336	341	Yolo	653	245
Imperial	1091	501	Napa	639	88	Santa Cruz	1431	494	Yuba	334	486
Inyo	147	598	Nevada	305	320	Shasta	684	528			
Kern	3427	60	Orange	5889	611	San Diego	Series 2	Book 1961,	Page 183887		

(which provisions, identical in all counties, are printed on the reverse hereof) hereby are adopted and incorporated herein and made a part hereof as fully as though set forth herein at length; that he will observe and perform said provisions; and that the references to property, obligations, and parties in said provisions shall be construed to refer to the property, obligations, and parties set forth in this Deed of Trust.

The undersigned Trustor requests that a copy of any Notice of Default and of any Notice of Sale hereunder be mailed to him at his address hereinbefore set forth.

STATE OF CALIFORNIA
COUNTY OF _____ } SS.

On _____ before me, the undersigned, a Notary Public in and for said State, personally appeared _____

personally known to me (or proved to me on the basis of satisfactory evidence) to be the person(s) whose name(s) is/are subscribed to the within instrument and acknowledged to me that he/she/they executed the same in his /her /their authorized capacity(ies), and that by his/her/their signature(s) on the instrument the person(s), or the entity upon behalf of which the person(s) acted, executed the instrument.
WITNESS my hand and official seal.

Signature _____

_____
Name (Typed or Printed)

(Seal)

ORT 100

OLD REPUBLIC TITLE COMPANY

SHORT FORM DEED OF TRUST AND ASSIGNMENT OF RENTS

Figure 8-8

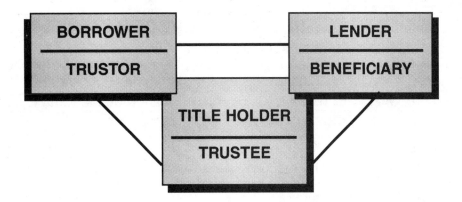

The lender of the money is called the "beneficiary" who holds the trust deed and note. A "beneficiary statement" shows the unpaid balance and the condition of the debt (must be provided within 30 days when requested).

EQUITABLE TITLE *is held by a trustor while he or she is repaying a trust deed and note.* It is **true** ownership in that the trustor may enjoy all customary rights of title and possession.

LEGAL TITLE, "Bare Naked Legal Title," *is held by a trustee until the terms of a trust deed and note have been fulfilled.* When the trustor has paid the note in full, the trustee will reconvey the bare naked legal title.

The trustee receives the naked legal title which is the power to sell the property if the trustor defaults, or reconveys title back to the trustor when paid in full.

3. Full Reconveyance (Proof of Payment in Full)

A **FULL RECONVEYANCE** *provides proof that a promissory note and the accompanying trust deed have been paid in full.* When the note has been paid in full, the beneficiary requests the trustee to grant a full reconveyance, which makes the trustor's legal title a part of the public record and gives evidence that the debt has been paid off. A full reconveyance must be recorded to give public notice, in the county records, that it has been paid. The reconveyance is paid for by the trustor. See **Figure 8-9** for more information about a full reconveyance and **Figure 8-10** for an example.

Figure 8-9

Full Reconveyance

A full reconveyance is a simple written document that offers proof that a loan on real property has been paid off in full. If a trust deed (loan on real property) is to be paid off in full, a request for full reconveyance is to be signed by the beneficiary and sent to the trustee for recording.

The trustor (borrower), who is in the process of paying off a loan secured by a note and deed of trust on a certain piece of real property, wants the following:

1. The return of the original note,

2. The return of the original trust deed, and

3. A "Reconveyance deed" should be recorded in the county recorder's office where the deed of trust is recorded.

When the trustor originally borrowed the money to purchase property or later obtained a loan secured by the property, he or she signed a promissory note and a trust deed. This trust deed, when recorded, became a specific lien. If the trustor tries to sell or refinance the property, this lien will show up on all title searches or title reports until the deed of trust has been "reconveyed."

So it is extremely important for the trustor to have the deed of trust and note returned along with having the beneficiary sign a "Request for Full Reconveyance." Under California Civil Code Section 2941, the beneficiary must forward a deed of reconveyance, within 90 days of receiving the "Request for Full Reconveyance," to the trustee. Violation of this law is a misdemeanor punishable by a $300 fine, plus damages, and/or six months in jail.

VIII. Default and Foreclosure of a Trust Deed

A. DEFAULT ON A TRUST DEED

In California, the procedure and remedy for nonpayment of a trust deed is well established by law. The trust deed is a lien on the property involved. The lender has the legal right to receive the trust deed payment on time. By law the lender can start default action after the 10- to 15-day grace period. A *GRACE PERIOD is a set number of days in which a lender will allow a payment to be late without any penalty*. The lender, at any time after the grace period, may start default action/foreclosure against the trustor. **Figure 8-11** shows the sequence of events that will follow if the trustor does not make the trust deed payments.

Figure 8-10

RECORDING REQUESTED BY

AND WHEN RECORDED MAIL TO

_____ SPACE ABOVE THIS LINE FOR RECORDER'S USE_____

TITLE ORDER NO.　　　TRUSTEE SALE NO.　　　COMPUTER NO.

FULL RECONVEYANCE

now duly appointed Trustee under Deed of Trust

EXECUTED BY:

TO:

TRUSTOR(S)
TRUSTEE

Recorded on　　　　　as Document no.　　　　　Book　　　　　Page
of Official Records in the office of the Recorder of　　　　　County,
California, having been requested in writing, by the holder of the obligation secured by said deed of trust, to reconvey the estate granted to trustee under said deed of trust, DOES HEREBY RECONVEY to the person or persons legally entitled thereto, without warranty, all the estate, title, and interest acquired by trustee under said deed of trust.
Brief description of property:

DATE:

BY: _____
　　　　　　　　Assistant Secretary

STATE OF CALIFORNIA　　　}　SS.

COUNTY OF _____}
On this the_____ day of_____ 19____,
before me the, the undersigned, a Notary Public in and for
said County and State, personally appeared _____

personally known to me or proved to me on the basis of
satisfactory evidence to be the person who executed the within
instrument as an Assistant Secretary, on behalf of the corporation therein named, and acknowledged to me that such
corporation executed the within instrument pursuant to its by-
laws or a resolution of its board of directors.

_____
Notary's Signature _____

SAFECO Stock No. **CA-BNL-0110**

Full Reconveyance

Figure 8-11

PAYMENT PAST DUE	3 MONTHS MINIMUM	21 DAYS MINIMUM	1 DAY
NOTICE OF DEFAULT RECORDED	REINSTATEMENT PERIOD (up to 5 days before sale)	PUBLISHING PERIOD (3 weeks)	TRUSTEE'S SALE

If a note and deed of trust is "silent" on the grace period, the law states it must be more than 10 days.

When a borrower defaults on his or her payments under the trust deed and note, the beneficiary's remedy is to start default action. The beneficiary notifies the trustee of the trustor's failure to make the payments. The trustee then records a notice of default, which will start the foreclosure action.

When the trustee is notified by the lender (beneficiary) of the trustor's nonpayment, the trustee records a "notice of default" (**See Figure 8-12**). This notice contains all the pertinent information about the default. Within 10 days after the recording, the borrower (trustor) and all people who have filed a "request for notice," such as junior lienholders, will receive (by certified or registered mail) notification from the trustee of the default. In addition, the notice of default must be published in a newspaper of general circulation once a week for three weeks.

A seller who agrees to carry back a second trust deed would have a "request for notice of default" recorded to protect his or her (the beneficiary of the second trust deed) interests.

B. TRUSTOR'S RIGHT OF REINSTATEMENT

1. Reinstatement Period (Three Months)

During the three-month reinstatement period after the notice of default is filed, the trustor may reinstate the loan. The **REINSTATEMENT PERIOD** *is the time within which the trustor may pay all past due payments.* To do this, the trustor must pay the beneficiary the following:

1. All past due payments, penalties, taxes, and interest.
2. Any other costs to the beneficiary.
3. All costs and fees owed to the trustee.

The trustor can reinstate a loan up until five days prior to foreclosure. If reinstated, it is again in good standing.

Figure 8-12

RECORDING REQUESTED BY

WHEN RECORDED MAIL TO

_____
_____
_____

SPACE ABOVE THIS LINE FOR RECORDER'S USE ——

TRUST ORDER NO.

Notice of Default and Election to Sell Under Deed of Trust

NOTICE IS HEREBY GIVEN: That _____ , a corporation, is Trustee, or successor
Trustee, or substituted Trustee under a deed of trust dated _____ , executed by _____
_____ as Trustor,
to secure certain obligations in favor of _____
_____
as Beneficiary, recorded _____ , in Book _____ , Page _____ , of Official
Records in the office of the Recorder of _____ County, California, describing land therein as:

said obligations including _____ note _____ for the _____ sum of $ _____ ,

That the beneficial interest under such deed and the obligations secured thereby have been transferred to the undersigned;
That a breach of, and default in, the obligations for which such deed is security has occurred in that payment has not been made of:

That by reason thereof, the undersigned, present beneficiary under such deed, has executed and delivered to said Trustee, or successor Trustee, or substituted Trustee a written Declaration of Default and Demand for sale, and has deposited with said Trustee, or successor Trustee, or substituted Trustee such deed and all documents evidencing obligations secured thereby, and has declared and does hereby declare all sums secured thereby immediately due and payable and has elected and does hereby elect to cause the trust property to be sold to satisfy the obligations secured thereby.

Dated _____

STATE OF CALIFORNIA }
COUNTY OF _____ } SS.
On _____
before me, the undersigned, a Notary Public in and for said County
and State, personally appeared
_____
_____
_____
known to me to be the person ____ whose name _____
subscribed to the within instrument and acknowledged that _____
executed the same.
WITNESS my hand and official seal.

(Seal) _____
Notary Public in and for said County and State
NOTARY—PLEASE PRINT OR TYPE YOUR NAME BELOW SIGNATURE

_____
_____
_____
_____
_____
_____
_____

THIS NOTICE MUST BE RECORDED BY ←
_____
TRUST ORDER NO. _____

If the trustor does not pay the past due payments, taxes, interest, and other charges within the three-month reinstatement period, the reinstatement rights are lost. This reinstatement period runs until five days before the date of sale. Sometimes in special circumstances, and always at the discretion of the lender, the trustor may still be allowed to reinstate the loan after this period. If the beneficiary decides to foreclose, however, he or she will start the process by recording a "notice of sale."

2. Notice Of Sale (21 Days)

The *NOTICE OF SALE is a recorded notice stating the time, place, property description, and type of sale.* Refer back to Figure 8-11, the notice of default. It also serves as the notice of sale. **The notice must be published in a newspaper of general circulation once a week, not more than seven days apart, during the 21-day publishing period.** A copy of the notice must also be posted on the property and in a public place, such as the city hall. Most title insurance companies also post a copy if they are acting as trustee.

3. The Trustee's Sale (Foreclosure Sale)

A trustee's sale is only for the real property backing up the trust deed.

The trustee's sale is held at the time and place stated in the notice of sale. At the public sale, the trustee states the purpose of the sale and describes the property to be sold. All bids must be in the form of cash or cashier's checks.

The first deed holder may bid up to the total amount of the debt without cash. Because it costs the first trust deed holder nothing more than what he or she is already owed, that person will usually make the first bid. The highest bidder obtains the property and will be issued a trustee's deed. Any money more than the amount owed is reimbursed to the trustor. The new owner is entitled to immediate possession.

A trustee's sale is an out of court procedure under the "power of sale" clause in the deed of trust and promissory note. It is the quickest and easiest way for a beneficiary to foreclose on a default of trust deed.

4. Judicial Court Foreclosure for a Trust Deed (Rare)

In rare cases, a beneficiary (lender) in California may want to foreclose by court action instead of the simpler trustee's sale. The reason would be to obtain a deficiency judgment if it was not a purchase money trust deed. See the purchase money section below for more information.

5. Deed In Lieu Of Foreclosure

A *DEED IN LIEU OF FORECLOSURE is a deed given by an owner (borrower) to a lender to prevent the lender from bringing foreclosure proceedings.* **The lender (beneficiary)**

becomes the new owner of the property. It is up to the lender to accept or reject such an offer. This could save the borrower's credit in some circumstances.

C. LIENS NOT ELIMINATED BY FORECLOSURE SALE

Most junior liens are eliminated by a foreclosure sale. The following liens are not necessarily eliminated:

1. Federal tax liens
2. State, county, and city taxes or assessments
3. Mechanic's liens for work begun before the trust deed was recorded

D. PURCHASE MONEY TRUST DEED OR MORTGAGE

A *PURCHASE MONEY INSTRUMENT is a trust deed or mortgage obtained during the purchase of a home (1-to-4 units, owner-occupied).* It is called a purchase money instrument **only when** it is obtained at the time of purchase, not on a refinanced loan. It is an automatic protection given to homeowners (nothing is signed and nothing is mentioned). This is important because if the property is forced into foreclosure, a purchase money trust deed holder, or mortgage lender, cannot obtain a deficiency judgment. (Deficiency judgments may be obtained on FHA and VA home loans because federal law supercedes state law.)

A *DEFICIENCY JUDGMENT is given when the security pledge for a loan does not satisfy the debt upon its default.* If a home was sold at a court foreclosure sale for $217,000 and $240,000 was owed on the property, a lender would have a $23,000 deficiency judgment against the borrower. If it were a purchase money instrument, however, there would be no deficiency judgment.

The purchase money instrument only protects owners of residential dwellings of 1-to-4 units where the owner lives in one unit. Owners of properties having more than four units or properties that do not have a purchase money instrument are not protected against possible deficiency judgments. **Remember:** deficiency judgments can be obtained only if the owner doesn't have a purchase money instrument and is foreclosed upon in a court foreclosure sale.

IX. Second Trust Deeds (Junior TDs)

When the current financial market is tight, a seller may have to take back a second trust deed as part of his or her equity in order to make the sale.

Even if a buyer qualifies for a loan to cover 80% of the cost of a home, he or she may still have a difficult time scraping together the 20% needed for the down payment. When a

buyer does not have enough cash to cover the gap between the sales price and the loan amount, another loan, or "second" trust deed, is sometimes obtained (often from the seller) and the interest charged the buyer is not governed by the usury law.

A. JUNIOR LIENS

Besides seconds, it is also possible for borrowers who qualify to obtain "third" or "fourth" trust deeds, but they are all commonly referred to as second trust deeds or junior liens. They all may be called second trust deeds but their priority is determined by the order in which they were recorded. *Any loan on real property obtained after the first trust deed and secured by a second, third, or subsequent trust deed, is known as a JUNIOR LIEN.* The most senior lien, on the other hand, is the first trust deed.

When a buyer wants to make a smaller cash down payment or an owner wants to convert equity into cash, the best source for a junior loan is a private lender.

Let's look at an example: Smith is buying a house with a sale's price of $250,000. She assumes the seller's loan on the property of $200,000. She applies to her company credit union and is given a second trust deed of $30,000, so all she needs is a cash down payment of $20,000, plus closing costs, to complete the transaction.

B. HOMEOWNER EQUITY LOANS

Second trust deeds are not only obtainable as part of the financing package when a property is first being purchased. Seconds and other junior liens may be arranged any time a qualified borrower wants to borrow money, for whatever reason, as long as there is sufficient equity and enough ready income to support the payments. *EQUITY is the fair market value of a property, minus the amount of money owed to lenders and all other lienholders. HOMEOWNER EQUITY LOANS are loans based on the homeowner's increase in equity caused by inflation, rising property values, and the reduction, by payments, of the existing loan balance.*

Let's suppose Smith, who purchased that new home for $250,000, finds herself in need of money after a few years. Fortunately, her property has increased in market value and is now worth more than $300,000. Even though Smith is already mortgaged up to her ears, she can borrow on her equity; the difference between what she owes and what her property is worth.

Second trust deed notes have a stated interest rate, so they are sold at a discount (reduction in value).

Homeowner equity loans are generally secured by second (junior) trust deeds. They are available from institutional lenders, small finance companies, and individuals who specialize in this area. Lenders will charge a higher interest rate on seconds and other junior trust deeds because they are less secure than primary financing.

C. HOLDER OF A SECOND TRUST DEED (Lender)

Sometimes when purchasing a property, additional funds will be required beyond the cash down payment and the first trust deed. As a result, the seller may loan the buyer more money through the use of a second trust deed. Usually the second trust deed has a higher rate of interest and a shorter payoff period because of the higher risk involved. The usual monthly payment is one percent of the loan.

Second trust deeds often require a balloon payment at the end of the term because they are not fully amortized. The holder of a second trust deed or any junior trust deed has the same rights as does the holder of the first deed of trust. He or she is entitled to his or her payment each month, as is the first trust deed holder. If the trustor defaults on the second, the second trust deed holder, just like the first trust deed holder, can start default action. In addition, if the trustor defaults on the first trust deed, the second trust deed holder can reinstate the first trust deed and start default action against the trustor. If the property's market value is higher than the total amount owed on the first trust deed, it is a wise move for the second trust deed holder to start his or her own default and sale action.

D. REQUEST FOR NOTICE

When a **REQUEST FOR NOTICE** *is recorded, the trustee is required to notify all persons who request notice if a "notice of default" is recorded on a particular property.* **See Figure 8-13.** Any person who has an interest in a particular trust deed, usually a second or third trust deed holder, should want to be informed if the buyer is not paying on the first deed of trust. This information not only informs the junior deed holders of nonpayment on the first trust deed, but it also allows them time to prepare to purchase the trust deed at the forthcoming trustee's sale. It will also give them time to start default actions on their own junior trust deeds.

This request for notice is recorded in the county recorder's office where the property is located. If a seller takes back a second or even a third trust deed, thereby becoming a junior trust deed holder on the property that person has just sold, that person would be wise to record a request for notice. Some request for notice forms are incorporated into the trust deed form, so the request for notice is automatically filed.

E. WRAP-AROUND—ALL INCLUSIVE TRUST DEEDS (AITD)

An *ALL INCLUSIVE TRUST DEED (WRAP-AROUND) is a second trust deed with a face value of both the new amount it secures and the balance due under the first trust deed.* A wrap-around trust deed can take the form of a land contract or a deed of trust. The wrap-around is seldom used except when a property is difficult to sell or credit is tight (high interest rates). This form of security may be used to increase the lender's (seller's) yield upon the sale of property and to provide easy financing for the buyer. Rather than having a new buyer assume an existing loan, the seller carries back a

Figure 8-13

RECORDING REQUESTED BY

AND WHEN RECORDED MAIL TO

NAME
ADDRESS
CITY &
    STATE

—— SPACE ABOVE THIS LINE FOR RECORDER'S USE ——

REQUEST FOR NOTICE

In accordance with section 2924b, Civil Code, request is hereby made that a copy of any notice of default

and a copy of any notice of sale under the deed of trust recorded   19

in Book   page   of official records of   County, (or filed for record

with recorder's serial No.

          County) California, executed by

as trustor in which

is named as beneficiary and

as trustee be mailed to   whose

address is

Signature ....

FOR NOTARY SEAL OR STAMP

STATE OF CALIFORNIA   SS.
COUNTY OF
On this the   day of   19   , before me,
the undersigned, a Notary Public in and for said County and State.
personally appeared

                      . personally known
to me or proved to me on the basis of satisfactory evidence to be the
person   whose name   subscribed to the within
instrument and acknowledged that
executed the same.

NOTARY SIGNATURE

Title Order No.   Escrow No.

STATE OF CALIFORNIA
COUNTY OF_____
On this the_____ day of _____ 19_____ before
me, the undersigned, a Notary Public in and for said County and State.
personally appeared_____
_____ , personally
known to me or proved to me on the basis of satisfactory evidence to
be the_____ President, and_____
_____ , personally
known to me or proved to me on the basis of satisfactory evidence to
be _____ Secretary of the corporation that executed the
within instrument on behalf of the corporation therein named, and
acknowledged to me that such corporation executed the within instrument pursuant to its by-laws or a resolution of its board of directors.

NOTARY SIGNATURE

wrap-around trust deed at a higher rate of interest (if the loan is assumable). The seller continues to pay off the old trust deed out of the payment received from the buyer. Since these payments are larger, the seller gets a margin of profit. The buyer, in turn, gets easy financing and avoids the new loan fees charged by institutional lenders. As always, an attorney should be consulted because wrap-around contracts may require special handling and will not be available with all loans.

Let's look at an example: Smith has a $300,000 property with an existing 6% interest loan of $150,000. He makes a $900 loan payment every month. Jones wants to buy the property and gives Smith $30,000 in cash down, while Smith carries a wrap-around trust deed for the remaining $270,000 owed. He charges Jones 7% interest payable in monthly installments of $1,132. When Smith receives his $1,132 each month, he uses $900 of it to pay off his 6% loan while pocketing the remaining $232. The seller is collecting interest on the existing lender's loan—money that is not his.

X. Land Contract
(Conditional Installment Sales Contract)

Trust deeds, mortgages, and land contracts are all methods of financing: they are financing instruments referred to as "security devices."

The **LAND CONTRACT** *is an instrument of finance in which the seller retains legal ownership of the property until the buyer has made the last payment.* It is usually called a land contract in California, but may also be referred to as a "contract of sale," "agreement of sale," "conditional sales contract," or an "installment sales contract." Since this is a contract between the buyer and seller, the requirements as to the down payment and other conditions of the land contract are negotiable.

When financing is hard to obtain, this can be an alternative to the usual financing methods. Although it is not widely used, it is a valid financing device. **See Figure 8-14.**

An installment sales contract (land contract) can be for both real and personal property. Mortgages and trust deeds are only for real property.

*An owner selling under a land contract is known as a **VENDOR**. A **VENDEE** is a buyer using a land contract.* A vendor can sell his or her store (real property) and store fixtures (personal property) to a vendee by use of a land contract. A land contract is a common way to sell a business.

With a conditional sales contract (land contract), the seller (vendor) gives the buyer (vendee) equitable title and possession but keeps legal title. The vendor is the lender and the vendee is the borrower.

Figure 8-14

RECORDING REQUESTED BY

AND WHEN RECORDED MAIL TO

Name

Street
Address

City &
State

SPACE ABOVE THIS LINE FOR RECORDER'S USE

FORM 1   **LONG FORM SECURITY (INSTALLMENT) LAND CONTRACT WITH POWER OF SALE**   D-120

THIS AGREEMENT, made and entered into this   day of   , 19   , by and
between   (Vendor's name),
whose address is
(hereinafter sometimes referred to as "Vendor"), and
     (Vendee's name), whose address is
     (hereinafter sometimes referred to as "Vendee"); and
STEWART TITLE, (hereinafter sometimes referred to as "Trustee.")
     W I T N E S S E T H :
WHEREAS, Vendor is now the owner of certain real property situated in the County of
State of California, commonly known as
     (property street address), and described as follows:

WHEREAS, Vendor has agreed to sell, and Vendee has agreed to buy said real property on the terms and conditions hereinafter set forth;
WHEREAS, Vendor shall retain legal title as a security interest in said real property until the payment of the balance of the purchase price has been paid by Vendee to Vendor as set forth below.
NOW, THEREFORE, THE PARTIES HERETO DO HEREBY AGREE AS FOLLOWS:
PURCHASE PRICE
1. Vendor agrees to sell, and Vendee agrees to buy all of the aforedescribed real property for the sum of
     (Total purchase price) ($),
lawful money of the United States, as hereinafter more fully set forth.

REQUEST FOR NOTICE OF DEFAULT
2. In accordance with Section 2924b, Civil Code, request is hereby made by the undersigned Vendor and Vendee that a copy of any Notice of Default and a copy of any Notice of Sale under Deed of Trust recorded_____in Book_____, Page_____, Official Records of _____ County, California, as affecting above described property, executed by _____as Trustor in which_____
is named as beneficiary, and_____as Trustee, be mailed to Vendor and Vendee at address in paragraph 3 below.
NOTICES AND REQUEST FOR NOTICE
3. Notices required or permitted under this agreement shall be binding if delivered personally to party sought to be served or if mailed by registered or certified mail, postage prepaid in the United States mail to the following:
Vendor: _____
     _____
     _____   Trustee: Stewart Title
Vendee: _____   505 North Brand, 12th Floor
     _____   Glendale, California 91203
     _____
Vendor and Vendee hereby request that notice of default and notice of sale hereunder be mailed to them at the above address.

PAYMENT OF PURCHASE PRICE
4. Vendee shall pay said purchase price of $_____as follows:
     (a) Vendee shall pay to Vendor the sum of $_____(Down Payment) as and for a down payment.
     (b) Vendee shall take subject to and pay the balance due on that certain note secured by a first trust deed on the above mentioned real property, the principal balance of which is $_____, together with interest thereon at the rate of
percent per annum, payable in installments of
$_____, (monthly payments amount; add "or more" if applicable) per month on the   day of each and
every month with the whole of the then outstanding balance thereof due on the   day of
19   . Each such payment includes payment of the following items under the terms of said note and trust deed:
     (1) Principal and interest;
     (2) Impounds for taxes;   (Strike out
     (3) Impounds for fire insurance;   inapplicable
     (4) Impounds for   items.)
Payments shall be made by Vendee directly to beneficiary of said first trust deed at the following address:

     (If a second trust deed exists, complete (c) below)
     (c) Vendee shall take subject to and pay the balance due on that certain note secured by a second trust deed on the above mentioned real property, principal balance of which is $_____ together with interest thereon at the rate of
percent per annum, payable in installments of $_____(monthly payment amount, add "or more"

274

With a land contract the buyer holds **equitable title**, like a borrower purchasing under a trust deed. He or she is entitled, though, to the full use and enjoyment of the property. **Legal title** is held by the seller until the land contract terms have been completely fulfilled. A grant deed to the property is given only when the land contract is paid off in full.

A land contract is also called a "real property sales contract," an "agreement of sale," an "agreement to purchase," or an "installment sales contract," or a "contract of sale."

Land contracts should be recorded. If the buyer were to default, his or her interest would show as a cloud on the title. To protect his or her interests, the vendee (buyer) should record the land contract.

If a buyer (vendee) defaults on a recorded land contract, the seller (vendor) should file a "quiet title action" to remove the "cloud on title."

Land contracts are legal documents that should be drawn by and discussed with an attorney before use. Legal problems associated with a land contract are: obtaining marketable title, non-recorded status, intervening liens, foreclosure, and quiet title action. As you can see, legal advice is necessary.

The seller keeps legal title (grant deed) under a land contract until all the terms of the contract are met. Buyers record land contracts to give constructive notice regarding their property rights.

XI. Truth in Lending Act Regulation "Z" and Other Acts

The purpose of the Federal Truth in Lending Act is for the lender to disclose the cost of credit terms to the buyer.

This disclosure must be presented to the borrower within 3 business days of receiving the borrower's loan application.

"Regulation Z" applies to dwellings with only one-to-four residential units. Agricultural loans are exempt from the truth in lending law as are business and commercial loans.

A. TRUTH IN LENDING

The Truth in Lending Act, known as Regulation Z, was enacted to protect the consumer by requiring that the lender (creditor) tell the borrower how much he or she is paying for credit. This enables the consumer to make comparisons between various credit sources. Regulation Z also states that the lender (creditor) must express all related financing costs as a percentage, known as the annual percentage rate (APR).

Regulation Z requires a creditor to make the following important financial disclosures:

1) Annual Percentage Rate (APR)*
2) Finance charges
3) Amount financed*
4) Total number of payments
5) Total sales price (credit sales)

*The two most important items, according to Regulation Z, are the APR and the amount financed.

Regulation Z is enforced by the Federal Trade Commission (FTC). The CAR® 3-page Mortgage Loan Disclosure Statement is used to implement Regulation Z (**See Figure 8-15**). **See Figure 8-16** for an example of the CAR® Seller Financing Addendum and Disclosure form.

A low down payment and a long-term loan will increase the total financing cost.

1. Annual Percentage Rate (APR)

APR is the measure or "relative cost of credit" expressed as a yearly rate. It is a percentage rate, NOT an interest rate. If the APR appears in an advertisement, NO other disclosure of terms need be stated because it includes all credit costs.

The ***ANNUAL PERCENTAGE RATE (APR)*** *represents the relationship between the total of the finance charges (interest rate, points, and the loan fee) and the total amount financed, expressed as a percentage.* It must be computed to the nearest one-quarter of one percent and must be printed on the loan form more conspicuously than the rest of the printed material.

Interest rates can be calculated by many different methods that can be very confusing to the borrower. The APR standardizes these figures, calculating all rates by the same formula. Borrowers should look for the APR figure (usually in a box) to compare and find the best APR available.

The APR includes all "finance charges," including assumption charges, but it does not include the 1) cost of a credit report and 2) appraisal fees, which are exempt.

2. Advertising Terms May Require Additional Disclosures

Anyone placing an advertisement for consumer credit must comply with the advertising requirements of the Truth in Lending Act. Disclosures must be made

Figure 8-15

CALIFORNIA
ASSOCIATION
OF REALTORS®

MORTGAGE LOAN DISCLOSURE STATEMENT (BORROWER)

(As required by the Business and Professions Code §10241 and Title 10, California Administrative Code, §2840)

_____
(Name of Broker/Arranger of Credit)

_____
(Business Address of Broker)

I. SUMMARY OF LOAN TERMS

A. PRINCIPAL AMOUNT . . . . $ _____

B. ESTIMATED DEDUCTIONS FROM PRINCIPAL AMOUNT

   1. Costs and Expenses (See Paragraph III-A) . . . . $ _____

   *2. Broker Commission/Organization Fee (See Paragraph III-B) . . . . $ _____

   3. Lender Origination Fee/Discounts (See Paragraph III-B) . . . . $ _____

   4. Additional compensation will/may be received from lender not deducted from loan proceeds.

       ☐ YES $ _____ (if known) or ☐ NO

   5. Amount to be Paid on Authorization of Borrower (See Paragraph III) . . . . $ _____

C. ESTIMATED CASH PAYABLE TO BORROWER (A less B) . . . . $ _____

II. GENERAL INFORMATION ABOUT LOAN

A. If this loan is made, Borrower will be required to pay the principal and interest at _____% per year, payable as follows: _____ payments of $ _____
    (number of payments)   (monthly/quarterly/annually)
and a **FINAL/BALLOON** payment of $ _____ to pay off the loan in full.

NOTICE TO BORROWER: IF YOU DO NOT HAVE THE FUNDS TO PAY THE BALLOON PAYMENT WHEN IT COMES DUE, YOU MAY HAVE TO OBTAIN A NEW LOAN AGAINST YOUR PROPERTY TO MAKE THE BALLOON PAYMENT. IN THAT CASE, YOU MAY AGAIN HAVE TO PAY COMMISSIONS, FEES AND EXPENSES FOR THE ARRANGING OF THE NEW LOAN. IN ADDITION, IF YOU ARE UNABLE TO MAKE THE MONTHLY PAYMENTS OR THE BALLOON PAYMENT, YOU MAY LOSE THE PROPERTY AND ALL OF YOUR EQUITY THROUGH FORECLOSURE. KEEP THIS IN MIND IN DECIDING UPON THE AMOUNT AND TERMS OF THIS LOAN.

B. This loan will be evidenced by a promissory note and secured by a deed of trust on property identified as (street address or legal description):
_____
_____

C. 1. Liens presently against this property (do not include loan being applied for):

Nature of Lien	Priority	Lienholder's Name	Amount Owing
_____	_____	_____	_____
_____	_____	_____	_____
_____	_____	_____	_____

   2. Liens that will remain against this property after the loan being applied for is made or arranged (include loan being applied for):

Nature of Lien	Priority	Lienholder's Name	Amount Owing
_____	_____	_____	_____
_____	_____	_____	_____
_____	_____	_____	_____

NOTICE TO BORROWER: Be sure that you state the amount of all liens as accurately as possible. If you contract with the broker to arrange this loan, but it cannot be arranged because you did not state these liens correctly, you may be liable to pay commissions, fees and expenses even though you do not obtain the loan.

REVISION DATE 10/2000   Print Date
MS-11 (PAGE 1 OF 3)

Borrower acknowledges receipt of copy of this page.
   Borrower's Initials (_____)(_____)

EQUAL HOUSING OPPORTUNITY

Reviewed by
Broker or Designee _____ Date _____

MORTGAGE LOAN DISCLOSURE STATEMENT (MS-11 PAGE 1 OF 3)

Property Address: _____ Date: _____

D. If Borrower pays all or part of the loan principal before it is due, a PREPAYMENT PENALTY computed as follows may be charged:

_____
_____
_____

E. Late Charges: ☐ YES, see loan documents   or ☐ NO

F. The purchase of credit life or credit disability insurance by a borrower is not required as a condition of making this loan.

G. Is the real property which will secure the requested loan an "owner-occupied dwelling?" ☐ YES____ or ☐ NO____
(Borrower initial opposite YES or NO)

An "owner-occupied dwelling" means a single dwelling unit in a condominium or cooperative or residential building of four or fewer separate dwelling units, one of which will be owned and occupied by a signatory to the mortgage or deed of trust for this loan within 90 days of the signing of the mortgage or deed of trust.

III. DEDUCTIONS FROM LOAN PROCEEDS

A. Estimated Maximum Costs and Expenses of Arranging the Loan to be Paid Out of Loan Principal:

	PAYABLE TO	
	Broker	**Others**
1. Appraisal fee	_____	_____
2. Escrow fee	_____	_____
3. Title insurance policy	_____	_____
4. Notary fees	_____	_____
5. Recording fees	_____	_____
6. Credit investigation fees	_____	_____
7. Other costs and expenses:		
_____	_____	_____
_____	_____	_____
_____	_____	_____
Total Costs and Expenses	$ _____	

*B. Compensation . . . . $ _____
  1. Brokerage Commission/Origination Fee . . . . $ _____
  2. Lender Origination Fee/Discounts . . . . $ _____

C. Estimated Payment to be Made out of Loan Principal on Authorization of Borrower

	PAYABLE TO	
	Broker	**Others**
1. Fire or other hazard insurance premiums	_____	_____
2. Credit life or disability insurance premiums (see Paragraph II-F)	_____	_____
3. Beneficiary statement fees	_____	_____
4. Reconveyance and similar fees	_____	_____
5. Discharge of existing liens against property:		
_____	_____	_____
_____	_____	_____
6. Other:		
_____	_____	_____
_____	_____	_____
_____	_____	_____
Total to be Paid on Authorization of Borrower	$ _____	

If this loan is secured by a first deed of trust on dwellings in a principal amount of less than $30,000 or secured by a junior lien on dwellings in a principal amount of less than $20,000, the undersigned licensee certifies that the loan will be made in compliance with Article 7 of Chapter 3 of the Real Estate Law.

*This loan **may / will / will not** (delete two) be made wholly or in part from broker-controlled funds as defined in Section 10241(j) of the Business and Professions Code.

REVISION DATE 10/2000   Print Date
MS-11 (PAGE 2 OF 3)

Borrower acknowledges receipt of copy of this page.
Borrower's Initials (_____)(_____)

Reviewed by
Broker or Designee _____ Date _____

EQUAL HOUSING OPPORTUNITY

MORTGAGE LOAN DISCLOSURE STATEMENT (MS-11 PAGE 2 OF 3)

Property Address: _____   Date: _____

*NOTICE TO BORROWER: This disclosure statement may be used if the Broker is acting as an agent in arranging the loan by a third person or if the loan will be made with funds owned or controlled by the broker. If the Broker indicates in the above statement that the loan "may" be made out of Broker-controlled funds, the Broker must notify the borrower prior to the close of escrow if the funds to be received by the Borrower are in fact Broker-controlled funds.

_____   _____
Name of Broker   Broker Representative

_____   _____
License Number   License Number

_____ OR _____
Signature of Broker   Signature

The Department of Real Estate License Information phone number is _____.

NOTICE TO BORROWER:

DO NOT SIGN THIS STATEMENT UNTIL YOU HAVE READ AND UNDERSTAND ALL OF THE INFORMATION IN IT. ALL PARTS OF THE FORM MUST BE COMPLETED BEFORE YOU SIGN.

Borrower hereby acknowledges the receipt of a copy of this statement.

DATED _____   _____
                                                                                  (Borrower)

                                                                _____
                                                                                  (Borrower)

<u>Broker Review:</u> Signature of Real Estate Broker after review of this statement.

DATED _____   _____
                                                                Real Estate Broker or Assistant Pursuant to Section 2725

REVISION DATE 10/2000   Print Date
MS-11 (PAGE 3 OF 3)

MORTGAGE LOAN DISCLOSURE STATEMENT (MS-11 PAGE 3 OF 3)

Figure 8-16

CALIFORNIA
ASSOCIATION
OF REALTORS®

SELLER FINANCING ADDENDUM AND DISCLOSURE
(California Civil Code §§2956-2967)

(C.A.R. Form SFA, Revised 10/02)

This is an addendum to the ☐ Residential Purchase Agreement, ☐ Counter Offer, or ☐ Other _____
_____, ("Agreement"), dated _____.
On property known as _____ ("Property"),
between _____ ("Buyer"),
and _____ ("Seller").
Seller agrees to extend credit to Buyer as follows:

1. **PRINCIPAL; INTEREST; PAYMENT; MATURITY TERMS:** ☐ Principal amount $ _____, interest at _____%
   per annum, payable at approximately $ _____ per ☐ month, ☐ year, or ☐ other _____,
   remaining principal balance due in _____ years.
2. **LOAN APPLICATION; CREDIT REPORT:** Within **5 (or** ☐ _____ **) Days** After Acceptance: **(a)** Buyer shall provide Seller a completed
   loan application on a form acceptable to Seller (such as a FNMA/FHLMC Uniform Residential Loan Application for residential one to four
   unit properties); and **(b)** Buyer authorizes Seller and/or Agent to obtain, at Buyer's expense, a copy of Buyer's credit report. Buyer shall
   provide any supporting documentation reasonably requested by Seller. Seller may cancel this Agreement in writing if Buyer fails to
   provide such documents within that time, or if Seller disapproves any above item within **5 (or** ☐ _____ **) Days** After receipt of each item.
3. **CREDIT DOCUMENTS:** This extension of credit by Seller will be evidenced by: ☐ Note and deed of trust; ☐ All-inclusive
   note and deed of trust; ☐ Installment land sale contract; ☐ Lease/option (when parties intend transfer of equitable title);
   OR ☐ Other (specify) _____

**THE FOLLOWING TERMS APPLY ONLY IF CHECKED. SELLER IS ADVISED TO READ ALL TERMS, EVEN THOSE NOT
CHECKED, TO UNDERSTAND WHAT IS OR IS NOT INCLUDED, AND, IF NOT INCLUDED, THE CONSEQUENCES THEREOF.**

4. ☐ **LATE CHARGE:** If any payment is not made within _____ **Days** After it is due, a late charge of either $ _____,
   or _____% of the installment due, may be charged to Buyer. **NOTE:** On single family residences that Buyer intends to occupy,
   California Civil Code §2954.4(a) limits the late charge to no more than 6% of the total monthly payment due and requires a grace
   period of no less than 10 days.
5. ☐ **BALLOON PAYMENT:** The extension of credit will provide for a balloon payment, in the amount of $ _____,
   plus any accrued interest, which is due on _____ (date).
6. ☐ **PREPAYMENT:** If all or part of this extension of credit is paid early, Seller may charge a prepayment penalty as follows (if
   applicable): _____. Caution: California Civil Code
   §2954.9 contains limitations on prepayment penalties for residential one-to-four unit properties.
7. ☐ **DUE ON SALE:** If any interest in the Property is sold or otherwise transferred, Seller has the option to require immediate
   payment of the entire unpaid principal balance, plus any accrued interest.
8.* ☐ **REQUEST FOR COPY OF NOTICE OF DEFAULT:** A request for a copy of Notice of Default as defined in California Civil
   Code §2924b will be recorded. **If Not**, Seller is advised to consider recording a Request for Notice of Default.
9.* ☐ **REQUEST FOR NOTICE OF DELINQUENCY:** A request for Notice of Delinquency, as defined in California Civil Code §2924e,
   to be signed and paid for by Buyer, will be made to senior lienholders. **If not**, Seller is advised to consider making a Request for
   Notice of Delinquency. Seller is advised to check with senior lienholders to verify whether they will honor this request.
10.* ☐ **TAX SERVICE:**
   A. If property taxes on the Property become delinquent, tax service will be arranged to report to Seller. **If not**, Seller is
   advised to consider retaining a tax service, or to otherwise determine that property taxes are paid.
   B. ☐ Buyer, ☐ Seller, shall be responsible for the initial and continued retention of, and payment for, such tax service.
11. ☐ **TITLE INSURANCE:** Title insurance coverage will be provided to **both** Seller and Buyer, insuring their respective interests
   in the Property. **If not**, Buyer and Seller are advised to consider securing such title insurance coverage.
12. ☐ **HAZARD INSURANCE:**
   A. The parties' escrow holder or insurance carrier will be directed to include a loss payee endorsement, adding Seller to
   the Property insurance policy. **If not**, Seller is advised to secure such an endorsement, or acquire a separate
   insurance policy.
   B. Property insurance **does not** include earthquake or flood insurance coverage, unless checked:
   ☐ Earthquake insurance will be obtained; ☐ Flood insurance will be obtained.
13. ☐ **PROCEEDS TO BUYER:** Buyer will receive cash proceeds at the close of the sale transaction. The amount received will be
   approximately $ _____, from _____ (indicate source of
   proceeds). Buyer represents that the purpose of such disbursement is as follows: _____.
14. ☐ **NEGATIVE AMORTIZATION; DEFERRED INTEREST:** Negative amortization results when Buyer's periodic payments are
   less than the amount of interest earned on the obligation. Deferred interest also results when the obligation does not
   require periodic payments for a period of time. In either case, interest is not payable as it accrues. This accrued interest
   will have to be paid by Buyer at a later time, and may result in Buyer owing more on the obligation than at its origination.
   The credit being extended to Buyer by Seller will provide for negative amortization or deferred interest as indicated below.
   (Check A, B, or C. CHECK ONE ONLY.)
   ☐ **A.** All negative amortization or deferred interest shall be added to the principal _____
   (e.g., annually, monthly, etc.), and thereafter shall bear interest at the rate specified in the credit documents (compound interest);
   OR ☐ **B.** All deferred interest shall be due and payable, along with principal, at maturity;
   OR ☐ **C.** Other _____

*(For Paragraphs 8-10) In order to receive timely and continued notification, Seller is advised to record appropriate notices and/or to
notify appropriate parties of any change in Seller's address.

SFA REVISED 10/02 (PAGE 1 OF 3) Print Date

Buyer's Initials (_____)(_____)
Seller's Initials (_____)(_____)

Reviewed by _____ Date _____

EQUAL HOUSING
OPPORTUNITY

SELLER FINANCING ADDENDUM AND DISCLOSURE (SFA PAGE 1 OF 3)

Property Address: _____ Date: _____

15. ☐ ALL-INCLUSIVE DEED OF TRUST; INSTALLMENT LAND SALE CONTRACT: This transaction involves the use of an all-inclusive (or wraparound) deed of trust or an installment land sale contract. That deed of trust or contract shall provide as follows:

    A. In the event of an acceleration of any senior encumbrance, the responsibility for payment, or for legal defense is: _____
_____ ; OR ☐ **Is not** specified in the credit or security documents.

    B. In the event of the prepayment of a senior encumbrance, the responsibilities and rights of Buyer and Seller regarding refinancing, prepayment penalties, and any prepayment discounts are: _____ ;
OR ☐ **Are not** specified in the documents evidencing credit.

    C. Buyer will make periodic payments to _____ (Seller, collection agent, or any neutral third party), who will be responsible for disbursing payments to the payee(s) on the senior encumbrance(s) and to Seller. **NOTE:** The Parties are advised to designate a neutral third party for these purposes.

16. ☐ TAX IDENTIFICATION NUMBERS: Buyer and Seller shall each provide to each other their Social Security Numbers or Taxpayer Identification Numbers.

17. ☐ OTHER CREDIT TERMS _____
_____

18. ☐ RECORDING: The documents evidencing credit (paragraph 3) will be recorded with the county recorder where the Property is located. **If not,** Buyer and Seller are advised that their respective interests in the Property may be jeopardized by intervening liens, judgments, encumbrances, or subsequent transfers.

19. ☐ JUNIOR FINANCING: There will be additional financing, secured by the Property, junior to this Seller financing. Explain: _____

20. SENIOR LOANS AND ENCUMBRANCES: The following information is provided on loans and/or encumbrances that will be **senior** to Seller financing. **NOTE:** The following are estimates, unless otherwise marked with an asterisk (*). If checked: ☐ A separate sheet with information on additional senior loans/encumbrances is attached

	1st	2nd
A. Original Balance	$ _____	$ _____
B. Current Balance	$ _____	$ _____
C. Periodic Payment (e.g. $100/month):	$ _____	$ _____/
Including Impounds of:	$ _____	$ _____/
D. Interest Rate (per annum)	_____%	_____%
E. Fixed or Variable Rate:	_____	_____
If Variable Rate: Lifetime Cap (Ceiling)	_____	_____
Indicator (Underlying Index)	_____	_____
Margins	_____	_____
F. Maturity Date	_____	_____
G. Amount of Balloon Payment	$ _____	$ _____
H. Date Balloon Payment Due	_____	_____
I. Potential for Negative Amortization? (Yes, No, or Unknown)	_____	_____
J. Due on Sale? (Yes, No, or Unknown)	_____	_____
K. Pre-payment penalty? (Yes, No, or Unknown)	_____	_____
L. Are payments current? (Yes, No, or Unknown)	_____	_____

21. BUYER'S CREDITWORTHINESS: (CHECK EITHER A OR B. Do not check both.) In addition to the loan application, credit report and other information requested under paragraph 2:

    A. ☐ No other disclosure concerning Buyer's creditworthiness has been made to Seller;

OR **B.** ☐ The following representations concerning Buyer's creditworthiness are made by Buyer(s) to Seller:

Borrower _____	Co-Borrower _____
1. Occupation _____	1. Occupation _____
2. Employer _____	2. Employer _____
3. Length of Employment _____	3. Length of Employment _____
4. Monthly Gross Income _____	4. Monthly Gross Income _____
5. Other _____	5. Other _____

22. ADDED, DELETED OR SUBSTITUTED BUYERS: The addition, deletion or substitution of any person or entity under this Agreement or to title prior to close of escrow shall require Seller's written consent. Seller may grant or withhold consent in Seller's sole discretion. Any additional or substituted person or entity shall, if requested by Seller, submit to Seller the same documentation as required for the original named Buyer. Seller and/or Brokers may obtain a credit report, at Buyer's expense, on any such person or entity.

Buyer's Initials (_____)(_____)
Seller's Initials (_____)(_____)

SFA REVISED 10/02 (PAGE 2 OF 3)

Reviewed by _____ Date _____

EQUAL HOUSING OPPORTUNITY

SELLER FINANCING ADDENDUM AND DISCLOSURE (SFA PAGE 2 OF 3)

Property Address: _____ Date: _____

23. **CAUTION:**

A. If the Seller financing requires a balloon payment, Seller shall give Buyer written notice, according to the terms of Civil Code §2966, at least 90 and not more than 150 days before the balloon payment is due if the transaction is for the purchase of a dwelling for not more than four families.

B. If **any** obligation secured by the Property calls for a balloon payment, Seller and Buyer are aware that refinancing of the balloon payment at maturity may be difficult or impossible, depending on conditions in the conventional mortgage marketplace at that time. There are no assurances that new financing or a loan extension will be available when the balloon prepayment, or any prepayment, is due.

C. If **any** of the existing or proposed loans or extensions of credit would require refinancing as a result of a lack of full amortization, such refinancing might be difficult or impossible in the conventional mortgage marketplace.

D. In the event of default by Buyer: (1) Seller may have to reinstate and/or make monthly payments on any and all senior encumbrances (including real property taxes) in order to protect Seller's secured interest; (2) Seller's rights are generally limited to foreclosure on the Property, pursuant to California Code of Civil Procedure §580b; and (3) the Property may lack sufficient equity to protect Seller's interests if the Property decreases in value.

If this three-page Addendum and Disclosure is used in a transaction for the purchase of a dwelling for not more than four families, it shall be prepared by an Arranger of Credit as defined in California Civil Code §2957(a). (The Arranger of Credit is usually the agent who obtained the offer.)

Arranger of Credit - (Print Firm Name) _____ By _____ Date _____

Address _____ City _____ State _____ Zip _____

Phone _____ Fax _____

BUYER AND SELLER ACKNOWLEDGE AND AGREE THAT BROKERS: (A) WILL NOT PROVIDE LEGAL OR TAX ADVICE; (B) WILL NOT PROVIDE OTHER ADVICE OR INFORMATION THAT EXCEEDS THE KNOWLEDGE, EDUCATION AND EXPERIENCE REQUIRED TO OBTAIN A REAL ESTATE LICENSE; OR (C) HAVE NOT AND WILL NOT VERIFY ANY INFORMATION PROVIDED BY EITHER BUYER OR SELLER. BUYER AND SELLER AGREE THAT THEY WILL SEEK LEGAL, TAX AND OTHER DESIRED ASSISTANCE FROM APPROPRIATE PROFESSIONALS. BUYER AND SELLER ACKNOWLEDGE THAT THE INFORMATION EACH HAS PROVIDED TO THE ARRANGER OF CREDIT FOR INCLUSION IN THIS DISCLOSURE FORM IS ACCURATE. BUYER AND SELLER FURTHER ACKNOWLEDGE THAT EACH HAS RECEIVED A COMPLETED COPY OF THIS DISCLOSURE FORM.

Buyer _____ Date _____
(signature)

Address _____ City _____ State _____ Zip _____

Phone _____ Fax _____ E-mail _____

Buyer _____ Date _____
(signature)

Address _____ City _____ State _____ Zip _____

Phone _____ Fax _____ E-mail _____

Seller _____ Date _____
(signature)

Address _____ City _____ State _____ Zip _____

Phone _____ Fax _____ E-mail _____

Seller _____ Date _____
(signature)

Address _____ City _____ State _____ Zip _____

Phone _____ Fax _____ E-mail _____

SURE TRAC
The System for Success™

Published by the
California Association of REALTORS®

EQUAL HOUSING OPPORTUNITY

SFA REVISED 10/02 (PAGE 3 OF 3)

Reviewed by _____ Date _____

SELLER FINANCING ADDENDUM AND DISCLOSURE (SFA PAGE 3 OF 3)

"clearly and conspicuously." If only the annual percentage (APR) rate is disclosed, additional disclosures are not required. If, however, an advertisement contains any one of the following terms, then the ad must also disclose other credit terms:

1. The amount or percentage of any down payment
2. The number of payments or period of repayment
3. The amount of any payment
4. The amount of any finance charge

When advertising a graduated payment loan, differences in monthly payments must be disclosed.

B. RIGHT TO CANCEL (Federal Notice of Right to Cancel)

Loans subsequent (future loans) have a 3-day right of rescission by the borrower (not original first trust deeds).

The **RIGHT TO CANCEL** *is the federal law that gives a borrower the right to rescind (cancel) any loan transaction only if it is a business loan or a second trust deed secured by the borrower's home.* The borrower has until midnight of the third business day following the signing to cancel.

A first trust deed loan to finance the purchase of the borrower's home carries no right of rescission. However, a first loan secured on the borrower's home for any other purpose, or a second loan on the same home, may be canceled within 3 business days. **See Figure 8-17**.

The borrower has the right to rescind when a loan is secured by a second trust deed on an owner-occupied single family residence already owned by the borrower.

C. EQUAL CREDIT OPPORTUNITY ACT

The **EQUAL CREDIT OPPORTUNITY ACT** *is a federal law prohibiting those who lend money from discriminating against borrowers based on their race, sex, color, religion, national origin, age, or marital status.* It is specifically designed to come to the aid of low income group members (who receive income from public assistance programs), women, and the elderly.

This law limits the lender's access to personal information regarding:

1. marriage and divorce,
2. receipt of alimony and child support, and
3. birth control and child bearing.

Figure 8-17

NOTICE OF RIGHT TO CANCEL
CALIFORNIA ASSOCIATION OF REALTORS® (CAR) STANDARD FORM

Name(s) of Customer(s)_____

Type of Loan _____

Amount of Loan _____ $_____

You have entered into a transaction which will result in a deed of trust or mortgage on your home. You have a legal right under federal law to cancel this transaction, without cost, within three business days from whichever of the following occurs last:

(1)   the date of the transaction, which is _____ : or

(2)   the date you received your Truth in Lending disclosures; or

(3)   the date you received this notice of your right to cancel.

If you cancel the transaction, the deed of trust or mortgage is also cancelled. Within 20 calendar days after we receive your notice, we must take the steps necessary to reflect the fact that the deed of trust or mortgage on your home has been cancelled, and we must return to you any money or property you have given to us or to anyone else in connection with this transaction.

You may keep any money or property we have given you until we have done the things mentioned above, but you must then offer to return the money or property. If it is impractical or unfair for you to return the property you must offer its reasonable value. You may offer to return the property at your home or at the location of the property. Money must be returned to the address below. If we do not take possession of the money or property within 20 calendar days of your offer, you may keep it without further obligation.

ACKNOWLEDGEMENT OF RECEIPT

I hereby acknowledge receipt of TWO copies of the foregoing Notice of Right to Cancel.

_____ , 19____   _____
(Date)   (Customer's Signature)

_____
(All joint owners must sign)

HOW TO CANCEL

If you decide to cancel this transaction, you may do so by notifying us in writing, at the following address:

_____
(Creditor's Name)
_____
(Address)
_____
(City, State, Zip Code)

You may use any written statement that is signed and dated by you and states your intention to cancel, or you may use this notice by dating and signing below. Keep one copy of this notice because it contains important information about your rights.

If you cancel by mail or telegram, you must send the notice no later than midnight of _____

_____ (or midnight of the third business day following
(date)

the latest of the three events listed above). If you send your written notice to cancel some other way, it must be delivered to the above address no later than that time.

_____ , 19____   _____
(Date)   (Customer's Signature)

OFFICE USE ONLY
Reviewed by Broker or Designee _____
Date _____

EQUAL HOUSING OPPORTUNITY
SF-Apr-90

FORM NRC-14

It can also require lenders to consider individuals on the merits of their personal credit, as distinct from the bad credit history of a joint account. It also insists that lenders respond quickly to loan applications and be prepared to explain any loan refusal.

D. SOLDIERS AND SAILORS CIVIL RELIEF ACT

The *SOLDIERS AND SAILORS CIVIL RELIEF ACT is a law passed by Congress to protect persons serving in the military, and their dependents, from loss of real property through foreclosure.*

In general, the law prohibits the sale or foreclosure of real estate owned by a military person without his or her expressed approval or a court order. It also extends foreclosure proceedings and the mortgage redemption period. Career soldiers are exempt.

XII. SUMMARY

Leverage is the practice of purchasing real estate using a small amount of your own money and a larger proportion of borrowed funds. Buyers generally **hypothecate** their property as security for a real estate loan, meaning they provide title as security for the loan, without giving up possession.

A **promissory note** is the basic instrument used to evidence the obligation or debt and can be a **straight note**, an **installment note with a balloon payment** or the most commonly used in California, a **fully amortized note**.

With the proper requirements, a promissory note can be a **fully negotiable instrument**, like a check, easily transferred to an innocent third party known as a **holder in due course**.

An **acceleration clause** speeds up the balance due based on the occurrence of a specific event. A buyer can assume a loan on a property by accepting responsibility (with the lender's consent) for the full payment of the loan, but cannot assume an existing loan that contains an **alienation clause** (where the entire balance becomes due when the property is sold, assigned, or transferred). A **subordination clause** allows a borrower to obtain additional loans on the property that have a higher priority. A **prepayment penalty** may only be charged during the first five years of a one-to-four unit home loan.

Real estate loans involve **simple interest**. The **nominal interest rate** is stated in the note, whereas the **effective interest rate** includes interest, points, and loan fees. The formula for finding interest is:

Interest = Principal x Rate x Time

With a **fixed interest rate loan**, the payments are the same for the life of the loan. **Amortization** is the repaying of a loan (principal and interest), in regular payments over the term of the loan. If the interest rate charges are higher than the monthly payment, it's called **negative amortization**. An **adjusted rate mortgage ("ARM"** or trust deed) has a fluxuating interest rate based on a specific index, meaning the payment amounts may also change.

A **point** equals 1% of the loan amount. **Usury** is charging more than the legally allowed percentage of interest.

The three financial instruments (security devices) used in California are: 1) **mortgages** (rare), 2) **trust deeds** (1st and 2nds are common), and 3) **land contracts** (uncommon). In California, the terms mortgage and trust deed are often used interchangeably, but in reality we are usually referring to trust deeds.

A **trust deed** (deed of trust loan) is personal property, and needs a **note** for security. It is not a negotiable instrument, but the note is. The **trustor** borrows the money from the **beneficiary**, who is the lender. A **trustee** is the third, disinterested party (usually a corporation) who holds title to the property on the condition it may have to be sold for the beneficiary if the trustor defaults. **Equitable title** is held by the trustor while repaying the trust deed and note in full, at which time he or she receives the legal or **"bare naked"** title. A **full reconveyance** provides proof that a promissory note and trust deed have been paid in full.

If a borrower defaults on a trust deed and note, the remedy is to start a **default action** (after a 10-15 day grace period). The sequence of events includes: 1) the recording of the default, 2) a 3-month minimum reinstatement period, 3) a three consecutive week minimum publishing period, and 4) a one-day trustee's sale (**foreclosure**).

Any loan on real property secured by a second, third, or subsequent trust deed is known as a **junior lien**. The best sources for junior liens are **private lenders**.

Homeowner equity loans are based on the increase in equity caused by inflation, rising property values, and the reduction, by payments, of the existing loan balance. They are generally secured by second (junior) trust deeds.

A **land contract** is also called a real property sales contract, an agreement of sale, an agreement to purchase, or an installment sales contract. It is an instrument of finance in which the **vendor** (seller) retains legal ownership of property until the **vendee** (buyer) has made the last payment. A **wrap-around**, or all inclusive trust deed, is a second trust deed with a face value of both the new amount it secures and the balance due under the first trust deed.

The **Truth in Lending Act (Regulation Z)** requires lenders to disclose the costs of credit terms to borrowers within three business days of receiving a loan application. The two most important terms are the **Annual Percentage Rate (APR)** and amount financed. APR is the "cost of credit" expressed in percentage terms.

A borrower has the **right to rescind** within three days when a loan is secured by a second trust deed and on an owner-occupied single family residence already owned by the borrower.

The **Equal Credit Opportunity Act** is a federal law prohibiting money lenders from discriminating against borrowers based on race, sex, color, religion, national origin, age, or marital status. The **Soldiers and Sailors Civil Relief Act** protects military personnel and their dependents from foreclosure.

XIII. TERMINOLOGY - CHAPTER 8

A. Acceleration Clause
B. Adjustable Rate Mortgage
C. Alienation Clause
D. Amortization
E. Amortization Book
F. Annual Percentage Rate
G. Assumption
H. Beneficiary
I. Default
J. Deficiency Judgment
K. Equal Credit Opportunity
L. Equitable Title
M. Equity
N. Grace Period
O. Graduated Payment Mortgage

P. Holder in Due Course
Q. Hypothecation
R. Interest
S. Junior Lien or Second Trust Deed
T. Land Contract
U. Legal Title
V. Leverage
W. Point
X. Prepayment Penalty
Y. Promissory Note
Z. Purchase Money Instrument
AA. Reconveyance Deed
BB. Reinstatement Period
CC. Request for Notice of Default
DD. Right to Cancel

EE. Straight Note
FF. Subordination Clause
GG. Trust Deed
HH. Trustee
II. Trustee's Sale
JJ. Trustor
KK. Truth in Lending Act
LL. Usury
MM. Vendee
NN. Vendor
OO. Wrap-Around (Trust Deed)

1.____ An instrument used to transfer title back from a trustee to the equitable owner of real estate.

2.____ A second trust deed for which the monthly payment includes the amount of monthly payment on the existing first trust deed.

3.____ Federal law granting women financial independence and preventing lenders from considering such negative credit aspects as the possibility of a woman having children and dropping out of the labor market.

4.____ A mortgage or deed of trust for which the payments increase over the term of the loan. The payments may increase as the buyer's earnings increase.

5.____ The amount for which the borrower is personally liable on a note and mortgage if the foreclosure sale does not bring enough to cover the debt.

6.____ A penalty under a note, mortgage, or deed of trust imposed when the loan is paid before it is due.

7.____ The total cost of financing expressed as one simple annual percentage rate. This rate must be clearly expressed on any loan agreement.

8.____ A promise in writing to pay a specified amount during a limited time, or on demand, to a named person.

9.____ Clause used in a deed of trust that gives the lender the right to demand payment in full upon the happening of a certain event.

10.____ Ownership by one who does not have legal title, such as a vendee under a land contract or, technically, a trustor under a deed of trust.

11.____ A sale at auction by a trustee under a deed of trust, pursuant to foreclosure proceedings.

12.____ A type of lien that is subordinate to a prior lien.

13.____ An instrument used in place of a mortgage in most western states that is based on the Spanish legal tradition. Property is transferred to a trustee by the borrower (trustor) in favor of the lender (beneficiary) and reconveyed upon payment in full.

14.____ A type of acceleration clause, calling for a debt under a mortgage or deed of trust, to be due in its entirety upon transfer of ownership.

15.____ The use of financing to allow a small amount of cash to purchase and control a large property investment.

16.____ A period of time past the due date for a payment (mortgage, insurance, etc.) during which a payment may be made and not considered delinquent.

17.____ Purchaser or buyer, especially on a land contract.

18.____ A nonamortized note for which the principal is due in a lump sum upon maturity.

19.____ Charging an illegal rate or amount of interest on a loan.

20.____ Payment of debt in regular, periodic installments of principal and interest, as opposed to interest only payments.

21.____ The seller of property under a land contract.

22.____ The kind of title held by the vendor under a land contract and the trustee under a deed of trust. They are still owed money by the buyer.

23.____ An installment contract for the sale of land. The seller (vendor) has legal title until paid in full. The buyer (vendee) has equitable title during the contract term.

24.____ A financing charge equal to one percent of the amount of the loan.

25.____ Money charged for the use of money.

26.____ A failure to perform the financial obligation to pay under a loan.

27.____ A holder of a check or note who takes the note in good faith, on the assumption it is valid.

28.____ The borrower under a deed of trust.

29.____ In a deed of trust, the person who acts as an intermediary between the trustor and the beneficiary.

30.____ A lender for whose benefit a trust is created in those states where trust deeds are commonly used instead of mortgages.

31.____ The ownership interest in real property; it is the market value minus any unpaid loan amount.

32.____ Agreement by the buyer to take over the financial responsibility for real property under the existing note and trust deed.

33.____ An agreement by which a lender substitutes a junior loan position for a senior loan position.

34.____ A schedule of monthly payments that varies according to interest rates and number of monthly payments.

35.____ Mortgage loans on which the interest rate is periodically adjusted to more closely coincide with current rates.

36.____ Regulation Z under the Federal Reserve regulations that requires a credit purchaser be advised, in writing, of all costs connected with the credit portion of their purchase.

37.____ The principle of using real property as security for a debt while the borrower retains possession.

38.____ A recorded form requiring the trustee to notify the trustor in the event of a default on the deed of trust to a property.

39.____ A limited amount of time during which the trustor has the right to pay all past due payments and charges due on a loan to bring it current.

40.____ Part of the Truth In Lending Law that allows a borrower to rescind a loan transaction until midnight of the third business day, on business loans and second trust deeds secured by a borrower's residence.

41.____ The original loan taken out when purchasing a property, not a refinanced or junior loan.

XIV. MULTIPLE CHOICE

1. How long is the trust deed reinstatement period after the notice of default has been filed?

    a. 2 months
    b. 3 months
    c. 4 months
    d. 1 month

2. If the beneficiary must foreclose on the property, the trustee will start the process by recording a:

    a. Notice of Sale.
    b. Notice of Default.
    c. Notice of Conveyance.
    d. None of the above.

3. A request for a notice of default on a first trust deed is for the benefit of the:

    a. trustee.
    b. vendee.
    c. beneficiary.
    d. trustor.

4. Any person who has an interest in a particular trust deed (i.e., second or third trust deed holders) should be sure to file a:

    a. trustee's notice.
    b. lender's notice.
    c. request for notice.
    d. deficiency notice.

5. In real estate terms, "alienation" means most nearly the opposite of:

    a. origination.
    b. acquisition.
    c. amortization.
    d. reconveyance.

6. A minimum of how many days must elapse between the first notice of sale and the actual date of the trustee's sale?

    a. 90
    b. 111
    c. 21
    d. None of the above

7. The figure that represents the relationship of the total finance charges to the total amount financed is known as the:

    a. lender's percentage rate.

    b. borrower's percentage rate.

    c. annual percentage rate.

    d. finance percentage rate.

8. What kind of instrument refers to real property that is sold on credit where the seller retains legal title until the debt is paid off?

    a. VA loan

    b. Pledge agreement

    c. Mortgage

    d. Conditional sales contract

9. One month's interest payment on a straight note amounts to $180. At 9% per annum interest rate, what is the face amount of the note?

    a. $26,000

    b. $24,000

    c. $20,000

    d. $27,000

10. Under the Equal Credit Opportunity Act, what information is the lender allowed to obtain regarding the borrower?

    a. Marital status

    b. Receipt of any alimony or child support money

    c. Length of time on the job

    d. Intentions regarding size of family

ANSWERS: 1. b; 2. b; 3. c; 4. c; 5. b; 6. c; 7. c; 8. d; 9. b; 10. c

Chapter 9
Financial Institutions

www.countrywide.com
Large Home Lender
www.wellsfargo.com
Wells Fargo

Inflation (when prices appreciate) protects both the lender and trustor. There is more equity protecting the lender if there is a default.

The real estate money market, like any other commodity market, changes constantly. Money for financing real estate may be plentiful in one month or quarter, then scarce and expensive in the next. The money market is no longer national, it has become a global market. A broker must be able to finance real estate transactions every month if he or she expects to remain in business. Because of this, a broker must be able to use all the standard financing methods and any unconventional methods that may fit the time and situation.

Before you advertise a property or present it to a prospect, try to visualize all the ways the property may be financed. The more alternatives available, the more likely you are to negotiate a sale. Real estate finance continues to become more variable and more complex as time goes on. This chapter will explain the sources of funds available from financial institutions, the government's role, and other creative prospects and information that will assist you when offering financing.

I. Our Ever Changing Economy (Economic Cycles)

General level of prices: When prices decrease, the value of money increases and when prices increase, the value of money decreases.

Because our government's spending and taxing policies shift with every new election, our economy is in a constant state of transition. From month-to-month, it is difficult to predict what amount of financing money will be available and what rate of interest will be charged. These influences, multiplied over a period of years, make it nearly impossible to accurately project long-term trends in the money supply.

INFLATION is the result of too much money chasing too few goods. When the economy is going very well, most people are making more money and spending it too freely, thereby driving up the price of real estate and other goods. The Fed, sensing that inflation is out of control, starts applying the brakes and starts restricting the amount of money available. This and higher interest rates decrease borrowing. If the Fed is forced to apply the brakes hard, deflation will occur. *DEFLATION is when prices of real estate, goods, and services go down.*

A "seller's market" is when prices rise due to shortages of available properties, and a "buyer's market" is when prices fall.

It is a *BUYER'S MARKET when the prices of real estate are down; terms are easy and there is usually a great deal of real estate listed for sale or rent.* Buyers have a choice; there is more to pick and choose from, at lower prices. In a *SELLER'S MARKET the prices of real estate are up and there is less real estate listed for sale or rent.* This is due to increased demand and lagging supplies.

Changes in consumerism, land use, and the real estate industry all affect real estate in future years.

A. THE FEDERAL RESERVE BANKING SYSTEM ("Fed")

The Federal Reserve has nothing directly to do with raising and lowering interest rates on government insured FHA loans or guaranteed VA loans; it works to stimulate or slow down the nation's entire economy.

The Federal Reserve Banking System is the single greatest influence on the cost and supply of money for real estate loans. It is the link between America's private financial institutions and the taxing and spending policies of the federal government. The *FEDERAL RESERVE BANKING SYSTEM (The "Fed") is the nation's central banking authority.* If the Fed makes money tight, thus restricting the amount of available loan funds, demand for the available funds increases, pushing interest rates higher. Conversely, if the Fed increases the amount of money in circulation, interest rates go down. In this way they keep centralized control over the interest rates for not only banks, but for all lending institutions.

A "tight money policy" from the Fed restricts loan activity and increases interest rates to mercifully slow down the economy, and thus prevents "overheating" the economy and higher, uncontrolled inflation.

These operations and the other important functions of the Federal Reserve System are supervised by the Federal Reserve Board. The ***FEDERAL RESERVE BOARD*** *is a committee appointed by the President, but is politically independent.* In regulating the amount and flow of loan money available to banks, the board has indirect but far-reaching influence over all lending institutions and the economy as a whole.

The Federal Reserve's monetary policies influence the supply of money by:

1. buying and selling government T-bonds and T-securities,
2. raising and lowering the reserve requirement,
3. raising and lowering the discount rate to member banks, and
4. margin requirements (percentage loaned on stocks and bonds).

www.federalreserve.gov/sitemap.htm **(Federal Reserve Board)**
www.ustreas.gov **(U.S. Treasury)**
www.occ.treas.gov **(Office of the Comptroller of the Currency)**
www.frbsf.org **(Federal Reserve Bank of San Francisco - 12th District)**

B. GROSS DOMESTIC PRODUCT *(Measures Economic Activity)*

We can monitor growth in our economy and the influence of the Fed by watching closely any changes in the gross domestic product. The ***GROSS DOMESTIC PRODUCT (GDP)*** *is the total value of all goods and services produced by an economy during a specific period of time.* It serves as a kind of monetary barometer that shows us the rate and areas of greatest growth.

The term Gross Domestic Product (GDP) is the measure of the total value of production (goods and services) from "our home economy"; specifically, the United States.

C. CHANGING INTEREST RATES *(Affect Real Estate)*

The economy goes in cycles. Interest rates go up and down. When interest rates go down, people will buy more homes. When interest rates go up, people will buy fewer homes, and have a harder time selling their homes. When interest rates go down, homes become more affordable.

If a homeowner has a high interest rate and the rate goes down, he or she may choose to refinance. *REFINANCING is the process of obtaining a new loan to pay off the old loan.* If interest rates fall dramatically, it is wise to consider refinancing. **In a tight money market, lenders may wave prepayment penalty clauses in order to lend out that money at a higher rate than old loans.**

II. Shopping for a Loan

All the variables of our changing economy come home in a very personal way when a borrower goes out to look for a loan. For the average person, borrowing the money necessary to buy a house is the largest financial obligation he or she is likely to assume in his or her lifetime. It's an extremely important decision, second only to the selection of the property itself. The salesperson should advise caution and careful consideration before a promissory note is signed. Shopping around for a loan from several different loan sources is an excellent idea. Even if the borrower has found financing that he or she feels is acceptable, talking to other lenders should never be discouraged. **Figure 9-1** provides a detailed discussion of the steps in obtaining a loan.

A. LOAN TO VALUE (Percent of Appraised Value Lender Will Loan)

LOAN TO VALUE is the percentage of appraised value the lender will loan the borrower to purchase the property. It is abbreviated as L-T-V or L to V. The lower the L to V, the higher the down payment has to be. The lower the L to V, the more equity is required.

Most lenders commonly request an 80 percent L-T-V ratio, but this varies depending on many factors. The lower the L-T-V, the greater the down payment (more equity funds are required).

B. ESTIMATE OF SETTLEMENT COSTS (RESPA)

The primary purpose of RESPA is to require lenders to make special disclosures, without cost to the borrowers, for loans involving the sale or transfer of one-to-four unit residential dwellings.

The lender must give the applicant the HUD booklet that explains closing costs and has until three business days after receipt of a loan application to provide a good faith estimate of the actual settlement costs to the borrower.

This disclosure (RESPA) must include:

1. the rate of interest,
2. points to be charged,
3. any additional loan fees and charges, and
4. escrow, title, and other allowable costs, which could add up to $1,000 or more above lender's estimates.

Figure 9-1

STEPS IN OBTAINING A LOAN

1. Application

After deciding that a real estate loan is necessary, the first step in obtaining the loan is filling out a loan application. It would be a good idea to shop around and check for the best rate and terms at various savings institutions before applying because, despite what many people suspect, every lender is different. Finding the right loan is as important as finding the right piece of real estate. The application will request detailed information regarding both the property and the borrower.

2. Analysis

The application generally receives a preliminary screening to determine if there are any obvious and glaring reasons why either the prospective borrower or the property could not qualify for a loan. This process is accomplished by credit scoring. This analysis is followed by a professional appraisal of the property and an in-depth investigation into the credit background of the applicant (in addition to credit scoring). The lender wants to know how likely the borrower is to meet monthly payments and pay back the loan. This is analyzed with reference to the borrower's "capacity" and "desire" to pay.

CAPACITY is determined based upon a borrower's savings, valuable property, and income and evaluated in terms of the reliability of these assets. Excellent evidence of capacity would be good collateral. *COLLATERAL is valuable property pledged as a guarantee for payment of a loan. DESIRE (to pay) is demonstrated by a good credit history reflecting the discipline to make monthly payments on time.* A background of late payments and loan defaults would make it difficult to get loan approval.

3. Processing

If loan analysis proves favorable and financing terms are acceptable to all parties, it is then time to get the terms of the agreement down on paper. Processing involves typing up the loan documents, preparing necessary disclosure statements, and issuing instructions to the escrow holder.

4. Escrow

All the paperwork of the loan transaction ends up in escrow along with all the other contracts involved in the purchase of real property. The trust deed and promissory note are signed and passed along to the escrow company where the deal is closed.

5. Servicing

Loan servicing involves mailing monthly loan statements, collecting payments, and seeing to it that all records are kept up to date. Some lenders service their own loans while others hire independent mortgage companies to handle the paperwork for them. Loan servicing also involves all correspondence for late and delinquent payments.

Qualifying for a Loan

All lenders set their own standards for evaluating who qualifies and who does not qualify for loan money. These standards are reflected in the interest rates charged. Some lenders have very strict requirements, while others will take a greater risk but charge a higher rate of interest—especially on second trust deeds. Real estate agents can obtain more specific guidelines simply by contacting local lenders.

Traditionally, lending institutions decided whether or not a borrower was qualified based upon a simple formula: the property should not cost more than two-and-a-half times the borrower's annual income. Today, however, many lenders recognize that this method can be very inadequate. It fails to take into account other debts that the borrower might be paying off and doesn't give the middle income property buyer, or those entering the housing market for the first time, much of a chance with today's high-cost real estate.

New rules of thumb consider a borrower's other debts along with the housing payments. Long term debts are added to these payments, and the sum is referred to as the borrower's total monthly expenses.

One standard rule was that a borrower's monthly expenses should be no more than 25 percent of all total monthly income. Now, in California, it is closer to 3½ to 1 ratio. Another rule, which is applied to borrowers who are not heavily in debt elsewhere, requires that their annual income be approximately 30 percent of the cost of the property. This is a variation on the traditional formula reflecting a more realistic attitude on the part of lenders.

Appraisal of the Property

Just as the borrower is evaluated during the loan process, lenders evaluate the property being purchased. They want to be certain that the price being paid reflects a fair market value. If a property is overpriced and the borrower defaults, it might be difficult for the lender to recoup the amount of the loan. This process of determining a property's fair market value is known as appraisal and is discussed in detail in Chapters 10 and 11.

Institutional lenders are not likely to lend the entire amount needed for the purchase of a property. Most often they will determine the fair market value and lend a set percentage of that amount. This "loan to value ratio" (L-T-V) is generally 80 percent to 90 percent at banks and savings banks and 70 percent if the loan comes from an insurance company. Collateral is required but most often the property itself (including any structures) is used as security for the loan.

The idea is to alert the borrower to, at the beginning of the loan process, how much cash besides the down payment will be needed to close escrow. Usually the lender will provide the complete estimated settlement cost form along with the loan application.

C. CREDIT SCORING (Access to Credit Profile)

CREDIT SCORING gives lenders a fast, objective measurement of your ability to repay a loan or make timely credit payments. It is based solely on information in consumer credit reports maintained at one of the credit reporting agencies. Factors comprising a credit score include:

> If a credit agency refuses to provide a copy of a credit report to an applicant who is denied credit, the applicant can:
> 1. file civil action against the credit agency;
> 2. negotiate a settlement; or
> 3. require the credit agency to pay all legal fees.

1. **Payment History** - What is your track record?
2. **Amounts Owed** - How much is too much?
3. **Length of Credit History** - How established is yours?
4. **New Credit** - Are you taking on more debt?
5. **Types of Credit Use** - Is it a "healthy" mix?

The most widely used credit bureau scores are developed by Fair, Isaac and Company. These are known as **FICO SCORES**. See **Figure 9-2** *for a fuller description of credit scoring, which is often difficult to explain.*

D. THE LOAN APPLICATION

The lender needs a loan application from the borrower so that the borrower's financial condition can be analyzed. **Figure 9-3** shows two pages of the FHLMC/FNMA application form that is used by most financial institutions. The application provides the lender with the following:

1. Information about property being financed
2. Information about borrower (and co-borrower, if any)
3. Sources of income and analysis
4. Monthly housing expenses (present and proposed)
5. Balance sheet
6. Other information relevant to the borrower's financial status

If a loan application section requests information regarding marital status or race, the applicant can refuse to complete this section.

E. EQUITY (Market Value Less Debt)

When shopping for a loan, the lender wants to determine your worth, or equity, so they will require you to fill out an accounting balance sheet as part of the application. *EQUITY is your net worth; it is the amount that is left after subtracting all that you owe (debt) from what you own (assets).* Lenders want to see your equity on paper. Equity shows them your ability to make the down payment and meet other expenses. It is

Figure 9-2

CREDIT SCORING

Over the past several years, lenders have increased their use of "credit scores," derived from information in a consumer's credit report, using a mathematical model to develop a three-digit score and determine whether or not to make a loan, and at what interest rate. The enactment of SB 1607 (Figueroa), CAR's landmark credit-scoring legislation, gives consumers access to their credit scores. In addition to providing consumers with their specific credit score and key reasons why a score was not better, the legislation also gives consumers the right to receive a copy of their credit scores when they request copies of their credit file.

WHAT IS CREDIT SCORING?

Credit scores are assigned numbers used by lenders to determine whether a consumer will get a loan and at what interest rate. Individual lenders often contract with a credit reporting agency such as Trans Union, Experian, or Equifax who compile consumer credit information. These companies then contract with a credit scoring company, more often than not, Fair, Isaacs and Company (www.fairisaac.com), who own the mathematical model used to create the score. They provide the lender with a list of "reason codes" that the lender can choose from when receiving scores for consumers applying for mortgages. The reason codes can include things like, "too few bank card accounts," "too many sub-prime accounts," etc. The credit scoring company uses information from a consumer's credit report, together with these reason codes and the mathematical formula to create an individual's credit score.

This new law will:

1. require lenders to provide consumers with their specific credit score, what credit information went into making up the score, and an explanation of how credit scores work in the loan approval process;

2. compel credit reporting agencies to correct inaccurate information in a timely manner; and

3. require credit reporting agencies to correct inaccurate information more quickly and provide consumers with additional legal recourse if an agency continues to report inaccurate information once they become aware that a mistake has been made.

www.transunion.com
TransUnion
www.experian.com/experian us.html
Experian
Equifax- www.equifax_com
Equifax

Figure 9-3

Uniform Residential Loan Application

This application is designed to be completed by the applicant(s) with the lender's assistance. Applicants should complete this form as "Borrower" or "Co-Borrower", as applicable. Co-Borrower information must also be provided (and the appropriate box checked) when ☐ the income or assets of a person other than the "Borrower" (including the Borrower's spouse) will be used as a basis for loan qualification or ☐ the income or assets of the Borrower's spouse will not be used as a basis for loan qualification, but his or her liabilities must be considered because the Borrower resides in a community property state, the security property is located in a community property state, or the Borrower is relying on other property located in a community property state as a basis for repayment of the loan.

I. TYPE OF MORTGAGE AND TERMS OF LOAN

Mortgage Applied for:	☐ VA ☐ Conventional ☐ Other: ☐ FHA ☐ FmHA	Agency Case Number	Lender Case No.

Amount $	Interest Rate %	No. of Months	Amortization Type:	☐ Fixed Rate ☐ GPM	☐ Other (explain): ☐ ARM (type):

II. PROPERTY INFORMATION AND PURPOSE OF LOAN

Subject Property Address (street, city, state, & ZIP)	No. of Units

Legal Description of Subject Property (attach description if necessary)	Year Built

Purpose of Loan	☐ Purchase ☐ Construction ☐ Other (explain): ☐ Refinance ☐ Construction-Permanent	Property will be: ☐ Primary Residence ☐ Secondary Residence ☐ Investment

Complete this line if construction or construction-permanent loan.

Year Lot Acquired	Original Cost $	Amount Existing Liens $	(a) Present Value of Lot $	(b) Cost of Improvements $	Total (a + b) $

Complete this line if this is a refinance loan.

Year Acquired	Original Cost $	Amount Existing Liens $	Purpose of Refinance	Describe Improvements ☐ made ☐ to be made Cost: $

Title will be held in what Name(s)	Manner in which Title will be held	Estate will be held in: ☐ Fee Simple ☐ Leasehold (show expiration date)

Source of Down Payment, Settlement Charges and/or Subordinate Financing (explain)

III. BORROWER INFORMATION

Borrower	Co-Borrower
Borrower's Name (include Jr. or Sr. if applicable)	Co-Borrower's Name (include Jr. or Sr. if applicable)

Social Security Number	Home Phone (incl. area code)	Age	Yrs. School	Social Security Number	Home Phone (incl. area code)	Age	Yrs. School

☐ Married ☐ Unmarried (include single, divorced, widowed) ☐ Separated	Dependents (not listed by Co-Borrower) no. / ages	☐ Married ☐ Unmarried (include single, divorced, widowed) ☐ Separated	Dependents (not listed by Borrower) no. / ages

Present Address (street, city, state, ZIP) ☐ Own ☐ Rent ____ No. Yrs.	Present Address (street, city, state, ZIP) ☐ Own ☐ Rent ____ No. Yrs.

If residing at present address for less than two years, complete the following:

Former Address (street, city, state, ZIP) ☐ Own ☐ Rent ____ No. Yrs.	Former Address (street, city, state, ZIP) ☐ Own ☐ Rent ____ No. Yrs.

Former Address (street, city, state, ZIP) ☐ Own ☐ Rent ____ No. Yrs.	Former Address (street, city, state, ZIP) ☐ Own ☐ Rent ____ No. Yrs.

IV. EMPLOYMENT INFORMATION

Borrower	Co-Borrower
Name & Address of Employer ☐ Self Employed	Yrs. on this job	Name & Address of Employer ☐ Self Employed	Yrs. on this job

	Yrs. employed in this line of work/profession		Yrs. employed in this line of work/profession

Position/Title/Type of Business	Business Phone (incl. area code)	Position/Title/Type of Business	Business Phone (incl. area code)

If employed in current position for less than two years or if currently employed in more than one position, complete the following:

Name & Address of Employer ☐ Self Employed	Dates (from - to)	Name & Address of Employer ☐ Self Employed	Dates (from - to)
	Monthly Income $		Monthly Income $
Position/Title/Type of Business	Business Phone (incl. area code)	Position/Title/Type of Business	Business Phone (incl. area code)

Name & Address of Employer ☐ Self Employed	Dates (from - to)	Name & Address of Employer ☐ Self Employed	Dates (from - to)
	Monthly Income $		Monthly Income $
Position/Title/Type of Business	Business Phone (incl. area code)	Position/Title/Type of Business	Business Phone (incl. area code)

Freddie Mac Form 65   Fannie Mae Form 1003

V. MONTHLY INCOME AND COMBINED HOUSING EXPENSE INFORMATION

Gross Monthly Income	Borrower	Co-Borrower	Total	Combined Monthly Housing Expense	Present	Proposed
Base Empl. Income *	$	$	$	Rent	$	
Overtime				First Mortgage (P&I)		$
Bonuses				Other Financing (P&I)		
Commissions				Hazard Insurance		
Dividends/Interest				Real Estate Taxes		
Net Rental Income				Mortgage Insurance		
Other (before completing, see the notice in "describe other income," below)				Homeowner Assn. Dues		
				Other:		
Total	$	$	$	Total	$	$

* Self Employed Borrower(s) may be required to provide additional documentation such as tax returns and financial statements.

Describe Other Income *Notice:* Alimony, child support, or separate maintenance income need not be revealed if the Borrower (B) or Co-Borrower (C) does not choose to have it considered for repaying this loan.

B/C		Monthly Amount
		$

VI. ASSETS AND LIABILITIES

This Statement and any applicable supporting schedules may be completed jointly by both married and unmarried Co-Borrowers if their assets and liabilities are sufficiently joined so that the Statement can be meaningfully and fairly presented on a combined basis; otherwise separate Statements and Schedules are required. If the Co-Borrower section was completed about a spouse, this Statement and supporting schedules must be completed about that spouse also.

Completed ☐ Jointly ☐ Not Jointly

ASSETS Description	Cash or Market Value	Liabilities and Pledged Assets. List the creditor's name, address and account number for all outstanding debts, including automobile loans, revolving charge accounts, real estate loans, alimony, child support, stock pledges, etc. Use continuation sheet, if necessary. Indicate by (*) those liabilities which will be satisfied upon sale of real estate owned or upon refinancing of the subject property.	Monthly Payt. & Mos. Left to Pay	Unpaid Balance
Cash deposit toward purchase held by:	$	**LIABILITIES**		
		Name and address of Company	$ Payt./Mos.	$
List checking and savings accounts below				
Name and address of Bank, S&L, or Credit Union				
		Acct. no.		
		Name and address of Company	$ Payt./Mos.	$
Acct. no.	$			
Name and address of Bank, S&L, or Credit Union				
		Acct. no.		
		Name and address of Company	$ Payt./Mos.	$
Acct. no.	$			
Name and address of Bank, S&L, or Credit Union				
		Acct. no.		
		Name and address of Company	$ Payt./Mos.	$
Acct. no.	$			
Name and address of Bank, S&L, or Credit Union				
		Acct. no.		
		Name and address of Company	$ Payt./Mos.	$
Acct. no.	$			
Stocks & Bonds (Company name/number & description)	$			
		Acct. no.		
		Name and address of Company	$ Payt./Mos.	$
Life insurance net cash value	$			
Face amount: $				
Subtotal Liquid Assets	$			
Real estate owned (enter market value from schedule of real estate owned)	$			
		Acct. no.		
Vested interest in retirement fund	$	Name and address of Company	$ Payt./Mos.	$
Net worth of business(es) owned (attach financial statement)	$			
Automobiles owned (make and year)	$			
		Acct. no.		
		Alimony/Child Support/Separate Maintenance Payments Owed to:	$	
Other Assets (itemize)	$	Job Related Expense (child care, union dues, etc.)	$	
		Total Monthly Payments	$	
Total Assets a.	$	Net Worth (a minus b) ➤	$	Total Liabilities b.	$

Freddie Mac Form 65

Fannie Mae Form 1003

common practice to ask buyers what the equity is in their current home in order to determine if they financially qualify for the price of a new home.

The equity (worth) you have in a home is its market value minus what you owe on it.

F. LIQUIDITY (Convert Assets into Cash)

LIQUIDITY *is the ability of a borrower to convert assets into cash so that debt obligation can be paid when due.* It is not enough to make money; there also must be the ability to pay bills on time. Real estate has very little liquidity. Depending on market conditions, it could take a very long time to sell a piece of real estate. On the other hand, income property may bring in more cash monthly than goes out for expenditures.

G. OPPORTUNITY COST (Cost of Non-Liquidity)

OPPORTUNITY COST *is the lost profit one could have made by the alternative investment action not taken.* It is the cost of non-liquidity. If you own a home, the lost return on that equity is referred to as opportunity cost.

III. Sources of Real Estate Funds

The remainder of this chapter will deal with the different institutions that lend money to finance the purchase of real property. Details concerning the types of lenders and how they make loans will be explained and different kinds of government loan participation are compared and discussed. In addition, the responsibilities of a broker acting as a loan agent or security dealer are outlined.

The three areas of demand for borrowing money are:

1. *Construction funds to build*
2. *To finance a purchase*
3. *For refinancing*

IV. Institutional Lenders

INSTITUTIONAL LENDERS *are very large corporations that lend the money of their depositors to finance real estate transactions.* Their principal function is to act as financial intermediaries; to transfer money from those who have funds to those who wish to borrow. **Figure 9-4** illustrates which groups are institutional and which are noninstitutional lenders.

Institutional lenders are big lenders who pool funds so they can lend to individual borrowers. They include: insurance companies, banks, and mutual saving banks.

Figure 9-4

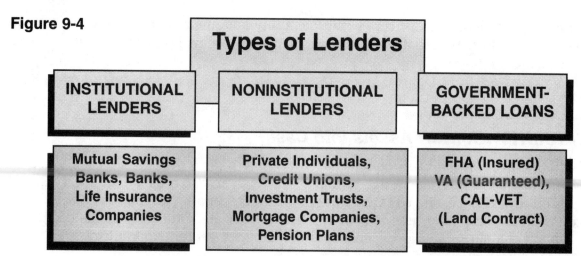

A. FEDERAL DEPOSIT INSURANCE CORPORATION (FDIC)

The *FEDERAL DEPOSIT INSURANCE CORPORATION (FDIC) is a government corporation that, for a fee, insures each account of a depositor up to $100,000.* All the deposits in savings banks and banks in California are insured by the FDIC because they pay for the premiums. If a depositor has more than the insured $100,000 in any one account, then he or she may lose that amount in excess of $100,000 if there is a savings bank or bank failure. It would be wise to put any excess in a different account or financial institution.

www.fdic.gov
Federal Deposit Insurance Corp.

B. MUTUAL SAVINGS BANKS (Greatest Source of Money for Home Loans)

In California, most of the home purchases are financed by mutual savings banks. They make more real estate loans than any other financial institution. This is because until recently all the money that savings banks lent out was in the form of real estate loans. Even with current changes in the banking industry, savings banks are still the primary home mortgage lenders. Savings banks are either federally or state licensed.

This is a brief description of how a mutual savings bank works: A person wishing to deposit funds in exchange for interest would open an account (i.e., savings, money market, or checking) at a mutual savings bank. These funds would then be invested in real estate loans, which yield higher rates of interest for the institution than is being paid out to depositors. This system allows savers to obtain interest from mutual savings bank accounts and at the same time provide a source of loan funds to home buyers. All mutual savings banks can make 80% loans on any amount that is acceptable to them. Mutual savings banks will occasionally make 90 and 95 percent (loan-to-value) loans if the loans are covered by private mortgage insurance.

Mutual savings banks primarily make loans on single family homes or condos that are owner-occupied. They will also make loans on apartment buildings and manufactured homes. Larger mutual savings banks will often make construction loans for a tract and then supply each owner with permanent, long-term financing.

Mutual savings banks, like banks and insurance companies, charge points and loan fees. Points will range from one to five percent (points) of the total loan amount. Loan fees are usually $300 to $500 while appraisal costs start at $200, but vary depending on the property. All institutional lenders tend to charge comparable points and fees according to economic conditions in the market place.

Mutual savings banks are primary sources for residential loans because they invest most of their money in home loans.

Figure 9-5 compares the lending priorities of mutual savings banks with banks and life insurance companies.

Figure 9-5

PRIORITIES OF INSTITUTIONAL LENDERS

MUTUAL SAVINGS BANKS (Residential Lenders)	BANKS (General Purpose Lenders)	LIFE INSURANCE COMPANIES (Big Money Lenders)
1. Single family homes and condos	1. Business and auto loans	1. Large shopping centers and office buildings
2. Apartment buildings	2. Conventional home loans	2. Hotels and industrial properties
3. Home improvement loans	3. Government backed FHA and VA home loans	3. FHA and VA home loans through mortgage companies (Government-backed loans)
4. Manufactured homes	4. Credit cards	
	5. Construction loans	

C. BANKS

Banks are *GENERAL PURPOSE LENDERS, which means they lend money for anything from real estate to sailboats.* Even so, they are the second largest lenders for real estate in California. All national banks are required to be members of the Federal Reserve System,

How Financial Institutions Determine Interest Rates

Financial institutions obtain funds from their depositors and pay a modest return in the form of interest or dividends to keep their depositors money invested with them. In order to make money, the spread that a financial institution must make between the interest rate it charges on loans and the interest rate paid to its depositors must be at least 2%. So if a bank pays 7% to depositors, it can only make loans at 9% or higher in order to stay in business.

while a state bank may be a member by choice. There is no great difference between real estate loans that a state bank makes and loans that the federal banks make. Interest rates and other loan terms are comparable to those offered by mutual savings banks.

Any commercial bank may lend money on real property if it is a first loan on that property. In general, there are four types of real estate financing:

1. **First Trust Deed Loans** — The bank finances long-term loans for existing land and the buildings.

2. **Construction Loans (or Interim Loans)** — Money is provided for the construction of a building, to be repaid when the construction is complete.

A construction loan (or interim loan) is a short-term loan.

3. **Take-Out Loans (Repayment of Interim Loan)** — Permanent long-term loans are made to pay off the interim lender upon completion of construction of commercial or apartment projects and are called "takeout loans" because they take out the interim lender.

When computing the unspecified maturity date on a construction loan, the repayment date is computed from the date of the note.

4. **Home Improvement Loans** — This type of loan is for repairing and modernizing existing buildings.

D. LIFE INSURANCE COMPANIES

A primary source for a very large loan is a life insurance company. Obtaining a small ($20,000) loan would be least likely from an insurance company.

Life insurance companies have more money to lend than either a bank or a savings bank. They are more conservative lenders and specialize in large loans for commercial projects, but they also make conventional loans on residential property. These companies supply

---

Truth in Savings Act

"Annual Percentage Yield" defined as APY

The Truth in Savings Act requires depository institutions to furnish "clear, complete, and uniform disclosures" of the terms of their savings and checking deposit accounts. It also requires institutions to pay interest on the consumer's daily balance. Certain practices are no longer permitted, such as advertising "Free Accounts" and then charging maintenance or per-check fees, or requiring minimum balances.

This Act introduces a standard method of expressing interest paid to depositors called "Annual Percentage Yield" or APY. This new method takes into account the interest rate and also the compounding. So if the APY is 4.46 percent, a hundred dollars will earn $4.46 in one year. The higher the APY, the more interest is paid.

---

most of the loan funds for properties where a great deal of capital is required (such as high-rise office buildings, shopping centers, industrial properties, and hotels).

Life Insurance companies seldom make construction loans.

Life insurance companies also invest large amounts of money in trust deeds that are either insured by the FHA or guaranteed by the VA. Mortgage companies make such loans for insurance companies. Quite often, these mortgage companies, in return for a servicing fee, collect the loan payments for the insurance company.

Life insurance companies are governed by the laws of the state in which they are incorporated, as well as the laws of the states in which they do business. There is no state restriction concerning the number of years for which a loan can be made. However, company policy usually restricts the term to no more than 30 years and requires a loan to be amortized.

When making loans, life insurance companies in California are restricted to a 75 percent maximum of market value of any given property. This is not a requirement if the loan is insured by the Federal Housing Administration (FHA) or guaranteed by the Veterans Administration (VA).

Life insurance companies use mortgage companies to obtain and service their trust deeds.

V. Noninstitutional Lenders

Noninstitutional lenders are smaller lenders which include: private lenders, mortgage companies, investment trusts, pension plans, and credit unions.

NONINSTITUTIONAL LENDERS *are individuals and organizations that lend on a private or individual basis.* Both institutional and noninstitutional lenders make loans that may be or may not be backed by one of the government loan programs.

CONVENTIONAL LOANS *are loans that are not insured or guaranteed by the United States government.*

Conventional loans are NOT insured or guaranteed by the federal government.

A. PRIVATE INDIVIDUALS

Any real estate loan by an individual is considered a private individual loan. Most individuals who lend money on real estate are sellers who take back a second trust deed as part of the real estate transaction. The seller will be a likely lender when the buyer needs a little more money to purchase a property. Most second trust deed loans are of this type and are the most important type of secondary financing in California.

When the current money market is tight, it often means that a seller will have to take back a second trust deed as part of the equity in his or her home. Many second loans on real estate, called junior loans (second trust deeds), are obtained from private investors.

Common second trust deed terms are:

1. The loan amount is usually relatively small (under $50,000).
2. There is a relatively high interest rate (8% to 15%).
3. The loan term is usually from 3 to 7 years, with payments on a monthly basis.
4. Loan payments are usually 1% of the original loan, and there is usually a balloon payment at the end of the term (if more than six years).
5. There is usually an acceleration clause that makes the entire loan due if any payment is missed or the property is transferred.

B. CREDIT UNIONS

A **CREDIT UNION** *is a co-operative association organized to promote thrift among its members and provide them with a source of credit.*

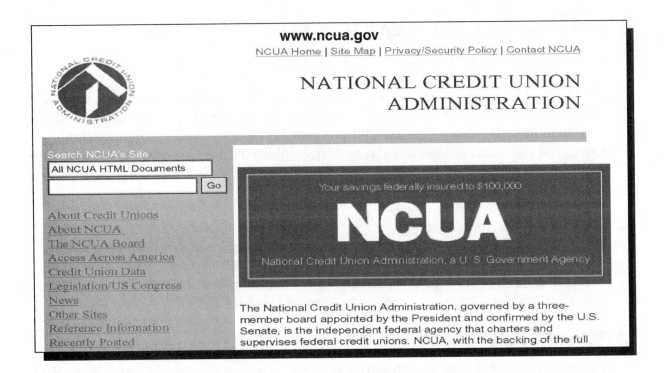

Under the Federal Credit Union Act of 1934, a credit union charter may be given to any group having a common bond of association or occupation—a factory, store, office, church, trade group, club, or fraternal organization.

Although there are thousands of credit unions across the country, they play a much smaller role than banks, savings banks, and insurance companies in financing real estate. The typical credit union is smaller than the average commercial bank or savings bank.

Most credit unions are incorporated and accumulate funds by selling shares to members. From this pool of funds, loans are made at an interest rate equal to or below the current market rate. Low interest rate loans to members are a big plus for credit unions.

The modern credit union offers savings plans, credit cards, ATM cards, travelers' checks, vehicle loans, signature loans, and real estate loans. All deposit accounts have FDIC insurance up to $100,000.

Recent changes in the law have enabled credit unions to make not only second trust deed loans, but also first trust deed loans. This source of real estate funding is expected to grow and expand in coming years.

C. REAL ESTATE INVESTMENT TRUST (REIT)

A REIT requires a minimum of 100 investors.

A **REAL ESTATE INVESTMENT TRUST (REIT)** *is a type of company that sells securities specializing in real estate ventures.* If the company distributes 90 percent or more of its income to its shareholders, it does not pay federal income taxes on that distribution. Because of these formalities, a real estate investment trust is taxed like any other real estate investment.

Real estate investment trusts are equity trusts or mortgage trusts.

An **EQUITY TRUST** *is a company that invests in real estate itself or several real estate projects.* The **MORTGAGE TRUST** *is a company that invests in mortgages and other types of real estate loans or obligations.* Now there are even combination trusts that invest in real estate and lend money in the form of real estate mortgages.

D. PENSION PLANS

A **PENSION PLAN** *is an investment organization that obtains funds from people before they retire and invests this money for their clients' retirement.* Company pension plans have become a popular source of real estate funds and are expected to grow even larger in the future. Enormous amounts of money, gathered through deductions from each pay period, are held by these plans. Those who administer pension money are becoming more and more inclined to invest it directly in large real estate projects rather than investing in the stock market or simply investing in savings institutions and insurance companies.

E. MORTGAGE BANKERS (COMPANIES)—Secondary Mortgage Market

The secondary mortgage market is a resale marketplace where smaller lenders sell their loans to larger lenders.

MORTGAGE BANKERS (COMPANIES) *usually lend their own money or roll it over so they can originate, finance, and close first trust deeds or mortgages secured by real estate. They then sell the loans to institutional investors and service the loans through a contractual relationship with the investors.* **Mortgage loan brokers (correspondents) are licensed by the DRE as real estate brokers and/or by the Department of Corporations as Residential Mortgage Lenders (RML) or California Finance Lenders (CFL).** In California, the brokerage function is one of the prime sources for loans on homes and income property, and they are the largest originator of FHA and VA trust deeds or mortgages. Sometimes private mortgage insurance is necessary to make a loan.

A mortgage banker establishes a good line of credit with a bank to obtain available funds. Mortgage companies like to make loans that can be sold easily on the secondary mortgage market (liquidity and marketability). "Warehousing" is the action of a mortgage banker collecting loans in a package prior to sale.

F. PRIVATE MORTGAGE INSURANCE (PMI)

PRIVATE MORTGAGE INSURANCE *is a guarantee to lenders that the upper portion of a conventional loan will be repaid if a borrower defaults and a deficiency occurs at the foreclosure sale.*

> **Let's look at an example:** *Smith is buying a property for $300,000 but he has only $15,000 for a down payment. He approaches lender Jones for financing. Lender Jones is eager to see this sale go through but he does not feel entirely comfortable putting up $285,000 when normally he would limit the loan to 80%, or $240,000. He is uncomfortable lending Smith the extra $45,000. He agrees to make the loan if Smith will pay for private mortgage insurance to cover the upper portion ($45,000) of the $285,000 loan.*

Private mortgage insurance is obtainable on properties with one-to-four units and generally covers the top 20% of the loan amount. The borrower generally pays an initial premium or an annual fee of one-half of one percent on the remaining principal balance.

VI. Government-Backed Loans

The government is very involved in helping people obtain homes. The three programs we will discuss have already helped millions to enjoy "owning a home," the American dream. FHA insurance (part of Housing and Urban Development - HUD) and VA guarantees are federal programs. They approve loans made by private lenders, but lend no actual money. The CAL-VET program makes direct loans to qualified borrowers from the state of California. See **Figure 9-6** and the chart in **Figure 9-7**.

Figure 9-6

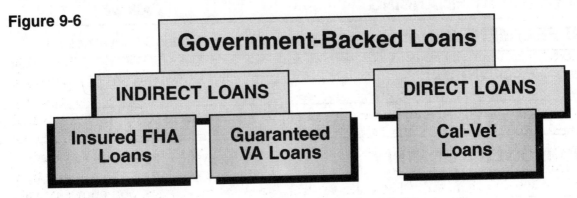

A. FHA INSURED LOANS (A Division of HUD)

Unlike conventional lenders, the Federal Housing Administration (FHA) does not make loans, but insures them.

Figure 9-7

Federal Housing Administration (FHA 203b "basic")

ELIGIBILITY	Anyone residing in the United States
SOURCE OF FUNDS	Approved Lenders
LOAN INSTRUMENT	**Trust Deed or Mortgage**
TERM	30 years
INTEREST RATE	Current interest rates plus mortgage insurance premiums paid up front, prior to close of escrow
MAXIMUM PURCHASE	**No Maximum**
MAXIMUM LOAN AMOUNT (For high cost areas)	97% of the maximum for the county average: house-condo $253,650; duplex $285,650; tri-plex $347,100; and 4-unit $400,500
DOWN PAYMENT	3% minimum cash investment; 100% over appraisal
SECONDARY FINANCING	**Allowed**
PREPAYMENT PENALTY	None (30 days' notice)
ASSIGNABLE	After 2 years, if owner-occupant
POINTS PAID BY	**Buyers or Sellers**
BORROWER'S MONTHLY PAYMENTS	Monthly principal and interest 29% to 41% of annual gross income
MONTHLY SALARY (AFTER FEDERAL TAXES)	Approximately 3 times total monthly payment

Veterans Administration VA	State of California CAL-VET
W.W. II, Korean Conflict, Vietnam Era, Persian Gulf War, or continuous active duty for 90 days (181 Peacetime)	W.W. II, Korean Conflict, Vietnam Era, Persian Gulf War, or certain medal winners
Approved Lenders	California Bond Issues
Trust Deed or Mortgage	**Conditional Sales Contract**
30-year maximum	30-year maximum
Set by Veterans Administration	Set by State of California, but may increase later
No Maximum by DVA (restricted by guarantee)	**None**
1-to-4 units, owner occupied, up to CRV. No loan maximum but usually under $240,000; Guarantee Maximum is $60,000	Manufactured Home - $70,000 (in Mobile Park) House - $322,700 Farm - $300,000
None required, lender may require down payment	Manufactured Home - 2% to 20% House - 2% to 20% Farm - 2% to 20%
Only up to amount of CRV	
None	None
After 3 years most qualify for loans	To a Cal-Vet, YES
Buyer or Seller	**Buyer**
Monthly principal and interest: 29% to 41% of annual gross income	Monthly principal and interest: 28% to 50% of annual gross income
Approximately 3 times total monthly payment	Approximately 2 times total monthly payment

Minimum Property Requirements (MPRs)

All of these government-backed finance programs have increased the number of houses and condominiums that people in California can afford to buy. They also have an indirect influence on the quality of homes constructed because they require that the home involved meet minimum property requirements as a prerequisite to financing. Minimum Property Requirements (MPR) are set standards of materials and construction required for FHA and VA loans. These requirements are often more restrictive than the building codes. As a real estate licensee, you should be familiar with the basic financing programs and qualification requirements. In addition, most mortgage companies will help you qualify the buyer and complete the necessary forms for FHA and VA loans.

Minimum Property Requirements (or MPR) are minimum quality standards established by the FHA and VA.

The FHA has two main programs that affect California homeowners and buyers: 1) Title I home improvement loans, and 2) Title II (Section 203b) purchase and construction loans. There are other types of FHA financing available. For information, contact a lender who specializes in FHA loans. See Figure 9-7.

www.hud.gov
Housing and Urban Development
www.hud.gov/oig/oigindex.html
Office of The Inspector General - OIG

1. FHA Title I: Home Improvement Loans

The FHA can make home improvement loans to a maximum of $25,000. The funds can be used only for home improvement purposes.

2. FHA Title II: Home Purchase or Build Loans

Section 203b program: Insures home loans (1-to-4 units) for anyone who is financially qualified. An FHA loan is based on the selling price when it is lower than the appraisal.

The maximum FHA loan amount varies from area-to-area in California and could change each year if median home prices change or Federal National Mortgage Association (FNMA) loan amounts change.

The maximum FHA loan amount is the lesser of 1) 95% of an area's median home price or 2) 75% of the Federal National Mortgage Association (FNMA) conforming loan amount.

The maximum loan amount is determined as follows:

1. On homes sold at over $125,000, the maximum loan-to-value ration is 97.15%.

2. On homes from $50,000 to $125,000, the maximum loan-to-value ration is 97.65%.

3. On homes below $50,000, the maximum loan-to-value ratio is 98.75%.

Obviously, different geographical areas warrant different maximum loans based on the median home values. Accessing the HUD's website at **www.hud.gov** will give the agent the latest quotes for the various counties.

www.comerica.com
Independent FHA Lender
www.fix.net/~chase/fha.html
Independent FHA lender

When assisting a home buyer in obtaining an FHA loan, a broker would most likely contact an institutional lender.

All FHA home buyers must obtain loans at an approved lender's office. The approved local lender (such as banks, insurance companies, and mortgage companies) will make the loan if the FHA qualifies the buyer. The FHA has many requirements for its different loan programs. Both the borrower and the property must meet these criteria. If either the borrower or the property does not meet the minimum standards, it would probably be better to look for a lender who deals in conventional rather than FHA loans.

FHA does not lend the money. Do not apply at a FHA office, but rather at an approved lender's office.

The FHA does not lend the money. It only insures the approved lender against foreclosure loss. The FHA collects a percentage of the loan for this insurance called the mortgage insurance premium. The *MORTGAGE INSURANCE PREMIUM (MIP) is the protection for the FHA that insures the lender for any loss if there is a foreclosure.* It is an up-front fee (paid by the borrower) in cash, or through insurance as part of the loan. If there is a foreclosure, FHA will take over the property and reimburse the lender for the cost of default.

MIP is the FHA insurance protection for the "lender" of the loan amount if the owner defaults.

An *FHA MORTGAGE LOAN CORRESPONDENT is a mortgagee approved by the Secretary of the Department Housing and Urban Development.* The loan correspondent has as his or her principle activity either 1) the origination of mortgages for sale or transfer to a sponsor or sponsors; or 2) satisfies the

definition of a supervised mortgagee contained in the regulations of the Secretary of the Department of Housing and Urban Development.

3. Advantages and Disadvantages of FHA Financing

The advantages and disadvantages of FHA financing include:

a. Advantages

1. Low down payment compared to conventional loans.
2. Loans are assumable. Loans require approval of the FHA and nonowner-occupied are prohibited.
3. No prepayment penalty is allowed by the FHA.
4. Minimum property requirements (MPRs) give the buyer a quality home.
5. A seller receives all cash because of the high loan-to-value ratio.

FHA-backed loans generally have lower interest rates than conventional loans.

b. Disadvantages

1. Lots of processing time and red tape.
2. Existing properties may require repairs necessary to meet minimum property requirements.

B. VETERANS ADMINISTRATION

1. VA Loans (Loan Guarantees to Approved Lenders)

The Congress of the United States has passed legislation to assist veterans in obtaining housing. A **VA LOAN** *is not a loan, but rather a guarantee to an approved institutional lender.*

a. Veteran's Eligibility

Veterans are eligible for a Veterans Administration (VA) loan guarantee if they served on active duty for 90 days or more (181 days during certain peacetime periods) and were honorably discharged.

Veterans who have served a minimum of 90 days continuous active duty (181 days during peacetime) or completed six years in the reserves or national guard qualify. Vets with service-related disabilities are NOT restricted by time requirements.

American citizens who served in the armed forces of our Allies in World War II may also apply. Widows or widowers of service people or veterans who were eligible at the time of death, but did not use their benefits, may apply to use their husbands'

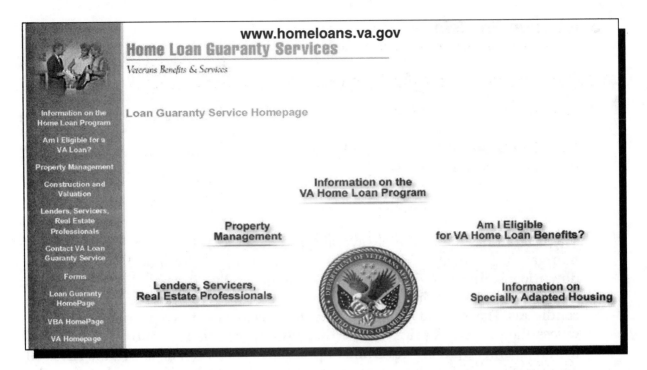

or wives' benefits. Also, the VA Adjudication Board, at its discretion, may give eligibility to any veteran who received other than an honorable discharge.

b. Veterans May be Entitled to More Than One Loan

A veteran may restore his or her eligibility and apply for an additional loan if the previous home was sold and its loan paid in full. Other veterans who are eligible for a new VA loan program may apply even if they have a prior VA loan, if the prior loan is not in default and if the veteran no longer owns the property. The previous VA loan need not be paid off. The veteran who purchased a home under a previous program may be eligible again under a new program.

2. Certificate of Reasonable Value (CRV)

A *CERTIFICATE OF REASONABLE VALUE (CRV) is an appraisal of the property to be purchased by the veteran.* The property is appraised by an independent fee appraiser who is appointed by the Veterans Administration. Although the appraisal may be paid for by the veteran, it is usually paid for by the seller. The CRV appraisal expires after six months.

The amount of down payment required for a VA loan is determined by the CRV.

3. VA Loan Provisions

VA loans require NO down payment on loans up to $240,000, but may require the veteran to pay an origination fee of up to 3% of the loan amount to an approved lender. In addition, the seller may have to pay discount points.

No down payment VA loans can be for any amount, but California lenders will only make a loan up to $240,000.

A CRV of $240,000 has a guarantee of $60,000 ($240,000 x 25%).

The veteran has the choice of several types of VA loans. They include fixed-rate mortgages, graduated payment mortgages, growing equity mortgages, and buy-down loans. The duration of a VA loan is generally 30 years. Discount points charged sellers and interest rates vary according to the current economic conditions. The main advantage to the veteran is that no down payment is needed, unless the property's price exceeds the VA's appraisal. This "no money down" feature is unique among government programs. Loans can be above the $240,000 guaranteed maximum loan amount, but require that the difference between the $240,000 maximum and the actual loan be in the form of a cash down payment.

4. Advantages and Disadvantages of VA Financing

The advantages and disadvantages of VA financing include:

a. Advantages

1. No down payment, but a funding fee paid by the veteran
2. Low interest rate because of the VA loan guarantee
3. No prepayment penalty is allowed by the VA

b. Disadvantages:

1. Buyer's creditworthiness is a requirement for assumption; VA must approve credit and a fee of up to $500 is required; assumption only after one year if owner-occupied or after two years if investor owned
2. Buyer or seller can pay discount points
3. Lengthy processing time and red tape

C. CALIFORNIA DEPARTMENT OF VETERAN'S AFFAIRS (CAL-VET)

1. Cal-Vet (Land Contract; Direct Loans)

Land contracts (real property purchase contracts) are used by the California Department of Veterans Affairs and legal title is held by Cal-Vet until the loan is paid in full.

The **CAL-VET** *loan program is administered by the California Department of Veterans Affairs.* As part of its comprehensive veterans program, the State of California has developed and operates a program to assist its veterans in purchasing a farm, home, or manufactured home. Home property must be a single family dwelling, condominium unit or apartment townhouse.

Cal-Vet will NOT loan on rental property purchases, but FHA-backed lenders will.

Funds for the Cal-Vet loans come from the sale of Veterans Bonds, voted into law by the people of California. All money lent to veterans is repaid through installments (including principal, property taxes, insurance, and interest) at a rate to cover all operating costs. The bonds are retired at maturity from veterans' loan payments without cost to the State of California.

Funds may not be immediately available for loans to all applicants. The availability of these funds is limited, therefore wartime veterans (especially those disabled with war-connected injuries) may be given higher priority when applying for these loans.

A veteran who intends to obtain a Cal-Vet loan should contact a representative of the Department of Veterans Affairs for complete California Farm and Home Purchase Plan information before committing to purchase a property. To apply for a loan, he or she should obtain the necessary information and forms from one of the California Department of Veterans Affairs offices throughout the state.

The Cal-Vet maximum for the purchase of a home is $322,700 and up to $300,000 for a farm. A farm loan, however, may not exceed 95 percent of the Cal-Vet appraisal. The veteran must pay to the seller the difference between the sales price and the Cal-Vet loan.

The loan term is determined by the amount of the loan and the age and income of each applicant. Most loans are for 30 years. New loan interest rates are usually lower than current market rates, but may vary according to economic conditions during the life of the loan.

A loan may be paid in full at any time. A Cal-Vet loan can be obtained for a manufactured home if the ownership of the land is included. The maximum manufactured home loan is $70,000 in a park and $90,000 on a single family lot.

The buyer pays for points with a Cal-Vet loan.

a. Eligibility

There is no residency requirement. All veterans are eligible for the Cal-Vet program.

To qualify, a California veteran must have served at least 90 days active duty in the armed forces of the United States and have been released from service under honorable conditions. A portion of his or her service must have been within one of the following war periods:

WORLD WAR II — December 7, 1941 to December 31, 1946
KOREAN CONFLICT — June 27, 1950 to January 31, 1955
VIETNAM ERA — August 5, 1964 to May 7, 1975
PERSIAN GULF WAR — August 2, 1990 to date yet to be determined

Also eligible is a California veteran who:

1. Participated in a campaign or expedition for which a medal was awarded by the government of the United States;
2. Was discharged with less than 90 days' active duty because of service-connected disability incurred during his or her qualifying service period.

A qualified veteran must apply for a Cal-Vet loan within 30 years following release from active military duty. However, those who were wounded or disabled during war or who were prisoners of war have an indefinite period in which to apply.

All veterans are eligible for the Cal-Vet program. The same person could be eligible for a FHA, a VA, and a Cal-Vet loan.

D. CALIFORNIA HOUSING FINANCE AGENCY (CHFA)

CALIFORNIA HOUSING FINANCE AGENCY (CHFA) is a state agency that sells bonds so that it can provide funds for low-income family housing on project or individual home basis. It is self-supporting and has political support across party lines. **Figure 9-8** explains CHFA in detail.

VII. Lending Corporations and the Secondary Mortgage Market

A. PRIVATE AND QUASI-GOVERNMENTAL CORPORATIONS

There were once three federal corporations that used cash to buy and sell trust deeds between financial institutions. These corporations are now either private or quasi-governmental and provide stability and flexibility for real estate financing in the United States. Each has different programs and areas of focus, but all work together to keep sufficient financing money available at lending institutions so they can make home loans.

B. SECONDARY MORTGAGE (TRUST DEED) MARKET

Lenders in the secondary market are concerned with the "liquidity and marketability" of loans.

The *SECONDARY MORTGAGE (TRUST DEED) MARKET provides an opportunity for financial institutions to buy from, and sell first mortgages (trust deeds) to, other financial institutions.* California has a growing real estate market that will pay higher interest rates than other parts of the country. Therefore, California's financial institutions will make trust deed loans and sell them to other institutions for a profit. The secondary mortgage market enables lenders to keep an adequate supply of money for new loans.

The secondary mortgage (trust deed) market is the market where lenders buy and sell mortgages. The secondary mortgage market is the transfer of mortgages among mortgagees.

1. Federal National Mortgage Association (Fannie Mae - Private)

The FNMA was created to increase the amount of funds available to finance housing.

The Federal National Mortgage Association (FNMA), which is commonly referred to as Fannie Mae, dominates the secondary mortgage market. Originally it bought and sold only FHA and VA trust deeds. In 1968 it became a private corporation and now sells securities over the stock exchange to get money so that it can buy and sell conventional loans in addition to government-backed notes.

Figure 9-8

www.calhfa.ca.gov

CHFA
California Housing Finance Agency

1121 "L" STREET 7TH FLOOR · SACRAMENTO, CA 95814 · (916) 322-3991

The **California Housing Finance Agency** is an exciting program providing real estate funds for low income families, encouraging homeownership over a wider spectrum than has been possible in recent years. This plan is being hailed as a boon from all quarters because it provides a desperately needed funding source and helps stimulate the real estate industry. At the same time, it is entirely self-supporting.

Bonds Issued

Seb Sterpa, past president of CAR, is credited with originating the idea for this program and promoting it to the governor and house speaker. The money for these loans is provided by the issuance of tax-free bonds by the state. These bonds sell quickly at a very favorable rate. Because this rate is below the current level, it enables approved lenders to provide loans with affordable rates of interest and still make a reasonable return.

Entirely Self-Supporting

Everyone benefits from this program. Housing in California has become more accessible to buyers with restricted resources. Young couples starting out are now able to enter the housing market. The market is stimulated by the influx of new participants. Investors who purchase the bonds enjoy this profitable form of investment. No tax money is involved and the program is entirely self-supporting.

Support Across Party Lines

Because of the universal benefits, this program claims support across traditional party lines. Democrats favor this program because of the opportunity it offers to the economically disadvantaged. Many Republicans in the state are delighted because of the boost these loans bring to the real estate industry and the state economy in general.

"Fannie Mae," the Federal National Mortgage Association (FNMA), helps set loan standards and helps to maintain the secondary mortgage market. The FNMA is NOT a demand source to borrow money.

www.fanniemaefoundation.org
Fannie Mae

2. Government National Mortgage Association (Ginnie Mae)

The **GOVERNMENT NATIONAL MORTGAGE ASSOCIATION (GNMA)** *is a government corporation referred to as Ginnie Mae. It sells secondary mortgages to the public and provides the federal government with cash.* These trust deeds are grouped together in pools, and shares are sold on the stock market exchange. All shares are federally guaranteed, making this one of the safest investments available.

www.ginniemae.gov/
Ginnie Mae

3. Federal Home Loan Mortgage Corporation (Freddie Mac)

The **FEDERAL HOME LOAN MORTGAGE CORPORATION (FHLMC)**, *commonly known as Freddie Mac, is a government corporation that issues preferred stock to the public.* It is supervised by the Federal Home Loan Bank Board. It helps savings banks maintain a stable and adequate money supply by purchasing their home loan mortgages and repackaging them for sale to investors. The savings banks use the money obtained to make new loans available for home buyers.

The Federal Home Loan Mortgage Corporation, commonly called "Freddie Mac," increases the availability of funds through its involvement in the maintenance of the secondary mortgage market.

www.freddiemac.com
Freddie Mac

C. FINAL WORD ON CONVENTIONAL LOANS (Risk—Loans Without Government Backing)

Since conventional loans are loans made without government backing or guarantees, they are riskier. Even if conventional loans have lower loan-to-value (LTV) ratios, which make them safer, government-backed loans are the safest. Because the government will payoff if there is a foreclosure, Fannie Mae and Freddie Mac currently have loan limits of $327,300 for a house or condo. *If the requested loan amount is higher than the Fannie Mae and Freddie Mac loan limit, it is called a JUMBO LOAN.*

Conventional loans have lower "loan-to-value" ratios, which offer greater protection for the lender. Despite the above, conventional loans generally have higher risk. Compared to FHA insured loans, conventional loans are riskier.

The higher the risk, the higher the interest rates.

More risk = higher interest rates
More risk = higher points

VIII. Real Estate Broker Can Make Loans

The broker or salesperson, as part of most real estate transactions, may help the buyer fill out a loan application for a financial institution or arrange financing for the buyer. In either case, there are certain restrictions that apply to a real estate licensee acting as a loan broker in buying, selling, or exchanging loans. Most of these loans are in the form of a trust deed since it is the usual financing instrument in California.

The "Mortgage Loan Broker Law" (sections 10240-10248 of Article 7) of the Business and Professions Code requires loan brokers to give a Mortgage Loan Disclosure Statement to all borrowers before they become obligated for the loan.

A. MORTGAGE LOAN DISCLOSURE STATEMENT

A real estate licensee negotiating a loan for a prospective borrower must present to that person a completed loan disclosure statement. This statement must be given to the borrower prior to his or her signing the loan documents. It is usually referred to as the Mortgage Loan Disclosure Statement.

A **MORTGAGE LOAN DISCLOSURE STATEMENT** *is a form that completely and clearly states all the information and charges connected with a particular loan.* It must be kept on file for three years. **See Figure 9-9.**

Loan broker must keep the Mortgage Loan Disclosure Statement (disclosure given to borrower) on file for three years for the commissioner's inspection.

Besides providing the borrower with the disclosure statement, the broker is prohibited from doing certain things and is restricted as to the amount of commission that he or she may charge the borrower.

Anyone negotiating real estate loans must be a real estate licensee. If you make collections on real estate loans and you make more than ten a year or collect more

Figure 9-9

CALIFORNIA
ASSOCIATION
OF REALTORS®

MORTGAGE LOAN DISCLOSURE STATEMENT
(BORROWER)

(As required by the Business and Professions Code §10241
and Title 10, California Administrative Code, §2840)

_____

(Name of Broker/Arranger of Credit)

_____

(Business Address of Broker)

I. SUMMARY OF LOAN TERMS

  A. PRINCIPAL AMOUNT . . . . $ _____

  B. ESTIMATED DEDUCTIONS FROM PRINCIPAL AMOUNT

    1. Costs and Expenses (See Paragraph III-A) . . . . $ _____

    *2. Broker Commission/Organization Fee (See Paragraph III-B) . . . . $ _____

    3. Lender Origination Fee/Discounts (See Paragraph III-B) . . . . $ _____

    4. Additional compensation will/may be received from lender not deducted from loan proceeds.

      ☐ YES $ _____ (if known) or ☐ NO

    5. Amount to be Paid on Authorization of Borrower (See Paragraph III) . . . . $ _____

  C. ESTIMATED CASH PAYABLE TO BORROWER (A less B) . . . . $ _____

II. GENERAL INFORMATION ABOUT LOAN

  A. If this loan is made, Borrower will be required to pay the principal and interest at _____% per year, payable
as follows: _____ payments of $ _____

      (number of payments)   (monthly/quarterly/annually)

  and a **FINAL/BALLOON** payment of $ _____ to pay off the loan in full.

  NOTICE TO BORROWER: IF YOU DO NOT HAVE THE FUNDS TO PAY THE BALLOON PAYMENT WHEN IT COMES DUE, YOU MAY HAVE TO OBTAIN A NEW LOAN AGAINST YOUR PROPERTY TO MAKE THE BALLOON PAYMENT. IN THAT CASE, YOU MAY AGAIN HAVE TO PAY COMMISSIONS, FEES AND EXPENSES FOR THE ARRANGING OF THE NEW LOAN. IN ADDITION, IF YOU ARE UNABLE TO MAKE THE MONTHLY PAYMENTS OR THE BALLOON PAYMENT, YOU MAY LOSE THE PROPERTY AND ALL OF YOUR EQUITY THROUGH FORECLOSURE. KEEP THIS IN MIND IN DECIDING UPON THE AMOUNT AND TERMS OF THIS LOAN.

  B. This loan will be evidenced by a promissory note and secured by a deed of trust on property identified as (street address or legal description):

  _____

  _____

  C. 1. Liens presently against this property (do not include loan being applied for):

Nature of Lien	Priority	Lienholder's Name	Amount Owing
_____	_____	_____	_____
_____	_____	_____	_____
_____	_____	_____	_____

    2. Liens that will remain against this property after the loan being applied for is made or arranged (include loan being applied for):

Nature of Lien	Priority	Lienholder's Name	Amount Owing
_____	_____	_____	_____
_____	_____	_____	_____
_____	_____	_____	_____

  NOTICE TO BORROWER: Be sure that you state the amount of all liens as accurately as possible. If you contract with the broker to arrange this loan, but it cannot be arranged because you did not state these liens correctly, you may be liable to pay commissions, fees and expenses even though you do not obtain the loan.

REVISION DATE 10/2000   **Print Date**
MS-11 (PAGE 1 OF 3)

Borrower acknowledges receipt of copy of this page.

Borrower's Initials (_____)(_____)

EQUAL HOUSING
OPPORTUNITY

Reviewed by

Broker or Designee _____ Date _____

MORTGAGE LOAN DISCLOSURE STATEMENT (MS-11 PAGE 1 OF 3)

Property Address: _____ Date: _____

D. If Borrower pays all or part of the loan principal before it is due, a PREPAYMENT PENALTY computed as follows may be charged:
_____
_____
_____

E. Late Charges: ☐ YES, see loan documents or ☐ NO
F. The purchase of credit life or credit disability insurance by a borrower is not required as a condition of making this loan.
G. Is the real property which will secure the requested loan an "owner-occupied dwelling?" ☐ YES_____ or ☐ NO_____
(Borrower initial opposite YES or NO)

An "owner-occupied dwelling" means a single dwelling unit in a condominium or cooperative or residential building of four or fewer separate dwelling units, one of which will be owned and occupied by a signatory to the mortgage or deed of trust for this loan within 90 days of the signing of the mortgage or deed of trust.

III. DEDUCTIONS FROM LOAN PROCEEDS

A. Estimated Maximum Costs and Expenses of Arranging the Loan to be Paid Out of Loan Principal:

	PAYABLE TO	
	Broker	**Others**
1. Appraisal fee	_____	_____
2. Escrow fee	_____	_____
3. Title insurance policy	_____	_____
4. Notary fees	_____	_____
5. Recording fees	_____	_____
6. Credit investigation fees	_____	_____
7. Other costs and expenses:		

_____   _____   _____
_____   _____   _____
_____   _____   _____

Total Costs and Expenses . . . . $ _____

*B. Compensation . . . . $ _____
1. Brokerage Commission/Origination Fee . . . . $ _____
2. Lender Origination Fee/Discounts . . . . $ _____

C. Estimated Payment to be Made out of Loan Principal on Authorization of Borrower

	PAYABLE TO	
	Broker	**Others**
1. Fire or other hazard insurance premiums	_____	_____
2. Credit life or disability insurance premiums (see Paragraph II-F)	_____	_____
3. Beneficiary statement fees	_____	_____
4. Reconveyance and similar fees	_____	_____
5. Discharge of existing liens against property:		

_____   _____   _____
_____   _____   _____

6. Other:
_____   _____   _____
_____   _____   _____
_____   _____   _____

Total to be Paid on Authorization of Borrower . . . . $ _____

If this loan is secured by a first deed of trust on dwellings in a principal amount of less than $30,000 or secured by a junior lien on dwellings in a principal amount of less than $20,000, the undersigned licensee certifies that the loan will be made in compliance with Article 7 of Chapter 3 of the Real Estate Law.

*This loan **may / will / will not** (delete two) be made wholly or in part from broker-controlled funds as defined in Section 10241(j) of the Business and Professions Code.

Borrower acknowledges receipt of copy of this page.
Borrower's Initials (_____)(_____)

Reviewed by
Broker or Designee _____ Date _____

MORTGAGE LOAN DISCLOSURE STATEMENT (MS-11 PAGE 2 OF 3)

Property Address: _____ Date: _____

*NOTICE TO BORROWER: This disclosure statement may be used if the Broker is acting as an agent in arranging the loan by a third person or if the loan will be made with funds owned or controlled by the broker. If the Broker indicates in the above statement that the loan "may" be made out of Broker-controlled funds, the Broker must notify the borrower prior to the close of escrow if the funds to be received by the Borrower are in fact Broker-controlled funds.

_____   _____
Name of Broker   Broker Representative

_____   _____
License Number   License Number

_____ OR _____
Signature of Broker   Signature

The Department of Real Estate License Information phone number is _____.

NOTICE TO BORROWER:

DO NOT SIGN THIS STATEMENT UNTIL YOU HAVE READ AND UNDERSTAND ALL OF THE INFORMATION IN IT. ALL PARTS OF THE FORM MUST BE COMPLETED BEFORE YOU SIGN.

Borrower hereby acknowledges the receipt of a copy of this statement.

DATED _____   _____
                                                          (Borrower)

_____
                                                          (Borrower)

<u>Broker Review</u>: Signature of Real Estate Broker after review of this statement.

DATED _____   _____
                                              Real Estate Broker or Assistant Pursuant to Section 2725

Published and Distributed by:
REAL ESTATE BUSINESS SERVICES, INC.
a subsidiary of the CALIFORNIA ASSOCIATION OF REALTORS®
525 South Virgil Avenue, Los Angeles, California 90020

Reviewed by
Broker or Designee _____ Date _____

EQUAL HOUSING OPPORTUNITY

REVISION DATE 10/2000   Print Date
MS-11 (PAGE 3 OF 3)

MORTGAGE LOAN DISCLOSURE STATEMENT (MS-11 PAGE 3 OF 3)

than $40,000, you must also be a licensed real estate broker. Many brokers establish a regular, ongoing business relationship with individuals or financial institutions that will loan money to prospective buyers.

B. BUSINESS AND PROFESSIONS CODE
(Commissions and Other Requirements)

1. Article 7 - Loan Broker Laws

On hard money loans (cash) of $30,000 and over for first trust deeds, and $20,000 and over for junior deeds of trust, the broker may charge as much as the borrower will agree to pay.

Brokers negotiating trust deed loans are subject to certain limitations regarding commissions and expenses and must meet other requirements set out by the real estate commissioner (see **Figure 9-10**). Legislation also requires that brokers provide both the borrower and the lender, on property for first trust deed loans under $30,000 and seconds under $20,000, with copies of the appraisal report. Anyone performing these services, whether soliciting borrowers or lenders in home loans secured by real property must have a real estate license. This restriction applies even if no advance fee is paid.

Loans on owner-occupied homes negotiated by brokers for a term of six years or less may not have a balloon payment. If nonowner occupied, loans are exempt from balloon payments when the term is less than three years. Neither of these restrictions apply to transactions where the seller extends credit to the buyer. When such transactions have balloon payments, the seller is obligated to notify the buyer 60 to 150 days before the payment is due. Also, the broker is obligated to inform the buyer regarding the likelihood of obtaining new financing.

a. Threshold Reporting (Big Lending - $2,000,000)

THRESHOLD REPORTING is the requirement of reporting annual and quarterly loan activity (review of trust fund) to the Department of Real Estate if, within the past 12 months, the broker has negotiated any combination of 20 or more loans to a subdivision or a total of more than $2,000,000 in loans. In addition, advertising must be submitted to the DRE for review. This regulation is intended to protect the public by over-seeing the loan activity of big lenders who are using their real estate broker's licenses.

2. Article 5 - Broker Restrictions

The licensee is prohibited from pooling funds. A broker may not accept funds except for a specifically identified loan transaction. Before accepting a lender's money, the broker must:

1. Own the loan or have an unconditional written contract to purchase a specific note.

2. Have the authorization from a prospective borrower to negotiate a secured loan.

3. Article 6 - Real Property Securities Dealer

A DRE broker's license and endorsement are required: A $100 fee plus a $10,000 surety bond. DRE permit is required to sell specific security.

No real estate investment type security shall be sold to the public without first obtaining a permit from the commissioner. A **COMMISSIONER'S PERMIT** *is the approval of the proposed real property security and plan of distribution.* If, in the commissioner's opinion, the security and proposed plan of distribution is fair, just, and equitable, he or she will authorize the sale, subject to any limiting conditions. A permit is not an endorsement or recommendation of the security; it is only a permit to sell. The application for the permit is extensive and may require supplementary filings. The duration of the permit is one year, and the permit may not be used in advertising unless it is used in its entirety.

A commissioner's permit requires a $10,000 surety bond.

a. Real Property Securities Dealer Endorsement

A **Real Property Securities Dealer (RPSD)** *is any person acting as principal or agent who engages in the business of selling real property securities (such as promissory notes or sales contracts).* RPSD dealers also accept or offer to accept funds for reinvestment in real property securities or for placement in a account. Before a licensed real estate broker may act in this capacity, he or she must obtain an RPSD endorsement on his or her broker's license. To obtain an RPSD endorsement on a broker's license, submit the appropriate endorsement fee ($100) along with proof of a properly executed $10,000 surety bond. (For information on Real Property Securities, call the DRE.)

Figure 9-10   Loan Broker Commission Limits

	Loans for Less Than 2 Years	Loans for 2 Years and Less Than 3 Years	Loans for 3 Years and Over	Transactions That are Exempt
First Trust Deeds	5 %	5 %	10 %	**Loans of $30,000 and over**
Junior Trust Deeds	5 %	10 %	15 %	**Loans of $30,000 and over**

"Equity Sharing"

A different financing and ownership idea

EQUITY SHARING (SHARED EQUITY FINANCING) is a contractual arrangement whereby an investor shares any equity gain with a homeowner. Since California has high housing costs that require a large down payment, many potential homeowners cannot qualify or do not have the cash for a down payment. The concept is that an investor puts up most of the down payment, and receives no interest deductions but shares in any equity gain when the property is sold. The homeowner gets his or her home quickly with a minimum down payment, with relaxed credit, and with full income tax write-offs. Consult an attorney or CPA before investing.

IX. SUMMARY

Inflation (when prices appreciate) protects both lender and trustor because there will be more equity protecting the lender in the case of a default. When prices decrease, the value of money increases and vice versa. In a **seller's market**, prices rise due to a shortage of properties available, whereas in a **buyer's market**, prices fall, terms are easy and properties plentiful.

The **Federal Reserve (Fed)** is the nation's central banking authority controls the availability of loan funds, but has nothing to do with raising or lowering interest rates. The Fed's influence on the economy is evidenced by changes in The **Gross Domestic Product (GDP)**.

The three areas of demand for borrowing money are: construction funds, financing a purchase, and refinancing. Moss lenders request an 80% **L-T-V (loan to value) ratio**. The lower the L-T-V, the greater the down payment.

The primary purpose of **RESPA** is to require lenders to make special disclosures, without cost to the borrower, for loans involving the sale or transfer of one-to-four residential dwellings. The **Truth in Savings Act** introduced a standard method of expressing interest paid to depositors called **Annual Percentage Yield (APY)**.

Large **Institutional lenders** who pool funds to lend to individual borrowers, include: insurance companies, savings banks, banks and mutual savings banks. Depositor's accounts in savings banks and banks are insured up to $100,000 by The **Federal Deposit Insurance Corporation (FDIC)**. Savings banks have the highest percentage of funds invested in real estate loans, followed by banks, which are **general purpose lenders**.

Smaller, **noninstitutional lenders** include: private lenders, mortgage companies, investment trusts, pension plans and credit unions. Private investors make many of the **second (junior) loans** on real estate. **Real estate investment trusts (REITs)** sell securities specializing in real estate ventures, and are of two types, 1) **equity trust** and 2) **mortgage trust**.

Mortgage bankers (companies) like to make loans that.can be sold easily on the **secondary mortgage market**, which is a resale marketplace for smaller lenders, to sell their loans to larger lenders. Lenders may be required to obtain **private mortgage insurance (PMI)** to protect the lender in case of default.

The **Federal Housing Administration (FHA)** is a division of **HUD** that **insures loans** but does not make them. **FHA Title 1** involves home improvement loans and **FHA Title II** insures home loan purchase or building loans. The **Mortgage Insurance Premium (MIP)** is the FHA insurance protection against owner default.

Veterans may qualify for a **Veterans' Administration (VA) Loan**, which is not really a loan, but a **loan guarantee** to approved institutional lenders. The amount of down payment on a VA loan is determined by the **Certificate of Reasonable Value (CRV)**. Vets may be required to pay origination fees and discount points. On the state level, **CAL-VET**, administered by the California Department of Veteran Affairs, will purchase a **land contract** and hold legal title to a property until the veteran pays off the loan in full.

The **secondary mortgage (trust deed) market**, is the market where lenders buy and sell mortgages. **Fannie Mae (FNMA)** buys and sells conventional loans. It helps set loan standards and maintain the secondary market, but is not a demand' source to borrow money. **Freddie Mac (FHLMC)** purchases home loan mortgages and repackages them for sale to, investors, freeing up savings banks to make new loans. Conventional loans are riskier than FHA loans; the higher the risk the higher the interest rates.

A loan broker must provide a borrower with a **Mortgage Loan Disclosure Statement**, clearly stating all information and charges connected with a loan, and keep it on file for three years. Brokers negotiating trust deed loans may charge whatever commission the buyer will pay on loans of $30,000+ for first trust deeds and $20,000+ for junior deeds of trust. A broker must make a **threshold report** if he or she negotiates more than $2 million in loans or 20+ subdivision loans. Other broker restrictions are covered by **Article 5**.

A **real property securities dealer (RPSD)** acts as a principal or agent engaged in the business of selling real property securities such as promissory notes or sales contracts. A DRE broker's license and endorsement are required including a $10,000 surety bond.

X. TERMINOLOGY - CHAPTER 9

A. Buyer's Market
B. California Housing Financing Agency (CHFA)
C. Cal-Vet Loans
D. Certificate of Reasonable Value (CRV)
E. Collateral
F. Conventional Loans
G. Credit Union
H. Equity Investment Trust
I. Fannie Mae
J. FDIC

K. Federal Reserve Board
L. Federal Reserve System (The "Fed")
M. Freddie Mac
N. Ginnie Mae
O. Gross Domestic Product (GDP)
P. Institutional Lender
Q. Minimum Property Requirements (MPRs)
R. Mortgage Banker
S. Mortgage Company

T. Mortgage Investment Trust
U. Mortgage Loan Disclosure Statement
V. Noninstitutional Lender
W. Private Mortgage Insurance (PMI)
X. Seller's Market
Y. Soft Money Fiancing
Z. VA Loans

1.____ A company providing mortgage financing with its own funds rather than simply bringing together lender and borrower, as does a mortgage broker. The mortgages are sold to investors within a short time.

2.____ (FHLMC) Federal Home Loan Mortgage Corporation. A federal Agency purchasing first mortgages, both conventional and federally insured, from members of the Federal Reserve System.

3.____ A company authorized to service real estate loans, charging a fee for this service.

4.____ The federal corporation that insures against loss of deposits in banks, up to a maximum amount (currently $100,000).

5.____ Insurance issued by a private insurance company against a loss by a lender in the event of default by a borrower (mortgagor). The premium is paid by the borrower and is included in the mortgage payment.

6.____ Loans made under a land contract directly from the California Department of Veterans Affairs, which has its own specific qualifications.

7.____ A mortgage or deed of trust not obtained under a government insured or guaranteed program.

8.____ The money value of all goods and services produced by a nation's economy for a given period of time.

9.____ Government National Mortgage Association: A federal corporation, working with the FHA, which offers special assistance in obtaining mortgages and purchases mortgages in the secondary market.

10.____ Banks, savings banks, loan associations, and other businesses which make loans to the public in the ordinary course of business, rather than individuals, or companies which may make loans to employees.

11.____ Housing loans to veterans by banks, savings banks, or other lenders that are guaranteed by the Veteran's Administration, enabling veterans to buy a residence with little or no down payment.

12.____ A private corporation that acts as a secondary market for the purchase of existing first mortgages, at a discount.

13.____ The central banking system that controls the amount of money and the rate of interest in the United States.

14.____ The powerful nine-member banking panel which controls the destiny of the United States' monetary system. Along with the President of the United States, the Chairman is one of the most powerful positions in the country.

15.____ A form that California law requires be given to the borrower, breaking down all the costs and fees of securing out a loan.

16.____ An agency, sponsored by the state of California, which sponsors special housing projects and certain types of loans.

17.____ The real estate pledged to back up a loan. The value of the real estate should be worth substantially more than the loan amount.

18.____ Smaller lenders such as sellers, credit unions, and pension plans that lend money on real estate.

19.____ An appraisal document stating the fair market value of real estate under a VA loan.

20.____ The minimal property standards for a property to qualify for an FHA loan.

21.____ A loan made by the seller to the buyer as part of the purchase transaction.

22.____ A market condition favoring the seller, when fewer homes are for sale than there are interested buyers.

23.____ A trust company specializing in making mortgages as an investment.

24.____ A trust company that specializes in taking an ownership position in other projects.

25.____ A market condition favoring the buyer, when more homes are for sale than there are interested buyers.

26.____ An organization whose members have a common bond of occupation. Considered a growing source of real estate funds.

XI. MULTIPLE CHOICE

1. Which of the following would NOT be considered institutional lenders?

    a. Savings banks
    b. Banks
    c. Life insurance companies
    d. Credit unions

2. A corporation, or an unincorporated association of 100 or more real estate investors that serves as a conduit for its investors is called a:

    a. pension plan.
    b. mortgage company.
    c. real estate investment trust (REIT).
    d. credit union.

3. The central banking system for the United States is the:

    a. United Banks.
    b. Federal Reserve.
    c. U.S. Banking Reserve.
    d. California Banking System.

4. Which is NOT a government-backed loan?

    a. FHA
    b. VA
    c. APR
    d. CAL-VET

5. To be eligible for a VA loan, a veteran must have served how much time on continuous active duty?

    a. 91 days
    b. 181 days (peacetime duty)
    c. 1 year
    d. 2 years

6. Which of the following is NOT a government lending corporation?

    a. Fannie Mae
    b. Ginnie Mae
    c. Big Mac
    d. Freddie Mac

7. If a real estate licensee negotiates a loan, he or she must give a Mortgage Loan Disclosure Statement to the:

   a. seller.
   b. borrower.
   c. lender.
   d. none of the above.

8. No real estate investment type security (like stock market securities) shall be sold without first obtaining a permit from the DRE commissioner. A commissioner's permit requires a:

   a. broker license endorsement.
   b. $100 fee.
   c. $10,000 surety bond.
   d. all of the above.

9. The total value of all goods and services produced by the U.S. during a specific period of time is called the:

   a. GDP.
   b. Federal Reserve.
   c. FSLIC.
   d. FDIC.

10. Why do buyers prefer FHA and VA loans?

   a. Low down payment
   b. Low interest rates
   c. No prepayment penalty
   d. All of the above

ANSWERS: 1. *d;* **2.** *c;* **3.** *b;* **4.** *c;* **5.** *b;* **6.** *c;* **7.** *b;* **8.** *d;* **9.** *a;* **10.** *d*

Chapter 10
Appraisal Basics

I. What is an Appraisal?

An **APPRAISAL** *is an opinion as to the monetary value of a particular property at a given date.* One of the most important factors for you to consider in deciding whether to sell or buy a home or any specific piece of real estate is its selling price. Each parcel of land (and the buildings on it) is unique. No two are exactly alike, so prices vary. The **MARKET PRICE (SELLING PRICE)** *is the total price, including down payment and financing, that a property actually brought when sold.* Market price is what it sold for, whereas market value is what it should have sold for in a competitive market.

> *An appraisal is an opinion of value (based on judgment and professional experience) for a specific property as of a certain date.*

The market value is what the property is actually worth. **MARKET VALUE** *is the price that a willing buyer will pay and a willing seller accept, both being fully informed and with the sale property exposed for a reasonable period.* The courtroom definition is even more technical:

"The highest price, estimated in terms of money, that a property will bring if it is exposed for sale in the open market, allowing a reasonable length of time to find a buyer who buys with full knowledge of all the uses to which it is adapted and for which the property is capable of being used."

In California, appraisers for federally insured (regulated) lending institutions must be licensed by the Office of Real Estate Appraisers. In effect, all appraisers must be licensed.

Current market value is not affected in any way by the original cost of the property. The market value of a particular property is an **opinion of value**, by an appraiser, based on analysis of actual and relevant data, as of a given date. Appraisers must have the required experience, education, and have passed one of the three California State Appraisal Exams. See end of Chapter 11.

Market value is primarily based upon the "willing buyer and willing seller" concept.

A. FOUR ESSENTIAL ELEMENTS OF VALUE

VALUE is a relationship between the thing desired and a potential purchaser. Four elements must be present to create and maintain value. The four essential elements of value are:

D   **1. Demand** — the desire, need, and ability to purchase
U   **2. Utility** — usefulness; ability to instill a desire for possession
S   **3. Scarcity** — in short supply, usually more expensive
T   **4. Transferability** — can change ownership, as with a deed.

Cost (or price) is NOT an element of value.

II. The Appraisal Process
(Four Logical Steps)

An appraisal is the solution to the problem of determining value. To solve this problem, an orderly procedure has been developed; it is called the appraisal process. The **APPRAISAL PROCESS** *is an orderly program by which the problem is defined, the work is planned, and the data is gathered, analyzed, and correlated to estimate the value.* Although the characteristics of real property differ, this is an orderly procedure for solving any appraisal problem. **See Figure 10-1**.

The appraisal process consists of four logical steps:

1. Defining and clarifying the problem (Chapter 10)
2. Gathering the data (Chapter 10)
3. Performing the three appraisal methods (Chapter 11)
4. Correlating the three methods and determining the final opinion of value. (Chapter 11)

A. DEFINITION OF THE APPRAISAL PROBLEM
(1st Step in the Appraisal Process)

The first step in the appraisal process must include a definition of what questions are to be answered during the appraisal. To begin with, the precise location of the property must be established. Next, the extent of ownership (fee simple or partial) to be appraised must be identified. The date and purpose of the appraisal (usually to establish market value) is then determined. Any limiting conditions (facts unknown to the appraiser) must be clarified. Finally, the appraiser will determine the fee for his or her services.

1. Purpose of an Appraisal

An appraisal can serve several purposes. Here is a partial list of the kinds of appraisals that you, as an owner or a potential owner, may need:

1. Market Value
2. Insurance Value
3. Loan Value
4. Tax Assessment Value
5. Rental Value
6. Value for certain Internal Revenue Service Purposes
7. Settlements
8. Salvage Value
9. Other

The usual reasons for an appraisal are: Transfer of ownership, obtaining a loan, condemnation, and insurance.

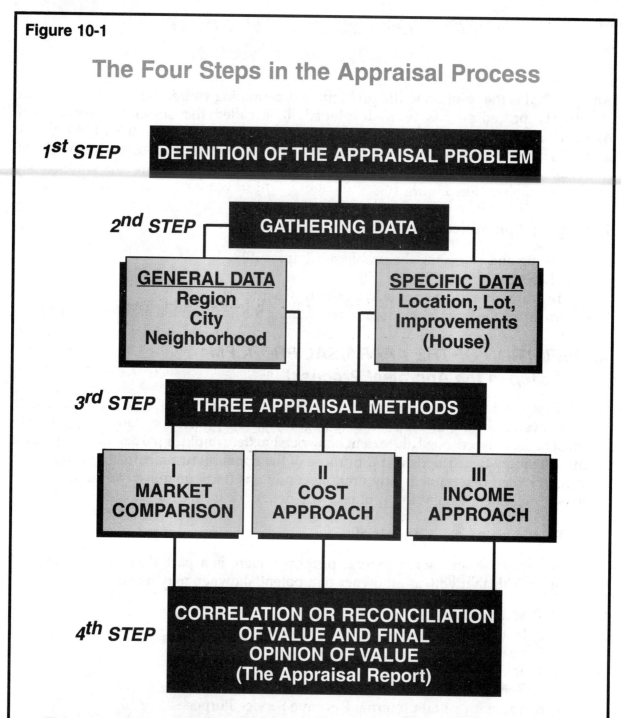

Figure 10-1

The Four Steps in the Appraisal Process

1st STEP — DEFINITION OF THE APPRAISAL PROBLEM

2nd STEP — GATHERING DATA

GENERAL DATA
Region
City
Neighborhood

SPECIFIC DATA
Location, Lot,
Improvements
(House)

3rd STEP — THREE APPRAISAL METHODS

I
MARKET
COMPARISON

II
COST
APPROACH

III
INCOME
APPROACH

4th STEP — CORRELATION OR RECONCILIATION
OF VALUE AND FINAL
OPINION OF VALUE
(The Appraisal Report)

This correlation or reconciliation is never an averaging of the three approaches. For instance, in a single family residential appraisal, the Income Approach is not as valuable as the Market Comparison Approach. This is one of the reasons why the experience and knowledge of the appraiser is so important in any appraisal.

2. Highest and Best Use

The first objective of an appraisal is to determine the highest and best use. The highest and best use increases productivity (net return) to the owner. Appraisers do a site analysis to determine highest and best use.

Before we can properly appraise a property, we must determine its highest and best use. *HIGHEST AND BEST USE is the use that will produce the maximum amount of profit or net return.* For example, should we build a house or an apartment on an available piece of land? From the standpoint of economics, it would be best to build that which brings the highest net return.

When the highest and best use is expected to change, the current use is called the "interim use."

B. GATHERING DATA (2nd Step in the Appraisal Process)

There are logical reasons why one home is worth more than another that appears comparable and why the choice of a neighborhood is as important, or even more important, than the house itself. There are also differences in location within a neighborhood that must be taken into accozunt. Differences in the actual building construction must also be considered. The background information needed for real estate appraisal is very broad, but there is a simple, sensible way to make a wise decision about buying a home or investment property. Start with the largest aspects and work toward the details. Look at:

1. GENERAL DATA

> a. Region
> b. City
> c. Neighborhood

2. SPECIFIC DATA (Site Analysis)

> a. Location
> b. Lot
> c. Improvements (House)

1. General Data (Region, City, Neighborhood)

The gathering of general data (regional, city or county, and neighborhood information) allows us to understand whether the area is prospering, holding its own, or declining and, if so, why.

a. Region (State is Divided into Regions)

A state can be divided into economic "regions" for analysis purposes. Example: San Diego, Los Angeles, Fresno, San Francisco, Sacramento, and Northern California.

The condition of the nation's economy can be reflected in the California real estate market and can affect the ease with which financing is available. But real estate markets are essentially regional and local. If the regional or local economy is expanding, people are working and can afford to buy homes because lending institutions are eager to grant loans. In a recession, jobs are less secure, confidence is low, and financing may not be as easy to obtain. So, the economic mood of the nation as a whole can indirectly affect the economic mood in California, but it is the local and regional economy that directly affects the mood in a particular real estate market.

A regional economy is affected by upturns and also downtrends. Not only do large areas reflect the national picture, but they also respond to more localized forces, such as the rapid growth of large cities and industrial complexes and the down-sizing of defense-related industries or even the weather in agricultural areas. California is divided into north and south regions and many sub-regions and cities.

California, like most large states, is a very geographically diverse state. Geographical considerations can easily affect an entire region. For example, if an area has snow for eight months of the year, the value of the property may be reduced when compared to regions that have year-round moderate or sunny climates.

b. City (or County)

A desirable city or county is a growing area where people can get good jobs and where people want to live. If the city is undesirable or even unsafe, people want to leave. Features to look for in cities, besides the availability of work and safety, are good public facilities, parks, good school systems, and active citizens who care and take part in the city's affairs.

c. Neighborhood

The neighborhood where you want to buy is more important than the house because it is the desirability of the area that sets value. An individual can change the appearance of his or her house but he or she alone cannot change the appearance of the neighborhood.

A **RESIDENTIAL NEIGHBORHOOD** is normally a limited area where the homes are physically similar and where the occupants have a certain degree of social and *economic background in common*. It may cover a few square miles or it may be only one block square. Boundaries may be defined by physical, social, or economic differences. The important thing is that your neighborhood is the environment in which you live day-in and day-out. THE NEIGHBORHOOD IN WHICH YOU LIVE IS USUALLY A MORE IMPORTANT FACTOR THAN THE HOUSE ITSELF! This is because the surroundings of a house influence the property value even more than the house itself does.

Neighborhoods influence homeowners' location decisions more than renters'. The reason is that many people rent apartments in neighborhoods in which they would never think of buying, because they plan to stay there for only a short time. Renters may rent in a less desirable area, but when they buy they will select a neighborhood they like.

A neighborhood has similar physical structures based on common social, economic, and political characteristics of the people. Owner-occupied homes lend economic stability to a neighborhood, as owners tend to take better care of property than renters.

The selection or acceptance of a neighborhood should come before the actual decision of whether to buy a particular house or not. The four primary forces that affect value of a neighborhood are shown in **Figure 10-2**.

Neighborhoods are always changing, sometimes at a fast pace, but usually at a slow, steady pace. The four considerations discussed in Figure 10-2 can change a prestigious area to a shabby neighborhood or vice versa. Each consideration can change the outlook for any neighborhood.

The four forces affecting value are: physical, social, economic, and political considerations.

2. Specific Data (Property Itself)

The most important economic characteristic is area preference (location).

There is plenty of land in the world, but the exact location of each parcel makes it unlike any other on earth. Its location is the major factor that determines its value.

a. Location

A low-income buyer would choose location as the prime factor in selecting a home because location has an important impact on transportation problems and costs of getting to work.

A **SITE** *is a particular parcel within a neighborhood*. Since each parcel is unique, the individual site that one selects for a home should be chosen with care. There are

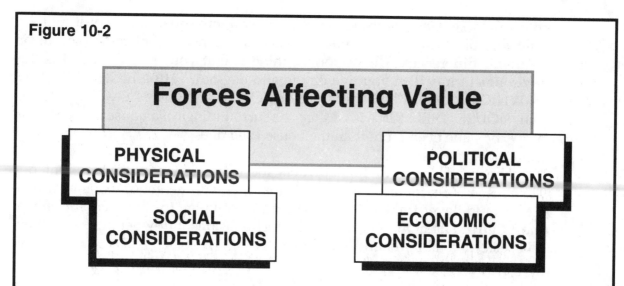

Forces Affecting Value

| PHYSICAL CONSIDERATIONS | POLITICAL CONSIDERATIONS |
| SOCIAL CONSIDERATIONS | ECONOMIC CONSIDERATIONS |

Figure 10-2

PHYSICAL CONSIDERATIONS

A neighborhood that is close to a commercial area is generally highly desirable. Being close to downtown areas, employment centers, and major shopping areas only adds to this desirability, as long as an owner is not located right next to such a facility. If the street patterns are curved and there are wide boulevards, the neighborhood also looks more attractive.

Access to transportation is necessary. The availability of freeways, transit systems, and convenient parking is an important consideration in making comparisons between various areas. However, this factor is less important in high-value suburban areas where estate living is desirable.

Balanced Land Use

The best efficiency and highest value come when there is a balance between different types of use. A city is a naturally attractive environment when it has a proper balance between residential, commercial, industrial, and recreational space.

Families are attracted to a neighborhood with good schools. Certain private or parochial schools may create a demand for homes in that area. Churches are also a definite benefit. Other institutions such as libraries, colleges, and universities may also enhance a community.

The first trip into a neighborhood may be impressive, or, on the other hand, it may be depressing. First impressions are important: the landscaping, architectural style, and the streets can create either impression. Well-maintained buildings create enhanced marketability.

Physical conditions such as lakes, beaches, rivers, or hilly areas may be either advantageous or disadvantageous depending on where they are. A feature such as a wooded hillside or lake front property would probably enhance a neighborhood, but a river that frequently floods the surrounding area is a disadvantage.

Invasion of a residential area by commercial or industrial usage around it is usually a disadvantage, especially if the neighborhood is exposed to noise or odors. A bar located across from a home is usually a devaluing factor. Some areas may be hazardous because of landslides or simply from heavy truck and auto traffic.

SOCIAL CONSIDERATIONS

Neighborhoods often consist of persons of similar income, education, cultural background and lifestyle. As such, the neighborhood may or may not appeal to certain individual buyers. Could a change in the social makeup of a neighborhood affect values? Whether or not such a change has any influence either positive or negative and the effect of any change is a field of inquiry that must be left to sociologists. Appraisers, lenders, and real estate agents are forbidden by both federal and state law to consider race, religion, sex, ethnicity, or lifestyle as factors of value. Only economic factors may be considered by real estate professionals.

BLIGHT *occurs as a result of a lack of property maintenance in a neighborhood.* This is generally due to an economic inability to provide maintenance on the part of the owners. The result is lowered property values.

GENTRIFICATION *is the rehabilitation of a blighted neighborhood.* It is generally a result of low property values attracting buyers who are economically able to upgrade and maintain the properties in the neighborhood.

ECONOMIC CONSIDERATIONS

Population growth is an indication of the economic health of a neighborhood. If more people want to live in an area, then it must be desirable: an economically alive neighborhood has well-maintained lawns and buildings, whereas in a deteriorating neighborhood the lack of maintenance is obvious and so is the lowered value of the homes.

The rents charged and income levels of the people indicate a community's prestige (or lack of it). **The larger the percentage of home ownership versus those renting, the more economically stable the area is**. If many rentals are vacant, you can surmise that renters are not interested in the area. New construction, on the other hand, indicates that the area is growing and its value is increasing.

POLITICAL CONSIDERATIONS

Property tax rates vary from area to area. Wealthy, more stable economic areas usually have a slightly higher tax rate because the residents are willing and have the ability to pay for more public services. In areas where the taxes are very high, potential buyers are often scared off. Special assessments for lighting, sewers, and street improvements may temporarily turn some people away, but they generally add to the property's total value.

Some cities use **zoning** and **building codes** as devices to ensure the continued stability of a neighborhood. If the desirability of the neighborhood warrants such regulation, then the city will continue to be a growing one. In the end, most city leaders politically control changes in their cities by enacting zoning and building codes.

several site selection factors that affect the value of the home, but the personal needs and objectives of the buyer should be of the utmost concern.

Site: the location of a plot of ground for a building.

b. Lot (Types)

There are six major types (**See Figure 10-3**) of lots:

1. Cul-de-sac (Lot A)
2. Corner (Lot B)
3. Key (Lot C)
4. T-Intersection (Lot D)
5. Interior (Lot E)
6. Flag (Lot F)

Figure 10-3

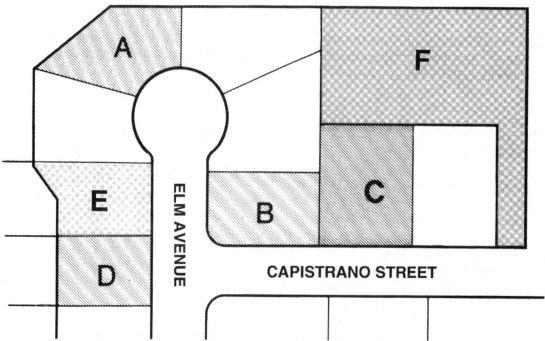

1. Cul-De-Sac Lot

The **CUL-DE-SAC LOT** *is a lot facing the turnaround portion of a dead-end street*. Figure 10-3 shows that Lot A is a cul-de-sac. The main advantage of a cul-de-sac lot is privacy and lack of traffic one gets by living on a "not a through" street. Due to its pie-shaped design, it has the disadvantage of a small front yard, but this is offset by generally having a large backyard. The design makes it more secluded and limits through traffic from both autos and pedestrians. Limited parking and front yard space does not stop it from rivaling the corner lot as one of the most desirable types of lots. A cul-de-sac lot's desirability may vary due to view, size, area, and family characteristics. Figure 10-3, Lot A, Cul-de-sac.

2. Corner Lot

The *CORNER LOT is a lot that is located at the intersection of two streets.* A corner site frequently has a higher value than a lot fronting only on one street. The appraiser must be careful to look at the local market in determining the actual effects of a corner influence on the surrounding lots. *CORNER INFLUENCE is the theory that a variety of forces affect corner lots (and also lots located near a corner) to a greater degree than most other lots.* A corner lot is generally more desirable if there is access to the backyard for items such as a trailer or camper. Other people like it because there are fewer homes nearby, which allows for more light, fresh air, and also more lot area for gardens and other types of landscaping.

The main disadvantage of a corner lot is the loss of privacy and higher cost, since both sides of the lot require off-site improvements, such as streets, curbs, gutters, and sidewalks. Also, zoning setbacks may reduce the buildable lot space. Usually commercial corner lots benefit because of easy access and added traffic exposure. Figure 10-3, Lot B, Corner.

3. Key Lot

The Key Lot is usually the least desirable lot because it has so many adjunct neighbors; it is bordered by more than three lots.

KEY LOT is a lot that is bordered on the side by the back of other lots that front on another street. Key lots are the least desirable lots because of the lack of privacy caused by the close proximity of several neighbors abutting the side of the property. Figure 10-3, Lot C, Key.

4. T-Intersection Lot

The *T-INTERSECTION LOT is an interior lot that is faced head-on by a street; it is the lot at the end of a dead-end street.* The streets form a "T" shape. It is an interior lot with one advantage and two disadvantages. The advantage is a clear view down the street, which gives a more spacious feeling. Intersection noise and annoying headlights at night are its disadvantages. Figure 10-3, Lot D, T-Intersection.

5. Interior Lot

An *INTERIOR LOT is a lot generally surrounded by other lots on three sides.* It is usually in the shape of a rectangle, but can be almost any shape. It is the

most common type of lot and it is preferred by most people. Interior lots have larger backyards than corner lots, which make them much better for recreational purposes. Since the front yards are smaller than those found on corner lots, they require less yard maintenance and benefit from less intersection noise. Because of typical long block design, interior lots are by far the most numerous. The disadvantages are limited backyard access and three or more adjoining neighbors. Figure 10-3, Lot E, Interior.

6. Flag Lot

A *FLAG LOT is a rear lot, in back of other lots, with a long, narrow access driveway.* This type of lot takes on the shape a flag. The flag lot's shape allows for a maximum of privacy and can be easily gated. In hilly areas, flag lots have some of the better views, while others can be pushed up against a steep mountain side. The value of a flag lot verses other types of lots depends on the circumstances. The same can be said about all other types of lots: their value depends on the specifics of each lot and the local market conditions. But it is up to the salesperson to gain a working knowledge of lot shapes and the pluses and minuses attributed to each type of lot. Figure 10-3, Lot F, Flag.

c. Physical Aspects of a Lot

The major physical aspects of the actual site are:

1. Size and shape
2. Slope, drainage, and soil (lot design layouts)
3. View, exposure to sun, and weather
4. Improvements (on-site and off-site)

1. Size and Shape of Lot

Lots or parcels can be subdivided into almost any shape imaginable, but most lots are rectangular and front onto a street. Any lot is valuable if it offers enough area to build a house that is compatible with the surroundings. In general, the more land or frontage on the street, the higher the value of the land. An example of a depth table will explain this concept. A *DEPTH TABLE is a percentage table that illustrates how the highest value is located in the front part of a lot.* **Figure 10-4** is an example of the "4-3-2-1" depth table.

The "4-3-2-1 rule" is best used by appraisers to determine the value of commercial properties on which the lots vary in depth.

The percentage of value for each ¼ or 25% section of the lot varies: 40%, 30%, 20%, to 10% in value for each quarter back from the front.

Figure 10-4

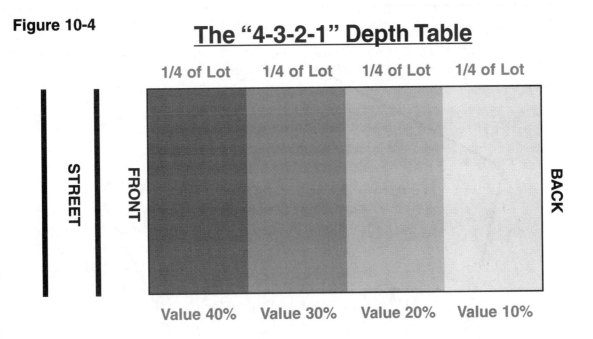

The "4-3-2-1" Depth Table

In Figure 10-4, the highest value is in the front portion of the lot. For example, a small backyard will not affect the value of the property as much as a small front yard. This is especially true with commercial property such as shopping centers where there is plenty of parking in the back, but most people prefer to park in the front. Remember, though, that the percentage and values of a depth table vary from property to property.

Front footage is a pricing tool used to sell commercial property.

Since the front portion of the lot has the most value, the more frontage there is, the better. *FRONT FOOTAGE is the width of the property in the front, along the street.* Generally speaking we can say that a house with a large front yard is worth more than the same house with a large backyard. But people do have different preferences, such as large backyards for swimming pools, tennis courts, or other recreational activities.

"Plottage" (assemblage) brings under single ownership two or more contiguous lots, previously owned separately, to increase the total value.

2. Lot Design Layouts

There are several ways to lay out lots in a parcel of land being subdivided. Zoning regulations usually state the minimum amount of square feet a lot can have, but a developer can get better prices if he or she divides the land wisely. **Figure 10-5** shows the same parcel of land twice. **Plan 1** is a good

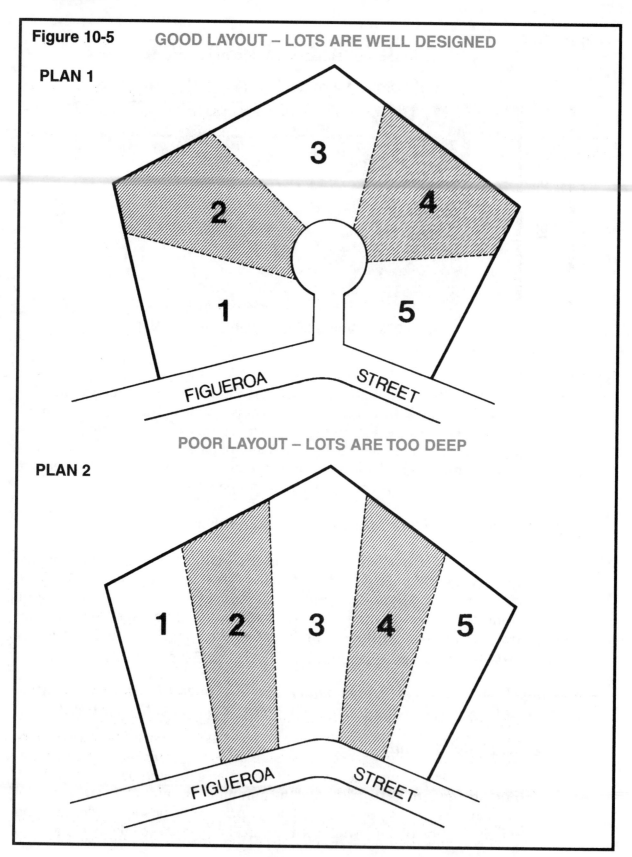

Figure 10-5 GOOD LAYOUT – LOTS ARE WELL DESIGNED

PLAN 1

3

2

4

1

5

FIGUEROA STREET

POOR LAYOUT – LOTS ARE TOO DEEP

PLAN 2

1 2 3 4 5

FIGUEROA STREET

design, giving a variety of desirable lots. **Plan 2** is a poor design, giving too little variation, too little front area and too much depth.

The layout of lots in a large subdivision is illustrated in **Figure 10-6**. Often a subdivision tract with fewer, well-planned lots will bring a higher total sales

Figure 10-6 TENTATIVE SUBDIVISION MAP

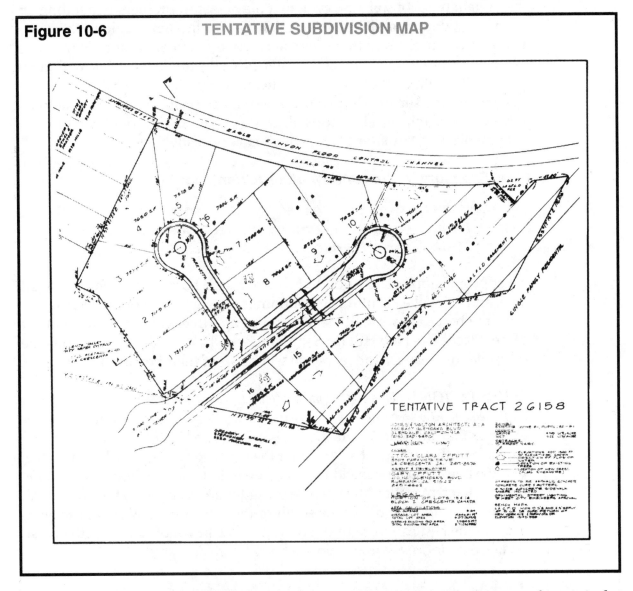

price than a poorly designed tract with more lots. The best tract layout is the one that considers all the costs involved and the marketability of all the lots. This kind of planning is not easy and requires the services of a specialist.

3. Slope, Drainage, and Soil

The slope of a lot will lower its value if it will be costly to improve. A lot that is higher or lower in relation to the street level may be costly to

improve because of possible slope and drainage problems. Erosion may also be a part of slope or drainage problems. These problems, however, can be easily offset by an excellent view or location.

The soil composition of a lot may or may not be of any great concern. There are certain types of soil, however, that may create a problem depending on your lifestyle or possible construction needs. In some regions there are certain peat moss areas that must be corrected before a foundation can be poured. In other areas the soil content can destroy a pipeline within 10 years. If you like gardens and plant life, it is wise to see how the plants are growing in the surrounding lots. Some hillside tracts are built on bedrock covered by a thin layer of topsoil; to dig a swimming pool might even require blasting with dynamite, which is very costly.

4. View, Exposure to Sun, and Weather (Orientation)

The south and west sides of streets are preferred by merchants: pedestrians seek the shady side and displayed merchandise is not damaged by the sun. The northeast corner is the least desirable.

Most people appreciate a good view from their homes; it is pleasant to sit back and enjoy the beautiful surroundings. In a new tract of homes, the lots with the best views usually sell first and apartments with views rent for more. Places like Nob Hill (in San Francisco), Lake Tahoe, and La Jolla are examples of areas that are expensive because of their beautiful views.

ORIENTATION *is planning the most advantageous place on a parcel of land for an improvement to be located.* The exposure of a house to the sun and weather elements may influence a person's decision to buy a house. If the wind usually blows from the northwest, it is best for the house to face the northwest. In this case the house can be a shield for backyard entertaining. The exposure to the sun is a different matter. Most people prefer the sun to shine on their backyard, so the backyard should face the south or the west. In this way the backyard receives the best exposure throughout the day. In windy areas on the coast, sheltered patios, away from cold sea breezes, are desirable.

Amenity properties are usually single-family residences.

AMENITIES *are those improvements or views that increase the desirability or enjoyment rather than the necessities of the residents.* For example, a view of the ocean, mountains, or city lights at night increase the value of a home. Amenity improvements would include jacuzzis, swimming pools, and tennis courts.

III. Improvements

Real estate is logically divided into land (site) and improvements. *IMPROVEMENTS are any buildings, walkways, pools, and other structures.* *CAPITAL IMPROVEMENTS are permanent improvements made to increase the useful life of the property or increase the property's value. They stay with the property.* These include off-site improvements (streets and utilities) and on-site improvements (buildings). *OFF-SITE IMPROVEMENTS are the improvements made to areas adjoining the parcel that add to the parcel's usefulness and sometimes its value.* Examples of off-site improvements are: streets, street lights, sewers, sidewalks, curbs, and gutters. These items generally add value to urban property but may be of little value in rural areas. Off-site improvements are usually paid for by the homeowners through the levying of special assessments. On the other hand, *ON-SITE IMPROVEMENTS are structures erected permanently for use on a site, such as buildings and fences.*

A. HOUSE STRUCTURE ILLUSTRATED

This section identifies different parts of a house. **Figure 10-7** is a diagram of a house that illustrates the 20 most used construction terms. **Figure 10-8** shows roof types. Each part is labeled and defined so that it can be identified. **Figure 10-9** lists construction and other terms.

B. HOME WARRANTY PLANS

A warranty plan is a good sales tool. It is usually paid for by the seller and assures the buyer that major repairs for defects will be fixed under the terms of the warranty contract. A buyer should sign a waiver if he or she turns down a home warranty or inspection.

A *WARRANTY PLAN is an insurance plan that provides financial protection against defects in any major home construction.* There are a growing number of such warranty plans in California. These warranty plans insure the new owner of an existing home against such things as malfunction of built-in appliances and defects in major systems such as structure, roof, heating, plumbing, and electrical wiring. For this protection, the previous owner or the buyer pays a fee that varies according to the type of coverage received. Some companies inspect the property (thereby giving notice of any existing defects). The CAR® deposit receipt informs buyers and sellers that there are warranty plans available. But this item, along with who pays for the warranty plan, is negotiable. **Note: All new homes automatically carry a one-year warranty, from the contractor, against labor or material defects.**

IV. Basic Appraisal Principles

There are several "principles of appraisal." These principles are valid economic concepts that are applied to the appraisal of real estate. A few of the basic principles are explained

Figure 10-7

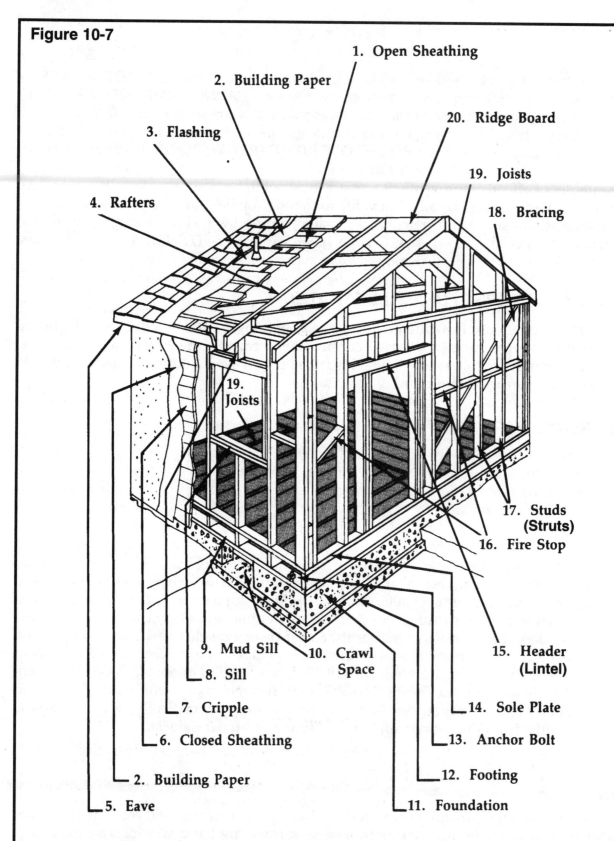

1. Open Sheathing
2. Building Paper
20. Ridge Board
3. Flashing
19. Joists
4. Rafters
18. Bracing
19. Joists
17. Studs (Struts)
16. Fire Stop
9. Mud Sill
10. Crawl Space
15. Header (Lintel)
8. Sill
7. Cripple
14. Sole Plate
6. Closed Sheathing
13. Anchor Bolt
2. Building Paper
12. Footing
5. Eave
11. Foundation

EXPLANATION OF DIAGRAM DETAILS

1. **Open Sheathing**   Boards nailed to rafters as foundation for the roof covering. Open sheathing is used with wood shingles.

2. **Building Paper**   Heavy waterproof paper used between sheathing and roof covering or siding.

3. **Flashing**   Sheet metal used to protect against water seepage.

4. **Rafters**   Sloping members of a roof used to support the roof boards and shingles (Maximum 24" apart).

5. **Eave**   Protruding underpart of roof overhanging exterior walls.

6. **Closed Sheathing**   Boards nailed to studding as foundation for exterior siding. "Closed" means butted together.

7. **Cripple**   Stud above or below a window opening or above a doorway.

8. **Sill**   Bottom portion lining doorway or window.

9. **Mud Sill**   Treated lumber (or redwood) bolted to the foundation.

10. **Crawl Space**   Unexcavated area under the house (Min. 18").

11. **Foundation**   Concrete base of house.

12. **Footing**   Expanded portion of concrete foundation.

13. **Anchor Bolt**   Large bolt used for fastening mud sill to foundation. Bolt is anchored into concrete foundation.

14. **Sole Plate**   Support on which the studs rest.

15. **Header (Lintel)**   The beam over a doorway or window.

16. **Fire Stop**   Blocking used to restrict flames from spreading to attic. May be placed horizontally or diagonally.

17. **Studs (Struts)**   Vertical 2" x 4" framework in the walls spaced 16" on center.

18. **Bracing**   Board running diagonally across the wall framing to prevent sway.

19. **Joists**   Structural parts supporting floor or ceiling loads. A beam which supports them would be called a girder.

20. **Ridge Board**   Highest point of construction in a frame building.

Figure 10-8

ROOF TYPES

Before purchasing a house, a potential buyer should carefully evaluate the structure, checking to see that its style of architecture is compatible with that of the surrounding neighborhood. This should also be an element of consideration when building a new house or remodeling.

Examining the type of roof, the way it is framed and finished, is one of the simplest ways to assess the architectural compatibility of a given house.

Pictured below are several of the most common roof types. One is likely to see examples of hip, gambrel, flat, gable, mansard, and pyramid roofs throughout California.

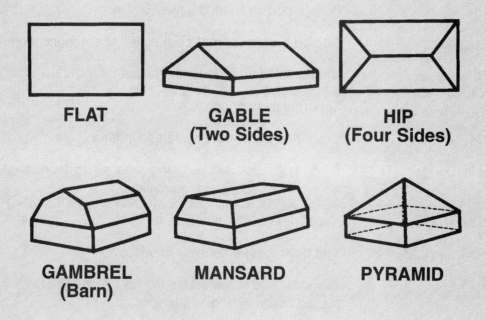

FLAT   GABLE   HIP
          (Two Sides)   (Four Sides)

GAMBREL   MANSARD   PYRAMID
(Barn)

Figure 10-9

Construction and Other Terms

Backfill – The replacement of excavated earth against a structure (wall).

Bearing Wall – A strong wall supporting any vertical load in addition to its own weight, usually a roof or floor above.

Boardfoot – A unit quantity for lumber equal to the volume of a board 12 x 12 x 1 inches.

BTU (British Thermal Unit) – A unit of measurement used to calculate heat - the quantity of heat required to raise one pound of water one degree Fahrenheit.

Capital Assets – Expenditures of a permanent nature that increase property values. Examples: buildings and street improvements.

Cash Flow – In investment property, the actual cash the investor will receive after deduction of operating expenses and debt servicing (loan payment) from his or her gross income.

Conduit – A flexible metal pipe used to protect the electrical wiring inside.

Dry Wall – Plaster walls that are installed in dry sheets.

EER (Energy Efficiency Ratio) – A measure of energy efficiency; the higher the EER, the higher the efficiency.

Elevation Sheet – A rendering which shows the front and side views of a building; it shows the exterior views.

Foundation Plan – Plan that shows footing, piers, and sub-flooring.

H2O Pressure – Testing water pressure by turning on all faucets and flushing all toilets.

HVAC – Heating, ventilation, and air conditioning system in a commercial property.

Hoskold Tables – Concept of a "sinking fund" as a compound interest-bearing account, into which the portion of the investment returned each year is reinvested immediately.

CONTINUED

Construction and Other Terms

Inwood Tables – Concept of using present value of income in a perpetuity table to help appraisers.

Kiosk – An information booth.

Local Building Inspector – Person who enforces construction standards.

Over-Improvement – Is an expenditure to a property that doesn't improve its value.

Percolation Test – A test to determine how well water is absorbed by the soil. (Used when installing a sewage system.)

Plot Plan – The placement of improvements (buildings) on a lot.

Potable Water – Drinkable water.

Property Residual, Building Residual, and Land Residual – All are methods of working backwards to find the unknown variable when appraising property.

R-Value – A measure used to calculate the heat resistance of insulation (the higher the better). Insulation is considered adequate if the temperature on the inside of an exterior wall is the same as the temperature on an interior wall.

Rehabilitation – The restoration of a property to a satisfactory condition without changing the interior or exterior design.

Soil Pipe – A pipe used to carry waste and sewage from a property.

Toxic Waste Report – A report evaluating how harmful the dangerous material is on a property.

Turnkey Project – Built, equipped, or installed complete and ready to occupy.

Unearned Increment – An increase in value of real estate due to no effort on the part of the owner; often caused by population increase.

Wainscoting – The wood lining of the lower portion of an interior wall with the upper portion wallpapered or covered with another material different from the lower portion.

so that you can understand the logic and reasons why a particular home is worth more than another. **Figure 10-10** shows you six of the basic appraisal principles.

Figure 10-10

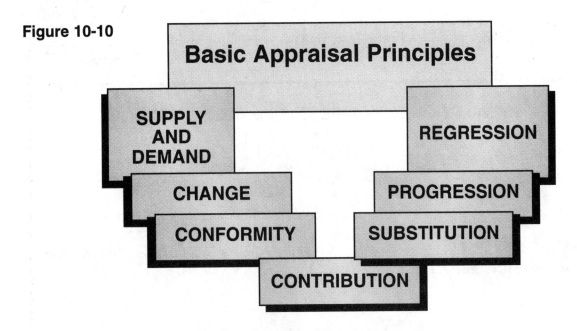

A. PRINCIPLE OF SUPPLY AND DEMAND

Scarcity is an economic characteristic of real estate. If the population of an area increases, the relative scarcity of housing will cause price increases.

The principle of supply and demand shows why "location" is important. The principle of *SUPPLY AND DEMAND states that as the supply of land decreases, the value of land increases, because more people are competing for the desirable land.* Living next to the Pacific Ocean is expensive because the land is scarce. Even small lots bring very high selling prices in these areas. To beach lovers, these are the most desirable neighborhoods because there are only so many ocean view lots. In areas where there are many lots available, like the desert, the supply is large and the price of a lot can be very low. Downtown high-rise commercial locations in cities like San Francisco, Los Angeles, and San Diego are scarce and therefore expensive.

Purchasing power and dollars follow demand.

B. PRINCIPLE OF CHANGE

The principle of *CHANGE is that real property is constantly changing.* Value is influenced by changes in such things as: population size, shopping centers, schools and colleges, freeways, economic and social trends. It is hard to see change on a day-to-day basis, but if you go back to the area where you grew up, the change is apparent.

A trend is a series of changes brought about by a chain of events (causes and effects).

The real property life cycle goes through three stages: development, maturity, and decline, which are illustrated in **Figure 10-11**.

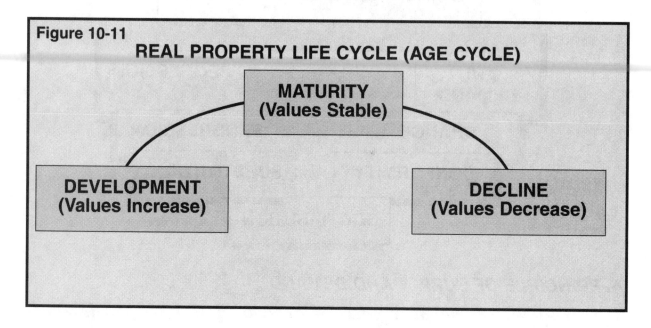

Figure 10-11
REAL PROPERTY LIFE CYCLE (AGE CYCLE)

MATURITY
(Values Stable)

DEVELOPMENT
(Values Increase)

DECLINE
(Values Decrease)

Change is evidenced by the fact that neighborhoods tend to pass through the three stages of the real estate life cycle.

1. Development (Integration)

This is the stage when the land is subdivided into lots, the streets are paved, and street lights are installed. Soon, homes are built and the community starts. As new people move in, landscaping and fences improve the homes.

The three steps in construction of a home are land and acquistion, development, and construction.

2. Maturity (Equilibrium)

The maturity stage starts when the homes become older and the children grow up and move away. Most of the residents are long-time homeowners and the community has a solid, well-established look.

3. Decline (Disintegration)

In this stage, the buildings show some wear and tear and the oldest buildings are starting to deteriorate. As the useful life of the property declines, lower social or economic groups move into the area. Large homes may be converted into multiple family use.

The life cycle of real property may take a few years, such as that of a mining town going "bust," or may span a century, such as that of a community that constantly revitalizes itself.

C. PRINCIPLE OF CONFORMITY

The principle of **CONFORMITY** *states that the maximum value is obtained when a reasonable degree of building similarity is maintained in the neighborhood.* So, if all the homes in an area are similar (not identical), the maximum value of real property is created. The word "similar" is the key. If all the tract homes are identical, as if they were all made with the same cookie cutter, the maximum value is not present.

The principle of conformity is one of the primary reasons for zoning regulations (discussed in Chapter 12). They protect the neighborhood from other nonconforming uses and from infiltration of incompatible structures. An attractive neighborhood would quickly decline in value if zoning did not help protect its conformity.

D. PRINCIPLE OF CONTRIBUTION

The principle of **CONTRIBUTION** *states that the value of a particular component is measured in terms of its contribution to the value of the whole property.* Consequently, cost does not necessarily equal value. It either adds more or less to the value of real property.

For example: If an apartment building produces a 10% return to investors, a $50,000 investment in a swimming pool, without an equal ($50,000 x 10%) $5,000 or higher increase in rents, would not be a good idea.

Thus, in some cases, a property's market value may not increase even if it has had additions, alterations, or has been rehabilitated. If the swimming pool were added, the property would be considered "over-built." The principle of contribution is also referred to as increasing and (decreasing) "diminishing returns" in economic textbooks.

An appraiser would apply the "principle of contribution" to determine if adding a swimming pool to a 30-unit apartment building would be economically justified.

E. PRINCIPLE OF SUBSTITUTION

With the principle of **SUBSTITUTION**, *a buyer will not pay more for a particular property if it costs less to buy a similar property of equal utility and desirability.* People prefer the less expensive price if all other things are considered equal. When appraisers use the principle of substitution, they compare properties to adjust for differences. The

maximum value of a property tends to be set by the cost of acquiring an equally desirable substitute property.

F. PRINCIPLE OF REGRESSION (Value Goes Down)

The principle of *REGRESSION states that between properties in the same neighborhood, the value of the best property will be adversely affected by the value of the other properties.* For example, if a house that would easily be worth $790,000 in a neighborhood of similar homes was to be built in a neighborhood of $210,000 homes, it would not sell for $790,000. Anyone in the market for a $790,000 house would not want to live in a tract where the average price of a house was $210,000. Because of its superior quality or size, the house would undoubtedly sell for more than the average house in the tract, but it would not approach $790,000.

The same principle applies to the over-improved home. When owners invest very large sums in major additions, lavish landscaping, and swimming pools, and the other residents do not improve their homes, the house is no longer similar to the others. The owners of the over-built house will not receive the full value for the cost of improvements they have made.

G. PRINCIPLE OF PROGRESSION (Value Goes Up)

In the principle of *PROGRESSION, the value of a lesser residence is increased in value by its location in a neighborhood of better homes.* This is the opposite of the principle of regression. A smaller, unattractive, and poorly maintained home in an exclusive area will sell for much more than if it were located in a comparable neighborhood. People who wish to live in an exclusive area would think of the smaller home as a bargain.

V. SUMMARY

An **appraisal** is an opinion of value (based on judgment and professional experience) for a specific property as of a certain date. Appraisers, who must be licensed in California, want "open market results," not prudent values or prices. The **value** of a property is determined by the elements of **demand, utility, scarcity,** and **transferability.** Cost is never one of these elements.

The **appraisal process** consists of four steps: 1) **defining the problem,** 2) **gathering the data,** 3) **performing the three appraisal methods,** and 4) **determining the final opinion of value.** Whether the reason for the appraisal is transfer of ownership, obtaining a loan, condemnation, or insurance, the first step is to do a **site analysis** to determine **highest and best use.**

The second step involves gathering data, including **general data** (region, city, and neighborhood) and **specific data** (location, lot, and improvements). The **neighborhood** is the most important general data. The **four forces** affecting value are: **physical, social, economic,** and **political considerations.** The most important economic characteristic is area preference (**location**).

Front footage is a pricing tool used to sell commercial property and a **4-3-2-1 depth table** is used when the lots vary in depth. **Plottage** (assemblage) refers to separately owned, contiguous lots brought under single ownership. The **shady south and west sides of streets** are preferred by merchants with the northeast corner being the least desirable.

There are several principles of appraisal, including that of **supply and demand,** and the **principle of change,** which is evident in the **real estate life cycle** of **development, maturity,** and **decline.** The **principle of conformity** states that the maximum value is obtained when building similarity is maintained in the neighborhood, and is one of the major reasons for **zoning regulations.**

The **principle of contribution** (or diminishing returns) states that the value of a particular component is measured in terms of its contribution to the value of the whole property. The **principle of substitution** states that a buyer will not pay more for a particular property if it costs less to buy a similar property of equal utility and desirability.

The **principle of regression** states that between properties in the same neighborhood, the value of the best property will be negatively affected by the value of the other properties. The opposite of regression is the **principle of progression,** where a lesser residence increases in value by its location in a neighborhood of better homes.

VI. TERMINOLOGY - CHAPTER 10

A. Appraisal
B. Appraisal Process
C. Change
D. Conformity
E. Corner Lot
F. Cul-de-Sac
G. Depth Table
H. Flag Lot

I. Frontage
J. Highest and Best Use
K. Interior Lot
L. Key Lot
M. Market Price
N. Market Value
O. Neighborhood
P. Off-Site Improvements

Q. Progression Principle
R. Regression Principle
S. Site
T. Supply and Demand
U. T-Intersection Lot
V. Warranty Plan

1.____ The appraisal principle that maintains the maximum value of a property is realized when a reasonable degree of similarity is present in the area where the property is located.

2.____ The least desirable type of lot because the back ends of other lots face one of its sides.

3.____ A general term describing people living or working together in an area of similar properties with similar social, economic, and political backgrounds.

4.____ The highest price a willing buyer would pay and a willing seller accept, both being fully informed, and the property exposed for a reasonable period of time. This value may be different from the price a property can actually be sold for at a given time.

5.____ Not a corner lot, but an inside lot; the most common type of lot.

6.____ Development of large parcels into smaller lots suitable for construction. This includes sidewalks, curbs, streets, sewers, streetlights, etc.

7.____ A lot at the U-shaped end of a street. Even though they are narrower in the front and wider in the back, these lots are popular because the street itself makes the area exclusive.

8.____ An opinion of real property value based upon a factual analysis by a qualified (licensed) person with education and experience.

9.____ The use of land that will bring the greatest economic return over a given time.

10.____ The price a property sells for, which may be higher or lower than its actual market value.

11.____ The orderly process of determining the fair market value of real property by: 1) defining the problem, 2) gathering the data, 3) applying the three methods of appraisal (cost approach, market comparison approach, income approach), and 4) correlating the information for a final estimate of value.

12.____ A general term for a lot or plot of land.

13.____ A lot with both the front and side facing different streets. Such a residential lot is generally more desirable because of its increased exposure to light and fresh air. A commercial lot benefits from better street access and exposure to traffic patterns.

14.____ An interior lot facing down a street into traffic. Such a lot benefits from the view down the open street but suffers from additional traffic noise and on-coming headlights at night.

15.____ A lot with a long, narrow entrance, forming the shape of a flag. While it has limited frontage, such a lot can be very desirable if the odd shape is accompanied by a spectacular view in the back.

16.____ A chart illustrating the principle that the greatest value exists in the front portion of the lot, and the value of the land decreases the further back from the street you go.

17.____ The linear measure of the front portion of a parcel facing a major street, walkway, lake, or ocean.

18.____ An insurance plan covering the major systems of a home such as electrical, heating, plumbing, and major appliances.

19.____ A principle of real estate appraisal suggesting that the value of property increases when there is more demand and a short supply in an area. Conversely, the value decreases when there is an abundant supply and less demand.

20.____ The concept that although changes may be imperceptible, neighborhoods are constantly changing. Population shifts and economic changes, along with many other variables, will constantly work to alter the value of property.

21.____ The real estate principle that a smaller, low quality home will gain value if larger, nicer homes are being built in the neighborhood .

22.____ The real estate principle that a larger, nicer home will not enjoy its full value if it is located in a neighborhood of smaller, low quality homes.

VII. MULTIPLE CHOICE

1. Vertical 2" x 4" framework in walls spaced 16" on center are:

   a. studs (struts).
   b. rafters.
   c. footing.
   d. cripple.

2. A bearing wall is defined as:

   a. an interior wall with a doorway.
   b. a solid wall of concrete.
   c. a wall made of studs and cross-bracing.
   d. a wall that supports a floor or ceiling.

3. The process of determining whether to build a house or an apartment building on a particular piece of land is known as:

   a. highest and best use.
   b. the market comparison approach.
   c. the cost process.
   d. the appraisal process.

4. All new homes in California automatically carry a warranty against labor or material defects for a period of:

   a. 6 months.
   b. 12 months.
   c. 8 months.
   d. 16 months.

5. A limited area, where the homes are physically similar and the residents have a certain degree of economic background in common, is known as a:

   a. city.
   b. township.
   c. housing tract.
   d. neighborhood.

6. "Backfill" is a term that most closely means:

   a. a special soil made of rock.
   b. to fill holes in concrete blocks.
   c. to refill excavated earth against a wall.
   d. placing grout between ceramic joints.

7. The beam over a window or door is called a:

    a. cripple.

    b. joist.

    c. stud.

    d. header.

8. What does it mean to buy a "turnkey" house?

    a. This is a technical construction term.

    b. The FHA will turn the keys over to the new buyer.

    c. A house that has been completed and is ready for occupancy.

    d. A federal subsidized housing program turns the key over to a low income family.

9. If a customer is deciding between two look-alike clothes dryers, the one with the highest energy efficiency rating (EER) is:

    a. more efficient.

    b. less efficient.

    c. producing more BTUs.

    d. requiring more voltage.

10. Conduit in the building trade would most likely be used by a(n):

    a. carpenter.

    b. electrician.

    c. plumber.

    d. roofer.

ANSWERS: *1. a; 2. d; 3. a; 4. b; 5. d; 6. c; 7. d; 8. c; 9. a 10. b*

Chapter 11
Appraisal Methods

Real estate salespeople need to know enough about appraisal techniques and practices so that they can determine, in advance, the approximate selling price of a property. Salespeople have the advantage of determining the "probable" sales price of a property quickly because they see what similar properties in their area sell for each day. They can be on top of the market because of their multiple listing service and close contact with other knowledgeable agents. They are constantly being updated as to the current listing and selling prices.

Figure 11-1 is an example of the Competitive Market Analysis Form. Once filled out, these "comps" are presented to sellers so they can see at a glance the selling prices of other houses or condos in their neighborhood. This enables the sellers to "price their listings" close to a realistic selling price.

An agent can download comparable sales information (comps) in a variety of forms by accessing an MLS website.

www.appraisalfoundation.org
Appraisal Foundation
www.asfmra.org/
American Society of Farm Managers and Rural Appraisers (ASFMRA)
http://aicanada.org
The Appraisal Institute of Canada

Figure 11-1

California Association of Realtors® (CAR) Standard Form

COMPETITIVE MARKET ANALYSIS

370

A salesperson or broker may establish a "sales price" for a property without an appraisal license, but a professional appraisal must be completed by a licensed or certified appraiser.

A state licensed (expert) appraiser will use all three of the valuation approaches to determine the value of a property, but will emphasize only one to establish the final value.

These approaches are:

> I. COMPARATIVE APPROACH (MARKET DATA METHOD)
> II. COST (REPLACEMENT) APPROACH
> III. CAPITALIZATION (INCOME) APPROACH

The appraisal is also an opinion of a value "range." Let us assume that a range of $450,000 to $500,000 is established from the three appraisal approaches mentioned above. By correlating the economic information from the three approaches, an experienced appraiser can estimate a more precise value. The results of the three approaches can be weighed and it can then be determined which method has provided the best information about the property. In this case, let's say that the appraiser felt he or she should emphasize the market comparison approach that was $490,000. The appraiser would state that, in his or her opinion, the property was worth $490,000; but the value "ranged" from $450,000 to $500,000.

I. Comparative Approach (Market Data Method)

Of the three approaches previously mentioned, the market comparison method is the one most frequently used. It is easy for an alert student to master this technique within a short time, and it is the most logical way to appraise a house.

The market data method uses the "principle of substitution" to compare similar properties.

The **MARKET DATA METHOD** *is a method of appraising real property by comparing the current selling prices of recently sold similar properties and adjusting those prices for any differences.* The comparative (market data method) approach uses the principle of substitution; a person will not pay more for a property if he or she can buy something similar for less.

Simply adjust the value of the comparable sales price. If a house is comparable except that it has a pool, sells for $640,000 and the value of the $40,000 pool is subtracted, the house we are appraising is valued at $600,000.

A. HOW TO ADJUST FOR A COMPARABLE SALE (Comps)

The term "Comps" is used to mean (similar) comparable properties.

The market data method is basically common sense. If your neighbor has a similar house to yours that he just sold for $400,000, then yours is worth about $400,000. The only problem is that adjustments must be made for any differences between the houses. For example, if a similar $400,000 house had a fireplace worth $8,000 and yours did not, then your house would be worth $392,000 ($400,000 - $8,000). Adjustments should be made to the selling price of the comparable house for any differences between the properties. **The usual adjustments are made for differences in location, age, lot size, building size, condition of the property, and any time difference between the sales.**

The unit of comparison in the market data approach for a house would be the "entire property." Subtract or add from or to the selling price of the comparable property to adjust for differences.

If the comparable property has an item not present in the subject property, the appraiser subtracts the value of the item from the comparable property's selling price. Likewise, if the subject property has an item not present in the comparable property, the appraiser adds the value of the item to the comparable property's selling price. After all these adjustments are made to the comparable selling price, the resulting figure gives the appraiser the subject property's value.

By comparing recent selling prices of properties in the same area, it is easy to see the trends in selling prices and why certain properties sell for more than others. The more comparable sales you gather, the more reliable the results. Real estate salespeople often refer to comparable sales as "comps."

An appraiser using the market date approach would be most interested in the date that the price was agreed upon.

Unsold properties are important when using the market data method. If a property has been listed "for sale" for a long time, it is usually overpriced. Such comparable "unsold properties" suggest an upper limit of value. Unsold listings can therefore help establish the highest comparable price. An experienced appraiser can easily estimate the amount of an adjustment. The adjustment is an estimate or opinion determined solely by the appraiser, and reflects his or her broad experience and education.

Comparable sales information can be obtained from many different sources. Brokers and salespeople are familiar with property sales prices in their area, so naturally they are a good source for appraisal data. In addition, most brokers are members of the local multiple listing service and have access to past sales information. Other people in the real estate field, such as loan officers, title insurance agents, and escrow officers can also supply comparable sales information.

It is essential that: 1) the information is from a reliable source, 2) there is an adequate number of comparable sales, and 3) the comparable sales are truly comparable.

The market data method is the most common approach for houses and condominiums. It is also the best method for appraising lots and vacant land (unimproved property).

Figures 11-2 shows the Uniform Residential Appraisal Report (URAR) that is accepted by Fannie Mae and Freddie Mac.

B. ADVANTAGES OF THE MARKET DATA METHOD

The market comparison approach is best for single family residences (houses or condos) and vacant land (lots).

This method is excellent for appraising single family homes. Here are the reasons why:

1. The market data method is easy to learn, and with a little experience it is easy to apply.
2. Since there are usually many recent comparable sales, the required information is readily available.
3. This method is used mostly for houses or condos, which makes this method the most relevant to us as homeowners, salespeople, or investors.

The most difficult part of the market data method is to adjust similar properties for differences. The market data method is limited when market conditions are rapidly changing.

Marketability and desirability of a property are the primary concerns when appraising a residential property.

C. DISADVANTAGES OF THE MARKET DATA METHOD

The disadvantages of using the market data method are concentrated into several areas which are listed below:

1. This method requires many recent comparable sales of similar properties.
2. This method is least reliable when there are rapid economic changes. If market prices are increasing rapidly, the comparables, which are based on past sales prices, lag behind. If prices are decreasing rapidly, the comparables, which are based on past sales prices, still remain high.
3. The market data method is less valid with certain income properties because a separate analysis of the income is required.

Listings set ceiling on market value, since they are asking prices.

Figure 11-2

UNIFORM RESIDENTIAL APPRAISAL REPORT

Property Description   **File No.**

Property Address		City		State	Zip Code

Legal Description   County

Assessor's Parcel No.   Tax Year   R.E. Taxes $ Special Assessments $

Borrower   Current Owner   Occupant: ☐ Owner ☐ Tenant ☐ Vacant

Property rights appraised ☐ Fee Simple ☐ Leasehold Project Type ☐ PUD ☐ Condominium (HUD/VA only) HOA$ /Mo.

Neighborhood or Project Name   Map Reference   Census Tract

Sale Price $ Date of Sale   Description and $ amount of loan charges/concessions to be paid by seller

Lender/Client   Address

Appraiser   Address

Location	☐ Urban	☐ Suburban	☐ Rural	Predominant	Single family housing		Present land use %	Land use change
				occupancy	PRICE $(000)	AGE (yrs)		
Built up	☐ Over 75%	☐ 25-75%	☐ Under 25%				One family ___	☐ Not likely ☐ Likely
Growth rate	☐ Rapid	☐ Stable	☐ Slow	☐ Owner	Low ___		2-4 family ___	☐ In process
Property values	☐ Increasing	☐ Stable	☐ Declining	☐ Tenant	High ___		Multi-family ___	To:
Demand/supply	☐ Shortage	☐ In balance	☐ Over supply	☐ Vacant (0-5%)	Predominant ___		Commercial ___	
Marketing time	☐ Under 3 mos.	☐ 3-6 mos.	☐ Over 6 mos.	☐ Vacant (over 5%)			___	

Note: Race and the racial composition of the neighborhood are not appraisal factors.

Neighborhood boundaries and characteristics: _____

Factors that affect the marketability of the properties in the neighborhood (proximity to employment and amenities, employment stability, appeal to market, etc.): _____

_____
_____
_____

Market conditions in the subject neighborhood (including support for the above conclusions related to the trend of property values, demand/supply, and marketing time - - such as data on competitive properties for sale in the neighborhood, description of the prevalence of sales and financing concessions, etc.):

_____
_____
_____
_____

Project Information for PUDs (If applicable) - - Is the developer/builder in control of the Home Owner's Association (HOA)? ☐ Yes ☐ No

Approximate total number of units in the subject project _____   Approximate total number of units for sale in the subject project _____

Describe common elements and recreational facilities: _____

Dimensions _____		Topography _____
Site area _____ Corner Lot ☐ Yes ☐ No		Size _____
Specific zoning classification and description _____		Shape _____
Zoning compliance ☐ Legal ☐ Legal nonconforming (Grandfathered use) ☐ Illegal ☐ No zoning		Drainage _____
Highest & best use as improved: ☐ Present use ☐ Other use (explain) _____		View _____

Utilities	Public	Other	Off-site Improvements	Type	Public Private	Landscaping _____
Electricity	☐		Street		☐ ☐	Driveway surface _____
Gas	☐		Curb/gutter		☐ ☐	Apparent easements _____
Water	☐		Sidewalk		☐ ☐	FEMA Special Flood Hazard Area ☐ Yes ☐ No
Sanitary sewer	☐		Street lights		☐ ☐	FEMA Zone ___ Map Date ___
Storm sewer	☐		Alley		☐ ☐	FEMA Map No. ___

Comments (apparent adverse easements, encroachments, special assessments, slide areas, illegal or legal nonconforming zoning use, etc.): _____

GENERAL DESCRIPTION	EXTERIOR DESCRIPTION	FOUNDATION	BASEMENT	INSULATION
No. of Units ___	Foundation ___	Slab ___	Area Sq. Ft. ___	Roof ☐
No. of Stories ___	Exterior Walls ___	Crawl Space ___	% Finished ___	Ceiling ☐
Type (Det./Att.) ___	Roof Surface ___	Basement ___	Ceiling ___	Walls ☐
Design (Style) ___	Gutters & Dwnspts. ___	Sump Pump ___	Walls ___	Floor ☐
Existing/Proposed ___	Window Type ___	Dampness ___	Floor ___	None ☐
Age (Yrs.) ___	Storm/Screens ___	Settlement ___	Outside Entry ___	Unknown ☐
Effective Age (Yrs.) ___	Manufactured House ___	Infestation ___		

ROOMS	Foyer	Living	Dining	Kitchen	Den	Family Rm.	Rec. Rm.	Bedrooms	# Baths	Laundry	Other	Area Sq. Ft.
Basement												
Level 1												
Level 2												

Finished area **above grade contains:**   Rooms: ___   Bedroom(s): ___   Bath(s): ___   Square Feet of Gross Living Area ___

INTERIOR	Materials/Condition	HEATING	KITCHEN EQUIP.	ATTIC	AMENITIES	CAR STORAGE:
Floors	___	Type ___	Refrigerator ☐	None ☐	Fireplace(s) # ___	None ☐
Walls	___	Fuel ___	Range/Oven ☐	Stairs ☐	Patio ___	Garage ___ # of cars
Trim/Finish	___	Condition ___	Disposal ☐	Drop Stair ☐	Deck ___	Attached ___
Bath Floor	___	COOLING	Dishwasher ☐	Scuttle ☐	Porch ___	Detached ___
Bath Wainscot	___	Central ___	Fan/Hood ☐	Floor ☐	Fence ___	Built-In ___
Doors	___	Other ___	Microwave ☐	Heated ☐	Pool ___	Carport ___
		Condition ___	Washer/Dryer ☐	Finished ☐		Driveway ___

Additional features (special energy efficient items, etc.): _____

Condition of the improvements, depreciation (physical, functional and external), repairs needed, quality of construction, remodeling/additions, etc.:

_____
_____
_____

Adverse environmental conditions (such as, but not limited to, hazardous wastes, toxic substances, etc.) present in the improvements, on the site, or in the immediate vicinity of the subject property: _____

Freddie Mac Form 70 6-93   PAGE 1 OF 2   Fannie Mae Form 1004 6-93

AC APPRAISALS

Valuation Section　　　　　　　　　　　　　　　　　　　　　　　　　File No. _____

| ESTIMATED SITE VALUE . . . . = $ _____ | Comments on Cost Approach (such as, source of cost estimate, site value, square foot calculation and for HUD, VA and FmHA, the estimated remaining economic life of the property): |

ESTIMATED REPRODUCTION COST-NEW-OF IMPROVEMENTS:

Dwelling _____ Sq. Ft. @ _____ = $ _____
_____ Sq. Ft. @ _____ = _____
_____ = _____
Garage/Carport _____ Sq. Ft. @ _____ = _____
Total Estimated Cost New . . . . = $ _____
　　　　　　Physical　　Functional　　External

Less

Depreciation _____ | _____ | _____ = $ _____
Depreciated Value of Improvements . . . . = $ _____
"As-is" Value of Site Improvements . . . . = $ _____
INDICATED VALUE BY COST APPROACH . . . . = $ _____

ITEM	SUBJECT	COMPARABLE NO. 1		COMPARABLE NO. 2		COMPARABLE NO. 3	
Address							
Proximity to Subject							
Sales Price	$	$		$		$	
Price/Gross Liv. Area	$	$		$		$	
Data and/or Verification Source							
VALUE ADJUSTMENTS	DESCRIPTION	DESCRIPTION	+(-) $ Adjustment	DESCRIPTION	+(-) $ Adjustment	DESCRIPTION	+(-) $ Adjustment
Sales or Financing Concessions							
Date of Sale/Time							
Location							
Leasehold/Fee Simple							
Site							
View							
Design and Appeal							
Quality of Construction							
Age							
Condition							
Above Grade Room Count	Total Bdrms Baths	Total Bdrms Baths		Total Bdrms Baths		Total Bdrms Baths	
Gross Living Area	Sq. Ft.	Sq. Ft.		Sq. Ft.		Sq. Ft.	
Basement & Finished Rooms Below Grade							
Functional Utility							
Heating/Cooling							
Energy Efficient Items							
Garage/Carport							
Porch, Patio, Deck, Fireplace(s), etc.							
Fence, Pool, etc.							
Net Adj. (total)		+ ☐ - $		+ ☐ - $		+ ☐ - $	
Adjusted Sales Price of Comparable		% Net % Grs $		% Net % Grs $		% Net % Grs $	

Comments on Sales Comparison (including the subject property's compatibility to the neighborhood, etc.): _____

ITEM	SUBJECT	COMPARABLE NO. 1	COMPARABLE NO. 2	COMPARABLE NO. 3
Date, Price, and Data Source, for prior sales within year of appraisal				

Analysis of any current agreement of sale, option, or listing of the subject property and analysis of any prior sales of subject and comparables within one year of the date of appraisal: _____

INDICATED VALUE BY SALES COMPARISON APPROACH . . . . $ _____

INDICATED VALUE BY INCOME APPROACH　(If Applicable) Estimated Market Rent $ _____ /Mo. x Gross Rent Multiplier _____ = $ _____

This appraisal is made ☐ "as is" ☐ subject to repairs, alterations, inspections or conditions listed below ☐ subject to completion per plans and specifications.

Conditions of Appraisal: _____

Final Reconciliation: _____

The purpose of this appraisal is to estimate the market value of the real property that is the subject of this report, based on the above conditions and the certification, contingent and limiting conditions, and market value definition that are stated in the attached Freddie Mac Form 439/Fannie Mae Form 1004B (Revised _____).

I (WE) ESTIMATE THE MARKET VALUE, AS DEFINED, OF THE REAL PROPERTY THAT IS THE SUBJECT OF THIS REPORT, AS OF _____

(WHICH IS THE DATE OF INSPECTION AND THE EFFECTIVE DATE OF THIS REPORT) TO BE $ _____

APPRAISER:	SUPERVISORY APPRAISER (ONLY IF REQUIRED):	
Signature _____	Signature _____	☐ Did ☐ Did Not
Name LEVIN P. MESSICK	Name _____	Inspect Property
Date Report Signed _____	Date Report Signed _____	
State Certification # _____ State	State Certification # _____	State
Or State License # _____ State	Or State License # _____	State

Freddie Mac Form 70　6-93　　　　　　　　　　　　　　PAGE 2 OF 2　　　　Fannie Mae Form 1004　6-93

II. Cost Approach
(Replacement Cost Method)

The **COST APPROACH** *is the process of calculating the cost of the land and buildings (as if they were new today) and then subtracting the accrued depreciation to arrive at the current value of the property.* To use the cost approach, the appraiser must be able to determine the new construction cost of replacing the building today, using current construction methods. Depreciation is estimated by the appraiser and is then subtracted from the estimated cost of the new building. The value of the lot and depreciated building is then added to find the market value.

The cost approach objective is to determine the land value plus the cost to replace the improvements new (minus depreciation) while maintaining the same utility value.

Of the three approaches, the cost approach tends to set what the appraisers call an "upper limit of value." Most home buyers or investors prefer a newer building over an older one if the price is about the same. The cost approach therefore tends to set the highest price that a knowledgeable person will pay for a property. Why not build if the construction cost of a newer building is close to the sales price of an older building?

In relation to the other appraisal methods, the cost approach tends to set the "upper limit of value" (highest price someone will pay).

The cost approach is most useful when appraising 1) new buildings and 2) special purpose or unique structures. Estimating depreciation is critical in this approach. As a building gets older, the depreciation becomes more difficult to estimate, eventually making the cost approach impractical. Since newer structures have little depreciation, the cost approach is the most suitable. The cost approach may also be preferred for special purpose or unique structures as they have few, if any, market comparable sales. Special purpose structures, such as an airplane factory, a city hall, or a church, are best appraised by the cost approach.

The cost approach is more appropriate for new buildings because there is almost no depreciation.

It is limited in its effectiveness for appraising old buildings because determining depreciation is the most difficult part of the cost approach for the appraiser.

Some properties **require** the use of the cost approach. If, for example, there have been no recent sales in an area, the market comparison approach cannot be used effectively. Furthermore, if there is no income (as for example, from government-owned properties), the appraiser must rely solely on the cost approach.

Value of the land plus (+) new cost of buildings today minus (-) depreciation equals (=) current market value of the property.

A. COSTS ARE BOTH DIRECT AND INDIRECT

Any method used for estimating cost requires the calculation of direct (hard) or indirect (soft) costs. Both types of costs are equally necessary for construction and must be measured accurately.

DIRECT COSTS are expenditures for labor and materials used in the construction of the improvement(s). A contractor's overhead and profit are generally treated as direct costs.

INDIRECT COSTS are expenditures other than material and labor costs. Examples are administrative costs, professional fees, financing costs, insurance, and taxes. Indirect costs are usually calculated separately from direct costs.

B. STEPS IN THE COST APPROACH

The steps used in the cost approach are easy to follow, but studying **Figure 11-3** will help to explain each step.

1. Estimate the value of the land (use the market comparison approach).
2. Estimate the replacement cost of the building as if it were new.
3. Deduct estimated depreciation from the replacement cost of the building.
4. Add the value of the lot (Step 1) and the replacement cost of a new building and subtract estimated depreciation (Steps 2 and 3) to find the total value (Step 4).

Figure 11-3

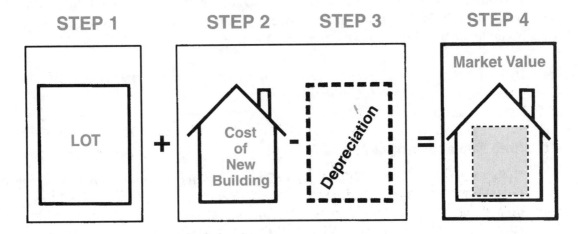

377

1. Step 1 - Appraise the Land (Lot) Separately

Appraise the land (lot) separately. The value of the vacant land is determined by comparing the lot of the property to be appraised with similar lots that have just been sold. The market comparison approach is used by the appraiser to estimate the lot value of the appraised property.

The cost approach requires the appraiser to identify land values separately by the use of the market data approach.

2. Step 2 - Estimate Replacement Cost

Estimate the replacement cost of the improvements to the land. This includes all the buildings and the landscaping improvements.

"Replacement cost" is the present cost to build a building having the same amount of utility.

a. Replacement Cost

REPLACEMENT COST is the cost of building a similar (having utility equivalent) new structure today using modern construction methods. These methods may differ from the original building techniques, but are becoming an important factor due to the ever increasing costs of new construction. As construction costs increase for new homes, the replacement cost of existing homes also increases. Therefore, well-located older homes will keep rising in value year after year, no matter how old they are, because the newer substitutes are so costly. This is not necessarily because of excellent upkeep, but because it is becoming impossible to find a newer home with the same features at a reasonable price. *REPRODUCTION OR REPLICATION COST is the cost of reproducing a structure (usually destroyed) at current prices using similar (older) style materials and methods as used in the original structure.* This method is rarely used, but it is the type, for example, used by Disneyland to recreate its historical Main Street.

The rarely used reproduction (replication) method is an exact replica ... it is the most expensive. New construction methods (replacement costs vs. replication costs) are almost always cheaper.

b. Three Replacement Methods

The *COMPARATIVE-UNIT METHOD is used to derive a cost estimate in terms of dollars per square foot or per cubic foot, based on known costs of similar structures and adjusted for time and physical differences.* The comparative-unit method represents a relatively uncomplicated, practical approach to a cost estimate and is widely used (illustrated below).

The **UNIT-IN-PLACE METHOD** *employs unit costs for the various building components such as foundations, floors, walls, windows, and roofs as installed and uses square foot, linear foot, or other appropriate units of measurement to estimate each component part.* These estimates include labor and overhead. To use this method, the appraiser must have specialized construction knowledge.

The **QUANTITY SURVEY METHOD** *involves detailed estimates of the quantities of raw materials used, such as brick, lumber, cement, the price of such materials, and the labor costs.* It is the most comprehensive and accurate method of cost estimating, but too complicated to fully explain here.

The Comparative-Unit Method (estimating dollars per square foot) is the most commonly used replacement cost method.

Although there are several ways to determine replacement cost, the simplest way is to *measure the outside of the building to determine SQUARE FOOTAGE.* After you determine the square footage, multiply it by the current cost of construction, per square foot, to get the value (as if it were new) of the building.

To determine square feet, use the formula: **LENGTH X WIDTH**

Square foot cost for a smaller house is higher than the square foot cost for a larger house. If other factors are equal, including square footage, the cost of building a two-story house is up to 50% cheaper than a one-story house.

The cubic foot method is used to appraise warehouses. To determine cubic feet, use the formula: **LENGTH X WIDTH X HEIGHT**

A warehouse building is appraised by the cubic foot but is usually rented by the square foot. Caution: the industrial land the warehouse is on is appraised by the square foot.

As construction costs vary from city-to-city and from builder-to-builder, many appraisers use cost engineers to help them determine the square foot cost of different types of construction. One of the most popular building cost information services is Marshall and Swift.

They annually compile a residential cost handbook that details the current cost of most types of residential construction in California.

3. Step 3 - Estimate and Deduct Depreciation

DEPRECIATION *is a reduction in the value of a property due to any cause.* The difference between replacement cost of a property and its market value is depreciation.

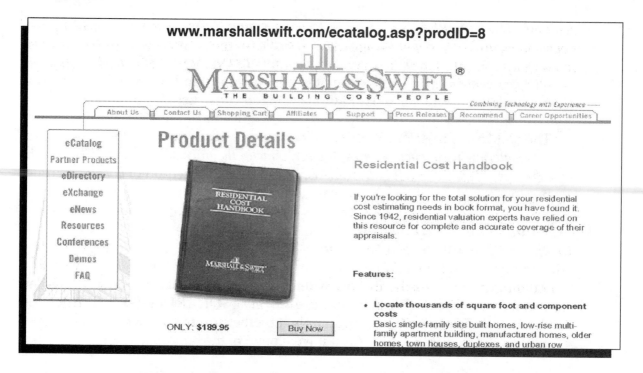

Depreciation is a loss in value from any cause. Depreciation is either curable (profitable to repair) or incurable (unprofitable to repair).

Estimate and deduct the depreciation from the replacement cost of the building being appraised. This accumulated depreciation is sometimes called accrued depreciation. *ACCRUED DEPRECIATION (OBSERVED) is the loss in value of improvements from any cause at the date of the appraisal.* Accrued depreciation is what has happened in the past, whereas the accrual for depreciation is the amount of future depreciation. There are five methods of estimating accrued depreciation:

1. Capitalized Income
2. Market
3. Straight-line (Most common and explained below)
4. Engineering
5. Breakdown

The straight-line method is explained here. For information on the other methods, please see Educational Textbook Company's, **Real Estate Appraisal**, by Walt Huber, Levin P. Messick, IFAC, and William Pivar (see **Order Form** at back of this book). The *STRAIGHT-LINE METHOD (AGE LIFE) assumes the value declines in equal amounts of depreciation each year, until it reaches zero.* A building with an economic life of 50 years would depreciate 2 percent (100 percent ÷ 50 years = 2 percent) in value each year. Actual age is the current (real) age of the building. When using the age life method, an appraiser will use an age other than the actual age of the building. This is known as the effective age. *EFFECTIVE AGE is* *determined by the condition of the building rather than the actual age.* If a building has been maintained, its effective age may be less than the actual age; if there has been inadequate maintenance, it may be greater. *ECONOMIC LIFE is the estimated number of years of anticipated usefulness of the improvements.*

"Effective age" is determined by the condition and usefulness of the property, not the actual age.

ACCRUAL FOR DEPRECIATION is the concept of estimating the amount of depreciation there will be in the future. The accrual for depreciation is used in the income approach, discussed in the next section.

To accurately estimate accrued depreciation, the appraiser must have experience, skill, and good judgment. He or she must not only estimate the physical wear and tear on the building, but also the losses in value due to outmoded styles, poor design, and neighborhood changes that tend to reduce the value of the improvements. A property can lose value through three different types of depreciation.

The three types of depreciation causes are: 1) physical, 2) functional, and 3) economic.

a. Physical Deterioration (Curable or Incurable)

PHYSICAL DETERIORATION is the loss in value due to wear and tear. As a building gets older, its age will start to show visibly. Since most types of physical deterioration (like a deteriorated driveway) can be repaired, we usually think of it as curable depreciation. On the other hand, severe structural deterioration may not be curable. So physical deterioration can be either curable or incurable. *CURABLE DEPRECIATION are repairs that add more to a building's value than they cost. INCURABLE DEPRECIATION refers to repairs that would be so expensive they are not economically feasible.*

Examples of physical deterioration (curable or incurable) are:

1. all forms of wear and tear
2. damage from dryrot and termites
3. negligent care (deferred maintenance)
4. depreciation that has already occurred

Obsolescence is not a method of calculating depreciation, but is a term meaning a "major cause" of depreciation.

b. Functional Obsolescence (Curable or Incurable)

FUNCTIONAL OBSOLESCENCE is the loss in value due to outmoded style or non-usable space. Examples of functional obsolescence would be a bedroom

that can be reached only by walking through another bedroom. By modern standards this is very inconvenient and reduces the value of the second bedroom. **Another devaluing factor is a home with a single car garage**. Functional depreciation is hard to cure. If the cost of curing the defect adds at least the same amount to the property's value, then it is worth the investment.

Types of functional obsolescence (curable or incurable) are:

    1. an out-dated kitchen
    2. antique fixtures
    3. a four-bedroom, one-bath home
    4. a one-car garage
    5. massive cornices

The cost approach would be the least useful for appraising older structures with many functional deficiencies.

c. Economic Obsolescence (Incurable)

If neighborhood commerical tenants are doing poorly, it is a sign of economic obsolescence.

> **ECONOMIC OBSOLESCENCE (ALSO REFERRED TO AS SOCIAL OBSOLESCENCE)** *is the loss in value due to changes in the neighborhood and is external to the property itself.* It is always incurable. If a freeway is built next to your property, your home will decrease in value because of the noise and nuisance factor. On the other hand, if the freeway is three blocks away, your house will increase in value because of improved freeway access. If social or economic factors (such as loss of jobs) cause a neighborhood to become shabby and run-down, the value of your property will decrease accordingly.

Since economic obsolescence results from "off the property" causes, it is always incurable. Economic (profitable) life remaining is the main concern when purchasing an older property.

Types of economic obsolescence (incurable) are:

    1. an over supply of similar or competitive units
    2. beyond the confines of the property
    3. aircraft noise
    4. adverse zoning and legislative acts
    5. economic recession
    6. departure of major industries from the area
    7. number of rental units increases

An example of "economic obsolescence" is seen when a city increases the amount of land needed for a front yard setback.

4. Step 4 - Value of the Property

The last step in the cost approach is to add the depreciated value of any improvements to the value of the land. This figure is the market value of the property using the cost approach.

C. ADVANTAGES OF THE COST APPROACH

The cost approach is best for new, unique architecture and public buildings.

The main advantages of the cost approach is that it can be used on: 1) newly constructed buildings, 2) unique structures, and 3) public buildings. Since there is little depreciation, if any, to calculate on newer buildings and there is available construction cost data, the value can be easily determined using the cost approach. Unique structures, public buildings, and one-of-a-kind structures have no comparables, so the cost approach may be the only logical way to appraise them.

"Cost equals value" when improvements are new and of the highest and best use.

D. DISADVANTAGES OF THE COST APPROACH

The disadvantages of using the cost approach are listed below:

1. There must be an accurate value of the site (land).
2. Since determining depreciation is more difficult as buildings age, the reliability of the depreciation estimate may be questioned.
3. This approach may be difficult to apply to condos or planned unit developments because the land, improvements and marketing costs are not always easy to determine just for appraising one unit.

The cost approach is limited (least reliable) for an older property. Older properties are harder to appraise because depreciation is difficult to estimate.

III. Capitalization Approach (Income Approach)

The income approach determines the "present worth of future net income." Capitalization is the process of converting income into value.

The **INCOME APPROACH** *is the process of analyzing the future net income from a property to determine its current market value.* Another word for this process is capitalization. The

appraiser, when using the income approach, is determining the present property value based upon the information he or she has on future income and expenses of that given property.

The actual process of capitalization is simple. Divide a capitalization rate into the yearly net income; the answer you obtain is the value of the property.

NET INCOME = **VALUE OF PROPERTY**
CAPITALIZATION RATE

$\dfrac{\$110,000}{10\%}$ = $\$1,100,000$

Rent producing (income) properties such as apartments, offices, warehouses, and manufacturing concerns can best be appraised by the income approach. This is because the people who invest in such projects are primarily interested in the income that they will receive. It is only natural that an investor would choose the property producing the highest return. The income approach allows a comparison of different types of income producing real estate and, at the same time, analyzes each as to the return of income to be received from that investment in the future.

The basis for the income approach is to determine the quality, quantity, and durability of the property's net income (future income).

A. STEPS IN THE INCOME APPROACH

There are five basic steps to establish value using the income approach:

1. Calculate the annual effective gross income.
2. Complete an operating expense statement.
3. Deduct related operating expenses from gross income to get net income.
4. Divide net income by the appropriate capitalization rate.
5. Result of dividing net income by capitalization rate.

Figure 11-4 illustrates the five steps.

1. Step 1 - Calculate the Annual Effective Gross Income

Rental income schedules for various units are best established by the market approach.

Calculate the annual effective gross income from the investment property. **EFFECTIVE GROSS INCOME** *is the gross income minus any vacancies or rental losses.* In the case of rental properties, the annual gross rental income will be the annual rent that an owner receives if he or she charges the going rental rates with no vacancies.

Figure 11-4

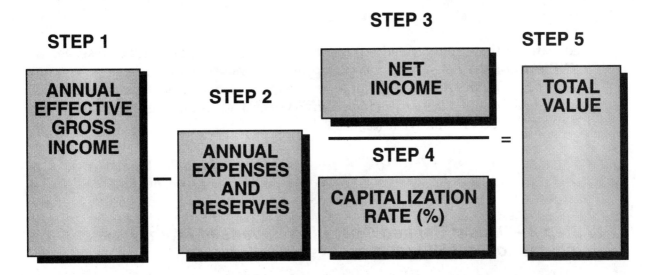

Sometimes managers charge rents that are below the market level, resulting in a very low number of vacancies. On the other hand, rents that are set too high usually yield a higher vacancy rate. The *VACANCY FACTOR is the loss in rents due to any cause.* This is commonly expressed as a percentage. The vacancy factor increases while trying to find a new tenant or because of cleaning, repairs, or non-paying renters.

Subtract deductions from the gross rental income for vacancies or any rental losses to arrive at the "effective gross income."

2. Step 2 - Complete an Operating Expense Statement

Complete an operating expense statement. The seven basic operating expense categories for this type of statement are listed below:

1. Property taxes
2. Insurance and licenses
3. Manager fees
4. Utilities
5. Maintenance and repairs
6. Services (i.e., gardener)
7. Replacement reserves

Management fees and replacement reserves must always be included in the basic operating expenses.

The expenses listed in the operating statement should represent the actual cost of each item. Though costs may vary, it is the appraiser's responsibility to determine what actual costs are on an annual basis.

Never deduct mortgage payments of principal or interest (cost of capital) from the operating expense statement. They are part of an investor's analysis, not an appraisal.

An item that may need explanation is the replacement reserve. A **REPLACEMENT RESERVE** *consists of funds set aside for the purpose of replacing items in the future.* An example of a replacement reserve cost would be a $2,000 water heater with a life expectancy of five years. The replacement reserve for this item would be $400 per year ($2,000 ÷ 5.)

"Variable costs" are operating expenses that can vary (utilities and repairs). "Fixed costs" remain constant; such as property taxes and fire insurance.

3. Step 3 - Deduct Related Operating Expenses From Gross Income to Get Net Income

To determine net income, simply deduct the related operating expenses (Step 2) from the annual effective gross income (Step 1).

To arrive at net income, deduct the above operating expenses from effective gross income.

4. Step 4 - Divide Net Income by the Appropriate Capitalization Rate

Divide the net income by the appropriate capitalization rate.

Rule: Always convert a monthly or quarterly net income into an annual net income before dividing by the capitalization rate.

Selection of a capitalization rate can be a delicate task. A one percent change in the capitalization rate, for example, can alter the estimated value of a property by up to ten percent or more. The capitalization rate is composed of a return to the investor "on" his or her original investment and "of" the amount to replace the building later.

For example, an investor may want an annual return of eight percent "on" his or her original investment, but two percent a year is needed to replace the building when its economic life is over. Determination of the appropriate capitalization rate takes skill and training.

The greater the risk, the greater the cap-rate. Leasing to a flower shop, for example, poses a greater risk of vacancy than a post office, therefore the cap rate would be higher.

There are several ways to select the proper capitalization rate. One way of selecting the appropriate capitalization rate is to sample similar recent apartment sales. Simply divide the net income by the sales price to obtain the capitalization rate used in that particular area.

Establishing the capitalization rate is the most difficult step for appraisers using the income approach.

The capitalization rate is composed of two parts: (1) a rate of return "on" the money invested and (2) a return "of" the asset that may be decreasing in value, but is rising in replacement cost. This is commonly referred to as the recapture rate, or depreciation. **See Figure 11-5**.

Figure 11-5

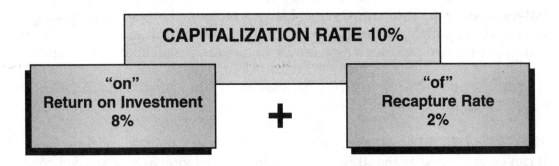

The capitalization rate is composed of two parts: the rate "on" the money invested (expected investor's return) and the annual rate "of" depreciation (recapture) on the improvements.

Capitalization rates can be determined by these advanced methods (not discussed here):

1. Comparison
2. Summation
3. Bands of Investment

The capitalization rate represents the integration of the 1) rate on income, expressed as interest, and the 2) rate of recapture, expressed as depreciation.

5. Step 5 - Result of Dividing Net Income by Capitalization Rate

This is the easiest and final step in the income approach. It is simply the result of dividing net income by the capitalization rate.

Net Income divided by Capitalization Rate = Market Value

Net income $65,000   = $650,000 Estimated Market Value
Capitalization Rate 10% (.10)

THE MARKET VALUE WHEN USING THE INCOME APPROACH IS $650,000

The appraised value increases when the "capitalization rate" is decreased.

B. GROSS RENT MULTIPLIER - GRM (Rule of Thumb)

GROSS RENT MULTIPLIER (GRM) is a multiplication rule of thumb used to convert the rental income into market value. If we use a gross rent multiplier of 125 times the monthly rent of $1,000, the property is worth approximately $125,000 (125 x $1,000). **See Figure 11-6** for more details. This is definitely not an accurate way to appraise a property, but it does give a quick estimate of value. Many professional investors use it as a screening device to eliminate undesirable investment opportunities. This monthly gross multiplier is often used for single-family homes and small apartment buildings.

A quick way to convert gross income into the approximate value is to use the gross rent multiplier.

The **GROSS (RENT)** *is the money received from a property before any expenses are deducted.* It can be expressed as monthly or annual income, as long as it is applied consistently.

The Gross Rent Multiplier (GRM) is based on "monthly rent only" and is used for residential properties. The "Gross Income Multiplier (GIM)" is used for commercial and industrial properties when part of the gross income comes from non-rental sources.

A desert cabin which rents for $600 per month just sold for $96,000. A similar property rents for $660 per month, so the market value is most likely to be near $105,600.

Remember the rule! Confirmed sales price ($96,000) divided by gross monthly rent ($600) equals gross rent multiplier of 160; then it follows that the gross rent multiplier of 160 times the rent ($660) of a similar property equals a $105,600 market value.

In the real estate investment field (commerical and industrial), it is common knowledge that the annual gross income multiplier of "x 6.2" is a good "rule of thumb" for an investment. For example, if the annual gross income from an apartment project is $40,000, its value should be approximately $248,000 ($40,000 x 6.2). The annual gross income multiplier varies from "x 5" to "x 12," depending upon the location of the property and the condition of the individual buildings. Remember: this is an approximation device and should be used only as a quick estimate—not in place of an actual appraisal.

Figure 11-6

Gross Rent Multiplier

The **GROSS RENT MULTIPLIER (GRM)** *is a rough, quick way of converting gross monthly rent into market value.* To obtain the gross rent multiplier, divide the monthly rent into the "sales" price. It is not a very accurate method, but it is a good estimator because it is so easy. The gross rent multiplier is best used for single or small multi-family residential properties.

<u>SALES PRICE</u> = GROSS RENT MULTIPLIER
    RENT

TYPICAL PROBLEMS:

If a house that rented for $600 a month sold for $78,000, what is the gross rent multiplier?

<u>$78,000 Sales price</u>   =   130 (Gross Rent Multiplier)
  Monthly Rent $600

If a similar house down the street is renting for $690, what would the selling price be?

Monthly Rent $690 x 130 (Gross Rent Multiplier) = $89,700.

CAN ANNUAL RENTS BE USED?

The gross rent multiplier is not a percentage, so it can be expressed as either a monthly or annual figure. If the above problem were expressed as an annual rent figure, the gross rent multiplier would have to be divided by 12. The annual gross rent multiplier is 10.83 (130 ÷ 12).

If a house that rents for $72,000 a year sold for $780,000, what is the annual gross multiplier?

<u>$780,000 Sales Price</u>   =   10.83 Annual Gross Rent Multiplier
Annual Rent $72,000

NOTE: Sometimes a different multiplier is used, the **Gross Income Multiplier (GIM)**, when the revenues being considered are not just from rental income (like coin-operated washers and dryers). The GIM is preferred for commercial and income properties.

C. ADVANTAGES OF THE INCOME APPROACH

The advantage of the income approach method is that no other method focuses solely on determining the present value of the future income stream from the subject property. It is a little different than the other two methods of determining value in that "If the purpose of the property is to generate income, use the income approach." For example a house that is zoned for commercial use may be valued at a much higher amount when used as an insurance office rather than as a house. The location may bring in a great deal of income; as a house the market value is low, but as an income-producing property the market value may be very high.

The "present worth of future benefits" is what the income approach is all about.

It is most often used for multi-family residential income property but could be used on any type of property that generates income.

D. DISADVANTAGES OF THE INCOME APPROACH

The disadvantage of the income approach is that it may be difficult to determine the proper capitalization rate. For example, it may be impossible to ascertain the cap-rate for a theme park or alligator farm. These other items used in the income approach may also be difficult to estimate: vacancy rate, economic rent, operation expenses, and reserve requirements.

IV. Correlation of Value (Bracketing)

The last and most important part of the appraisal process is the correlation (sometimes referred to as reconciliation) of the three approaches to value. *CORRELATION is the process of selecting the most appropriate approach for the particular appraisal job and giving it the most consideration in pinpointing the final value.* Although all three methods are used in appraisal, one is usually most appropriate for a specific appraisal problem.

In general, the "market comparison approach" is best for single-family homes or lots; the "cost approach" is best for new, unique or unusual structures; and the "income approach" is best for properties that can be used to generate income.

V. Final Estimate of Value (Appraisal Report)

The appraisal report is the documentation of the appraiser's findings. It can be a prepared fill-in form. However, if it is complicated or subject to close interpretation, the report should be written in a narrative form with supporting data contained in supplemental exhibits. In practice most appraisal reports are written.

There are two main types of written appraisal reports:

1. Short form (a form with checks and explanations)
2. Narrative report (most complete and extensive)

A narrative report is the most comprehensive and complete appraisal report, and contains such headings as "Introduction," "Site and Improvements Analysis," and "Supporting Data."

Whether the report is a simple one-page report or an extensive volume, the following information should be presented:

1. An adequate description for the property that is being appraised.

2. A statement as to the purpose and scope of the appraisal.

3. An adequate description of the neighborhood.

4. The date on which the value is estimated.

5. The qualifying conditions and assumptions.

6. The factual data, maps, and photos with their analysis and interpretations.

7. The processing of the data by one or more of the three approaches to value (correlation).

8. The estimate of value.

9. The name, address, type of license (and any certifications), and signature of the appraiser.

There is NO information about the buyer's or seller's financial condition on an appraisal report.

A. COST OF AN APPRAISAL

Appraisal costs can vary from relatively small amounts to thousands of dollars. The cost of an appraisal may be affected by its purpose, the qualifications of the appraiser, and how detailed the appraisal. An appraisal used to document a court case could cost several thousand dollars.

Many community colleges and universities offer courses in appraisal or investment properties to acquaint you with the techniques involved in the income approach.

http://www.cccco.edu/
Information on the California Community Colleges

It would be impractical to spend thousands of dollars for a home appraisal just to determine a selling price. If you are thinking about selling your home, your local real estate broker will probably do this at no cost. Local brokers are familiar with your area and are knowledgeable about current sales prices of similar homes in your neighborhood. On the other hand, appraisal of large parcels, commercial buildings, and apartment houses, or appraisals to be used in court, may require the services of a highly skilled appraiser. Although the fees are higher, they reflect the experience and ability of the appraiser. The appraisal fee and an outline of what is to be accomplished in the appraisal should be set in advance. It is unethical to set an appraisal fee as a percentage of the determined value. This may influence the appraiser to increase the value.

Appraisal Report Copies

A lender must provide a notice to a loan applicant stating that the applicant is entitled to a copy of the appraisal report if the applicant requests and pays for the report.

The notice must be provided on any loan secured by residential property and on purchase money financing (or refinancing of purchase money debt) on non-residential property.

VI. Licensing, Fee Appraisers, and Appraisal Organizations

A. APPRAISAL LICENSE AND CERTIFICATION

All appraisers are required to be licensed or certified. See **Figure 11-7**. The license/certification categories are:

1. LICENSED APPRAISER
2. CERTIFIED RESIDENTIAL APPRAISER
3. CERTIFIED GENERAL APPRAISER

Figure 11-7

(CALIFORNIA)
OFFICE OF REAL ESTATE APPRAISERS (OREA) LICENSES

TRAINEE LICENSE

Education: A minimum of 90 hours of appraisal related education covering the specific topics required by the Appraiser Qualifications Board (AQB), including the 15-hour National Uniform Standards of Professional Appraisal Practice (USPAP) course.
Experience: None
Exam: Must pass the AQB approved residential examination.
Scope: Must work under the technical supervision of a licensed appraiser. May assist on any appraisal within the scope of practice of the supervising appraiser.

Assists supervising appraiser

RESIDENTIAL LICENSE

Education: A minimum of 90 hours of appraisal related education covering the specific topics required by AQB, including the 15-hour National USPAP course.
Experience: A minimum of 2,000 hours of acceptable appraisal experience.
Exam: Must pass the AQB approved residential examination.
Scope: May appraise 1-to-4 unit residential property up to a transaction value of $1 million and non-residential property up to $250,000.

Residential limit $1 million – nonresidental limit $250,000

CERTIFIED RESIDENTIAL LICENSE

Education: A minimum of 120 hours of appraisal related education covering the specific topics required by AQB, including the 15-hour National USPAP course.
Experience: A minimum of 2,500 hours and two and one-half years of acceptable appraisal experience.
Exam: Must pass the AQB approved certified residential examination.
Scope: May appraise all 1-to-4 unit residential property without regard to transaction value, and non-residential property up to a transaction value of $250,000.

No $ limit on residential – $250,000 limit on nonresidential

CERTIFIED GENERAL LICENSE

Education: A minimum of 180 hours of appraisal related education covering the specific topics required by AQB, including the 15-hour National USPAP course.
Experience: A minimum of 3,000 hours and two and one-half years of acceptable appraisal experience. At least 1,500 hours of the experience must be non-residential properties.
Exam: Must pass the AQB approved certified general examination.
Scope: May appraise all types of real estate. Ex: Required for a $550,000 strip mall.

All types of property – no $ limits

B. FEE APPRAISERS

While the Standards permit an appraiser to appraise a property in which he or she has an interest, as long as the fact is disclosed to the lender/client in writing, it would be highly unusual for it to be accepted by any lender/client.

A **FEE APPRAISER is** *an independent, self-employed appraiser; he or she appraises for a fee or charge.* In California a license or certification is required to appraise real estate as a profession. Other appraisers are dependent on large corporations or organizations for their employment. Gas, electric, telephone, and other utility companies have appraisal departments. Banks, savings banks, mortgage companies, and other lenders often have in-house appraisal staffs. Most cities and counties have large appraisal staffs in their assessors' offices. There are also various state agencies, such as Cal-Trans, that maintain appraisal staffs.

A fee appraiser is self-employed; he or she appraises for a fee or charge. Remember: appraisers and real estate agents are concerned with the marketability of residential properties.

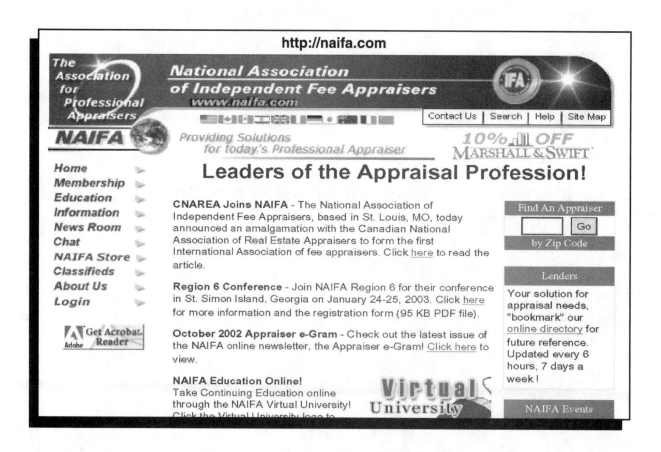

C. PROFESSIONAL APPRAISAL ASSOCIATIONS

American Society of Appraisers (ASA)
P.O. Box 17265
Washington, D.C. 20041-0265
www.appraisers.org

American Society of Farm Managers and Rural Appraisers (ASFMRA)
9505 Cherry Street, Suite 508
Denver, CO 80222
www.asfmra.org

Appraisal Institute (AI)
875 North Michigan Avenue, Suite 2400
Chicago, IL 60611-1980
www.appraisalinstitute.org

Appraisal Institute of Canada
1111 Portage Avenue
Winnipeg, MB, Canada R3GO58
www.aicanada.org

International Association of Assessing Officers (IAAO)
1313 East 60th Street
Chicago, IL 60637
www.iaao.org

International Right of Way Association (IRWA)
13650 Gramercy Place
Gardena, CA 90249
www.irwaonline.org

National Association of Independent Fee Appraisers (NAIFA)
7501 Murdoch Avenue
St. Louis, MO 63119
www.naifa.com

National Association of Master Appraisers (NAMA)
303 West Cypress Street
P.O. Box 12617
San Antonio, TX 78212-0617
www.masterappraisers.com

VII. SUMMARY

A **licensed appraiser** will use three different approaches to establish **final value**. These include the: 1) **comparative (market data) approach**, 2) **cost (replacement) approach**, and 3) **capitalization (income) approach**.

The **market data method** (or **sales comparison approach**) takes the current selling prices of similar or comparable properties (comps) and adjusts for any differences. The **principle of substitution** is applied, assuming a person will not pay more for a property when something similar is available for less.

The **cost approach** or (**replacement cost method**) determines the current market value of a property by adding the value of the land plus (+) replacement or reproduction cost of buildings today, minus (-) depreciation, maintaining the same amount of utility.

In step one of the cost approach, the appraiser finds the value of the land using the market data approach. In step two, the **reproduction** or **replacement cost** is calculated. The three replacement methods include the **comparative-unit method** (most commonly used), the **unit-in-place method**, and the **quantity survey method**. In step three, **depreciation** is factored in. The three types of depreciation are: 1) **physical**, 2) **functional**, and 3) **economic** and can be either **curable** (profitable to repair) or **incurable** (unprofitable to repair). In step four the depreciated value of improvements is added to the value of the land to find the **market value** of the property.

The **capitalization** (or **income**) **approach** is concerned with the present worth of future benefits. The basic formula to determine total value is: **Annual effective gross income minus (-) annual expenses and reserves equals (=) net income**. Then **divide the net income by the capitalization rate to find (=) market value**. The **cap rate** is the percentage rate that an investor expects to earn "on" a real estate investment. A quick rule of thumb to convert gross income into approximate value is to use the **gross rent multiplier**, which is based on monthly rent and is used for residential properties. The **gross income multiplier** is based on annual rents and is used for commercial properties.

Correlation (or **reconciliation**) is the process of selecting the most appropriate approach for the appraisal job. Generally, the market comparison approach is best for single-family homes or lots; the cost approach is best for new, unique or unusual structures; and the income approach is best for properties that can be used to generate income. The **final estimate of value** (or **appraisal report**) is then generated, the **narrative report** being the most comprehensive and complete.

The **cost of an appraisal** can be effected by its purpose, how detailed it is, and the experience of the appraiser. All appraisers must be licensed or certified, the categories being **trainee license**, **residential license, certified residential license**, and **certified general license**. A **fee appraiser** is self employed, and charges a fee for his or her services. Although highly unusual, it is technically permissible for a fee appraiser to appraise a property in which he or she owns an interest as long as it is disclosed in writing. It is the **marketability of real property** that concerns appraisers and real estate agents.

VIII. TERMINOLOGY - CHAPTER 11

A. Accrual for Depreciation
B. Accrued Depreciation
C. Actual Age
D. Correlation
E. Cost Approach
F. Curable Depreciation
G. Depreciation
H. Direct Cost

I. Economic Life
J. Economic Obsolescence
K. Effective Age
L. Effective Gross Income
M. Functional Obsolescence
N. Gross Rent Multiplier
O. Income Approach
P. Incurable Depreciation

Q. Indirect Costs
R. Market Comparison
S. Physical Deterioration
T. Replacement
U. Replacement Reserve
V. Reproduction Cost
W. Square Footage
X. Vacancy Factor

1.____ The estimated percentage of vacancies in a rental property, such as in an apartment building.
2.____ The use of different appraisal methods to reach an estimate of the value of a property. The methods must be weighed as to which is most appropriate for the type of property being appraised.
3.____ The theoretical cost of replacing a building with one of equivalent usefulness.
4.____ A simple method of using gross monthly or yearly rents to obtain an approximate value of an income property.
5.____ The need to replace part of a structure because new improvements have come along that make the older structure inefficient by comparison. For example, a one-bathroom, eight-bedroom house.
6.____ An appraisal method, estimating the replacement cost of a structure, less depreciation, plus land value.
7.____ Loss of desirability and useful life of a property through economic forces, such as zoning changes, traffic pattern changes, etc., rather than wear and tear.
8.____ A decrease in the value of real property improvements for any reason.
9.____ An appraisal method to determine the present value today of rental property by estimating the income it will generate over the life of the structure.
10.____ A way of measuring real property in 1 ft. by 1 ft. segments.
11.____ The method of estimating the value of real property by adjusting the sales price of comparable properties for differences.
12.____ Gradual physical wear and tear on a structure that decreases its value.
13.____ Periodically setting money aside to replace systems and appliances in a building. For example, a landlord putting aside a portion of monthly rents toward a new roof or water heater.
14.____ The chronological age of a structure as opposed to its effective or economic life.
15.____ Accumulation of depreciation.
16.____ Construction costs (material and labor).
17.____ The cost of reproducing a property (usually one that has been destroyed) at current prices using the same materials.
18.____ Repairs that would be so expensive they are not economically feasible.
19.____ Age of a structure as estimated by its condition rather than its actual age.
20.____ Repairs that are economically logical to do.
21.____ Costs other than labor and materials.
22.____ Amount of depreciation in the future, not past.
23.____ The "profitable" life of an improvement. Generally shorter than the physical life.
24.____ Gross income of a building if fully rented, less an allowance for estimated vacancies.

IX. MULTIPLE CHOICE

1. An army base moved out of an area, which caused unemployment and housing values to drop. This is referred to as:

  a. economic obsolescence.
  b. functional obsolescence.
  c. physical obsolescence.
  d. none of the above.

2. In the appraisal of residential property, the cost approach is most useful in the case of:

  a. single-family dwellings.
  b. older, greatly depreciated properties.
  c. middle-aged properties.
  d. new structures.

3. Which is the best method for appraising single-family homes?

  a. Market approach
  b. Income approach
  c. Cost approach
  d. Correlation approach

4. The appraiser must determine the construction expense of replacing a building today, using current construction methods, with the:

  a. market approach.
  b. cost approach.
  c. income approach.
  d. expense approach.

5. Wear and tear on the roof of an urban office building would constitute:

  a. physical deterioration.
  b. functional obsolescence.
  c. economic depreciation.
  d. commercial damages.

6. If an appraiser lowered the value of a house due to functional obsolescence, he would be referring to:

  a. termites.
  b. economic decline in the neighborhood.
  c. single-car garage.
  d. damage to the foundation.

7. Loss of value due to changes in the neighborhood and external to the property is called:

    a. economic obsolescence.

    b. physical deterioration.

    c. functional obsolescence.

    d. income obsolescence.

8. A mathematical rule of thumb used to convert the rental value into market value is known as the:

    a. correlation multiplier.

    b. net multiplier.

    c. gross rent multiplier.

    d. evaluation process.

9. A water heater costs $1,000 and is expected to last five years. The $200 a year that would be put aside for this expense is called the:

    a. maintenance cost.

    b. plumbing reserve.

    c. replacement reserve.

    d. operating expense.

10. Which of the following would NOT normally be appraised by the income method?

    a. Apartments

    b. Government land

    c. Warehouses

    d. Offices

ANSWERS: *1. a; 2. d; 3. a; 4. b; 5. a; 6. c; 7. a; 8. c; 9. c; 10. b*

Chapter 12
Subdivisions and Government Control

I. Doctrine of Police Power

There are over 35 million people in California as of the year 2003; we are adding over 1,700 new residents each day.

With a population of more than thirty-five million people, California has more people than any other state. That means we have approximately 12.5% of the United States population. Since we are such a fast growing and mobile state, the problems encountered can be tremendous. The state and local governments have the responsibility (under the doctrine of police power) to enact and enforce legislative acts to protect the general public. This public protection in the real estate area prevents fraud, misrepresentation, and deceit.

A. POLICE POWER

Police power is the right of public officials to control the use of private property for the health, safety, and general welfare of the public.

POLICE POWER *is the power to make rulings to control the "use and taking of private property" for the protection of the public's health, safety, and welfare.* Police power allows the state, county, or city to protect its citizens by controlling how land is being used.

Police power provides for the regulation of lot design and physical improvements for the orderly and proper development of the community, the construction of streets, highways and parking facilities adequate for our car-oriented society, and the certainty of an adequate water supply. It ensures the protection of life and property by police and firemen, the maintenance of the purity of air we breathe, the control of noise, the disposal of sewage and waste, and the provision under public or private regulation for essential utility services. **Figure 12-1** shows seven basic areas of government control at either the state or local level.

Figure 12-1

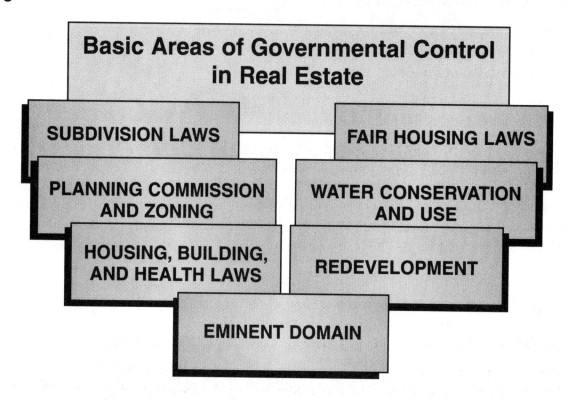

II. The Basic Subdivision Laws

*A **SUBDIVISION** is a parcel of land divided into five or more parcels with the intent to sell, lease, or finance them now or in the future. It can also be some form of common or mutual ownership rights in one parcel. A **condominium** is sometimes referred to as a "one lot subdivision."* There are two basic laws under which subdivisions are controlled in California:

    A. Subdivision Map Act (City or County)
    B. Subdivided Lands Law (Department of Real Estate)

These two laws were enacted for different purposes, and were adopted to achieve the objective for which each was designed.

A. SUBDIVISION MAP ACT (Enforced by Local City or County)

The *primary objective of the SUBDIVISION MAP ACT is to provide an outline of the methods for the subdivision filing procedure at the city or county level and to make sure subdividers comply with the city's or county's master plan.* This law permits the local government of the city or county to enact subdivision ordinances. Thus, the direct control of the kind and type of subdivision for each community, and the public physical improvements to be installed, is left to the local city (if incorporated) or county (if unincorporated).

This act has two major objectives:

1. To coordinate the subdivision plans including lot design, street patterns, drainage, and sewers with the community pattern (master plan) as laid out by the local planning authorities.

2. To ensure, by the filing of the subdivision maps, that parts of the subdivision area will be dedicated to the city or county for public purposes. These dedications include public streets and other public areas, dedicated by the subdivision so that they will not be an unmanageable future burden upon the taxpayers of the community.

State law now requires that each community (city or county government) shall enact local subdivision ordinances. Before the Department of Real Estate will approve the subdivision, a tentative subdivision map must be approved by the local government.

The Subdivision Map Act gives "cities and counties" control over the physical design of a subdivision.

B. SUBDIVIDED LANDS LAW (State Law Enforced by the DRE)

This law is statewide in its operation and is directly administered by the California Real Estate Commissioner. The basic objective of the *SUBDIVIDED LANDS LAW is to protect the purchasers of property in new subdivisions from fraud, misrepresentation, or deceit in the marketing of subdivided lots, parcels, condominiums, or other undivided property interests in the state of California.*

No subdivision unit can be offered for sale in California unless the commissioner has issued a subdivision public report. This applies not only to tracts located in California, but also to subdivided lands lying partly outside the state's boundaries. The public report is a factual account of the subdivided property.

The report is not issued until the commissioner is satisfied that the subdivider has met all the statutory requirements, with particular emphasis on the establishment and facilities included in the offering, and demonstrates that the lots or parcels can be used for the purpose for which they are being offered.

The Subdivision Lands Law (public report) requirements apply when a parcel is divided into five or more lots (units).

III. Public Report (Consumer Information)

The public report (issued by the Department of Real Estate) is required reading by any purchaser.

As provided by the Subdivided Lands Law, purchasers of a home in a new subdivision must receive a Public Report from the California Real Estate Commissioner's office. A **PUBLIC REPORT** *is a formal disclosure report of the important facts regarding a subdivision.* It is, in a sense, a developer's "permit" to sell. It is not, however, a recommendation pro or con. **Figures 12-2** illustrates a five-page public report. The report makes clear the physical characteristics of the land, so that the buyer can know exactly what he or she is buying. The buyer is told the size, arrangement, and location of the lot and exactly what off-site improvements and recreation facilities to expect.

A subdivider must give a copy of the Commissioner's Public Report to anyone who requests one.

There may be two public reports. The optional preliminary report may be submitted to the Department of Real Estate for tentative approval. The required final report must be

Figure 12-2

Department of Real Estate
of the
State of California

FINAL SUBDIVISION PUBLIC REPORT

In the matter of the application of

ROLLINGWOOD GREEN ASSOCIATES, INC.
a California Corporation

FILE NO. : 025053SA-F00

ISSUED : SEPTEMBER 21, 1988

EXPIRES : SEPTEMBER 20, 1993

for a Final Subdivision Public Report on

ROLLINGWOOD GREEN (PHASE TWO)

SACRAMENTO COUNTY, CALIFORNIA

JAMES A. EDMONDS, JR.
Commissioner

by ___S.S. Turpen___
Deputy Commissioner

CONSUMER INFORMATION

❖ THIS REPORT IS NOT A RECOMMENDATION OR ENDORSEMENT OF THE SUBDIVISION; IT IS INFORMATIVE ONLY.

❖ BUYER OR LESSEE MUST SIGN THAT (S)HE HAS RECEIVED AND READ THIS REPORT.

❖ A copy of this subdivision public report along with a statement advising that a copy of the public report may be obtained from the owner, subdivider, or agent at any time, upon oral or written request, *must* be posted in a conspicuous place at any office where sales or leases or offers to sell or lease interests in this subdivision are regularly made. *[Reference Business and Professions (B&P) Code Section 11018.1(b)]*

This report expires on the date shown above. All material changes must be reported to the Department of Real Estate. *(Refer to Section 11012 of the B&P Code; and Chapter 6, Title 10 of the California Administrative Code, Regulation 2800.)* Some material changes may require amendment of the Public Report; which Amendment must be obtained and used in lieu of this report.

Section 12920 of the California Government Code provides that the practice of discrimination in housing accommodations on the basis of race, color, religion, sex, martial status, national origin, physical handicap or ancestry, is against public policy.

Under Section 125.6 of the B&P Code, California real estate licensees are subject to disciplinary action by the Real Estate Commissioner if they discriminate or make any distinction or restriction in negotiating the sale or lease of real property because of the race, color, sex, religion, ancestry, national origin, or physical handicap of the client. If any prospective buyer or lessee believes that a licensee is guilty of such conduct, (s)he should contact the Department of Real Estate.

READ THE ENTIRE REPORT ON THE FOLLOWING PAGES BEFORE CONTRACTING TO BUY OR LEASE AN INTEREST IN THIS SUBDIVISION.

RE 618 (Rev. 12/87)

Page 1 of 5   File No. 025053SA-F00

COMMON INTEREST DEVELOPMENT
GENERAL INFORMATION

The project described in the attached Subdivision Public Report is known as a common-interest development. Read the Public Report carefully for more information about the type of development. The development includes common areas and facilities which will be owned and/or operated by an owners' association. Purchase of a lot or unit automatically entitles and obligates you as a member of the association and, in most cases, includes a beneficial interest in the areas and facilities. Since membership in the association is mandatory, you should be aware of the following information before you purchase:

Your ownership in this development and your rights and remedies as a member of its association will be controlled by governing instruments which generally include a Declaration of Restrictions (also known as CC&R's), Articles of Incorporation (or association) and bylaws. The provisions of these documents are intended to be, and in most cases are, enforceable in a court of law. Study these documents carefully before entering into a contract to purchase a subdivision interest.

In order to provide funds for operation and maintenance of the common facilities, the association will levy assessments against your lot or unit. If you are delinquent in the payment of assessments, the association may enforce payment through court proceedings or your lot or unit may be liened and sold through the exercise of a power of sale. The anticipated income and expenses of the association, including the amount that you may expect to pay through assessments, are outlined in the proposed budget. Ask to see a copy of the budget if the subdivider has not already made it available for your examination.

CALIFORNIA
DEPARTMENT
OF REAL ESTATE

RE 646 (Rev. 2/86)

A homeowner association provides a vehicle for the ownership and use of recreational and other common facilities which were designed to attract you to buy in this development. The association also provides a means to accomplish architectural control and to provide a base for homeowner interaction on a variety of issues. The purchaser of an interest in a common-interest development should contemplate active participation in the affairs of the association. He or she should be willing to serve on the board of directors or on committees created by the board. In short, "they" in a common interest development is "you". Unless you serve as a member of the governing board or on a committee apointed by the board, your control of the operation of the common areas and facilities is limited to your vote as a member of the association. There are actions that can be taken by the governing body without a vote of the members of the association which can have a significant impact upon the quality of life for association members.

Until there is a sufficient number of purchasers of lots or units in a common interest devolopment to elect a majority of the governing body, it is likely that the subdivider will effectively control the affairs of the association. It is frequently necessary and equitable that the subdivider do so during the early stages of development. It is vitally important to the owners of individual subdivision interests that the transition from subdivider to resident-owner control be accomplished in an orderly manner and in a spirit of cooperation.

When contemplating the purchase of a dwelling in a common interest development, you should consider factors beyond the attractiveness of the dwelling units themselves. Study the governing instruments and give careful thought to whether you will be able to exist happily in an atmosphere of cooperative living where the interests of the group must be taken into account as well as the interests of the individual. Remember that managing a common interest development is very much like governing a small community . . . the management can serve you well, but you will have to work for its success. [B & P Code Section 11018.1(c)]

SPECIAL NOTES

1. IF YOU HAVE RECEIVED A PRELIMINARY PUBLIC REPORT FOR THIS SUBDIVISION, YOU ARE ADVISED TO CAREFULLY READ THIS FINAL PUBLIC REPORT SINCE IT CONTAINS INFORMATION THAT IS MORE CURRENT AND PROBABLY DIFFERENT THAN THAT INCLUDED IN THE PRELIMINARY REPORT.

2. IF YOU ENTER INTO AN AGREEMENT TO PURCHASE OR LEASE AN INTEREST IN THE PROPERTY COVERED BY THIS PUBLIC REPORT, AND YOU SIGNED A RESERVATION AGREEMENT UNDER THE AUTHORITY OF A SHORT FORM PRELIMINARY PUBLIC REPORT, YOU HAVE A RIGHT TO RESCIND (CANCEL) THE AGREEMENT AND TO THE RETURN OF ANY MONEY OR OTHER CONSIDERATION THAT YOU HAVE GIVEN TOWARD THE PURCHASE OR LEASE UNTIL MIDNIGHT OF THE FIFTH CALENDAR DAY FOLLOWING THE DAY YOU EXECUTE THE CONTRACT TO PURCHASE OR LEASE. YOU MAY EXERCISE THIS RIGHT WITHOUT GIVING ANY REASON FOR YOUR ACTION AND WITHOUT INCURRING ANY PENALTY OR OBLIGATION BY NOTIFYING THE DEVELOPER (OR THE DEVELOPER'S AUTHORIZED REPRESENTATIVE) OF SUCH CANCELLATION BY TELEGRAM, MAIL, OR OTHER WRITTEN NOTICE SENT OR DELIVERED NOT LATER THAN MIDNIGHT OF THE FIFTH CALENDAR DAY FOLLOWING THE DATE THE CONTRACT WAS SIGNED. THE NOTIFICATION SHOULD BE SENT TO:

   ROLLINGWOOD GREEN ASSOCIATES, INC.,
   A CALIFORNIA CORPORATION
   ATTN: JAMES D. FLOOD
   9274 MADISON AVENUE
   ORANGEVALE, CA 95662

3. THIS PUBLIC REPORT COVERS ONLY RESIDENTIAL LOTS 19 THROUGH 40, INCLUSIVE, GARAGE LOTS 19G THROUGH 33G, INCLUSIVE, AND COMMON AREA LOT C.

4. THIS PROJECT IS A COMMON-INTEREST SUBDIVISION OF THE TYPE REFERRED TO AS A "PLANNED DEVELOPMENT". IT INCLUDES COMMON AREAS AND COMMON FACILITIES WHICH WILL BE MAINTAINED BY AN INCORPORATED OWNERS ASSOCIATION.

5. THE ASSOCIATION HAS THE RIGHT TO LEVY ASSESSMENTS AGAINST YOU FOR THE MAINTENANCE OF THE COMMON AREAS AND OTHER PURPOSES. YOUR CONTROL OF OPERATIONS AND EXPENSES IS LIMITED TO THE RIGHT OF YOUR ELECTED REPRESENTATIVES TO VOTE ON CERTAIN PROVISIONS AT MEETINGS.

6. WARNING: WHEN YOU SELL YOUR LOT TO SOMEONE ELSE, YOU MUST GIVE THAT PERSON A COPY OF THE DECLARATION OF RESTRICTIONS, ARTICLES OF INCORPORATION, THE BYLAWS AND A TRUE STATEMENT CONCERNING ANY DELINQUENT ASSESSMENTS, PENALTIES, ATTORNEYS' FEES OR OTHER CHARGES, PROVIDED BY THE CC&R'S OR OTHER MANAGEMENT DOCUMENTS ON THE LOT AS OF THE DATE THE STATEMENT WAS ISSUED.

   NOTE: IF YOU FORGET TO DO THIS, IT MAY COST YOU A PENALTY OF $500.00 -- PLUS ATTORNEY'S FEES AND DAMAGES (SEE CIVIL CODE SECTION 1368).

   THE SUBDIVIDER MUST MAKE AVAILABLE TO YOU, COPIES OF THE ASSOCIATION GOVERNING INSTRUMENTS, A STATEMENT CONCERNING ANY DELINQUENT ASSESSMENTS AND RELATED CHARGES AS PROVIDED BY THE GOVERNING INSTRUMENTS AND, IF AVAILABLE, A CURRENT FINANCIAL AND RELATED STATEMENTS (SEE BUSINESS AND PROFESSIONS CODE SECTION 11018.6).

INTERESTS TO BE CONVEYED: You will receive fee title to a specified lot, together with a membership in the "Rollingwood Green Homeowners Association" and rights to use the common area.

LOCATION AND SIZE: This subdivision is located in Sacramento County at Madison Avenue near Hazel Avenue.

This is the second increment which consists of approximately 1.306 acres divided into twenty-two residential lots, and including the common area which consists of Lot "C".

Common facilities consisting of lighting, paving and landscaping will be constructed on the common area.

This increment is part of a total project which, if developed as proposed, will consist of a total of three increments containing 58 residential lots within the overall projected development.

There is no assurance that the total project will be completed as proposed.

MANAGEMENT AND OPERATION: The Rollingwood Green Homeowners Association, which you must join, manages and operates the common areas in accordance with the Restrictions, Articles of Incorporation, and the Bylaws.

MAINTENANCE AND OPERATIONAL EXPENSES: The subdivider has submitted budgets for the maintenance and operation of the common areas and for long-term reserves when the subdivision is substantially completed (built-out budget), and an interim budget applicable to this increment. These budgets were reviewed by the Department of Real Estate in October, 1986. You should obtain copies of these budgets from the subdivider.

EASEMENTS: Easements for utilities, planting, rights of way, and other purposes are shown on the Title Report and Subdivision Map recorded in the Office of the Sacramento County Recorder, Book 176 of Maps, Map No. 19 on July 14, 1987.

RESTRICTIONS: This subdivision is subject to Restrictions recorded in the Office of the Sacramento County Recorder, Book 8608-01, Page 522 et. seq., on August 1, 1986 and Declaration of Annexation, Book 8708-11, Page 2018 on August 11, 1987.

> FOR INFORMATION AS TO YOUR OBLIGATIONS AND RIGHTS, YOU SHOULD READ THE RESTRICTIONS. THE SUBDIVIDER SHOULD MAKE THEM AVAILABLE TO YOU.

TAXES: The maximum amount of any tax on real property that can be collected annually by counties is 1% of the full cash value of the property. With the addition of interest and redemption charges on any indebtedness, approved by voters prior to July 1, 1978, the total property tax rate in most counties is approximately 1.25% of the full cash value. In some counties, the total tax rate could be well above 1.25% of the full cash value. For example, an issue of general obligation bonds previously approved by the voters and sold by a county water district, a sanitation district or other such district could increase the total tax.

ASSESSMENTS: This subdivision lies within the boundaries of the Fair Oaks Irrigation District and the Sacramento Municipal Utilities District and is subject to any taxes, assessments and obligations thereof.

CONDITIONS OF SALE - INTEREST TO BE CONVEYED: If your purchase involves financing, a form of deed of trust and note will be used. The provisions of these documents may vary depending upon the lender selected.

> BEFORE SIGNING, YOU SHOULD READ AND THOROUGHLY UNDERSTAND ALL LOAN DOCUMENTS.

Page 4 of 5   File No. 025053SA-F00

PURCHASE MONEY HANDLING: The subdivider must impound all funds received from you in an escrow depository until legal title is delivered to you. (Refer to Sections 11013, 11013.1 and 11013.2(a) of the Business and Professions Code.)

The subdivider advises that individual escrows will not close until 51 percent of the lots have been sold (applies only to lot purchasers obtaining financing from a lender imposing such a requirement).

If the escrow has not closed on your lot within twelve (12) months of the date of your escrow opening, you may request return of your deposit.

The subdivider has no such interest in the escrow company which is to be used in connection with the sale or lease of lots in this subdivision.

SOILS CONDITIONS: A Soils Report is available at Sacramento County Department of Public Works, 827 7th Street, Room 105, Sacramento, CA 95814.

GEOLOGIC CONDITIONS: THE UNIFORM BUILDING CODE, CHAPTER 70, PROVIDES FOR LOCAL BUILDING OFFICIALS TO EXERCISE PREVENTIVE MEASURES DURING GRADING TO ELIMINATE OR MINIMIZE DAMAGE FROM GEOLOGIC HAZARDS SUCH AS LANDSLIDES, FAULT MOVEMENTS, EARTHQUAKE SHAKING, RAPID EROSION OR SUBSIDENCE. THIS SUBDIVISION IS LOCATED IN AN AREA WHERE SOME OF THESE HAZARDS MAY EXIST. SOME CALIFORNIA COUNTIES AND CITIES HAVE ADOPTED ORDINANCES THAT MAY OR MAY NOT BE AS EFFECTIVE IN THE CONTROL OF GRADING AND SITE PREPARATION.

STREETS AND ROADS: The paved areas within this project will be maintained by the homeowner association. The costs of repair and maintenance of these paved areas are included in the budget and are a part of your regular assessment.

FIRE PROTECTION: The Fair Oaks Fire Protection District advises as follows:

"The above mentioned subdivision is within the Fair Oaks Fire Protection District. The project will be provided with a full range of fire and life safety services. Certain fees for service may be imposed for services provided, pursuant to Ordinance 85-1.

The closest fire station is approximately one and one half miles away.

This project will be served by public water and fire hydrants are required to be installed by the developer.

WATER: Fair Oaks Irrigation District.

GAS: Pacific Gas & Electric.

ELECTRIC: Sacramento Municipal Utilities District.

TELEPHONE: Pacific Bell.

For further information in regard to this subdivision, you may call or examine the documents at the Department of Real Estate, Subdivisions North, 2201 Broadway, Sacramento, California, 95818, (916) 739-3631.

Page 5 of 5   File No. 025053SA-F00

issued and given to the buyer. The **PRELIMINARY PUBLIC REPORT (PINK)** *is a tentative public report that must be given to each prospective purchaser*. The report is printed on pink paper, making it easily recognizable. It is given to a buyer when he or she makes a reservation to purchase or lease a lot, unit, or parcel in a subdivision.

Preliminary reports allow subdividers to obtain reservations only. They CANNOT sell and the deposit is fully refundable. Any preliminary report issued will expire when the final report is published or after one year passes, whichever is first.

A prospective purchaser must be given a copy of the preliminary report and sign a receipt to that effect. A copy of the reservation agreement is signed by the prospective buyer and the money deposited with a neutral escrow company. **The reservation to buy or lease must contain a clause allowing the buyer the option to cancel his or her reservation at any time and immediately have the deposit returned**. Any preliminary report issued will expire when the final report is published or after one year passes, whichever occurs first. The subdivider must keep receipts taken for any public report on file for three years.

A "Desist and Refrain Order" is issued by the Real Estate Commissioner to stop sales for violations.

The **FINAL PUBLIC REPORT (WHITE)**, *"Real Estate Commissioner's Final Subdivision Public Report," is the official report that must be given to the buyer*. The buyer must receive a copy of the final public report even if he or she has a preliminary public report. After having enough time to read it, the buyer must sign a receipt stating that the report has been received. There is a five-year time limit on the report, and it can be updated and renewed.

Important! Do NOT buy into any new subdivision unless you have read the report and have checked out all questions that you may have.

Note – The public report process only applies to the first sale of each lot. Later resales are exempt.

A. PUBLIC REPORT RECEIPTS

Subdivider must keep receipt of public report for a three-year period.

The receipt stating that the buyer has received a copy of any public report, and had the opportunity to read it, must be kept on file by the owner, his or her agent, or the subdivider. Receipts for any public reports are subject to inspection by the commissioner for a three-year period. An approved reservation agreement form is furnished by the Department of Real Estate (**See Figure 12-3**). This form, or a form similar to it, is to be used when taking reservations and deposits under a preliminary public report or deposits under the final public report.

Figure 12-3

REGULATION 2795.1

REQUIRED RECEIPT FOR PUBLIC REPORT

The following form shall be duplicated and used by the owner, subdivider or agent as the prospective purchaser's receipt for the copy of the Public Report which was given to said prospective purchaser.

It shall also be used pertinent to all prospective purchasers who sign a reservation agreement under the authority of a Preliminary Public Report or a Short Form Preliminary Public Report.

The receipt is to be kept on file by the subdivider or his/her representative/agent for three years

---

RECEIPT FOR PUBLIC REPORT

The Laws and Regulations of the Real Estate Commissioner require that you as a prospective purchaser or lessee be afforded an opportunity to read the public report for this subdivision before you make any written offer to purchase or lease a subdivision interest or before any money or other consideration toward purchase or lease of a subdivision interest is accepted from you.

In the case of a preliminary subdivision public report, you must be afforded an opportunity to read the report before a written reservation or any deposit in connection therewith is accepted from you.

DO NOT SIGN THIS RECEIPT UNTIL YOU HAVE RECEIVED A COPY OF THE REPORT AND HAVE READ IT.

I have read the Commissioner's Public Report on

"CENTURY PARK PLACE"

054916LA-A04   37164, Phase 4, Lot 1
    (File No.)   (Tract No. or Name)

I understand the report is not a recommendation or endorsement of the subdivision, but is for information only.

The date of the public report which is received and read is: _6/7/XX_ .

Vic Lester
                    Name
1207 Arden Street
                    Address
_6/7/XX_
                    Date

A subdivider must comply with the minimum housing standards that are the most rigid or stringent. If there is a discrepancy between local and state building codes, the highest standard of safety will prevail. A developer is responsible for streets, curbs, and utilities in a new subdivision.

B. MATERIAL CHANGES (Notify Commissioner)

Change in price is NOT a material fact.

Any material change in the subdivision or its handling after the filing is made, or the public report is issued, must be reported to the Commissioner of Real Estate. This not only includes physical changes, such as changes in the lot or street lines, but any new condition or development that may affect the value of the subdivision or the terms of how it is offered to the public.

The owner of a standard type subdivision or planned development must report to the commissioner the sale of five or more parcels. The sale to a single purchaser of two or more units in a community apartment, condominium, or stock cooperative project must also be reported. Failure to report material changes not only violates the law, but may furnish a basis for rescission, by court action, of purchases.

If a person purchases, or has an option to purchase, five or more lots in a subdivision, whether contiguous or not, the subdivider must immediately notify the Department of Real Estate with the name and address. The reason for this is that another subdivision has been created within the original subdivision, so a new Final Public Report will be required.

IV. Subdivision Defined by Law

Although the definitions of the Subdivided Lands Law and the Subdivision Map Act are in many ways similar, there are some differences. Both define a subdivision as improved or unimproved land divided for the purpose of sale, leasehold, or financing into several parcels. They are applied not only to residential land, but include lands used for any purpose, including business, industry, recreation, or agriculture.

There are several differences between the two Acts. In general, the Subdivided Lands Law applies to five or more units while the Subdivision Map Act applies to two or more units.

Full compliance with all the provisions of the Subdivision Map Act and the Subdivided Lands Law is required by law. Subdividers and their professional consultants should be thoroughly familiar with the provisions of the state laws and with the specific city and county provisions that affect the particular community in question. Many variations are found in local subdivision ordinances due to the great diversity of communities and conditions throughout the state. (See **Figure 12-4** for a summary of subdivision laws.)

Figure 12-4   **Subdivision Laws Summarized**

Subdivision Map Act	Subdivided Land Act
Two or more lots or parcels	Five or more lots or parcels
Land must be contiguous units	No contiguity requirement
No exemption for 160 acres and larger	160 and larger parcels are exempt
Administered by local officials	Administered by the California Real Estate Commissioner
No public report required	Public report required

A. LAND PROJECTS (State Law)

In recent years, lots in some subdivisions located in sparsely populated areas have been sold by intensive promotional efforts that tend to obscure the gamble involved in such speculations. Such subdivisions are referred to as land projects. A *LAND PROJECT is a remote subdivision of 50 or more vacant lots in a rural area (having fewer than 1,500 registered voters within two miles).*

Certain laws have been established to protect the public from these risky ventures. By law, any contract to buy or lease in a land project may be rescinded without cause, by written notice, before midnight on the fourteenth day after the sales contract is signed.

B. OUT OF STATE BUYERS (Federal Law)

Subdividers of large subdivisions to be sold interstate are registered with HUD.

Under the Federal Interstate Land Sales Full Disclosure Act, such sales are subject to special registration and control. A contract for the purchase or lease of a lot of this kind is voidable at the option of the buyer if the contract is made without prior inspection of the site. The buyer has seven days after receiving the public report to rescind the contract.

V. Common Interest Development (CID)

A *COMMON INTEREST DEVELOPMENT (CID) is a project where there are common areas used by all—excepting separate interests for the use of individual living units and managed by a nonprofit association.* The four basic types of common interest ownership, which are defined as subdivisions, include:

A. Planned Development (PD)
B. Community Apartment Project
C. Condominiums (including Timesharing)
D. Stock Cooperative

To be defined as subdivisions by the Department of Real Estate as part of the Subdivided Lands Law, a planned unit development must have five or more lots, but all the other types only need two units.

A. PLANNED DEVELOPMENT (PD)

"Common area" means to own as one.

A **PLANNED DEVELOPMENT**, *sometimes referred to as a planned unit development (PUD), is a subdivision where lots are owned separately, but certain areas are owned in common by all owners.* Generally, an owner's association is elected by all the owners to manage and maintain the common areas.

The **COMMON AREA** *is that part of a lot or unit in a subdivision that is shared equally by all owners (undivided interest).* An **UNDIVIDED INTEREST** *is the right of any owner to use any part of the project.*

An example of a PD (or PUD) is a subdivided tract of homes, each on its own lot, that share a swimming pool on a separate lot, which is owned in common by all the tract owners.

B. COMMUNITY APARTMENT PROJECTS

COMMUNITY APARTMENT PROJECTS *are two or more apartments, defined as a subdivision, where the operation, maintenance, and control is usually exercised by a governing board elected by the owners of the fractional interests.* An owner receives an undivided interest in the land together with an exclusive leasehold right to occupy a unit. There is only one property tax bill for the entire project.

Purchasers receive only a leasehold interest in an apartment, while a condominium purchaser gets a deed (fee interest) to a unit.

C. CONDOMINIUM (Most Common Type)

A condominium owner gets a deed (fee interest) to a unit and a separate tax bill.

A **CONDOMINIUM** *is the ownership of the land and buildings in common with other owners plus the individual ownership of specific air spaces.* A "condominium" is a type of ownership; a "townhouse" is a type of architecture. In a PD, the property owner owns the living unit as well as the lot. Condominiums may be used for residential, industrial, or commercial purposes, although the residential type is most commonly seen in California. Condominium projects having two or more units are defined as subdivisions.

A condominium is the ownership of unit (airspace) and shared ownership of the land and all improvements. Each "condo" has a separate grant deed, trust deed, and tax bill. You "own what you see"; the airspace between the paint on one wall to the paint on the other wall.

In effect, a condominium buyer owns, in fee simple, the air space in which his or her particular unit is situated. He or she receives a separate tax bill for private airspace and percentage share of the common area. Each airspace unit is given a grant deed, and the owner can acquire a title insurance policy. The common area is managed by an elected governing board.

With the sale of a condominium, the seller must provide the buyer with a copy of the:

1. CC&Rs (covenants, conditions, restrictions)
2. By-laws (governing rules of the association)
3. Financial statement (the condo association's most recent)

1. Timesharing

TIMESHARING *is a form of ownership where each investor holds a share in a specific unit or home and possesses the right to occupy that home for a specified period each year.* **See Figure 12-5.**

Fifty-two owners (usually less because of downtime for maintenance) may each own a specific one-week share in one unit at a resort property.

D. STOCK COOPERATIVE (Corporation is the Owner)

A **STOCK COOPERATIVE** *is a corporation that is formed to own the land and improved real property.* A stock cooperative either owns or leases real property. The buyer does not receive a grant deed but owns a share of the corporation and the right to occupy a certain unit. The right to occupy can be transferred only with the share of stock in the corporation.

There is one property tax bill in the name of the corporation. A Stock cooperative is a forerunner of the condominium.

VI. Subdivision Advertising

Guidelines for subdividers in advertising and promotions have been developed by the Department of Real Estate. The pamphlet contains filing procedures, requirements and prohibitions on advertising. Since misleading advertising is watched very carefully, it is now a requirement that the public report must be given to each advertising media selected by the subdivider. In addition, a true copy of any advertising proposed for use in connection with a land project offering must be submitted as part of the documentation required prior to the issuance of the public report.

Figure 12-5

TIMESHARING:

Pro or Con? — You Decide! A chalet at Lake Tahoe...a condo in Palm Springs...beachfront property in La Jolla...

TIMESHARING is a form of ownership where each investor holds a share in a specific unit or home and possesses the right to occupy that home for a specified period each year. For instance, fifty-two owners may each own a one-week share in the property. Each is given a grant deed and each has the right to sell his or her share, rent out the week, or stay there for one seven-day period every year. The ownership week is fixed but it is possible to trade with other owners. Similarly, there are timesharing groups across the country and around the world which allow investors to exchange time with owners of comparable properties in other desirable locations.

Advantages

The advantages to this kind of ownership are obvious. The buyer has a vacation home without the expense of purchasing the complete home outright. This kind of plan provides access to some of the most unique and scenic property in the world. Once these very special locations are sold, they are gone: they cannot be replaced in the marketplace.

Disadvantages

On the negative side, these properties tend to be disproportionately high priced. For instance, if you multiplied the cost of one share in a week-based timeshare by and even 50, it would total much more than the market value of the property purchased. Those selling timeshares are burdened with tremendous marketing expenses. Rather than selling once, each property must be sold many times, complete with financing and paperwork.

Restrictions

A brokerage license is required to sell a timeshare package but, just as with other forms of home sales, owners have the right to transfer their ownership shares without a real estate license and have a 72-hour right of rescission.

VII. Environmental Laws

In recent years there has been increasing attention focused on the problems of our environment. These problems include energy, water pollution, air pollution, population growth, preservation of wild life, waste disposal and the quality of life in general. In response, the federal, state and local governments have passed laws and made regulations to help protect us and our environment.

An *ENVIRONMENTAL IMPACT REPORT (EIR) is a study of how a subdivision will affect the ecology of a subdivision's surroundings.* An EIR may be required by either city or county authorities prior to their approval of the subdivision map, but some projects may be exempt. In rare cases, the responsibility for the preparation of the EIR will belong to the Department of Real Estate.

> *A negative declaration (nothing found) on an EIR report is good. It indicates that the subdivision does NOT harm the environment.*

The voters of California passed Proposition 20 that established the state Coastal Commission to preserve the coastline. This commission has set construction standards for private and public projects within 1,000 yards of the Pacific Ocean or any other body of water. Its purpose is to establish land use planning, which has considerable economic, social, and political overtones. As part of this law, the commission had to establish a long-range coastal plan. No one seems to agree on the economic effects of Proposition 20, but it did have the result of reducing the number and size of coastal construction projects and required an average of six weeks to pass a project through the commission.

A. LEAD-BASED PAINT DISCLOSURE (Federal Government)

Lead-Based Paint Disclosure Pamphlet
Residential Lead-Based Paint Hazard Reduction Act

The seller or lessor must provide the buyer or lessee with a lead hazard information pamphlet (including disclosure form) and disclose the known presence of any lead-based paint.

The CAR® Residential Purchase Agreement and Deposit Receipt contains a Lead Warning Statement and a statement, to be signed by the buyer, that the buyer has read the warning statement. Also, CAR® has a **Lead-Based Paint Hazards Disclosure, Acknowledgment, and Addendum Form (Figure 12-6)** that can be made a part of a Residential Purchase Agreement, Residential Lease or Month-To-Month Rental Agreement, or some other contract.

The agent, on behalf of the seller or lessor, must ensure compliance with the requirements of the law. The purchaser has a 10-day opportunity to inspect before becoming obligated under the contract.

Figure 12-6

CALIFORNIA
ASSOCIATION
OF REALTORS®

LEAD-BASED PAINT AND LEAD-BASED PAINT HAZARDS DISCLOSURE, ACKNOWLEDGMENT AND ADDENDUM
For Pre-1978 Housing Sales, Leases, or Rentals
(C.A.R. Form FLD, Revised 1/03)

The following terms and conditions are hereby incorporated in and made a part of the: ☐ California Residential Purchase Agreement, ☐ Residential Lease or Month-to-Month Rental Agreement, or ☐ other: _____
_____,dated _____, on property known as: _____ ("Property")
in which _____ is referred to as Buyer or Tenant
and _____ is referred to as Seller or Landlord.

LEAD WARNING STATEMENT (SALE OR PURCHASE) Every purchaser of any interest in residential real property on which a residential dwelling was built prior to 1978 is notified that such property may present exposure to lead from lead-based paint that may place young children at risk of developing lead poisoning. Lead poisoning in young children may produce permanent neurological damage, including learning disabilities, reduced intelligent quotient, behavioral problems and impaired memory. Lead poisoning also poses a particular risk to pregnant women. The seller of any interest in residential real property is required to provide the buyer with any information on lead-based paint hazards from risk assessments or inspections in the seller's possession and notify the buyer of any known lead-based paint hazards. A risk assessment or inspection for possible lead-based paint hazards is recommended prior to purchase.

LEAD WARNING STATEMENT (LEASE OR RENTAL) Housing built before 1978 may contain lead-based paint. Lead from paint, paint chips and dust can pose health hazards if not managed properly. Lead exposure is especially harmful to young children and pregnant women. Before renting pre-1978 housing, lessors must disclose the presence of lead-based paint and/or lead-based paint hazards in the dwelling. Lessees must also receive federally approved pamphlet on lead poisoning prevention.

1. SELLER'S OR LANDLORD'S DISCLOSURE

I (we) have no knowledge of lead-based paint and/or lead-based paint hazards in the housing other than the following:
_____
_____
_____
_____

I (we) have no reports or records pertaining to lead-based paint and/or lead-based paint hazards in the housing other than the following, which, previously or as an attachment to this addendum have been provided to Buyer or Tenant:
_____
_____
_____

I (we), previously or as an attachment to this addendum, have provided Buyer or Tenant with the pamphlet "Protect Your Family From Lead In Your Home" or an equivalent pamphlet approved for use in the State such as "The Homeowner's Guide to Environmental Hazards and Earthquake Safety."

For Sales Transactions Only: Buyer has 10 days, unless otherwise agreed in the real estate purchase contract, to conduct a risk assessment or inspection for the presence of lead-based paint and/or lead-based paint hazards.

I (we) have reviewed the information above and certify, to the best of my (our) knowledge, that the information provided is true and correct.

_____
Seller or Landlord   Date

_____
Seller or Landlord   Date

FLD REVISED 1/03 (PAGE 1 OF 2) Print Date

Buyer's Initials (_____)(_____)
Seller's Initials (_____)(_____)

Reviewed by _____ Date _____

EQUAL HOUSING OPPORTUNITY

LEAD-BASED PAINT AND LEAD-BASED PAINT HAZARDS DISCLOSURE (FLD-11 PAGE 1 OF 2)

Property Address: _____ Date _____

2. LISTING AGENT'S ACKNOWLEDGMENT

Agent has informed Seller or Landlord of Seller's or Landlord's obligations under §42 U.S.C. 4852d and is aware of Agent's responsibility to ensure compliance.

I have reviewed the information above and certify, to the best of my knowledge, that the information provided is true and correct.

_____   By _____
Agent (Broker representing Seller)Please Print   Associate-Licensee or Broker Signature   Date

3. BUYER'S OR TENANT'S ACKNOWLEDGMENT

I (we) have received copies of all information listed, if any, in 1 above and the pamphlet "Protect Your Family From Lead In Your Home" or an equivalent pamphlet approved for use in the State such as "The Homeowner's Guide to Environmental Hazards and Earthquake Safety." **If delivery of any of the disclosures or pamphlet referenced in paragraph 1 above occurs after Acceptance of an offer to purchase, Buyer has a right to cancel pursuant to the purchase contract. If you wish to cancel, you must act within the prescribed period.**

For Sales Transactions Only: Buyer acknowledges the right for 10 days, unless otherwise agreed in the real estate purchase contract, to conduct a risk assessment or inspection for the presence of lead-based paint and/or lead-based paint hazards; OR, (if checked) ☐ Buyer waives the right to conduct a risk assessment or inspection for the presence of lead-based paint and/or lead-based paint hazards.

I (we) have reviewed the information above and certify, to the best of my (our) knowledge, that the information provided is true and correct.

_____   _____   _____   _____
Buyer or Tenant   Date   Buyer or Tenant   Date

4. COOPERATING AGENT'S ACKNOWLEDGMENT

Agent has informed Seller or Landlord, through the Listing Agent if the property is listed, of Seller's or Landlord's obligations under §42 USC 4852d and is aware of Agent's responsibility to ensure compliance.

I have reviewed the information above and certify, to the best of my knowledge, that the information provided is true and correct.

_____   By _____
Agent (Broker obtaining the Offer)   Associate-Licensee or Broker Signature   Date

SURE TRAC
The System for Success™

Published by the
California Association of REALTORS®

FLD REVISED 1/03 (PAGE 2 OF 2)

Reviewed by _____ Date _____

EQUAL HOUSING OPPORTUNITY

LEAD-BASED PAINT AND LEAD-BASED PAINT HAZARDS DISCLOSURE (FLD-11 PAGE 2 OF 2)

B. GEOLOGICAL HAZARD ZONES

Before any real estate development or large structure is built in California, a geological report must be submitted. This report must be compiled by a registered geologist and given to the city in which the development is planned. In the case of a development in an unincorporated area, the report is submitted to the county in which the planned development is located.

If the state geologist approves it, the city or county department may waive such a report as long as there is no earthquake fault activity.

The California Geological Survey (formerly called the Division of Mines and Geology) has mapped every earthquake fault that has hazardous potential or recent activity. These special study zones are found throughout California and new ones are added to the map (**Figure 12-7**).

Any person buying within such a zone should be informed either by the seller or the real estate licensee of this fact. A buyer who is thinking of building should be cautioned as to the regulations and requirements that may have to be met to develop the land. See **Figure 12-8** for specifics on the Alquist-Priolo Special Studies Zones Act. There are approximately 205 different Geological Survey areas in California. If you want more information about these hazardous zones or copies of the maps, they can be obtained for a small fee.

CALIFORNIA GEOLOGICAL SURVEY
801 K Street, MS 14-33
Sacramento, CA 95814-3532
(916) 445-5716
(916)327-1853 (Fax)
www.consrv.ca.gov/dmg/index.htm

VIII. Planning Commission

The primary responsibility of a *CITY or COUNTY PLANNING COMMISSION is to prepare and adopt comprehensive, long-term general plans for the physical development of its area of jurisdiction.* These city or county organizations gather information, cite other examples, and come up with their own innovations in an attempt to make some order out of the chaos into which a city may have fallen. Commissions have discovered that preplanning exactly which types of buildings can go where, before they are constructed, saves more time and money than all the zoning laws made after the building is done. Such planning commissions make predictions to guarantee that today's residential, commercial, and industrial areas will not collide in the future due to expansion of both areas.

Zoning is the basic or primary tool used by a planning commission to implement a general plan.

Figure 12-7

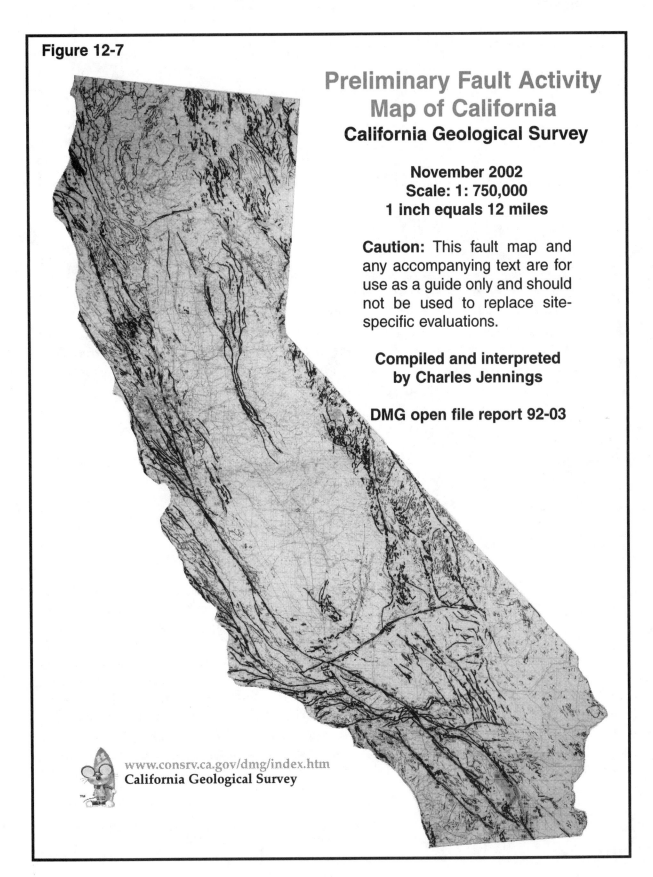

Preliminary Fault Activity
Map of California
California Geological Survey

November 2002
Scale: 1: 750,000
1 inch equals 12 miles

Caution: This fault map and any accompanying text are for use as a guide only and should not be used to replace site-specific evaluations.

Compiled and interpreted by Charles Jennings

DMG open file report 92-03

www.consrv.ca.gov/dmg/index.htm
California Geological Survey

Figure 12-8

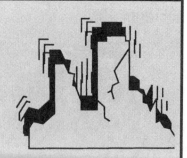

Earthquake Zones

Alquist-Priolo Special Studies Zones Act

It is a zoning act designed to control the development in the vicinity (1/4 mile on each side) of hazardous earthquake faults for the benefit of public safety for the entire state of California.

The purpose of the Alquist-Priolo Special Studies Zones Act is to assist governmental jurisdictions in the exercise of their responsibility to prohibit the development of structures for human occupancy on top of active earthquakes faults as defined by the state geological survey maps. Developments or structures in existence prior to May 4, 1975, are not affected.

An earthquake zone normally extends one-quarter of a mile or more in width, centered on the trace of a fault, and includes an area that may be hazardous for development or construction of a structure for human occupancy due to surface faulting or fault creep.

Maps for Special Studies Zone

These maps can be consulted at any district office of the California Geological Survey (formerly named the Division of Mines and Geology). Individuals can obtain copies of these maps at many different local jurisdictions. As a practical matter, the local Multiple Listing Office is one of the most convenient locations to see a map.

"Any person who is acting as a agent for a seller of real estate that is located within a delineated special studies zone, or the seller if acting without an agent, shall disclose the fact that the property is located within a delineated special studies zone."

Note – Most agents and sellers have a professional company prepare these disclosures for the buyers.

A. MASTER PLAN

Every city and county must have a planning commission. The primary purpose of a Master Plan is to set forth existing and future matters concerning seismic safety, districts, streets, and highways.

Entire new cities can be pre-planned so that zoning laws exist only to enforce and execute the city's master plan. The *MASTER PLAN is a comprehensive guide through which zoning establishes an ideal plan for the city's development in the future. DIRECTIONAL GROWTH is the actual growth path of urban development. Properties in the direction of growth tend to increase in value especially if the growth is steady and rapid.* It is used, by smart investors, to determine where future development will be most profitable. A good example of preplanning is the Irvine Ranch in Orange County, where there is a balance between residential, recreational, commercial, and manufacturing areas.

The essential elements of a master plan are:

1. The designation of proposed general distribution, location, and extent of land uses within certain areas.
2. The determination of general traffic patterns, including the extensions of existing and proposed transportation routes, terminals, and other public utility facilities.
3. The setting of standards of population density and building units per acre of various districts and the estimation of future population growth trends. A number of other elements may also be included.

IX. Zoning (Use)

Zoning is the city or county exercise of "police power;" rulings are made to control the use of private property for the protection of the public's health, safety, and welfare. The power to zone is given by the U.S. Constitution.

ZONING LAWS regulate the use of property by prescribing what uses that land can be put to and by establishing uniformity throughout the community. For example, zoning laws may indicate that a specific property can be used only as a single family home, multiple family housing, or for commercial or industrial use. It is possible for the planning commission to change zoning. It can change an area from commercial to residential or change a residential area from R-4 to R-1. This is called down zoning. *DOWN ZONING means the land will have less use density. INCLUSIONARY ZONING requires builders of new residential housing to provide a certain number of low- and moderate-income units.* No permit will be obtained if the builder does not agree. Sometimes a builder will, in lieu of setting aside inclusionary units, contribute to a fund used to provide low- and moderate-income housing.

If zoning conflicts with deed restrictions, the most restrictive control.

Zoning laws use the "police power" granted to every county and city to regulate the use, planning, and setbacks of land. Such regulations protect the health, safety, comfort and general welfare of the community. These ordinances are public restrictions to the uses of private property. Counties and cities can set higher standards, which can be much higher than the minimums set by the state. For example, zoning which regulates the use of lands and buildings may specify the following:

1. Location and type of building
2. Height of the structure
3. Size of the building
4. Percentage of a lot the building may occupy
5. Setback requirements from front, back, and sides of the property boundaries.

Owners, subdividers, and government agencies can petition for zone changes.

Figure 12-9 is an example of a Los Angeles zoning plan. You will notice that there are many symbols that indicate the regulated uses for all the different parts of Los Angeles.

Each symbol represents a different type of zone, but it is possible to make the following generalization about some of the common zoning symbols:

A — This symbol usually indicates an *agricultural* area such as farm or ranch land. In a few isolated areas a symbol beginning with "A" stands for an airport.

C — The "C" symbol represents *commercial* areas. In these areas anything from an office building to a community shopping center may exist. There are other, more specific, "C" symbols regulating the construction of such commercial properties.

A "strip commercial development" is a single line of store buildings constructed along a major transportation route.

M — Stands for *manufacturing*. Industrial complexes must be built only in zones classified "M."

P — Although there are many different interpretations of the "P" symbol, the most important categories it covers are *parking lots* and *parks*.

R — The "R" symbol stands for *Residential* and is probably the most important symbol to the real estate person. This symbol (and its derivations) designates those areas in which *homes, condominiums,* or *apartments* may be built or maintained.

Each of these symbols is usually followed by a number, for example "R" may be followed by 1, 2, 3, or 4. The number indicates a higher density or use for that particular zone. The following will help explain each use:

R1 - is for a *single-family* dwelling

Figure 12-9

SUMMARY OF ZONING REGULATIONS
CITY OF LOS ANGELES

CLASSIFICATION	ZONE	USE	MAXIMUM HEIGHT STORIES	MAXIMUM HEIGHT FEET	REQUIRED YARDS FRONT	REQUIRED YARDS SIDE	REQUIRED YARDS REAR	MINIMUM AREA PER LOT	MINIMUM AREA PER DWELLING UNIT	MINIMUM LOT WIDTH	PARKING SPACE	EAGLE PRISMACOLOR PENCIL CHART
AGRICULTURAL	A1	AGRICULTURAL ONE-FAMILY DWELLINGS-PARKS-PLAY-GROUNDS-COMMUNITY CENTERS GOLF COURSES-TRUCK GARDENING-EXTENSIVE AGRICULTURAL USES	3	45 FT.	25 FT.	25 FT MAXIMUM 10% LOT WIDTH 3 FT. MINIMUM	25 FT	5 ACRES	2½ ACRES	300 FT.	TWO SPACES PER DWELLING UNIT	909 GRASS GREEN
AGRICULTURAL	A2	AGRICULTURAL A1 USES	3	45 FT.	25 FT	25 FT. MAXIMUM 10% LOT WIDTH 3 FT. MINIMUM	25 FT	2 ACRES	1 ACRE	150 FT	TWO SPACES PER DWELLING UNIT	912 APPLE GREEN
AGRICULTURAL	RA	SUBURBAN LIMITED AGRICULTURAL USES	3	45 FT.	25 FT	10'-1&2 STORIES 11'-3 STORIES	25 FT	17,500 SQ.FT ✱	17,500 SQ FT ✱	70 FT. ✱	TWO GARAGE SPACES PER DWELLING UNIT	910 TRUE GREEN
ONE FAMILY RESIDENTIAL	RE40	RESIDENTIAL ESTATE ONE-FAMILY DWELLINGS PARKS PLAYGROUNDS COMMUNITY CENTERS TRUCK GARDENING	3	45 FT.	25 FT.	10 FT	25 FT	40,000 SQ.FT ✱	40,000 SQ.FT. ✱	80 FT. ✱	TWO GARAGE SPACES PER DWELLING UNIT	950 GOLD
ONE FAMILY RESIDENTIAL	RE20				25 FT.	10 FT	25 FT	20,000 SQ.FT ✱	20,000 SQ.FT. ✱	80 FT. ✱		
ONE FAMILY RESIDENTIAL	RE15				25 FT.	10 FT. MAXIMUM 10% LOT WIDTH 5 FT. MINIMUM	25 FT.	15,000 SQ.FT. ✱	15,000 SQ.FT. ✱	80 FT. ✱		
ONE FAMILY RESIDENTIAL	RE11				25 FT.	5'-1&2 STORIES 6'-3 STORIES	25 FT.	11,000 SQ.FT. ✱	11,000 SQ.FT. ✱	70 FT. ✱		
ONE FAMILY RESIDENTIAL	RE9				25 FT.	5 FT. MAXIMUM 10% LOT WIDTH 3 FT MINIMUM	25 FT.	9,000 SQ.FT. ✱	9,000 SQ.FT. ✱	65 FT ✱		
ONE FAMILY RESIDENTIAL	RS	SUBURBAN ONE-FAMILY DWELLINGS-PARKS PLAYGROUNDS-TRUCK GARDENING	3	45 FT.	25 FT	5'-1&2 STORIES 6'-3 STORIES	20 FT	7,500 SQ FT	7,500 SQ.FT	60 FT.	TWO GARAGE SPACES PER DWELLING UNIT	911 OLIVE GREEN
ONE FAMILY RESIDENTIAL	R1	ONE-FAMILY DWELLING RS USES	3	45 FT	20 FT.	5'-1 & 2 STORIES 6'-3 STORIES	15 FT	5,000 SQ FT	5,000 SQ.FT.	50 FT.	TWO GARAGE SPACES PER DWELLING UNIT	916 CANARY YELLOW
ONE FAMILY RESIDENTIAL	RW1	ONE-FAMILY RESIDENTIAL WATERWAYS ZONE	3	45 FT.	10 FT.	4' PLUS 1' EACH STORY ABOVE 2ᴺᴰ 10% LOT WIDTH	15 FT	2,300 SQ FT	2,300 SQ FT	28 FT	TWO GARAGE SPACES PER DWELLING UNIT	914 CREAM
ONE FAMILY RESIDENTIAL	RW2	TWO-FAMILY RESIDENTIAL WATERWAYS ZONE							1,150 SQ.FT.			
MULTIPLE RESIDENTIAL	R2	TWO-FAMILY DWELLING R1 USES TWO-FAMILY DWELLINGS	3	45 FT.	20 FT.	5'-1&2 STORIES 6'-3 STORIES	15 FT	5,000 SQ FT	2,500 SQ.FT	50 FT.	TWO SPACES ONE IN A GARAGE	917 YELLOW ORANGE
MULTIPLE RESIDENTIAL	RD1.5	RESTRICTED DENSITY MULTIPLE DWELLING ZONE TWO-FAMILY DWELLING APARTMENT HOUSES MULTIPLE DWELLINGS	HEIGHT DISTRICT NO. 1 3 STORIES 45 FT. / HEIGHT DISTRICT NOS. 2,3 OR 4 6 STORIES 75 FT.		20 FT.	6 FT	20 FT.	6,000 SQ FT	1,500 SQ FT	60 FT	ONE SPACE EACH DWELLING UNIT OF LESS THAN THREE ROOMS ONE AND ONE HALF SPACES EACH DWELLING UNIT OF THREE ROOMS TWO SPACES EACH DWELLING UNIT OF MORE THEN THREE ROOMS ONE SPACE EACH GUEST ROOM (FIRST THIRTY)	940 SAND
MULTIPLE RESIDENTIAL	RD2							8,000 SQ FT	2,000 SQ FT	60 FT		
MULTIPLE RESIDENTIAL	RD3				20 FT	10 FT	25 FT	12,000 SQ. FT.	3,000 SQ. FT.	70 FT		
MULTIPLE RESIDENTIAL	RD4								4,000 SQ. FT.			
MULTIPLE RESIDENTIAL	RD5								5,000 SQ.FT.			
MULTIPLE RESIDENTIAL	RD6								6,000 SQ.FT.			
MULTIPLE RESIDENTIAL	R3	MULTIPLE DWELLING R2 USES APARTMENT HOUSES MULTIPLE DWELLINGS			15 FT	5'-1 & 2 STORIE 6'-3 STORIES	15 FT	5,000 SQ.FT.	800 TO 1,200 SQ. FT.	50 FT		918 ORANGE
MULTIPLE RESIDENTIAL	R4	MULTIPLE DWELLING R3 USES CHURCHES HOTELS-SCHOOLS	UNLIMITED ✱		15 FT	5' PLUS 1' EACH STORY ABOVE 2ᴺᴰ 16 FT MAX	15' PLUS 1' EACH STORY ABOVE 3ᴿᴰ 20 FT. MAX.	5,000 SQ FT	400 TO 800 SQ. FT	50 FT		943 BURNT OCHRE
MULTIPLE RESIDENTIAL	R5	MULTIPLE DWELLING R4 USES CLUBS-HOSPITALS LODGES-SANITARIUMS	UNLIMITED ✱		15 FT.	5' PLUS 1' EACH STORY ABOVE 2ᴺᴰ 16 FT. MAX.	15' PLUS 1' EACH STORY ABOVE 3ᴿᴰ 20 FT MAX	5,000 SQ.FT.	200 TO 400 SQ. FT	50 FT.		946 DARK BROWN

✱ SEE HEIGHT DISTRICTS AT THE BOTTOM OF PAGE 2

● FOR TWO OR MORE LOTS THE INTERIOR SIDE YARDS MAY BE ELIMINATED, BUT 4 FT IS REQUIRED ON EACH SIDE OF THE GROUPED LOTS.

✱ "H" HILLSIDE OR MOUNTAINOUS AREA DESIGNATION MAY ALTER THESE REQUIREMENTS IN THE RA-H OR RE-H ZONES. SUBDIVISIONS MAY BE APPROVED WITH SMALLER LOTS, PROVIDING LARGER LOTS ARE ALSO INCLUDED EACH LOT MAY BE USED FOR ONLY ONE SINGLE-FAMILY DWELLING SEE MINIMUM WIDTH & AREA REQUIREMENTS BELOW

ZONE COMBINATION	MINIMUM TO WHICH NET AREA MAY BE REDUCED	MINIMUM TO WHICH LOT WIDTH MAY BE REDUCED
RA-H	14,000 SQ FT	63 FT
RE 9 -H	7,200 SQ FT	60 FT
RE11-H.	8,800 SQ FT	63 FT
RE15-H	12,000 SQ FT	72 FT
RE 20-H	16,000 SQ FT	72 FT
RE 40-H	32,000 SQ FT	NO REDUCTION

SHEET 1 OF 2   CP FORM 10

PREPARED BY CITY PLANNING DEPARTMENT

SUMMARY OF ZONING REGULATIONS
CITY OF LOS ANGELES

CLASSIFICATION	ZONE	USE	MAXIMUM HEIGHT		REQUIRED YARDS			MINIMUM AREA PER LOT AND UNIT	MINIMUM LOT WIDTH	LOADING SPACE	PARKING SPACE	EAGLE PRISMACOLOR PENCIL CHART
			STORIES	FEET	FRONT	SIDE	REAR					
RESIDENTIAL USES (EXCEPT HOTELS) PROHIBITED UNLESS CONDITIONAL USE IS APPROVED BY ZONING ADMINISTRATOR — COMMERCIAL	**CR**	LIMITED COMMERCIAL — BANKS, CLUBS, HOTELS, CHURCHES, SCHOOLS, BUSINESS & PROFESSIONAL OFFICES, PARKING AREAS	6	75 FT.	10 FEET	5'-10' CORNER LOT, RESIDENTIAL USE OR ADJOINING AN "A" OR "R" ZONE. SAME AS R4 ZONE	15' PLUS 1' EACH STORY ABOVE 3rd	SAME AS R4 FOR DWELLINGS OTHERWISE NONE LOT ABUTS ALLEY		HOSPITALS, HOTELS INSTITUTIONS, AND WITH EVERY BUILDING WHERE LOT ABUTS ALLEY	ONE SPACE FOR EACH 500 SQ. FT. OF FLOOR AREA	939 / FLESH
	C1	LIMITED COMMERCIAL — LOCAL RETAIL STORES, OFFICES OR BUSINESSES, HOTELS, LIMITED HOSPITALS AND/OR CLINICS, PARKING AREAS				3'-5' CORNER LOT OR ADJOINING AN "A" OR "R" ZONE RESIDENTIAL USE SAME AS R4 ZONE	15' PLUS 1' EACH STORY ABOVE 3rd RESIDENTIAL USE OR ABUTTING AN "A" OR "R" ZONE OTHERWISE NONE	SAME AS R3 FOR DWELLINGS EXCEPT 5000 SQ FT PER UNIT IN C1-H ZONES — OTHERWISE NONE		50 FEET FOR RESIDENCE USE OTHERWISE NONE	MINIMUM LOADING SPACE 400 SQUARE FEET ADDITIONAL SPACE REQUIRED FOR BUILDINGS CONTAINING MORE THAN 50,000 SQUARE FEET OF FLOOR AREA	ONE SPACE FOR EACH 400 SQUARE FEET OF FLOOR AREA IN ALL BUILDINGS ON ANY LOT MUST BE LOCATED WITHIN 750 FEET OF BUILDING	929 / PINK
	C1.5	LIMITED COMMERCIAL — C1 USES — DEPARTMENT STORES, THEATRES, BROADCASTING STUDIOS, PARKING BUILDINGS, PARKS & PLAYGROUNDS							SAME AS R4 FOR DWELLINGS OTHERWISE NONE				928 / BLUSH
	C2	COMMERCIAL — C1.5 USES — RETAIL BUSINESSES WITH LIMITED MANUFACTURING, AUTO SERVICE STATION & GARAGE, RETAIL CONTRACTORS BUSINESSES, CHURCHES, SCHOOLS	UNLIMITED ✱		NONE	NONE FOR COMMERCIAL BUILDINGS RESIDENTIAL USES — SAME AS IN R4 ZONE	NONE FOR COMMERCIAL BUILDINGS RESIDENTIAL USES — SAME AS IN R4 ZONE			NONE REQUIRED FOR APARTMENT BUILDINGS 20 UNITS OR LESS	SEE CODE FOR ASSEMBLY AREAS, HOSPITALS AND CLINICS	922 / SCARLET RED
	C4	COMMERCIAL — C2 USES — (WITH EXCEPTIONS, SUCH AS AUTO SERVICE STATIONS, AMUSEMENT ENTERPRISES, CONTRACTORS BUSINESSES, SECOND-HAND BUSINESSES)										924 / CRIMSON RED
	C5	COMMERCIAL — C2 USES — LIMITED FLOOR AREAS FOR LIGHT MANUFACTURING OF THE CM-ZONE TYPE										925 / CRIMSON LAKE
	CM	COMM'L MANUFACTURING — WHOLESALE BUSINESSES, STORAGE BUILDINGS, CLINICS, LIMITED MANUFACTURING, C2 USES — EXCEPT HOSPITALS, SCHOOLS, CHURCHES						SAME AS R3 FOR DWELLINGS OTHERWISE NONE				905 / AQUA-MARINE
RESIDENTIAL USES PROHIBITED IN ALL INDUSTRIAL ZONES — INDUSTRIAL	**MR1**	RESTRICTED INDUSTRIAL — CM USES — LIMITED COMMERCIAL & MANUFACTURING USES, HOSPITALS, CLINICS, SANITARIUMS, LIMITED MACHINE SHOPS			15 FT.	NONE FOR INDUSTRIAL OR COMMERCIAL BUILDINGS RESIDENTIAL USES — SAME AS IN R4 ZONE	NONE FOR INDUSTRIAL OR COMMERCIAL BUILDINGS RESIDENTIAL USES — SAME AS IN R4 ZONE			HOSPITALS, HOTELS INSTITUTIONS, AND WITH EVERY BUILDING WHERE LOT ABUTS ALLEY	ONE SPACE FOR EACH 500 SQUARE FEET OF FLOOR AREA IN ALL BUILDINGS ON ANY LOT MUST BE LOCATED WITHIN 750 FEET OF BUILDING	901 / INDIGO BLUE
	MR2	RESTRICTED LIGHT INDUSTRIAL — MR1 USES — ADDITION INDUSTRIAL USES, MORTUARIES, AGRICULTURE						SAME AS R4 FOR DWELLINGS OTHERWISE NONE	50 FEET FOR RESIDENCE USE OTHERWISE NONE	MINIMUM LOADING SPACE 400 SQUARE FEET ADDITIONAL SPACE REQUIRED FOR BUILDINGS CONTAINING MORE THAN 50,000 SQUARE FEET OF FLOOR AREA		906 / COPEN-HAGEN BLUE
	M1	LIMITED INDUSTRIAL — CM USES — LIMITED INDUSTRIAL & MANUFACTURING USES — NO "R" ZONE USES, NO HOSPITALS, SCHOOLS OR CHURCHES	UNLIMITED ✱									904 / LIGHT BLUE
	M2	LIGHT INDUSTRIAL — M1 USES — ADDITIONAL INDUSTRIAL USES, STORAGE YARDS OF ALL KINDS, ANIMAL KEEPING — NO "R" ZONE USES			NONE					NONE REQUIRED FOR APARTMENT BUILDINGS 20 UNITS OR LESS	SEE CODE FOR ASSEMBLY AREAS, HOSPITALS AND CLINICS	902 / ULTRA-MARINE
	M3	HEAVY INDUSTRIAL — M2 USES — ANY INDUSTRIAL USES — NUISANCE TYPE — 500 FT. FROM ANY OTHER ZONE — NO "R" ZONE USES				NONE	NONE	NONE —NOTE— "R" ZONE USES PROHIBITED	NONE			931 / PURPLE
PARKING	**P**	AUTOMOBILE PARKING — SURFACE & UNDERGROUND — PROPERTY IN A "P" ZONE MAY ALSO BE IN AN "A" OR "R" ZONE. PARKING PERMITTED IN LIEU OF AGRICULTURAL OR RESIDENTIAL USES						NONE UNLESS ALSO IN AN "A" OR "R" ZONE	NONE UNLESS ALSO IN AN "A" OR "R" ZONE	—	—	967 / COLD GREY LIGHT
	PB	PARKING BUILDING — AUTOMOBILE PARKING WITHIN OR WITHOUT A BUILDING	✱✱	—	0', 5', OR 10' DEPENDING ON ZONING IN BLOCK AND ACROSS STREET	5' PLUS 1' EACH STORY ABOVE 2nd IF ABUTTING OR ACROSS STREET FROM "A" OR "R" ZONE	5' PLUS 1' EACH STORY ABOVE 2nd IF ABUTTING AN "A" OR "R" ZONE, TO A 15' MAXIMUM	NONE	NONE			936 / SLATE GREY
SPECIAL	**SL**	SUBMERGED LAND ZONE — COMMERCIAL SHIPPING, NAVIGATION, FISHING, RECREATION										919 / SKY BLUE
	(T)	TENTATIVE CLASSIFICATION — USED IN COMBINATION WITH ZONE CHANGE ONLY - DELAYS ISSUANCE OF BUILDING PERMIT UNTIL SUBDIVISION OR PARCEL MAP RECORDED										
	(F)	FUNDED IMPROVEMENT CLASSIFICATION — AN ALTERNATE MEANS OF EFFECTING ZONE CHANGES AND SECURING IMPROVEMENTS (WHEN NO SUBDIVISION OR DEDICATIONS ARE INVOLVED)										
	(Q)	QUALIFIED CLASSIFICATION — USED IN COMBINATION WITH ZONE CHANGES ONLY EXCEPT WITH RA, RE, RS OR R1 ZONES - RESTRICTS USES OF PROPERTY AND ASSURES DEVELOPMENT COMPATIBLE WITH THE SURROUNDING PROPERTY										

SUPPLEMENTAL USE DISTRICTS: G ROCK AND GRAVEL • O OIL DRILLING • S ANIMAL SLAUGHTERING • RPD RESIDENTIAL PLANNED DEVELOPMENT • K HORSE-KEEPING

(ESTABLISHED IN CONJUNCTION WITH ZONES)

HEIGHT DISTRICT		
✱	Nº 1	FLOOR AREA OF MAIN BUILDING MAY NOT EXCEED THREE TIMES THE BUILDING AREA OF THE LOT
	Nº 1L	SAME AS Nº 1 AND MAXIMUM HEIGHT - 6 STORIES OR 75 FT.
	Nº 1-VL	SAME AS Nº 1 AND MAXIMUM HEIGHT - 3 STORIES OR 45 FT.
	Nº 2	FLOOR AREA OF MAIN BUILDING MAY NOT EXCEED SIX TIMES THE BUILDABLE AREA OF THE LOT
	Nº 3	FLOOR AREA OF MAIN BUILDING MAY NOT EXCEED TEN TIMES THE BUILDABLE AREA OF THE LOT
	Nº 4	FLOOR AREA OF MAIN BUILDING MAY NOT EXCEED THIRTEEN TIMES THE BUILDABLE AREA OF THE LOT

MAXIMUM PB ZONE HEIGHTS		
✱✱	Nº 1	2 STORIES AND ROOF
	Nº 2	6 STORIES
	Nº 3	10 STORIES
	Nº 4	13 STORIES

NOTE: ALL INFORMATION GENERAL - FOR SPECIFIC DETAILS CHECK WITH DEPARTMENT OF BUILDING AND SAFETY

SHEET 2 OF 2

PREPARED BY CITY PLANNING DEPARTMENT

R2 - is for *two dwelling* units

R3 - is for *multiple dwellings* depending on square footage and height of apartment buildings, condominiums, etc. **The typical zoning for multiple family residential units is R-3.**

R4 - is for *higher density multiple dwellings with certain square footage*

R5 - *requirements and maximum height allowable* concerning motels, hotels, and high-rise apartments or condominiums.

Zoning restrictions reduce the buildable area by requiring setbacks from the front, back, and sides of the lot lines.

Figure 12-10 is a math problem using setbacks to determine the buildable area of a lot. Remember that all the above explanations are general and may vary. You should investigate any individual symbol for its exact meaning in your city or county before interpreting it.

Title insurance does NOT give protection for zoning changes.

A. ZONING REGULATION (Controls Use)

Zoning is police power that controls only the "use" of the property, NOT ownership.

Most planning commissions, boards, or city councils have an established procedure for a change of zoning. As part of a logical procedure, four steps are usually followed. They are:

1. Giving public notice of any proposed zoning changes.
2. Calling a public hearing where interested people can voice their opinions before any changes are made.
3. Adoption or rejection of a zoning regulation.
4. If rejected, an appeal can be made to the city council, which can overrule the planning commission.

Once zoning regulations are enacted, the objecting parties have the right to appeal to the courts on the basis that the ordinance may be arbitrary or unreasonable. The usual grounds for appeal is equal protection under the ordinance. Zoning ordinances have been held invalid when it was shown that a monopoly would be created, the new ordinance rendered an adjoining lot worthless, or when it prohibited an existing business that did not create a nuisance.

Although the intent of zoning is to create reasonable uniformity, total uniformity is not required. Spot zoning might benefit the public in some cases. *SPOT ZONING is a small area that is zoned differently from the surrounding area.* For example, controlled use of commercial stores and service stations can enhance the value and utility of the residential area.

Figure 12-10

SETBACK PROBLEM
(ZONING REGULATIONS)

BUILDABLE AREA is the maximum allowable area of a lot that a city or county allows for a building after deducting setbacks from the front, back, and sides.

DETERMINING USABLE AREA

Question: What is the buildable space of a lot 150 feet by 50 feet if the city zoning regulation requires deducting a 20-foot setback from the front and deducting 4 feet from each side and the back?

150 Feet x 50 Feet

4-Foot Setback

20-Foot Setback

Buildable Area?

4-Foot Setback

4-Foot Setback

Answer:

Width: 50 feet minus (4 feet on both the left and right side) = ?
50 feet - 8 Feet = **42 feet buildable width**

Length: 150 feet minus (20-foot front setback and a 4-foot rear setback) = ?
150 feet - 24 feet = **126 feet buildable length**

   TOTAL:
   Width X Length = Area
   42 feet X 126 feet = Area
   42 feet X 126 feet = **5,292 square feet**

B. NONCONFORMING USE

As conditions in the area change, the zoning of existing parcels may also change. The change may cause some of the existing structures to become nonconforming. *NONCONFORMING USE is a property that is not used according to the current zoning, but which existed legally before zoning changes were enacted.* An example of nonconforming use is an apartment building with one parking space per unit where zoning changes require two parking spaces per unit. It is a general policy to let nonconforming uses continue for a time if conformity creates unnecessary hardships. However, the growing trend is for cities to charge large fees for nonconforming properties as a source of income.

A "grandfather" clause allows an owner to continue using his or her property in a way prohibited by the new zoning (non-conforming use).

C. VARIANCE (For Private Hardship)

One way to provide reasonable conformity is to allow zoning variances. A *VARIANCE is an exception to the existing zoning regulations in cases of special need for circumstances that might create serious hardship for property owners.* Zoning restrictions such as setbacks may be removed by petitioning for a variance.

Variance is for one lot; re-zoning is for many lots.

For example, if an individual wants to construct a building that does not comply with the local zoning rule, he or she may petition for a variance. When filing this petition, the individual must prove that the construction of the building will not be detrimental to the public. Variances are often granted with special conditions such that both plans and construction be approved and initiated within a specified time.

D. CONDITIONAL USE PERMIT (For Public Benefit)

A *CONDITIONAL USE PERMIT is an exception to the current zoning for the public welfare or benefit.* Variances, on the other hand, are based on hardship.

Since zoning ordinances may be altered, most title insurance policies do not insure against zoning changes. For a small fee, an endorsement may be added to the title insurance policy that covers any losses due to zoning changes. Zoning is an environmental control that attempts to ensure uniform land use while also meeting the occasional special needs of the community.

X. Housing, Building, and Health Laws

The basic control of housing, building, and health standards is held at the state level. Although building codes and health standards are usually enforced by the local county

and city agencies, contractors, factory home builders, and house builders are always regulated at the state level.

Regulatory authority of the housing and construction industry is accomplished by the state contractor's license laws, the local building codes, and the State Housing Law.

A. STATE HOUSING LAW

California has adopted a State Housing Law that sets the minimum construction and occupancy requirements for all apartments, hotels and other dwellings. It should be noted that any city or county may impose more stringent requirements if it so wishes. Construction regulations under this law are handled by local building inspectors. Occupancy and sanitation regulations are enforced by local health officers.

B. LOCAL BUILDING CODES

If there is a building code conflict, the highest construction standard controls.

Most cities and counties have additional, more stringent construction standards than the state. The *BUILDING CODE is the basic minimum construction standard for a structure.* This code includes regulation of all the basic methods, materials, and components of a structure from the foundation to the plumbing and electrical system. Local building inspectors enforce both the state and local building codes.

The local building inspector enforces construction standards (codes).

New construction or building alterations require a building permit. A *BUILDING PERMIT is an approved building application that includes plans, specifications, and a plot plan.* After an examination of the application, plans and any revisions of the plans, the building permit is issued. No construction or alteration can be started until the building permit has been issued.

C. GOVERNMENT FINANCING REQUIREMENTS

To obtain certain forms of government financing toward the purchase of a home, various construction requirements must be met. These **Minimum Property Requirements (MPRs)** are usually more restrictive than state housing or local building codes. This indirect type of regulation must be considered if any FHA, VA, or Cal-Vet financing is needed.

D. FACTORY-BUILT HOUSING LAW

The state has preempted local building codes concerning factory-built housing (prefabricated homes). These are homes that are built in sections in a factory and assembled on site. Each section is checked at the factory by state inspectors. Local inspectors oversee only the site hookup of water lines and other on-site facilities.

1. Manufactured Housing

Real estate licensees can sell a manufactured home that is over one year old, whereas licensed manufactured home dealers can sell new or used manufactured homes.

> **MANUFACTURED HOUSING,** *is a transportable structure in one or more eight-foot (or more) wide by 40-foot (or more) long sections that will cover 320 or more square feet that meets HUD Code Standards.* Built on a permanent chassis, it is designed to be used with or without permanent foundation when connected to the necessary utilities. If sold in California, it must meet the California Department of Housing standards.

Real estate salespeople can also sell, lease, or finance manufactured homes as soon as they have been transformed into real property (wheels removed, placed on a foundation and having a building permit).

Real Estate brokers can sell manufactured homes once they are considered real property. A real estate broker must report all sales of manufactured homes within ten calendar days to the Department of Housing and Community Development (HCD). Registration cards, title, and fees are also sent there.

A new manufactured home dealer must be licensed by the Department of Housing and Community Development (HCD).

New manufactured homes, a growing industry, can only be sold by licensed manufactured home dealers. The **Manufactured Home Purchase Agreement and Joint Escrow Instructions (And Receipt For Deposit)** Form is available from CAR® (**Figure 12-11**).

A licensee must withdraw any advertisement of a manufactured home within 48 hours after notice that it is no longer available for sale.

E. CONTRACTOR'S STATE LICENSE LAW

Contractors are licensed at the state level by the Contractor's State License Board, whose main purpose is to protect the public against incompetent building contractors and subcontractors. This protection is achieved by requiring construction to be done only by licensed persons. This includes subcontract work as well as general and engineering contract work.

The construction field is divided into general engineering, general building and specialty contracting. A license is required to perform work in any of these categories.

Figure 12-11

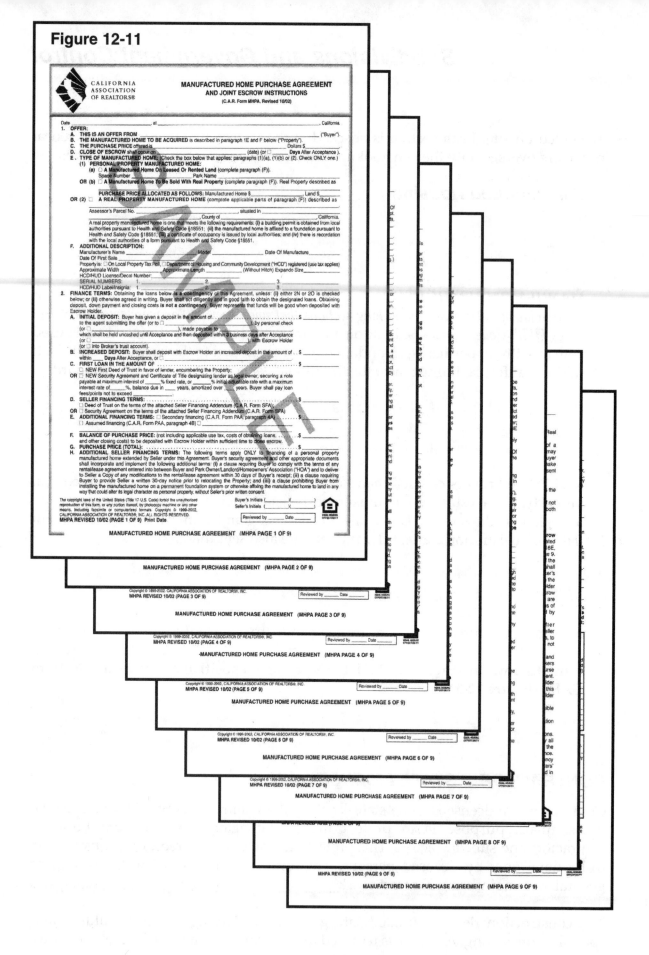

Examinations are prepared on legal matters affecting construction and cost estimation. Each applicant is further required to have a certain amount of actual experience in his or her particular field. Only construction work done on one's own home without intent to sell or lease may be undertaken without a license, but still requires a building permit.

The state housing law, administered by the codes and standards division, is designed to provide that minimum construction and occupancy standards are met.

F. HEALTH AND SANITATION (County Function)

The California State Department of Health regulates a statewide health program. Even though the state regulates it, local health officials are required by law to be appointed in every city or county. These officials enforce either state or local health laws, whichever is stricter. Health inspectors also act as health advisors. They can close down any proposed development that may cause contamination of the water supply or drainage systems, as well as any development that would cause improper sewage disposal. Furthermore, the sanitary condition of all housing is subject to control by the health authorities.

XI. Eminent Domain

A. EMINENT DOMAIN (Involuntary Taking—Condemnation)

INVOLUNTARY CONVERSION is the legal conversion of real property to personal property (money) without the voluntary act of the owner. This occurs when property is taken by eminent domain (condemnation).

Eminent domain is an involuntary conversion process, which means that the owner receives money and is allowed to buy another property, within three years, without incurring taxes.

The owner is allowed to convert back to real property (buy another property) without paying tax on the gain from the condemnation. This must be done within a three-year period and the prices of the old and new property are considered to form a new tax base. (Tax laws are complicated and subject to change, so professional tax advice is always wise.)

EMINENT DOMAIN is the right of the federal or state government to take private property from a landowner (with the fair market value paid as compensation to that owner) for the "public good." The use of the right of eminent domain is often referred to as "condemnation" or "expropriation." In most condemnation cases, the main issue is the amount of just compensation required to be paid to the property owner. If a portion of a parcel is condemned, then there may be severance damages. *SEVERANCE DAMAGE is the compensation paid an owner for "devalued remaining property" as the result of an eminent domain action.*

In some instances, the property owner will feel that the property is so devalued that he or she will file an inverse condemnation action. *INVERSE CONDEMNATION is an action whereby the property owner files suit to force the government to take all of the property, not just a part.*

Eminent domain or condemnation is the process of taking private property for compensation. It is not police power.

Some examples of private property being taken through eminent domain to benefit the general public are: improvement committees (urban renewal), K-12 schools, colleges, and public utilities.

Eminent domain is the power of the government to take private property for public use, by paying the fair market value for it.

B. REDEVELOPMENT (City and County Agencies)

REDEVELOPMENT is the process of purchasing land in a run-down area (blighted) and constructing new buildings, parks, and other new construction. Early efforts at redevelopment were made by organizations such as syndication groups, realty boards, and large insurance companies. However, the difficulty of assembling the necessary parcels by negotiation alone proved to be an impossible task. There was need for a government agency that could exercise its right of eminent domain to bring, by process of law, the court condemnation orders. Redevelopment organizations have been replaced by redevelopment agencies. *REDEVELOPMENT AGENCIES are city or county-run organizations that direct the spending of federal and state money.* The cities or counties have found a new way to rebuild their areas with government money.

C. MUTUAL WATER COMPANY

A *MUTUAL WATER COMPANY is organized by water users in a given district to supply ample water at a reasonable rate.* It is usually a corporation in which the owner of each parcel of land is given a share of stock. The stock is appurtenant to the land; that is, each share of stock is attached to the land and cannot be sold separately. This enables the water company to develop uniformity and prevents speculation in the shares of stock.

Stock in a mutual water company is appurtenant to the land; it is real property.

No cash dividends are declared by these companies, but credits are given to water users if surpluses occur. On the other hand, assessments may be levied if operating revenues are not sufficient. Directors are elected by the stockholders, who usually employ one officer to operate the company, supervise the clerical help, and advise stockholders regarding any water problems.

XII. Fair Housing Laws

California first passed the Unruh Civil Rights Act (no discrimination in business, including real estate agents' services) and then the Rumford Act (no discrimination in housing). These were later reinforced by the Federal Civil Rights Act of 1968.

California was among the first states with fair housing laws. Our first law was the **Unruh Civil Rights Act (no discrimination in business)**, then the **Rumford Act (no discrimination in housing)**, and later these were reinforced with the Federal Civil Rights Act of 1968 (expanded in 1988). **Figure 12-12** describes the different types of civil rights violations.

A. STATE LAW - UNRUH CIVIL RIGHTS ACT
(No Discrimination in Business)

The Unruh Civil Rights Act was the first civil rights act in California; it prohibits "steering" and "block busting" as a real estate business practice.

California first passed the Unruh Civil Rights Act that declares:

"All persons within the jurisdiction of this state are free and equal, and no matter what their race, color, religion, ancestry, or national origin, they are entitled to the full and equal accommodations, advantages, facilities, privileges, or services in all business establishments of every kind whatsoever. . ."

B. STATE LAW - RUMFORD ACT
(California Fair Employment and Housing Act)

The Rumford Act (no discrimination in housing) established the Commission of Fair Employment and Housing to investigate and take action against property owners, financial institutions, and real estate licensees who engage in discriminatory practices.

It clearly defines discrimination as the refusal to sell, rent, or lease housing accommodations, including misrepresentation as to availability, offering inferior terms, and cancellations on the basis of race, color, religion, sex, family status, national origin, ancestry, and age. It also outlaws sale or rental advertisements containing discriminatory information.

Owners of three single-family homes and owner-occupied buildings that are four units or less are exempt from Fair Housing Laws under the "Mom and Pop" provision.

Figure 12-12

FAIR HOUSING VIOLATIONS AND POSSIBLE REMEDIES

REDLINING — The refusal of a loan or insurance based upon a property's location (zip code).

STEERING — Showing a client property in only one type of neighborhood, such as a Caucasian buyer in a Caucasian neighborhood, and the refusal to communicate the availability of housing in other neighborhoods.

OWNER TELLS AGENT NOT TO SHOW PROPERTY TO MINORITY — The agent is relieved of the duty to show the property to anyone, including a minority who has requested to see the property.

CONTRACT REFUSED TO BUYER BECAUSE OF RACE — ADVISE BUYER of the right to complain to the Fair Employment and Housing (FEH) and WARN SELLER that he or she has violated fair housing laws.

RACE RESTRICTIONS — Any race restriction is UNENFORCEABLE. It has NO LEGAL effect upon a transaction.

PANIC SELLING OR BLOCK BUSTING AND PANIC PEDDLING — An agent intentionally incites existing homeowners to sell their properties by saying that property values will fall because persons of a different race or religion have targeted a move into their neighborhood.

SALE OF PROPERTY—AGENT ASKED TO DISCRIMINATE — Agent must REFUSE the listing.

C. STATE LAW - HOLDEN ACT
(Housing Financial Discrimination Act)

The Housing Financial Discrimination Act of 1977 (Holden Act) prohibits financial institutions from engaging in discriminatory loan practices called "redlining."

In remedying such violations, the state may force a landowner to proceed with the rental or sale in question, provide comparable housing accommodations if the original is no longer available or pay punitive damages up to $1,000. Under the **Housing Financial Discrimination Act of 1977 (Holden Act)**, the practice of redlining is specifically outlawed. *REDLINING is the practice by financial institutions of denying loans or varying finance terms based on the location of a given property, regardless of the credit worthiness of the borrower.* This law explicitly forbids discrimination because of the race of the borrower or the racial composition of the neighborhood in which the borrower's prospective home is located.

The Holden Act (no redlining) covers 1-to-4 units (at least one owner-occupied) used for residential purposes, but an owner seeking a home improvement loan need not occupy the property.

A grievance under the Holden Act is directed to the U.S. Department of Business, Transportation, and Housing. Lending institutions in violation of the Holden Act may be required to pay for damages, limited to $1,000 for each offense.

D. FEDERAL LAWS (Federal Civil Rights Act of 1968)

Federal law prohibits discrimination on the part of owners of property and their agents based on the **U.S. Supreme Court case** *Jones v. Mayer* (after the Civil War) and Title VIII of the Civil Rights Act of 1968.

For all practical purposes, discrimination laws evolved from the U.S. Supreme Court Case Jones vs. Mayer, Title VIII of the Civil Rights Act of 1968 and the 13th Amendment to the U.S. Constitution.

At the federal level, the Federal Civil Rights Act of 1968 reinforced the Unruh and Rumford Acts: 1) Any discrimination that the two acts did not prohibit was explicitly outlawed. **THERE ARE NO EXCEPTIONS**; 2) It makes it illegal for real estate licensees to engage in discriminatory practices regardless of any instructions the agent may have received from the seller or landlord. If asked to discriminate in the sale of a property, the salesperson must refuse to accept the listing; 3) It bars real estate boards or multiple listing services from discriminating by denying participation or restricting terms and conditions of membership; 4) It requires a fair housing poster to be displayed at all real estate offices and subdivision model homes. **The poster (Figure 12-13) must also be displayed at all financial institutions or by mortgage lenders who make loans to the general public.**

437

Figure 12-13

Equal Housing Lender

We Do Business In Accordance With The Federal Fair Housing Law

(Title VIII of the Civil Rights Act of 1968, as Amended by the Housing and Community Development Act of 1974)

IT IS ILLEGAL TO DISCRIMINATE AGAINST ANY PERSON BECAUSE OF RACE, RELIGION, CREED, COLOR, NATIONAL ORIGIN, ANCESTRY, PHYSICAL HANDICAP, MEDICAL CONDITION, FAMILIA STATUS, SEX, OR AGE TO:

- ■ Deny a loan for the purpose of purchasing, constructing, improving, repairing or maintaining a dwelling or

- ■ Discriminate in fixing of the amount, interest rate, duration, application procedures or other terms or conditions of such a loan.

IF YOU BELIEVE YOU HAVE BEEN DISCRIMINATED AGAINST, YOU MAY SEND A COMPLAINT TO:

U.S. DEPARTMENT OF HOUSING AND URBAN DEVELOPMENT
Assistant Secretary for Fair Housing and Equal Opportunity Washington, D.C. 20410

or call your local HUD Area or Insuring Office.

The only time an agent can refuse to show a property to a buyer is when the owner's have informed the agent that they will be out of town and, during their absence, the broker has been instructed not to show the property to anyone.

Note – A lender who charges an additional fee per annum for processing loans to non-English speaking applicants because the lender must hire non-English speaking employees, is practicing discrimination.

1. Federal Civil Rights Act Expanded in 1988 (HUD Can Initiate Housing Discrimination Cases)

A 1988 federal law allows the U.S. Government to take court action if it believes discrimination exists in home sales or apartment rentals. Landlords are explicitly forbidden to discriminate against families with children under 18 years of age. The only exemptions from this would be in retirement communities where most of the residents are more than 55 years of age.

This federal law also extends protections to handicapped home buyers or tenants. As of 1991, builders of all new apartment buildings were required to include ground floor rooms suitable for use by residents in wheelchairs.

The Housing and Urban Development (HUD) Department is authorized to bring enforcement action against sellers and landlords who defy this law. Fines of up to $10,000 have been authorized for first time violators, up to $25,000 for a second offense within five years and up to $50,000 for a third offense within seven years. Those accused of violating this tough statute would face an administrative judge unless they specifically requested a jury trial.

Complaints should be filed with Housing and Urban Development (HUD). Fair Employment and Housing will enforce any action.

To sum up: Real estate licensees must not discriminate, and to that end should NOT accept restrictive listings or make, print, or publish any notice, statement or advertisement with respect to a sale or rental of a dwelling that suggests discrimination.

E. THE REAL ESTATE COMMISSIONER AND "NAR" ALSO ENFORCE ANTI-DISCRIMINATION

The Real Estate Commissioner

Regulations of the Real Estate Commissioner

(10177 of the Business and Professions Code)

Regulations have been issued by the real estate commissioner that cover any discrimination with regard to housing. Disciplinary action will be taken against any real estate licensee who violates these regulations. This could include a suspension, fine, revocation of license, or prosecution by the local district attorney. See Chapter 14 for more about the Commissioner's Regulations.

The National Association of Realtors®

Code of Ethics

The National Association of Realtors® (NAR) Code of Ethics and Fair Practices forbids discrimination against any minority group. Any violation by a real estate licensee could subject that licensee to disciplinary action from the local board of Realtors®.

Article 10 states that the Realtor® shall not deny equal service (or be a party to any plan or agreement to deny service) to any person for reasons of race, color, religion, handicap, family status or national origin.

www.realtor.com
National Association of Realtors®

XIII. SUMMARY

There are two basic subdivision laws, including the **Subdivision Map Act** (2 or more lots) which gives cities and counties control over the physical design of a subdivision, and the **Subdivided Lands Law** (5 or more lots) which protects the purchasers of property in new subdivisions from fraud, misrepresentation, or deceit in the marketing of subdivisions.

The subdivided lands law requires a subdivider to give a buyer a copy of the public report disclosing important facts about the subdivision. A **preliminary public report** allows property reservations before the final report is issued, and a **final public report**, which must be kept by the subdivider for a three year period, is the official report that must be given to the buyer. In addition to the public reports an **environmental impact report (EIR)** may be necessary and disclosure of location within a **special studies zone** (earthquake zone).

A **master plan** is a comprehensive guide through which zoning establishes an ideal plan for the city's development in the future. **Zoning** is the city or county's exercise of **police power**, which are rulings made to control the use (not the ownership) of private property for the protection of the public's health, safety, and welfare.

Eminent domain (or **condemnation**) is the right of the government to take private property from a landowner (in exchange for fair market value) for the "public good." If any remaining property is devalued because of the condemnation, the government may pay severance damage. If the property is so devalued that a property owner feels the government should take all of the property, he or she may file an action called **inverse condemnation**.

California was one of the first states with **fair housing laws**. These include the **Unruh Civil Rights Act**, which prohibits steering and blockbusting in real estate, and the **Rumford Act**, which established the **Department of Fair Employment and Housing** to address housing discrimination. In addition, the **Holden Act (Housing Financial Discrimination Act of 1977)** prohibits financial institutions from engaging in discriminatory loan practices called **redlining**.

Federal law also prohibits discrimination on the part of owners of property and their agents based on the Supreme Court Case *Jones vs. Mayer*, **Title VIII of the Civil Rights Act of 1968**, and the **13th Amendment**. In 1988, the Federal Civil Rights Act was in expanded to allow HUD to enforce actions against sellers and landlords who defy the law. The **DRE** and **NAR** also enforce anti-discrimination laws.

XIV. TERMINOLOGY - CHAPTER 12

A. Building Code
B. Building Permit
C. Civil Rights Act of 1968
D. Common Area
E. Community Apartment Project
F. Conditional Use Permit
G. Condominium
H. Eminent Domain
I. Environmental Impact Report

J. Holden Act
K. Jones v. Mayer
L. Land Project
M. Manufactured Homes
N. Master Plan
O. Mutual Water Company
P. Nonconforming Use
Q. Planned Development (PD)
R. Planning Commission
S. Public Report

T. Redevelopment Agency
U. Redlining
V. Rumford Act
W. Severance Damages
X. Spot Zoning
Y. Subdivided Lands Law
Z. Subdivision Map Act
AA. Unruh Act
BB. Variance
CC. Zoning Laws

1.____ A comprehensive zoning plan to help a city grow in an orderly and sound manner, both economically and ecologically.

2.____ A water company in which the owners are the customers.

3.____ A permit given by a local government to construct a building or make improvements.

4.____ A report given to a prospective purchaser(s) in a new subdivision.

5.____ Zoning on a parcel-by-parcel basis, rather than a comprehensive general or master plan. Considered poor planning.

6.____ The outlining in red on a map of certain "high risk" areas where lenders will not extend credit, regardless of the qualifications of the applicants (illegal practice).

7.____ The local government board which must approve proposed building projects according to zones; it must answer to the county board or city council.

8.____ A subdivision where there is private ownership of individual lots as well as common ownership of another lot, usually a swimming pool or a recreation room.

9.____ A report of the probable effect of a development on the ecology of the surrounding area. The report is prepared by an independent company and follows federal, state, or local guidelines.

10.____ An isolated rural subdivision, operating under federal guidelines, with certain rights of rescission.

11.____ Permission to change a portion of zoning requirements without changing the entire zoning.

12.____ Loss in value to the remaining property when part of a parcel is condemned and seized by the government for public use.

13.____ A corporation formed for the purpose of holding title to a building. Each shareholder receives the right to occupy a dwelling unit but must pay property taxes and insurance in common with the other owners.

14.____ The area owned in common by all the owners of condominiums or planned unit developments.

15.____ A property that does not conform to the current zoning of the area. Usually, the property was built in conformity and then the zoning was changed.

16.____ A structure of two or more units, the interior spaces of which are individually owned; the balance of the property is owned in common by the owners of the individual units.

17.____ A comprehensive set of laws that control the construction of buildings, including design, materials used, repair, remodeling, and other similar factors.

18.____ Generally, the improvement of land in accordance with a city renewal project.

19.____ A governmental right to acquire private property for public use by condemnation, and the payment of just compensation.

20.____ Homes that are not truly mobile but are constructed in the same manner as trailers, as opposed to conventional, on-site construction.

21.____ Laws that require cities and counties to specify the uses allowable for real property in different areas or zones.

22.____ An act requiring developers to obtain local government (city or county) approval for the detailed construction plan of their subdivision.

23.____ A specific exception to zoning laws, granted for the general good of the community.

24.____ A law requiring an acknowledgment from the Department of Real Estate that a subdivision has met the minimum requirements for filing the necessary reports.

25.____ Established far-reaching federal anti-discrimination laws. Requires that fair housing posters be displayed at real estate offices and lending institutions.

26.____ Civil War-era court case that was the basis for current civil rights laws.

27.____ State fair housing law established to eliminate redlining.

28.____ Established the California Fair Employment and Housing Act.

29.____ The state fair housing law that disallowed discrimination in business, including real estate agent's services.

XV. MULTIPLE CHOICE

1. The law that permits the local government at the city or county level to enact subdivision ordinances is called the:

    a. State Redevelopment Act.
    b. Subdivision Map Act.
    c. Subdivided Lands Act.
    d. Fair Housing Act.

2. The receipt stating that the buyer has received a copy of any public report must be kept on file by an owner for:

    a. 1 year.
    b. 120 days.
    c. 3 years.
    d. 5 years.

3. Any material change in a subdivision after the public report is issued must be reported to the:

    a. Real Estate Commissioner.
    b. Department of Corporations.
    c. Fair housing Administration.
    d. State Department of Subdivisions.

4. A study of how a subdivision will affect the ecology of a subdivision's surroundings is called a(n):

    a. Coastal Commission Report.
    b. Environmental Impact Report.
    c. Pollution Control Report.
    d. Subdivision Impact Report.

5. Unless provided for in the policy, title insurance will NOT protect against:

    a. recorded liens.
    b. zoning changes.
    c. forgeries.
    d. acts of minors.

6. Real estate brokers CANNOT sell manufactured homes that:

    a. are new.
    b. have been registered for more than one year.
    c. are permanently stationed in a housing park.
    d. have their axles removed.

7. What is eminent domain often referred to as?

    a. Police Power

    b. Condemnation

    c. Spot zoning

    d. Easement appurtenant

8. The Rumford Act established:

    a. the Unruh Civil Rights Act.

    b. the Department of Fair Employment and Housing.

    c. the Housing Financial Discrimination Act.

    d. HUD.

9. Display of the fair housing poster became mandatory under the:

    a. Housing Financial Discrimination Act.

    b. Rumford Act.

    c. Civil Rights Act of 1968.

    d. Garn Act.

10. Which of the following may NOT generally exercise the power of eminent domain?

    a. Improvement committees

    b. Private individuals

    c. Public education institutions

    d. Utility companies

ANSWERS: 1. b; 2. c; 3. a; 4. b; 5. b; 6. a; 7. b; 8. b; 9. c; 10. b

Chapter 13
Taxation of Real Estate

Taxes are an important aspect of all real estate transactions. Property owners are taxed annually on the property they own. In addition, there are other state and federal taxes that must be paid in order to buy, sell, or give away real property. **Figure 13-1** illustrates the five taxes with which every taxpayer, investor, and salesperson should be familiar. The amount of tax and who must pay the tax are often major factors to consider in the transfer of real estate.

I. Property Taxes

A city or county receives most of its operating revenue from the assessment and collection of real property taxes. *REAL PROPERTY TAXES are taxes determined according to the value of the real property, and are paid annually or semi-annually.* These taxes are called ad valorem taxes. An *AD VALOREM TAX is a tax that is charged in proportion to the value of the property.* Property taxes are based on the concept that taxes should be assessed in accordance with a person's ability to pay. In the case of real estate, the higher the value of the property, the higher the property taxes.

"Ad valorem" means taxed "according to value." Real property is reassessed each time it is transferred (sold) at 100% of its selling price (or market value, if it is higher).

Figure 13-1

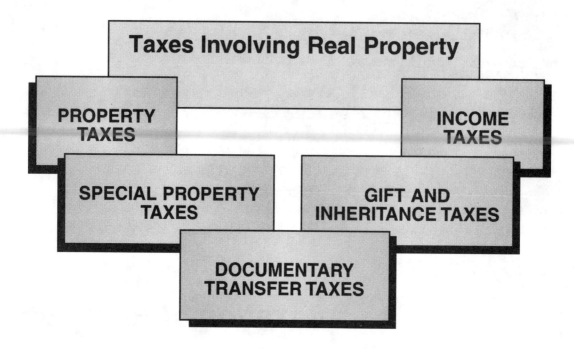

The **COUNTY ASSESSOR** *is the county officer who has the responsibility of determining the assessed valuation of land, improvements, and personal property used in business.* The county assessor determines the value of both county and city properties, except in a few cities that use their own assessors. In Los Angeles County, the City of Pasadena has its own assessor who assesses the property in that city. San Francisco is unique because the city and county are combined, so the city and county assessor's functions are combined.

www.co.la.ca.us/assessor
L. A. County Assessor

In general all real property, except that which is owned by the government, and all tangible personal property except inventory used in a business, is subject to property tax assessment in California. **Intangible personal property, such as shares of stock, goodwill of a business opportunity, and promissory notes, as well as household furnishings and personal effects of individuals, are not assessed or taxed**.

County Assessor assesses; County Tax Collector collects; County Board of Supervisors sets tax rate.

The **COUNTY TAX COLLECTOR** *is the county officer who collects the real property taxes.* He or she only collects taxes; the county tax collector has nothing to do with determining how much tax is levied. If the real property taxes are not paid, the county tax collector will eventually require that the property be sold at a tax sale.

www.cacttc.org/start.html
List of Assessors

A. PROPOSITION 13

PROPOSITION 13 limits the amount of taxes to a maximum of 1%* of the March 1, 1975, market value of the property plus the cumulative increase of 2% in market value each year thereafter. Improvements made after March 1, 1975, are added to the value in the year they are made. If ownership has changed after March 1, 1975, the tax is limited to 1%* of the market value plus the 2% cumulative increase each succeeding year. (In some cases, property values came down, lowering taxes instead of raising them by 2%.) Any state-allowed exemptions are deducted after figuring the basic tax. **See Figure 13-2.**

*Voted indebtedness may increase this rate beyond 1%, from area-to-area, with voter approval.

B. REAL PROPERTY TAX BASE IS TRANSFERABLE (PROPS 60 & 90)

Under the following conditions (based on Propositions 60 and 90), homeowners may be permitted to transfer their current Proposition 13 tax base with them when they buy a new home:

1. Homeowners over the age of 55, and
2. Home purchased within two years of original sale, and
3. Replacement home of equal or lesser value, and
4. New home must be in the same county; or another participating county (check first).

Propositions 60 and 90 allow "empty-nesters" to purchase new homes (one at a time) while holding on to their low tax base, thus freeing up larger multiple bedroom homes for younger families.

ASSESSED VALUATION is set at 100% of the property's selling price or fair market value, whichever is higher, plus a 2% increase for every year the property has been owned, but only as far back as March 1, 1975. The tax rate is set at 1% of fair market value (or selling price, whichever is higher) plus any voter-approved indebtedness. Properties that are transferred and new construction are subject to a new appraisal based upon the current market value or selling price, whichever is higher. Existing structures are given a new assessment each year as of January 1. New construction and transfers are assessed immediately upon the first day of the next month. **See Figures 13-3 and 13-4** for an example of a property tax bill.

C. PROPERTY TAXES BECOME A SPECIFIC LIEN

Property taxes due upon real property are, in effect, liens against that specific property. Business personal property taxes (trade fixtures) also become liens against that specific real property on the same tax bill. For example, the furniture in

Figure 13-2   **PROPOSITION 13**

That Article XII A is added to the Constitution to read:

Section 1.

(a) The maximum amount of any ad valorem tax on real property shall not exceed one percent (1%)* of the full cash value of such property. The one percent (1%)* tax to be collected by the counties and apportioned according to law to the districts within the counties.

(b) The limitation provided for in subdivision (a) shall not apply to ad valorem taxes or special assessments to pay the interest and redemption charges on any indebtedness approved by the voters prior to the time this section becomes effective.

Section 2.

(a) The full cash value means the county assessors valuation of real property as shown on the 1975-76 tax bill under "full cash value," or thereafter, the appraised value of real property when purchased, newly constructed, or a change in ownership has occurred after the 1975 assessment. All real property not already assessed up to the 1975-76 tax levels may be reassessed to reflect that valuation.

(b) The fair market value base may reflect from year to year the inflationary rate not to exceed two percent (2%) for any given year or reduction as shown in the consumer price index or comparable data for the area under taxing jurisdiction.

Section 3.

From and after the effective date of this article, any changes in state taxes enacted for the purpose of increasing revenues collected pursuant thereto whether by increased rates or changes in methods of computation must be imposed by an Act passed by not less than two-thirds of all members elected to each of the two houses of the Legislature, except that no new ad valorem taxes on real property, or sales or transaction taxes on the sales of real property may be imposed.

Section 4.

Cities, counties, and special districts, by a two-thirds vote of the qualified electors of such district, may impose special taxes on such district, except ad valorem taxes on real property or a transaction tax or sales tax on the sale of real property within such city, county, or special district.

Section 5.

This article shall take effect for the tax year beginning on July 1 following the passage of this Amendment, except Section 3 which shall become effective upon the passage of this article.

Section 6.

If any section, part, clause, or phrase hereof is for any reason held to be invalid or unconstitutional, the remaining sections shall not be affected but will remain in full force and effect.

> *Voted indebtedness may increase this rate beyond 1% from local area to area with voter approval.*

Figure 13-3

2003 ANNUAL PROPERTY TAX BILL 2003

CITIES, COUNTY, SCHOOLS AND ALL OTHER TAXING AGENCIES IN LOS ANGELES COUNTY

SECURED PROPERTY TAX FOR FISCAL YEAR JULY 1, 2003 TO JUNE 30, 2004

MARK J. SALADINO, TREASURER AND TAX COLLECTOR

FOR ASSISTANCE CALL (213) 974-2111 OR (888) 807-2111

ASSESSOR'S ID. NO. CK
DETAIL OF TAXES DUE FOR **4225 007 032 03 000** 87

AGENCY	AGENCY PHONE NO.	RATE		AMOUNT
GENERAL TAX LEVY				
ALL AGENCIES		1.000000	$	829.18
VOTED INDEBTEDNESS				
COUNTY		.000992	$	.82
CITY-LOS ANGELES		.050574		41.93
METRO WATER DIST		.006100		5.06
FLOOD CONTROL		.000462		.38
COMMNTY COLLEGE		.019857		16.47
UNIFIED SCHOOLS		.077145		63.97
DIRECT ASSESSMENTS				
CITY LND/LT 96-1	(213) 847-9579		$	14.59
LA STORMWATER	(213) 473-8098			5.03
CITY 911 FUND	(213) 978-1099			7.58
FLOOD CONTROL	(626) 458-3945			6.31
COUNTY PARK DIST	(213) 738-2983			15.03
CITY LT MTC	(213) 847-5507			.69
TRAUMA/EMERG SRV	(866) 587-2862			27.60
LA WEST MOSQ AB	(310) 915-7370			3.97

PROPERTY IDENTIFICATION
ASSESSOR'S ID.NO.: 4225 007 032 03 000
OWNER OF RECORD AS OF JANUARY 1, 2003
SAME AS BELOW

MAILING ADDRESS

Wolfgang Hubie
100 Internet Highway
Culver City, CA 90230

ELECTRONIC FUND TRANSFER (EFT) NUMBER
ID#:19 4225 007 032 7 YEAR:03 SEQUENCE:000 7
PN: 7095
For American Express, Mastercard and Visa payments call (888) 473-0835 and have available the EFT number listed above. Service fees will be charged.
For check payments, please write the EFT number above on your check.

SPECIAL INFORMATION

PROPERTY LOCATION AND/OR PROPERTY DESCRIPTION
100 Internet Highway   Culver City
TRACT NO 31507 CONDOMINIUM   UNIT 2

TOTAL TAXES DUE		**$1,038.61**
FIRST INSTALLMENT TAXES DUE NOV. 1, 2003		**$519.31**
SECOND INSTALLMENT TAXES DUE FEB. 1, 2004		**$519.30**

VALUATION INFORMATION

ROLL YEAR 03-04	CURRENT ASSESSED VALUE	TAXABLE VALUE
LAND	43,828	43,828
IMPROVEMENTS	39,090	39,090

ASSESSOR'S REGIONAL OFFICE
REGION #07 INDEX: TRA:00067
WEST DISTRICT OFFICE
6120 BRISTOL PARKWAY
CULVER CITY CA 90230
(310)665-5300

ACCT. NO.:   PRINT NO.: 565806 BILL ID.:

TOTAL		82,918
LESS EXEMPTION:		
NET TAXABLE VALUE		82,918

THERE WILL BE A $50.00 CHARGE FOR ANY CHECK RETURNED BY THE BANK.
KEEP THIS UPPER PORTION FOR YOUR RECORDS. YOUR CANCELLED CHECK IS YOUR RECEIPT.

furnished apartments is taxed as business personal property and is usually included on the property tax bill.

Property taxes for the following fiscal year become a lien against the real property on January 1 of the current year. Officially, the first installment for half of the taxes

Figure 13-4

DETACH AND MAIL THIS STUB WITH YOUR 2ND INSTALLMENT PAYMENT | ANNUAL | 2003

Wolfgang Hubie
100 Internet Highway
Culver City, CA 90230

ASSESSOR'S ID. NO. CK PK

4225 007 032 03 000 87 2

2ND INSTALLMENT DUE   INDICATE AMOUNT PAID

$519.30

PAYMENT DUE 02/01/04
IF NOT RECEIVED OR POSTMARKED BY 04/10/04
REMIT AMOUNT OF $581.23

MAKE CHECKS PAYABLE TO: LOS ANGELES COUNTY TAX COLLECTOR
P.O. BOX 54018
LOS ANGELES, CA 90054-0018

87846

DO NOT INCLUDE NOTES WITH YOUR PAYMENT
DO NOT STAPLE OR CLIP PAYMENT STUB OR CHECK

0480300074225007032000005193000000581284620412

2ND

DETACH AND MAIL THIS STUB WITH YOUR 1ST INSTALLMENT PAYMENT
IF PAYING BOTH INSTALLMENTS, USE THIS STUB ONLY | ANNUAL | 2003

Wolfgang Hubie
100 Internet Highway
Culver City, CA 90230

ASSESSOR'S ID. NO. CK PK

4225 007 032 03 000 87 1

1ST INSTALLMENT DUE   INDICATE AMOUNT PAID

$519.31

FOR MAILING ADDRESS CHANGE
PLEASE MARK BOX BELOW AND
COMPLETE FORM ON REVERSE SIDE
OF THIS PAYMENT COUPON.

PAYMENT DUE 11/01/03
IF NOT RECEIVED OR POSTMARKED BY 12/10/03
REMIT AMOUNT OF $571.24

MAKE CHECKS PAYABLE TO: LOS ANGELES COUNTY TAX COLLECTOR
P.O. BOX 54018
LOS ANGELES, CA 90054-0018

17859

DO NOT INCLUDE NOTES WITH YOUR PAYMENT
DO NOT STAPLE OR CLIP PAYMENT STUB OR CHECK

0310300074225007032000005193100000571248591210

1ST

---

becomes due on November 1 and is delinquent after 5pm on December 10. The second installment is due on February 1 and is delinquent if not paid by 5pm on April 10. If either December 10 or April 10 falls on a Saturday, Sunday, or legal holiday, the delinquency date is extended to the close of the next business day.

D. PROPERTY TAX TIME TABLE

The city or county fiscal year starts on July 1 and ends on June 30. All revenues and expenditures are planned for this period of time. **Figure 13-5** illustrates all the important dates that are associated with property taxes. Assessable property is evaluated by the assessor on January 1st for the upcoming year in the name of the property's legal owner on that date. Most cities allow the county assessor to evaluate the property in both the county and the incorporated parts of the county, which are

Figure 13-5   PROPERTY TAX TIME TABLE

January 1	July 1	November 1	February 1
Property tax becomes a lien on real property	Fiscal year starts	1st installment is due and delinquent after December 10 at 5:00 P.M.	2nd installment is due and delinquent after April 10 at 5:00 P.M.

the cities. In a few rare cases as stated earlier, cities may use their own assessors. County assessors complete their assessment rolls by July 1, the beginning of the government (fiscal) year.

Important tax dates can be remembered "**N**o **D**arn **F**ooling **A**round" as follows:

N November 1 (first installment)
D December 10 (first installment is delinquent)
F February 1 (second installment)
A April 10 (second installment is delinquent)

The government fiscal tax year is July 1 through June 30.

E. PROPERTY TAX PRORATION PROBLEM

Proration question: Who owes whom how much?

If the seller of the subject property has paid both the 1st and 2nd installments of the property taxes for a total annual bill of $2,760, what is the proration of property taxes for both the seller and buyer if the buyer takes possession on May 1?

Remember: Escrow prorates property taxes using old (seller's) assessed value (tax bill).

The first step is to determine the amount of taxes per month. The annual tax bill of $2,760 is divided by 12 months to determine that the monthly tax is $230. Since the seller paid the property taxes through the month of June (the end of the fiscal tax year, which is July 1 through June 30), and the buyer took possession on May 1, two months of paid property taxes are owed the seller. The buyer would owe the seller

for two months (May and June) that were already paid by the seller. This amount would be $460 (2 x $230).

When a property is sold, the buyer will receive one new property tax bill, but it may be followed by other updated property tax bills referred to as supplemental property tax bills. **See Figure 13-6**.

Figure 13-6

SUPPLEMENTAL PROPERTY TAX BILLS

The law (SB 813) requires reassessment of property **immediately** when it changes ownership or when new construction is completed. While the amount of the supplemental assessment is still determined in accordance with Proposition 13, the actual effect is to "speed up" reassessment of property. In fact, prior to the change in the law, property was generally not reappraised until January 1.

The Office of Assessor enters the new property value onto the assessment roll as of the first of the month following the month in which the property changes ownership or new construction is completed.

Depending upon the date you purchase property or the date construction is completed, you will receive **one or more** supplemental tax bills in addition to your regular tax bill. Taxes on the supplemental tax roll become a lien against the real property on the date of change in ownership or the date new construction is completed.

F. HOMEOWNER'S PROPERTY TAX EXEMPTION

Homeowner's property tax exemption is $7,000 of assessed valuation. NOT the same as a homestead exemption.

The *HOMEOWNER'S PROPERTY TAX EXEMPTION is a deduction on the property tax bill of the first $7,000 of assessed value of an owner-occupied property.*

A homeowner's exemption on your home does the following:

1. All personal property of the homeowner is exempt from property taxes.

2. A resident owner receives a $7,000 homeowner's exemption in assessed value if the property is the principal residence on the 1st of March.

The time to file for the homeowner's exemption is from January 1 to April 15 in order to receive the full exemption. Once the exemption is filed, it remains on the property until the homeowner terminates it. If the exemption is terminated, a new claim form must be obtained from, and filed with, the assessor to regain eligibility.

Qualifying residential property that is owner-occupied receives a $7,000 homeowner's exemption. For example, an assessed value of $300,000 minus the homeowner's exemption of $7,000 is $293,000.

G. HOMEOWNER'S AND RENTER'S PROPERTY TAX REBATE
(Senior Citizens and Disabled Persons)

This is a property tax relief law for any resident who is 62 years of age or older as of January 1, and has a household income of not more than $12,000 for the calendar year. The applicant must have owned and occupied his or her home within the fiscal year. Persons under the age of 62 who are totally disabled also qualify for this rebate. A similar program provides a rebate to elderly and disabled persons who rent their homes or apartments.

All relief is in the form of a property tax rebate granted to the applicant. The amount of the property tax rebate is a percentage of household income on the first $8,500 of assessed valuation. The exact amount of rebate is determined by the Senior Citizen's Property Tax Assistance branch of the State Franchise Tax Board.

Rebate applicants pay property taxes as usual during the year and their application must be filed between May 16 and August 31. The claim form is processed and the rebate checks are sent directly to the applicant. The form may be obtained from the local Franchise Tax Board office.

SENIOR CITIZEN'S PROPERTY TAX ASSISTANCE
P. O. BOX 1588
SACRAMENTO, CALIFORNIA 95807

H. DISABLED AND SENIOR CITIZEN'S PROPERTY TAX POSTPONEMENT

Seniors who are 62 years of age or older and have a household income of $24,000 or less may qualify for this tax postponement assistance program. This program offers them the option of having the state pay all or part of the taxes on their homes. In return, a lien is placed on the property for the amount that the state has to pay. This lien becomes payable when the taxpayer moves or dies. In effect, the homeowner is relieved of his or her tax burden in exchange for a lien his or her home to be paid upon death. California has extended this program to include persons under the age of 62 who are legally disabled. **Further information is available from the State Controller.**

I. VETERAN'S EXEMPTION

Any California resident who served in the military during a time of war is entitled to an annual $4,000 property tax exemption against the assessed value of one property. This exemption also applies to the widow, widowed mother, or pensioned father of a

deceased veteran. However, the exempted property is limited to an assessed value of less than $5,000 for a single veteran or $10,000 if he or she is married. For disabled California veterans who qualify, however, the assessment limit can be raised up to $100,000.

A veteran cannot have a veteran's exemption and a homeowner's property tax exemption on the same property.

J. TAX EXEMPT PROPERTY

In California there are some properties that are partially or totally tax exempt. All real property that is owned by the federal, state, county, or city government is automatically tax exempt. This is a huge benefit to the federal government, as it owns 45% of California land. Eastern states benefit because only about 10% of their land is owned by the federal government. **A lessee with possessory interest in oil and gas rights on government owned property is not exempt from property taxes**.

Since California has many national and state parks, the majority of land in this state is tax exempt. Any property that is used exclusively by non-profit organizations for religious, charitable, medical, or educational purposes is also tax exempt. In addition, 50 percent of all growing crops, young orchard trees, immature timber, and young grapevines are tax exempt.

Property of non-profit organizations used for religious, charitable, medical, or educational purposes is tax exempt.

K. PROPERTY TAX APPEALS

Over-assessments can be taken to the appeals board.

People who feel that the assessment of their property is not correct may appeal the assessment. Appeals would be directed to the Board of Equalization (the property tax assessment appeals board) in the county in which the property is located between July 2 and August 26 (in most counties). After it considers the case, the Board may reduce an assessment, or it may increase it, or it may issue a new assessment if the property has not been assessed before.

In most small and many medium sized counties, the County Board of Supervisors serves as the Board of Equalization. In larger counties with a larger number of properties to assess, a special Tax Appeals Board is usually established. This board has no control over tax rates in general but is the government body that makes individual assessment decisions on individual properties.

If a property owner wishes to protest the real property tax assessment, he or she can do so by contacting the appeals board office for detailed information. This Board of Equalization agency may reduce an assessed value that has been appealed.

L. DELINQUENT TAX SALE (Book Sale)

Each year, on or before June 8, the county tax collector publishes a list of tax delinquent properties. This is his or her "notice of intent to sell" all such properties on which the property taxes have not been paid for one year. *Strictly speaking, this is not a true sale but is a formality called a* **BOOK SALE**, *that starts a five-year redemption period*. If the property is not redeemed within five years, it will be deeded over to the state.

Properties may be redeemed by anyone upon the payment of taxes, interest, costs, and redemption penalties. The tax collector gives a receipt called a "certificate of redemption" as evidence of payment. If the owner cannot pay for all past due taxes and costs at once, he or she may pay them in five annual installment payments, providing all current taxes are paid.

If taxes are NOT paid on or before June 30, the property is sold to the state. This sale starts the running of the redemption period which is five years.

M. SECOND SALE (After Five Years)

After five years, if the property has not been redeemed, the delinquent property is deeded to the state. This is the official sale, and the former owner may now redeem the property only if the state has not sold the property at public auction.

www.sdtreastax.com/taxsalefaqs.html

FREQUENTLY ASKED QUESTIONS   HOME | E-MAIL

COUNTY OF SAN DIEGO TREASURER - TAX COLLECTOR

Quick Links   Go

INFORMATION ON SAN DIEGO COUNTY'S ANNUAL PUBLIC AUCTION (ORAL) TAX SALE

- Where and when will the next Public Auction Tax Sale for San Diego County be held?
- How can I obtain a list of properties to be offered at the next Tax Sale?
- Can I mail in, or submit, a sealed bid for a property in the public auction tax sale?
- Can I obtain a property available at the public auction tax sale by paying the delinquent taxes thereon prior to the tax sale date?
- How do I find or "see" a property I'd like to bid upon at the tax sale?
- How must I pay for a property at the tax sale?
- Can I go to my bank to get to get the cash or certified funds after I'm the successful bidder?
- What are the conditions of payment for property at the tax sale?
- How do I obtain information on Tax Lien Certificate Sales?
- Do liens or encumbrances on tax sale properties transfer to the new owner through a Tax sale property purchase?
- Are Internal Revenue Service liens different from other liens?
- How can I determine what use I can make of a tax sale property before I purchase it?
- How soon can I take possession of a property after my purchase at the tax sale?
- How is the minimum bid on a tax sale property determined?
- Is a tax sale publicly advertised?
- When does the right of redemption on a tax-defaulted parcel subject to the power to sell, cease?
- How will title in the deed to the purchaser be vested?

Although property taxes are NOT paid, an owner can remain in possession and could redeem for 5 years.

N. SALE TO THE PUBLIC

The county tax collector will sell the state-owned properties to other taxing agencies or to the highest bidder at a public tax auction. The minimum bid is established by the tax collector and approved by the county board of supervisors. All such sales are for cash at the time of the sale. The purchaser then receives a tax deed. Most title insurance companies will insure the tax deed sale after one year has elapsed. But, if any difficulties are encountered, the buyer may clear title through a "quiet title" court action.

II. Special Assessment Tax

A **SPECIAL ASSESSMENT TAX** *is levied by a city council or a county board of supervisors, with the voters' approval, for the cost of specific local improvements such as streets, sewers, irrigation, or drainage.* **Assessments differ from property taxes in that property taxes finance the general functions of government and go into the general fund, whereas a special assessment is levied once (usually) by the city, county, or "improvement district" for a particular work or improvement.**

The official body that levies a special assessment is called a **SPECIAL ASSESSMENT DISTRICT BOARD.** According to state law, any self-governing area such as a city or county may establish a special assessment district for the purpose of levying a special assessment.

As a rule, a district issues its own bonds to finance particular improvements such as water distribution systems, parking facilities, street lighting, and many other types of developments. To repay the funds borrowed through the bonds issued, these districts have the power to assess all lands included in the district on an ad valorem basis. Such loans constitute liens on the land until paid. These liens can be foreclosed by sale similar to a tax sale and have priority over private property interests.

Special assessments are for improvements only. If you purchase a lot for $40,000 and assume a $1,200 assessment bond, your cost basis for income tax purposes would be $41,200.

A. IMPROVEMENT BOND ACT OF 1915

The **IMPROVEMENT BOND ACT OF 1915** *finances street and highway improvements through an assessment to property owners based upon the frontage they enjoy facing the improved street.* It allows property owners, through the issuance of municipal bonds, up to 30 years to pay off their portion of the improvement assessment. The seller and the broker must give the buyer a disclosure notice of assessment amount and the amount applicable to the property.

B. THE MELLO-ROOS COMMUNITY FACILITIES ACT

The Mello-Roos Community Facilities Act is another type of improvement bond. **Figure 13-7** explains Mello-Roos in detail.

III. Documentary Transfer Tax

$.55 per $500 is paid only on the new amount of money (cash down and new financing), not on any assumed financing.

The **DOCUMENTARY TRANSFER TAX** *is a tax that is applied to the consideration paid or money borrowed when transferring property, except for any remaining loans or liens on the property.* This tax is computed at the rate of 55 cents for each $500 or $1.10 per $1,000 of consideration or any fraction thereof that exceeds $100. The consideration is any amount of cash payment plus any new loans. However, this tax does not apply to any liens or encumbrances that remain on the property as part of the transfer. If a house were sold for $230,000 and a buyer assumed the old loan of $30,000, the documentary transfer tax would be $220.

$$\frac{\$200,000}{\$500} \times \$.55 = \$220$$

The documentary transfer tax is charged to the seller and is handled as part of the escrow. According to state law the county is allowed to charge this tax. However, a city within a county can charge that county for one-half of this tax. Therefore, in most cities, the county collects the documentary transfer tax and gives half of it to the city. Based on the information found at the county recorder's office, the documentary transfer tax can be used to determine a previous sale price of a property. Simply divide 55 cents into the amount of the documentary transfer tax and multiply by $500. If any loans have been assumed by the new owner, also add that amount to arrive at the total prior sale price of the property.

If any old loans or liens are to remain on the property, this fact must be stated on the deed or on a separate paper filed with the deed. Then add the value of the cash down payment and any new loans together with any remaining loan on the property to find the total selling price.

— CITY TRANSFER TAXES —

The city of Los Angeles initiated a transfer tax to be paid by sellers when a property is sold. The current charge is $4.50 per $1,000 of selling price.

— WATCH FOR A VERSION OF THIS TAX IN YOUR CITY —

Figure 13-7

Mello-Roos Liens
DISCLOSURE REQUIRED

Failure to disclose allows buyer a 3-day right of rescission, and results in agent disciplinary action.

MELLO-ROOS LIENS are municipal bonds issued to fund streets, sewers, and other infrastructure needs before a housing development is built. This financial device allows developers to raise money to complete off-site improvements in a house or condo subdivision. The developer is usually responsible for making payments on the bond until the home is sold. The homeowner then becomes responsible for payment via a special tax.

The Mello-Roos Community Facilities Act is a way that a city or governmental district can skirt the property tax limitations of Proposition 13. The city can include the cost and maintenance of infrastructure items in the property tax bill as a special tax, which is allowed to go above the limits of Proposition 13.

This has been a boon for developers who need help financing their projects and for municipalities anxious to upgrade new developments under the restrictions of Proposition 13. The downside is that if something goes wrong with the economy or the project, the municipality may have to foreclose on the developer.

The primary responsibility for disclosure of any Mello-Roos bonds lies with the seller.

A broker must disclose to property buyers that a project is subject to a Mello-Roos special tax levy. If the agent fails to provide this disclosure, he or she is subject to discipline by the Real Estate Commissioner. A disclosure notice of the amount assessed and the amount of special tax applicable to the property is required on the sale or lease (for more than five years) of property subject to this lien. Failure to give notice before signing the sales contract permits the buyer or tenant a three-day right of rescission after receipt of the notice.

Warning: Whereas property taxes are totally deductible from state and federal income taxes, Mello-Roos taxes may only be partially deductible depending upon whether they are for maintenance or improvements. Consult with your C.P.A. before claiming such a deduction.

IV. Gift and Estate Taxes

For federal purposes, the transfer of property by a gift or inheritance is taxed. Exemptions may reduce the taxes and sometimes eliminate them. **Figure 13-8** illustrates the federal taxes encountered by transferring property as a gift or by inheritance.

A gift of real estate may avoid federal estate taxes. So if a person wants to give a property away, it will most likely escape (the future) federal estate taxes. But, if you are to avoid federal gift taxes, usually only a fractional interest in the property should be given away each year. For example, you could give a son and daughter each a 1/30 interest in your home every year for 15 years to give the house to your children.

Figure 13-8

A. FEDERAL GIFT TAXES

Estate taxes and income taxes on appreciated property may be avoided by giving it away or by donating it to a non-profit organization; see a CPA or tax expert for advice.

Frequently, as an individual family matures, the value of the real property owned by the family increases, and the owning family may consider bestowing it as a gift. When a family gives property, whether real or personal, to another individual, there may be federal gift taxes that must be paid. If the value of the property is higher than an exempt amount, the donor must pay a gift tax. A **DONOR** *is the person or persons giving the property as a gift. Generally, people give their property away to relatives on a systematic basis so that taxes are avoided.* The **DONEE** *is the person or persons who receive the property as a gift.* The federal gift tax law also provides for a $11,000 annual exemption per donee.

B. FEDERAL ESTATE TAX

A **FEDERAL ESTATE TAX** *return must be filed for the estate of every resident of the United States whose gross estate exceeds $1,000,000 ($1,500,000 in 2004, $2,000,000 in 2006) in*

value at the date of death. Estate tax exemptions will gradually increase the size of estates that are exempt from $1,000,000 to being repealed in 2010. However, the estate tax can be restored in 2011.

C. NO STATE GIFT AND INHERITANCE TAXES

California State Inheritance Tax
  None (Repealed June 8, 1982)

California State Gift Tax
  None (Repealed June 8, 1982)

V. Federal, State, and Local Income Taxes

The annual Federal Income Tax Form 1040 (**See Figure 13-9**) and the State Income Tax Form 540 are bookkeeping or accounting summaries of the prior year's financial facts. These facts are a history and cannot be altered at the time of filing the income tax return.

www.irs.ustreas.gov
Internal Revenue Service (IRS)
www.ftb.ca.gov
Franchise Tax Board (FTB)

California has both state and federal income taxes. (**See Figure 13-10**). That's right! California residents pay both income taxes, which ranks us among the most taxed people in the United States. It is no wonder that Californians are very interested in understanding the effects of income taxes on both their personal residence and income-producing property.

Tax matters should be considered prior to buying and continued during ownership until the estate's ultimate disposition.

We will discuss only the most basic concepts of reducing the income tax bite for the average citizen. A basic knowledge of the requirements necessary to take advantage of federal and state income tax incentives is helpful. Arranging the purchase of real estate in a manner that reduces your personal income taxes is the purpose of tax planning. This may allow you to reduce the income taxes you pay, or at least postpone such taxes.

Tax shelters are the reduction in income taxes. Now is the time to start tax planning for your future income tax returns.

Figure 13-11 shows the five main areas of the federal and state income tax laws that are incentives to owning real estate. Each area will be explained only to give the general concepts or ideas behind the laws. To obtain the exact meaning and clauses of the law,

Figure 13-9

Form **1040** Department of the Treasury—Internal Revenue Service **20XX**

U.S. Individual Income Tax Return IRS Use Only—Do not write or staple in this space.

For the year Jan. 1–Dec. 31, 1992, or other tax year beginning , 1992, ending , 19 | OMB No. 1545-0074

Label

(See instructions on page 10.)

Use the IRS label. Otherwise, please print or type.

L A B E L H E R E

Your first name and initial — Last name — Your social security number

If a joint return, spouse's first name and initial — Last name — Spouse's social security number

Home address (number and street). If you have a P.O. box, see page 10. — Apt. no.

City, town or post office, state, and ZIP code. If you have a foreign address, see page 10.

For Privacy Act and Paperwork Reduction Act Notice, see page 4.

Presidential Election Campaign (See page 10.)

Do you want $1 to go to this fund? . . . . Yes | No

If a joint return, does your spouse want $1 to go to this fund? . Yes | No

Note: Checking "Yes" will not change your tax or reduce your refund.

Filing Status

(See page 10.)

Check only one box.

1 Single

2 Married filing joint return (even if only one had income)

3 Married filing separate return. Enter spouse's social security no. above and full name here. ▶

4 Head of household (with qualifying person). (See page 11.) If the qualifying person is a child but not your dependent, enter this child's name here. ▶

5 Qualifying widow(er) with dependent child (year spouse died ▶ 19). (See page 11.)

Exemptions

(See page 11.)

6a ☐ **Yourself.** If your parent (or someone else) can claim you as a dependent on his or her tax return, **do not** check box 6a. But be sure to check the box on line 33b on page 2

b ☐ Spouse

c Dependents:

(1) Name (first, initial, and last name)	(2) Check if under age 1	(3) If age 1 or older, dependent's social security number	(4) Dependent's relationship to you	(5) No. of months lived in your home in 1992

If more than six dependents, see page 12.

No. of boxes checked on 6a and 6b ___

No. of your children on 6c who:
- lived with you ___
- didn't live with you due to divorce or separation (see page 13) ___

No. of other dependents on 6c ___

d If your child didn't live with you but is claimed as your dependent under a pre-1985 agreement, check here ▶ ☐

Add numbers entered on lines above ▶

e Total number of exemptions claimed

Income

Attach Copy B of your Forms W-2, W-2G, and 1099-R here.

If you did not get a W-2, see page 9.

Attach check or money order on top of any Forms W-2, W-2G, or 1099-R.

7 Wages, salaries, tips, etc. Attach Form(s) W-2 . . . . . . | 7

8a Taxable interest income. Attach Schedule B if over $400 . . . . | 8a

b Tax-exempt interest income (see page 15). DON'T include on line 8a | 8b |

9 Dividend income. Attach Schedule B if over $400 . . . . . . | 9

10 Taxable refunds, credits, or offsets of state and local income taxes from worksheet on page 16 | 10

11 Alimony received . . . . | 11

12 Business income or (loss). Attach Schedule C or C-EZ . . . . | 12

13 Capital gain or (loss). Attach Schedule D . . . . | 13

14 Capital gain distributions not reported on line 13 (see page 15) . | 14

15 Other gains or (losses). Attach Form 4797 . . . . | 15

16a Total IRA distributions . | 16a | b Taxable amount (see page 16) | 16b

17a Total pensions and annuities | 17a | b Taxable amount (see page 16) | 17b

18 Rents, royalties, partnerships, estates, trusts, etc. Attach Schedule E | 18

19 Farm income or (loss). Attach Schedule F . . . . | 19

20 Unemployment compensation (see page 17) . . . . . . | 20

21a Social security benefits | 21a | b Taxable amount (see page 17) | 21b

22 Other income. List type and amount—see page 18 . . . . . . | 22

23 Add the amounts in the far right column for lines 7 through 22. This is your **total income** ▶ | 23

Adjustments to Income

(See page 18.)

24a Your IRA deduction from applicable worksheet on page 19 or 20 | 24a

b Spouse's IRA deduction from applicable worksheet on page 19 or 20 | 24b

25 One-half of self-employment tax (see page 20) . . . | 25

26 Self-employed health insurance deduction (see page 20) | 26

27 Keogh retirement plan and self-employed SEP deduction | 27

28 Penalty on early withdrawal of savings . . . . . . | 28

29 Alimony paid. Recipient's SSN ▶ | 29

30 Add lines 24a through 29. These are your **total adjustments** . . . . . ▶ | 30

Adjusted Gross Income

31 Subtract line 30 from line 23. This is your **adjusted gross income.** *If this amount is less than $22,370 and a child lived with you, see page EIC-1 to find out if you can claim the "Earned Income Credit" on line 56* . . . . . ▶ | 31

Cat. No. 11320B

Form **1040**

Figure 13-10

CALIFORNIA vs. FEDERAL INCOME TAX:
Emphasis is on the Federal

California state income tax laws tend to conform with federal laws in most respects. There are, however, several important income tax exceptions listed below:

1. State does not tax Social Security benefits.
2. State has no capital gains rates; just ordinary income rates.
3. State does not allow tax breaks for IRA plans (simple).
4. State does not tax lottery winnings.

The state taxes at a lower rate (a maximum of 9.3 percent) but tends to be more restrictive on deductions. State taxes paid are themselves deductible from the federal return.

Most state and local tax laws are considered by many insiders to be antiquated. Tax reform on these levels has become a much slower process than that by the federal government. Focus is on the federal government which taxes at higher rates and sets the tone for state and local taxes. For more detailed information on preparing personal income taxes, a tax attorney or CPA should be consulted.

Figure 13-11

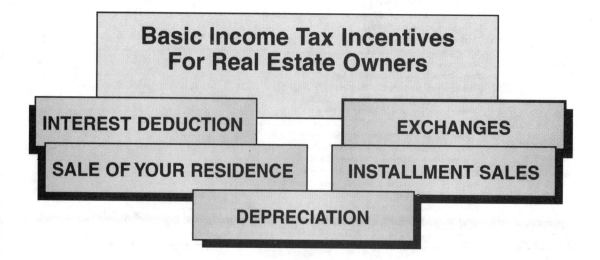

Basic Income Tax Incentives For Real Estate Owners

INTEREST DEDUCTION

EXCHANGES

SALE OF YOUR RESIDENCE

INSTALLMENT SALES

DEPRECIATION

an owner or investor should seek the help of a Certified Public Accountant for advice on the accounting, or an attorney who is familiar with tax problems. Remember, these are only generalizations, and our income tax laws are more complex than the basic concepts presented here.

VI. Taxes on Personal Residence

Homeowners can annually deduct these three items from their income taxes based on their personal residence:

1. Mortgage Interest on Loan (Trust Deeds)
2. Property Taxes
3. Prepayment Penalties

By the way, you cannot deduct the cost of personal residence repairs from your federal taxes, except for uninsured casual losses. For example, if your roof blows off and you have no insurance to cover it, the replacement cost can be deducted from your federal income taxes.

A. DEDUCTION OF INTEREST

Deduction of interest on your home loan from your income taxes is one of the major tax advantages of owning real estate. Buying a first and second home provides the average family with the biggest buffer against income taxes that it is likely to enjoy. Despite recent income tax reforms, the federal tax laws still provide incentives to those who purchase a first and even a second home. When buying these homes you may finance up to $1 million ($1,000,000) with all the interest paid out during the year fully tax deductible. An additional deduction is available on the interest from home equity loans, taken for any purpose, even buying a second home, of up to $100,000 in principal. The $1,000,000 and $100,000 debit limit is a total applied against both first and second homes together or one owner-occupied home taken separately.

B. DEDUCTION OF PROPERTY TAXES

Property taxes on your 1st and 2nd homes are deductible from your income taxes. This makes us feel better about paying local property taxes.

C. DEDUCTION OF PREPAYMENT PENALTIES

Prepayment penalties are also deductible from your income taxes. If you pay off or drastically reduce your home loan balance, there may be a prepayment penalty.

Interest, property taxes, and prepayment penalties paid on your personal residence can be deducted from your income taxes.

D. SALE OF YOUR RESIDENCE

When selling a personal residence, the seller can deduct up to $250,000 ($500,000 if married) of any financial gain (profit) for each spouse. This could be used only once every two years.

Federal income tax laws allow a taxpayer to exclude up to $250,000 of gain for each individual ($500,000 if married and on the title). This benefit may only be used once every two years for a residence.

While the law allows this deduction once every two years, you must reside in the home for two out of the last five years to qualify. In other words, if you live in the home for a year, then rent it out for four years, you would have to move back in for another year in order to take advantage of this tax break.

You can deduct a loss on sale of a personal residence if you have turned it into income producing property by renting it.

The only way to deduct a loss on a personal residence is to turn that property into income-producing property first by renting it. Then any loss based on its sale is deductible because it is income-producing property, not a personal residence.

VII. Taxes for Income Producing Properties

Investors of income producing properties can annually deduct these items from their income taxes:

1. Mortgage Interest on Loans (no maximum)
2. Property Taxes
3. Prepayment Penalties

In addition they can deduct:

4. Operating Expenses
5. Depreciation of Improvements

In addition to deducting mortgage interest (no maximum), property taxes, and prepayment penalties, income property owners can deduct operating expenses and depreciation. Owners CANNOT deduct losses due to vacancies.

A. DEPRECIATION OF BUSINESS PROPERTY (Federal and State)

DEPRECIATION FOR TAX PURPOSES is a yearly tax deduction for wear, tear, and obsolescence on investment property that is deducted from the taxpayer's income on his or her income tax form. This deduction applies only to investment property or property used in a business, not on a taxpayer's personal residence. Apartment buildings, commercial buildings, and any building improvements to investment property can be depreciated. The land itself cannot be depreciated.

Only the buildings and other improvements on income, trade, or business property can be depreciated, NOT the land.

One can only depreciate property that is improved. Since land cannot be depreciated, only the improvements can be depreciated. Currently, the straight-line method is the accepted way to depreciate buildings and other improvements.

Residential (homes and apartments) property depreciation schedule:
   Minimum 27.5 years (Straight-line)

Commercial improvements depreciation schedule:
   Minimum 39 years (Straight-line).

The amount of depreciation must be spread uniformly over the useful life of the property, with the same amount deducted each year (straight-line depreciation). Since most buildings in these inflationary times actually increase in value, depreciation is usually just a technique for postponing income taxes until the property is sold.

> **Example:** If you own a cabin in the desert that you rent to vacationers and the cabin cost $100,000 and the land value is $25,000, this leaves improvements of $75,000. Divide this $75,000 by 30 years giving you a depreciation of $2,500 for each year of the 30 years. If we had used a 27.5 year formula, the yearly depreciation amount would be slightly higher.

Remember: A property owner can deduct depreciation on income, trade, or business real property, NOT on a residence.

B. ADVANTAGES OF "SALE-LEASEBACK"
(Buyer Gets to Depreciate New Building Cost)

If the owner of a business sells her building for cash, and then leases it back, the seller becomes a lessee and the buyer the lessor.

The advantage to the seller: all lease payments can be deducted from income taxes and he or she receives cash for the building.

The advantage to the buyer: he or she can use the purchase price as the new basis for depreciation and establish a new depreciation schedule.

Seller, now renter, deducts 100% of future rents paid. Buyer can depreciate new cost of buildings (even if they have been depreciated previously).

VIII. Sale of Real Property

A. CAPITAL ASSETS (Gains and Losses)

In real estate a capital asset includes your personal residence (including your second home) and any other real estate because they are long-term investments. When you sell your home or other real estate, there is either a capital gain or loss. **CAPITAL GAINS** *are taxed at a lower rate than is ordinary income*, but **CAPITAL LOSSES** *can be deducted from capital gains*. A capital gain is taxed at a lower rate than is ordinary income. It is in the public interest to foster investment in land and buildings and other long-term assets so that businesses are encouraged to expand. This in turn creates more job opportunities for everyone.

Congress and the President, the same group that promised tax simplification, has established four capital gains tax rates as follows:

20% maximum capital gains tax rate if held for more than 18 months
15% maximum capital gains tax rate if held for more than 7 years
10% capital gains tax rate if net income is less than $50,000
5% capital gains tax rate (over 7 years) if net income is less than $50,000

Gains are taxed at the lower capital gains tax rates (lower than ordinary income tax rates).

There should be a tax benefit to encourage entrepreneurs to risk investing long-term in things such as equipment, stocks, bonds, and real estate in order to obtain capital gains or losses. Other countries, like Japan and Germany, have very low capital gain tax rates which encourage investment in companies so that more career opportunities are generated for their employees. The size of the nation's "economic pie," which everyone enjoys, increases.

B. FEDERAL INCOME TAX RATES

As the old saying goes, "Nothing in life is certain, except death and taxes." One other certainty is the constant change in federal tax rates. Income tax rates are progressive. **PROGRESSIVE TAXES** *are taxes where the rates (percentage paid) increase as the amount to be taxed increases.* So as you make more money, not only does the amount increase, but the rate at which income is taxed also increases. The end effect is that higher income families (the exact ones who usually own businesses and can expand job opportunities) pay most of the income taxes.

MARGINAL TAX RATE is the rate that the next dollar earned puts you into.

REGRESSIVE TAXES use the same rate no matter how much is spent or earned. Sale tax is an example of a regressive tax. The rate is the same, so in effect the poor pay a higher percent of their income.

Income tax rates are progressive. Sale taxes are regressive.

C. ACCOUNTING FOR THE SALE OF REAL ESTATE

The method of determining a profit or loss on the sale of real property is spelled out by the Internal Revenue Service. Steps 1 and 2 must be completed before determining the profit or loss on a sale (Step 3).

"Adjusted cost basis" is the base cost, plus capital improvements, minus depreciation and sale expenses. A broker's commission is an expense of the sale.

(1) Cost Basis (Purchase price)	**$500,000**
+ Improvements	**200,000**
$700,000	
- Depreciation (tax records)	**30,200**
= Adjusted Cost Basis	**$669,800**
(2) Sale price	**$1,000,000**
- Sale Expenses	**32,500**
= Adjusted Sale Price	**$967,500**
(3) Adjusted Sale Price	**$967,500**
- Adjusted Cost Basis	**669,800**
= Gain	**$297,700**

IX. Installment Sales and Exchanges

A. INSTALLMENT SALES OF REAL ESTATE

An **INSTALLMENT SALE** *is the sale of real estate in which the payments for the property extend over more than one calendar year.* Installment sales are used to spread a gain over two or more calendar years so that the entire gain is not taxed all in the first year. Our income tax system has progressive rates, which means that the higher the income, the higher the income tax rate for that year. If a person can spread a gain over more than one calendar year, the same income may be taxed at a lower rate.

By doing this the seller avoids the disadvantages of paying for his or her entire gain in one year and thereby has a substantial savings on his or her income taxes. This method is usually used when selling large tracts of land held for a period of time or large buildings owned by one individual.

Installment sales are used because a gain is only taxed in the year that it is received. Spreading the gain over several years may drop you into a lower tax bracket (marginal tax rate).

A sale of a large lot for $100,000 all at once might force you into a higher tax rate. So by having an installment sale of $25,000 for each of the next four years, you may substantially reduce the total income taxes paid. An installment sale may be a good way to defer income taxes if your income varies from year-to-year; just arrange to get larger installment payments in years when your ordinary income is low.

B. EXCHANGES TAX-DEFERRED (Federal and State) (Section 1031 of the I.R.S. Code)

In an exchange, the adjusted cost basis of the old property becomes the basis of the new property.

An **EXCHANGE** *is a transfer of real estate where one party trades property for another's property.* The property must be of "like kind" in nature or character, not in use, quality, or grade. The exchange may be a straight trade (tax-free) or one party may receive cash in addition to the property (partially tax-free). An exchange can be income tax free, partially taxed, or fully taxed, depending on the cost factors in each particular exchange. Exchanges are too detailed to explain here, but it is a way of deferring or possibly eliminating income taxes on the transfer of real estate.

To defer all current taxes, a party in an exchange would need to receive a more valuable building with a larger loan on it than the current property and pay compensation to the other party for any difference in the equities. *Any net cash or net mortgage relief that a participant in an exchange might receive in addition to the actual property is known as BOOT.* All boot is taxable to the extent of the gain in this partially tax-free exchange. **See Figure 13-12**.

"Boot" is cash or debt relief. Receiver has recognized gain. If there is NO boot in an exchange, the old basis is the new basis.

Exchanges are popular among apartment owners and commercial property investors. This is because these owners are usually in high-income tax bracket, and exchanging enables them to move up to a more valuable property without paying taxes on the gain. People in higher income tax brackets usually keep their money invested in real estate, and they find exchanges to be a way of selling and buying simultaneously.

Figure 13-12

Tax Deferred Exchanges

Boot is defined as cash or mortgage relief.

In a tax-free exchange, boot is defined as cash or mortgage relief given in addition to the property. Boot is the amount received to balance the equities in the exchange. Brokers often encounter the term "boot" when talking with a client about income taxes.

The person receiving boot has a net gain and has to pay taxes on it. When no boot is given or received, then the basis remains the same.

In a tax free exchange, properties must be of a "like kind" in nature or character, not in use, quality or grade. "Tax free" merely means to DEFER the payment of taxes until a later time. Since you can move your equity to another property, it is almost like buying and selling without paying income taxes.

The actual techniques used to understand exchanging are too complex to be explained here, but many six-hour seminars and exchange clubs are available to interested people.

X. We Are Now Tax Collectors (Federal and State Income Tax Laws— Escrow Usually Takes Care of This)

A. FEDERAL TAX COLLECTION REQUIREMENTS AND EXEMPTIONS (If a Foreigner)

Persons buying property from foreign investors (sellers) are required to set aside 10% of the purchase price for the Internal Revenue Service. This 10% withholding is kept by the IRS to ensure that property capital gains taxes are paid on the transaction. Both the buyer and broker share liability. If this amount is not withheld, the broker may be liable for the full amount of the tax not paid.

In effect, this law holds brokers responsible to check the citizenship of all sellers and see to it that the buyer retains either a 10% deposit, an affidavit from the seller stating that he or she is not a foreigner, or a waiver from the IRS. Residential property purchased for under $300,000 to be used as the buyer's residence is exempted from this withholding. The key points for licensees to remember are these:

1. **Inquire** into the citizenship of all sellers of residential or commercial properties priced at $300,000 or more, even if a foreigner holds only partial or syndicate interest.

2. **Require** a statement of citizenship as part of the listing agreement and then follow up in escrow by having the seller or sellers sign a sworn affidavit.

3. **Do not discriminate.** Require this information of all sellers in transactions of $300,000 or more. Even if someone does not appear to be an alien, they might hold foreign citizenship.

The CAR® Seller's Affidavit of Nonforeign Status and/or California Residency Form is a form for the seller to sign (**Figure 13-13**) swearing that he or she is not a nonresident alien. If the seller completes the lower portion of this sworn statement, the buyer and broker may no longer be liable for any portions of unpaid taxes.

Figure 13-14 shows a Buyer's Affidavit Form available from CAR. This form states that the sales price is less than $300,000 and that the property will be used as a residence. It is signed by the buyer under penalty of perjury. If these two considerations can be met, the buyer is immediately exempted from the withholding requirement. If neither of these forms can truthfully be completed, then the broker should see to it that 10% of the sales price is withheld in escrow or that the proper waiver is obtained from the IRS. The escrow officer will help you with this matter.

B. STATE TAX COLLECTION REQUIREMENTS AND EXEMPTIONS (If a Foreigner or Resident of Another State)

Persons buying property from foreign or out-of-state investors may be required to set aside 3.3% of the sales price for the Franchise Tax Board. If this amount is not withheld, the broker and buyer may be liable for the full amount of income taxes not paid. Escrow usually handles this, but the buyer and broker are responsible.

The exemptions from the buyer withholding 3.3% of the sales price for the Franchise Tax Board are:

1. Sales price is $100,000 or less.
2. Property is seller's principle residence, under certain conditions.
3. Seller signs California Residency Declaration.
4. Seller receives a waiver—Franchise Tax Board Form 567A.

Both of these laws put the burden on the buyer, NOT the seller. Escrow officers will help with these requirements. Buyer and broker must retain the documentation for 5 years.

Figure 13-13

CALIFORNIA
ASSOCIATION
OF REALTORS®

SELLER'S AFFIDAVIT OF NONFOREIGN STATUS AND/OR CALIFORNIA WITHHOLDING EXEMPTION
FOREIGN INVESTMENT IN REAL PROPERTY TAX ACT (FIRPTA) AND CALIFORNIA WITHHOLDING LAW
(Use a separate form for each Transferor)
(C.A.R. Form AS, Revised 1/03)

USE ONLY FOR ESCROWS CLOSING ON OR AFTER JANUARY 1, 2003

Internal Revenue Code ("IRC") Section 1445 provides that a transferee of a U.S. real property interest must withhold tax if the transferor is a "foreign person." California Revenue and Taxation Code Section 18662 provides that a transferee of a California real property interest must withhold tax if the transferor: **(i)** is an individual (unless certain exemptions apply); or **(ii)** is any entity other than an individual ("Entity") if the transferor's proceeds will be disbursed to a financial intermediary of the transferor, or to the transferor with a last known street address outside of California. California Revenue and Taxation Code Section 18662 includes additional provisions for corporations.

I understand that this affidavit may be disclosed to the Internal Revenue Service and to the California Franchise Tax Board by the transferee, and that any false statement I have made herein (if an Entity Transferor, on behalf of the Transferor) may result in a fine, imprisonment or both.

1. **PROPERTY ADDRESS** (the address of the property being transferred): _____
   _____

2. **TRANSFEROR'S INFORMATION:**
   Full Name _____
   Telephone No. _____
   Address _____
   (Use HOME address for individual transferors. Use OFFICE address for Entities: corporations, partnerships, limited liability companies, trusts and estates.)
   Social Security No., Federal Employer Identification No., or California Corporation No. _____

3. **AUTHORITY TO SIGN:** If this document is signed on behalf of an Entity Transferor, THE UNDERSIGNED INDIVIDUAL DECLARES THAT HE/SHE HAS AUTHORITY TO SIGN THIS DOCUMENT ON BEHALF OF THE TRANSFEROR.

4. **FEDERAL LAW:** I, the undersigned individual, declare under penalty of perjury that, for the reason checked below, if any, I am exempt (or if signed on behalf of an Entity Transferor, the Entity is exempt) from the federal withholding law (FIRPTA):
   ☐ (For individual Transferors) I am not a nonresident alien for purposes of U.S. income taxation.
   ☐ (For corporation, partnership, limited liability company, trust, and estate Transferors) The Transferor is not a foreign corporation, foreign partnership, foreign limited liability company, foreign trust, or foreign estate, as those term are defined in the Internal Revenue Code and Income Tax Regulations.

5. **CALIFORNIA LAW:** I, the undersigned individual, declare under penalty of perjury that, for the reason checked below, if any, I am exempt (or if signed on behalf of an Entity Transferor, the Entity is exempt) from the California withholding law:
   ☐ The total sale price for the property is $100,000 or less.
   For individual and revocable/grantor trust Transferors only:
   ☐ The property being transferred is in California and was my principal residence within the meaning of IRC Section 121.
   ☐ The property is being, or will be, exchanged for property of like kind within the meaning of IRC Section 1031.
   ☐ The property has been compulsorily or involuntarily converted (within the meaning of IRC1033) and I intend to acquire property similar or related in service or use to be eligible for non-recognition of gain for California income tax purposes under IRC Section 1033.
   ☐ The transaction will result in a loss for California income tax purposes.
   For Entity Transferors only:
   ☐ (For corporation Transferors) The Transferor is a corporation qualified to do business in California, or has a permanent place of business in California at the address shown in paragraph 2 ("Transferor's Information").
   ☐ (For limited liability company ("LLC") or partnership Transferors) The Transferor is an LLC or partnership and recorded title to the property being transferred is in the name of the LLC or partnership and the LLC or partnership will file a California tax return to report the sale and withhold on foreign and domestic nonresident partners as required.
   ☐ (For irrevocable trust Transferors) The Transferor is an irrevocable trust with at least one trustee who is a California resident and the trust will file a California tax return to report the sale and withhold when distributing California source taxable income to nonresident beneficiaries as required.
   ☐ (For estate Transferors) The Transferor is an estate of a decedent who was a California resident at the time of his/her death and the estate will file a California tax return to report the sale and withhold when distributing California source taxable income to nonresident beneficiaries as required.
   ☐ (For tax-exempt Entity and nonprofit organization Transferors) The Transferor is exempt from tax under California or federal law.

By_____ Date _____
(Transferor's Signature) (Indicate if you are signing as the grantor of a revocable/grantor trust.)

_____   _____
Typed or printed name   Title (If signed on behalf of entity Transferor)

SURE TRAC
The System for Success™

Published by the
California Association of REALTORS®

Reviewed by _____ Date _____

EQUAL HOUSING OPPORTUNITY

AS REVISED 1/03 (PAGE 1 OF 1) Print Date

SELLER'S AFFIDAVIT OF NONFOREIGN STATUS AND/OR CALIFORNIA WITHHOLDING EXEMPTION (AS PAGE 1 OF 1)

Figure 13-14

CALIFORNIA
ASSOCIATION
OF REALTORS®

BUYER'S AFFIDAVIT
**That Buyer is acquiring property for use as a residence
and that sales price does not exceed $300,000.**
(FOREIGN INVESTMENT IN REAL PROPERTY TAX ACT)

1. I am the transferee (buyer) of real property located at _____
_____.

2. The sales price (total of all consideration in the sale) does not exceed $300,000.

3. I am acquiring the real property for use as a residence. I have definite plans that I or a member of my family will reside in it for at least 50 percent of the number of days it will be in use during each of the first two 12 month periods following the transfer of the property to me. I understand that the members of my family that are included in the last sentence are my brothers, sisters, ancestors, descendents, or spouse.

4. I am making this affidavit in order to establish an exemption from withholding a portion of the sales price of the property under Internal Revenue Code §1445.

5. I understand that if the information in this affidavit is not correct, I may be liable to the Internal Revenue Service for up to 10 percent of the sales price of the property, plus interest and penalties.

Under penalties of perjury, I declare that the statements above are true, correct and complete.

Date _____   Signature _____

                                Typed or Printed Name _____

Date _____   Signature _____

                                Typed or Printed Name _____

IMPORTANT NOTICE: An affidavit should be signed by each individual transferee to whom it applies. Before you sign, any questions relating to the legal sufficiency of this form, or to whether it applies to a particular transaction, or to the definition of any of the terms used, should be referred to an attorney, certified public accountant, other professional tax advisor, or the Internal Revenue Service.

FORM AB-11 REVISED 2/91

XI. Other Taxes Paid by Brokers

A. BUSINESS LICENSE TAXES (City Income Taxes)

A city may levy a tax against real estate brokerage firms, which is based upon the gross receipts, through a BUSINESS LICENSE TAX. In most areas of California, this annual city business license tax is a nominal amount that usually starts at about $100. Other city taxes may also include employee payroll taxes.

A city tax on a real estate brokerage firm's gross receipts is called a business license tax.

XII. SUMMARY

Real property taxes are determined by the value of the real property (ad valorem) and are reassessed each time a property is sold at 1% of its selling price. The **County Assessor** assesses taxes, the **County Tax Collector** collects them, and the **County Board of Supervisors** sets the rates. **Proposition 13** limits the amount of taxes to 1% of the 1975 market value of the property plus a cumulative increase of 2% in market value each year thereafter, called **assessed valuation**.

Property taxes due are, in effect, liens against that specific property. Important tax dates include **November 1** (first installment), **December 10** (first installment is delinquent), **February 1** (second installment) and **April 10** (second installment is delinquent), or **No Darn Fooling Around.**

If taxes are not paid on or before June 30, the property is sold to the state, beginning a 5-year **redemption period**. After five years, the delinquent property is deeded to the state and sold at a **public tax auction**.

The **homeowner's property tax exemption** is $7000 of assessed valuation. And, although California has no exemption for low income families, it does have senior citizen and disabled person tax rebates and postponements, as well as veterans' and non-profit organizations' tax exemptions.

Local improvement taxes for off-site improvements like streets, sewers, irrigation, etc. are called **special assessment taxes**. Additional taxes that may be incurred include: **documentary transfer taxes, Mello-Roos liens** (for which disclosure is required), **city transfer taxes, gift and estate taxes, federal gift taxes** and **federal estate taxes.**

Interest, property taxes and prepayment penalties paid on a personal residence can be deducted from income taxes. Federal income tax allows a taxpayer to exclude up to $250,000 of gain for each individual ($500,000 if married and on title). When you sell your home (capital asset) a capital gain or loss results. **Capital gains** are taxed at a lower rate than ordinary income tax rates.

A loss on a sale of a personal residence can also be deducted if it is turned into **income producing property** by renting it. Income property owners can deduct **mortgage interest**, **property taxes**, and **prepayment penalties**, as well as **operating expenses** and **depreciation**, but not losses due to vacancies. If a business owner sells a building for cash, then leases it back (a **sale-leaseback**), the seller becomes the lessee and the buyer the lessor, and the seller can deduct 100% of future rents paid.

Federal taxes are **progressive**, meaning the percentage paid increases as the amount to be taxed increases, which is the opposite of sales taxes which are regressive.

In addition to depreciation, two major tax benefits of owning income producing property are **installment sales** (gain is only taxed in the year it is received) and **1031 tax-deferred exchanges** (a means of deferring or eliminating income taxes on property transfers). Cash or debt relief gained in a tax deferred exchange is known as **boot**.

Persons buying property from **foreign investors** are required to set aside 10% of the purchase price for the IRS, to insure the property capital gains taxes are paid on the transaction. An additional 3.3% of the sales price for the Franchise Tax Board may also have to be withheld. In both cases, the burden is on the buyer and broker, not the seller. Brokers may also have to pay a **business license tax**, which is a city tax based on gross receipts.

XIII. TERMINOLOGY - CHAPTER 13

A. Ad Valorem
B. Assessed Valuation
C. Boot
D. County Assessor
E. County Collector
F. Depreciation for Tax Purposes
G. Documentary Transfer Tax
H. Donee

I. Donor
J. Exchange
K. Federal and State Income Tax
L. Federal Estate Tax
M. Federal Gift Tax
N. Homeowners Property Tax Exemption
O. Installment Sale
P. Proposition 13

Q. Real Property Taxes
R. Renter's Credit
S. Special Assessment
T. Two Out of the Last 5 Years
U. $250,000

1.____ Value placed upon property, for property tax purposes, by the tax assessor.
2.____ The sale of property in installments that spreads tax on profit from a sale of property over a number of years.
3.____ A tax charged according to the value of the property.
4.____ One who gives a gift.
5.____ Federal taxes paid on the giving of gifts.
6.____ One who receives a gift.
7.____ In a tax-deferred exchange, any cash or other property included in the transaction to make the exchange an even proposition.
8.____ The trading of parcels of real property to obtain tax benefits that might not be available in a normal sale. Generally considered tax-deferred, not tax-exempt.
9.____ An annual tax that applies to real estate that is based on the assessed valuation of the property.
10.____ The person, in a given political division within a state, who is responsible for collecting property taxes.
11.____ One who estimates the value of property for property tax purposes.
12.____ A renter's deduction allowed from state income taxes payable, under certain conditions.
13.____ A loss in value of improvements as an accounting procedure: used as a deduction on income taxes.
14.____ A lien assessed against real property in a given district, by a public authority to pay costs of special public improvements.
15.____ A tax on the sale of real property, usually based on the sales price and paid on or before the recordation of the deed.
16.____ A tax against the property of a deceased, based on the value of the estate.
17.____ Limits the amount of taxes to a maximum of 1% of the March 1, 1975 market value of the property plus the cumulative increase of 2% in market value each year thereafter.
18.____ Personal taxes paid annually on your taxable income.
19.____ A deduction of up to $7,000 from an owner-resident's assessed valuation on his or her property tax bill. Must be filed between March 1 and April 15 each year, to receive the full deduction.
20.____ The length of time a couple must live in their house to qualify for a $500,000 exclusion.
21.____ The amount that is exempt if a single person sells his or her house.

XIV. MULTIPLE CHOICE

1. The second installment on property taxes would be considered delinquent on:

    a. July 11.
    b. April 11.
    c. December 11.
    d. March 11.

2. The first installment on property taxes becomes due on:

    a. June 30.
    b. April 15.
    c. March 1.
    d. November 1.

3. Of the following, which one would best describe income taxes?

    a. Regressive
    b. Progressive
    c. Marginal
    d. Repressive

4. A tax that is charged in proportion to the value of the property is referred to as a(n):

    a. ad valorem tax.
    b. progression tax.
    c. progressive tax.
    d. excise tax.

5. Proposition 13 set property taxes at what percent of the selling price or fair market value (whichever is higher)?

    a. 1%
    b. 2%
    c. 5%
    d. 10%

6. A person can exclude $250,000 of profit from federal income taxes if he or she lives in the house for:

    a. one year.
    b. two out of the last five years.
    c. five years.
    d. ten years.

7. On what date does the county or city fiscal year begin?

    a. January 1
    b. December 10
    c. July 1
    d. April 10

8. The documentary transfer tax is how much per $500 of new loans and considerations?

    a. 6%
    b. $1.10
    c. $.55
    d. None of the above

9. Which of the following taxes is for specific improvements?

    a. Special assessments
    b. Property taxes
    c. Inheritance taxes
    d. Estate taxes

10. The person who gives a gift is called a:

    a. trustor.
    b. donee.
    c. donor.
    d. none of the above.

ANSWERS: 1. b; 2. d; 3. b; 4. a; 5. a; 6. b; 7. c; 8. c; 9. a; 10. c

Licensing, Education, and Associations

I. Department of Real Estate (DRE)

In California, all real estate agreements are under the jurisdiction of the *CALIFORNIA DEPARTMENT OF REAL ESTATE (DRE), which is the regulatory agency for real estate in California*. The main purpose of this department is to protect the public by enactment and enforcement of laws relating to real estate and by establishing requirements for real estate salespersons' or brokers' licenses.

> *Any person who is actively involved in a real estate transaction at the service of another, in expectation of receiving a commission, must be licensed.*

The California Department of Real Estate is responsible for regulating real estate brokerage matters and the enforcement of real estate laws. These laws help protect both the individual citizen and the real estate profession. There are obvious benefits derived by shielding citizens from dishonest or incompetent real estate licensees. The reputation of the real estate profession is upheld by making sure that all practicing salespeople and brokers are both honest and capable of performing their jobs properly.

The Real Estate Commissioner, deputies, and clerks (as employees of the Department of Real Estate) are NOT allowed to have an interest in any real estate company or brokerage firm.

The California Department of Real Estate is governed by the Real Estate Commissioner. The Commissioner, who sets all the rules and regulations for the Department of Real Estate, receives his or her power from the state legislature. The legislature, in turn, used police power to create the position of Commissioner. *POLICE POWER is the right to enact and enforce laws beneficial to the health, safety, morals, and general welfare of the public.*

A. REAL ESTATE COMMISSIONER (Appointed by the Governor)

The governor appoints the Real Estate Commissioner, who is defended by the state Attorney General. The Real Estate Commissioner issues rules and regulations that have the force and effect of law.

www.ca.gov
Welcome to California - Online Services

In addition to his or her position as chairperson of the State Real Estate Advisory Commission, the *REAL ESTATE COMMISSIONER is the chief executive of the Department of Real Estate.* It is the Commissioner's duty, therefore, to mold the department's policy, create regulations, and to enforce Real Estate Law (found in the Business and Professions Code) so that both real estate purchasers and real estate licensed agents benefit from his or her rulings. The Commissioner's other duties include:

1. Deciding the business policy of the State Department of Real Estate.

2. Informing the Governor and other state officials as to what services the department can render to the state and provide them with descriptions of the department's licenses.

3. Recommending changes in policy that may have been deemed necessary for the good of the public and the business of real estate in California.

4. Regulating of the sales of subdivisions.

5. Deciding if applicants for real estate licenses have met all the experience and education requirements.

6. Investigating complaints against allegedly incompetent license holders.

7. Investigating complaints against those performing acts without the required license.

The Commissioner does not take the place of a court of law, does not give legal advice, and does not settle commission (payment for real estate services) disputes. Commission disputes are settled by arbitration or civil lawsuits in local courts.

The Real Estate Commissioner has the power to call formal hearings to discuss any issue concerning an applicant for a license, a current license holder, or a subdivider. The Commissioner may subsequently suspend, revoke or deny a license. He or she could also halt sales (desist and refrain order) in a subdivision. Remember: The Commissioner cannot take the place of a court of law.

A licensee can be disciplined by the Real Estate Commissioner, but the local District Attorney prosecutes for the Real Estate Commissioner.

B. REAL ESTATE ADVISORY COMMISSION

The *REAL ESTATE ADVISORY COMMISSION recommends and makes suggestions to the Commissioner*. The Advisory Commission has ten members, all appointed by the Commissioner and serving at his or her pleasure. Six members must be licensed California real estate brokers and four must be chosen from the general public; they are not paid a salary, but their actual and necessary expenses are reimbursed. They meet with and advise the Commissioner on matters relating to the Department of Real Estate's function and to the real estate profession in the state.

The Commissioner is required to call Advisory Committee meetings at least four times a year, and the proceedings of all meetings must be made public. At such meetings, the views and suggestions of the public and of the licensees of the Department are heard.

II. Real Estate License Requirements

As mentioned in the preceding section, the Real Estate Commissioner's main purpose is the regulation of the real estate business in the state of California. This regulation is accomplished by imposing mandatory licenses on those individuals who choose to work in the field of real estate. Who is required to have these licenses? In short, any person who is actively involved in a real estate transaction at the service of another, in the expectation of receiving a commission, must be licensed.

A. WHO MUST HAVE A LICENSE

A person is required to have a license if he or she:

1. sells or offers to sell, buys or offers to buy, and solicits buyers or sellers.

2. solicits or obtains listings.

3. negotiates the purchase, sale, or exchange of real property or business opportunities.

4. leases or rents, collects rents, or negotiates the sale, purchase, or exchange of leases.

5. assists in the purchase of leases on lands owned by the state or federal government.

6. negotiates loans, collects payments, or performs services for borrowers or lenders.

Any person found to be involved in such actions without a license may be guilty of breaking the Real Estate Law, under which stiff penalties can be imposed.

B. WHEN A LICENSE IS NOT REQUIRED

It should be noted that there are a few exceptions to these regulations. The following people, because of the nature of their work, are exempt from the licensing regulations (NO LICENSE REQUIRED):

1. Employees of lending institutions
2. Lenders making federally insured or guaranteed loans
3. Certain agricultural associations
4. Licensed personal property brokers
5. Cemetery authorities
6. Collectors of loans made on real property
7. Certain clerical help

A person who is not a real estate salesperson or broker may solicit for the sale of real property (according to Section 10133 of the Real Estate Law) as long as he or she is:

1. the owner.
2. holding power of attorney for the owner.

3. an attorney at law acting on behalf of the owner.

4. a receiver or court appointee.

5. a trustee, selling under a deed of trust.

C. OBTAINING THE SALESPERSON'S LICENSE

The candidate for a real estate salesperson's license examination must:

1. be 18 years of age to apply for a license, although there is no age restriction for taking the exam;

2. provide Proof of Legal Presence in the United States; if not a California resident, refer to "Out-of-State Applicants" on DRE Web site;

3. be honest and truthful;

4. complete a college-level Real Estate Principles course; and

5. pass the required examination. (Governmental Photo ID required)

For further information, call or write any district office of the Department of Real Estate. Ask for the pamphlet, *Instructions to License Applicants* (**See Figure 14-1**). At the same time, ask for the examination application and a license application.

The salesperson exam takes "three hours, fifteen minutes," has 150 questions, and requires a 70% correct score to pass.

PROOF OF LEGAL PRESENCE IN THE UNITED STATES

The **Personal Responsibility and Work Opportunity Act** (the "Act") requires states to eliminate a broad array of public benefits for illegal immigrants. The definition of a public benefit includes professional and occupational licenses issued to individuals by state agencies. For purposes of the Department of Real Estate, the term "public benefit" applies to original and renewal real estate salesperson and broker licenses, prepaid rental listing service licenses, and a payment from the Real Estate Recovery Account.

To implement the provisions of the Act, the Department has adopted Regulation 2718. This regulation requires **proof of legal presence in the United States from all applicants for a license**, and from applicants for payment from the Real Estate Recovery Account. This requirement applies to applicants for both original and renewal licenses.

---

1. Conditional Salesperson's License (The 18-Month License)

To obtain a conditional salesperson's license (18-month), the applicant must 1) complete a college level Real Estate Principles course; 2) pass the DRE salesperson's exam; and 3) pay the necessary fees. A *CONDITIONAL SALESPERSON'S LICENSE is the license of a person who has only taken the Real*

Chapter 14

Figure 14-1

DEPARTMENT OF REAL ESTATE

PRINCIPAL OFFICE

All offices open 8-5 weekdays

SACRAMENTO
2201 Broadway, Sacramento, CA 95818-2500 (916-227-0931)

 www.dre.ca.gov

DISTRICT OFFICES

LOS ANGELES Suite 350 (213-620-2072)
320 W. 4th St. Los Angeles, CA 90013-1105

OAKLAND Suite 702 (510-622-2552)
1515 Clay St. Oakland, CA 94612-1402

SAN DIEGO Suite 3064 (619-525-4192)
1350 Front St., San Diego, CA 92101-3687

FRESNO Rm. 3070 (559-445-5009)
2550 Mariposa Mall, Fresno, CA 93721-2273

Estate Principles course. This license expires 18 months after issuance unless the salesperson has submitted evidence to the DRE of the completion of one Real Estate Practice course and one other college level (broker-required) real estate course.

2. Four-Year Salesperson's License (Regular, Renewable License)

To obtain a regular four-year salesperson's license, the applicant must:

1. complete a college level **Real Estate Principles course, a Real Estate Practice course**, and one other approved college level (broker-required) course;

2. pass the DRE salesperson's exam; and

3. pay the necessary fees.

With a conditional salesperson's license, the licensee must furnish, within 18 months, transcript evidence to the DRE that he or she has successfully completed Real Estate Practice and one other (broker-required) three semester-unit (or equivalent quarter-unit) course.

If an applicant has already completed a college level Real Estate Principles course, a Real Estate Practice course, and at least one other (broker-required) approved course, he or she can apply for the regular four-year salesperson's license.

3. Salesperson's Examination

To pass, an applicant must achieve a score of at least 70% in the three-hour, fifteen minute salesperson's exam, which has 150 multiple choice questions. Exams are usually scheduled during the morning or afternoon. A non-refundable fee is required to take the test. If you fail, you may take the exam as often as you wish, but you must pay for each exam application. See **Figures 14-2 and 14-3** for the salesperson's and broker's requirements.

The use of silent, battery-operated, pocket-sized **electronic calculators** that are non-programmable and do not have a printout capability is permitted.

4. Notification of Examination Results

You will be notified of your examination results mail, normally within five working days after the examination. You can also check your examination results using the DRE exam Web site (**https://secure.dre.ca.gov/SecureASP/ExamResults.asp**).

To pass the examination, you must correctly answer at least 70% of the questions. The examination is qualifying in nature; applicants who pass are not informed of their score. You will be notified of the actual score and the percentage of questions answered correctly in each of the seven subject areas only when unsuccessful. Those who pass will receive an application for a license. Those who do not receive a passing grade will automatically receive a reexamination form.

You may not apply for a reexamination until after notification of failure of a prior test. Another application fee payment will be required.

There is no limitation to the number of reexaminations you may take during the two-year period following the date of the filing of the original application. If you wish to take additional examinations after the two-year period, you must complete a new application.

5. Electronic Fingerprint Requirement (Salesperson and Broker)

Applicants for the salesperson's license must apply for a license within one year from the exam date.

If you have taken Principles and Practice, plus one other required course and have passed the examination, you are qualified to apply for a four-year renewable license. You must pay $129 for an active license and $56 (paid to scan service provider—fee may vary) for the live scan set of your fingerprints. The fee is $178 for the conditional 18-month license, if you have completed Principles, but not the other two required courses.

Figure 14-2

EXAMINATION—SUBJECT AREAS	SALESPERSON EXAM	BROKER EXAM
1. Property Ownership and Land Use Controls and Regulations	**18%**	**15%**
Classes of property; Property characteristics; Encumbrances; Types of ownership; Descriptions of property; Government rights in land; Public controls; Environmental hazards and regulations; Private controls; Water rights; Special categories of land		
2. Laws of Agency	**12%**	**12%**
Law, definition, and nature of agency relationships, types of agencies, and agents; Creation of agency and agency agreements; Responsibilities of agent to seller/buyer as principal; Disclosure of agency; Disclosure of acting as principal or other interest; Termination of agency; Commission and fees		
3. Valuation and Market Analysis	**12%**	**11%**
Value; Methods of estimating value		
4. Financing	**13%**	**13%**
General concepts; Types of loans; Sources of financing; How to deal with lenders; Government programs; Mortgages/deeds of trust/notes; Financing/credit laws; Loan brokerage		
5. Transfer of Property	**9%**	**10%**
Title insurance; Deeds; Escrow; Reports; Tax aspects; Special processes		
6. Practice of Real Estate and Mandated Disclosures	**24%**	**27%**
Trust account management; Fair housing laws; Truth in advertising; Record keeping requirements; Agent supervision; Permitted activities of unlicensed sales assistants; DRE jurisdiction and disciplinary actions; Licensing, continuing education requirements and procedures; California Real Estate Recovery Fund; General ethics; Technology; Property management/landlord-tenant rights; Commercial/industrial/income properties; Specialty areas; Transfer disclosure statement; Natural hazard disclosure statements; Material facts affecting property value; Need for inspection and obtaining/verifying information		
7. Contracts	**12%**	**12%**
General; Listing agreements; Buyer broker agreements; Offers/purchase contracts; Counter offers/multiple counter offers; Leases; Agreements; Promissory notes/securities		

Dept. of Real Estate % of Exam Questions Testing Emphasis

For more information:

www.dre.ca.gov
(Department of Real Estate Home Page)

www.dre.ca.gov/salesqs.htm
(Salesperson Examination Content and Test Questions)

Figure 14-3

SALESPERSON AND BROKER COURSES
(The statutory required college-level courses)

The statutory required college-level courses for people wishing to qualify for either the real estate salesperson or broker license examination.

APPLICANTS FOR THE SALESPERSON'S EXAM

1. To qualify to take an examination for a real estate **salesperson's** license, an applicant must have completed the **REAL ESTATE PRINCIPLES** college level course.

2. In order for the applicant to obtain the original four-year salesperson's license, he or she must also, either prior to the salesperson's exam or within 18 months after issuance of the conditional salesperson's license, complete the **REAL ESTATE PRACTICE** course and one additional basic real estate course selected from among the following:

Real Estate Appraisal	**Escrows**
Accounting	**Property Management**
Business Law	**Real Estate Office Administration**
Legal Aspects of Real Estate	**Mortgage Loan Brokering and Lending**
Real Estate Financing	**Computer Applications in Real Estate**
Real Estate Economics	**Common Interest Development (2004)**

3. **Salespersons** who qualify to take the examination by completing only the **Real Estate Principles** course shall have their licenses automatically suspended, effective 18 months after issuance of the conditional license, unless the **Real Estate Practice** course and one additional course have been completed within that time.

APPLICANTS FOR THE BROKER'S EXAM

1. An applicant for the broker's license examination must have completed eight courses in addition to the experience requirements. These eight courses must include the following five:

Real Estate Practice	**Real Estate Appraisal**
Legal Aspects of Real Estate	**Real Estate Economics (or Accounting)**
Real Estate Financing	

2. The remaining three courses are to be selected from the following:

Real Estate Principles	**Advanced Legal Aspects of R. E.**
Business Law	**Advanced Real Estate Finance**
Property Management	**Advanced R. E. Appraisal**
Escrows	**Computer Applications in Real Estate**
R. E. Office Administration	**Common Interest Development (2004)**
Mortgage Loan Brokering and Lending	

Upon completion of the real estate license exam, a copy of RE Form 237 (the Live Scan Service Request Form) will be mailed to all applicants. A list of providers of the live scan fingerprinting technique is available through the DRE website (**www.dre.ca.gov**).

D. OBTAINING THE BROKER'S LICENSE (Renewable Four-Year License)

A **BROKER'S LICENSE** *is required of any individual who wants to operate a real estate office.* The candidate for a real estate broker's license examination must:

1. be 18 years of age to apply for a license, although there is no age restriction for taking the exam.

2. provide Proof of Legal Presence in the United States.

3. if not a California resident, refer to "Out-of-State Applicants" on DRE Web site.

4. have had previous experience (two years or college education).

5. complete the required eight broker courses.

6. be honest and truthful.

7. pass the required DRE examination. (Governmental Photo ID required)

1. Broker's Qualifying Experience

A candidate must also be able to prove that he or she has experience in real estate before applying for a broker's license. Generally, two years of full-time work (104 forty-hour weeks) as a salesperson is required. This two-year requirement may be replaced by an equivalent amount of part-time salesperson work. Such experience must have been completed within the five years immediately preceding the date of application.

Sometimes the State Real Estate Commissioner will accept experience in fields other than real estate sales. These fields include contract work, lease, escrow, title insurance, bonds, mortgage company, or experience in another area directly involved in real estate.

Besides direct experience in these fields, education may qualify as full or partial experience. For example, the commissioner has ruled that any individual with a four-year college degree is exempt from the two-year experience requirement. But, all candidates **must** complete the eight required real estate courses, regardless of their educational degree. A community college graduate with the required real estate courses needs only one year of experience.

All students are encouraged to submit an equivalency request with the Department of Real Estate. All decisions made by the commissioner are final.

B.S. or B.A. (four-year degree) = 2 years of experience
A.A. (two-year degree) = 1 year of experience

Most California colleges and universities offer courses and majors in real estate. (**See Figure 14-4.**)

The broker's 200-question exam takes five hours to complete. The applicant must answer 75% of the questions correctly to pass.

2. Broker's Required Education (Eight Courses)

Applicants for the real estate broker's license examination must have successfully completed the eight statutory-required, college-level courses. The required salesperson's courses can be found on the list of required broker's courses, but the number of required courses is different: three for the regular salesperson's license and eight for the broker's license. An applicant's choice of eight (broker-required) courses must be taken by all broker candidates. Refer back to Figure 14-3.

Once all of these requirements have been completed, a candidate may apply to take the broker's examination. By filing the examination fee, plus proof of 2 years' experience or the equivalent thereof, and transcripts showing that the eight statutory classes have been completed, the applicant will receive his or her admission card for the test. The cost of a broker's license is $165.

E. RENEWAL OF LICENSE - EVERY FOUR YEARS
(Salesperson and Broker)

Broker's and salesperson's licenses can be renewed; a conditional (18-month) salesperson's license CANNOT.

Once the license has expired, no licensed activity can be performed by the salesperson until the license has been renewed. The late renewal period (often referred to as the "grace" period) simply allows the licensee to renew on a late basis without retaking the examination; it does not allow the licensee to conduct licensed activity during the late renewal period. The license renewal fee for a salesperson is $120 if filed on time and $180 if filed late. A broker's renewal costs $165 if on time and $248 if late.

Whenever a real estate salesperson enters the employ of a real estate broker, or whenever the salesperson is terminated, the broker shall immediately notify the Department of Real Estate in writing.

F. CONTINUING EDUCATION (CE) REQUIREMENT
(45 Hours Every Four Years to Renew Your License)

The continuing education requirement (45 hours every 4 years for license renewal) is NOT the same as the requirement for statutory broker courses.

Figure 14-4

ADVANCED EDUCATION IN REAL ESTATE

As the study of real estate becomes more complex and more intertwined with other business disciplines, students of real estate find it rewarding to continue their studies beyond those levels required to enter the field as a salesperson or broker. Many real estate professionals, after obtaining their A.A. degrees from one of our 108 community colleges, have gone on to pursue bachelor's and master's degrees.

CALIFORNIA STATE UNIVERSITY SYSTEM

Bakersfield	Northridge
Channel Islands	Pomona*
Chico	Sacramento*
Dominguez Hills	San Bernardino
Fresno	San Diego*
Fullerton	San Francisco
Hayward	San Jose
Humboldt	San Luis Obispo
Long Beach	San Marcos
Los Angeles	Sonoma
Maritime Academy	Stanislaus
Monterey Bay	

*Regional centers for RELUI
Real Estate and Land Use Institute
Cal State University, Sacramento
Sacramento, CA 95819

UNIVERSITY OF CALIFORNIA SYSTEM

Berkeley**	Riverside
Davis	San Diego
Irvine	San Francisco
Los Angeles***	Santa Barbara
Merced	Santa Cruz

The U.C. Berkeley Fisher Center for Real Estate and Urban Economics (FCREUE) publishes a newsletter, **Quarterly Report, which may be obtained by instructors and school libraries by writing (on college stationery) to, or contacting: Haas Real Estate Group or FCREUE: Haas School of Business, University of California Berkeley, CA 94720-1900; Tel: (510) 643-6105; Fax: (510) 643-7357; Email: creue@haas.berkeley.edu .

***U.C.L.A. offers information on recent trends in real estate. For more information, contact the Richard S. Ziman Center for Real Estate, 110 Westwood Plaza, Los Angeles, CA 90095; Phone: (310) 206-9424; Fax: (310) 206-5455; ziman.center@anderson.ucla.edu

EXTENSION COURSES

The UC and Cal State University campuses also offer extension programs for persons interested in a more in-depth study of certain areas of real estate without the constraints of a degree program. Classes are generally offered in the evening or on weekends.

All real estate licensees are required to attend 45 clock hours of Commissioner-approved courses, seminars, or conferences during the four-year period preceding license renewal. Three of these hours must be in an Ethics course and three hours must be in Agency. On a salesperson's license first renewal, only the Ethics and Agency courses are required. Thereafter, however, the 45-clock-hour requirement continues indefinitely with every renewal. **Figure 14-5** shows distribution of continuing education courses.

Figure 14-5

45 Hours of Required Continuing Education

A three-hour continuing education course in Agency and a three-hour continuing education course in Ethics and Professional Conduct is a necessary part of the 45 hours. The required 45 hours of continuing education include:

3 hours of Ethics and Professional Conduct
3 hours of Agency
3 hours of Trust Fund Accounting and Handling
3 hours of Fair Housing
33 hours of Consumer Protection

45 TOTAL HOURS (Required)

---

1. "Six-Hour Continuing Education (CE) Survey" Course

The "Six-Hour CE Survey" course can replace the 12-hour combination of four separate 3-hour courses in (Ethics, Agency, Trust Fund Handling, and Fair Housing), starting with your second license renewal. So if a licensee takes the *Six-hour CE Survey* course, he or she still needs an additional 39 hours of CE to complete the 45 total hours required every four years at license renewal time.

G. OTHER REAL ESTATE-RELATED LICENSES

1. Prepaid Rental Listing Service License

A *PREPAID RENTAL LISTING SERVICE (PRLS) license is required when running a business that supplies prospective tenants with listings of residential real property for rent or lease while collecting a fee for such service.* Negotiation of the rental of property is not a part of this activity. An individual may obtain, without examination, a two-year license to conduct PRLS activities.

Prior to issuance of the PRLS license, the applicant must submit, and have approved by the DRE, a contract to be entered into between the licensee and client (prospective tenant). Fingerprints and a $2,500 surety bond are required for each business location.

2. Real Property Securities Dealer (RPSD) Endorsement

A *REAL PROPERTY SECURITIES DEALER (RPSD)* *is any person acting as a* *principal or agent who engages in the business of selling real property securities (such as* *promissory notes or sales contracts).* RPSDs also accept, or offer to accept, funds for reinvestment in real property securities or for placement in an account. Before a licensed real estate broker may act in the capacity of a RPSD, he or she must obtain an RPSD endorsement on his or her broker's license. To obtain an RPSD endorsement on a broker's license, submit the appropriate endorsement fee along with proof of a properly executed $10,000 surety bond. (For information on Real Property Securities, see Chapter 9 or call the DRE.)

www.corp.ca.gov
Department of Corporations

III. Business Opportunity Brokerage

In a sale of an existing business (Business Opportunity), the real *property is transferred by "deed" and the personal property is* *transferred by a "bill of sale." If money is owed on the business, the* *proper financial statements are filed with the Secretary of State's office.*

Your real estate license also authorizes you to practice in the specialized field of "Business Opportunities." This is a different area of real estate, and requires knowledge and experience beyond that which is needed for real property transactions. The business opportunity broker's transactions usually include the three items shown in **Figure 14-6**.

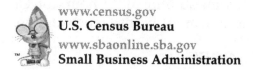

www.census.gov
U.S. Census Bureau
www.sbaonline.sba.gov
Small Business Administration

A. BUSINESS OPPORTUNITY SALE

A common definition of a *BUSINESS* is *an establishment whose main purpose is the buying* *and reselling of goods, or the performance of services, with the intention of making a profit.* A *BUSINESS OPPORTUNITY* is *the sale or lease of a business, including the goodwill of an* *existing business.* It involves the sale of personal property and must also conform to the rules and laws that govern the transfer of chattels (personal property). The most common

Figure 14-6

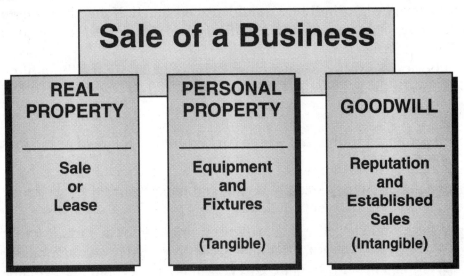

types of business opportunities are small, locally owned neighborhood businesses like grocery stores, liquor stores, laundromats, service stations, and restaurants.

The three documents in a personal property security transaction are: 1) a promissory note; 2) a security agreement; and 3) compliance with the UCC-1 financing statement.

B. BUSINESS OPPORTUNITY LISTING

A business opportunity salesperson should have a working knowledge of business practices and a thorough understanding of accounting or bookkeeping principles. The seller of the business must give you all the pertinent information as part of the listing agreement. The accuracy of the information, however, should be validated by the listing broker.

Business opportunities can involve the transfer of both real and personal property and usually use one escrow.

The business opportunity listing should include all the information necessary for a real property sale. But, in addition, it should include:

1. name of business and owner.
2. nature and location of business.
3. price and terms of sale.
4. encumbrances and items that are to be assumed by the buyer.

In addition if there is a lease, the terms should be stated. The important income information should detail the gross income, expenses, and net income. If there is

competition in the area, it should be so stated. The usual business hours each day and the square footage of the building should also be stated. If the current employees are expected to stay, salary and any existing fringe benefits should be explained in detail.

Buyers of businesses differ. They are usually motivated by the thought of becoming their own boss or the need for a steady income, and they usually fall into one of these two categories:

1. The experienced individual with a background in the field or business he or she is buying.

2. The new buyer who is usually young and inexperienced.

The experienced individual will usually need only the basic facts in order to decide whether to purchase or not. The inexperienced buyer needs more help but is sometimes hesitant to ask questions, so all pertinent facts should be explained in detail to that person. He or she should also be informed of applicable laws that govern that particular business. See **Figure 14-7** for information about buying a bar or liquor store.

C. BULK SALES (Transfer of Business Inventory) (Notice to Creditors Required)

A **BULK TRANSFER** *is any sale of a substantial part of the 1) inventory, items purchased for resale; 2) other supplies and equipment associated with a business.* Division 6 of the Uniform Commercial Code (UCC) requires the purchaser (transferee) in a bulk transfer to give the seller's (transferor's) creditors fair warning that a sale of all or a major part of the inventory is about to take place.

1. Buyer (Transferee) Must Comply with the UCC

If a retail or wholesale merchant transfers a substantial part of his or her materials, supplies, merchandise, or inventory, the transferee involved in the transfer must give notice by:

1. Twelve business days prior to transfer, recorded notice with the County Recorder's Office.

2. Twelve business days prior to transfer, published notice in a newspaper of general circulation in the county or judicial district.

3. Twelve business days prior to transfer, delivered notice (by hand or registered mail) to the County Tax Collector.

Figure 14-7

(ABC)
ALCOHOLIC BEVERAGE CONTROL

Any California real estate licensee who is interested in negotiating business opportunity transactions should be familiar with the legal controls on the transfer of licenses for the sale of alcoholic beverages.

The Department of Alcoholic Beverage Control (ABC) administers the Alcoholic Beverage Control Act and issues all licenses there under.

Alcoholic beverage licenses are issued to qualified adults, partnerships, fiduciaries, and corporations for use at a particular premises, which also has to be approved by the ABC. The ABC may refuse to issue a license to any person who has a criminal record or has violated the ABC Act. The premises may be disapproved for various reasons, including over concentration of alcoholic beverage licenses in the area, the creation of a police problem, or the proximity to a school, playground, or church.

With the sale of a business opportunity involving a liquor license, you cannot automatically assume that the ABC will permit the transfer. An escrow is legally required and no consideration may be paid out before the license and the sale of the business is approved. Each application and transfer is subject to protest by local officials and private parties within 30 days of the posted notice of intention to sell alcoholic beverages.

New licenses for bars (on-sale) and liquor stores (off-sale) are usually obtained through a lottery type system in each county. The maximum sales price for a new license is $6,000, but after a period of five years from the date of the original issuance, this restriction is lifted and the purchase price is usually considerably more.

DEPARTMENT OF ALCOHOLIC BEVERAGE CONTROL
1901 BROADWAY
SACRAMENTO, CALIFORNIA

www.abc.ca.gov
Alcoholic Beverage Control)

2. Protection for Creditors

This notice must include:

1. notification that the transfer is going to take place.
2. the name and any business addresses used by the seller.
3. the location and a description of the property.
4. the place and date of the transfer.

If all of the conditions of the bulk transfer notice are not met, any transfer of bulk is fraudulent and void against creditors, but valid between buyer and seller.

D. CALIFORNIA SALES TAXES (Selling Retail)

SALES TAXES are taxes imposed on the sale of tangible personal property by retailers. This is important to brokers and salespeople who are in transactions involving the sale of businesses where sales of tangible personal property is involved. A seller's permit from the State Board of Equalization is the permit that allows sellers to buy at wholesale without paying sales tax as long as they collect sales taxes from their customers and forward these taxes to the State Board of Equalization. Before selling a business, escrow should check to see if there are any past due sales taxes.

IV. Real Estate Law and Regulations

California laws affecting real estate are included in several different acts and codes. The **CALIFORNIA REAL ESTATE LAW** *is the portion of the Business and Professions Code that refers to licensing and subdivisions.* On the other hand, the **COMMISSIONER'S REGULATIONS** *are rules that form part of the California Administrative Code established and enforced by the Commissioner of Real Estate.* All licensees should be familiar with the Real Estate Law, the Commissioner's Regulations, and (as mentioned before) the Subdivided Lands Act administered by the Commissioner.

A. ENFORCEMENT OF REAL ESTATE LAW

Licensing and regulatory law is effective only to the extent that it is enforced. The Commissioner, as the chief officer of the Department of Real Estate, is duty bound to enforce the provisions of the Real Estate Law. The Commissioner may, by his or her own choice, and must upon a verified complaint in writing, investigate the actions of any person engaged in the real estate business or acting in the capacity of a licensee within this state. He or she has the power to suspend any real estate license or to revoke it permanently. The Commissioner also has the authority to deny a license to an applicant if the applicant does not meet the full requirements of the law. If, through the screening process (including the fingerprint record) of an applicant for license, it is found that he or she has a criminal record or some other record that may adversely reflect on his or her character, an investigation is made by the commissioner's staff. A formal hearing may be ordered to determine whether or not the applicant meets the requirements of honesty, truthfulness, and good reputation.

B. HEARINGS FOR LICENSE VIOLATIONS

One function of Real Estate Law is to hold a hearing when there is a question as to the rights of persons to obtain or keep their real estate licenses. The Department of Real Estate and other licensing agencies must conduct hearings with strict regard for the rules set forth in the Administrative Procedure Act. Before denying, suspending, or revoking any license, the licensee is served a statement, and the Commissioner acts as the complainant. The licensee, or respondent as he or she is known in the hearing procedures, may appear with or without counsel. The hearing is conducted according to rules of evidence in civil matters.

A decision is made by the hearing officer based upon his or her findings. The Commissioner may reject or accept the proposed decision or reduce the proposed penalty, and then make his or her official decision. The respondent has the right of appeal to the courts. If the testimony substantiates the charges and they appear to be sufficiently serious, the license of the respondent is suspended or revoked. After a license is revoked, the person affected may not apply for reinstatement until one year has passed.

C. LICENSES: REVOKE, RESTRICT, SUSPEND

The real estate commissioner can revoke, restrict, or suspend the license of any real estate agent for misconduct.

REVOKE — take away the license.
RESTRICT — to limit the use of the license.
SUSPEND — to take away the license for a period of time.

1. Child Support Obligations (150-Day License)

The DRE will not issue or renew a full-term license if the applicant is on a list of persons (obligors) who have not complied with a court order to provide child support payments. The DRE will issue them a 150-day license. The Department of Child Support Services compiles a list of delinquencies of over four months, and active licensees who appear on the list have 150 days to get current or have their licenses suspended. The license will not be issued or suspension revoked until a release is furnished from the district attorneys' office.

V. Common Real Estate Law Violations

Section 10176 of the Business and Professions Code is the legal guideline for the licensee engaged in the practice and performance of any of the acts within the scope of the Real

Estate Law. **Section 10177** of the Business and Professions Code applies to situations where the licensee involved was not necessarily acting as an agent or as a licensee.

All agents must adhere to the ethical and legal requirements of Section 10176 and Section 10177 of the Business and Professions Code, which include violations such as misrepresentation and failure to disclose hidden relationships.

A. SECTION 10176: LICENSEE ACTING IN A LICENSEE CAPACITY

This section of the Real Estate Law is for violations by those licensees who are acting within the scope of their licenses. (**See Figures 14-8 and 14-9**.)

B. SECTION 10177: LICENSEE NOT NECESSARILY ACTING AS A LICENSEE

Section 10177 applies to situations where the affected party was not necessarily acting in the capacity of an agent or as a real estate licensee. (**See Figure 14-10.**) The vast majority of brokers and salespeople are honest and perform their services in a straightforward manner. Occasionally, a section of the Real Estate Law may be violated inadvertently and without intent. In such cases the Commissioner would most likely consider restriction of the real estate license. On the other hand, a flagrant violation would most likely cause a revocation of the license.

It is "blind advertising" if an agent gives the impression that he or she is the owner of the property for sale. The Real Estate Commissioner does NOT approve of pocket listings (kept within real estate office)— they are not part of the professional code and guidelines.

C. REGULATIONS OF THE COMMISSIONER
(Found in the Administrative Code)

The Regulations of the Real Estate Commissioner have the force and effect of the law itself.

Real Estate Law empowers the Commissioner to issue regulations to aid in the administration and enforcement of the law. These regulations, which are known formally as the Regulations of the Real Estate Commissioner, have the force and effect of the law itself. Licensees and prospective licensees should be familiar with these regulations. The California Department of Real Estate produces a factual law book entitled *Real Estate Law* (Real Estate Law and Regulations of the Real Estate Commissioner), which can be obtained from their office.

Figure 14-8

Business & Professions Code 10176
(Real Estate Licensee <u>Acting</u> As Licensee)

Grounds for Revocation or Suspension

Misrepresentation - 10176(a)

The licensee must disclose to his or her principal all material facts that the principal should know. Failure to do so or lying is cause for disciplinary action. A great majority of the complaints received by the commissioner allege misrepresentation on the part of the broker or his or her salespeople.

False Promise - 10176(b)

A false promise is a false statement about what the promisor is going to do in the future. Many times a false promise is provided by showing the promise was impossible to perform and that the person making the promise knew it was impossible.

Continued and Flagrant Misrepresentation by Agents - 10176(c)

This section gives the commissioner the right to discipline a licensee for a continued and flagrant course of misrepresentation or making of false promises through real estate agents or salespeople.

Divided Agency - 10176(d)

This section requires a licensee to inform all his or her principals if he or she is acting as agent for more than one party in a transaction.

Commingling - 10176(e)

Commingling takes place when a broker has mixed the funds of his or her principals with his or her own money. A broker should keep all funds separate.

(Continued)

Figure 14-9

Business & Professions Code 10176
(Real Estate Licensee <u>Acting</u> As Licensee)
Grounds for Revocation or Suspension

Definite Termination Date - 10176(f)

A specified termination date, in writing, is required for all exclusive listing transactions.

Secret Profit - 10176(g)

Secret profit cases usually arise when the broker makes a low offer, usually through a "dummy" purchaser, when he or she already has a higher offer from another buyer. The difference is the secret profit.

Listing Option - 10176(h)

This section requires a licensee, when he or she has used a form which is both an option and a listing, to obtain the written consent of his or her principal approving the amount of such profit before the licensee may exercise the option. This does not apply where a licensee is using an option only.

Dishonest Dealing - 10176(i)

Dishonest dealing is a catch-all section used when the acts of the person required a license but he or she did not have a license.

Signatures of Prospective Purchasers - 10176(j)

Brokers must obtain a written (business opportunities) authorization to sell from an owner before securing the signature of a prospective purchaser to the agreement. This section strikes at what was once a common practice in some areas in the sale of business opportunities, where the prospective purchaser was forced to deal with the broker who furnished him or her the listing.

Figure 14-10

Business and Professions Code 10177
(R.E. Licensee Not Necessarily Acting as a Licensee)

Grounds for Revocation or Suspension

Obtaining License by Fraud - Section 10177(a)

This section gives the Commissioner the power to take action against a licensee for misstatements of fact in an application for a license and in those instances where licenses have been procured by fraud, misrepresentation, or deceit.

Convictions - Section 10177(b)

This section permits proceedings against a licensee after a criminal conviction for either a felony or a misdemeanor which involves moral turpitude (anything contrary to justice, honesty, modesty, or good morals).

False Advertising - Section 10177(c)

This section makes licensees who are parties to false advertising subject to disciplinary action. The ban extends to subdivision sales as well general property sales.

Violations of Other Sections - Section 10177(d)

This section gives the Department authority to proceed against the licensee for violation of any of the other sections of the Real Estate Law, the regulations of the commissioner, and the subdivision laws.

Misuse of Trade Name - Section 10177(e)

Only active members of the national association or local associations of real estate boards are permitted to use the term "Realtor." This is a term belonging exclusively to such members, and no licensee may advertise or hold himself or herself out as a "Realtor®" without proper entitlement.

Conduct Warranting Denial - Section 10177(f)

This is a general section of the Real Estate Law and almost any act involving crime or dishonesty will fall within it. An essential requirement for the issuance of a license is that the applicant be honest, truthful, and of good reputation.

Negligence or Incompetence - Section 10177(g)

Demonstrated negligence or incompetence, while acting as a licensee, is just cause for disciplinary action. The department proceeds in those cases where the licensee is so careless or unqualified that to allow him or her to handle a transaction would endanger the interests of his or her clients or customers. (Continued)

Business and Professions Code 10177
(R.E. Licensee Not Necessarily Acting as a Licensee)

Grounds for Revocation or Suspension

Supervision of Salespersons - Section 10177(h)

A broker is subject to disciplinary action if he or she fails to exercise reasonable supervision over the activities of his or her salespersons.

Violating Government Trust - Section 10177(i)

Prescribes disciplinary liability for using government employment to violate the confidential nature of records thereby made available.

Other Dishonest Conduct - Section 10177(j)

Specifies that any other conduct which constitutes fraud or dishonest dealings may subject the ones involved to license suspension or revocation.

Restricted License Violation - Section 10177(k)

Makes violation of the terms, conditions, restrictions, and limitations contained in any order granting a restricted license grounds for disciplinary action.

Inducement of Panic Selling (Blockbusting) - Section 10177(l)

It is a cause for disciplinary action to solicit or induce a sale, lease, or the listing for sale or lease, of residential property on the grounds of loss of value because of entry into the neighborhood of a person or persons of another race, color, religion, ancestry, or national origin.

Violation of Franchise Investment Law - Section 10177(m)

Violates any of the provisions of the Franchise Investment Law or any regulations of the Corporations Commissioner pertaining thereto.

Violation of Securities Law - Section 10177(n)

Violates any of the provisions of the Corporations Code or any regulations the Commissioner of Corporations relating to securities as specified.

Violation of Securities Law - Section 10177(o)

Failure to disclose to buyer the nature and extent of ownership interest licensee has in property in which the licensee is an agent for the buyer. Also, failure to disclose ownership on the part of licensee's relative or special acquaintance in which licensee has ownership interest.

Importance of Section 10176 and Section 10177
REGULATIONS OF THE COMMISSIONER

The Real Estate Commissioner is empowered to adopt Regulations for the administration and enforcement of the Real Estate Law and the Subdivided Lands Law. Duly adopted regulations become part of the California Code of Regulations and, in effect, have the force and authority of the law itself. Therefore, all licensees, prospective licensees, and subdividers should be thoroughly familiar with the Real Estate Commissioner's Regulations.

10176. The Commissioner may, upon his own motion, and shall, upon the verified complaint in writing of any person, investigate the actions of any person engaged in the business or acting in the capacity of a real estate licensee within this state, and he or she may temporarily suspend or permanently revoke a real estate license at any time where the licensee, while a real estate licensee, in performing or attempting to perform any of the acts within the scope of this chapter, has been guilty of any act listed in this Section.

10177. The Commissioner may suspend or revoke the license of any real estate licensee or may deny the issuance of a license to an applicant or may suspend or revoke the license of, or deny the issuance of a license to, a corporate applicant if an officer, director, or person owning or controlling 10 percent or more of the corporation's stock has done any of the acts listed in this section.

 www.dre.ca.gov
California Department of Real Estate

VI. Real Estate General Fund

*All the money collected from license and exam fees goes into the **REAL ESTATE GENERAL FUND**.* Eight percent of this money is used for the operating expenses of the Department of Real Estate. Twenty percent of the Real Estate General Fund is set aside as follows:

1. Eight percent to the Real Estate Education and Research Fund;
2. Twelve percent to the Recovery Fund.

The **RECOVERY FUND** *was established for the payment of damages and arbitration awards to people who have suffered financial loss due to the wrongful act of a licensee in a real estate transaction.* To qualify for these funds, plaintiffs must first obtain a judgment in civil court (or through arbitration) against a licensee on the grounds of fraud, misrepresentation, deceit, or conversion of trust funds. If after reasonable effort the judgment remains uncollected, a claim may be filed with the Commissioner's office.

A license is suspended until the fund is reimbursed (plus interest). The total liability of the recovery fund in any one transaction is $20,000, and the total series of judgments against any individual licensee is limited to $100,000.

California is one of the few states that actively helps protect the public against fraudulent acts by real estate licensees.

VII. Trade and Professional Associations

A *TRADE OR PROFESSIONAL ASSOCIATION is a voluntary, non-profit organization made up of independent firms in the same industry.* It is formed to promote progress, aid in solving the industry's problems, and enhance its service to the community. We will discuss the role of local boards of Realtors®, the California Association of Realtors® (CAR), the National Association of Realtors® (NAR) and its Code of Ethics, and the term Realtist.

A "Realtor®" is a member of NAR, real estate trade association.

A. LOCAL REAL ESTATE BOARDS

The *LOCAL BOARD OF REALTORS is a voluntary organization of real estate licensees in a particular community.* A broker is entitled to full membership, a salesperson may be an associate member, and a non-realtor (who is in a real estate related field) may be an affiliate member. For example, an affiliate member might work for a title insurance company, an escrow company, a lender, or any other business having an interest in local real estate activities.

Local boards usually provide a multiple listing service for their members so that all members can be equally informed. Most local boards provide services such as distribution of educational material, seminars, library services, and other worthwhile services for the local Realtors®.

www.bhbr.com
(Beverly Hills, California, Board of Realtors)

B. CALIFORNIA ASSOCIATION OF REALTORS® (CAR)

The *CALIFORNIA ASSOCIATION OF REALTORS® is the state division of the National Association of Realtors®.* It is a voluntary organization whose membership includes local realty boards throughout the state and individual members who are not affiliated with any particular local board. With the exception of NAR, CAR is the largest Realtor® organization in the United States, with over 100,000 members in California.

The objectives of the California Association of Realtors® are:

1. To promote high standards and unite its members.
2. To safeguard the property-buying public.
3. To foster legislation for the benefit and protection of the real estate field.
4. To cooperate in the economic growth and development of the state.

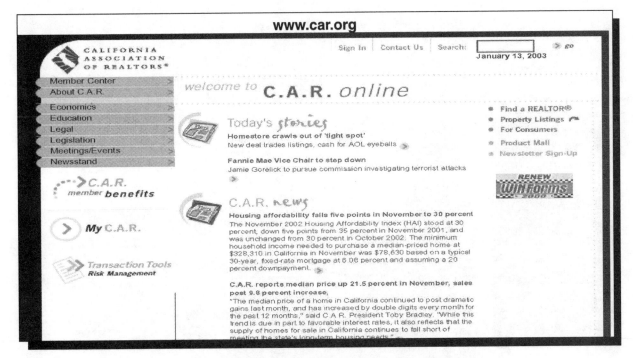

California Association of Realtors®
525 South Virgil Avenue
P. O. Box 76917
Los Angeles, California 90076

CAR has many standing committees that meet at director's meetings, seminars, and annual conventions. These committees specialize in specific areas such as education, ethics, legislation, political affairs, real property taxation, professional standards, and many other areas. There are also many divisions of CAR.

Most of the people who are successful salespeople are also members of the California Association of Realtors®. We suggest you become a member of this or some other trade association when you are serious about selling real estate.

C. NATIONAL ASSOCIATION OF REALTORS® (NAR)

The *NATIONAL ASSOCIATION OF REALTORS® is the national trade association for all the state associations and local boards of Realtors® in the United States.* NAR unifies the real estate industry at the national level. It encourages legislation favorable to the real estate industry and enforces professional conduct standards on behalf of its members across the nation.

1. Trade Name

Only active members of the National Association of Realtors® (NAR) or the California Association of Realtors® (CAR), through their local real estate boards, are permitted to use the term Realtor®. This is a term belonging exclusively to

such members, and no licensee may advertise or present himself or herself to be a Realtor® if not associated with such a group.

Use of the term "Realtor®" without proper group affiliation is grounds for revocation of your license.

The National Association of Realtors® has affiliated institutes, societies, and councils that provide a wide-ranging menu of programs and services that assist members in increasing skills, productivity, and knowledge. (**See Figure 14-11.**)

2. Code of Ethics

See Figure 14-12 for the National Association of Realtors® Code of Ethics. These guidelines show not only how one should act but also how one must act.

The National Association of Realtors® and its state and local divisions form a composite organization of brokers whose objective is to forward the interests of brokers, encourage education of practitioners and the public, raise the standard of real estate practice and increase the esteem in which brokers are held by their fellow citizens. To this end, a code of ethics has been formulated and adopted. It is the generally accepted code of ethics for real estate people and every Realtor® swears to abide by it.

"Under all is the land" are the beginning words of the NAR Code of Ethics.

Figure 14-11

NAR Affiliates

1. American Society of Real Estate Counselors (ASREC)

This division of NAR offers the CRE (Counselor of Real Estate) designation.

2. Commercial Investment Real Estate Institute (CIREI)

CIREI enhances the professional development of those engaged in commercial investment real estate. Offers the CCIM (Certified Commercial Investment Member) designation.

3. Institute of Real Estate Management (IREM)

IREM is committed to enhancing the knowledge and professionalism of the real estate management industry.

 www.ccim.com

4. Realtors® National Marketing Institute (RNMI)

RNMI promotes professional competence in real estate sales and brokerage, and real estate brokerage management. It has two councils:

A. Council of Real Estate Brokerage Managers

Recognized throughout the industry as the professional peer organization for managers of residential, commercial, industrial, relocation, appraising and property management companies. The CRB designation is available for members who meet experience requirements and complete a series of courses.

 www.crb.com

B. Counselors of Real Estate

The Counselors of Real Estate is a professional membership organization established exclusively for leading real property advisors.

 www.cre.org

5. Realtors® Land Institute (RLI)

RLI brings together real estate professionals interested in the improvement of their professional competence in activities related to land. They offer the ALC (Accredited Land Consultant) designation. Requirements include course study as well as minimum experience.

(Continued)

NAR Affiliates

6. Real Estate Buyer's Agent Council (REBAC)

REBAC (Real Estate Buyer's Agent Council) serves Realtors® members who wish to devote all or part of their business to the practice of buyer's agency.

7. Society of Industrial and Office Realtors® (SIOR)

An international organization whose members specialize in a variety of commercial real estate activities. They offer the SIOR designation.

 www.sior.com

8. Women's Council of Realtors® (WCR)

WCR offers opportunities for developing leadership skills as well as a Referral and Relocation Certification (RRC). This is the only referral and relocation certification offered by NAR.

9. Professional Real Estate Executive (PRE)

The PRE designation is available for corporate real estate executives who meet experience and course completion criteria.

 www.realtor.org
NAR - All these affiliates can be accessed here

10. Leadership Training Graduate (LTG)

The LTG (Leadership Training Graduate) designation requires experience plus completion of four leadership training requirements.

11. The Institute of Real Estate Management (REM)

This is an organization, within NAR, of professional property managers. They offer a number of designations including:

A. Certified Property Manager (CPM)

This is generally considered the highest property management designation an individual can earn. It requires intensive course work and a year of candidacy and completion of management plan for a property.

B. Accredited Reside Manager (ARM)

While the CPM designation requires a broad spectrum of experience, the ARM is exclusively residential. There are educational and experience requirements as well as an examination.

C. Accredited Management Organization (AMO)

Rather than an individual recognition, it is a firm's recognition. The firm must have a CPM in charge of management, and he or she must complete a course in managing a management company.

Figure 14-12

Code of Ethics and Standards of Practice of the National Association of REALTORS®
Effective January 1, 2002

Where the word REALTORS® is used in this Code and Preamble, it shall be deemed to include REALTOR-ASSOCIATE®s.

While the Code of Ethics establishes obligations that may be higher than those mandated by law, in any instance where the Code of Ethics and the law conflict, the obligations of the law must take precedence.

Preamble...

Under all is the land. Upon its wise utilization and widely allocated ownership depend the survival and growth of free institutions and of our civilization. REALTORS® should recognize that the interests of the nation and its citizens require the highest and best use of the land and the widest distribution of land ownership. They require the creation of adequate housing, the building of functioning cities, the development of productive industries and farms, and the preservation of a healthful environment.

Such interests impose obligations beyond those of ordinary commerce. They impose grave social responsibility and a patriotic duty to which REALTORS® should dedicate themselves, and for which they should be diligent in preparing themselves. REALTORS®, therefore, are zealous to maintain and improve the standards of their calling and share with their fellow REALTORS® a common responsibility for its integrity and honor.

In recognition and appreciation of their obligations to clients, customers, the public, and each other, REALTORS® continuously strive to become and remain informed on issues affecting real estate and, as knowledgeable professionals, they willingly share the fruit of their experience and study with others. They identify and take steps, through enforcement of this Code of Ethics and by assisting appropriate regulatory bodies, to eliminate practices which may damage the public or which might discredit or bring dishonor to the real estate profession. REALTORS® having direct personal knowledge of conduct that may violate the Code of Ethics involving misappropriation of client or customer funds or property, willful discrimination, or fraud resulting in substantial economic harm, bring such matters to the attention of the appropriate Board or Association of REALTORS®. (Amended 1/00)

Realizing that cooperation with other real estate professionals promotes the best interests of those who utilize their services, REALTORS® urge exclusive representation of clients; do not attempt to gain any unfair advantage over their competitors; and they refrain from making unsolicited comments about other practitioners. In instances where their opinion is sought, or where REALTORS® believe that comment is necessary, their opinion is offered in an objective, professional manner, uninfluenced by any personal motivation or potential advantage or gain.

The term REALTORS® has come to connote competency, fairness, and high integrity resulting from adherence to a lofty ideal of moral conduct in business relations. No inducement of profit and no instruction from clients ever can justify departure from this ideal. In the interpretation of this obligation, REALTORS® can take no safer guide than that which has been handed down through the centuries, embodied in the Golden Rule, "Whatsoever ye would that others should do to you, do ye even so to them."

Accepting this standard as their own, REALTORS® pledge to observe its spirit in all of their activities and to conduct their business in accordance with the tenets set forth below.

Duties to Clients and Customers
Article 1

When representing a buyer, seller, landlord, tenant, or other client as an agent, REALTORS® pledge themselves to protect and promote the interests of their client. This obligation to the client is primary, but it does not relieve REALTORS® of their obligation to treat all parties honestly. When serving a buyer, seller, landlord, tenant or other party in a non-agency capacity, REALTORS® remain obligated to treat all parties honestly. (Amended 1/01)

Standard of Practice 1-1

REALTORS®, when acting as principals in a real estate transaction, remain obligated by the duties imposed by the Code of Ethics. (Amended 1/93)

Standard of Practice 1-2

The duties the Code of Ethics imposes are applicable whether REALTORS® are acting as agents or in legally recognized non-agency capacities except that any duty imposed exclusively on agents by law or regulation shall not be imposed by this Code of Ethics on REALTORS® acting in non-agency capacities. As used in this Code of Ethics, "client" means the person(s) or entity(ies) with whom a REALTOR® or a REALTOR®'s firm has an agency or legally recognized non-agency relationship; "customer" means a party to a real estate transaction who receives information, services, or benefits but has no contractual relationship with the REALTOR® or the REALTOR®'s firm; "agent" means a real estate licensee (including brokers and sales associates) acting in an agency relationship as defined by state law or regulation; and "broker" means a real estate licensee (including brokers and sales associates) acting as an agent or in a legally recognized non-agency capacity. (Adopted 1/95, Amended 1/99)

Standard of Practice 1-3

REALTORS®, in attempting to secure a listing, shall not deliberately mislead the owner as to market value.

Standard of Practice 1-4

REALTORS®, when seeking to become a buyer/tenant representative, shall not mislead buyers or tenants as to savings or other benefits that might be realized through use of the REALTOR®'s services. (Amended 1/93)

Standard of Practice 1-5

REALTORS® may represent the seller/landlord and buyer/tenant in the same transaction only after full disclosure to and with informed consent of both parties. (Adopted 1/93)

Standard of Practice 1-6

REALTORS® shall submit offers and counter-offers objectively and as quickly as possible. (Adopted 1/93, Amended 1/95)

NATIONAL ASSOCIATION OF REALTORS®

The Voice for Real Estate®

www.realtor.org/realtororg.nsf/pages/narcode
DRE Code of Ethics

Standard of Practice 1-7

When acting as listing brokers, REALTORS® shall continue to submit to the seller/landlord all offers and counter-offers until closing or execution of a lease unless the seller/landlord has waived this obligation in writing. REALTORS® shall not be obligated to continue to market the property after an offer has been accepted by the seller/landlord. REALTORS® shall recommend that sellers/landlords obtain the advice of legal counsel prior to acceptance of a subsequent offer except where the acceptance is contingent on the termination of the pre-existing purchase contract or lease. (Amended 1/93)

Standard of Practice 1-8

REALTORS® acting as agents or brokers of buyers/tenants shall submit to buyers/tenants all offers and counter-offers until acceptance but have no obligation to continue to show properties to their clients after an offer has been accepted unless otherwise agreed in writing. REALTORS® acting as agents or brokers of buyers/tenants shall recommend that buyers/tenants obtain the advice of legal counsel if there is a question as to whether a pre-existing contract has been terminated. (Adopted 1/93, Amended 1/99)

Standard of Practice 1-9

The obligation of REALTORS® to preserve confidential information (as defined by state law) provided by their clients in the course of any agency relationship or non-agency relationship recognized by law continues after termination of agency relationships or any non-agency relationships recognized by law. REALTORS® shall not knowingly, during or following the termination of professional relationships with their clients: 1) reveal confidential information of clients; or 2) use confidential information of clients to the disadvantage of clients; or 3) use confidential information of clients for the REALTOR®'s advantage or the advantage of third parties unless: a) clients consent after full disclosure; or b) REALTORS® are required by court order; or c) it is the intention of a client to commit a crime and the information is necessary to prevent the crime; or d) it is necessary to defend a REALTOR® or the REALTOR®'s employees or associates against an accusation of wrongful conduct. Information concerning latent material defects is not considered confidential information under this Code of Ethics. (Adopted 1/93, Amended 1/01)

Standard of Practice 1-10

REALTORS® shall, consistent with the terms and conditions of their real estate licensure and their property management agreement, competently manage the property of clients with due regard for the rights, safety and health of tenants and others lawfully on the premises. (Adopted 1/95, Amended 1/00)

Standard of Practice 1-11

REALTORS® who are employed to maintain or manage a client's property shall exercise due diligence and make reasonable efforts to protect it against reasonably foreseeable contingencies and losses. (Adopted 1/95)

Standard of Practice 1-12

When entering into listing contracts, REALTORS® must advise sellers/landlords of: 1) the REALTOR®'s general company policies regarding cooperation with and compensation to subagents, buyer/ tenant agents and/or brokers acting in legally recognized non-agency capacities; 2) the fact that buyer/tenant agents or brokers, even if compensated by listing brokers, or by sellers/landlords may represent the interests of buyers/tenants; and 3) any potential for listing brokers to act as disclosed dual agents, e.g. buyer/tenant agents. (Adopted 1/93, Renumbered 1/98, Amended 1/99)

Standard of Practice 1-13

When entering into buyer/tenant agreements, REALTORS® must advise potential clients of: 1) the REALTOR®'s general company policies regarding cooperation and compensation; and 2) any potential for the buyer/tenant representative to act as a disclosed dual agent, e.g. listing broker, subagent, landlord's agent, etc. (Adopted 1/93, Renumbered 1/98, Amended 1/99)

Standard of Practice 1-14

Fees for preparing appraisals or other valuations shall not be contingent upon the amount of the appraisal or valuation. (Adopted 1/02)

Article 2

REALTORS® shall avoid exaggeration, misrepresentation, or concealment of pertinent facts relating to the property or the transaction. REALTORS® shall not, however, be obligated to discover latent defects in the property, to advise on matters outside the scope of their real estate license, or to disclose facts which are confidential under the scope of agency or non-agency relationships as defined by state law. (Amended 1/00)

Standard of Practice 2-1

REALTORS® shall only be obligated to discover and disclose adverse factors reasonably apparent to someone with expertise in those areas required by their real estate licensing authority. Article 2 does not impose upon the REALTOR® the obligation of expertise in other professional or technical disciplines. (Amended 1/96)

Standard of Practice 2-2

(Renumbered as Standard of Practice 1-12 1/98)

Standard of Practice 2-3

Renumbered as Standard of Practice 1-13 1/98

Standard of Practice 2-4

REALTORS® shall not be parties to the naming of a false consideration in any document, unless it be the naming of an obviously nominal consideration.

Standard of Practice 2-5

Factors defined as "non-material" by law or regulation or which are expressly referenced in law or regulation as not being subject to disclosure are considered not "pertinent" for purposes of Article 2. (Adopted 1/93)

Article 3

REALTORS® shall cooperate with other brokers except when cooperation is not in the client's best interest. The obligation to cooperate does not include the obligation to share commissions, fees, or to otherwise compensate another broker. (Amended 1/95)

Standard of Practice 3-1

REALTORS®, acting as exclusive agents or brokers of sellers/ landlords, establish the terms and conditions of offers to cooperate. Unless expressly indicated in offers to cooperate, cooperating brokers may not assume that the offer of cooperation includes an offer of compensation. Terms of compensation, if any, shall be ascertained by cooperating brokers before beginning efforts to accept the offer of cooperation. (Amended 1/99)

Standard of Practice 3-2

REALTORS® shall, with respect to offers of compensation to another REALTOR®, timely communicate any change of compensation for cooperative services to the other REALTOR® prior to the time such REALTOR® produces an offer to purchase/lease the property. (Amended 1/94)

Standard of Practice 3-3

Standard of Practice 3-2 does not preclude the listing broker and cooperating broker from entering into an agreement to change cooperative compensation. (Adopted 1/94)

Standard of Practice 3-4

REALTORS®, acting as listing brokers, have an affirmative obligation to disclose the existence of dual or variable rate commission arrangements (i.e., listings where one amount of commission is payable if the listing broker's firm is the procuring cause of sale/lease and a different amount of commission is payable if the sale/lease results through the efforts of the seller/landlord or a cooperating broker). The listing broker shall, as soon as practical, disclose the existence of such arrangements to potential cooperating brokers and shall, in response to inquiries from cooperating brokers, disclose the differential that would result in a cooperative transaction or in a sale/lease that results through the efforts of the seller/landlord. If the cooperating broker is a buyer/tenant representative, the buyer/tenant representative must disclose such information to their client before the client makes an offer to purchase or lease. (Amended 1/02)

Standard of Practice 3-5

It is the obligation of subagents to promptly disclose all pertinent facts to the principal's agent prior to as well as after a purchase or lease agreement is executed. (Amended 1/93)

Standard of Practice 3-6

REALTORS® shall disclose the existence of an accepted offer to any broker seeking cooperation. (Adopted 5/86)

Standard of Practice 3-7

When seeking information from another REALTOR® concerning property under a management or listing agreement, REALTORS® shall disclose their REALTOR® status and whether their interest is personal or on behalf of a client and, if on behalf of a client, their representational status. (Amended 1/95)

Standard of Practice 3-8

REALTORS® shall not misrepresent the availability of access to show or inspect a listed property. (Amended 11/87)

Article 4

REALTORS® shall not acquire an interest in or buy or present offers from themselves, any member of their immediate families, their firms or any member thereof, or any entities in which they have any ownership interest, any real property without making their true position known to the owner or the owner's agent or broker. In selling property they own, or in which they have any interest, REALTORS® shall reveal their ownership or interest in writing to the purchaser or the purchaser's representative. (Amended 1/00)

Standard of Practice 4-1

For the protection of all parties, the disclosures required by Article 4 shall be in writing and provided by REALTORS® prior to the signing of any contract. (Adopted 2/86)

Article 5

REALTORS® shall not undertake to provide professional services concerning a property or its value where they have a present or contemplated interest unless such interest is specifically disclosed to all affected parties.

Article 6

REALTORS® shall not accept any commission, rebate, or profit on expenditures made for their client, without the client's knowledge and consent. When recommending real estate products or services (e.g., homeowner's insurance, warranty programs, mortgage financing, title insurance, etc.), REALTORS® shall disclose to the client or customer to whom the recommendation is made any financial benefits or fees, other than real estate referral fees, the REALTOR® or REALTOR®'s firm may receive as a direct result of such recommendation. (Amended 1/99)

Standard of Practice 6-1

REALTORS® shall not recommend or suggest to a client or a customer the use of services of another organization or business entity in which they have a direct interest without disclosing such interest at the time of the recommendation or suggestion. (Amended 5/88)

Article 7

In a transaction, REALTORS® shall not accept compensation from more than one party, even if permitted by law, without disclosure to all parties and the informed consent of the REALTOR®'s client or clients. (Amended 1/93)

Article 8

REALTORS® shall keep in a special account in an appropriate financial institution, separated from their own funds, monies coming into their possession in trust for other persons, such as escrows, trust funds, clients' monies, and other like items.

Article 9

REALTORS®, for the protection of all parties, shall assure whenever possible that agreements shall be in writing, and shall be in clear and understandable language expressing the specific terms, conditions, obligations and commitments of the parties. A copy of each agreement shall be furnished to each party upon their signing or initialing. (Amended 1/95)

Standard of Practice 9-1

For the protection of all parties, REALTORS® shall use reasonable care to ensure that documents pertaining to the purchase, sale, or lease of real estate are kept current through the use of written extensions or amendments. (Amended 1/93)

Duties to the Public

Article 10

REALTORS® shall not deny equal professional services to any person for reasons of race, color, religion, sex, handicap, familial status, or national origin. REALTORS® shall not be parties to any plan or agreement to discriminate against a person or persons on the basis of race, color, religion, sex, handicap, familial status, or national origin. (Amended 1/90) REALTORS®, in their real estate employment practices, shall not discriminate against any person or persons on the basis of race, color, religion, sex, handicap, familial status, or national origin. (Amended 1/00)

Standard of Practice 10-1

REALTORS® shall not volunteer information regarding the racial, religious or ethnic composition of any neighborhood and shall not engage in any activity which may result in panic selling. REALTORS® shall not print, display or circulate any statement or advertisement with respect to the selling or renting of a property that indicates any preference, limitations or discrimination based on race, color, religion, sex, handicap, familial status, or national origin. (Adopted 1/94)

Standard of Practice 10-2

As used in Article 10 "real estate employment practices" relates to employees and independent contractors providing real-estate related services and the administrative and clerical staff directly supporting those individuals. (Adopted 1/00)

Article 11

The services which REALTORS® provide to their clients and customers shall conform to the standards of practice and competence which are reasonably expected in the specific real estate disciplines in which they engage; specifically, residential real estate brokerage, real property management, commercial and industrial real estate brokerage, real estate appraisal, real estate counseling, real estate syndication, real estate auction, and international real estate.

REALTORS® shall not undertake to provide specialized professional services concerning a type of property or service that is outside their field of competence unless they engage the assistance of one who is competent on such types of property or service, or unless the facts are fully disclosed to the client. Any persons engaged to provide such assistance shall be so identified to the client and their contribution to the assignment should be set forth. (Amended 1/95)

Standard of Practice 11-1

When REALTORS® prepare opinions of real property value or price, other than in pursuit of a listing or to assist a potential purchaser in formulating a purchase offer, such opinions shall include the following: 1) identification of the subject property 2) date prepared 3) defined value or price 4) limiting conditions, including statements of purpose(s) and intended user(s) 5) any present or contemplated interest, including the possibility of representing the seller/landlord or buyers/tenants 6) basis for the opinion, including applicable market data 7) if the opinion is not an appraisal, a statement to that effect. (Amended 1/01)

Standard of Practice 11-2

The obligations of the Code of Ethics in respect of real estate disciplines other than appraisal shall be interpreted and applied in accordance with the standards of competence and practice which clients and the public reasonably require to protect their rights and interests considering the complexity of the transaction, the availability of expert assistance, and, where the REALTOR® is an agent or subagent, the obligations of a fiduciary. (Adopted 1/95)

Standard of Practice 11-3

When REALTORS® provide consultive services to clients which involve advice or counsel for a fee (not a commission), such advice shall be rendered in an objective manner and the fee shall not be contingent on the substance of the advice or counsel given. If brokerage or transaction services are to be provided in addition to consultive services, a separate compensation may be paid with prior agreement between the client and REALTOR®. (Adopted 1/96)

Standard of Practice 11-4

The competency required by Article 11 relates to services contracted for between REALTORS® and their clients or customers; the duties expressly imposed by the Code of Ethics; and the duties imposed by law or regulation. (Adopted 1/02)

Article 12

REALTORS® shall be careful at all times to present a true picture in their advertising and representations to the public. REALTORS® shall also ensure that their professional status (e.g., broker, appraiser, property manager, etc.) or status as REALTORS® is clearly identifiable in any such advertising. (Amended 1/93)

Standard of Practice 12-1

REALTORS® may use the term "free" and similar terms in their advertising and in other representations provided that all terms governing availability of the offered product or service are clearly disclosed at the same time. (Amended 1/97)

Standard of Practice 12-2

REALTORS® may represent their services as "free" or without cost even if they expect to receive compensation from a source other than their client provided that the potential for the REALTOR® to obtain a benefit from a third party is clearly disclosed at the same time. (Amended 1/97)

Standard of Practice 12-3

The offering of premiums, prizes, merchandise discounts or other inducements to list, sell, purchase, or lease is not, in itself, unethical even if receipt of the benefit is contingent on listing, selling, purchasing, or leasing through the REALTOR® making the offer. However, REALTORS® must exercise care and candor in any such advertising or other public or private representations so that any party interested in receiving or otherwise benefiting from the REALTOR®'s offer will have clear, thorough, advance understanding of all the terms and conditions of the offer. The offering of any inducements to do business is subject to the limitations and restrictions of state law and the ethical obligations established by any applicable Standard of Practice. (Amended 1/95)

Standard of Practice 12-4

REALTORS® shall not offer for sale/lease or advertise property without authority. When acting as listing brokers or as subagents, REALTORS® shall not quote a price different from that agreed upon with the seller/landlord. (Amended 1/93)

Standard of Practice 12-5

REALTORS® shall not advertise nor permit any person employed by or affiliated with them to advertise listed property without disclosing the name of the firm. (Adopted 11/86)

Standard of Practice 12-6

REALTORS®, when advertising unlisted real property for sale/lease in which they have an ownership interest, shall disclose their status as both owners/landlords and as REALTORS® or real estate licensees. (Amended 1/93)

Standard of Practice 12-7

Only REALTORS® who participated in the transaction as the listing broker or cooperating broker (selling broker) may claim to have "sold" the property. Prior to closing, a cooperating broker may post a "sold" sign only with the consent of the listing broker. (Amended 1/96)

Article 13

REALTORS® shall not engage in activities that constitute the unauthorized practice of law and shall recommend that legal counsel be obtained when the interest of any party to the transaction requires it.

Article 14

If charged with unethical practice or asked to present evidence or to cooperate in any other way, in any professional standards proceeding or investigation, REALTORS® shall place all pertinent facts before the proper tribunals of the Member Board or affiliated institute, society, or council in which membership is held and shall take no action to disrupt or obstruct such processes. (Amended 1/99)

Standard of Practice 14-1

REALTORS® shall not be subject to disciplinary proceedings in more than one Board of REALTORS® or affiliated institute, society or council in which they hold membership with respect to alleged violations of the Code of Ethics relating to the same transaction or event. (Amended 1/95)

Standard of Practice 14-2

REALTORS® shall not make any unauthorized disclosure or dissemination of the allegations, findings, or decision developed in connection with an ethics hearing or appeal or in connection with an arbitration hearing or procedural review. (Amended 1/92)

Standard of Practice 14-3

REALTORS® shall not obstruct the Board's investigative or professional standards proceedings by instituting or threatening to institute actions for libel, slander or defamation against any party to a professional standards proceeding or their witnesses based on the filing of an arbitration request, an ethics complaint, or testimony given before any tribunal. (Adopted 11/87, Amended 1/99)

Standard of Practice 14-4

REALTORS® shall not intentionally impede the Board's investigative or disciplinary proceedings by filing multiple ethics complaints based on the same event or transaction. (Adopted 11/88)

Duties to REALTORS®

Article 15

REALTORS® shall not knowingly or recklessly make false or misleading statements about competitors, their businesses, or their business practices. (Amended 1/92)

Standard of Practice 15-1

REALTORS® shall not knowingly or recklessly file false or unfounded ethics complaints. (Adopted 1/00)

Article 16

REALTORS® shall not engage in any practice or take any action inconsistent with the agency or other exclusive relationship recognized by law that other REALTORS® have with clients. (Amended 1/98)

Standard of Practice 16-1

Article 16 is not intended to prohibit aggressive or innovative business practices which are otherwise ethical and does not prohibit disagreements with other REALTORS® involving commission, fees, compensation or other forms of payment or expenses. (Adopted 1/93, Amended 1/95)

Standard of Practice 16-2

Article 16 does not preclude REALTORS® from making general announcements to prospective clients describing their services and the terms of their availability even though some recipients may have entered into agency agreements or other exclusive relationships with another REALTOR®. A general telephone canvass, general mailing or distribution addressed to all prospective clients in a given geographical area or in a given profession, business, club, or organization, or other classification or group is deemed "general" for purposes of this standard. (Amended 1/98)

Article 16 is intended to recognize as unethical two basic types of solicitations:

First, telephone or personal solicitations of property owners who have been identified by a real estate sign, multiple listing compilation, or other information service as having exclusively listed their property with another REALTOR®; and Second, mail or other forms of written solicitations of prospective clients whose properties are exclusively listed with another REALTOR® when such solicitations are not part of a general mailing but are directed specifically to property owners identified through compilations of current listings, "for sale" or "for rent" signs, or other sources of information required by Article 3 and Multiple Listing Service rules to be made available to other REALTORS® under offers of subagency or cooperation. (Amended 1/93)

Standard of Practice 16-3

Article 16 does not preclude REALTORS® from contacting the client of another broker for the purpose of offering to provide, or entering into a contract to provide, a different type of real estate service unrelated to the type of service currently being provided (e.g., property management as opposed to brokerage). However,

information received through a Multiple Listing Service or any other offer of cooperation may not be used to target clients of other REALTORS® to whom such offers to provide services may be made. (Amended 1/93)

Standard of Practice 16-4

REALTORS® shall not solicit a listing which is currently listed exclusively with another broker. However, if the listing broker, when asked by the REALTOR®, refuses to disclose the expiration date and nature of such listing; i.e., an exclusive right to sell, an exclusive agency, open listing, or other form of contractual agreement between the listing broker and the client, the REALTOR® may contact the owner to secure such information and may discuss the terms upon which the REALTOR® might take a future listing or, alternatively, may take a listing to become effective upon expiration of any existing exclusive listing. (Amended 1/94)

Standard of Practice 16-5

REALTORS® shall not solicit buyer/tenant agreements from buyers/tenants who are subject to exclusive buyer/tenant agreements. However, if asked by a REALTOR®, the broker refuses to disclose the expiration date of the exclusive buyer/tenant agreement, the REALTOR® may contact the buyer/tenant to secure such information and may discuss the terms upon which the REALTOR® might enter into a future buyer/tenant agreement or, alternatively, may enter into a buyer/tenant agreement to become effective upon the expiration of any existing exclusive buyer/tenant agreement. (Adopted 1/94, Amended 1/98)

Standard of Practice 16-6

When REALTORS® are contacted by the client of another REALTOR® regarding the creation of an exclusive relationship to provide the same type of service, and REALTORS® have not directly or indirectly initiated such discussions, they may discuss the terms upon which they might enter into a future agreement or, alternatively, may enter into an agreement which becomes effective upon expiration of any existing exclusive agreement. (Amended 1/98)

Standard of Practice 16-7

The fact that a client has retained a REALTOR® as an agent or in another exclusive relationship in one or more past transactions does not preclude other REALTORS® from seeking such former client's future business. (Amended 1/98)

Standard of Practice 16-8

The fact that an exclusive agreement has been entered into with a REALTOR® shall not preclude or inhibit any other REALTOR® from entering into a similar agreement after the expiration of the prior agreement. (Amended 1/98)

Standard of Practice 16-9

REALTORS®, prior to entering into an agency agreement or other exclusive relationship, have an affirmative obligation to make reasonable efforts to determine whether the client is subject to a current, valid exclusive agreement to provide the same type of real estate service. (Amended 1/98)

Standard of Practice 16-10

REALTORS®, acting as agents of, or in another relationship with, buyers or tenants, shall disclose that relationship to the seller/landlord's agent or broker at first contact and shall provide written confirmation of that disclosure to the seller/landlord's agent or broker not later than execution of a purchase agreement or lease. (Amended 1/98)

Standard of Practice 16-11

On unlisted property, REALTORS® acting as buyer/tenant agents or brokers shall disclose that relationship to the seller/landlord at first contact for that client and shall provide written confirmation of such disclosure to the seller/landlord not later than execution of any purchase or lease agreement.

REALTORS® shall make any request for anticipated compensation from the seller/landlord at first contact. (Amended 1/98)

Standard of Practice 16-12

REALTORS®, acting as agents or brokers of sellers/landlords or as subagents of listing brokers, shall disclose that relationship to buyers/tenants as soon as practicable and shall provide written confirmation of such disclosure to buyers/tenants not later than execution of any purchase or lease agreement. (Amended 1/98)

Standard of Practice 16-13

All dealings concerning property exclusively listed, or with buyer/tenants who are subject to an exclusive agreement shall be carried on with the client's agent or broker, and not with the client, except with the consent of the client's agent or broker or except where such dealings are initiated by the client. (Adopted 1/93, Amended 1/98)

Standard of Practice 16-14

REALTORS® are free to enter into contractual relationships or to negotiate with sellers/landlords, buyers/tenants or others who are not subject to an exclusive agreement but shall not knowingly obligate them to pay more than one commission except with their informed consent. (Amended 1/98)

Standard of Practice 16-15

In cooperative transactions REALTORS® shall compensate cooperating REALTORS® (principal brokers) and shall not compensate nor offer to compensate, directly or indirectly, any of the sales licensees employed by or affiliated with other REALTORS® without the prior express knowledge and consent of the cooperating broker.

Standard of Practice 16-16

REALTORS®, acting as subagents or buyer/tenant agents or brokers, shall not use the terms of an offer to purchase/lease to attempt to modify the listing broker's offer of compensation to subagents or buyer's agents or brokers nor make the submission of an executed offer to purchase/lease contingent on the listing broker's agreement to modify the offer of compensation. (Amended 1/98)

Standard of Practice 16-17

REALTORS® acting as subagents or as buyer/tenant agents or brokers, shall not attempt to extend a listing broker's offer of cooperation and/or compensation to other brokers without the consent of the listing broker. (Amended 1/98)

Standard of Practice 16-18

REALTORS® shall not use information obtained from listing brokers through offers to cooperate made through multiple listing services or through other offers of cooperation to refer listing brokers' clients to other brokers or to create buyer/ tenant relationships with listing brokers' clients, unless such use is authorized by listing brokers. (Amended 1/02)

Standard of Practice 16-19

Signs giving notice of property for sale, rent, lease, or exchange shall not be placed on property without consent of the seller/landlord. (Amended 1/93)

Standard of Practice 16-20

REALTORS®, prior to or after terminating their relationship with their current firm, shall not induce clients of their current firm to cancel exclusive contractual agreements between the client and that firm. This does not preclude REALTORS® (principals) from establishing agreements with their associated licensees governing assignability of exclusive agreements. (Adopted 1/98)

Article 17

In the event of contractual disputes or specific non-contractual disputes as defined in Standard of Practice 17-4 between REALTORS® (principals) associated with different firms, arising out of their relationship as REALTORS®, the REALTORS® shall submit the dispute to arbitration in accordance with the regulations of their Board or Boards rather than litigate the matter.

In the event clients of REALTORS® wish to arbitrate contractual disputes arising out of real estate transactions, REALTORS® shall arbitrate those disputes in accordance with the regulations of their Board, provided the clients agree to be bound by the decision. The obligation to participate in arbitration contemplated by this Article includes the obligation of REALTORS® (principals) to cause their firms to arbitrate and be bound by any award. (Amended 1/01)

Standard of Practice 17-1

The filing of litigation and refusal to withdraw from it by REALTORS® in an arbitrable matter constitutes a refusal to arbitrate. (Adopted 2/86)

Standard of Practice 17-2

Article 17 does not require REALTORS® to arbitrate in those circumstances when all parties to the dispute advise the Board in writing that they choose not to arbitrate before the Board. (Amended 1/93)

Standard of Practice 17-3

REALTORS®, when acting solely as principals in a real estate transaction, are not obligated to arbitrate disputes with other REALTORS® absent a specific written agreement to the contrary. (Adopted 1/96)

Standard of Practice 17-4

Specific non-contractual disputes that are subject to arbitration pursuant to Article 17 are:

1) Where a listing broker has compensated a cooperating broker and another cooperating broker subsequently claims to be the procuring cause of the sale or lease. In such cases the complainant may name the first cooperating broker as respondent and arbitration may proceed without the listing broker being named as a respondent. Alternatively, if the complaint is brought against the listing broker, the listing broker may name the first cooperating broker as a third-party respondent. In either instance the decision of the hearing panel as to procuring cause shall be conclusive with respect to all current or subsequent claims of the parties for compensation arising out of the underlying cooperative transaction. (Adopted 1/97)

2) Where a buyer or tenant representative is compensated by the seller or landlord, and not by the listing broker, and the listing broker, as a result, reduces the commission owed by the seller or landlord and, subsequent to such actions, another cooperating broker claims to be the procuring cause of sale or lease. In such cases the complainant may name the first cooperating broker as respondent and arbitration may proceed without the listing broker being named as a respondent. Alternatively, if the complaint is brought against the listing broker, the listing broker may name the first cooperating broker as a third-party respondent. In either instance the decision of the hearing panel as to procuring cause shall be conclusive with respect to all current or subsequent claims of the parties for compensation arising out of the underlying cooperative transaction. (Adopted 1/97)

3) Where a buyer or tenant representative is compensated by the buyer or tenant and, as a result, the listing broker reduces the commission owed by the seller or landlord and, subsequent to such actions, another cooperating broker claims to be the procuring cause of sale or lease. In such cases the complainant may name the first cooperating broker as respondent and arbitration may proceed without the listing broker being named as a respondent. Alternatively, if the complaint is brought against the listing broker, the listing broker may name the first cooperating broker as a third-party respondent. In either instance the decision of the hearing panel as to procuring cause shall be conclusive with respect to all current or subsequent claims of the parties for compensation arising out of the underlying cooperative transaction. (Adopted 1/97)

4) Where two or more listing brokers claim entitlement to compensation pursuant to open listings with a seller or landlord who agrees to participate in arbitration (or who requests arbitration) and who agrees to be bound by the decision. In cases where one of the listing brokers has been compensated by the seller or landlord, the other listing broker, as complainant, may name the first listing broker as respondent and arbitration may proceed between the brokers. (Adopted 1/97)

The Code of Ethics was adopted in 1913. Amended at the Annual Convention in 1924, 1928, 1950, 1951, 1952, 1955, 1956, 1961, 1962, 1974, 1982, 1986, 1987, 1989, 1990, 1991, 1992, 1993, 1994, 1995, 1996, 1997, 1998, 1999, 2000, and 2001.

Explanatory Notes

The reader should be aware of the following policies which have been approved by the Board of Directors of the National Association:

In filing a charge of an alleged violation of the Code of Ethics by a REALTOR®, the charge must read as an alleged violation of one or more Articles of the Code. Standards of Practice may be cited in support of the charge.

The Standards of Practice serve to clarify the ethical obligations imposed by the various Articles and supplement, and do not substitute for, the Case Interpretations in Interpretations of the Code of Ethics.

Modifications to existing Standards of Practice and additional new Standards of Practice are approved from time to time. Readers are cautioned to ensure that the most recent publications are utilized.

D. REALTIST DEFINED

"Realtist" is the name for a member of the National Association of Real Estate Brokers (NAREB).

The National Association of Real Estate Brokers, or "Realtist," is the oldest minority trade association in the United States. *Although composed principally of African Americans and other minority real estate professionals, the **REALTIST** organization is an integrated entity open to all practitioners who are committed to achieving "democracy in housing."*

The organization has local boards in the largest cities in most states. The organization in this state, called the California Association of Real Estate Brokers, has four board affiliations:

1. Associated Real Property Brokers, Oakland
2. Consolidated Real Estate Brokers, Sacramento
3. Consolidated Realty Board, Los Angeles
4. Logan Heights Realty Board, San Diego

National Association of Real Estate Brokers
9831 Greenbelt Road
Lanham, Maryland 20706

A Realtist must be a member of a local board as well as a member of the national organization. Both on the local and national levels, Realtists work for better housing in the communities they serve. In many instances, individuals are both Realtors® and Realtists by virtue of dual membership.

E. NATIONAL ASSOCIATION OF HISPANIC REAL ESTATE PROFESSIONALS (NAHREP)

The National Association of Hispanic Real Estate Professionals (NAHREP) is a national non-profit trade association made up primarily of Hispanic members. This association was created to establish a venue where members can congregate, exchange ideas, and formulate an agenda beneficial to the collective well-being of the Hispanic segment of the industry. The mission statement of NAHREP is "To increase the Hispanic homeownership rate by empowering the real estate profesionals that serve Hispanic consumers."

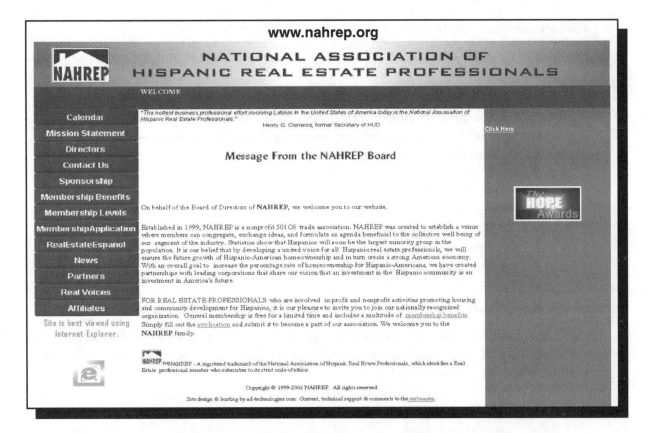

National Association of Hispanic Real Estate Professionals
1650 Hotel Circle North, Suite 215-A
San Diego, CA 92108

F. ASIAN REAL ESTATE ASSOCIATION OF AMERICA (AREAA)

The Asian Real Estate Association of America is a national trade association committed to enhancing business opportunities and success of real estate professionals serving the Asian American community. AREAA is dedicated to promoting homeownership opportunities among the many Asian American communities throughout the nation.

G. INDEPENDENT BOARDS

There are also several "independent" boards in California, some of which are large in membership and influential in their communities. Most of these boards are organized for some particular purpose, such as a multiple listing service. Many members of independent boards are also members of boards affiliated with CAR. Examples of independent boards are:

1. Chinese American Real Estate Professionals Association of Southern California
2. Chinese Real Estate Association of America

519

3. Korean Real Estate Brokers of Southern California
4. W.I.R.E. - Women in Real Estate

H. OTHER ASSOCIATIONS

In addition to the above-mentioned organizations, there are many trade associations and professional bodies that are related to the real estate business, such as:
1. American Bankers Association
2. American Savings and Loan Institute
3. Building Owners and Managers Association
4. Mortgage Bankers Association
5. National Association of Home Builders
6. National Association of Mutual Savings Banks
7. Prefabricated Home Manufacturers Institute

I. REAL ESTATE INSTRUCTOR AND LICENSING ASSOCIATIONS

In addition to the above mentioned organizations, there are real estate instructor organizations and other professional bodies that are related to real estate education and licensing. **See Figure 14-13**.

J. NO AFFILIATION NECESSARY

A real estate licensee need not be a member of any trade or professional association. In this case, he or she is simply referred to as a salesperson or broker. There is no compulsion for any licensee of the Department of Real Estate to join or affiliate with any local or state organization. That decision is strictly individual and personal.

Figure 14-13

REAL ESTATE TEACHERS' GROUPS

California Real Estate Educators Association (CREEA)

Real estate instructors from throughout the state have come together with the formation of CREEA, the California Real Estate Educators Association. This organization constitutes a chapter of REEA, the Real Estate Educators Association, a private trade association, which is international in scope. REEA has a reputation throughout the world for its comprehensive representation.

California Real Estate
Education Association
P.O. Box 1230
Costa Mesa, CA 92628
714-751-2787 Ext. 211

Real Estate Educators Association (REEA)
407 Wekiva Springs Road, Suite 241
Longwood, FL 32779
407-834-6688

www.creea.org (CREEA)
www.reea.org (REEA)
www.ccsf.edu/Resources/Real_Estate_Education_Center/
(California Community Colleges Real Estate Education Center)
www.arello.org (Association of Real Estate License Law Officials - ARELLO)

CALIFORNIA COMMUNITY COLLEGES
REAL ESTATE EDUCATION CENTER

The California Community Colleges Real Estate Education Center is a real estate instructors group sponsored by the California Department of Real Estate. The Center publishes a quarterly newsletter and sponsors educators' conferences three times a year in cooperation with the California Community College Chancellor's office. The newsletter, called *The Informer*, is a useful reference source to keep educators up to date on new laws and real estate practices. The conferences are held in the San Francisco Bay area, the Los Angeles area, and the San Diego area. For information about *The Informer* and Endowment Fund contact:

Tom Gruenig, Director
California Community Colleges
Real Estate Education Center
City College of San Francisco - Downtown Campus
800 Mission Street
San Francisco, California 94103
415-267-6550

Association of Real Estate
License Law Officials (ARELLO)
P. O. BOX 230159
Montgomery, AL 36123-0159

VIII. SUMMARY

A person who is actively involved in a real estate transaction at the service of another, in the expectation of receiving a commission must be licensed by the **Department of Real Estate (DRE)**, which is the regulatory agency for real estate in California. The DRE is governed by the **Real Estate Commissioner**, who is appointed by the governor and defended by the state Attorney General. The Commissioner does not settle commission disputes, take the place of a court of law, nor give legal advice, but the rules and regulations he or she issues do have the force and effect of law.

To obtain a **salesperson's license**, a candidate must: be 18 or over, honest and truthful, complete college level Real Estate Principles course and pass the state exam. The salesperson exam takes 3 hours and 15 minutes, has 150 questions and requires a 70% or better to pass.

A **conditional salespersons' license** can be obtained after taking the Real Estate Principles course. The license expires after 18 months, unless the salesperson completes the Real Estate Practice course and one other college-level (broker-required) real estate course. Once the two additional course are completed, the salesperson can apply for the (regular renewable) **four-year salesperson's license**. Applicants must apply for a license within one year from passing the exam date, at which time he or she will have to submit an **electronic fingerprint scan**.

A **broker's license** is required to operate a real estate office. A broker must be 18 years old, have had two years previous experience or college education, complete the required 8 broker courses, be honest and truthful, and pass the required examination. A four year degree (B.S. or B.A) = 2 years experience, and a two year degree (A.A.) = one year of experience.

The **continuing education requirement** of 45 hours every four years for a license renewal, includes three hours each of **Ethics, Agency, Trust Fund Handling**, and **Fair Housing**. After a second license renewal, these four three-hour courses can be replaced with a **six-hour CE survey course**.

In a sale of a business, (**Business Opportunity**) the real property is transferred by deed and the personal property by bill of sale. The three documents in a **personal security transaction** are: 1) a promissory note; 2) a security agreement; and 3) compliance with the UCC-1 financing statement. A **bulk transfer** involves the sale of a substantial part of the 1) inventory, items purchased for resale; 2) other supplies and equipment associated with the business. If tangible personal property is involved, escrow should check to be sure there are no past sales taxes due to the **State Board of Equalization**.

California Real Estate Law is the portion of the **Business and Professions Code** that refers to licensing and subdivision. The **Commissioners' Regulations** are rules that form part of the **California Administrative Code** and are enforced by the Real Estate Commissioner. The Commissioner can revoke, restrict, or suspend the license of any real estate agent for misconduct.

All agents must adhere to **Section 10176** (acting in a licensee capacity) and **Section 10177** of the **Business and Professions Code**, which have the force and effect of the law itself.

IX. TERMINOLOGY - CHAPTER 14

A. Broker's License
B. Business
C. Business Opportunity and Bulk Sales
D. California Association of Realtors®
E. Commissioner's Code of Ethics (2785)
F. Commissioner's Regulations

G. Continuing Education Requirements
H. Department of Real Estate (DRE)
I. Local Board of Realtors®
J. NAR Code of Ethics
K. NARELLO
L. National Association of Realtors® (NAR)

M. Police Power
N. Real Estate Advisory Commission
O. Real Estate Law
P. Realtist
Q. Realtor®
R. Recovery Fund
S. Trade Association

1.____ A national trade association of real estate professionals who call themselves Realtors®.

2.____ The sale of a business.

3.____ The right of the government to enact laws for the protection of the general public. Laws such as zoning ordinances, building codes, and health and safety requirements are common in real estate.

4.____ Any legitimate activity by which people expect to earn money.

5.____ The division of the state government responsible for the licensing and regulation of persons engaged in the real estate business. Heading the department is the Real Estate Commissioner.

6.____ Composed of ten members, it recommends and makes suggestions to the Commissioner.

7.____ A voluntary, nonprofit organization made up of independent firms in the same industry. CAR and NAR are examples.

8.____ A license that allows a person to represent, for compensation, one or more parties in a real estate transaction.

9.____ Established to compensate people who have suffered financial loss due to the wrongful act of a real estate licensee.

10.____ Rules that form part of the California Administrative Code. Established regulations are enforced by the Commissioner of Real Estate.

11.____ The portion of the Business and Professions Code that refers to licensing and subdivisions.

12.____ A local voluntary organization in a given community, made up of real estate licensees.

13.____ The state division of the National Association of Realtors.

14.____ The 45 clock hours of Commissioner-approved courses that must be taken by all real estate licensees during the four-year period preceding license renewal.

15.____ The association made up of real estate license law officials.

16.____ Standards of professional conduct and business practices established by the commissioner to enhance the professionalism of the California real estate industry.

17.____ A term reserved for active members of the National Association of Realtors or the California Association of Realtors.

18.____ Members of the National Association of Real Estate Brokers.

19.____ In order to be a realtor, a person must swear to uphold this code.

X. MULTIPLE CHOICE

1. The Real Estate Commissioner is:

    a. appointed by the Governor.
    b. appointed by the Legislature.
    c. appointed by the Board of Governors.
    d. elected by members of CAR.

2. Which of the following would be required to have a real estate license?

    a. A person who solicits or obtains listings.
    b. A person who is a cemetery owner.
    c. A person who is an employee of a lending institution.
    d. A person who collects loan payments made on real property.

3. How many clock hours of continuing education are required for renewal of a real estate license?

    a. 10
    b. 20
    c. 45
    d. 60

4. The salesperson's examination process consists of:

    a. 150 multiple choice question test.
    b. photo identification required for entry.
    c. three-and-a-quarter-hour exam period.
    d. all of the above.

5. Bulk sales of inventory supplies and associated equipment requires, by law, notice to the:

    a. creditors.
    b. Department of Real Estate.
    c. Department of Motor Vehicles.
    d. buyers.

6. The name for a member of a real estate trade association that consists of predominantly African-American and other minority members is a:

    a. realtor®.
    b. realist.
    c. salesperson.
    d. realtist.

7. With regard to the recovery fund, what is the total maximum payable for one salesperson's offense?

   a. $20,000
   b. $40,000
   c. $50,000
   d. $100,000

8. To secure a salesperson's license, a person is NOT required to:

   a. be 18 years old.
   b. pass the exam.
   c. be a U.S. citizen.
   d. file a set of fingerprints.

9. A real estate licensee may sell a business in addition to real estate. This is called:

   a. business opportunities.
   b. business sales.
   c. resale license.
   d. none of the above.

10. Any person who is a salesperson or broker must also be a(n):

   a. realtor®.
   b. realtist.
   c. independent board member.
   d. none of the above.

ANSWERS: 1. a; 2. a; 3. a; 4. c; 5. d; 6. d; 7. d; 8. c; 9. a; 10. d

Chapter 15
Real Estate Math

Real estate, as you have learned, can be an extremely profitable profession. The licensee who is able to compute quickly and accurately the mathematics underlying most transactions will be in a better position to capitalize on opportunities as they arise.

This chapter will illustrate and explain some basic mathematical skills useful to a career in real estate. Familiarity with fundamental arithmetic and a few simple formulas along with plain common sense will provide the necessary background. Such knowledge will not only assist in the practice of real estate, but should also prove advantageous in passing the licensing exam. **Figure 15-1** is a table of common measurements.

It might also prove to your advantage to bring a calculator with you when taking the salesperson's examination. The state permits applicants to use electronic calculators as long as they are battery operated, non-programmable, silent, and without printout capability. Such a device will free you from tedious and time-consuming arithmetic work in order to concentrate on the reasoning behind the problems you will encounter.

Figure 15-1

MEASUREMENTS

(A SALESPERSON SHOULD BE FAMILIAR WITH THESE)

LINEAR

1 foot (ft) = 12 inches (in.)
1 yard (yd) = 3 feet (ft.)
1 rod = 16.5 ft = 5.5 yd
1 mile = 5,280 ft = 1,760 yd = 320 rods

SQUARE

1 sq. ft. = 144 sq. in.
1 sq. yd. = 9 sq. ft.
1 acre = 43,560 sq. ft. = 4,840 sq. yd. = 160 sq. rods

CUBIC

1 cu. ft. = 1,728 cu. in.
1 cu. yd. = 27 cu. ft.

LAND DESCRIPTION

1 link = 7.92 inches
1 rod = 25 links
1 chain = l00 links = 66 ft. = 4 rods
1 mile = 80 chains
1 Acre = 43,560 sq. ft.
1 Township = 36 sections = 36 square miles = 23,040 acres
1 section = 1 mile square = 640 acres = 1/36 of a township
1 circle = 360 degrees (°)
1 quadrant = 90 degrees (°)
1 degree (°) = 60 minutes (´)
1 minute (´) = 60 seconds (")

I. Area Measurement

LAND AREA is the surface space between lot lines measured in square feet.

A. AREA OF A RECTANGULAR LOT

A RECTANGULAR LOT is a four-sided parcel whose opposite sides are equal in length and right angles are formed by the intersection of the sides. The dimensions of a rectangle are equal on two sides. Most lots encountered will be rectangular in shape.

1. How Do We Get "Square" Measurement?

The area of a rectangular or square lot is determined by multiplying the length by the width. The result is expressed in square feet, square yards, or some similar expression. The formula is:

$$A = L \times W$$

$$AREA = LENGTH \times WIDTH$$

EXAMPLE: How many square feet would there be in a rectangular parcel 100 feet long and 50 feet wide?

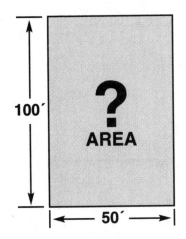

$A = L \times W$

$AREA = LENGTH \times WIDTH$

$AREA = 100\ FEET \times 50\ FEET$

$A = 100 \times 50$

$A = 5,000\ SQUARE\ FEET$

ANSWER: The area of this lot is calculated to be 5,000 square feet.

B. AREA OF A TRIANGULAR LOT

A TRIANGULAR LOT is a three-sided parcel.

In order to determine the area of a triangular parcel, we must know the measurements of its base and height.

The *BASE OF A TRIANGULAR LOT* is the side that is horizontal. The *HEIGHT OF A TRIANGULAR LOT* is the perpendicular distance from the base to the highest point.

The area of a triangular parcel is determined by multiplying the base by the height, and then dividing by two. This is normally expressed by the formula:

$$A = \frac{B \times H}{2}$$

$$AREA = \frac{BASE \times HEIGHT}{2}$$

Here is a sample exercise for you to try:

>   **EXAMPLE:** How many square feet would there be in a triangular lot with a 150 foot base and a height of 100 feet?

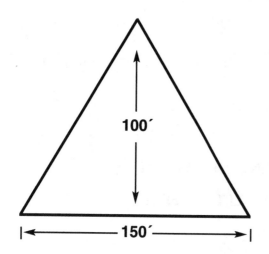

$$A = \frac{B \times H}{2}$$

$$AREA = \frac{BASE \times HEIGHT}{2}$$

$$AREA = \frac{150\ FEET \times 100\ FEET}{2}$$

$$A = \frac{150 \times 100}{2}$$

$$A = \frac{15,000}{2}$$

$$A = 7,500\ SQUARE\ FEET$$

>   **ANSWER:** The area of this lot is 7,500 square feet.

C. AREA OF AN IRREGULAR LOT

An *IRREGULAR LOT is a parcel that does not consist of a single known shape.* Often the area of an irregular or circular parcel cannot be measured accurately without the help of a land measurement expert, such as a surveyor. Many times, though, an irregular lot is simply made up of a series of rectangles and triangles, the combined measures of which make up the measure of the whole. In these cases the square footage of the parcel can be determined through the use of techniques already described in this chapter.

The area of an irregular parcel is determined by breaking the lot up into the various rectangles and triangles which comprise it, and totaling their areas.

1. An Irregular Lot Problem

EXAMPLE: What would be the total area of the irregular lot shown below? Use the dimensions given to calculate your answer.

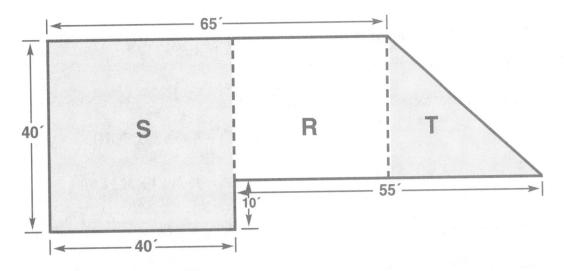

ANSWER: The irregular lot is broken up into a square, a rectangle, and a triangle. The area of the parcel is the total of the areas of each of these.

TOTAL AREA = AREA (S) + AREA (R) + AREA (T)

TOTAL AREA = AREA SQUARE + AREA RECTANGLE + AREA TRIANGLE

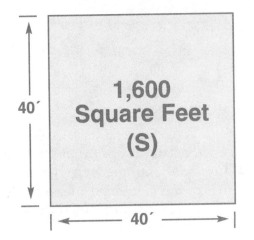

AREA (S) = L x W

AREA (S) = LENGTH x WIDTH

AREA (S) = 40 FEET x 40 FEET

AREA (S) = 40 x 40

AREA (S) = 1,600 SQUARE FEET

The area of the square (S) is 1,600 square feet.

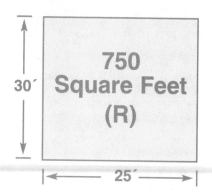

AREA (R) = L x W

AREA (R) = LENGTH x WIDTH

AREA (R) = 30 FEET x 25 FEET

AREA (R) = 30 x 25

AREA (R) = 750 SQUARE FEET

The area of the rectangular (R) is 750 square feet.

AREA (T) = $\dfrac{B \times H}{2}$

AREA (T) = $\dfrac{BASE \times HEIGHT}{2}$

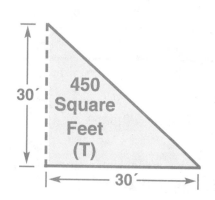

AREA (T) = $\dfrac{30\ FEET \times 30\ FEET}{2}$

AREA (T) = $\dfrac{30 \times 30}{2}$

AREA (T) = $\dfrac{900}{2}$

AREA (T) = 450 SQUARE FEET

The area of the triangle (T) is 450 square feet.

Irregular Problem Solution

AREA (S) = 1,600 SQUARE FEET

AREA (R) = 750 SQUARE FEET

AREA (T) = 450 SQUARE FEET

TOTAL AREA = AREA (S) + AREA (R) + AREA (T)

TOTAL AREA = 1,600 + 750 + 450

TOTAL AREA = 2,800 SQUARE FEET

ANSWER: The total area of this irregular lot is 2,800 square feet.

CONVERSION: SQUARE FEET TO SQUARE YARDS

Many questions on area will ask that you present the answer in square yards, rather than square feet. Conversion of square feet to square yards is a simple matter of dividing the answer by nine, because there are nine square feet in a square yard.

(3 feet x 3 feet = 9 square feet or 1 square yard)

Square yards, likewise, may be converted into square feet through multiplication by nine.

SQUARE YARDS = SQUARE FEET
9

SQUARE FEET = SQUARE YARDS x 9

D. VOLUME OF A STRUCTURE

STRUCTURAL VOLUME is the square or cubic measure of the space within a structure. Structural volume measurement is generally used when renting space in a warehouse type structure. Square measure is the area of the floor space, and it is determined through the use of the same techniques that apply to finding the square footage of a lot. *CUBIC MEASURE is the area volume or total air space.* The cubic volume of a structure is determined by multiplying the interior length by the width and the height. This can be expressed by the formula:

$$V = L \times W \times H$$

VOLUME = LENGTH x WIDTH x HEIGHT

EXAMPLE: How many cubic feet would there be in a room that is 15 feet long, 10 feet wide, and 10 feet high?

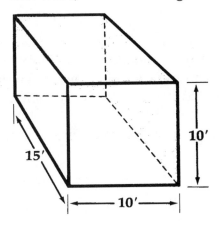

V = L x W x H
VOLUME = LENGTH x WIDTH x HEIGHT
VOLUME = 15 FEET x 10 FEET x 10 FEET
VOLUME = 15 x 10 x 10
VOLUME = 150 x 10
VOLUME = 1,500 CUBIC FEET

ANSWER: The cubic volume of this room would be 1,500 cubic feet.

II. Percentage Problems

The majority of math problems that you will encounter in real estate involve the use of percent. It is important, therefore, for you to understand certain general rules about percentage problems before dealing with any of the particular types.

There are three factors in any percentage problem:

1. The amount *PAID (P) is the amount invested.*
2. The *RATE (%) is the percentage.*
3. The amount *MADE (M) is the amount earned.*

In percentage problems, **one** of the three factors is missing. There are three rules for finding the missing factor:

1. To find the amount **PAID (P)**, divide **MADE (M)** by the **RATE (%)**
2. To find the amount **MADE (M)**, multiply **PAID (P)** by **RATE (%)**
3. To find the **RATE (%)**, divide **MADE (M)** by **(PAID (P)**.

A. OTHER FACTOR TERMS

MADE	PAID	% RATE
Return	Investment	Rate of return
Profit	Cost	Rate of profit
Commission	Price	Rate of commission
Net income	Value	Rate of capitalization
Interest	Principal	Rate of interest

Whenever you are working a percent problem, you will be dealing with one of these equations or a modification of one of them. The typical percent problem will supply you with two of the variables. You may easily determine the third through the use of the proper equation.

B. HUBER'S PYRAMID

If you feel that you might have trouble committing the percent equations to memory, you might want to make use of Huber's percent problem pyramid instead. Shown in **Figure 15-2**, this diagram points out what operation is required to find each of the variables.

To use the Huber Pyramid, simply cover the chamber you are trying to find and then perform the required math:

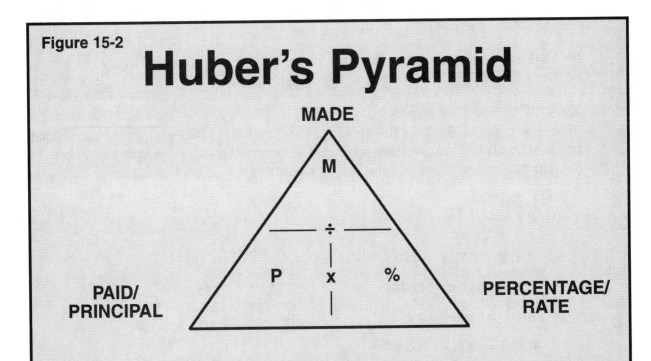

Figure 15-2

Huber's Pyramid

MADE

M

÷

P **X** **%**

**PAID/
PRINCIPAL**

**PERCENTAGE/
RATE**

The Huber Pyramid consists of three sections, or chambers (which can be modified to four chambers for certain problems). The top chamber is the **MADE (M)** chamber. It is separated from the other two chambers by a division sign. The bottom left chamber is the **PAID** or **PRINCIPAL (P)** chamber. The bottom right chamber is the **RATE (%)** chamber. It is separated from the **PAID** chamber by a **multiplication sign**.

1. To find M, cover M and multiply P x %

2. To find P, cover P and divide M by %

3. To find %, cover % and divide M by P

When doing a math problem involving three or more variables, first draw the Huber Pyramid and plug in the available figures, then perform the required action.

Your success in solving percentage problems will depend largely on your ability to spot and identify the three variables as they are presented. In most problems the **PAID** and the **MADE** will both be labeled as money. But the **PAID** (generally the larger amount) will usually be given as a base amount such as a price, investment, or loan balance. The **MADE**, on the other hand (generally the smaller amount), will be a sum made or lost from the **PAID**. Returns, profits, net income, taxes, interest, and commissions are all common labels identifying the **MADE**. The rate is easy to identify because it will always be given as some form of a percentage (%).

Here is a sample percent exercise for you to try:

EXAMPLE: Your agency purchases a lot for $9,000. In selling it later, you made a profit of $3,000. What was your percentage of profit?

ANSWER: The first step is to identify the variables. The principal (paid) is the purchase price of $9,000. The result (made) is the $3,000 margin of profit that resulted from the transaction. The rate is the percentage that we are asked to determine. To find it we use the rate equation.

$$\% = \frac{M}{P}$$

RATE = MADE ÷ PAID

RATE = $3,000 ÷ $9,000

RATE = 3,000 ÷ 9,000

RATE = .3333 = 33.33%

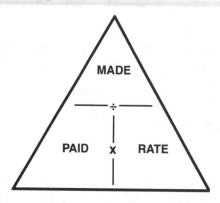

So, your agency made a 33.33% profit on the transaction.

Figure 15-3

DECIMAL TO PERCENT

.095 = 9.5%

1.2 = 120%

.009 = .9%

The above problem was looking for the rate (a percentage). The decimal number .3333 is not a percentage and so it had to be converted into a percentage in the final step of the sample exercise.

To convert a decimal number into a percentage, you simply move the decimal point two spaces to the right, adding zeros if needed. **Figure 15-3** gives some examples of this type of conversion.

In problems where you are asked to compute the results (paid) and the principal (made) it will be necessary for you to multiply or divide by the rate. In these cases you will have to convert the percentage into a decimal before completing the operation. This is done by reversing the process above: Move the decimal point two spaces to the left, and drop the percent sign. This changes a percent into its equivalent decimal form. **Figure 15-4** demonstrates this process.

Figure 15-4

PERCENT TO DECIMAL

8.5% = .085

50.% = .5

110% = 1.1

Another simple way to remember percents is to relate them to dollars and cents.

10 cents	=	.10	10%	=	.10
50 cents	=	.50	50%	=	.50
$1.50	=	1.50	150%	=	1.50

C. DETERMINING COMMISSIONS AND SELLING PRICE

A *COMMISSION RATE is a percentage of the selling price that is used to calculate the commission. The COMMISSION is the dollar amount received by a real estate agent for completing the sale.* A real estate agent wants to know how much he or she will be paid for doing his or her job. Most real estate salespeople are paid on a commission basis. As a licensed real estate agent, one of your most pleasant duties will be determining your commission.

When dealing with math problems in real estate, it is important to translate "words" into "math words" and "math symbols."

WORD	MATH WORD	MATH SYMBOL
OF (Means)	MULTIPLY	x
IS (Means)	EQUALS	=

In commission problems you are supplied with the principal (**PAID**), which is the property selling price, and the rate (**%**), which is the rate of commission, and asked to find the result (**MADE**), the agent's commission. Such problems use the result equation: $M = P \times \%$.

EXAMPLE: You have completed the sale of a $100,000 home. The rate of commission is 6%. How much money have you made?

$M = P \times \%$

MADE = PAID x RATE

MADE = $100,000 x 6% (.06)

MADE = $6,000

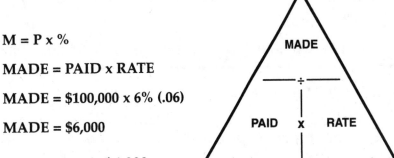

ANSWER: Your commission is $6,000.

1. Splitting Commissions

Most often when you have completed a sale, your brokerage will not be entitled to the entire commission. If you were representing the seller, for example, you might very likely split your commission with a broker and salesperson for the buyer. You will have earned a percentage of the amount earned by your broker, depending on the percentage both of you have agreed to in advance. The rates here are negotiable and usually vary with your experience and success.

When determining the splits of a commission, you use the result **(MADE)** equation. The total commission represents the principal **(PAID)** and the percentage **(RATE)** is whatever rate of commission was agreed to between the parties. **Figure 15-5** illustrates how a commission might be split.

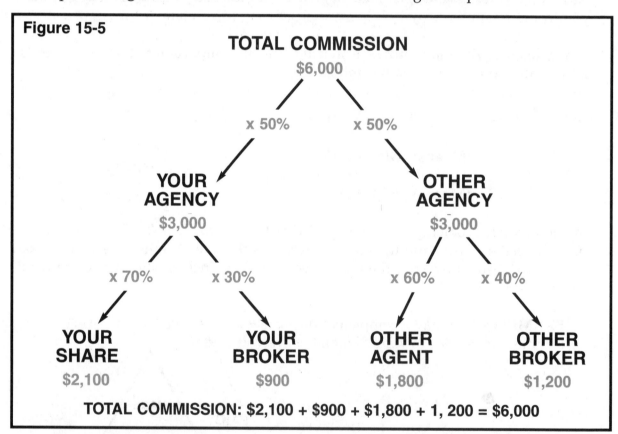

Figure 15-5

TOTAL COMMISSION
$6,000

x 50%   x 50%

YOUR AGENCY $3,000   **OTHER AGENCY** $3,000

x 70%   x 30%   x 60%   x 40%

YOUR SHARE $2,100   **YOUR BROKER** $900   **OTHER AGENT** $1,800   **OTHER BROKER** $1,200

TOTAL COMMISSION: $2,100 + $900 + $1,800 + 1,200 = $6,000

D. PROFIT AND LOSS

When dealing with profit and loss problems, you must establish the value, or cost, before profit (+), or loss (-).

The terms "value" and "cost" are interchangeable in real estate math problems; **it is what you paid for the property**.

Key terms when working profit and loss problems:

1. **SELLING PRICE** - the dollar value after the profit or loss has been added or subtracted from the original cost.

2. **COST** - the dollar value before the profit or loss has been added or subtracted. Cost is often stated as **purchase price** or **original price**.

3. **1 + % PROFIT** - in a profit problem, the percent used in the formula will **always** be greater than 100%; in other words, the original cost (100%) plus the percent of profit. If you sold your property for 40% more than you paid for it, your selling price (100% + 40% = 140%) would be the cost x 140 % (1.40). To find the amount of profit (+40%), you would subtract the cost from the selling price.

4. **1 - % LOSS** - for a loss problem, the percent used will **always** be less than 100%; in other words, the original cost (100%) minus the percent of loss. If you sold your property for 25% less than what you paid for it, your selling price (100% - 25% = 75%) would be the cost x 75% (.75). To find the amount of loss (- 25%), you would subtract the **selling price** from the cost.

The key to working these types of problems is to determine what percent to use.

EXAMPLE: Ms. Smith sold her home for $250,000, which was 8% more than she paid for the property. How much did Ms. Smith pay for the property?

SOLUTION: Remember that profit is **always a % of cost**. If we use the Huber Pyramid, we know the Selling price (MADE) is $250,000 and the rate (%) is 108% (100% + 8%). To find the cost (PAID), we would divide **MADE by %**.

ANSWER: (rounded) $250,000 divided by 108% (1.08) = **$231,481**
Ms. Smith paid $231,481 for her property.

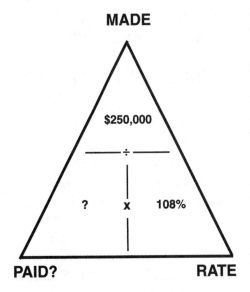

Let's try another problem:

EXAMPLE: Mr. Bush bought a new home on January 14 for $280,000. On July 6, he was transferred to a new city and sold his home for $270,000. What was his percent of loss?

REMEMBER: the percent of loss is based on what the home cost, not what it sold for.

SOLUTION: First we determine the amount of loss: $280,000 - $270,000 = $10,000.

Now we plug in the figures: MADE ($10,000) divided by PAID ($280,000) = percent (%) of loss.

ANSWER: Mr. Bush's percent of loss was 4% (.03572, or .04).

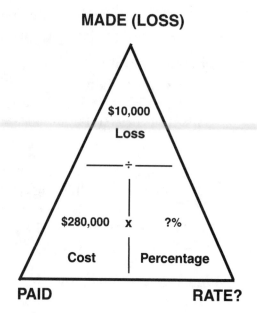

Remember: In profit problems, percent will always be greater than 100%. In loss problems, percent will always be less than 100%.

E. PRINCIPAL AND INTEREST CALCULATIONS

Use a 30-day month (banker's month) in calculating interest payments; thus 1 year = 360 days (statutory year).

Great amounts of capital are necessary to complete most real estate transactions. As a licensed real estate agent, financing will often be one of the major concerns of your clients. It will be advantageous, therefore, for you to be able to provide loan counseling as a part of your services. Essential to this service will be your ability to readily calculate principal and interest payments.

INTEREST is a fee paid for the use of other people's money, stated in dollars and cents. When one leases an apartment, he or she pays rent to the landlord for the use of the property. Similarly, when one borrows money he or she pays "rent" to the lender for the use of the money. This "rent" is called interest. *SIMPLE INTEREST is the term used to describe interest on the unpaid balance.*

Most interest problems will supply you with the principal **(PAID)**, which is the amount borrowed, and the rate **(%)**, which is the percentage being charged. You are asked to determine the interest **(MADE)**. We learned this formula earlier:

$$M = P \times R \, (\%)$$

There is an extra variable that is a factor in all interest problems: time. The duration of the loan determines how much interest is owed at the annual rate. One year equals one, one month equals 1/12, and one day equals 1/360. In order to take this factor into consideration, we modify the MADE equation slightly, with **MADE (M)** becoming **INTEREST (I)**:

$$I = P \times R \times T$$

INTEREST (MADE) = PRINCIPAL (PAID) x RATE (%) x TIME

When doing principal and interest problems, you are trying to find one of four unknowns: **INTEREST (I), PRINCIPAL (P), INTEREST RATE (R),** or **TIME (T)**.

We will use this modified Huber Pyramid to work these types of problems:

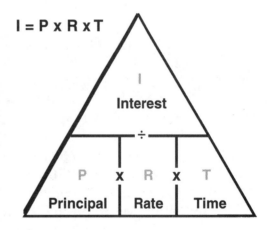

Remember: To use the Huber Pyramid, simply cover the chamber you are trying to find and then perform the required math.

1. Interest Problem

Interest is the payment made for using other people's money. The formula for finding interest is:

$$I = P \times R \times T$$

Here is a sample exercise for you to try:

Chapter 15

EXAMPLE: What would be the interest due on a loan of $10,000, borrowed at 9%, for a period of 2 years?

I = P x R x T

INTEREST = PRINCIPAL x RATE x TIME

INTEREST = $10,000 x 9% x 2 YEARS

INTEREST = $10,000 x .09 x 2

INTEREST = $900 x 2

INTEREST = $1,800

ANSWER: The interest would be $1,800.

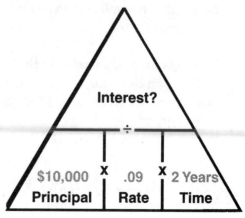

2. Principal Problem

As used in real estate finance problems, **PRINCIPAL** *is the amount borrowed in dollars.* To find the principal (amount borrowed), we would use the following formula:

$$P = \frac{I}{R \times T}$$

EXAMPLE: Mr. Johnson has a trust deed loan with annual interest payments of $5,200. If the rate of interest is 10%, how much did he borrow?

SOLUTION: We know that the interest (I) is $5,200, the rate (%) is 10% (.10) and the time (T) is 1 year. Using the above formula:

$$P = \frac{\$5,200}{.10 \times 1} = \frac{\$5,200}{.10} = \$52,000$$

ANSWER: Mr. Johnson borrowed $52,000.

3. Interest Rate Problem

The **INTEREST RATE** *is the percent of interest charged.* The purpose of principal and interest problems is to determine what we are paying **(INTEREST)** for the use of the amount borrowed **(PRINCIPAL)** and expressing that amount as a percentage **(INTEREST RATE)**. We use the following formula to find the interest rate:

$$R = \frac{I}{P \times T}$$

EXAMPLE: Ms. Bishop borrows $150,000 from 1ST Bank to purchase a condominium. If, after the first year, she owes the lender $15,000 interest, what is the rate of interest?

SOLUTION: We know that the **INTEREST (I)** is $15,000, the **PRINCIPAL (P)** is $150,000 and the **TIME (T)** is one year.

Using the above formula:

$$R = \frac{\$15,000}{\$150,000 \times 1} = \frac{\$15,000}{\$150,000} = (.10) \text{ or } 10\%$$

ANSWER: Ms. Bishop's rate of interest is 10%.

Unless stated otherwise, the interest rate is assumed to be in annual terms.

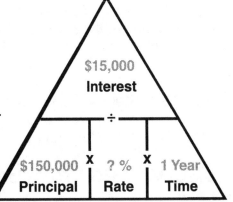

Figure **15-6** explains some useful terms in calculating interest rate problems.

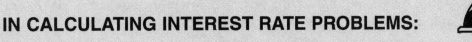

Figure 15-6

IN CALCULATING INTEREST RATE PROBLEMS:

Annual = once a year
Semiannual = twice a year at 6 month intervals
Biannual = twice a year
Bimonthly = 6 times a year (every 2 months)
Monthly = 12 times a year
Semimonthly = twice a month
Biennial = once every 2 years
1 Year = 12 months = 52 weeks = 360 days
1 Month = 30 days

4. Time Problem

TIME is used for periods less than or greater than one year. Time is expressed as a fraction or percent of a year (1/12th or .0833) if a payment is to be made monthly. As stated earlier, **interest rates** are assumed to be annual unless otherwise stated. However the payment of **principal and interest** is usually done on a monthly basis. The previous problems used a one year time period. If the time period is more or less than a year, then **TIME (T)** takes on a different value:

Monthly payment: T = 1/12 or .0833

Semiannual payment: T = 1/2 or .5

EXAMPLE: Mr. Philips borrows $200,000 at 9.5 % interest. What is the monthly interest payment?

SOLUTION: PRINCIPAL (P) is $200,000, **RATE (R)** is 9.5% and **TIME (T)** is 1/12 or .0833.

$$I = P \times R \times T$$

I = $200,000 x .095 x .0833 = $1,583

ANSWER: Mr. Philips makes a monthly interest payment of $1,583.

F. DISCOUNT POINTS ("Points")

1 discount point = 1% of the loan amount

DISCOUNT POINTS *are charges made by a lender to increase the yield on a loan: one point equals 1% of the loan.*

EXAMPLE: Mr. and Mrs. Majors are purchasing a house for $155,000. They will put $30,000 down and borrow the rest, which will include a 4 point charge by the savings bank. How much will the points cost them?

SOLUTION: First we must determine the amount being borrowed:

$155,000 - $30,000 = $125,000

Next we compute the discount rate:

1 point = 1% of the loan amount = .01 x $125,000 = $1,250

Finally, we calculate the amount of discount:

4 x $1,250 = $5,000

ANSWER: The Majors will pay $5,000 for the discount points from the borrowed $125,000.

III. Determining Prorations

Buyer's ownership starts on the day of closing.

PRORATION *is the process of proportionately dividing (prorating) expenses or income to the precise date that escrow closes, or any other date previously agreed upon.* Its purpose is to apportion income and expense items correctly between the parties of a sale. These are divided (or **prorated**) in proportion to the time that each owned or will own the property. In analyzing proration problems, you will need to determine **who** will be credited with a dollar amount at closing. The next thing that you need to consider is **how much** will be credited.

Items that are normally prorated include mortgage interest, taxes, fire insurance premiums, rent, and assessments. In some areas, prorations are also known as **adjustments** or **apportionments**.

Proration involves dividing the dollar amount associated with the time an expense or income occurred between two parties (the buyer and seller). Rent and interest are usually paid in one month intervals, property taxes are paid every six months or once a year, and fire insurance premiums can be for one, two or even as many as five years. A important question that must be answered is who gets credit for an item. The rules are simple.

On an escrow statement a CREDIT is something that is received and a DEBIT is something that is owed.

BUYER'S AND SELLER'S SETTLEMENT STATEMENTS

(Also See Chapter 7)

DOUBLE-ENTRY BOOKKEEPING *is the balancing procedure used to complete a settlement statement.* (Accountants will find this the opposite of true accounting.) The statement consists of two parts: a **buyer's statement** and a **seller's statement**. Each of these is divided into a **debit column** and a **credit column**.

A **DEBIT** *is something that is owed.* A debit entry for a buyer is anything charged against or subtracted from his or her account. The purchase price of the property is an example of something debited to the buyer. A debit entry for a seller means the same thing. Unpaid property taxes are a good example.

A **CREDIT** *is something that is received.* A credit entry for a buyer is anything received or added to his or her account. The deposit made on the property is a good example of something credited to the buyer. A good example of a credit entry for the seller would be prepaid property taxes.

If an item was **paid** before closing, the buyer's closing statement will be debited and the seller's statement will be credited. If **income** was received before closing, the buyer's statement will be credited and the seller's statement will be debited. Though items on closing statements follow no set order of entry, **the purchase price is usually the first entry and the amount due from/to buyer to close, and the amount due to/from seller to close are the last entries**.

A. RENTS (INCOME)

In determining the proration of rents, it is important to remember that all escrow companies use a **30-day base month** (banker's month) and a **360-day statutory year**. The portion of income that is granted to each party can be represented as a fraction. The denominator will be 30, while the numerator will vary depending upon what day in the month escrow closes. It is important to remember that the buyer's ownership starts on the day of closing.

> **EXAMPLE:** If the escrow closes on the 21st day of the month, how would you divide a prepaid rent of $1,500 between the seller and the buyer?

> **ANSWER:** The seller's share would be 20/30 of the whole, because he holds ownership through the 20th day. The share of the other 10 days (10/30) would go to the buyer.

> **SELLER'S SHARE**
>
> **BUYER'S SHARE**
>
> $\dfrac{20}{30} \times 1{,}500 = \$1{,}000$
>
> $\dfrac{10}{30} \times 1{,}500 = \$500$

So, the seller would receive $1,000 of the rent money, while the buyer would be prorated $500.

B. PROPERTY TAXES (EXPENSES) - BUYER'S AND SELLER'S

Property taxes are prorated either from July 1, the beginning of the fiscal year, or January 1, the middle of the fiscal year. Since each of these two installments covers a six-month period, the portion of the expense prorated to each party is represented as a fraction with a denominator of 6. The numerator varies depending upon what month in the six-month period escrow closes.

> **EXAMPLE:** The second installment of property tax on a home is $500. The seller has paid this tax, which covers a six-month period ending July 1. If he sells this property and escrow closes on April 1, how much of the $500 is his share in the expense? How much would the buyer have to reimburse?

> **ANSWER:** The seller's share would be 3/6 of the tax bill, while the buyer would also be responsible for 3/6. This is because both the seller and the buyer owned the property for three months during the six-month period.

SELLER'S SHARE	BUYER'S SHARE
$\dfrac{3}{6} \times 500 = \$250$	$\dfrac{3}{6} \times 500 = \$250$

Each would be responsible for $250 of the property tax; the buyer having to reimburse the seller, who already paid the entire property tax bill.

IV. Depreciation (For Tax Purposes)

DEPRECIATION (for income taxes) is a diminishing (loss) in the value of buildings and other improvements. All new depreciation schedules for normal income tax purposes involving real property must be straight-line.

A. STRAIGHT-LINE DEPRECIATION

STRAIGHT-LINE DEPRECIATION is a method of computing depreciation on assets other than land for income tax purposes in which the difference between the original cost and salvage value is deducted in installments evenly over the life of the asset. It is based upon the assumption that depreciation is dependent solely on the passage of time. Depreciation is spread uniformly over the useful life of a property (building).

When doing depreciation problems, it is important to remember that land does NOT depreciate.

To find depreciation using the straight-line method use:

ANNUAL DEPRECIATION (A) = $\dfrac{\text{VALUE (COST) OF IMPROVEMENTS (V)}}{\text{ECONOMIC LIFE (E)}}$

or simplified:

$$A = \frac{V}{E}$$

Let's try a problem using straight-line depreciation:

EXAMPLE: Mr. and Mrs. Roberts purchased some real property for $475,000. The land was valued at $200,000. The improvements had an estimated economic life of 27.5 years. What would be the depreciated value of the property after 17 years?

ANSWER: We must first determine the value of the depreciable asset (improvements) because land is not depreciated.

$475,000 (land and improvements)
- 200,000 (land)
$275,000 (COST of improvements)

$$\underline{A} = V = A = \underline{\$275,000} = \$10,000 \text{ depreciation per year}$$
$$E \qquad\qquad 27.5$$

$10,000 x 17 years = $170,000 accumulated depreciation
$275,000 - $170,000 = $105,000 depreciated value of the improvements only
$105,000 + $200,000 (value of land) = $305,000

$305,000 is the depreciated value of the property.

The IRS allows a minimum of 27.5 years straight-line depreciation on residential properties and 39 years on commercial properties.

V. How to Find the Value of a Parcel

 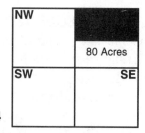

Problem: The NW¼ of the SW¼ of Section 7 is valued at $800 per acre. The N½ of the NE¼ of Section 4 is valued at $500 per acre. What is the difference in value between the two parcels?

Solution:

1 section = 640 acres
¼ section = 160 acres
¼ of ½ section = 40 acres   40 acres x $800 per acre = $32,000
½ of ¼ section = 80 acres   80 acres x $500 per acre = $40,000
$40,000 - $32,000 = $8000

Answer: $8,000

I wish you the best of luck in your real estate career, whether it be as a homeowner, investor or salesperson. The future is yours!

Walter Roy Huber

 www.etcbooks.com
Educational Textbook Company

VI. SUMMARY

A licensee must be able to compute quickly and accurately the basic mathematics underlying most real estate transactions. A person who understands math will be better able to capitalize on opportunities as they arise. The Department of Real Estate may ask about 10 math questions on the license exam. It is better to be prepared than to guess.

This chapter illustrates some of the basic mathematical skills useful for a career in real estate. Familiarity with fundamental arithmetic and a few simple formulas, along with plain common sense, will provide the necessary background. Such knowledge will not only assist in the practice of real estate, but should also prove advantageous in passing the licensing exam. You should know the following common measurements:

LINEAR

1 foot (ft) = 12 inches (in.)
1 yard (yd) = 3 feet (ft.)
1 rod = 16.5 ft = 5.5 yd
1 mile = 5,280 ft = 1,760 yd = 320 rods

SQUARE

1 sq. ft. = 144 sq. in.
1 sq. yd. = 9 sq. ft.
1 acre = 43,560 sq. ft. = 4,840 sq. yd. = 160 sq. rods

CUBIC

1 cu. ft. = 1,728 cu. in.
1 cu. yd. = 27 cu. ft.

LAND DESCRIPTION

1 link = 7.92 inches
1 rod = 25 links
1 chain = 100 links = 66 ft. = 4 rods
1 mile = 80 chains
1 Acre = 43,560 sq. ft.
1 Township = 36 sections = 36 square miles = 23,040 acres
1 section = 1 mile square = 640 acres = 1/36 of a township
1 circle = 360 degrees (°)
1 quadrant = 90 degrees (°)
1 degree (°) = 60 minutes (′)
1 minute (′) = 60 seconds (″)

The agent needs to know measurements. The buyer wants to know how much land and building space he or she is buying. **Area measurements (length times width)** in square feet gives him or her that information.

Land area is the surface space between lot lines measured in square feet. **Building area** is the space enclosed by the exterior walls, measured in square feet.

Rectangular Lot: 4-sided parcels. Opposite sides are equal in length and right angles are formed by the intersection of the sides. Area equals Length times Width: **A = L x W.**

Triangular Lot: 3-sided parcel. Area equals Base (horizontal side) times Height (perpendicular distance from base to highest point) divided by 2: **A = B x H ÷ 2.**

Irregular Lot: Parcel that does not consist of a single known shape. Area is determined by breaking lot into rectangles and triangles and totalling the areas: **Total Area = Area (S) + Area (R) + Area (T).**

Structural Volume is the cubic measure of the space within a structure. Structural volume measurement is generally used when renting space in a warehouse type structure. **Cubic Measure** is determined by multiplying the interior length by the width and the height: **V = L x W x H.**

The majority of math problems that you will encounter in real estate involve the use of **percentages**. It is important, therefore, for you to understand certain general rules about percentage problems before dealing with any of the particular types.

Percentage problems: Factors are: (1) Amount invested is the amount **Paid (P)**; (2) The rate is the **Percentage (%)**; and (3) The amount **Made (M)** is the amount earned. One of the three factors is usually missing. To compute the missing factor:

    Amount Paid (P)   = **Amount Made (M) ÷ Percentage Rate (%)**
    Amount Made (M) = **Amount Paid (P) x Percentage (%)**
    Percentage Rate (%) = **Amount Made (M) ÷ Amount Paid (P)**

The **commission** is the dollar amount received by a real estate agent for completing the sale. A real estate agent wants to know how much he or she will be paid for doing his or her job. Most real estate salespeople are paid on a commission basis. As a licensed real estate agent, one of your most pleasant duties will be determining your commission.

Determining Commissions and Selling Price: The **Commission Rate** is a percentage of selling price. The **Commission** is the dollar amount received for completing the sale:

Commission = Principal Paid x Percentage Rate

Profit and Loss: Profit is the excess of revenues over expenses. **Loss** is the excess of expenses over revenues. **Profits = Revenues minus Expenses**.

Large amounts of capital are necessary to complete most real estate transactions. As a licensed real estate agent, financing will often be one of the major concerns of your clients. It will be advantageous for you to be able to provide loan counseling as a part of your services. Your ability to readily calculate **principal and interest payments** will be essential to this service.

Interest is a fee paid for the use of other people's money stated in dollars and cents. When one leases an apartment, he or she pays rent to the landlord for the use of the property. Similarly, when one borrows money he or she pays "rent" to the lender for the use of the money. This "rent" is called **interest. Simple interest** is the term used to describe interest on the unpaid balance.

Principal and Interest Calculations: Interest is the fee paid for the use of other people's money. **Interest (Amount Made) = Principal (Amount Paid) x Percentage Rate (%) x Time (T)**.

Determining Prorations: Dividing expenses (property taxes) or income (rents) to a specified date, close of escrow or other agreed upon date, in proportion to time each owned or will own the property is called **proration**. In determining the proration of rents, it is important to remember that all escrow companies use a **30-day base month** (banker's month) and a **360-day statutory year**. The portion of income that is granted to each party can be represented as a fraction. The denominator will be 30, while the numerator will vary depending upon what day in the month escrow closes. **It is important to remember that the buyer's ownership starts on the day of closing**.

> **EXAMPLE:** If the escrow closes on the 21st day of the month, how would you divide a prepaid rent of $1,500 between the seller and the buyer? The seller's share would be 20/30 of the whole, because he holds ownership through the 20th day. The share of the other 10 days (10/30) would go to the buyer.

Straight-line depreciation is the difference between original cost of improvements and salvage value that is deducted in even installments over the life of the asset. When doing depreciation problems, it is important to remember that land does not depreciate, just the cost of improvements depreciate. The IRS allows straight-line depreciation of 27.5 years on residential properties and 39 years on commercial properties.

Annual Depreciation (A) = Cost of Improvements - salvage value (V) ÷ Economic Life (E)

It might also prove to your advantage to bring an **electric calculator** with you when taking the salesperson's examination. The state permits applicants to use electronic calculators as long as they are battery operated, non-programmable, silent, and without printout capability. It will free you from tedious and time-consuming arithmetic work in order to concentrate on the reasoning behind the problems you will encounter.

VII. TERMINOLOGY - CHAPTER 15

A. Area
B. Commission
C. Credit
D. Cubic Area
E. Debit
F. Depreciation

G. Discount Points (Points)
H. Interest
I. Interest Rate
J. Irregular Lot
K. Principal (Amount Paid)
L. Proration

M. Rectangular Lot
N. Result (Amount Made)
O. Straight-Line Depreciation
P. Triangular Lot

1.____ The amount of money borrowed.

2.____ Money owed; it is shown as what on the settlement statement.

3.____ The up-front charge by a lender to obtain and to increase the yield on a loan.

4.____ The amount paid to a real estate broker usually expressed as a percentage of the sale price.

5.____ To divide property taxes, insurance premiums, rental income, etc. between buyer and seller proportionately to time of use or the date of closing.

6.____ Decrease in value to real property improvements by any cause.

7.____ The rent or charge for the use of money.

8.____ The surface of land or building. Length (in feet) times width (in feet).

9.____ The area of this shaped lot is obtained by multiplying base times height and dividing by 2.

10.____ Money received; it is shown as what on the settlement statement.

11.____ Principal (paid) times rate (%) equals?

12.____ The percentage paid for the use of borrowed money. Usually expressed as an annual percentage.

13.____ Equal amount of depreciation each year. A loss in the value of improvements, used as an accounting (income tax) procedure.

14.____ A lot with an unusual shape.

15.____ The result of multiplying length times width times height.

16.____ Four-sided figure with opposite sides equal in length and intersecting corners forming right angles.

VIII. MULTIPLE CHOICE

1. Ms. Donaldson exchanged her fourplex (fair market value $100,000 with a loan of $52,000) for a larger building (fair market value $150,000 with a loan of $42,000). Using only the above figures, how much money did Donaldson have to pay to complete the exchange?

   a. $48,000
   b. $52,000
   c. $60,000
   d. $108,000

2. Carol borrowed $5,200 and signed a straight note with an interest rate of 7% per annum. If she paid $1,125 in interest during the term of the note, what was the term of the note?

   a. 22 months
   b. 27 months
   c. 32 months
   d. 37 months

3. A woman owns a rental unit that nets her $450 per month. She realizes a 10% return on her investment each year. What is her investment in the property?

   a. $45,000
   b. $48,500
   c. $54,000
   d. None of the above

4. The assessed value of a piece of property is $48,700. The tax is $1.02 per $100 of assessed valuation. The tax is:

   a. $496.74.
   b. $489.60.
   c. $584.40.
   d. $594.14.

5. How much would have to be invested at 7% in order to provide an investor with $640 monthly income?

   a. $9,143
   b. $91,429
   c. $109,714
   d. $53,760

6. The second quarter interest on a $7,600 term loan at 8% interest is:

   a. $76.
   b. $152.
   c. $608.
   d. none of the above.

7. An apartment complex cost $450,000. It brings in a net income of $3,000 per month. The owner is making what percentage of return on her investment?

    a. 7%

    b. 8%

    c. 11%

    d. 12%

8. Broker Jones negotiates a lease for 3,000 square feet of warehouse storage space at a monthly rental of $0.50 per square foot. Jones commission is 8% of the first year's gross. Jones will receive:

    a. $1,180.

    b. $1,340.

    c. $1,440.

    d. none of the above.

9. Frank holds a five-year trust deed and note that was paid off at 7.2% interest per annum. If the total interest he received from the borrower was $4,140, what, approximately, was the original amount of the loan?

    a. $11, 500

    b. $29,700

    c. $33,650

    d. $57,500

10. A builder constructed a home for $350,000 and sold it for a 20% profit. What is the amount of profit?

    a. $17,500

    b. $20,000

    c. $35,000

    d. $70,000

ANSWERS: 1. c; 2. d; 3. c; 4. a; 5. a; 6. b; 7. b; 8. c; 9. a; 10. d

A

ALTA Title Policy (American Land Title Association): A type of title insurance policy issued by title insurance companies which expands the risks normally insured against under the standard type policy to include unrecorded mechanic's liens; unrecorded physical easements; facts a physical survey would show; water and mineral rights; and rights of parties in possession, such as tenants and buyers under unrecorded instruments.

ALTA Owner's Policy (Standard Form B1962, as amended 1969): An owner's extended coverage policy that provides buyers or owners the same protection the ALTA policy gives to lenders.

Abatement of Nuisance: Extinction or termination of a nuisance.

Absolute Fee Simple Title: Absolute or fee simple title is one that is absolute and unqualified. It is the best title one can have.

Abstract of Judgment: A condensation of the essential provisions of a court judgment.

Abstract of Title: A summary or digest of the conveyances, transfers, and any other facts relied on as evidence of title, together with any other elements of record which may impair the title.

Abstraction: A method of valuing land. The indicated value of the improvement is deducted from the sale price.

Acceleration Clause: Clause in trust deed or mortgage giving lender right to call all sums owing him to be immediately due and payable upon the happening of a certain event.

Acceptance: When the seller's or agent's principal agrees to the terms of the agreement of sale and approves the negotiation on the part of the agent and acknowledges receipt of the deposit in subscribing to the agreement of sale, that act is termed an acceptance.

Access Right: The right of an owner to have ingress and egress to and from his property.

Accession: Gaining title when property is added to a property by another or a natural action.

Accretion: An addition to land from natural causes as, for example, from gradual action of the ocean or river waters.

Accrued Depreciation: The difference between the cost of replacement new as of the date of the appraisal and the present appraised value.

Accrued Items of Expense: Those incurred expenses which are not yet payable. The seller's accrued expenses are credited to the purchaser in a closing statement.

Acknowledgment: A formal declaration before a duly authorized officer by a person who has executed an instrument that such execution is his act and deed.

Acoustical Tile: Blocks of fiber, mineral or metal, with small holes or rough textured surface to absorb sound, used as covering for interior walls and ceilings.

Acquisition: The act or process by which a person procures property.

Acre: A measure of land equaling 160 square rods, or 4,840 square yards, or 43,560 square feet, or a tract about 208.71 feet square.

Adjustments: A means by which characteristics of a residential property are regulated by dollar amount or percentage to conform to similar characteristics of another residential property.

Affiant: A person who has made an affidavit.

Administrator: A person appointed by the probate court to administer the estate of a person deceased.

Ad Valorem: A Latin phrase meaning, "according to value." Usually used in connection with real estate taxation.

Advance: Transfer of funds from a lender to a borrower in advance on a loan.

Advance Commitment: The institutional investor's prior agreement to provide long-term financing upon completion of construction.

Advance Fee: A fee paid in advance of any services rendered.

Adverse Possession: Claiming based on the open and notorious possession and occupancy, usually under an evident claim or right, in denial or opposition to the title of another claimant.

Affidavit: A statement or declaration reduced to writing sworn to or affirmed before some officer who has authority to administer an oath or affirmation.

Affidavit of Title: A statement in writing, made under oath by seller or grantor, acknowledged before a Notary Public in which the affiant identifies himself and his marital status certifying that since the examination of title on the contract date there are no judgments, bankruptcies or divorces, or unrecorded deeds, contracts, unpaid repairs or improvements or defects of title known to him and that he is in possession of the property.

Affirm: To confirm, to aver, to ratify, to verify.

AFLB: Accredited Farm and Land Broker.

Agency: The relationship between principal and agent which arises out of a contract, either expressed or implied, written or oral, wherein the agent is employed by the principal to do certain acts dealing with a third party.

Agent: One who represents another from whom he has derived authority.

Agreement of Sale: A written agreement or contract between seller and purchaser in which they reach a meeting of minds on the terms and conditions of the sale.

Air Rights: The rights in real property to use the air space above the surface of the land.

Alienation: The transferring of property to another; the transfer of property and possession of lands, or other things, from one person to another.

Allodial Tenure: A real property ownership system where ownership may be complete except for those rights held by government. Allodial is in contrast to feudal tenure.

Alluvion (Alluvium): Soil deposited by accretion. Increase of earth on a shore or bank of a river.

Amenities: Satisfaction of enjoyable living to be derived from a home; conditions of agreeable living or a beneficial influence arising from the location or improvements.

AMO: Accredited Management Organization.

Amortization: The liquidation of a financial obligation on an equal installment basis; also, recovery: over a period, of cost or value.

Amortized Loan: A loan that is completely paid off, interest and principal, by a series of regular payments that are equal or nearly equal. Also called a **Level Payments Loan**.

Annuity: A series of assured equal or nearly equal payments to be made over a period of time or it may be a lump sum payment to be made in the future.

Anticipation, Principle of: Affirms that value is created by anticipated benefits to be derived in the future.

Appraisal: An estimate and opinion of value; a conclusion resulting from the analysis of facts.

Appraiser: One qualified by education, training and experience who is hired to estimate the value of real and personal property based on experience, judgment, facts, and use of formal appraisal processes.

Appurtenance: Something annexed to another thing which may be transferred incident to it. That which belongs to another thing, as a barn, dwelling, garage, or orchard is incident to the land to which it is attached.

Architectural Style: Generally the appearance and character of a building's design and construction.

ASA: American Society of Appraisers.

Asbestos: A fibrous insulation and construction material that causes serious lung problems.

Assessed Valuation: A valuation placed upon property by a public officer or board, as a basis for taxation.

Assessed Value: Value placed on property as a basis for taxation.

Assessment: The valuation of property for the purpose of levying a tax or the amount of the tax levied.

Assessor: The official who has the responsibility of determining assessed values.

Assignment: A transfer or making over to another of the whole of any property, real or personal, in possession or in action, or of any estate or right therein.

Assignor: One who assigns or transfers property.

Assigns; Assignees: Those to whom property shall have been transferred.

Assumption Agreement: An undertaking or adoption of a debt or obligation primarily resting upon another person.

Assumption Fee: A lender's charge for changing over and processing new records for a new owner who is assuming an existing loan.

Assumption of Mortgage: The taking of title to property by a grantee, wherein he assumes liability for payment of an existing note secured by a mortgage or deed of trust against the property; becoming a co-guarantor for the payment of a mortgage or deed of trust note.

Attachment: Seizure of property by court order, usually done to have it available in event a judgment is obtained in a pending suit.

Attest: To affirm to be true or genuine; an official act establishing authenticity.

Attorney in Fact: One who is authorized to perform certain acts for another under a power of attorney; power of attorney may be limited to a specific act or acts, or be general.

Avulsion: The sudden tearing away or removal of land by action of water flowing over or through it.

Axial Growth: City growth which occurs along main transportation routes. Usually takes the form of star-shaped extensions outward from the center.

B

Backfill: The replacement of excavated earth into a hole or against a structure.

Balloon Payment: Where the final installment payment on a note is greater than the preceding installment payments and it pays the note in full, such final installment is termed a balloon payment.

Bargain and Sale Deed: Any deed that recites a consideration and purports to convey the real estate; a bargain and sale deed with a covenant against the grantor's acts is one in which the grantor warrants that he himself has done nothing to harm or cloud the title.

Baseboard: A board placed against the wall around a room next to the floor.

Base and Meridian: Imaginary lines used by surveyors to find and describe the location of private or public lands.

Base Molding: Molding used at top of baseboard.

Base Shoe: Molding used at junction of baseboard and floor. Commonly called a carpet strip.

Batten: Narrow strips of wood or metal used to cover joints, interiorly or exteriorly; also used for decorative effect.

Beam: A structural member transversely supporting a load.

Bearing Wall or Partition: A wall or partition supporting any vertical load in addition to its own weight.

Bench Marks: A location indicated on a durable marker by surveyors.

Beneficiary: (1) One entitled to the benefit of a trust; (2) One who receives profit from an estate, the title of which is vested in a trustee; (3) The lender on the security of a note and deed of trust.

Bequeath: To give or hand down by will; to leave by will.

Bequest: That which is given by the terms of a will (applies to personal property).

Betterment: An improvement upon property which increases the property value and is considered as a capital asset or distinguished from repairs or replacements where the original character or cost is unchanged.

Bill of Sale: A written instrument given to pass title of personal property from vendor to the vendee.

Binder: An agreement to consider a down payment for the purchase of real estate as evidence of good faith on the part of the purchaser. Also, a notation of coverage on an insurance policy, issued by an agent, and given to the insured prior to issuing of the policy.

Blacktop: Asphalt paving used in streets and driveways.

Blanket Mortgage: A single mortgage which covers more than one piece of real estate.

Blighted Area: A declining area in which real property values are seriously affected by destructive economic forces, such as encroaching inharmonious property usages, infiltration of lower economic inhabitants, and/or rapidly depreciating buildings.

Board Foot: A unit of measurement of lumber; one foot wide, one foot long, one inch thick; 144 cubic inches.

Bona Fide: In good faith, without fraud.

Bond: An obligation under seal. A real estate bond is a written obligation issued on security of a mortgage or trust deed.

Bracing: Framing lumber nailed at an angle in order to provide rigidity.

Breach: The breaking of a law, or failure of duty, either by omission or commission.

Breezeway: A covered porch or passage, open on two sides, connecting house and garage or two parts of the house.

Bridge Loan (Gap Loan/Swing Loan): Short-term loan between construction loan and permanent financing.

Bridging: Small wood or metal pieces used to brace floor joists.

Broker: A person employed by another, to carry on any of the activities listed in the license law definition of a broker, for a fee.

B.T.U. (British Thermal Unit): The quantity of heat required to raise the temperature of one pound of water one degree Fahrenheit.

Building Code: A systematic regulation of construction of buildings within a municipality established by ordinance or law.

Building Line: A line set by law a certain distance from a street line in front of which an owner cannot build on his lot. (**Setback Line**)

Building Paper: A heavy waterproofed paper used as sheathing in wall or roof construction as a protection against air passage and moisture.

Built-In: Cabinets or similar features built as part of the house.

Bundle of Rights: Beneficial interests or rights.

Buy-Down Loan: A loan where the seller pays points to a lender so that the lender can offer below market financing.

Buyer's Agent: An agent representing the buyer rather than the seller.

C

CCIM: Certified Commercial Investment Member.

CC&Rs: Abbreviation for covenants, conditions, and restrictions.

CPM: Certified Property Manager, a designation of the Institute of Real Estate Management.

Capital Assets: Assets of a permanent nature used in the production of an income, such as: land, buildings, machinery, and equipment, etc. Under income tax law, it is usually distinguishable from "inventory" which comprises assets held for sale to customers in ordinary course of the taxpayers' trade or business.

Capital Gain: Income from a sale of an asset rather than from the general business activity. Capital gains are generally taxed at a lower rate than ordinary income.

Capitalization: In appraising, determining value of property by considering net income and percentage of reasonable return on the investment. Thus, the value of an income property is determined by dividing annual net income by the capitalization rate (see below).

Capitalization Rate: The rate of interest which is considered a reasonable return on the investment, and used in the process of determining value based upon net income. It may also be described as the yield rate that is necessary to attract the money of the average investor to a particular kind of investment. In the case of land improvements which depreciate to this yield rate is added a factor to take into consideration the annual amortization factor necessary to recapture the initial investment in improvements.

Casement Window: Frames of wood or metal, which swing outward.

Cash Flow: The net income generated by a property before depreciation and other noncash expenses.

Caveat Emptor: "Let the buyer beware." The buyer must examine the goods or property and buy at his own risk.

Certificate of Reasonable Value (CRV): The federal Veterans Administration appraisal commitment of property value.

Chain: A unit of measurement used by surveyors. A chain consists of 100 links equal to 66 feet.

Chain of Title: A history of conveyances and encumbrances affecting the title from the time the original patent was granted, or as far back as records are. available.

Change, Principle of: Holds that it is the future, not the past, which is of prime importance in estimating value.

Characteristics: Distinguishing features of a (residential) property.

Chattel Mortgage: A claim on personal property (instead of real property) used to secure or guarantee a promissory note. (See definitions of **Security Agreement** and **Security Interest**.)

Chattel Real: A personal property interest related to real estate, such as a lease on real property.

Chattels: Goods or every species of property movable or immovable which are not real property.

Circuit Breaker: An electrical device which automatically interrupts an electric circuit when an overload occurs; may be used instead of a fuse to protect each circuit and can be reset.

Civil Rights Act of 1866: The first fair housing act (applied to race only).

Civil Rights Act of 1968: Our fair housing act.

Clapboard: Overlapping boards usually thicker at one edge used for siding.

Closing Statement: An accounting of funds made to the buyer and seller separately.

Cloud on the Title: Any conditions revealed by a title search which affect the title to property; usually relatively unimportant items but which cannot be removed without a quitclaim deed or court action.

Collar Beam: A beam that connects the pairs of opposite roof rafters above the attic floor.

Collateral: This is the property subject to the security interest. (See definition of **Security Interest**)

Collateral Security: A separate obligation attached to contract to guarantee its performance; the transfer of property or of other contracts, or valuables, to insure the performance of a principal agreement.

Collusion: An agreement between two or more persons to defraud another of his rights by the forms of law, or to obtain an object forbidden by law.

Color of Title: That which appears to be good title but which is not title in fact. Example: title under a forged deed.

Commercial Acre: A term applied to the remainder of an acre of newly subdivided land after the area devoted to streets, sidewalks, and curbs, etc., has been deducted from the acre.

Commercial Paper: Bills of exchange used in commercial trade.

Commission: An agent's compensation for performing the duties of his agency; in real estate practice, a percentage of the selling price of property, percentage of rentals, etc.

Commitment: A pledge or a promise or firm agreement.

Common Law: The body of law that grew from customs and practices developed and used in England "Since the memory of man runneth not to the contrary." (Based on court decisions not statutes)

Community: A part of a metropolitan area that has a number of neighborhoods that have a tendency toward common interests and problems.

Community Property: Property accumulated during marriage that is owned equally by husband and wife.

Compaction: Ability of the soil to support a structure. Compaction tests are important as to filled land.

Comparable Sales: Sales which have similar characteristics as the subject property and are used for analysis in the appraisal process.

Compensator Damages: Damages to reimburse an injured party for the actual loss suffered.

Competent: Legally qualified.

Competition, Principle of: Holds that excess profits tend to breed competition.

Component: One of the features making up the whole property.

Compound Interest: Interest paid on original principal and also on the accrued and unpaid interest which has accumulated.

Conclusion: The final estimate of value, realized from facts, data, experience and judgment.

Condemnation: The act of taking private property for public use. Also a declaration that a structure is unfit for use.

Condition: A qualification of an estate granted which can be imposed only in conveyances. They are classified as conditions precedent and conditions subsequent.

Condition Precedent: A condition that requires certain action or the happening of a specified event before the estate granted can take effect. **Example:** most installment real estate sale contracts require all payments to be made at the time specified before the buyer may demand transfer of title.

Condition Subsequent: When there is a condition subsequent in a deed, the title vests immediately in the grantee, but upon breach of the condition the grantor has the power to terminate the estate if he wishes to do so. **Example:** A condition in the deed prohibiting the grantee from using the premises as a liquor store.

Conditional Commitment: A commitment of a definite loan amount for some future unknown purchaser of satisfactory credit standing.

Condominium: A system of individual fee ownership of units in a multifamily structure, combined with joint ownership of common areas of the structure and the land. (Sometimes referred to as a **Vertical Subdivision.**)

Conduit: Usually a metal pipe in which electrical wiring is installed.

Conduits: Individuals or firms that purchase loans from originators to resell to investors.

Confession of Judgment: An entry of judgment upon the debtor's voluntary admission or confession.

Confirmation of Sale: A court approval of the sale of property by an executor, administrator, guardian or conservator.

Confiscation: The seizing of property without compensation.

Conforming Loans: Loans that meet the purchase requirement of Fannie Mae and Freddie Mac.

Conformity, Principle of: Holds that the maximum value is realized when a reasonable degree of homogeneity of improvements is present.

Conservation: The process of utilizing resources in such a manner which minimizes their depletion.

Consideration: Anything of value given to induce entering into a contract; it may be money, personal services, or anything having value.

Constant: The percentage which, when applied directly to the face value of a debt, develops the annual amount of money necessary to pay a specified net rate of interest on the reducing balance and to liquidate the debt in a specified time period. For example, a 6% loan with a 20 year amortization has a constant of approximately 8.5%. Thus, a $10,000 loan amortized over 20 years requires an annual payment of approximately $850.00.

Contingent Remainder: A remainder interest that can be defeated by the happening of an event.

Construction Loans: Loans made for the construction of homes or commercial buildings. Usually funds are disbursed to the contractor builder during construction and after periodic inspections. Disbursements are based on an agreement between borrower and lender.

Constructive Eviction: Breach of a covenant of warranty or quiet enjoyment, e.g., the inability of a lessee to obtain possession because of a paramount defect in title, or a condition making occupancy hazardous. A lessee can treat it as cause to void a lease.

Constructive Notice: Notice given by the public records.

Consummate Dower: A widow's dower interest which, after the death of her husband, is complete or may be completed and become an interest in real estate.

Contour: The surface configuration of land.

Contour Lines: Liens on a map that indicate elevation. When liens are close together, it indicates a steep stoop but if the lines are far apart, it indicates the land is relatively level.

Contract: An agreement, either written or oral, to do or not to do certain things.

Contribution, Principle of: Holds that maximum real property values are achieved when the improvements on the site produce the highest (net) return commensurate with the investment.

Consumer Goods: These are goods used or bought for use primarily for personal, family or household purposes.

Conventional Mortgage: A mortgage securing a loan made by investors without governmental underwriting, i.e., which is not FHA insured or VA guaranteed.

Conversion: Change from one character or use to another. Also, the wrongful appropriation of funds of another.

Conveyance: This has two meanings. One meaning refers to the process of transferring title to property from one person to another. In this sense it is used as a verb. The other meaning refers to the document used to effect the transfer of title (usually some kind of deed). In this last sense, it is used a noun.

Cooperative Ownership: A form of apartment ownership. Ownership of shares in a cooperative venture which entitles the owner to use, rent, or sell a specific apartment unit. The corporation usually reserves the right to approve certain actions such as a sale or improvement.

Comer Influence Table: A statistical table that may be used to estimate the added value of a corner lot.

Corporation: A group or body of persons established and treated by law as an individual or unit with rights and liabilities or both, distinct and apart from those of the persons composing it. A corporation is a creature of law having certain powers and duties of a natural person. Being created by law it may continue for any length of time the law prescribes.

Corporeal Rights: Possessory rights in real property.

Correction Lines: A system for compensating inaccuracies in the Government rectangular Survey System due to the curvature of the earth. Every fourth township line, 24 mile intervals, is used as a correction line on which the intervals between the north and south range lines are remeasured and corrected to a full 6 miles.

Correlate the Findings: Interpret the data and value estimates to bring them together to a final conclusion of value.

Correlation: To bring the indicated values developed by the three approaches into mutual relationship with each other.

Correlative User: Rights of an owner to reasonable use of nonflowing underground water.

Cost: A historical record of past expenditures, or an amount which would be given in exchange for other things.

Cost Approach: One of three methods in the appraisal process. An analysis in which a value estimate of a property is derived by estimating the replacement cost of the improvements, deducting therefrom the estimated accrued depreciation, then adding the market value of the land.

Counterflashing: Sheet metal used around chimneys, at roof line and in roof valleys to prevent moisture entry.

Covenant: Agreements written into deeds and other instruments promising performance or nonperformance of certain acts or stipulating certain uses or nonuses of the property.

CPM: Certified Property manger. IREM's highest designation.

Crawl Hole: Exterior or interior opening permitting access underneath building, as required by building codes.

CRB: Certified Residential Broker.

CRE: Counselor of Real Estate. Members of American Society of Real Estate Counselors.

CRS: Certified Residential Specialist (A NAR designation).

Cubage: The number or product resulting by multiplying the width of a thing by its height and by its depth or length.

Curable Depreciation: Items of physical deterioration and functional obsolescence which are customarily repaired or replaced by a prudent property owner.

Curtail Schedule: A listing of the amounts by which the principal sum of an obligation is to be reduced by partial payments and of the dates when each payment will become payable.

Curtesy: The right which a husband has in a wife's estate at her death.

D

Damages: The indemnity recoverable by a person who has sustained an injury, either in his person, property, or relative rights, through the act or default of another.

Data Plant: An appraiser's file of information on real estate.

Debenture: Bonds issued without specific security.

Debtor: This is the party who "owns" the property which is subject to the security interest.

Deciduous Trees: Trees that lose their leaves in the autumn and winter. (Regarded as hardwoods)

Deck: Usually an open area on the roof, or off a ground or higher floor. Similar areas are called porch, patio, lanai, veranda.

Dedication: A conveyance of land by its owner for some public use, accepted for such use by authorized public officials on behalf of the public.

Deed: Written instrument which, when properly executed and delivered, conveys title.

Deed in Lieu of Foreclosure: Mortgagor gives a quit claim deed to mortgagee. There could be a problem as to junior liens.

Deed Restrictions: This is a limitation in the deed to a property that dictates certain uses that may or may not be made of the property.

Default: Failure to fulfill a duty or promise or to discharge an obligation; omission or failure to perform any act.

Defeasance Clause: The clause in a mortgage that gives the mortgagor the right to redeem his property upon the payment of his obligations to the mortgagee.

Defeasible Fee: Sometimes called a "base fee" or "qualified fee"; a fee simple absolute interest in land that is capable of being terminated upon the happening of a specified event.

Deferred Maintenance: Existing but unfulfilled requirements for repairs and rehabilitation.

Deficiency Judgment: A judgment given when the foreclosure sale of the security pledge, for a loan does not satisfy the debt.

Depreciation: Loss of value in real property brought about by age, physical deterioration or functional or economic obsolescence. Broadly, a loss in value from any cause.

Depth Table: A statistical table that may be used to estimate the value of the added depth of a lot.

Desist and Refrain Order: An order directing a person to desist and refrain from committing an act in violation of the real estate law.

Desk Cost: The cost of operation of a real estate office expressed on a per salesperson basis.

Deterioration: Impairment of condition. One of the causes of depreciation and reflecting the loss in value brought about by wear and tear, disintegration, use in service, and the action of the elements.

Devisee: One who receives a bequest made by will.

Devisor: One who bequeaths by will.

Directional Growth: The location or direction toward which the residential sections of a city are destined or determined to grow.

Discount: An amount deducted in advance from the principal before the borrower is given the use of the principal. (See **Points**)

Disintermediation: The relatively sudden withdrawal of substantial sums of money savers have deposited with savings and loan associations, commercial banks, and mutual savings banks. This term can also be considered to include life insurance policy purchasers borrowing against the value of their policies. The essence of this phenomenon is financial intermediaries losing within a short period of time billions of dollars as owners of funds held by those institutional lenders exercise their prerogative of taking them out of the hands of these financial institutions.

Disposable Income: The after-tax income a household receives to spend on personal consumption.

Dispossess: To deprive one of the use of real estate.

Documentary Transfer Tax: A state enabling act allowing a county to adopt a documentary transfer tax to apply on all transfer of real property located in the county. Notice of payment is entered on face of the deed or on a separate paper filed with the deed.

Dominant Tenement: Estate benefited by an easement right of use.

Donee: A person to whom a gift is made.

Donor: A person who makes a gift.

Dower: The right which a wife has in her husband's estate at his death.

Dual Agency: An agent who has agency duties to both buyer and seller.

Duress: Unlawful constraint exercised upon a person whereby he is forced to do some act against his will.

E

Earnest Money: Down payment made by a purchaser of real estate as evidence of good faith.

Easement: Created by grant or agreement for a specific purpose, an easement is the right, privilege or interest which one party has in land of another. **Example:** right of way

Easement by Necessity: Easement granted when lands were formerly under a single owner and there is not other ingress or egress.

Easement by Prescription: An easement obtained by open, notorious and hostile use.

Easement In Gross: Easement personal to the easement holder where there is no dominant tenement.

Eaves: The lower part of a roof projecting over the wall.

Economic Life: The period over which a property will yield a return on the investment, over and above the economic or ground rent due to land.

Economic Obsolescence: A loss in value due to factors away from the subject property but adversely affecting the value of the subject property.

Economic Rent: The reasonable rental expectancy if the property were available for renting at the time of its valuation.

Effective Age of Improvement: The number of years of age that is indicated by the condition of the structure.

Effective Date of Value: The specific day the conclusion of value applies.

Effective Interest Rate: The percentage of interest that is actually being paid by the borrower for the use of the money.

Electromagnetic Fields: Possible harmful magnetic fields surrounding high capacity electrical transmission lines.

Eminent Domain: The right of the government to acquire property for necessary public or quasi-public use by condemnation; the owner must be fairly compensated. The right of the government to do this and the right of the private citizen to get paid is spelled out in the 5th Amendment to the United States Constitution.

Encroachment: Trespass, the building of a structure or construction of any improvements, partly or wholly on the property of another.

Encumbrance: Anything which affects or limits the fee simple title to property, such as mortgages, easements or restrictions of any kind. Liens are special encumbrances which make the property security for the payment of a debt or obligation, such as mortgages and taxes.

Environmental Impact Report: A report as to the effect of a proposed development on the environment.

Equity: The interest or value which an owner has in real estate over and above the liens against it; branch of remedial justice by and through which relief is afforded to suitors in courts of equity.

Equity of Redemption: The right to redeem property during or after the foreclosure period, such as a mortgagor's right to redeem within a set period after foreclosure sale (some states).

Erosion: The wearing away of land by the action of water, wind or glacial ice.

Escalation: The right reserved by the lender to increase the amount of the payments and/or interest upon the happening of a certain event.

Escalator Clause: A clause in a contract or lease providing for the upward or downward adjustment of payments.

Escheat: The reverting of property to the State when heirs capable of inheriting are lacking.

Escrow: The deposit of instruments and funds with instructions to a third neutral party to carry out the provisions of an agreement or contract; when everything is deposited to enable carrying out the instructions, it is called a complete or perfect escrow.

Estate: As applied to the real estate practice, the term signifies the quantity of interest, share, right, equity, of which riches or fortune may consist, in real property. The degree, quantity, nature, and extent of interest which a person has in real property.

Estate of Inheritance: An estate which may descend to heirs. All freehold estates are estates of inheritance, except estates for life.

Estate for Life: A freehold estate, not of inheritance, but which is held by the tenant for his own life or the life or lives of one or more other persons, or for an indefinite period which may endure for the life or lives of persons in being and beyond the period of life.

Estate from Period-to-Period: An interest in land where there is no definite termination date but the rental period is fixed at a certain sum per week, month, or year. Also called a **Periodic Tenancy**.

Estate at Sufferance: An estate arising when the tenant wrongfully holds over after the expiration of his term. The landlord has the choice of evicting the tenant as a trespasser or accepting such tenant for a similar term and under the conditions of the tenant's previous holding. Also called a tenancy at sufferance.

Estate of Will: The permissive occupation of lands and tenements by a tenant for an indefinite period, without a rental agreement.

Estate for Years: An interest in lands by virtue of a contract for the possession of them for a definite and limited period of time. A lease with a definite termination date may be said to be an estate for years.

Estate Tax: Inheritance tax.

Estimate: To form a preliminary opinion of value.

Estimated Remaining Life: The period of time (years) it takes for the improvements to become valueless.

Estoppel: A doctrine which bars one from asserting rights which are inconsistent with a previous position or representation.

Ethics: That branch of moral science, idealism, justness, and fairness, which treats of the duties which a member of a profession or craft owes to the public, to his clients or patron, and to his professional brethren or members.

Eviction: Dispossession by process of law. The act of depriving a person of the possession of lands, in pursuance of the judgment of a court.

Exclusive Agency Listing: A written instrument giving one agent the right to sell property for a specified time but reserving the right of the owner to sell the property himself without the payment of a commission.

Exclusive Right to Sell Listing: A written agreement between owner and agent giving agent the right to collect a commission if the property is sold by anyone during the term of his agreement.

Execute: To complete, to make, to perform, to do, to follow out; to execute a deed, to make a deed, including especially signing, sealing, and delivery; to execute a contract is to perform the contract, to follow out to the end, to complete.

Executor: A person named in a will to carry out its provisions as to the disposition of the estate of a person deceased.

Expansion Joint: A fiber strip used to separate units of concrete to prevent cracking due to expansion as a result of temperature changes.

Expenses: Certain items which may appear on a closing statement in connection with a real estate sale.

F

Facade: Front of a building.

Facilitator: A person who acts to bring parties to an agreement but is the agent of neither.

Fair Market Value: This is the amount of money that would be paid for a property offered on the open market for a reasonable period of time with both buyer and seller knowing all the uses to which the property could be put and with neither party being under pressure to buy or sell.

Farm Service Agency (FSA): An agency of the Department of agriculture. Primary responsibility is to provide financial assistance for farmers and others living in rural areas where financing is not available on reasonable terms from private sources.

Federal Deposit Insurance Corporation (FDIC): Agency of the federal government which insures deposits at commercial banks and savings banks.

Federal Home Loan Bank (FHLB): A district bank of the Federal Home Loan Bank system that lends only to member savings and loan associations.

Federal Home Loan Bank Board (FHLBB): The administrative agency that charters federal savings and loan associations and exercises regulatory authority over the FHLB system.

Federal Housing Administration (FHA): An agency of the federal government that insures mortgage loans.

Federal National Mortgage Association (FNMA - "Fannie Mae"): A private corporation whose primary function is to buy and sell FHA and VA mortgages in the secondary market.

Fee: An estate of inheritance in real property.

Fee Simple: In modern estates, the terms "Fee" and "Fee Simple" are substantially synonymous. The term "Fee" is of Old English derivation. "Fee Simple Absolute" is an estate in real property, by which the owner has the greatest power over the title which it is possible to have, being an absolute estate. In modern use, it expressly establishes the title of real property in the owner, without limitation or end. He may dispose of it by sale, or trade or will, as he chooses.

Fee Simple Determinable: An estate that ends automatically when a condition is breached.

Feudal Tenure: A real property ownership system where ownership rests with a sovereign who, in turn, may grant lesser interests in return for service or loyalty. In contrast to allodial tenure where ownership is complete.

Feuds: Grants of land.

Fidelity Bond: A security posted to insure the honesty of a person.

Fiduciary: A person in a position of trust and confidence, as between principal and broker; broker as fiduciary owes certain loyalty which cannot be breached under the rules of agency.

Filtering Down: The process of housing passing down to successively lower income groups.

Financial Intermediary: Financial institutions such as commercial banks, savings and loan associations, mutual savings banks and life insurance companies which receive relatively small

sums of money from the public and invest them in the form of large sums. A considerable portion of these funds are loaned on real estate.

Financing Statement: This is the instrument which is filed in order to give public notice of the security interest in personal property and thereby protect the interest of the secured parties in the collateral. See definitions of Security Interest and Secured Party.

Finder's Fee: A fee for introducing the parties to a transaction.

Finish Floor: Finish floor strips are applied over wood joists, and plywood before finish floor is installed; finish floor is the final covering on the floor: wood, linoleum, cork, tile or carpet .

Fire Stop: A horizontal board between studs placed to prevent the spread of fire and smoke through such a space.

First Mortgage: A legal document pledging collateral for a loan (see "mortgage") that has first priority over all other claims against the property except taxes and bonded indebtedness.

Fiscal Controls: Federal tax and expenditure policies used to control the level of economic activity.

Fixity of Location: The physical characteristic of real estate that subjects it to the influence of its surroundings.

Fixtures: Appurtenances attached to the land or improvements, which usually cannot be removed without agreement as they become real property; examples: plumbing fixtures built into the property.

Flashing: Sheet metal or other material used to protect a building from seepage of water.

Footing: The base or bottom of a foundation wall, pier, or column.

Foreclosure: Legal procedure whereby property pledged as security for a debt is sold to pay the debt in event of default in payments or terms.

Forfeiture: Loss of money or anything of value, due to failure to perform .

Foundation: The supporting portion of a structure below the first floor construction, or below grade.

Franchise: A specified privilege awarded by a government or business firm which awards an exclusive marketing.

Fraud: The intentional and successful employment of any cunning, deception, collusion, or artifice, used to circumvent, cheat or deceive another person, whereby that person acts upon it to the loss of his property and to his legal injury.

Freehold: An estate of indeterminable duration, e.g., fee simple or life estate.

Frontage: Land bordering a street.

Front Foot: Property measurement for sale or valuation purposes; the property measures by the front foot on its street line--each front foot extending the depth of the lot.

Front Money: The minimum amount of money necessary to initiate a real estate venture.

Frostline: The depth of frost penetration in the soil. Varies in different parts of the country. Footings should be placed below this depth to prevent movement.

Fructus Naturales: Naturally growing plants and trees.

Functional Obsolescence: A loss of value due to adverse factors built into the structure which affect the utility of the structure.

Funding Fee: A fee paid to the Department of Veterans Affairs for a VA loan.

Furring: Strips of wood or metal applied to a wall or other surface to even it, to form an air space, or to give the wall an appearance of greater thickness.

Future Benefits: The anticipated benefits the present owner will receive from his property in the future.

G

Gable Roof: A pitched roof with sloping sides.

Gambrel Roof: A curb roof, having a steep lower slope with a flatter upper slope above.

General Lien: A lien on all the property of a debtor.

General Warranty Deed: The warranty deed where the seller guarantees that the title is marketable.

Gift Deed: A deed for which the consideration is love and affection and where there is no material consideration.

Girder: A large beam used to support beams, joists and partitions.

Grade: Ground level at the foundation.

Graduated Lease: Lease which provides for a varying rental rate, often based upon future determination; sometimes rent is based upon result of periodical appraisals; used largely in long-term leases.

Grant: A technical term made use of in deeds of conveyance of lands to import a transfer.

Grant Deed: A deed in which "grant" is used as the word of conveyance. The grantor impliedly warrants that he has not already conveyed to any other person, and that the estate conveyed is free from encumbrances done, made or suffered by the grantor or any person claiming under him, including taxes, assessments, and other liens.

Grantee: The purchaser; a person to whom a grant is made.

Grantor: Seller of property; one who signs a deed.

GRI: Graduate, Realtors Institute.

Grid: A chart used in rating the borrower risk, property, and the neighborhood.

Gross Income: Total income from property before any expenses are deducted.

Gross Domestic Product (GDP): The total value of all goods and services produced in a economy during a given period of time.

Gross Rate: A method of collecting interest by adding total interest to the principal of the loan at the outset of the term.

Gross Rent Multiplier: A figure which, times the gross income of a property, produces an estimate of value of the property.

Ground Lease: An agreement for the use of the land only, sometimes secured by improvements placed on the land by the user.

Ground Rent: Earnings of improved property credited to earnings of the ground itself after allowance is made for earnings of improvements; often termed economic rent.

Growing Equity Mortgage (GEM): A mortgage with payments that increase in steps resulting in a rapid payback.

H - I

Habendum Clause: The "to have and to hold" clause in a deed.

Hard Money Loan: A cash loan by a noninstitutional lender.

Header: The horizontal beam above doors or windows.

Highest and Best Use: An appraisal phrase meaning that use which at the time of an appraisal is most likely to produce the greatest net return to the land and/or buildings over a given period of time; that use which will produce the greatest amount of amenities or profit. This is the starting point for appraisal.

Hip Roof: A pitched roof with all sides sloping to the eaves.

Holder in Due Course: One who has taken a note, check or bill of exchange in due course:

1. Appears good on its face
2. Before it was overdue;
3. In good faith and for value;
4. Without knowledge that it has been previously dishonored without notice of any defect at the time it was negotiated to him.

Holdover Tenant: Tenant who remains in possession of leased property after the expiration of the lease term.

Homestead: A home upon which the owner or owners have recorded a Declaration of Homestead. As provided by Statutes in some states; protects home against judgments up to specified amounts.

Hundred Percent Location: A city retail business location which is considered the best available for attracting business.

Hypothecate: To give a thing as security without the necessity of giving up possession of it.

Impounds: A trust-type account established by lenders for the accumulation of funds to meet taxes and, future insurance policy premiums required to protect their security. Impounds are usually collected with the note payment.

Inchoate Right of Dower: A wife's interest in the real estate of her husband during his life which upon his death may become a dower interest.

Income Approach: One of the three methods in the appraisal process; an analysis in which the estimated net income from the subject residence is used as a basis for estimating value by dividing the net by a capitalization rate.

Incompetent: One who is mentally incompetent, or because of age or not incarceration lacks contractual capacity.

Incorporeal Rights: Nonpossessory rights in real estate.

Increment: An increase. Most frequently used to refer to the increase of value of land that accompanies population growth and increasing wealth in the community. The term unearned increment is used in this connection since values are supposed to have increased without effort on the part of the owner.

Indenture: A formal written instrument made between two or more persons.

Indorsement: The act of signing one's name on the back of a check or note, with or without further qualification.

Injunction: A writ or order issued under the seal of a court to restrain one or more parties to a suit or proceeding from doing an act which is deemed to be inequitable or unjust in regard to the rights of some other party or parties in the suit or proceeding.

Input: Data, information, etc., that is fed into a computer or other system.

Installment Contract: Purchase of real estate wherein the purchase price is paid in installments over a long period of time, title is retained by seller, upon default the payments are forfeited. Also known as a land contract.

Installment Note: A note which provides that payments of a certain sum or amount be paid on the dates specified in the instrument.

Installment Reporting: A method of reporting capital gains by installments for successive tax years to minimize the impact of the totality of the capital gains tax in the year of the sale.

Instrument: A written legal document; created to effect the rights of the parties.

Interest: The charge in dollars for the use of money for a period of time. In a sense, the "rent" paid for the use of money.

Interest Rate: The percentage of a sum of money charged for its use.

Interim Loan: A short-term loan until long-term financing is available.

Intermediate Theory: That a mortgage is a lien but title transfers to mortgagee automatically upon default.

Interstate Land Sales Full Disclosure Act: Disclosure requirements for unimproved land sales made in interstate commerce.

Intestate: A person who dies having made no will, or one which is defective in form in which case his estate descends to his heirs at law or next of kin.

Involuntary Alienation: Involuntary transfer such as foreclosure for eminent domain.

Involuntary Lien: A lien imposed against property without consent of an owner; example: taxes, special assessments, federal income tax liens, etc.

Inwood Tables: Concept of using present value of income in a perpetuity table to help appraisers.

IREM: Institute of Real Estate Management. Part of NAR.

Irrevocable: Incapable of being recalled or revoked; unchangeable.

J

Jalousie: A slatted blind shutter or window, like a venetian blind but used on the exterior to protect against rain as well as to control sunlight.

Jamb: The side post or lining of a doorway, window or other opening.

Joint Note: A note signed by two or more persons who have equal liability for payment.

Joint Tenancy: Joint ownership by two or more persons with right of survivorship; all joint tenants own equal interest and have equal rights in the property and are formed at the same time by the same instrument.

Joint Venture: Two or more individuals or firms joining together on a single project as partners.

Joist: One of a series of parallel horizontal beams to which the boards of a floor and ceiling laths are nailed, and supported in turn by larger beams, girders, or bearing walls.

Judgment: The final determination of a court of competent jurisdiction of a matter presented to it; money judgments provide for the payment of claims presented to the court, or are awarded as damages, etc.

Judgment Lien: A legal claim on all of the property of a judgment debtor in the county where recorded, which enables the judgment creditor to have the property sold for payment of the amount of the judgment.

Junior Mortgage: A mortgage second in lien to a previous mortgage.

Jurisdiction: The authority by which judicial officers take cognizance of and decide causes; the power to hear and determine a cause; the right and power which a judicial officer has to enter upon the inquiry.

L

Laches: Delay or negligence in asserting one's legal rights.

Land Contract: A contract ordinarily used in connection with the sale of property in cases where the seller does not wish to convey title until all or a certain part of the purchase price is paid by the buyer; often used when property is sold on small down payment.

Landlord: One who rents his property to another.

Lateral Support: The support which the soil of an adjoining owner gives to his neighbors' land.

Lath: A building material of wood, metal, gypsum, or insulating board fastened to the frame of a building to act as a plaster base.

Lead Base Paint Disclosure: Federally mandated disclosure for residential property built prior to 1978.

Lease: A contract between owner and tenant, setting forth conditions upon which tenant may occupy and use the property, and the term of the occupancy.

Leasehold Estate: A tenant's right to occupy real estate during the term of the lease. This is a personal property interest.

Legal Description: A description recognized by law; a description by which property can be definitely located by reference to government surveys metes and bounds or approved recorded maps.

Lessee: One who contracts to rent property under a lease contract.

Lessor: An owner who enters into a lease with a tenant.

Level Payment Mortgage: A loan on real estate that is paid off by making a series of equal (or nearly equal) regular payments. Part of the payment is usually interest on the loan and part of it reduces the amount of the unpaid balance of the loan. Also sometimes called an **Amortized Mortgage**.

Leverage: Maximizing net by using borrowed funds.

Lien: A form of encumbrance which usually makes property security for the payment of a debt or discharge of an obligation. **Example:** judgments, taxes, mortgages, deeds of trust, etc.

Lien Theory: A mortgage theory that a mortgage creates only a lien.

Life Estate: An estate or interest in real property which is held for the duration of the life of some certain person.

Limited Partnership: A partnership composed of some partners whose contribution is financial and liability is are limited to their investment.

Lintel: A horizontal board that supports the load over an opening such as a door or window.

Lis Pendens: Suit pending, usually recorded so as to give constructive notice of pending litigation.

Liquidated Damages: A sum agreed upon by the parties to be full damages if an agreement is breached.

Listing: An employment contract between principal and agent authorizing the agent to perform services for the principal involving the latter's property; listing contracts are entered into for the purpose of securing persons to buy, lease or rent property. Employment of an agent by a prospective purchaser or lessee to locate property for purchase or lease may be considered a listing.

Loan Administration: Also called **Loan Servicing**. Mortgage bankers not only originate loans, but also "service" them from origination to maturity of the loan.

Loan Application: The loan application is a source of information on which the lender bases his decision to make the loan, defines the terms of the loan contract; gives the name of the borrower, place of employment, salary, bank accounts, and credit references; and, describes the real estate that is to be mortgaged. It also stipulates the amount of loan being applied for, and repayment terms.

Loan Closing: When all conditions have been met, the loan officer authorizes the recording of the trust deed or mortgage. The disbursal procedure of funds is similar to the closing of a real estate sales escrow. The borrower can expect to receive less than the amount of the loan, as title, recording, service, and other fees may be withheld, or he can expect to deposit the cost of these items into the loan escrow. This process is sometimes called "funding" or "settlement."

Loan Commitment: Lender's contractual commitment to a loan based on the appraisal and underwriting.

Loan To Value Ratio (LTV): The percentage of a property's value that a lender can or may loan to a borrower. For example, if the ratio is 80% this means that a lender may loan 80% of the property's appraised value to a borrower.

Long-Term Gain: Capital gain on sale of property held over 18 months.

Louver: An opening with a series of horizontal slats set at an agle to permit ventilation without admitting rain, sunlight, or vision.

M

MAI: Designates a person who is a member of the Appraisal Institute.

Margin of Security: The difference between the amount of the mortgage loan(s) and the appraised value of the property.

Marginal Land: Land which barely pays the cost of working or using.

Market Data Approach: One of the three methods in the appraisal process. A means of comparing similar type residential properties, which have recently sold, to the subject property.

Market Price: The price paid regardless of pressures, motives or intelligence.

Market Value: (1) The price at which a willing seller would sell and a willing buyer would buy, neither being under abnormal pressure; (2) as defined by the courts, is the highest price estimated in terms of money which a property will bring if exposed for sale in the open market allowing a reasonable time to find a purchaser with knowledge of property's use and capabilities for use.

Marketable Title: Merchantable title; title free and clear of objectionable liens or encumbrances.

Material Fact: A fact is material if it is one which the agent should realize would be likely to affect the judgment of the principal in giving his consent to the agent to enter into the particular transaction on the specified terms.

Mechanics' Lien: A lien created by statute which exists against real property in favor of persons who have performed work or furnished materials for the improvement of the real estate.

Meridians: North-south surveyor lines which intersect base lines to form a starting point for the measurement of land.

Metes and Bounds: A term used in describing the boundary lines of land, setting forth all the boundary lines together with their terminal points and angles.

Mid-Term Gain: Gain on sale of property held over one year but less than 18 months.

Mile: 5,280 feet.

Mineral, Oil, and Gas Rights: The right to minerals, oil and gas in the ground and the implied easement to enter to mine or drill.

Minor: All persons under 18 years of age who are not emancipated.

Misplaced Improvement: Improvements on land which do not conform to the most profitable use of the site.

Mitigation of Damages: Duty of lessor to attempt to rent to keep defaulting tenant's damages down.

Manufactured Home: A home constructed and then transported on its own chassis.

Modular: A building composed of modules constructed on an assembly line in a factory. Usually, the modules are self-contained.

Moldings: Usually patterned or curved strips used to provide ornamental variation of outline or contour, such as cornices, bases, window and door jambs.

Monetary Controls: Federal Reserve tools for regulating the availability of money and credit to influence the level of economic activity.

Monument: A fixed object and point established by surveyors to establish land locations.

Moratorium: The temporary suspension, usually by statute, of construction or the enforcement of a debt.

Mortgage: An instrument recognized by law by which property is hypothecated to secure the payment of a debt or obligation; procedure for foreclosure in event of default is established by statute.

Mortgage Guaranty Insurance: Insurance against financial loss available to mortgage lenders from Mortgage Guaranty Insurance Corporation (MGIC), a private company organized in 1956.

Mortgage Loan Broker: A broker who charges borrowers for loans arranged.

Mortgagee: One to whom a mortgagor gives a mortgage to secure a loan or performance of an obligation, a lender. (See definition of Secured Party.)

Mortgagor: One who gives a mortgage on his property to secure a loan or assure performance of an obligation; a borrower. (See definition of **Debtor**.)

Multiple Listing: A listing, usually an exclusive right to sell, taken by a member of an organization composed of real estate brokers, with the provisions that all members will have the opportunity to find an interested client; a cooperative listing.

Mutual Water Company: A water company organized by or for water users in a given district with the object of securing an ample water supply at a reasonable rate; stock is issued to users.

NAREB: National Association of Real Estate Brokers.

NAR: National Association of Realtors®.

Narrative Appraisal: A summary of all factual materials, techniques and appraisal methods used by the appraiser in setting forth his value conclusion.

Negative Amortization: Loan payments that do not cover the interest due so that the loan principal increases.

Negative Declaration: A statement that a development will not adversely effect the environment.

Negotiable: Capable of being negotiated; assignable, or transferable in the ordinary course of business.

Net Listing: A listing which provides that the agent may retain as compensation for his services all sums received over and above a net price to the owner. (Illegal in many states)

Nominal Interest Rates: The percentage of interest that is stated in loan documents.

Notary Public: An appointed officer with authority to take the acknowledgment of persons executing documents, to sign the certificate, and affix his seal.

Note: A signed written instrument acknowledging a debt and promising payment.

Notice: Actual knowledge acquired by being or knowing of the occurrence.

Notice of Nonresponsibility: A notice provided by law designed to relieve a property owner from responsibility for the cost of work done on the property or materials furnished therefor; when contracted by a tenant or vendee on a land contract notice must be verified, recorded and posted.

Notice to Quit: A notice to a tenant to vacate rented property.

Nuncupative Will: Oral will. Not generally valid.

Obligating Advance: Required advance on a construction loan as work progresses.

Obsolescence: Loss in value due to reduced desirability and usefulness of a structure because its design and construction become obsolete.

Occupancy Permit: Required from building inspector prior to occupancy of a new unit.

Offset Statement: Statement by owner of property or owner of lien against property, setting forth the present status of liens against said property.

Open-End Mortgage: A mortgage containing a clause which permits the mortgagor to borrow additional money without rewriting the mortgage.

Open Housing Law: See Civil Rights Act of 1968.

Open Listing: An authorization given by a property owner to a real estate agent wherein said agent is given the non-exclusive rights to secure a purchaser; open listings may be given to any number of agents without liability to compensate any except the one who first secures a buyer ready, willing and able to meet the terms of the listing, or secures the acceptance by the seller of a satisfactory offer.

Opinion of Title: An attorney's evaluation of the condition of the title to a parcel of land after his examination of the abstract of title to the land.

Option: A right given for a consideration to purchase or lease a property upon specified terms within a specified time.

Oral Contract: A verbal agreement; one which is not reduced to writing.

Orientation: Placing a house on its lot with regard to its exposure to the rays of the sun, prevailing winds, privacy from the street and protection from outside noises.

Overhang: The part of the roof extending beyond the walls, to shade buildings and cover walks.

Over Improvement: An improvement which is not the highest and best use for the site on which it is placed by reason of excess size or cost. An improvement that will not reasonably contribute to income or market value.

P

Packaged Mortgage: A mortgage covering both real and personal property.

Parquet Floor: Hardwood flooring laid in squares or patterns.

Participation: In addition to base interest on mortgage loans on income properties, a percentage of ownership is given to the lender.

Partition Action: Court proceedings by which co-owners seek to sever their joint ownership.

Partnership: A contract of two or more persons to unite their property, labor or skill, or some of them, in prosecution of some joint or lawful business, and to share the profits in certain proportions.

Party Wall: A wall erected on the line between two adjoining properties, which are under different ownership, for the use of both properties.

Patent: Conveyance of title to government land.

PCPs: A carcinogenic substance used in insulating fluids in electrical transformers.

Penalty: An extra payment or charge required of the borrower for deviating from the terms of the original loan agreement. Usually levied for being late in making regular payment or for paying off the loan before it is due.

Penny: The term, as applied to nails, serves as a measure of nail length and is abbreviated by the letter "d."

Percentage Lease: Lease on the property, the rental for which is determined by amount of business done by the lessee; usually a percentage of gross receipts from the business with provision for a minimum rental.

Perimeter Heating: Baseboard heating, or any system in which the heat registers are located along the outside walls of a room, especially under the windows.

Personal Property: Any property which is not real property.

Physical Deterioration: Impairment of condition. Loss in value brought about by wear and tear, disintegration, use, and actions of the elements.

Pier: A column of masonry, usually rectangular in horizontal cross section, used to support other structural members.

Pitch: The incline or rise of a roof.

Planned Unit Development (PUD): A land use design with rivate unit ownership but having of common areas.

Plate: A horizontal board placed on a wall or supported on posts or studs to carry the trusses of a roof or rafters directly; a shoe, or base member as of a partition or other frame; a small flat horizontal board placed on or in a wall to support girders, joists, rafters, etc.

Pledge: The depositing of personal property by a debtor with a creditor as security for a debt or engagement.

Pledgee: One who is given a pledge or a security. (See definition of **Secured Party**.)

Pledgor: One who offers a pledge or gives security. (See definition of **Debtor**.)

Plottage Increment: The appreciation in unit value created by joining smaller ownerships into one large single ownership.

Plywood: Laminated wood made up in panels; several thickness of wood glued together with grain at different angles for strength.

Point of Beginning (POB): Beginning point for a metes and bounds description.

Points: Each point is one percent of the loan. They are charged by lenders to make the loan more attractive. For buyers they are treated as prepaid interest.

Police Power: The right of the State to enact laws and regulations enforce them for the order, safety, health, morals, and general welfare of the public.

Power of Attorney: An instrument authorizing a person to act as the agent of the person granting it, and a general power authorizing the agent to act generally in behalf of the principal. A special power limits the agent to a particular or specific act, as a landowner may grant an agent special power of attorney to convey a single and specific parcel of property. Under the provisions of a general power of attorney, the agent having the power may convey any or all property of the principal granting the general power of attorney.

Prefabricated House: A house manufactured, and sometimes partly assembled, before delivery to building site.

Prepaid Items of Expense: Prorations of prepaid items of expense which are credited to the seller in the closing statement.

Prepayment: Provision made for loan payments to be larger than those specified in the note.

Prepayment Penalty: Penalty for the payment of a mortgage or trust deed note before it actually becomes due if the note does not provide for prepayment.

Present Value: The lump sum value today of an annuity. A $100 bill to be paid to someone in one year is worth less than if it were a $100 bill to be paid to someone today. This is due to several things, one of which is that the money has time value. How much the $100 bill to be paid in one year is worth today will depend on the interest rate that seems proper for the particular circumstances. For example, if 6% is the appropriate rate, the $100 to be paid one year from now would be worth $94.34 today.

Presumption: A rule of law that courts and judges shall draw a particular inference from a particular fact, or from particular evidence, unless and until the truth of such inference is disproved.

Prima Facie: Presumptive on its face.

Principal: This term is used to mean either the employer of an agent or the amount of money borrowed or the amount of the loan.

Principal Note: The promissory note which is secured by the mortgage or trust deed.

Prior Appropriation: The superior rights of the first user of flowing water (in some states).

Private Mortgage Insurance (PMI): A policy of Private Mortgage Insurance usually required for a conventional loan where the down payment is less than 20 percent.

Privity: Mutual relationship to the same rights of property, contractual relationship.

Procuring Cause: That cause originating from series of events that, without break in continuity, results in the prime object of an agent's employment producing a final buyer.

Progression, Principle of: The worth of a lesser valued residence tends to be enhanced by association with many higher valued residences in the same area.

Promissory Note: Following a loan commitment from the lender, the borrower signs a note, promising to repay the loan under stipulated terms. The promissory note establishes liability for its repayment.

Property: The rights of ownership. The right to use, possess, enjoy, and dispose of a thing in every legal way and to exclude everyone else from interfering with these rights. Property is generally classified into two groups, personal property and real property.

Proprietary Lease: The lease that goes with stock in a cooperative authorizing occupancy of a specific unit.

Proration: Adjustments of interest, taxes, and insurance, etc., on a prorate basis as of the closing date. Fire insurance is normally paid for in advance. If a property is sold during this time, the seller wants a refund on that portion of the advance payment that has not been used at the time the title to the property is transferred.

Proration of Taxes: To divide or prorate the taxes equally or proportionately to time of use.

Proximate Cause: That cause of an event is that which, in a natural and continuous sequence unbroken by any new cause, produced that event, and without which the event would not have happened. Also, the procuring cause.

Public Trustee: The county public official whose office has been created by statute, to whom title to real property, in certain states, e.g., Colorado, is conveyed by Trust Deed for the use and benefit of the beneficiary, who usually is the lender.

Punitive Damages: Damages in excess of compensatory damages to punish the wrongdoer for an outrageous action.

Purchase and Installment Sale-Back: Involves purchase of the property upon completion of construction and immediate sale-back on a long-term installment contract.

Purchase of Land, Leaseback, and Leasehold Mortgages: An arrangement whereby land is purchased by the lender and leased back to the developer with a mortgage negotiated on the resulting leasehold of the income property constructed. The lender receives an annual ground rent, plus a percentage of income from the property.

Purchase and Leaseback: Involves the purchase of property subject to an existing mortgage and immediate leaseback.

Purchase Money Mortgage or Trust Deed: A trust deed or mortgage given as part or all of the purchase consideration for property. In some states the purchase money mortgage or trust deed loan can be made by a seller who extends credit to the buyer of property or by a third party lender (typically a financial institution) that makes a loan to the buyer of real property for a portion of the purchase price to be paid for the property. (In many states there are legal limitations upon mortgagees and trust deed beneficiaries collecting deficiency judgments against the purchase money borrower after the collateral hypothecated under such security instruments has been sold through the foreclosure process. Generally no deficiency judgment is allowed if the collateral property under the mortgage or trust deed is residential property of four units or less with the debtor occupying the property as a place of residence.)

Q - R

Quantity Survey: A highly technical process in arriving at cost estimate of new construction, and sometimes referred to in the building trade as the price takeoff method. It involves a detailed estimate of the quantities of raw material lumber, plaster, brick, cement, etc. used, as well as the current price of the material and installation costs. These factors are all added together to arrive at the cost of a structure. It is usually used by contractors and experienced estimators.

Quarter Round: A molding that presents a profile of a quarter circle.

Quiet Enjoyment: Right of an owner to the use of the property without interference of possession.

Quiet Title: A court action brought to establish title; to remove a cloud on the title.

Quitclaim Deed: A deed to relinquish any interest in property which the grantor may have, without claiming to have an interest.

Radiant Heating: A method of heating, usually consisting of coils or pipes placed in the floor, wall, or ceiling.

Radon: A colorless odorless, naturally occurring hazardous gas.

Rafter: One of a series of boards of a roof designed to support roof loads. The rafters of a flat roof are sometimes called roof joists.

Range: A strip of land six miles wide determined by a government survey, running in a north-south direction.

Ratification: The adoption or approval of an act performed on behalf of a person without previous authorization.

Real Estate Board: An organization whose members consist primarily of real estate brokers and salespeople.

Real Estate Settlement Procedures Act (RESPA): A federal disclosure law effective June 20, 1975 requiring new procedures and forms for settlements (closing costs) involving federally related loans.

Real Estate Trust: A special arrangement under Federal and State law whereby investors may pool funds for investments in real estate and mortgages and yet escape corporation taxes.

Realtist: A real estate broker holding active membership in a real estate board affiliated with the National Association of Real Estate Brokers.

Realtor®: A real estate broker holding active membership in a real estate board affiliated with the National Association of Realtors®.

Recapture: The rate of interest necessary to provide for the return of an investment. Not to be confused with interest rate, which is a rate of interest on an investment.

Reconveyance: The transfer of the title of land from one person to the immediate preceding owner. This particular instrument of transfer is commonly used when the performance or debt is satisfied under the terms of a deed of trust, when the trustee conveys the title he has held on condition back to the owner.

Recording: The process of placing a document on file with a designated public official for everyone to see. This public official is usually a county officer known as the County Recorder. He designates the fact that a document has been given to him by placing his stamp upon it indicating the time of day and the date when it was officially placed on file. Documents filed with the Recorder are considered to be placed on open notice to the general public of that county. Claims against property usually are given a priority on the basis of the time and the date they are recorded with the most preferred claim status going to the earliest one recorded and the next claim going to the next earliest one recorded, and so on. This type of notice is called "constructive notice" or "legal notice."

Redemption: Buying back one's property after a judicial sale.

Refinancing: The paying-off of an existing obligation and assuming a new obligation in its place.

Reformation: An action to correct a mistake in a deed or other document.

Rehabilitation: The restoration of a property to satisfactory condition without drastically changing the plan, form, or style of architecture.

Release Clause: This is a stipulation that upon the payment of a specific sum of money to the holder of a trust deed or mortgage, the lien of the instrument as to a specific described lot or area shall be removed from the blanket lien on the whole area involved.

Release Deed: An instrument executed by the mortgagee or the trustee reconveying to the mortgagor the real estate which secured the mortgage loan after the debt has been paid in full. Upon recording it cancels the mortgage lien created when the mortgage or trust deed was recorded.

Reliction: The addition to land by the permanent recession of water.

Remainder: An estate which takes effect after the termination of the prior estate, such as a life estate.

Remainder Depreciation: The possible loss in value of an improvement which will occur in the future.

Replacement Cost: The cost to replace the structure with one having utility equivalent to that being appraised, but constructed with modern materials, and according to current standards, design and layout.

Reproduction Costs: The cost of replacing the subject improvement with one that is the exact replica, having the same quality of workmanship, design and layout.

Request for Notice of Default: Recorded request so junior lienholder will be notified of foreclosure action.

Request for Notice of Delinquency: When filed, mortgagee must notify junior lienholder that mortgagor is delinquent in payments.

Required Provider: A lender requiring particular service providers.

Rescission of Contract: The abrogation or annulling of contract; the revocation or repealing of contract by mutual consent by parties to the contract, or for cause by either party to the contract.

Reservation: A right retained by a grantor in conveying property.

Restriction: The term as used relating to real property means the owner of real property is restricted or prohibited from doing certain things relating to the property, or using the property for certain purposes. Property restrictions fall into two general classifications--public and private. Zoning ordinances are examples of the former type. Restrictions may be created by private owners, typically by appropriate clauses in deeds, or in agreements, or in general plans of entire subdivisions. Usually they assume the form of a covenant, or promise to do or not to do a certain thing. They cover a multitude of matters including use for residential or business purposes, e.g. houses in tract must cost more than $150,000 etc.

Retrospective Value: The value of the property as of a previous date.

Reversion: The right to future possession or enjoyment by the person, or his heirs, creating the preceding estate.

Reversionary Interest: The interest which a person has in lands or other property, upon the termination of the preceding estate.

Ridge: The horizontal line at the junction of the top edges of two sloping roof surfaces. The rafters at both slopes are nailed to a ridge board at the ridge.

Ridge Board: The board placed on edge at the ridge of the roof to support the upper ends of the rafters; also called roof tree, ridge piece, ridge plate or ridgepole.

Right of First Refusal: A right to buy or lease only if an owner wishes to sell or lease to another party. (Rights holder must match the offer.)

Right of Survivorship: Right to acquire the interests of a deceased joint owner; distinguishing feature of a joint tenancy.

Right of Way: A privilege operating as an easement upon land, whereby the owner does by grant, or by agreement, give to another the right to pass over his land, to construct a roadway, or use as a roadway, a specific part of his land, or the right to construct through and over his land, telephone, telegraph, or electric power lines, or the right to place underground water mains, gas mains, sewer mains, etc.

Riparian Rights: The right of a landowner to flowing water on, under, or adjacent to his land.

Riser: The upright board at the back of each step of a stairway. In heating, a riser is a duct slanted upward to carry hot air from the furnace to the room above.

Risk Analysis: A study made, usually by a lender, of the various factors that might affect the repayment of a loan.

Risk Rating: A process used by the lender to decide on the soundness (syn) of making a loan and to reduce all the various factors affecting the repayment of the loan to a qualified rating of some kind.

S

Sales Contract: A contract by which buyer and seller agree to terms of a sale.

Sale-Leaseback: A situation where the owner of a piece of property wishes to sell the property and retain occupancy by leasing it from the buyer.

Sandwich Lease: A leasehold interest which lies between the primary lease and the operating lease.

Sash: Wood or metal frames containing one or more window panes.

Satisfaction: Discharge of mortgage or trust deed lien from the records upon payment of the evidenced debt.

Satisfaction Piece: An instrument for recording and acknowledging payment of an indebtedness secured by a mortgage.

Scribing: Fitting woodwork to an irregular surface.

Seal: An impression made to attest the execution of an instrument in some states, particular documents require seals.

Secondary Financing: A loan secured by a second mortgage or trust deed on real property. These can be third, fourth, fifth, sixth—on and on ad infinitum.

Secured Party: This is the party having the security interest. Thus the mortgagee, the conditional seller, the beneficiary, etc., are all now referred to as the secured party.

Security Agreement: An agreement between the secured party and the debtor which creates the security interest.

Security Interest: A term designating the interest of the creditor in the personal property of the debtor in all types of credit transactions. It thus replaces such terms as the following: chattel mortgage; pledge; trust receipt; chattel trust; equipment trust; conditional sale; inventory lien; etc.

Section: Section of land is established by government survey and contains 640 acres.

Seizin: Possession of real estate by one entitled thereto.

Separate Property: Property owned by a husband or wife which is not jointly owned.

Septic Tank: An underground tank in which sewage from the house is reduced to liquid by bacterial action and drained off.

Servicing: Supervising and administering a loan after it has been made. This involves such things as: collecting the payments, keeping accounting records, computing the interest and principal, foreclosure of defaulted loans, and so on.

Servient Tenement: The estate being used by an easement holder.

Setback Ordinance: An ordinance prohibiting the erection of a building or structure between the curb and the setback line.

Severalty Ownership: Owned by one person only. Sole ownership.

Shopping Center, Regional: A large shopping center with 250,000 to 1,000,000 or more square feet of store area, serving 200,000 or more people.

Shake: A handsplit shingle, usually edge grained.

Sharing Appreciation Mortgage: A loan where a lender shares in the value appreciation. It usually requires a sale or appraisal at a future date.

Sheathing: Structural covering usually boards, plywood, or wallboards, placed over exterior studding or rafters of a house.

Sheriff's Deed: Deed given by court order in connection with sale of property to satisfy a judgment.

Short-Term Gain: Gain on sale where property was held for one year or less.

Sill: The lowest part of the frame of a house, resting on the foundation and supporting the uprights of the frame (mud sill). The board or metal forming the lower side of an opening, as a door sill, window sill, etc.

Sinking Fund: Fund set aside from the income from property which, with accrued interest, will eventually pay for replacement of the improvements.

SIR: Society of Industrial Realtors®.

Soft Money Loan: Seller financing where cash does not change hands.

Soil Pipe: Pipe carrying waste out from the house to the main sewer line.

Sole or Sole Plate: A member, usually a 2 by 4, on which wall and partition studs rest.

Span: The distance between structural supports such as walls, columns, piers, beams, girders, and trusses.

Special Assessment: Legal charge against real estate by a public authority to pay cost of public improvements such as: street lights, sidewalks, street improvements, etc.

Special Warranty Deed: A deed in which the grantor warrants or guarantees the title only against defects arising during his ownership of the property and not against defects existing before the time of his ownership.

Specific Liens: Liens which attach to only a certain specific parcel of land or piece of property.

Specific Performance: An action to compel performance of an agreement, e.g., sale of land.

Standard-Depth: Generally the most typical lot depth in the neighborhood.

Standby Commitment: The mortgage banker frequently protects a builder by a "standby" agreement, under which he agrees to make mortgage loans at an agreed price for many months in the future. The builder deposits a "standby fee" with the mortgage banker for this service. Frequently, the mortgage banker protects himself by securing a "standby" from a long-term investor for the same period of time, paying a fee for this privilege.

Starker Exchange: A delayed tax deferred exchange.

Statute of Frauds: State law which provides that certain contracts must be in writing in order to be enforceable at law. Examples: real property lease for more than one year; agent's authorization to sell real estate.

Statutory Warranty Deed: A short form warranty deed which warrants by inference that the seller is the undisputed owner and has the right to convey the property and that he will defend the title if necessary. This type of deed protects the purchaser in that the conveyor covenants to defend all claims against the property. If he fails to do so, the new owner can defend said claims and sue the former owner.

Straight-Line Depreciation: Definite annual sum to recover the cost of improvements.

Strict Foreclosure: Foreclosure without a sale if the debt has not been paid after statutory notice. The court transfers title to the mortgagee. (A few states).

String, Stringer: A timber or other support for cross members. In stairs, the diagonal support on which the stair treads rest.

Studs or Studding: Vertical supporting timbers in the walls and partitions.

Subjacent Support: The duty of an excavator or miner to support the surface.

"Subject To" Mortgage: When a grantee takes a title to real property subject to mortgage, he is not responsible to the holder of the promissory note for the payment of any portion of the amount due. The most that he can lose in the event of a foreclosure is his equity in the property. See also **Assumption of Mortgage**. In neither case is the original maker of the note released from his responsibility.

Sublease: A lease given by a lessee.

Subordinate: To make subject to, or junior to.

Subordination Clause: Clause in a junior or a second lien permitting retention of priority for prior liens. A subordination clause may also be used in a first deed of trust permitting it to be subordinated to subsequent liens as, for example, the liens of construction loans.

Subpoena: A process to cause a witness to appear and give testimony.

Subrogation: The substitution of another person in place of the creditor, to whose rights he succeeds in relation to the debt. The doctrine is used very often where one person agrees to stand surety for the performance of a contract by another person.

Substitution, Principle of: Affirms that the maximum value of a property tends to be set by the cost of acquiring an equally desirable and valuable substitute property, assuming no costly delay is encountered in making the substitution.

Sum of the Years Digits: An accelerated depreciation method.

Supply and Demand, Principle of: Affirms that price or value varies directly, but not necessarily proportionally with demand, and inversely, but not necessarily proportionately with supply.

Surety: One who guarantees the performance of another: Guarantor. A surety bond guarantees contract performance.

Surplus Productivity, Principle of: Affirms that the net income that remains after the proper costs of labor, organization and capital have been paid, which surplus is imputable to the land and tends to fix the value thereof.

Survey: The process by which a parcel of land is measured and its area is ascertained.

Syndicate: A partnership organized for participation in a real estate venture. Partners may be limited or unlimited in their liability.

T

Tacking One: Adding the use of use owners to obtain the continuous use period of an easement by prescription title by adverse possession.

Takeout Loan: The permanent loan arranged by the owner or builder developer for a buyer. The construction loan made for construction of the improvements is usually paid from the proceeds of this loan.

Tax-Free Exchange: Income property exchanged on for other income property which does not have to pay a capital gain tax at the time.

Tax Roll: Total of taxable property assessments in taxing district.

Tax Sale: Sale of property by a taxing authority after a period of nonpayment of taxes.

Tax Shelter: Use of depreciation to shelter income from taxation.

Teaser Rate: An initial rate on an adjustable rate loan less than the index figure plus margin. It is usually only given for a relatively short period of time.

Tenancy in Common: Ownership by two or more persons who hold undivided interest, without right of survivorship; interests need not be equal.

Tenants by the Entireties: Under certain state laws, ownership of property acquired by a husband and wife during marriage which is jointly owned and cannot be separately transferred. Upon death of one spouse, it becomes the property of the survivor.

Tentative Map: The Subdivision Map Act requires subdividers to submit initially a tentative map of their tract to the local planning commission for study. The approval or disapproval of the planning commission is noted on the map. Thereafter a final map of the tract embodying any changes requested by the planning commission is required to be filed with the planning commission.

Tenure in Land: The mode or manner by which an estate in lands is held.

Termites: Ant-like insects which feed on wood.

Termite Shield: A shield, usually of noncorrodible metal, placed on top of the foundation wall or around pipes to prevent passage of termites.

Testator: One who leaves a will in force at his death.

Threshold: A strip of wood or metal beveled on each edge and used above the finished floor under outside doors.

Third Party Originator: A party that prepares loan packages for borrowers for submission to lenders.

Time Is the Essence: A requirement that performance be punctual and that any delay will breach the contract.

Title: Evidence that owner of land is in lawful possession thereof, an instrument evidencing such ownership.

Title Insurance: Insurance written by a title company to protect property owner against loss if title is imperfect.

Title Report: A report which discloses condition of the title, made by a title company preliminary to issuance of title insurance.

Title Theory: Mortgage arrangement whereby title to mortgaged real property vests in the lender.

Topography: Nature of the surface of land; topography may be level, rolling, mountainous.

Torrens Title: System of title records provided by state law (no longer used in California).

Tort: A wrongful act; wrong, injury; violation of a legal right.

Township: A division by government survey that is six miles long, six miles wide and containing 36 sections, each one mile square.

Trade Fixtures: Articles of personal property annexed to real property, but which are necessary to the carrying on of a trade and are removable by the owner.

Treads: Horizontal boards of a stairway on which one steps.

Trim: The finish materials in a building, such as moldings, applied around openings (window trim, door trim) or at the floor and ceiling (baseboard, cornice, picture molding).

Trust Account: An account separate and apart and physically segregated from broker's own funds, in which broker is required by law to deposit all funds collected for clients.

Trust Deed: Just as with a mortgage, this is a legal document by which a borrower pledges certain real property or collateral as guarantee for the repayment of a loan. However, it differs from the mortgage in a number of important respects. For example, instead of there being two parties to the transaction, there are three. There is the borrower who gives the trust deed and who is called the trustor. There is the third, neutral party (just as there is with an escrow) who receives the trust deed and who is called the trustee. And, finally, there is the lender who is called the beneficiary since he is the one who benefits from the pledge arrangement in that in the event of a default the trustee can sell the property and transfer the money obtained at the sale to him as payment of the debt.

Trustee: One who holds property in trust for another to secure the performance of an obligation.

Trustor: One who deeds his property to a trustee to be held as security until he has performed his obligation to a lender under terms of a deed of trust.

U - V

Under Improvement: An improvement which, because of its deficiency in size or cost, is not the highest and best use of the site.

Underwriting: The technical analysis by a lender to determine if a borrower should receive a loan.

Undue Influence: Taking any fraudulent or unfair advantage of another's weakness of mind, or distress or necessity.

Unearned Increment: An increase in value of real estate due to no effort on the part of the owner; often due to increase in population.

Uniform Commercial Code (UCC): Establishes a unified and comprehensive scheme for regulation of security transactions in personal property, superseding the existing statutes on chattel mortgages, conditional sales, trust receipts, assignment of accounts receivable and others in this field.

Unit-in-place Method: The cost of erecting a building by estimating the cost of each component part, i.e. foundations, floors, walls, windows, ceilings, roofs, etc. (including labor and overhead).

Urban Property: City property; closely settled property.

Usury: On a loan, claiming a rate of interest greater than that permitted by law.

Utilities: Refers to services rendered by utility companies, such as: water, gas, electricity, telephone.

Utility: The ability to give satisfaction and/or excite desire for possession.

Valid: Having force, or binding force; legally sufficient and authorized by law.

Valley: The internal angle formed by the junction of two sloping sides of a roof.

Valuation: Estimated worth or price. Estimation. The act of valuing by appraisal .

Vendee: A purchaser; buyer.

Vendor: A seller; one who disposes of a thing in consideration of money.

Veneer: Thin sheets of wood glued to other wood products to form a surface.

Vent: A pipe installed to provide a flow of air to or from a drainage system or to provide a circulation of air within such system to protect trap seals from siphonage and back pressure.

Verification: Sworn statement before a duly qualified officer to correctness of contents of an instrument.

Vested: Bestowed upon someone; secured by someone, such as a title to property.

Vested Remainder: A certain remainder interest.

Void: To have no force or effect; that which is unenforceable.

Voidable: That which is capable of being adjudged void, but is not void unless action is taken to make it so.

Voluntary Lien: Any lien placed on property with consent of, or as a result of, the voluntary act of the owner.

W - Z

Wainscoting: The covering of an interior wall with wood (usually panels), tiles, etc., from the floor to a point about half way to the ceiling. The remaining portion is painted, wallpapered or covered with another material different from the lower portion.

Waive: To relinquish, or abandon; to forego a right to enforce or require anything.

Warranty Deed: A deed used to convey real property which contains warranties of title and quiet possession, and the grantor thus agrees to defend the premises against the lawful claims of third persons. It is commonly used in many states but in others the grant deed has supplanted it due to the practice of securing title insurance policies which have reduced the importance of express and implied warranty in deeds.

Waste: The destruction, removal material alteration of, or injury to premises by a tenant for life or years.

Water Table: Distance from surface of ground to a depth at which natural groundwater is found.

Wrap-Around Mortgage: A second trust deed with a face value of both the new amount it secures and the balance due under the first trust deed. A wrap-around can take the form of a land contract or a deed of trust.

Yield: The interest earned by an investor on his investment (or bank on the money it has lent). Also called Return.

Yield Rate: The yield expressed as a percentage of the total investment. Also called Rate of Return.

Zone: The area set off by the proper authorities for specific use; subject to certain restrictions or restraints.

Zoning: Act of city or county authorities specifying type of use to which property may be put in specific areas.

Glossary

Appendix A: Matching Terminology Answers

Chapter 1

1. P
2. K
3. V
4. I
5. L
6. N
7. E
8. H
9. M
10. F
11. U
12. Q
13. G
14. A
15. R
16. T
17. S
18. C
19. D
20. O
21. J
22. B

Chapter 2

1. K
2. N
3. P
4. Q
5. O
6. T
7. C
8. V
9. G
10. I
11. DD
12. M
13. J
14. A
15. W
16. H
17. S
18. E
19. BB

20. X
21. D
22. Y
23. AA
24. EE
25. F
26. CC
27. U
28. R
29. Z
30. L
31. B

Chapter 3

1. J
2. P
3. N
4. U
5. X
6. B
7. Q
8. Y
9. D
10. E
11. H
12. T
13. V
14. A
15. S
16. CC
17. G
18. C
19. W
20. F
21. AA
22. M
23. K
24. I
25. DD
26. Z
27. L
28. R
29. O
30. BB

Chapter 4

1. C
2. S
3. D
4. U
5. A
6. Y
7. AA
8. H
9. N
10. V
11. E
12. P
13. Z
14. M
15. I
16. J
17. R
18. F
19. W
20. L
21. O
22. Q
23. BB
24. B
25. K
26. G
27. T
28. X

Chapter 5

1. HH
2. H
3. Q
4. CC
5. N
6. W
7. X
8. D
9. B
10. U
11. L
12. Y
13. C

14. J
15. M
16. T
17. E
18. JJ
19. LL
20. BB
21. AA
22. Z
23. A
24. K
25. F
26. GG
27. V
28. FF
29. DD
30 EE
31. R
32. I
33. O
34. II
35. P
36. KK
37. S
38. G

Chapter 6

1. T
2. M
3. P
4. C
5. J
6. N
7. O
8. X
9. I
10. E
11. H
12. V
13. U
14. F
15. A
16. G
17. K

18. D
19. S
20. Q
21. B
22. Y
23. W
24. R
25. Z
26. L

Chapter 7

1. N
2. F
3. B
4. L
5. H
6. G
7. A
8. C
9. D
10. J
11. E
12. M
13. K
14. I
15. O

Chapter 8

1. AA
2. OO
3. K
4. O
5. J
6. X
7. F
8. Y
9. A
10. L
11. II
12. S
13. GG
14. C
15. V
16. N

17. MM
18. EE
19. LL
20. D
21. NN
22. U
23. T
24. W
25. R
26. I
27. P
28. JJ
29. HH
30. H
31. M
32. G
33. FF
34. E
35. B
36. KK
37. Q
38. CC
39. BB
40. DD
41. Z

Chapter 9

1. R
2. M
3. S
4. J
5. W
6. C
7. F
8. O
9. N
10. P
11. Z
12. I
13. L
14. K
15. U
16. B
17. E

18. V
19. D
20. Q
21. Y
22. X
23. T
24. H
25. A
26. G

Chapter 10

1. D
2. L
3. O
4. N
5. K
6. P
7. F
8. A
9. J
10. M
11. B
12. S
13. E
14. U
15. H
16. G
17. I
18. V
19. T
20. C
21. Q
22. R

Chapter 11

1. X
2. D
3. T
4. N
5. M
6. E
7. J
8. G
9. O

10. W
11. R
12. S
13. U
14. C
15. B
16. H
17. V
18. P
19. K
20. F
21. Q
22. A
23. I
24. L

Chapter 12

1. N
2. O
3. B
4. S
5. X
6. U
7. R
8. Q
9. I
10. L
11. BB
12. W
13. E
14. D
15. P
16. G
17. A
18. T
19. H
20. M
21. CC
22. Z
23. F
24. Y
25. C
26. K
27. J

28. V
29. AA

18. P
19. J

Chapter 13

1. B
2. O
3. A
4. I
5. L
6. H
7. C
8. J
9. Q
10. E
11. D
12. R
13. F
14. S
15. G
16. M
17. P
18. K
19. N
20. T
21. U

Chapter 15

1. K
2. E
3. G
4. B
5. L
6. F
7. H
8. A
9. P
10. C
11. N
12. I
13. O
14. J
15. D
16. M

Chapter 14

1. L
2. C
3. M
4. B
5. H
6. N
7. S
8. A
9. R
10. F
11. O
12. I
13. D
14. G
15. K
16. E
17. Q

Order Department

Sometimes our textbooks are hard to find!

If your bookstore does not carry our textbooks, send us a check or money order and we'll mail them to you with our 30-day money back guarantee.

Other great books from Educational Textbook Company:

California Real Estate Principles, 10th ed., by Huber	$65.00	____
How To Pass The Real Estate Exam (850 Exam Questions), by Huber	$40.00	____
California Real Estate Law, by Huber & Tyler	$50.00	____
Real Estate Finance, by Huber & Messick	$50.00	____
Real Estate Economics, by Huber & Pivar	$50.00	____
Real Estate Appraisal, by Huber, Messick, & Pivar	$50.00	____
Mortgage Loan Brokering, by Huber & Pivar	$50.00	____
Property Management, by Huber & Pivar	$50.00	____
Escrow I: An Introduction, by Huber	$50.00	____
California Real Estate Practice, by Huber & Lyons	$50.00	____
Computer Real Estate Applications, Huber & Grogan	$50.00	____
California Business Law, by Huber, Owens, & Tyler	$65.00	____
Hubie's Power Prep CD – 100 Questions - Vol. 1, by Huber	$50.00	____

Subtotal ____
Add shipping and handling @ $5.00 per book ____
Add California sales tax @ 8.25% ____
TOTAL ____

Allow 2-3 weeks for delivery

Name: _____

Address: _____

City, State, Zip: _____

Phone: _____

Check or money order: Educational Textbook Company, P.O. Box 3597, Covina, CA 91722

For faster results, order by credit card from the Glendale Community College Bookstore:

1-818-240-1000 x3024